State of the Apes

Killing, Capture, Trade and Conservation

C000263091

The illegal trade in live apes, ape meat and body parts occurs across all ape range states and poses a significant and growing threat to the long-term survival of wild ape populations worldwide. What was once a purely subsistence and cultural activity, now encompasses a global multi-million-dollar trade run by sophisticated trans-boundary criminal networks. The challenge lies in teasing apart the complex and interrelated factors that drive the ape trade, while implementing strategies that do not exacerbate inequality. This volume of *State of the Apes* brings together original research and analysis with topical case studies and emerging best practices, to further the ape conservation agenda around killing, capture and trade.

This title is available as an open access eBook via Cambridge Core and at www.stateof theapes.com.

State of the Apes

Series editors

Helga Rainer   Arcus Foundation

Alison White   Arcus Foundation

Annette Lanjouw   Arcus Foundation

The world's primates are among the most endangered of all tropical species. All great ape species – gorilla, chimpanzee, bonobo and orangutan – are classified as either Endangered or Critically Endangered. Furthermore, nearly all gibbon species are threatened with extinction. Whilst linkages between ape conservation and economic development, ethics and wider environmental processes have been acknowledged, more needs to be done to integrate biodiversity conservation within broader economic, social and environmental communities if those connections are to be fully realized and addressed.

Intended for a broad range of policymakers, industry experts and decision-makers, academics, researchers and NGOs, the *State of the Apes* series will look at the threats to these animals and their habitats within the broader context of economic and community development. Each publication presents a different theme, providing an overview of how these factors interrelate and affect the current and future status of apes, with robust statistics, welfare indicators, official and various other reports providing an objective and rigorous analysis of relevant issues.

State of the Apes

Killing, Capture, Trade and Conservation

iv

CAMBRIDGE
UNIVERSITY PRESS

University Printing House, Cambridge CB2 8BS, United Kingdom

Cambridge University Press is part of the University of Cambridge.

It furthers the University's mission by disseminating knowledge in the pursuit of education, learning and research at the highest international levels of excellence.

www.cambridge.org

Information on this title:
www.cambridge.org/9781108487948
DOI: 10.1017/9781108768351

First published 2020

Printed in the United Kingdom by TJ Books Limited, Padstow Cornwall

A catalogue record for this publication is available from the British Library

ISBN 978-1-108-48794-8 Hardback
ISBN 978-1-108-73826-2 Paperback

Credits

Editors
Helga Rainer, Alison White and Annette Lanjouw

Production Coordinator
Alison White

Editorial Consultant and Copy-editor
Tania Inowlocki

Designer
Rick Jones, StudioExile

Cartographer
Jillian Luff, MAP*grafix*

Fact-checker and Reference Editor
Eva Fairnell

Proofreader
Sarah Binns

Indexer
Caroline Jones, Osprey Indexing

Cover photographs:

Background: © Jabruson

Bonobo: © Takeshi Furuichi

Gibbon: © IPPL

Gorilla: © Annette Lanjouw

Orangutan: © Jurek Wajdowicz, EWS

Chimpanzee: © Nilanjan Bhattacharya/Dreamstime.com

Foreword

Understanding the impact of human behavior on the environment and the countless species facing serious threats to their survival is critical to developing intelligent and flexible approaches that will enable us to live within our planetary boundaries, sustaining the diversity of life and lives. The *State of the Apes* series brings together data and knowledge about the impact of human activities on apes and their habitat. By identifying potential solutions to avoid or minimise harm, it serves as an important resource for surmounting the many challenges confronting us and all other species on this planet. Across their range, ape populations are declining as a result of habitat loss and degradation, hunting and disease; all ape species face the threat of extinction. Understanding the scope and the impact that killing, capture and trade have on the different ape species across Africa and Asia, and how these threats affect their conservation, as well as the well-being of individual animals, is vital to finding solutions for their protection.

The fourth volume in the *State of the Apes* series focuses on one of the most direct threats to apes: hunting. This activity, which is a threat in almost all areas where non-human apes are found, results in their killing, often with the aim of using their body parts for food, medicine or other purposes, or live capture and trade to keep the animals as pets, for props in the entertainment industry or displayed in collections. All apes are protected under the law in every country where they exist: the killing, capture and trade in apes is therefore illegal. Despite this, apes are hunted in every country where they occur naturally, albeit for different and often complex reasons. In some cases, people hunt for cultural reasons, but often it is motivated by economic drivers, either to earn cash, obtain food or to remove an animal that is perceived as a nuisance, destroying crops.

Apes are among the most charismatic groups of species in tropical forests across Africa and Asia. They are intelligent, sentient, social and emotional beings, and given their close genetic similarity and shared evolutionary history with humans, they are often fascinating to people. This fascination or attraction has been one of the factors that has given rise to the threats apes currently face. It is largely based on their "almost-human" aspect that great apes and gibbons are captured to fuel the entertainment industry and to supply the vibrant pet trade and animal collections.

The impact of hunting on the individual apes concerned are also severe, leading to traumatized animals that experience fear, loneliness, pain, confusion and isolation from other individuals of their species. Most apes are social animals, spending years with their mother and natal group, learning how to survive and interact in the wild. When kept in captivity in artificial, stressful conditions, they experience trauma that lasts a lifetime. The hunting and killing or capture of apes, and their trade, has severe impacts on the conservation of these highly threatened species, who often exist in fragmented populations in forest patches that have already been seriously degraded by industrial agriculture, extractive industries and infrastructure projects. The removal of even a few individuals can have significant impacts on a species' future. Their survival is, quite literally, in our hands.

Nadya Hutagalung
United Nations Environment Program
(UNEP) and Great Apes Survival
Partnership (GRASP) Ambassador/
TV personality

Contents

Section 1
Killing, Capture, Trade and Conservation

Section 2
The Status and Welfare of Great Apes and Gibbons

Other Titles in this Series

Arcus Foundation. 2018. *State of the Apes: Infrastructure Development and Ape Conservation.* Cambridge: Cambridge University Press.

Arcus Foundation. 2015. *State of the Apes: Industrial Agriculture and Ape Conservation.* Cambridge: Cambridge University Press.

Arcus Foundation. 2014. *State of the Apes: Extractive Industries and Ape Conservation.* Cambridge: Cambridge University Press.

Other Language Editions

Bahasa Indonesia

Arcus Foundation. 2020. *Negara Kera: Pembunuhan, Penangkapan, Perdagangan, dan Konservasi.*

Arcus Foundation. 2018. *Negara Kera: Pembangunan Infrastruktur dan Konservasi Kera.*

Arcus Foundation. 2015. *Negara Kera: Pertanian Industri dan Konservasi Kera.*

Arcus Foundation. 2014. *Negara Kera: Industri Ekstraktif dan Konservasi Kera.*

Chinese

类人猿现状 ：捕杀、捕捉、贸易和保护

类人猿现状 ：基础设施开发与类人猿保护

French

Arcus Foundation. 2020. *La Planète des grands singes : La destruction, la capture, le trafic et la conservation.*

Arcus Foundation. 2018. *La planète des grands singes : Le développement des infrastructures et la conservation des grands singes.*

Arcus Foundation. 2015. *La planète des grands singes : L'agriculture industrielle et la conservation des grands singes.*

Arcus Foundation. 2014. *La planète des grands singes : Les industries extractives et la conservation des grands singes.*

The Arcus Foundation

The Arcus Foundation is a private grant-making foundation that advances social justice and conservation goals. The Foundation works globally and has offices in New York City, USA and Cambridge, UK. For more information visit:

- arcusfoundation.org.

Or connect with Arcus at:

- twitter.com/ArcusGreatApes; and
- facebook.com/ArcusGreatApes.

Great Apes and Gibbons Program

The long-term survival of humans, great apes and gibbons is dependent on how we respect and care for other animals and our shared natural resources. The Arcus Foundation seeks to increase respect for and recognition of the rights and value of great apes and gibbons, and to strengthen protection from threats to their habitats. The Arcus Great Apes and Gibbons Program supports conservation and policy advocacy efforts that promote their survival in the wild and in sanctuaries that offer high-quality care, safety and freedom from invasive research and exploitation.

Contact details

New York office:

44 West 28th Street, 17th Floor
New York, New York 10001, United States

+1 212 488 3000 / phone
+1 212 488 3010 / fax

**Cambridge office
(Great Apes and Gibbons Program):**

Nine Hills Road
Cambridge CB2 1GE
United Kingdom

+44 (0)1223 653040 / phone

Notes to Readers

Acronyms and abbreviations

A list of acronyms and abbreviations can be found at the back of the book, starting on p. 282.

Annexes

All annexes can be found at the back of the book, starting on p. 263, except for the Abundance Annex, which is available from the *State of the Apes* website:

- www.stateoftheapes.com.

Glossary

There is a glossary of scientific terms and keywords at the back of the book, starting on p. 285.

Chapter cross-referencing

Chapter cross-references appear throughout the book, either as direct references in the body text or in brackets.

Ape Abundance Estimates

Definitive, up-to-date abundance estimates are not available for all ape species. The most recent Abundance Annex, which can be accessed at stateoftheapes.com, presents estimates at the site level and uses abundance classes to indicate population ranges. In this volume, the Apes Overview and some chapters feature abundance information based on other geographic scales, drawn from a variety of sources, including forthcoming Red List assessments. Consequently, some figures may not align exactly.

Ape Range Maps

The ape range maps throughout this edition show the extent of occurrence (EOO) of each species. An EOO includes all known populations of a species contained within the shortest possible continuous imaginary boundary. It is important to note that some areas within these boundaries are unsuitable and unoccupied.

The Arcus Foundation commissioned the ape distribution maps in the Apes Overview, Figures AO1 and AO2, to provide the most accurate and up-to-date illustration of range data. These maps were created by the Max Planck Institute for Evolutionary Anthropology, who manage the A.P.E.S. portal and database. This volume also features maps created by contributors who used ape range data from other sources. As a consequence, the maps may not all align exactly.

Acknowledgments

As with all volumes in the *State of the Apes* series, pulling together the content for this publication has been an extensive undertaking. Our aim is not only to encourage the critical engagement of all stakeholders, including conservation organizations, civil society, industry, donor and financial institutions, and governments, but also to increase support for great apes and gibbons. We would like to express our gratitude to everyone who played a role, from those who attended our stakeholder meeting, to our contributors and reviewers, to all those involved in the production and translation of the book. Thank you for your input, knowledge, advice, expertise, support, flexibility and patience!

Jon Stryker and the Arcus Foundation Board of Directors have been instrumental in enabling us to produce this publication series. We thank them for their ongoing support of our efforts to bring an overview of critical ape conservation issues to important audiences. We also thank Katrina Halliday and the team at Cambridge University Press for their commitment to this series.

In addition to the thematic content, each publication provides an overview of the status of apes, both in their natural habitats and in captivity. We are very grateful to the captive-ape organizations that provided detailed information and to all the great ape and gibbon scientists who contribute their valuable data to build the A.P.E.S. database. Such collaborative efforts are key to effective conservation action.

Particular thanks go to the following individuals and organizations: Marc Ancrenaz, Duncan Brack, Dirck Byler, Susan M. Cheyne, Lauren Coad, Gunung Gea, Charlotte Houpline, Tatyana Humle, Fiachra Kearney, Hjalmar S. Kühl, Noëlle Kümpel, Fabian Leendertz, Legal Atlas, Linda May, Max Planck Institute, Adam Phillipson, Martha

Robbins, Maribel Rodriguez, Julie Sherman, Tenekwetche Sop, Marie Stevenson and Sabri Zain.

We are grateful to the authors and contributors of this volume, including those who provided essential data. They are named at the end of each chapter. We could not have produced this book without them. We also extend thanks to our reviewers for providing constructive feedback and helping to ensure the quality of individual chapters and the book as a whole. They are: Katharine Abernethy, Graham L. Banes, Elizabeth L. Bennett, Tom Blomley, Luke Bond, Liana Chua, Rosie Cooney, Isabel Esterman, David Favre, Anna Frostic, Jessica Graham, Justin Kenrick, Tien Ming Lee, Peter J. Li, Neil Maddison, Fiona Maisels, Vincent Nijman, Colman O'Criodain, Alex Piel, Rajindra Puri, Cindy Rizzo, Steve Ross, Nadine Ruppert, Judith Shapiro, Willie Shubert, Serge A. Wich, Elizabeth A. Williamson, Karen Winfield and Stefan Ziegler.

Credits appear alongside all photographs in this volume, many of which were generously contributed by the photographers. We are also thankful to the organizations that allowed us to include extracts from previously published books, journals, reports and internal documents.

To ensure that the *State of the Apes* series is accessible to as many stakeholders, decision- and policy-makers as possible, it is published under an open access agreement with Cambridge University Press and translated into multiple languages. This volume will be available in Bahasa Indonesia, Chinese (Mandarin) and French thanks to our translators, graphic designers and proofreaders: Alboum Associates, Nelly Aubaud Davies, Exile: Design & Editorial Services, Xuezhu Huff, MAPgrafix, Anton Nurcahyo, Owlingua, Hélène Piantone, Erica Taube, Beth Varley and Rumanti Wasturini. The *State of the Apes* editions are available in all languages on the dedicated website (state oftheapes.com); our thanks go to the Arcus Communications team for managing this site, especially Angela Cave, Sebastian Naidoo and Bryan Simmons.

Many others contributed in various ways, such as by providing introductions, anonymous input and strategic advice, or by helping with essential, if sometimes tedious, administrative tasks. We also thank all those who provided much-appreciated moral support.

Helga Rainer, Alison White and Annette Lanjouw
Editors

Apes Overview

Apes Index

All information is drawn from the *Handbook of the Mammals of the World. Volume 3. Primates* (Mittermeier, Rylands and Wilson, 2013), unless otherwise cited.

Bonobo (*Pan paniscus*)

Distribution and Numbers in the Wild

The bonobo is only present in the Democratic Republic of Congo (DRC), bio-geographically separated from chimpanzees and gorillas by the Congo River (see Figure AO1). The population size is unknown, as only 30% of the species' historic range has been surveyed; however, estimates from the four geographically distinct bonobo strongholds suggest a minimum population of 15,000–20,000 individuals, with numbers decreasing (Fruth *et al.*, 2016).

The bonobo is included in Appendix I of the Convention on International Trade in Endangered Species of Wild Fauna and Flora (CITES) and is categorized as endangered on the International Union for Conservation of Nature (IUCN) Red List (Fruth *et al.*, 2016; see Box AO1). The causes of population decline include poaching; habitat loss and degradation; disease; and people's lack of awareness that hunting and eating bonobos is unlawful. Poaching, which is mainly carried out as part of the commercial wild meat trade and for some medicinal purposes, has been exacerbated by the ongoing effects of armed conflict, such as military-sanctioned hunting and the accessibility of modern weaponry and ammunition (Fruth *et al.*, 2016).

Physiology

Male adult bonobos reach a height of 73–83 cm and weigh 37–61 kg, while females are slightly smaller, weighing 27–38 kg. Bonobos are moderately sexually dimorphic and similar in size and appearance to chimpanzees, although with a smaller head and lither appearance. The reported maximum life span in the wild is 50 years (Hohmann, Robbins and Boesch, 2006; Robson and Wood, 2008).

The bonobo diet is mainly frugivorous (more than 50% fruit), supplemented with leaves, stems, shoots, pith, seeds, bark, flowers, honey and fungi. Only a very small part of their diet consists of animal matter—such as insects, small reptiles, birds and medium-sized mammals, including other primates.

Social Organization

Bonobos live in fission–fusion communities of up to 100 individuals, consisting of multiple males and females. When foraging, they split into smaller mixed-sex subgroups, or parties, averaging 5–23 individuals.

Male bonobos cooperate with and tolerate one another; however, lasting bonds between adult males are rare, in contrast to the bonds between adult females, which are strong and potentially last for years. A distinguishing feature of female bonobos is that they are co-dominant with males and form alliances against certain males within the community. Among bonobos, the bonds between mother and son are the strongest, prove highly important for the social status of the son and last into adulthood.

Together with chimpanzees, bonobos are the closest living relatives to humans, sharing 98.8% of human DNA (Smithsonian Institute, n.d.; Varki and Altheide, 2005).

Chimpanzee (*Pan troglodytes*)

Distribution and Numbers in the Wild

Chimpanzees are widely distributed across equatorial Africa, with discontinuous populations from southern Senegal to western Uganda and Tanzania (Humle *et al.*, 2016b; see Figure AO1).

Chimpanzees are listed in CITES Appendix I, and all four subspecies are categorized as either endangered or critically endangered on the IUCN Red List. There are approximately 114,200–317,000 central chimpanzees (*Pan troglodytes troglodytes*); 17,600–96,700 western chimpanzees (*Pan t. verus*); 170,000–250,000 eastern chimpanzees (*Pan t. schweinfurthii*); and probably fewer than

9,000 Nigeria–Cameroon chimpanzees (*Pan t. ellioti*) (Heinicke *et al.*, 2019; Humle *et al.*, 2016a; Maisels *et al.*, 2016; Oates *et al.*, 2016; Plumptre *et al.*, 2010, 2016a; Strindberg *et al.*, 2018). All populations are believed to be declining, but the rate has not yet been quantified for all (Humle *et al.*, 2016b). An assessment of the rate of population change for the western chimpanzee from 1990 to 2014 found a 6% annual decline, corresponding to a population decline of 80.2% over the study period (Kühl *et al.*, 2017).

Decreases in chimpanzee numbers are mainly attributed to increased poaching for the commercial wild meat trade, habitat loss and degradation, and disease (Humle *et al.*, 2016b).

Physiology

Male chimpanzees are 77–96 cm tall and weigh 28–70 kg, while females measure 70–91 cm and weigh 20–50 kg. They share many facial expressions with humans, although forehead musculature is less pronounced and they have more flexible lips. Chimpanzees live for up to 50 years in the wild.

Chimpanzees are mainly frugivorous. Some communities include 200 species of food items in a diet of fruit supplemented by bark, flowers, fungi, honey, leaves, pith, seeds, shoots and stems, and animal prey, such as ants and termites, but also small mammals, including other primates. Chimpanzees are the most carnivorous of all the apes.

Social Organization

Chimpanzees show fission–fusion, multi-male–multi-female grouping patterns. A large community includes all individuals who regularly associate with one another; such communities comprise an average of 35 individuals, with the largest-known group exceeding 150, although this size is rare. The community separates into smaller, temporary subgroups, or parties. The parties can be highly fluid, with members moving in and out quickly or a few individuals staying together for a few days before rejoining other members of the community.

Typically, home ranges are defended by highly territorial males, who may attack or even kill neighboring chimpanzees. Male chimpanzees are dominant over female chimpanzees and are generally the more social sex, sharing food and grooming each other more frequently. Chimpanzees are noted for their sophisticated forms of cooperation, such as in hunting and territorial defense; the level of cooperation in social hunting activities varies across communities, however.

Gorilla (*Gorilla* species (spp.))
Distribution and Numbers in the Wild

The western gorilla (*Gorilla gorilla*) is distributed throughout western equatorial Africa and has two subspecies: the western lowland gorilla (*Gorilla g. gorilla*) and the Cross River gorilla (*Gorilla g. diehli*). The eastern gorilla (*Gorilla beringei*) is found in the DRC and across the border in Uganda and Rwanda. There are two subspecies of the eastern gorilla: the mountain gorilla (*Gorilla b. beringei*) and Grauer's gorilla (*Gorilla b. graueri*) (see Figure AO1).

Three of the four gorilla taxa are listed as critically endangered on the IUCN Red List (Bergl *et al.*, 2016; Hickey *et al.*, 2018; Maisels *et al.*, 2018; Plumptre *et al.*, 2016b). The first range-wide population estimate for the western lowland gorilla was undertaken in 2013 and gives a total population of nearly 362,000 while as few as 250–300 Cross River gorillas remain in the wild (Bergl *et al.*, 2016; Dunn *et al.*, 2014; Strindberg *et al.*, 2018). The most recent population estimate for Grauer's gorilla is 3,800, which indicates a 77% loss since 1994 (Plumptre *et al.*, 2016c). Mountain gorillas are estimated to number at least 1,000 individuals (Granjon *et al.*, 2020; Hickey *et al.*, 2019). The main threats to both species are poaching for the commercial wild meat trade, habitat destruction and degradation, and disease (for the western gorilla, the Ebola virus in particular) (Maisels, Bergl and Williamson, 2018; Plumptre, Robbins and Williamson, 2019). The Grauer's gorilla is also threatened by civil unrest (Plumptre, Robbins and Williamson, 2019). A predicted threat is the impact of climate change on the gorilla's forest habitats (Maisels, Bergl and Williamson, 2018; Plumptre, Robbins and Williamson, 2019).

Physiology

The adult male of the eastern gorilla is slightly larger (159–196 cm, 120–209 kg) than the western gorilla (138–180 cm, 145–191 kg). Both species are highly sexually dimorphic and females are about half the size of males. Their lifespan ranges from 30 to 40 years in the wild. Mature males are known as "silverbacks" due to the development of a gray saddle on their back when they attain maturity.

The gorillas' diet consists predominantly of ripe fruit and terrestrial, herbaceous vegetation. More herbaceous vegetation is ingested while fruit is scarce, in line with seasonality and fruit availability, and protein gain comes from tree leaves and bark;

gorillas do not eat meat but occasionally consume ants and termites. Mountain gorillas have less fruit in their environment than lowland gorillas, so they feed mainly on leaves, pith, stems, bark and, occasionally, ants.

Social Organization

Western gorillas live in stable groups with multiple females and one adult male (silverback); in contrast, eastern gorillas are polygynous and can be polygynandrous, with groups that comprise one or more silverbacks, multiple females, their offspring and immature relatives. The average group consists of ten individuals, but eastern gorillas can live in groups of up to 65 individuals, whereas the maximum group size for the western gorilla is 22. Gorillas are not territorial and home ranges overlap extensively. Chest beats and vocalizations typically are used when neighboring silverbacks come into contact, but intergroup encounters may escalate into physical fights. Groups that live in the same areas normally adopt a strategy of mutual avoidance.

Orangutan (*Pongo* spp.)

Distribution and Numbers in the Wild

The orangutan range is now limited to the forests of Sumatra and Borneo, but these great apes were once present throughout much of southern Asia (Wich *et al.*, 2008, 2012a; see Figure AO2).

Survey data indicate that in 2015 fewer than 14,000 Sumatran orangutans (*Pongo abelii*) and around 100,000 Bornean orangutans (*Pongo pygmaeus* spp.) remained in the wild (Ancrenaz *et al.*, 2016; GRASP and IUCN, 2018; Singleton *et al.*, 2017; Voigt *et al.*, 2018; Wich *et al.*, 2016). As a result of continuing habitat loss and hunting, both the Sumatran orangutan and the Bornean orangutan are classified as critically endangered (Ancrenaz *et al.*, 2016; Singleton *et al.*, 2017). Both species are listed in Appendix I of CITES.

In November 2017, a new species of orangutan was described in three forest fragments in Sumatra's Central, North and South Tapanuli districts, which are part of the Batang Toru Ecosystem (Nater *et al.*, 2017). The Tapanuli orangutan (*Pongo tapanuliensis*) has a total distribution of about 1,100 km² (110,000 ha) and a population size of fewer than 800 individuals (Wich *et al.*, 2019). It is classified as critically endangered (Nowak *et al.*, 2017)

The main threats to all orangutan species are habitat loss and fragmentation, and killings due to human–ape conflict, hunting and the international live animal trade (Ancrenaz *et al.*, 2016; Gaveau *et al.*, 2014; Singleton *et al.*, 2017; Wich *et al.*, 2008). For the Bornean orangutan, additional threats include forest fires and people's lack of awareness that they are protected by law (Ancrenaz *et al.*, 2016). For the Sumatran orangutan, the current most important threat is a land use plan issued by the government of Aceh in 2013. The plan does not recognize the Leuser Ecosystem as a National Strategic Area, a legal status that prohibits cultivation, development and other activities that would degrade the ecosystem's environmental functions (Singleton *et al.*, 2017). For the Tapanuli orangutan, industrial development poses a serious threat, from gold and silver mining and existing extensive logging permits, to proposed hydroelectric projects (Nowak *et al.*, 2017; Wich *et al.*, 2019).

Physiology

Adult males can reach a height of 94–99 cm and weigh 60–85 kg (flanged) or 30–65 kg (unflanged). Females are 64–84 cm tall and weigh 30–45 kg, meaning that they are far smaller than males and that orangutans are highly sexually dimorphic. In the wild in Sumatra, the life expectancy is 58 years for males and 53 years for females. No accurate data exist for the Bornean orangutan.

Fully mature males develop a short beard and protruding cheek pads, termed "flanges." Some male orangutans experience "developmental arrest," maintaining a female-like size and appearance for many years past sexual maturity; they are known as "unflanged" males. Orangutans are the only great ape to exhibit male bimaturism.

The orangutan diet consists mainly of fruit, but they also eat leaves, shoots, seeds, bark, pith, flowers, eggs, soil and invertebrates such as termites and ants. Carnivorous behavior has also been observed, but at a low frequency (preying on species such as slow lorises).

Social Organization

The mother–offspring unit is the only permanent social unit among orangutans, yet social groupings between independent individuals do occur, although their frequency varies across populations and taxa; they are more common in the two Sumatran species than the Bornean species. While females are usually relatively tolerant of each other, flanged males are intolerant of other flanged and unflanged males (Wich, de Vries and Ancrenaz, 2009). Orangutans on Sumatra are generally more social than those on Borneo and live in overlapping home ranges, with flanged males emitting "long calls" to alert others to their location (Delgado and Van Schaik, 2000; Wich, de Vries and Ancrenaz, 2009). Orangutans are characterized by an extremely slow life history, with the longest interbirth interval of any primate species, an average of 7.6 years (van Noordwijk *et al.*, 2018).

Gibbons (*Hoolock* spp.; *Hylobates* spp.; *Nomascus* spp.; *Symphalangus* spp.)

All four genera of gibbon generally share ecological and behavioral attributes, such as social monogamy in territorial groups; vocalization through elaborate song (including complex duets); frugivory and brachiation (moving through the canopy using only the arms). Gibbons primarily consume fruit but have a varied diet including insects, flowers, leaves and seeds. Female gibbons have a single offspring every 2.5–3 years (S. Cheyne, personal communication, 2017). Gibbons are diurnal and sing at sunrise and sunset; they dedicate a significant part of the day to finding fruit trees within their territories.

Hoolock genus

Distribution and Numbers in the Wild

Three species comprise the *Hoolock* genus: the western hoolock (*Hoolock hoolock*), the eastern hoolock (*Hoolock leuconedys*) and the newly discovered Gaoligong or Skywalker hoolock (*Hoolock tianxing*) (Fan *et al.*, 2017; Fan, Turvey and Bryant, 2019). The Mishmi Hills hoolock (*Hoolock h. mishmiensis*), the most recently discovered subspecies of western hoolock, was officially named in 2013 (Choudhury, 2013).

The western hoolock's distribution spans Bangladesh, India and Myanmar. The eastern hoolock lives in China and Myanmar (see Figure AO2). To date, the Gaoligong hoolock has only been seen in eastern Myanmar and south-western China (Fan *et al.*, 2017). The Gaoligong hoolock comprises an estimated nine subpopulations and about 200 individuals in China. No recent population estimates exist for Myanmar (P.-F. Fan, personal communication, 2019). Previous, unconfirmed estimates—dating from the time when the Gaoligong hoolock was still identified as the eastern hoolock—suggest that, in 2009, Myanmar may have been home to as many as 40,000 individuals (Geissmann *et al.*, 2013).

With an estimated population of 15,000 individuals, the western hoolock is listed as endangered on the IUCN Red List (Brockelman, Molur and Geissmann, 2019). The eastern hoolock has a population of 10,000–50,000 and is listed as vulnerable on the IUCN Red List (Brockelman and Geissmann, 2019). Both species are listed in CITES Appendix I, with the main threats identified as habitat loss and fragmentation, and hunting for food, pets, tourism and medicinal purposes. The Gaoligong hoolock is categorized as endangered on the IUCN Red List (Fan, Turvey and Bryant, 2019).

Physiology

An individual hoolock can have a head and body length of 45–81 cm and weigh 6–9 kg, with males slightly heavier than females. Like most gibbons, the *Hoolock* genus is sexually dichromatic, with the pelage (coat) of females and males differing in terms of patterning and color. Pelage also differs across species: unlike the western hoolock, the eastern one features a white preputial tuft and a complete separation between the white brow markings.

The diet of the western hoolock is primarily frugivorous, supplemented with vegetative matter such as leaves, shoots, seeds, moss and flowers. While little is known about the diet of the eastern hoolock, it most likely resembles that of the western hoolock.

Social Organization

Hoolocks live in family groups of 2–6 individuals, consisting of a mated adult pair and their offspring. They are presumably territorial, although no specific data exist. Hoolock pairs vocalize a "double solo" rather than the more common "duet" of various gibbons.

Hylobates genus

Distribution and Numbers in the Wild

Nine species are currently included in the *Hylobates* genus, although there remains some dispute about whether Abbott's gray gibbon (*Hylobates abbottii*), the Bornean gray gibbon (*Hylobates funereus*) and Müller's gibbon (*Hylobates muelleri*) represent full species (see Table AO1).

This genus of gibbon occurs discontinuously in tropical and subtropical forests from southwestern China (extirpated?), through Indochina, Thailand and the Malay Peninsula to the islands of Sumatra, Borneo and Java (Wilson and Reeder, 2005; see Figure AO2). The overall estimated minimum population for the *Hylobates* genus is about 400,000–480,000. The least abundant species is the moloch gibbon (*Hylobates moloch*) and most abundant, collectively, are the "gray gibbons" (Abbott's, the Bornean and Müller's gibbons), although no accurate population numbers are available for Abbott's gray gibbon.

All *Hylobates* species are listed as endangered on the IUCN Red List and are in CITES Appendix I. Three hybrid zones occur naturally and continue to coexist with the unhybridized species in the wild. The main collective threats facing the genus are deforestation, hunting and the illegal pet trade (S. Cheyne, personal communication, 2017).

Physiology

Average height for both sexes of all species is approximately 46 cm and their weight ranges between 5 kg and 7 kg. With the exception of the pileated gibbon (*Hylobates pileatus*), species in the genus are not sexually dichromatic, although the lar gibbon (*Hylobates lar*) has two color phases, which are not related to sex or age.

Gibbons are mainly frugivorous. Figs are an especially important part of their diet and are supplemented by leaves, buds, flowers, shoots, vines and insects, while small animals and bird eggs form the protein input.

Social Organization

Hylobates gibbons are largely socially monogamous, forming family units of two adults and their offspring; however, polyandrous and polygynous units have been observed, especially in hybrid zones. Territorial disputes are predominantly led by males, who become aggressive towards other males, whereas females tend to lead daily movements and ward off other females.

Nomascus genus

Distribution and Numbers in the Wild

Seven species make up the *Nomascus* genus (see Table AO1).

The *Nomascus* genus, which is somewhat less widely distributed than the *Hylobates* genus, is present in Cambodia, Lao People's Democratic Republic, Viet Nam and southern China, including Hainan Island (see Figure AO2). Population estimates exist for some taxa: there are approximately 5,000 western black crested gibbons (*Nomascus concolor*), about 200 Cao Vit gibbons (*Nomascus nasutus*) and 23 Hainan gibbons (*Nomascus hainanus*). Population estimates for the white-cheeked gibbons (*Nomascus leucogenys* and *Nomascus siki*) are available for some sites, and overall numbers are known to be severely depleted. The yellow-cheeked gibbons (*Nomascus annamensis* and *Nomascus gabriellae*) have the largest populations among the *Nomascus* gibbons.

All species are listed in CITES Appendix I; in the IUCN Red List, four are categorized as critically endangered (*Nomascus concolor, nasutus, hainanus* and *leucogenys*) and two as endangered (*Nomascus siki* and *N. gabriellae*), while one—the northern yellow-cheeked crested gibbon (*Nomascus annamensis*)—is yet to be assessed (IUCN, 2019). Major threats to these populations include hunting for food, pets and for medicinal purposes, as well as habitat loss and fragmentation.

Physiology

Average head and body length across all species of this genus, for both sexes, is approximately 47 cm; individuals weigh around 7 kg. All *Nomascus* species have sexually dimorphic pelage; adult males are predominantly black while females are a buffy yellow. Their diet is much the same as that of the *Hylobates* genus: mainly frugivorous, supplemented with leaves and flowers.

Social Organization

Gibbons of the *Nomascus* genus are mainly socially monogamous; however, most species have also been observed in polyandrous and polygynous groups. More northerly species appear to engage in polygyny to a greater degree than southern taxa. Copulations outside monogamous pairs have been recorded, although infrequently.

Symphalangus genus

Distribution and Numbers in the Wild

Siamang (*Symphalangus syndactylus*) are found in several forest blocks across Indonesia, Malaysia and Thailand (see Figure AO2); the species faces severe threats to its habitat across its range. No accurate estimates exist for the total population size. The species is listed in CITES Appendix I and is classified as endangered on the IUCN Red List (Nijman and Geissmann, 2008).

Physiology

The siamang's head and body length is 75–90 cm, and adult males weigh 10.5–12.7 kg, while adult females weigh 9.1–11.5 kg. The siamang is minimally sexually dimorphic, and the pelage is the same across sexes: black. The species has a large inflatable throat sac.

Siamang rely heavily on figs and somewhat less on leaves—a diet that allows them to be sympatric with *Hylobates* gibbons in some locations, since the latter focus more on fleshy fruits. The siamang diet also includes flowers and insects.

Social Organization

Males and females call territorially, using their large throat sacs, and males will give chase to neighboring males. One group's calls will inhibit other groups nearby, and they will consequently take turns to vocalize. The groups are usually based on monogamous pairings, although polyandrous groups have been observed. Males may also adopt the role of caregiver for infants.

Ape Socioecology

This section presents an overview of the socioecology of the different non-human apes: bonobos; chimpanzees; eastern and western gorillas; gibbons (including siamangs); and Bornean, Sumatran and Tapanuli orangutans. The information provided in this section is largely drawn from Emery Thompson and Wrangham (2013), Mittermeier, Rylands and Wilson (2013), Reinartz, Ingmanson and Vervaecke (2013), Robbins (2011), Robbins and Robbins (2018), Wich *et al.* (2009), Williamson and Butynski (2013a, 2013b), and Williamson, Maisels and Groves (2013).

Gorillas live in ten Central African countries (Maisels, Bergl and Williamson, 2018; Plumptre, Robbins and Williamson, 2019). Chimpanzees are the most wide-ranging ape species in Africa, occurring across 21 countries, while bonobos are restricted to the Democratic Republic of Congo (DRC) (Fruth *et al.*, 2016; Humle *et al.*, 2016b). Orangutans are found in Asia—in both Indonesia and Malaysia—and are the only ape to have two distinct male types (Ancrenaz *et al.*, 2016; Nowak *et al.*, 2017; Singleton *et al.*, 2017). Gibbons are the most geographically widespread group of apes. Currently, 20 species of gibbon in four genera are recognized across Asia: 9 *Hylobates* species, 7 *Nomascus* species, 3 *Hoolock* species and the single *Symphalangus* species (Fan *et al.*, 2017; IUCN, 2019; Thinh *et al.*, 2010).

Social Organization

Apes vary considerably in their social organization. While orangutans lead semi-solitary

BOX AO1

IUCN Red List Categories and Criteria, and CITES Appendices

The IUCN Species Survival Commission assesses the conservation status of each species and subspecies using IUCN Red List Categories and Criteria. As all great apes and gibbons are categorized as Vulnerable, Endangered or Critically Endangered, this box presents details on a selection of the criteria for these three categories (see Table AO1). A summary of the five criteria is provided in Annex 1. Full details of the IUCN Red List Categories and Criteria (in English, French and Spanish) can be viewed and downloaded at:

https://www.iucnredlist.org/resources/categories-and-criteria.

Detailed guidelines on their use are available at:

https://www.iucnredlist.org/resources/redlistguidelines.

Appendices I, II and III to the Convention on International Trade in Endangered Species of Wild Fauna and Flora (CITES) are lists of species afforded different levels or types of protection from overexploitation.

All non-human apes are in **Appendix I**, which comprises species that are the most endangered among CITES-listed animals and plants. CITES prohibits international trade in species that are threatened with extinction, except under specified circumstances, including for certain types of scientific research. Such exceptional trade requires both an import permit and an export permit, or a re-export certificate—which authorities will grant only if they determine that the transfers will not have a nega-

Table AO1

Principal Criteria for the Red List Categories: Vulnerable, Endangered and Critically Endangered

IUCN Red List Category	Risk of extinction in the wild	Number of mature individuals in the wild	Rate of population decline over the past 10 years or 3 generations (whichever is longer)
Vulnerable	High	<10,000	>30%
Endangered	Very high	<2,500	>50%
Critically Endangered	Extremely high	<250	>80%

tive impact on the survival of the species in the wild, that the specimens to be transferred have been acquired legally and that the trade is not for primarily commercial purposes—so long as the transfers do not contravene national legislation (see Chapters 6 and 8). Article VII of the Convention provides for a number of exemptions to this general prohibition. For more information, see https://www.cites.org/eng/disc/text.php#VII.

Table AO2

Great Apes and Gibbons

GREAT APES		
Pan genus		
Bonobo	*Pan paniscus*	■ Democratic Republic of Congo (DRC)
Central chimpanzee	*Pan troglodytes troglodytes*	■ Angola ■ Cameroon ■ Central African Republic ■ DRC ■ Equatorial Guinea ■ Gabon ■ Republic of Congo
Eastern chimpanzee	*Pan troglodytes schweinfurthii*	■ Burundi ■ Central African Republic ■ DRC ■ Rwanda ■ South Sudan ■ Tanzania ■ Uganda
Nigeria–Cameroon chimpanzee	*Pan troglodytes ellioti*	■ Cameroon ■ Nigeria
Western chimpanzee	*Pan troglodytes verus*	■ Ghana ■ Guinea ■ Guinea-Bissau ■ Ivory Coast ■ Liberia ■ Mali ■ Senegal ■ Sierra Leone
Gorilla genus		
Cross River gorilla	*Gorilla gorilla diehli*	■ Cameroon ■ Nigeria
Grauer's gorilla	*Gorilla beringei graueri*	■ DRC
Mountain gorilla	*Gorilla beringei beringei*	■ DRC ■ Rwanda ■ Uganda
Western lowland gorilla	*Gorilla gorilla gorilla*	■ Angola ■ Cameroon ■ Central African Republic ■ Equatorial Guinea ■ Gabon ■ Republic of Congo
Pongo genus		
Northeast Bornean orangutan	*Pongo pygmaeus morio*	■ Indonesia ■ Malaysia
Northwest Bornean orangutan	*Pongo pygmaeus pygmaeus*	■ Indonesia ■ Malaysia
Southwest Bornean orangutan	*Pongo pygmaeus wurmbii*	■ Indonesia
Sumatran orangutan	*Pongo abelii*	■ Indonesia
Tapanuli orangutan	*Pongo tapanuliensis*	■ Indonesia

GIBBONS (excluding subspecies)		
Hoolock genus		
Eastern hoolock	*Hoolock leuconedys*	■ China ■ Myanmar
Gaoligong hoolock (a.k.a. Skywalker hoolock)	*Hoolock tianxing*	■ China ■ Myanmar
Western hoolock	*Hoolock hoolock*	■ Bangladesh ■ India ■ Myanmar
Hylobates genus		
Abbott's gray gibbon	*Hylobates abbotti*	■ Indonesia ■ Malaysia
Agile gibbon (a.k.a. dark-handed gibbon)	*Hylobates agilis*	■ Indonesia ■ Malaysia
Bornean gray gibbon (a.k.a. northern gray gibbon)	*Hylobates funereus*	■ Brunei ■ Indonesia ■ Malaysia
Bornean white-bearded gibbon (a.k.a. Bornean agile gibbon)	*Hylobates albibarbis*	■ Indonesia
Kloss's gibbon (a.k.a. Mentawai gibbon)	*Hylobates klossii*	■ Indonesia
Lar gibbon (a.k.a. white-handed gibbon)	*Hylobates lar*	■ Indonesia ■ Lao People's Democratic Republic (PDR) ■ Malaysia ■ Myanmar ■ Thailand
Moloch gibbon (a.k.a. Javan gibbon, silvery gibbon)	*Hylobates moloch*	■ Indonesia

lives, some gibbons form family groups with monogamous pairs, and African great apes —bonobos, chimpanzees and gorillas—a part of larger social groupings.

Bonobos and chimpanzees form multi-male and multi-female dynamic communities or groups that can fission into smaller groups (known as parties) or fuse to form larger ones. These parties can vary in size throughout the day and depending on food availability and the presence of reproductively active females (Wrangham, 1986). Parties, especially in chimpanzees, tend to be smaller during periods of fruit scarcity (Furuichi, 2009). Adult female chimpanzees often spend time alone with their offspring or in a party with other females, while adult female bonobos tend to associate more extensively with their adult sons. Chimpanzee communities average 35 members, with some even exceeding 150 members (Mitani, 2009; Mittermeier, Rylands and Wilson, 2013). Bonobo communities usually comprise 30–80 individuals (Fruth, Williamson and Richardson, 2013). In both species, females are typically the dispersing sex, emigrating from their native community to a neighboring one upon sexual maturity, which bonobos reach between the ages of 6 and 13, while chimpanzees do so between the ages of 8 and 14 (Furuichi *et al.*, 1998; Walker *et al.*, 2018).

▶ Müller's gibbon (a.k.a. Müller's gray gibbon, southern gray gibbon)	*Hylobates muelleri*	■ Indonesia
Pileated gibbon (a.k.a. capped gibbon, crowned gibbon)	*Hylobates pileatus*	■ Cambodia ■ Lao PDR ■ Thailand
***Nomascus* genus**		
Cao Vit gibbon (a.k.a. eastern black crested gibbon)	*Nomascus nasutus*	■ China ■ Viet Nam
Hainan gibbon (a.k.a. Hainan black crested gibbon, Hainan black gibbon, Hainan crested gibbon)	*Nomascus hainanus*	■ China (Hainan Island)
Northern white-cheeked crested gibbon (a.k.a. northern white-cheeked gibbon, white-cheeked gibbon)	*Nomascus leucogenys*	■ Lao PDR ■ Viet Nam
Northern yellow-cheeked crested gibbon (a.k.a. northern buffed-cheeked gibbon)	*Nomascus annamensis*	■ Cambodia ■ Lao PDR ■ Viet Nam
Southern white-cheeked crested gibbon (a.k.a. southern white-cheeked gibbon)	*Nomascus siki*	■ Lao PDR ■ Viet Nam
Southern yellow-cheeked crested gibbon (a.k.a. red-cheeked gibbon, buff-cheeked gibbon, buffy-cheeked gibbon)	*Nomascus gabriellae*	■ Cambodia ■ Viet Nam
Western black crested gibbon (a.k.a. black crested gibbon, black gibbon, concolor gibbon, Indochinese gibbon)	*Nomascus concolor*	■ China ■ Lao PDR ■ Viet Nam
***Symphalangus* genus**		
Siamang	*Symphalangus syndactylus*	■ Indonesia ■ Malaysia ■ Thailand

Sources: Mittermeier, Rylands and Wilson (2013); personal communication in 2019 with Susan Cheyne, Serge Wich and Elizabeth A. Williamson

Gorillas live in stable, cohesive social units, or groups, with a median size of ten. Most groups consist of one or more "silverback" males with several females and their offspring. Mountain gorillas differ, in that they frequently contain more than 20 individuals and have a multi-male structure (Robbins and Robbins, 2018). Their largely vegetation-based diet enables mountain gorillas to live in areas with limited amounts of fruit and to maintain stable groups. Western gorillas typically form one-male groups with one silverback, although multi-male and all-male groups (non-reproductive groups that contain no females) occur occasionally. Multi-male groups contain more than one silverback, but only rarely contain more than two.

Gorillas are among the few primate species in which both males and females disperse from their natal groups. Males emigrate to become solitary when they are blackbacks or young silverbacks (about 13–15 years of age). Males may be solitary for several years before forming a group. Male western gorillas tend to acquire groups around age 18, a few years later than mountain gorillas, who typically become dominant around 15 years of age. Western gorilla males almost exclusively follow the path of becoming solitary and forming new groups when females join them. Mature males never join established groups, so multi-male groups are extremely rare among western gorillas. When the silverback of a one-male group dies, the group disintegrates, as the adult females and immature offspring join a solitary male or another group. In contrast to western gorillas, about 40% of mountain gorilla groups are multi-male. Mountain gorilla males follow one of two strategies to become the leader of a

Figure AO1

Ape Distribution in Africa[1]

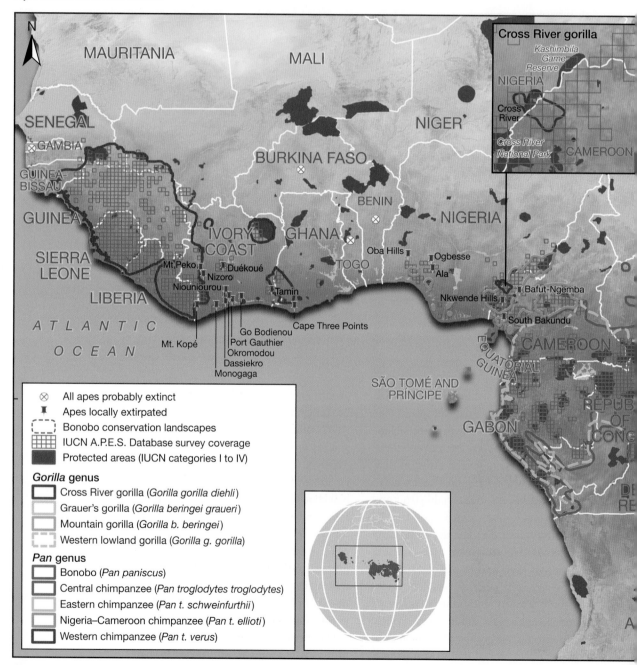

group: either they remain in the group and attempt a takeover from within, or they emigrate to become solitary males and eventually form new groups (Robbins and Robbins, 2018).

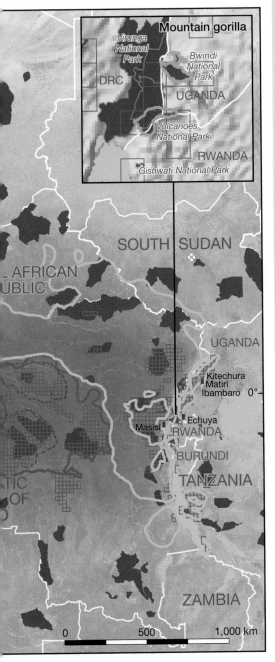

Orangutans are semi-solitary and have loosely defined communities. The basic social unit is a single individual, although adult females are usually found with one baby or one baby and an adolescent. Flanged adult males, characterized by fatty cheek pads and large size, lead a semi-solitary existence and are rather intolerant of other flanged males and, to a lesser degree, unflanged ones (Emery Thompson, Zhou and Knott, 2012; Utami-Atmoko et al., 2009b). Smaller, unflanged adult males are more tolerant of other orangutans. Adult females are the most social individuals and sometimes travel together for a few hours to several days, especially in Sumatra, where orangutans occasionally congregate when food is abundant (Wich et al., 2006). Male orangutans are the dispersing sex: upon reaching sexual maturity, they leave the area where they were born to establish their own range.

Gibbons are highly territorial and live in semi-permanent family groups, defending a territory to the exclusion of other gibbons. Both male and female gibbons disperse from their natal groups and establish their own territories (Leighton, 1987). Gibbons have been typified as forming socially monogamous family groups. Other studies, however, have revealed they are not necessarily sexually monogamous (Palombit, 1994). Notable exceptions include extra-pair copulations (mating outside of the pair bond), departure from the home territory to take up residence with neighboring individuals and male care of infants (Lappan, 2008; Palombit, 1994; Reichard, 1995). Research also indicates that the more northerly Cao Vit, Hainan and western black crested gibbons commonly form polygynous groups (Fan and Jiang, 2010; Fan et al., 2010; Zhou et al., 2008). There is no consensus regarding the underlying reasons for these variable social and mating structures; they may be natural or a by-product of small

Figure AO2

Ape Distribution in Asia[2]

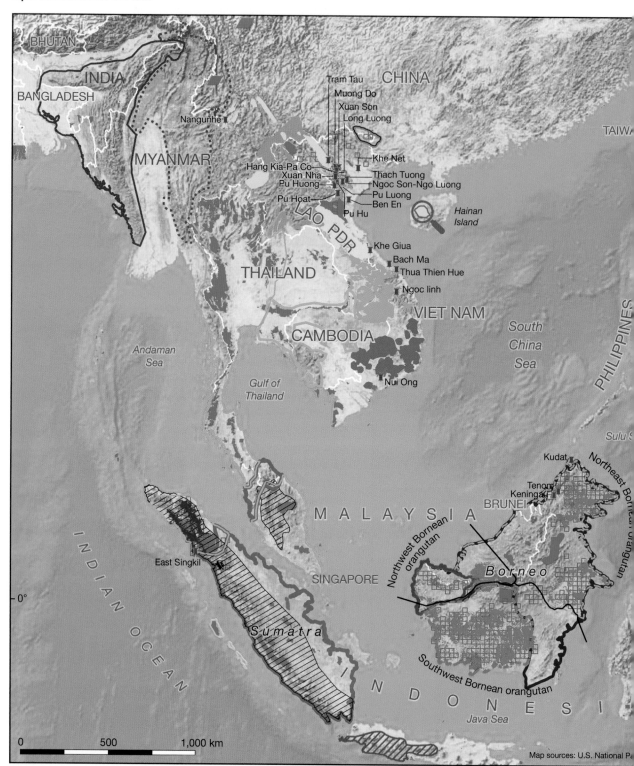

Map sources: U.S. National Pa...

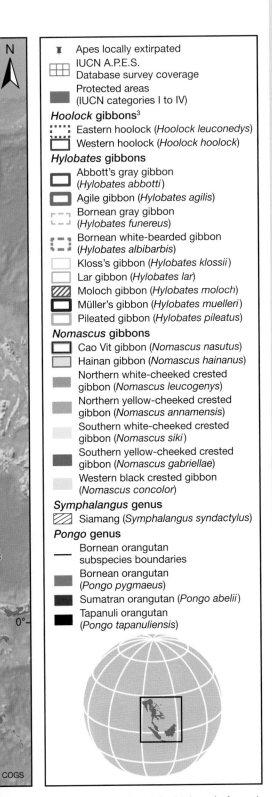

Legend:

⚗ Apes locally extirpated

⊞ IUCN A.P.E.S. Database survey coverage

▮ Protected areas (IUCN categories I to IV)

Hoolock gibbons[3]

⋯ Eastern hoolock (*Hoolock leuconedys*)

▭ Western hoolock (*Hoolock hoolock*)

Hylobates gibbons

▭ Abbott's gray gibbon (*Hylobates abbotti*)

▭ Agile gibbon (*Hylobates agilis*)

⌐ Bornean gray gibbon (*Hylobates funereus*)

▦ Bornean white-bearded gibbon (*Hylobates albibarbis*)

▭ Kloss's gibbon (*Hylobates klossii*)

▭ Lar gibbon (*Hylobates lar*)

▨ Moloch gibbon (*Hylobates moloch*)

▬ Müller's gibbon (*Hylobates muelleri*)

▭ Pileated gibbon (*Hylobates pileatus*)

Nomascus gibbons

▭ Cao Vit gibbon (*Nomascus nasutus*)

▦ Hainan gibbon (*Nomascus hainanus*)

▬ Northern white-cheeked crested gibbon (*Nomascus leucogenys*)

▬ Northern yellow-cheeked crested gibbon (*Nomascus annamensis*)

▭ Southern white-cheeked crested gibbon (*Nomascus siki*)

▬ Southern yellow-cheeked crested gibbon (*Nomascus gabriellae*)

▭ Western black crested gibbon (*Nomascus concolor*)

Symphalangus genus

▨ Siamang (*Symphalangus syndactylus*)

Pongo genus

— Bornean orangutan subspecies boundaries

▬ Bornean orangutan (*Pongo pygmaeus*)

▬ Sumatran orangutan (*Pongo abelii*)

▬ Tapanuli orangutan (*Pongo tapanuliensis*)

Note: Active collection of population data is ongoing for apes in various locations across their entire range. Updated information is available on the A.P.E.S. Portal (IUCN SSC, n.d.).

population sizes, compression scenarios or suboptimal habitats. Group demography only changes in the event of a death of one of the adults; there is no regular immigration into or emigration from these social groups. Gibbons in fragments are isolated from other groups and thus their dispersal is compromised, which can threaten the long-term sustainability of these populations. There is insufficient information about dispersal distances for sub-adult gibbons to determine maximum distances over which gibbons can disperse (perhaps with assistance of canopy bridges).

Habitat Type and Status

Most apes live in closed, moist, mixed tropical forest, occupying a range of various forest types, including lowland, swamp, seasonally inundated, gallery, coastal, submontane, montane and secondary regrowth forests. Some bonobo populations and eastern and western chimpanzees also live in forest–savannah mosaic landscapes. The largest populations of great apes are found below 500 m elevation, in the vast swamp forests of Asia and Africa (Williamson *et al.*, 2013). Bonobos have a discontinuous distribution at 300–700 m above sea level across undulating terrain in the DRC, south of the Congo River (Fruth *et al.*, 2016; Fruth, Williamson and Richardson, 2013). Eastern chimpanzees and eastern gorillas can range above 2,000 m altitude; orangutans can be found at above 1,000 m in both Sumatra and Borneo (Payne, 1988; Wich *et al.*, 2016; Williamson *et al.*, 2013).

Most chimpanzees and bonobos inhabit evergreen forests, but some populations also exist in deciduous woodland and drier savannah-dominated habitats interspersed with gallery forest. Although many populations inhabit protected areas, a great number of chimpanzee communities occur outside. Indeed, the majority of chimpanzees in

West Africa—in countries such as Guinea, Liberia and Sierra Leone—are present outside protected areas, and approximately 80% of central chimpanzees and western gorillas live outside of protected areas in Central Africa (Brncic, Amarasekaran and McKenna, 2010; Kormos et al., 2003; Strindberg et al., 2018; Tweh et al., 2015). Nowadays half of the wild orangutan population in Indonesian Borneo is surviving outside of protected forests, in areas that are prone to human development and transformation (Wich et al., 2012b). Gibbons range from montane to lowland peat swamp habitats, up to 1,700 m elevation (Guan et al., 2018). Many gibbons exist outside protected areas (Cheyne et al., 2016; Geissmann et al., 2013; Sarma, Krishna and Kumar, 2015).

Diet

Great apes are adapted to a plant diet, but all taxa consume insects, and some kill and eat small mammals. All apes may also target cultivars—that is, crops in fields or fruit and trees in orchards and plantations—especially when wild foods are scarce, but also because these may be preferred, since they are highly nutritious and easy to access. Succulent fruits are the main source of nutrition for all great apes, except at altitudes where mountain gorillas occur and few fleshy fruits are available. Although mainly fruit eaters, bonobos consume more terrestrial herbaceous vegetation, as well as aquatic plants, than chimpanzees (Fruth et al., 2016). Gorillas across their range rely more heavily than any other ape species on herbaceous vegetation, such as the leaves, stems and pith of understory vegetation, as well as leaves from shrubs and trees (Doran-Sheehy et al., 2009; Ganas et al., 2004; Masi, Cipolletta and Robbins, 2009; Wright et al., 2015; Yamagiwa and Basabose, 2009). Early research suggested that gorillas ate very little fruit, a finding that can be attributed to the fact that initial studies of their dietary patterns were conducted in the Virunga Volcanoes, the only habitat in which gorillas eat almost no fruit as it is virtually unavailable; these conclusions were adjusted once detailed studies were conducted on gorillas living in lower altitude habitats (Doran-Sheehy et al., 2009; Masi, Cipolletta and Robbins, 2009; Watts, 1984; Wright et al., 2015). While gorillas incorporate a notable amount of fruit into their diets when it is available, they are less frugivorous than chimpanzees, consuming vegetative matter even at times of high fruit availability (Head et al., 2011; Morgan and Sanz, 2006; Yamagiwa and Basabose, 2009).

Mountain gorillas are primarily terrestrial. Although western gorillas are more arboreal, they still primarily travel on the ground and not through the tree canopy. Wherever gorillas and chimpanzees are sympatric, dietary divisions between the species limit direct competition for food (Head et al., 2011). If the area of available habitat is restricted, such mechanisms for limiting competition are compromised (Morgan and Sanz, 2006). During certain periods of fruit scarcity, African apes concentrate on terrestrial herbs, leaves or bark.

Similarly, in Asia, orangutans feed primarily on fruits, but they consume more bark and young leaves when fruit sources become scarce; orangutans adapt their diet to what is available in the forest. Sumatran orangutans are more frugivorous than their Bornean relatives. In Borneo, they are known to feed on more than 1,500 plant species from 453 genera and 131 families (Russon et al., 2009). The list continues to grow as more data are collected. The resilience of the species and its ability to cope with drastic habitat changes are further illustrated by records of species presence in acacia plantations in East Kalimantan (Meijaard et al., 2010); a mosaic of mixed agriculture in Sumatra (Campbell-Smith et al., 2011); oil palm plantations in Borneo (Ancrenaz et al., 2015); and in forests exploited for timber (Ancrenaz et al., 2010; Wich et al., 2016). In these disturbed landscapes, Bornean orangutans rely more on young shoots and leaves than in primary forest.

Gibbons are reliant on forest ecosystems for food. Gibbon diets are characterized by high levels of fruit intake, dominated by figs and supplemented with young and mature leaves, as well as flowers, although siamangs are more folivorous (Bartlett, 2007; Cheyne, 2008; Elder, 2009; Palombit, 1997). Reliance on other protein sources, such as insects, bird eggs and small vertebrates, is probably underrepresented in the literature. The diet composition changes with the seasons and habitat type; flowers and young leaves dominate during the dry season in peat-swamp forests, while figs dominate in dipterocarp forests (Cheyne, 2010; Fan and Jiang, 2008; Lappan, 2009; Marshall and Leighton, 2006). While gibbons have not been observed to forage on crops (either on plantations or small-scale farms), it is possible that gibbons do exploit disturbed areas if necessary.

Home and Day Range

Foraging in complex forest environments requires spatial memory and mental mapping. Daily searches for food are generally restricted to a particular location, an area of forest that an individual ape or group knows well. Chimpanzees are capable of memorizing the individual locations of thousands of trees over many years (Normand and Boesch, 2009); the other ape species are likely to possess similar mental capacities. The area used habitually by an individual, group or community of a species is referred to as a home range. Establishing a home range helps apes to secure access to resources within it (Delgado, 2010; Mittermeier, Rylands and Wilson, 2013).

Chimpanzee home ranges can vary dramatically, ranging from around 10 to 90 km² (1,000–9,000 ha), depending on the habitat and resource distribution; populations in dryer and more open habitats exhibit larger home ranges (Herbinger, Boesch and Rothe, 2001; Pruetz and Herzog, 2017). Male chimpanzees are typically highly territorial and patrol the boundaries of their ranges. Parties of males may attack members of neighboring communities and some populations are known for their aggression (Williams et al., 2008). Victors benefit by gaining females or increasing the size of their range. Chimpanzees are generally highly intolerant of neighboring groups and inter-group encounters can result in lethal attacks among males in particular (Mitani, Watts and Amsler, 2010; Watts et al., 2006; Wilson et al., 2014). The frequency of such encounters can be exacerbated by shifts in home ranges linked to habitat loss, changes in habitat quality and disruptions in the chimpanzees' environment (such as road construction or logging).

The home range of bonobos also varies significantly, between 20 and 60 km² (2,000–6,000 ha), typically with extensive overlap between the ranges of different communities (Fruth, Williamson and Richardson, 2013). Bonobos do not engage in territorial defense or cooperative patrolling; encounters between members of different communities are more often characterized by excitement rather than conflict (Hohmann et al., 1999).

Eastern gorillas range over areas of 6–34 km² (600–3,400 ha), and western gorilla home ranges average 10–20 km² (1,000–2,000 ha)—and potentially up to 50 km² (5,000 ha) (Caillaud et al., 2014; Head et al., 2013; Robbins, 2011; Seiler et al., 2018; Williamson and Butynski, 2013a, 2013b). Gorillas are not territorial; they have overlapping home ranges that they do not actively defend. There is evidence, however, that they have distinct, exclusive core areas (the parts used the most by a group), suggesting that groups do partition their habitat (Seiler *et al.*, 2017).

As the density of gorillas increases, the degree of home range overlap can increase dramatically, as can the frequency of intergroup encounters, which may lead to increased fighting, injuries and mortality (Caillaud *et al.*, 2014). Encounters between groups can occur without visual contact; instead, silverback males exchange vocalizations and chestbeats until one or both groups move away. Most encounters between groups involve more than auditory contact and can escalate to include aggressive displays or fights (Bradley *et al.*, 2004; Robbins and Sawyer, 2007). Physical aggression is rare, but if contests escalate, fighting between silverbacks can be intense. In some cases, injuries sustained during intergroup interactions have become infected and led to deaths (Rosenbaum, Vecellio and Stoinski, 2016; Williamson, 2014).

A male orangutan's range encompasses several (smaller) female ranges. As high-status flanged males are able to monopolize both food and females to a degree, they may temporarily reside in a relatively small area—4–8 km² (400–800 ha) for Bornean males—even though the actual size of their home range could be much larger than 10 km² (1,000 ha). Orangutan home-range overlap is usually extensive, but flanged male orangutans establish personal space by emitting long calls. As long as distance is maintained, physical conflicts are rare; however, close encounters between adult males trigger aggressive displays that sometimes lead to fights. If an orangutan inflicts serious injury on his opponent, infection of the wounds can result in death (Knott, 1998).

African apes are semi-terrestrial and often rest on the ground during the daytime; in contrast, orangutans are almost exclusively arboreal, although the Bornean species use terrestrial locomotion more often than previously thought (Ancrenaz *et al.*, 2014). Bornean flanged adult males and adult females move an average of 200 m each day; unflanged adult males usually cover twice that distance. Sumatran orangutans move farther, but still less than 1 km each day on average (Singleton *et al.*, 2009). Orangutans can walk on the ground for considerable distances in all types of natural and human-made habitats, especially in Borneo (Ancrenaz *et al.*, 2014; Loken, Boer and Kasyanto, 2015; Loken, Spehar and Rayadin, 2013). Consequently, they are able to cross open artificial infrastructures to a certain extent. In Sabah, for example, orangutans have been seen crossing sealed and dust roads as long as the traffic is not too heavy. Increased terrestriality in orangutans increases sanitary concerns and the risk of contracting diseases to which they are not usually exposed in the tree canopy. At this stage, there is a dearth of information about such sanitary and health risks.

Territorial apes whose habitats are destroyed encounter great difficulties establishing a new territory nearby, where other animals are already established. Indeed, animals whose territory has been destroyed slowly die off. Unflanged adult males do not seem to have a strictly defined territory and move over large distances (Ancrenaz *et al.*, 2010).

The semi-terrestrial African apes range considerably longer distances and the most frugivorous roam several kilometers each day: mountain gorillas travel about 500 m–1 km per day; bonobos and western lowland gorillas average 2 km but sometimes reach 5–6 km; and chimpanzees travel 2–3 km, although they occasionally venture out on 10-km excursions. Savannah-dwelling chimpanzees generally range farther daily than their forest-dwelling counterparts. The distance travelled by gorillas declines with increasing availability of understory vegetation, varying between approximately 500 m and 3 km per day. As a result of their dietary patterns, they are restricted to moist forest habitats (at altitudes ranging from sea level to more than 3,000 m) and are not found in forest–savannah mosaics or gallery forests inhabited by chimpanzees and bonobos (Robbins, 2011).

Hylobates gibbon territories average 0.42 km² (42 ha), but there is considerable variation. The more northerly *Nomascus* taxa maintain larger territories—from about 0.13 to 0.72 km² (13–72 ha)—possibly in line with lower resource abundance at certain times of year in these more seasonal forests (Bartlett, 2007; Fan *et al.*, 2013). Less seasonal forests have increased resource abundance, yet gibbon density and territory size may not be directly correlated with these factors (Bryant *et al.*, 2015; Hamard, Cheyne and Nijman, 2010; Zhang *et al.*, 2014).

Nesting

Most apes not only feed in trees, but also rest, socialize and sleep in them, although gorillas are largely terrestrial. Being large-brained, highly intelligent mammals, they need long periods of sleep. All great apes build nests or beds in which they spend the night; bonobos and chimpanzees may also build daytime nests in trees or on the ground to rest, while gorillas nest primarily on the ground. All weaned great ape individuals will build a nest to sleep in at night. Tree nests are usually constructed between 10 and 20 m above ground (Fruth, Tagg and Stewart, 2018). Variation in nesting height is influenced by environmental variables such as rainfall, temperature, habitat structure, availability of material, predator presence, and demographic parameters such as the sex or the age of the individual, as well as social factors such as transferred habits (Fruth and Hohmann, 1996). All great apes may reuse nests, although the frequency of reuse depends largely on the availability of sleeping site locations and material for construction (Fruth, Tagg and Stewart, 2018). Bonobos prefer to nest in areas with abundant food, while sleeping site association with fruiting trees is more variable in chimpanzees (Fruth, Tagg and Stewart, 2018; Serckx *et al.*, 2014). However, both chimpanzees and bonobos show preferences when it comes to nesting in specific tree species (Fruth, Tagg and Stewart, 2018).

Reproduction

Male great apes reach sexual maturity between the ages of 8 and 18 years, with chimpanzees attaining adulthood at 8–15 years, bonobos at 10, eastern gorillas around 12–16 and western gorillas at 18 (Williamson *et al.*, 2013). Orangutan males mature between the ages of 8 and 16 years, but they may not develop flanges for another 20 years (Utami-Atmoko *et al.*, 2009a). Female apes become reproductively active between the ages of 6 and 12 years: gorillas at 6–7 years, chimpanzees at 7–8, bonobos at 9–12 and orangutans at 10–11. They tend to give birth to their first offspring between the ages of 8 and 16: gorillas at 10 (with an average range of 8–14 years), chimpanzees at 13.5 years (with a mean of 9.5–15.4 years at different sites), bonobos at 13–15 years and orangutans at 15–16 years (van Noordwijk *et al.*, 2018).

Pregnancy length in gorillas and orangutans is about the same as for humans; it is slightly shorter in chimpanzees and bonobos, at 7.5–8 months (van Noordwijk *et al.*, 2018; Wallis, 1997). Apes usually give birth to one infant at a time, although twin births do occur (Goossens *et al.*, 2011). Births are not seasonal; however, conception requires females to be in good health. Chimpanzees and bonobos are more likely to ovulate when fruit is abundant, so in some populations there are seasonal peaks in the number of conceiving females, with contingent peaks in birth rate during particular months (Anderson, Nordheim and Boesch, 2006; Emery Thompson and Wrangham, 2008). Bornean orangutans living in highly seasonal dipterocarp forests are most likely to conceive during mast fruiting events, when fatty seeds are plentiful (Knott, 2005). Sumatran orangutans do not face such severe constraints (Marshall et al., 2009). Meanwhile, gorillas are less dependent on seasonal foods and show no seasonality in their reproduction.

Gibbon females have their first offspring at around 9 years of age. Data from captivity suggest that gibbons become sexually mature as early as 5.5 years of age (Geissmann, 1991). Interbirth intervals are in the range of 2–4 years, and gestation lasts about seven months (Bartlett, 2007). Captive individuals have lived upwards of 40 years; gibbon longevity in the wild is unknown but thought to be considerably shorter. Since gibbons mature relatively late and have long interbirth intervals, their reproductive lifetime may be only 10–20 years (Palombit, 1992). Population replacement in gibbons is therefore relatively slow.

All apes have slow reproductive rates; mothers invest considerable time in a single offspring and infants are slow to develop and mature. Infants sleep with their mothers until they are weaned (4–5 years in African apes; 5–6 years in Bornean orangutans; 7 years in Sumatran orangutans) or a sibling is born. Weaning marks the end of infancy for African apes around the age of 3–6 years, but orangutan infants remain dependent on their mothers until they reach 7–9 years of age (van Noordwijk et al., 2009). Females cannot become preg-

nant while an infant is nursing because suckling inhibits the reproductive cycle (Stewart, 1988; van Noordwijk et al., 2013). Consequently, births are widely spaced, occurring on average every 4–7 years in African apes, every 6–8 years in Bornean orangutans and every 9 years in Sumatran orangutans. Interbirth intervals can be shortened if a member of the same species—typically an unrelated adult male—kills unweaned offspring (Harcourt and Greenberg, 2001; Hrdy, 1979). Infanticide has not been observed in orangutans or bonobos, but if a female gorilla or chimpanzee with an infant transfers to a different group, her offspring is likely to be killed by a male in her new group, resulting in early resumption of her reproductive cycle (Knott et al., 2019; Watts, 1989).

Long-term research on mountain gorillas and chimpanzees has allowed female lifetime reproductive success to be evaluated. The mean birth rate is 0.2–0.3 births per adult female per year, or one birth for every adult female every 3.3–5.0 years. Mountain gorilla females produce an average of 3.6 offspring during their lifetimes; similarly, chimpanzees produce 1.0–4.3 offspring who survive into adulthood (Emery Thompson, 2013; Robbins et al., 2011).

Key points to be noted are that: 1) documenting the biology of long-lived species takes decades of research due to their slow rates of reproduction, and 2) ape populations that have declined in numbers are likely to take several generations to recover (generation time among apes is 18–25 years) (IUCN, 2019). These factors make apes far more vulnerable than smaller, faster-breeding species. Orangutans have the slowest life history of any mammal, with later age at first reproduction, longer interbirth intervals and longer generation times than African apes; as a result, they are the most susceptible to loss (Wich, de Vries and Ancrenaz, 2009; Wich et al., 2009).

Acknowledgments

Principal authors: Annette Lanjouw,[4] Helga Rainer[5] and Alison White[6]

Socioecology section: Marc Ancrenaz,[7] Susan M. Cheyne,[8] Tatyana Humle,[9] Benjamin M. Rawson,[10] Martha M. Robbins[11] and Elizabeth A. Williamson[12]

Endnotes

1   The Arcus Foundation commissioned the ape distribution maps (Figures AO1 and AO2) for *State of the Apes*, so as to provide accurate and up-to-date illustrations of range data. This volume also features maps created by contributors who used ape range data from different sources. As a consequence, the maps may not all align exactly.

2   See Endnote 1.

3   The newly identified Gaoligong or Skywalker hoolock (*Hoolock tianxing*) does not appear on the map, as there is no detailed distribution information for the species. To date, it has only been seen in eastern Myanmar and south-western China.

4   Arcus Foundation (www.arcusfoundation.org/).

5   Arcus Foundation (www.arcusfoundation.org/).

6   Independent consultant.

7   HUTAN–Kinabatangan Orang-utan Conservation Programme (www.hutan.org.my).

8   Borneo Nature Foundation (www.borneonaturefoundation.org).

9   University of Kent (www.kent.ac.uk/sac).

10   WWF-Vietnam (vietnam.panda.org/).

11   Max Planck Institute for Evolutionary Anthropology (www.eva.mpg.de).

12   University of Stirling (www.stir.ac.uk/about/faculties/natural-sciences/).

Photo: Ape hunting and trade refer to the illegal capture, killing, transport, sale and possession of live apes, their body parts or meat. © Paul Hilton/Earth Tree Images

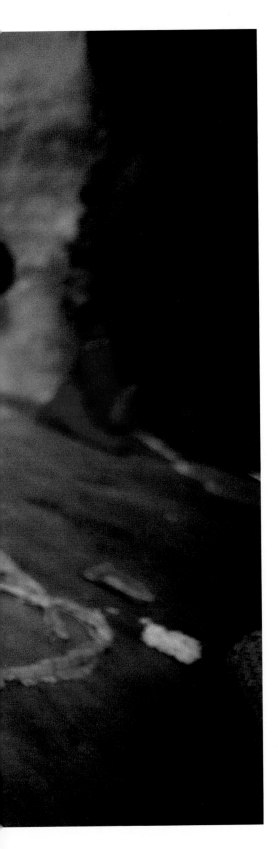

INTRODUCTION

Section 1: Killing, Capture, Trade and Conservation

This, the fourth in the *State of the Apes* series, focuses on the impact of killing, capture and trade on ape conservation and welfare. The first three volumes of *State of the Apes* briefly considered these issues in relation to extractive industries, industrial agriculture and infrastructure development (Arcus Foundation, 2014, 2015, 2018). This volume explores these relationships more explicitly, featuring in-depth analysis of the hunting of and trade in apes, the impact on wild ape populations and captured individuals, the relevant legal and regulatory framework, the cultural and socioeconomic drivers behind ape hunting, and the responses to these drivers, including conservation initiatives and law enforcement efforts.

Trade in live apes, parts and products occurs across multiple scales, from the local to the global. The drivers of this trade are dynamic, reflecting evolving consumer preferences and economic fluctuations. Illegal hunting and the ape trade thrive under a variety of circumstances, including when law enforcement is inadequate; corruption is rampant; law enforcement officials are not trained to identify trafficked species or conduct meaningful investigations; infrastructure development permits better access to forests, markets and transportation; people associate ape meat consumption or owning a pet with status; and enhanced connectivity allows for the spread of social media. These and other factors complicate efforts to curb the demand for apes and to protect ape populations. As a result, interventions to date have not been enough to halt their overall slide towards extinction.

With the aim of helping conservationists, local communities, international agencies and other stakeholders reverse that trend, this volume of *State of the Apes* provides collected insights, tools and techniques for use in strategies to stem the demand for apes, as well as the supply. Ultimately, this volume is a call to engage with the complex drivers of the hunting, buying and selling of apes with a view to securing their conservation and well-being over the long term.

The *State of the Apes* Series

Commissioned by the Arcus Foundation, the *State of the Apes* series strives to raise awareness of the impacts of human activities on all great ape and gibbon populations. Apes are vulnerable to a range of threats that are primarily driven by humans, including hunting that supplies the trade in wild meat, body parts and live animals; deforestation and degradation of habitat; and the transmission of disease. Interactions between humans and apes continue to increase as development and human population growth drive further incursions into spaces that apes inhabit. By using apes as an example, this publication series aims to underscore the importance of wider species conservation.

State of the Apes covers all non-human ape species, namely bonobos, chimpanzees, gibbons, gorillas and orangutans, as well as

their habitats. Ape ranges are found throughout the tropical belt of Africa and South and Southeast Asia. Robust statistics on the status and welfare of apes are derived from the Ape Populations, Environments and Surveys (A.P.E.S.) Portal (IUCN SSC, n.d.). Abundance estimates for the different ape taxa are presented in the Abundance Annex, available on the *State of the Apes* website at www.stateoftheapes.com. The annex is updated with each new volume in the series, to allow for comparisons over time. Details on the socioecology and geographic range of each species are provided in the Apes Overview.

Each volume in the *State of the Apes* series is divided into two sections. Section 1 focuses on the thematic topic of interrogation, which in this case is killing, capture and trade. The immediate objectives are to provide accurate information on the current situation, present various perspectives and, wherever applicable, highlight best practice. In the longer term, the key findings and messages are intended to stimulate debate, multi-stakeholder collaboration and changes to policies and practice that can facilitate the reconciliation of economic development and the conservation of biodiversity. Section 2 is included in every volume to present details relating to the broader status and welfare of apes, both in their natural habitat and in captivity.

An Overview of the Ape Trade

The hunting of apes and the trade in live apes, their meat, body parts and products involve a series of illegal activities, from the killing or capture of individuals, to their transport and sale (see Box I.1). The live trade entails the capture, trafficking and sale of living wild apes (see Chapter 4); the wild meat trade supplies fresh or smoked ape meat for human consumption, while traffickers of body parts and products offer their goods for cultural, medicinal or symbolic use (see Chapter 3). The drivers of ape hunting and trade vary across species, locations and socio-economic conditions. On the supply side, strong economic incentives motivate the illegal trade in protected species, particularly for the live trade (see Figure I.1), while poor law enforcement, corruption and challenges in species identification (including of body parts) hamper efforts to curtail the trade (Clough and May, 2018; Stiles *et al.*, 2013).

The hunting of apes and the associated trade have direct and indirect impacts on their conservation and well-being. The primary direct impact is population decline or local extinction in areas where they are hunted (Tranquilli *et al.*, 2012). Hunting also affects ape behavior and ecology, leading to changes in social grouping, communication and interaction, as well as feeding and ranging behaviors. Among chimpanzees, human pressure in the form of hunting and habitat destruction can also increase the degree of intergroup conflict and lead to a higher rate of intraspecific killing (Williams *et al.*, 2008). Indirectly, hunting affects ecosystem functions in ape habitats, for example by limiting the reproduction of flora that are reliant on apes for seed dispersal and by having an impact on the abundance of chimpanzee prey species, such as monkeys (Effiom *et al.*, 2013; McGraw, 2007).

Determining the level of threat that the illegal trade poses to global ape populations is challenging, as many activities along the supply chain are conducted covertly. Threat levels may be ascertained by type of illegal trade or by ape species. The live ape trade attracts the most media attention and therefore greater efforts are focused on curtailing it (Shukman and Piranty, 2017); it remains unclear, however, which of the three types of trade—that in live animals, body parts or wild meat—poses the greatest threat to global ape populations (O. Drori and K. Ammann, personal communication, 2017).

Determining threat levels across species is similarly difficult, due largely to limited data, but some studies have been able to show that the killing of apes accounts for a significant loss of life. An interview-based survey in Borneo, for example, estimated that between 630 and 1,357 orangutans were killed between September 2008 and

---

BOX I.1

Hunting vs. Killing and Capture: A Note on Terminology

"Poaching"—which is illegal by definition—and "hunting" can involve the killing, injury (which may be fatal) or capture of wild animals. Ape body parts and products may be harvested for food; medicines or substances perceived to have medicinal properties; use in ritual or traditional practices; or personal fulfillment. Captured apes may be kept or supplied into the live animal trade, including for use in entertainment facilities, as photo props in the tourism industry and as pets (Etiendem, Hens and Pereboom, 2011; Fa, Currie and Meeuwig, 2003; Hastie and McCrea-Steele, 2014).

The terms "poaching" and "hunting" are often associated with the acquisition of meat or parts, and thus with the death of an animal. As this volume demonstrates, however, many apes are captured alive. Regardless of whether apes are killed or captured, their removal from the wild has implications for the survival of the species in their natural habitats (Stiles et al., 2013).

Apes are also killed for non-harvesting reasons, such as in retaliation for crop-raiding or damaging property, or in connection with fear for personal or community safety. Such killings are not always perceived as the results of hunting (Davis et al., 2013).

As the title of this volume indicates, the key hunting-related threats to the viability and well-being of ape populations are killing and capture.

FIGURE I.1

Value Changes from Forest to Foreign Buyer for Bonobos, Chimpanzees, Gorillas and Orangutans

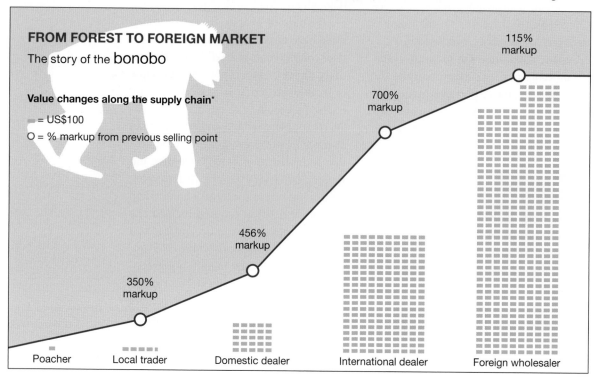

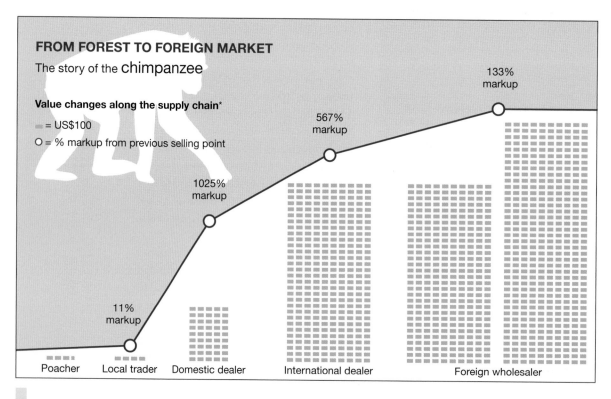

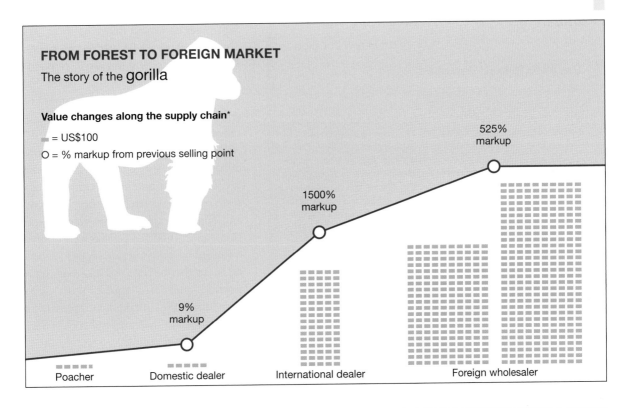

FROM FOREST TO FOREIGN MARKET
The story of the gorilla

Value changes along the supply chain*

■ = US$100
O = % markup from previous selling point

525%
markup

1500%
markup

9%
markup

Poacher　　　Domestic dealer　　　International dealer　　　Foreign wholesaler

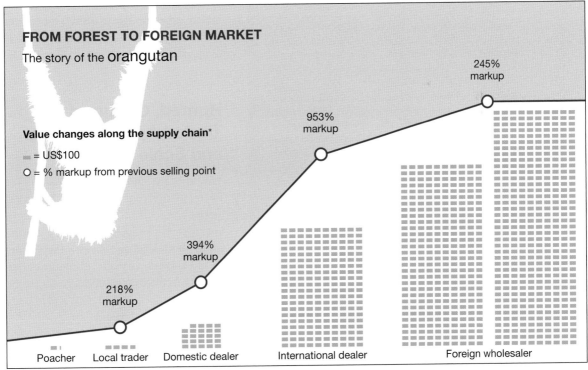

FROM FOREST TO FOREIGN MARKET
The story of the orangutan

245%
markup

953%
markup

Value changes along the supply chain*

■ = US$100
O = % markup from previous selling point

394%
markup

218%
markup

Poacher　Local trader　Domestic dealer　　　International dealer　　　Foreign wholesaler

Note: * The original research uncovered a range of prices at each point in the supply chain. For graphical purposes, the study utilized the upper value for each segment of the supply chain.
Source: Clough and May (2018, pp. 8, 9, 25). © Global Financial Integrity 2018

GLOBAL FINANCIAL INTEGRITY

The Apes Seizure Database

The Apes Seizure Database was launched at the 17th Conference of the Parties of the Convention on International Trade in Endangered Species of Wild Fauna and Flora (CITES) in October 2016 to address a significant lack of verified qualitative data on the scale of the illegal trade in great apes, including live animals, body parts and meat (CITES, 2016; GRASP, n.d.-a). Developed by the Great Apes Survival Partnership (GRASP) and the United Nations Environment Programme World Conservation Monitoring Centre (UNEP-WCMC), it is the first global online database to gauge the scale and scope of poaching and illegal trade in great apes (GRASP, n.d.-b; UNEP-WCMC, n.d.). The aim is to assist national authorities, civil society and businesses to monitor the trade patterns, develop longer-term strategies and channel resources effectively to combat the trade.

As requested by the CITES Standing Committee, GRASP and the Primate Specialist Group of the International Union for Conservation of Nature Species Survival Commission prepared a report on the status of great apes and the relative impact of illegal trade and other pressures on their status (GRASP and IUCN, 2018). Recommendations from this report, including the call on CITES parties to contribute to the Apes Seizure Database, are reflected in an amendment to the resolution on great apes, adopted at the 18th Conference of the Parties, in August 2019 (CITES, 2019b).

Great ape sanctuaries, protected area authorities and other such actors are the key providers of relevant and case-specific seizure information. All data, once submitted, is validated by a great ape expert panel, the Technical Advisory Group. The database is hosted at database.un-grasp.org, but given the sensitive nature of the data, access to the database is restricted. GRASP and UNEP-WCMC manage the data providers' user rights, while only staff members of GRASP and UNEP-WCMC have access to all reported data.

Phase 1, including the development of basic technical infrastructure, is nearly completed and the database is operational. Ongoing activities include the development of an interactive user manual to attract regular submissions of new data, as well as refinement of a robust data validation process, the cornerstone of an independent and credible platform.

As data become truly useful when they are analyzed and overlaid with other contextual information, Phase 2 of the database, which is contingent on new funding, is to provide the following capabilities:

- the creation of automatic, web-based, geospatial data analysis tools to identify the state, trends and hot spots regarding poaching and illegal trade, including a public annual report to highlight main findings;
- the development of a sampling and export protocol to identify seized great apes or body parts using genetic data, as a way of supporting analysis of illegal activities and enabling repatriation of live apes to their country of origin, potentially with the help of the facial recognition algorithm "ChimpFace," developed by Conservation X Labs (Timmins, 2019); and
- geographic and sectoral expansion of the database to increase involvement of West African stakeholders, customs organizations and other actors that are currently under-represented.

September 2009, and that roughly 2,000–3,000 animals were killed per year on average within the lifetimes of the survey respondents (Meijaard et al., 2011, 2012). Given that fewer than 105,000 Bornean orangutans remain in the wild, these harvest rates are categorically unsustainable (Ancrenaz et al., 2016; IUCN SSC, n.d.; see Box 1.3). Similarly, in Africa, an investigation into the scale of the wild meat trade in the Cross-Sanaga rivers region that stretches across Cameroon and Nigeria estimated that about 2,400 chimpanzees and 700 gorillas were hunted on an annual basis (Fa et al., 2006). In view of the fact that the Nigeria–Cameroon chimpanzee population comprises 3,500–9,000 individuals, this offtake rate represents a major threat to their survival (IUCN SSC, n.d.; Oates et al., 2016).

The complicity of corrupt authorities thwarts attempts to monitor the scale of the problem, while motivations for hunting and trade are also challenging to counter. Recent initiatives have sought to address the current lack of verified qualitative data on the scale of illegal trade in great apes (see Box 1.2).

Hunted, Captured and Traded Apes: Typology and Scale

Wild apes are hunted, captured and traded for many different purposes, which vary across species and regions. The trade in apes is part of a much larger global wildlife trade—both legal and illegal—that occurs in and between virtually all countries (see Box 1.3). Its three main subcategories are the trade in live apes, in wild meat and in body parts, as discussed below.

The Live Ape Trade

The live trade entails the illegal capture of living wild apes—typically infants—for sale on the local or international market. Locally traded apes are primarily used as pets; they may serve as playthings for hunters' families, status symbols for rich and influential personalities, highlights of private zoos or ranches, or exotic tokens and even "rescues" (Caldecott, Miles and Annan, 2005; Nijman, 2005b; Stiles, 2016). Internationally traded apes are generally used as prestige pets or in entertainment, such as ape boxing attrac-

tions in Asia (Kerr, 2017). They may also be used to attract tourists to amusement parks, safaris and circuses. The use of apes—particularly gibbons—as photo props for tourist photo sessions on Asian beaches is also widespread (Stiles *et al.*, 2013).

Due to inadequate law enforcement, the trade in live apes is very difficult to measure, although some studies have investigated certain aspects of it (Nijman, 2005b;

FIGURE I.2

Main International Routes for Illegal Trafficking of Great Apes

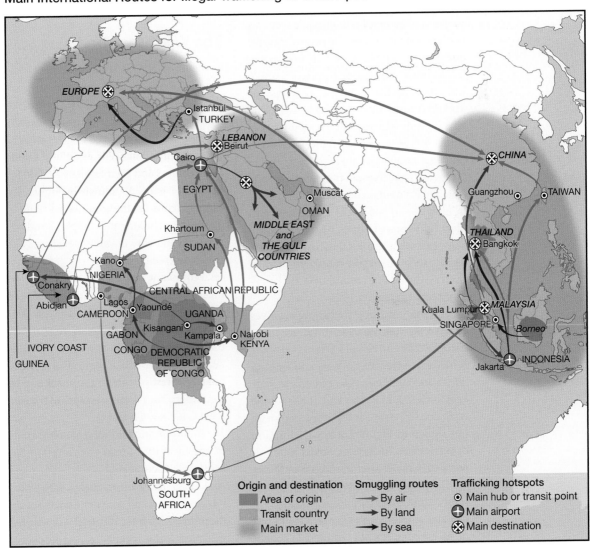

Source: Stiles *et al.* (2013, p. 32), based on the original map by Riccardo Pravettoni

Nijman *et al.*, 2017). In many cases, estimates of the scale of the trade are based on confiscations and the number of apes held in sanctuaries, even though these figures probably represent only a small portion of the trade (Stiles *et al.*, 2013). For a detailed assessment of the trade in live apes, see Chapter 4.

The international live trade is sophisticated, lucrative and involves many rich and powerful players, including collectors, middlemen and transporters. In Africa, apes appear to be captured and "stocked" so that demand can be met without significant delay (O. Drori and K. Ammann, personal communication, 2017). Transportation methods vary along the supply chain; when it comes to air travel, smugglers use private, charter and commercial planes of well-known airline companies, including Togo-based ASKY, Ethiopian Airlines, Kenya Airways and Turkish Airlines, often moving between carriers (K. Ammann, personal communication, April 2017; Stiles, 2016). Traffickers tend to rely on a number of approaches to enable transfer of apes: they use fraudulent permits from the Convention on International Trade in Endangered Species of Wild Fauna and Flora (CITES; see Chapter 6); they integrate apes with other species that may be traded legally, such as certain monkeys; or they smuggle them using concealment in a carry-on or cargo container (Stiles, 2016).

International ape trafficking involves complex networks of actors in various countries (See Box 1.4). Figure I.2 shows key trade routes that originate in West and Central Africa and Southeast Asia and link to markets in China, Malaysia and Thailand; the Arabian Gulf states; and Europe. Although not shown in Figure I.2, key destination countries also include ex-Soviet states, as revealed in undercover investigations (Stiles, 2016). Ape transport networks are in a constant state of flux, responding to changes in demand, as well as surveillance, law enforcement, the complicity of corrupt CITES officials and flight scheduling.

Little is known about how orangutans are trafficked along Asian trade routes. Evidence suggests they may be transported by boat from ports in Borneo to Singapore and then by road or rail to Kuala Lumpur or Bangkok (Stiles, 2016). Orangutan traffickers are also known to take boats to Jakarta and then planes to Bangkok, Muscat, Guangzhou and other Chinese cities. While most of the live trade in gibbons appears to be domestic rather than international, limited evidence indicates that the Middle East and Singapore are destinations for this species (C. Kalaweit, personal communication, April 2017).

The Wild Meat Trade

Across most ape range countries of tropical Africa and Asia, the wild meat trade involves the sale of fresh or smoked ape meat for human consumption. The meat is usually butchered and either used to meet subsistence consumption needs, especially among local hunters and their families, or sold for economic gain. As shown in Figure I.3, supply chains for the commercial trade in ape meat can be long and complex. Products generally increase in value at each stage of the chain (see Figure I.1).

Within ape range states, the rate of ape meat consumption is generally associated with cost and taste, as well as status, particularly in urban areas (Nijman, 2005a). The international trade in ape meat, which is far more lucrative than the local one, is also linked to prestige, culture and status among consumers. For a detailed analysis of the wild meat trade, see Chapter 3.

The domestic and international trade in ape meat for human consumption has been well documented across Africa and Asia.[1] Less clear is the frequency with which it is consumed, and whether food is always the primary driver for killing apes, or whether wild meat is also acquired as a by-product of the trade in body parts or live animals, such

FIGURE I.3

A Wild Meat Supply Chain

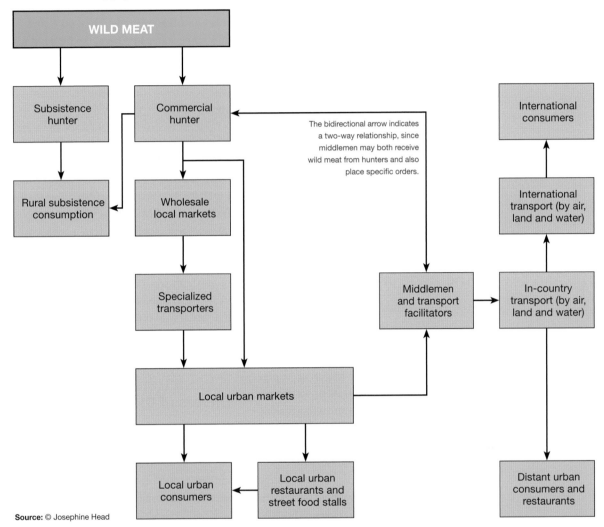

Source: © Josephine Head

as when hunters kill mothers to capture their young. People who kill orangutans do so primarily for food, while traditional medicine and the live infant trade account for just 3% of the killings each (Davis *et al.*, 2013). In West and Central Africa consumption of ape meat is widespread and ape meat is regularly found for sale in local markets. It is not known what proportion of ape meat is exported from Africa, as data on the international trade is limited, but a 2006 study of illegal markets in Brussels, Chicago, London,

Los Angeles, Montreal, New York, Paris and Toronto identified 27 records of chimpanzee and gorilla parts for sale (Brown, 2006). A few years later, in 2011, wild meat tested on a market stall in central England was found to be from a chimpanzee (Ellicott, 2011).

Anecdotal evidence suggests that ape meat that is exported to the United States and Europe is part of the wider illegal trade in wild meat. Customs data on confiscations of wild ape meat in Swiss airports between 2011 and 2013 indicate that the vast majority came from Africa, while less that 2% arrived with passengers from Asia or the Middle East (Wood *et al.*, 2014). Evidence suggests that in the UK, the illegal wildlife trade operates through established smuggling routes of organized criminals (see Box I.5). Based on one report, 50% of those prosecuted for wildlife trade have previous drug- and firearm-related convictions (Cook, Roberts and Lowther, 2002). While various studies examine the international wild meat trade, assessing what percentage of internationally traded wild meat comes from primates, and specifically apes, remains challenging (Brashares *et al.*, 2011; Chaber *et al.*, 2010; Wood *et al.*, 2014).

The Trade in Parts

The trade in ape body parts occurs in countries of origin and beyond. Commonly traded parts—such as heads, hands, feet and bones—tend to be ascribed cultural or symbolic significance. Within ape range states their consumption or possession is linked to a range of beliefs, including making children stronger, healing fractures, curing arthritis, improving agility and protecting houses against fire (CITES and GRASP, 2006; Nforngwa, 2017; Zhou *et al.*, 2005). Although not covered in this volume, there is a suggestion that ape skulls are considered prized trophies in Western countries, particularly the United States, while in China, bones are in high demand for use in traditional medicine (Nforngwa, 2017). For more details on the trade in ape body parts, see Chapter 3.

Experts disagree on the scale of the trade in ape body parts. Some investigators of wildlife trafficking point to a rapid increase in demand, indicating that gorillas and chimpanzees are being hunted vigorously to feed a growing international trade in skulls and other body parts. They argue that this trade has all but supplanted the meat-based black market. Others maintain that the market is

old, that the associated crimes are relatively uncommon, and that the body parts are simply by-products of the trade in wild meat and live animals. They note that in ape-range states in Africa, the demand for hands and bones for medicinal purposes is scattered, small-scale and largely opportunistic (O. Drori and K. Ammann, personal communication, 2017).

Supply chains for the wild ape meat and body parts tend to overlap. Body parts from Africa largely transit through Cameroon, Nigeria and the West African coast, while much of the Asian trade originates in Indonesia and Malaysia (Stiles, 2016). The international supply chains begin with small-scale poachers in African and Southeast Asian forests, who supply game to a network of dealers, traders and traffickers, who smuggle the body parts—often alongside butchered wild meat—to final destinations, including in China, Europe and the United States (Brown, 2006).

Drivers of the Ape Trade

People become involved in the wild ape trade for various reasons, many of which depend on personal and local conditions, such as limited economic opportunities, a lack of affordable alternative protein sources, poverty, conflict and insecurity, cultural beliefs, urbanization and the commercialization of the illegal trade at the regional level (De Merode and Cowlishaw, 2006; Kümpel *et al.*, 2010). Other drivers of the trade include new and improved infrastructure that provides increased access to markets via shipping and flight routes, corruption and technology (Cook, Roberts and Lowther, 2002; Stiles, 2016). The extent to which the trades in live animals, wild meat and body parts influence each other is difficult to assess, not only because of the dearth of reliable, comprehensive data, but also because of the dynamic nature of these markets.

Chapter 2 presents a detailed exploration of the cultural drivers of the live ape trade, including cultural norms (Malone *et al.*, 2003; Nijman *et al.*, 2017). Such dynamics are also influenced and facilitated by social media (see Box I.6). Ape meat consumption is variously driven by taste, customs, tradition and the desire for prestige. People acquire ape body parts as trophies or for use in traditional healing and religious practices (CITES and GRASP, 2006; Nforngwa, 2017; Zhou *et al.*, 2005). Economic gain and local value are also key drivers of the illegal trade. In comparison to the trade in meat and parts, the trade in live infant and juvenile apes is the more lucrative, with an average annual value of between US$2.1 million and US$8.8 million (Clough and May, 2018). In some regions ape meat that is consumed locally can be significantly more affordable and more widely available than chicken, pork or beef (Bassett, 2005; Olupot, McNeilage and Plumptre, 2009; Willcox and Nambu, 2007). The socioeconomic factors driving the illegal ape trade are examined in Chapters 3 and 4.

Photo: Drivers of the ape trade at the regional level include limited economic opportunities in rural areas, a lack of affordable alternative protein sources, poverty, conflict and insecurity, cultural beliefs, urbanisation and the commercialisation of the illegal trade. © David Greer

BOX I.3

The Global Wildlife Trade

Wildlife trade—the sale or exchange of animals, plants, fungi, their parts or their derivatives—affects a wide variety of species around the globe and is conducted within and between virtually all countries (Broad, Mulliken and Roe, 2003; Nijman, 2010; Phelps et al., 2010; Rosen and Smith, 2010). The various market segments vary in scale; trades range from the exchange of a small sum for a single animal or plant within a village to the global commercial timber industry worth billions of US dollars per year. The illegal trade in wildlife may appear to overshadow the legal trade, particularly since a few charismatic mammals—such as elephants, pangolins, rhinos and tigers—seem to attract disproportionate funding, policy attention, public awareness campaigns and research (Sas-Rolfes et al., 2019; Scheffers et al., 2019; World Bank Group, 2016). Although much of the trade in wildlife is legal and regulated with long-term sustainability goals in mind, illegal trade persists and, in some areas, it is flourishing (Bergin and Nijman, 2020). The trade in wildlife, both legal and illegal, acts as a significant barrier to the conservation of wild populations of animals, threatens ecosystems through the introduction of non-native species, and can pose a risk to human and animal health by facilitating disease transmission (Karesh et al., 2005; Nijman, 2010; Westphal et al., 2008).

While there are no reliable estimates of the value or volumes of all wildlife trade—that is, totals for the domestic and international, as well as the legal and illegal trade—data are available for the international portion of the legal trade. The United Nations International Trade Statistics Database, known as UN Comtrade, is a global depository for trade data. States report their statistics, including volume and import value, on thousands of articles and products using Harmonized System codes, such as 01061100 for live primates (Chan et al., 2015; Nijman, 2017; World Customs Organization, 2017). In contrast, the trade database of the Convention on International Trade in Endangered Species of Wild Fauna and Flora (CITES) only contains data relating to species that are listed on one of the three CITES appendices, and reporting can be biased (CITES, n.d.-b; Phelps et al., 2010). The database currently lists dozens of trade terms for the form in which a species can be traded—such as "ears," "live," and "plate"—which makes it difficult to identify how many individuals are involved in any trade; complicating matters is a lack of consistency in the use of these terms.

Based on UN Comtrade import data, the wildlife trade-monitoring network TRAFFIC estimated the value of global wildlife imports in 2009 at more than US$323 billion, which suggests that the current annual value of the legal trade exceeds US$400 billion (Newton and Cantarello, 2014). Timber and fisheries, excluding aquaculture, account for more than 50% and 30% of this value, respectively, and ornamental plants

Table I.1

The Monetary Value of Examples of the Global Legal Wildlife Trade

Wildlife traded		Value (US$ million)*
Live animals	Birds (caged and birds of prey)	62
	Primates	110
	Ornamental fish	376
Animal products for decoration and clothing	Mammal furs and fur products	5,828
	Ornamental coral and shells	125
	Reptile skin	372
Animal products for food	Game meat	534
	Frog legs	58
	Edible snails	87
	Fisheries (excluding aquaculture)	100,199
Plants	Medicinal	1,457
	Ornamental plants	16,079
	Timber	169,910

Notes: * Values originally reported in euros for the year 2005; converted to US dollars and corrected for inflation to 2020 values (EUR 1 = US$1.1; cumulative rate of inflation = 32.5%).

Data source: Engler and Parry-Jones (2007, table 1)

and non-wood forest products account for around 5% each (see Table I.1). CITES trade data does not provide insight into the monetary value of the trade, but analysis of 40 years of import records reveals that, in terms of individuals, plants dominate with 86%, while reptiles form the next-largest group (7%) and fish make up less than 1% (Harfoot *et al.*, 2018).

The United Nations Office on Drugs and Crime estimates that the illegal wildlife trade, excluding illicit timber and unregulated fisheries, is worth US$8–10 billion, while timber accounts for another US$7 billion and illegal and unregulated fisheries possibly double that (Newton and Cantarello, 2014). Since most of the public attention and enforcement efforts are focused on a few illegally traded mammals, seizure data reflect that bias: all together, big cats, elephants (ivory), pangolins and rhinos (horn) make up 25% of the monetary value of global seizures. Reptiles—both live animals and their parts—account for 15%. Meanwhile, the 33 species of rosewood[2] make up 35% of the value of these seizures and agarwood[3] accounts for 6% (UNODC, 2016). The illegal wildlife trade is a way for organized criminal networks to generate profits by extracting high-value animals and plants, yet it is also central to livelihood strategies in some of the poorest and most marginalized communities in the world (Broad, Mulliken and Roe, 2003).

Monetary value aside, it is clear that the international trade in wildlife has increased over time. Rapidly expanding human populations, increased per capita wealth, changing consumer preferences for wild meat and exotic pets, improvements in infrastructure and logistics, increased internet connectivity and more widespread access to mobile devices, as well as easier access to harvest areas, mean that more wildlife is traded at present than ever before. At the national level, the wildlife trade is regulated to varying degrees, depending on a country's legislation (see Chapter 6). In some countries, wildlife is regarded as common property under the law; in others, all wild animals and forest products are the property of the state. At the international level, CITES governs the trade in about 6,000 animals and 30,000 plant species. CITES Appendix I precludes commercial international trade in about 1,000 of these species, two-thirds of which are animals; Appendix II allows regulated international trade in the remaining species. While CITES provides an international regulatory framework, each state party has to adopt its own legislation to ensure that CITES is implemented at the national level. All species of primate are included on either Appendix I or II of CITES, and all species of great ape and gibbon are listed in Appendix I; all primates are thus subject to CITES trade regulations (CITES, 2019a, n.d.-a).

Despite these regulations, primates are traded in their millions every year, for wild meat and medicinal use, as pets and for use in biomedical research (Nijman and Healy, 2016). As with all wildlife trade, curbing this illegal trade is unlikely to be addressed through a one-size-fits-all solution.

Tackling the Illegal Trade: A Typology of Responses

Conservationists, animal welfare activists and others are using a wide range of approaches to address the threat of hunting and trade. Interventions range from law enforcement activities, protected area management and conservation education, to community engagement, the development of alternative livelihoods and tourism (see Chapter 5). While some of these approaches have made a positive impact—as exemplified by the effects of ecotourism on mountain gorillas in Rwanda and Uganda (Robbins *et al.*, 2011)—none have proven effective on a wider scale.

Law Enforcement

All apes are protected under international and national law; it is illegal to hunt, trade or consume them. Law enforcement has therefore been an integral part of conservation actions, and a central pillar in efforts to reduce ape hunting across Africa and Asia and the trade in live apes, their meat and their parts in range countries and beyond. Law enforcement takes various forms at different levels—from the creation of national parks and associated patrols by rangers, to checkpoints on main roads, legal and regulatory frameworks and undercover investigations by independent organizations working in collaboration with governments.

The Eco Activists for Governance and Law Enforcement (EAGLE) network is one such independent organization. Operating across eight West and Central African countries, EAGLE aims to develop civic activism and collaborate with governments and civil society to improve the application of national and international environmental legislation through investigations, arrests, prosecutions and publicity. Evidence shows

Photo: Law enforcement occurs in different forms and at different levels – from the creation of national parks and associated patrols by rangers, to checkpoints on main roads, legal and regulatory frameworks and undercover investigations by independent organisations working in collaboration with governments. Armed EcoGuard, Campo Ma'an National Park, Cameroon. © Jabruson (www.jabruson. photoshelter.com)

that their approach and actions are having some impact. In 2019, for example, the network enabled 171 arrests for wildlife crime, 144 of which were prosecuted and 99 of which led perpetrators to be sentenced to jail (EAGLE, 2019, n.d.).

Law enforcement is an integral part of conservation management. Since it does not address the primary motivations behind the illegal ape trade or offer alternative livelihoods to those involved, however, it works bests as part of a wider approach to tackling the trade (Milner-Gulland and Bennett, 2003). When used in isolation, law enforcement is rarely sufficient and has the potential to turn public opinion against wildlife and conservation. Despite these limitations, law enforcement still tends to be prioritized over behavior change and community engagement (see Chapter 5). Meanwhile, much work also remains to be done to improve legal and regulatory frameworks (see Chapter 6).

Behavior Change

In recent years, there has been an increasing focus on effecting individual behavior change as a way to reduce the threat to apes from hunting and trade (Baker, Jah and Connolly, 2018). Traditional approaches, such as conservation education in schools, focus exclusively on informing individuals about these threats and the importance of conserving apes, yet they do not address people's motivations for hunting, trading or consumption. Conservationists have therefore looked for alternatives to this limited model and sought to take a more evidence-based approach (Chausson *et al.*, 2019). Best practice for behavior change involves conducting baseline surveys to estimate the level of ape meat consumption and truly assessing the context to uncover the motivations behind that consumption (van Vliet and Mbazza, 2011). Findings can be used to inform the best approach to influencing behavior in a particular locality.

Targeted interventions that aim to bring about behavior change (known as "social marketing", see Box I.4, Chapter 3 and Annex II) are becoming increasingly popular among conservationists. They have been referred to as "conservation marketing," defined as "the ethical application of market-

ing strategies, concepts and techniques to influence attitudes, perceptions and behaviours of individuals, and ultimately societies, with the objective of advancing conservation goals" (Wright *et al.*, 2015). While the use of conservation marketing for protecting apes has been limited to date, its use with respect to products such as ivory, rhino horn, shark fin and tiger bone has been more widespread (Box I.4 and Annex II; Greenfield and Veríssimo, 2019). Examples of conservation marketing designed to protect apes

BOX I.4

The Wild for Life Campaign

In 2015, the United Nations General Assembly and the UN Environment Assembly requested that the United Nations, led by the UN Environment Programme (UNEP), raise broad global awareness of the social, economic and environmental implications of the illegal trade in wildlife and reduce demand for illegally traded wildlife products (UNEP 2016; UNGA 2015).

Campaign

The following year, UNEP launched a global digital campaign in nine languages[4]—with UN partners, governments, businesses, civil society and key opinion leaders—to build a dynamic platform for change.

The campaign built on the insight that people protect what they love and that they tend to love what they know. Around the world, news stories about the legal killing of Cecil the lion and the illegal killing of Satao the elephant highlighted the fact that while thousands of unnamed lions, elephants and myriad other species are poached or illegally trafficked every day, those with names get the public's attention (Dell'amore, 2014; Wildlife Watch, 2018). This confirmed that if wildlife crime was to be relevant to people, it had to be personal. So was born Wild for Life: Wildlife Crime Just Got Personal. The campaign's aim is to mobilize the public to communicate a simple message to governments: endangered species have our attention and our protection, and we expect the government to act to stop the poaching crisis.

The campaign underscores that cultural beliefs, entertainment, fashion, investment, sport and traditional medicine should not contribute to the illegal trade or result in existential threats to protected species. It asks participants to use their own spheres of influence to end the illegal trade, however it touches or affects them.

Wild for Life was designed as a social first strategy, with going viral as a key objective. UNEP deployed a portfolio of celebrity goodwill ambassadors and influencers, each of whom represented a species. Together, they have reached more than 500 million users across social media platforms.[5] Now, more than 30 celebrities champion 26 species, including the elephant, helmeted hornbill, jaguar, lion, manta ray, orangutan, rosewood, sea turtle, sunbear, Tibetan antelope and tiger (Wild for Life, n.d.).

Species were chosen based on how they are affected by wildlife crime, and the dedicated website expands on the variety of factors that threaten them. Most of the represented species appear in CITES Appendix I, which prohibits all forms of international commercial trade in listed species. Website activities are designed around personal connections and include:

- a quiz to let people find their kindred species;
- an algorithm that blends a person's own image with that of a species and then shares the composite image on social media to inspire others to get involved; and
- pledges to help stop wildlife crime through personal spheres of influence.

Successes

By the end of 2018, Wild for Life had reached 1.5 billion people and mobilized millions to participate in the process of making commitments and taking action to end the illegal trade in wildlife and forest products. More than 4.5 million had engaged in the campaign—as evidenced by likes, shares and comments. More than 50,000 had found their kindred species and pledged. More than 20 non-governmental partners were supporting the campaign and it has received a number of industry awards.[6]

Most critically, many of the species in the campaign have maintained or received greater protection from CITES and governments, including elephants, helmeted hornbills, pangolins, rhinos, rosewood and snow leopards; bans on illegal products, including ivory and rhino horn, are being upheld and expanded across the world.

What's Next

With the aim of building and maintaining momentum in phase 2 of the campaign, Wild for Life will identify and raise awareness of emerging threats; advocate wildlife-friendly policies; add new species, including chimpanzees and gorillas; and develop new user journeys to deepen connections. The aim is to achieve a higher level of commitment to robust, targeted and measurable social and behavior change communication campaigns to address wildlife crime drivers and shift norms, thereby reducing demand while supporting stronger enforcement and legislation. To achieve these goals, UNEP is creating an open-source Communication to Combat Wildlife Crime Toolkit with outreach action plans that countries can develop and implement. More information is available at https://wildfor.life.

include campaigns on social media and local radio, as well as the use of "entertainment–education" programs that focus on incorporating environmental storylines into popular soaps on radio and television (Baker, Jah and Connolly, 2018; see Box 3.3).

Community Engagement

Community engagement is a bottom-up approach to conservation that seeks to empower communities to be stewards of their own resources. It includes local people in decision-making processes and land management with a view to ensuring their buy-in and support for conservation action (Vermeulen *et al.*, 2009; see Chapter 3). Community engagement can also involve providing support for the development of alternative livelihoods, such as farming, fishing or employment as community rangers (Horwich *et al.*, 2010). Where tourism is present, it can support small-scale industry such as retail, accommodation, entertainment and catering (Macfie and Williamson, 2010).

Criminal Networks

In recent years, the trafficking of wildlife has drawn global attention at the highest levels of government, largely due to growing evidence of the involvement of organized criminal networks and the devastating impact on plants and animals, including apes (INTERPOL-UNEP, 2016; see Box I.5). In the past decade, an increasing number of large-scale ivory seizures helped to shed light on the role of organized crime; the complex logistics involved in moving such large volumes of contraband point to the systematic corruption of officials along the trafficking chain. The establishment and maintenance of efficient systems for the illicit trade of large volumes over great geographic distances typically requires significant funds, planning,

organization and intelligence. Such systems also necessitate investment in secure facilities for storage and staging purposes; they rely on high levels of collusion and corruption, and the ability to exploit trading links and networks effectively and covertly between range states and end-use markets (CITES, 2007).

Many wildlife crime syndicates also engage in other kinds of criminal activities. Investigators have found links between the poaching of abalone—a marine mollusc eaten as a delicacy—and a growing addiction crisis in South African coastal communities, where drugs are frequently exchanged for illegally harvested abalone (De Greef and Raemaekers, 2014). Similarly, rhino horn syndicates have shown involvement in other crimes, such as drug and diamond smuggling, human trafficking and trading in other wildlife products, such as elephant ivory, abalone, lion bones and live game (Milliken and Shaw, 2012).

While much more is known about the links between criminal networks and the trade in products such as ivory and rhino horn, there is increasing evidence that ape traffickers utilize similarly sophisticated networks. Investigations by ProFauna Jakarta and others have revealed a complex and extensive network of smugglers working in close cooperation with customs officials, police and airport personnel in the illegal trade in orangutans in Java. This group of organized criminals is suspected of involvement in the export of at least two dozen orangutans in the first few months of 2003 (H. Baktiantoro, personal communication, 2003). The Last Great Ape Organization (LAGA) has uncovered similarly complex networks in both Central and West Africa (O. Drori, personal communication, 2017).

Another indication of links between ape trafficking and diverse criminal activities is the frequency with which apes are discovered in mixed shipments alongside other illegal items. They are usually trafficked with other live animals so that smugglers can use the same shipping and concealment methods, which differ from those used for other commodities. A well-known example of a mixed shipment is that of a trafficker in Cameroon who was arrested while in possession of a young chimpanzee as well as four large sacks of marijuana, each weighing at least 50 kg, and a quantity of cocaine (Stiles *et al.*, 2013). The trafficker had been employing at least five poachers and, before his arrest, he regularly traded in other protected primate species. In addition, TRAFFIC reports that 176 shipments that were seized between 2012 and 2018 involved apes as well as other protected species, such as pythons, turtles, birds and other primates (TRAFFIC International, 2018; see Figure I.4). Javan wildlife markets are notorious for selling a wide array of protected species, including orangutans and gibbons, and some larger markets[7] seem to hold key positions in a loose criminal network that transports animals to and within Java (Nijman *et al.*, 2017).

Ape Trafficking as a Transnational Organized Crime[8]

The term "wildlife trafficking" refers to the illegal sourcing, movement and disposal of live or dead wildlife, or their parts or products, usually for commercial purposes. Ape trafficking can include "one-off" events—such as the individual transfer and sale of an ape as a pet; in contrast, this box focuses on organized commercial trafficking, referred to as transnational organized crime (TOC). Trafficking usually entails the movement of wildlife across an international border without the requisite documentation. TOC networks vary in nature, from highly organized and hierarchical structures to dispersed, loose affiliations of people who come together to make profit. Facilitation networks, which operate alongside TOC networks, assist in or turn a blind eye to the commission of related crimes including poaching, bribery, the falsification or illegal acquisition of transfer documents, customs fraud, money laundering and wire fraud. Facilitators may include corrupt customs officers, police officers, CITES officials, members of the judiciary or other government officials. Irrespective of the type of network, key points where transactions occur are frequently referred to as nodes.

From a law enforcement perspective, the complexity of ape trafficking networks presents both challenges and opportunities. While building a case for prosecution of crimes can be extremely time-consuming, TOC networks tend to have multiple points of vulnerability (POV) at which actionable, verifiable information may be gathered and exploited to disrupt activities. Legal and regulatory options may be available to law enforcement officials at each POV, so long as these can be mapped with a fair degree of accuracy. In areas where wildlife laws are inadequate or poorly enforced, but money laundering or other legislation is

Figure I.4

Live Protected Species Most Commonly Seized alongside Apes, 2012–18

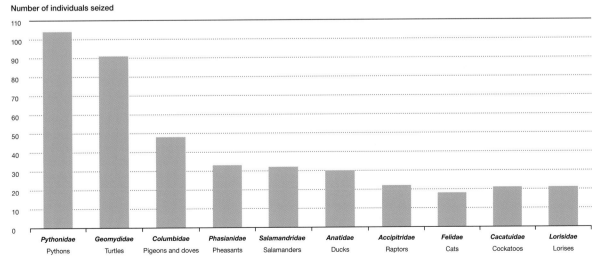

Number of individuals seized

Source: TRAFFIC International (2018)

strong, prosecution could focus on various predicate crimes that tend to be committed at POVs (see Chapter 6).

With the right resources and skill sets, intelligence that can underpin a strong transnational case need not be difficult to obtain. As many ape trafficking networks operate in countries with low enforcement levels, or where high-level government officials and politicians are readily corruptible, their network security is rarely high. Political interference can, however, hamper efforts to collect intelligence.

Understanding and Mapping Ape Trafficking

There is value in mapping TOC ape trafficking networks. Fine-resolution mapping in particular allows for the identification of key source, logistical, financial or corruption nodes that can provide a tangible output around which to discuss and plan disruption options. The mapping of trafficking routes only results in a static snapshot of a dynamic problem, however. Such mapping is based on seizure data only, which provides a limited picture of the true nature of ape trafficking networks and can give rise to incorrect assumptions about wildlife crime. Under ideal circumstances, mapping would be based on real-time, ongoing intelligence from inside a network and a series of local and regional overlays would provide context to help law enforcement officials understand how the network functions.

Successful TOC networks are agile, intimately understand their operating environment, adapt to it and exploit social, economic, governance and cultural loopholes. These networks understand—and are built on—the motivations of vendors and purchasers, be they private zoo owners or traditional healers. When informed by a solid understanding of all such factors, the mapping of ape trafficking networks can allow for the planning of an effective disruption, whereby an entire network can be pulled apart and its ape trafficking activities stopped.

Counter-trafficking Efforts: A Call for Dynamism and Innovation

Like most wildlife trafficking, ape trafficking comprises a set of activities that are fluid and highly responsive to legal, regulatory and public pressure. Yet, in contexts where regulatory and law enforcement institutions are underfunded, inefficient or unresponsive, where corruption fuels illegal activities, or where wildlife issues are not at the top of the political agenda, TOC actors tend to thrive and counter-trafficking efforts grind to a halt. Indeed, the success rate of disruption efforts is extremely low. Since not all wildlife crimes can be stopped by prosecution, innovative methods are required to detect, disrupt, deter and dismantle organized criminal networks.

Counter-trafficking experience to date suggests that programs must be flexible enough to engage in rapid, coordinated intervention activities at local and transnational POVs, across diverse, secure partnerships. To keep apace with—and get one step ahead of—TOC networks, counter-trafficking programs must be at least as dynamic and adaptable. A starting point could be to consider program principles that enable dynamism, such as building in rules for radical program adaptation; aggressively challenging assumptions on what will work and what will not; bringing diverse areas of expertise into the dialog that may well challenge accepted operating norms; and experimenting and being prepared to take significantly larger risks. Ultimately, the true success of any innovative strategies to disrupt TOC networks needs to be measured against the conservation goals and long-term viability of wild ape populations.

BOX 1.6

Social Media and Online Trafficking

Around the world, about 3.5 billion people use social media. Facebook accounts for the largest share of users, with close to 2 billion registered users. Nearly 400 million daily active users are in Asia, Facebook's largest region, whose market share is larger than anywhere else in the world (Kemp, 2019). In 2018, Instagram, the Facebook-owned photo-sharing app, became one of the most popular social networks worldwide, reaching 1 billion monthly active accounts, most of which are in Southeast Asia (Clement, 2019). Given its popularity and scope, it is unsurprising that the Internet is playing an increasingly important role in the illegal ape trade. In addition to enabling low-cost, anonymous access to markets, these platforms also create new live ape markets (see Chapter 4).

Social media networks such as Facebook and Instagram can be more appealing to traders than traditional commercial trade platforms or open markets, largely because they allow trade to be conducted free of charge and with a very high degree of anonymity. In addition, social media networks allow users to create special interest groups that provide a layer of control and accessibility that is governed by those managing the group. Such groups generally admit new members only through invites, making it difficult for any non-member to acquire information about the group or view its contents. In this way, social network sites and specialist forums help to perpetuate the illicit wildlife trade, both through legal and illegal means. They do so directly, by enabling trade exchanges, and indirectly, by allowing discussions about the trade (Smith and Cheyne, 2017; Stiles, 2016). To protect their identities further, sellers tend to instruct potential buyers in online groups to communicate via private or direct message on encrypted messaging apps such as WhatsApp and WeChat.

A 2014 investigation into the online wildlife trade revealed that Russia, Ukraine and the Middle East were the worst offenders for advertising live apes online

(Hastie and McCrea-Steele, 2014). A similar investigation focused on the United Arab Emirates and found more than 200 live apes on more than 80 Instagram, Facebook and website accounts over an 18-month period between 2015 and 2016 (Stiles, 2016). Many were for sale and some sellers openly listed prices.

Internet scamming has also played a role in the online ape trade, particularly in Nigeria. In 2006 LAGA brought about the arrest of scammers in Nigeria who had advertised the sale of apes and ape skulls that were not actually in their possession; interested parties never received any products for their money, which was simply pocketed. Following the arrest, the scammers realized that they could make more money by actually supplying the skulls instead of pretending that they would. They subsequently became significant traffickers of ape body parts (O. Drori, personal communication, 2017).

Researchers have attempted to understand the drivers of the online ape trade, and tools and resources such as databases, data mining and facial recognition have been used to enhance online monitoring (Hernandez-Castro and Roberts, 2015; Smith and Cheyne, 2017; Stiles, 2017; Timmins, 2019; Zainol *et al.*, 2018). However, challenges to investigating and prosecuting online traffickers include difficulties inherent in the identification of suspects, the origin of species and the applicable legislation. Currently there are no global legal studies on how countries deal with these issues, but approaches may differ across ape range states. For example, Malaysia only prohibits the advertisement of illegally imported wildlife, but not of native gibbons or orangutans from Malaysian Borneo (Parliament of Malaysia, 2008, art. 12). Similarly, Indonesia lacks specific provisions on advertising, and online sales are not explicitly included in the country's legislative definition of what constitutes a "sale" (Ministry of Forestry, 1990, art. 21). Filling these legal gaps will require new laws or amendments to existing legislation. Further analysis of legal tools is needed to determine how the law may best serve the purpose of combating online trafficking (see Chapter 6).

FOLLOW

20 likes   86w

اخوي القرد للبيع ؟

أنت كويتي

لا اماراتيه

للبيع

كم طالب في

تواصل واتساب يكون افضل

طيب توصلون الرياض

Translation

My friend, is the monkey for sale?

Are you Kuwaiti?

No, Emirati

For sale.

How much is the asking price?

Best to continue the conversation on WhatsApp.

OK. Do you deliver to Saudi Arabia?

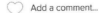 Add a comment... ○ ○ ○

Photo: Social network sites and specialist forums help to perpetuate the illicit wildlife trade, both through legal and illegal means, either directly by enabling trade exchanges or indirectly where discussions around the species in trade have been taking place. Chimpanzee for sale. Screenshot courtesy of PEGAS.

Photo: If shifts in the protection of ape populations are to be made, concerned stakeholders, ranging from local communities to international agencies, will have to make concerted efforts that build on a range of strategies. © Jabruson (www.jabruson.photoshelter.com)

Chapter Highlights

The first six chapters of this volume of *State of the Apes* interrogate the interface between ape conservation and killing, capture and trade. **Chapter 1** looks specifically at the impact of killing, capture and trade on apes and their habitat. **Chapter 2** assesses the role that cultural drivers play in the trade in apes and the responses to them. The next two chapters discuss the socioeconomic drivers of the trade in meat and parts (**Chapter 3**) and the live animal trade (**Chapter 4**), as well as current efforts to control them. **Chapter 5** presents the approaches for tackling illegal hunting and trade at its source, including through community engagement and behavior change. **Chapter 6** analyzes national and international legal and regulatory frameworks that are relevant to the killing, capture and trade in apes.

Section 2 provides updates on the conservation of apes in their natural habitat, in Africa and Asia (**Chapter 7**), and on the status and welfare of apes in captivity (**Chapter 8**). See the Introduction to Section 2 for the highlights of these two chapters (pages 196–197).

Chapter 1: Impact on Apes and Their Habitat

This chapter assesses the impacts of killing, capture and trade on the ecology and well-being of apes and their habitats. It examines to what extent hunting-induced declines in the number of apes affect their socioecology and their overall conservation, including the survival chances of local groups of apes and wider populations. It also explores the knock-on effects of hunting and trading in apes on the ecological functioning of

forests, the likelihood of disease transmission between apes and humans, ethical and legal considerations, and the impact on legal and illegal ape-based economies.

Chapter 2: Cultural Drivers and Responses

In focusing on the cultural drivers of the trade in apes, as well as the responses to them, the chapter offers particular insight into the demand for ape parts in Cameroon, based on a study commissioned by the Arcus Foundation. It considers shifting cultural practices that are increasing the vulnerability of apes, such as taboo degradation regarding the consumption of ape meat. The chapter highlights the ways in which anthropological research can contribute to ape conservation planning; it also details legal and other opportunities for integrating culture and conservation to protect ape habitat.

Chapter 3: Socioeconomics and the Trade in Ape Meat and Parts

After placing wild meat hunting in its historical context, this chapter offers available data on current offtakes in Africa and Asia. It evaluates the consequences of the trade in ape meat and parts, focusing on resulting declines in wild ape populations as well as the role of wild meat in human food security. In discussing socioeconomic drivers of wild meat hunting, it underscores that while poverty may encourage people to poach for commercial reasons, they tend to do so in response to demand from wealthier communities. The chapter also maps out a commodity chain for great ape meat; identifies ways to curb wild meat trafficking on airplanes; and highlights approaches that can reduce consumer demand for ape meat and parts, including through the promotion of

alternative protein sources, awareness raising of the ecological consequences of unsustainable harvesting, improvements to legal frameworks and law enforcement, and the provision of economic incentives to stop hunting and consuming.

Chapter 4: Socioeconomics and the Trade in Live Apes

This chapter examines the demand for live apes, especially from zoos and wild animal parks in China, the marketing and entertainment sectors of the United States and Thailand, and residents of rural Borneo, where misconceptions about apes and their needs fuel a desire to "rescue" orangutans. The chapter also reviews how the use of live apes in the entertainment industry affects the discourse of ape conservation. It considers how social media influences demand and enables supply, particularly by engaging new audiences and conferring value on ape ownership (see Box I.6). In addition, it discusses collaborative counter-trafficking efforts among animal rights organizations and social media companies, including education projects for social media users, and suggests additional approaches to reducing the demand for live apes.

Chapter 5: Responses at Source

In contrast to Chapter 2–4, which focus on the drivers of the ape trade, this chapter provides an overview of ways to curb the killing, capture and trade in apes, primarily within their natural habitat. It briefly reviews legal concerns—which are discussed at length in Chapter 6—and offers details on efforts to strengthen site-based law enforcement and community engagement in the context of ape conservation. The chapter argues in favor of a combination of site-specific approaches to tackle the ape trade, citing serious drawbacks of strategies that are built exclusively on top-down law enforcement. It also stresses the need to ensure that individuals and communities perceive engagement in the illegal wildlife trade as more costly and less beneficial than conservation, so that they are more likely to be protectors than poachers of apes.

Chapter 6: The Legal and Regulatory Environment

This chapter scrutinizes the legal and regulatory frameworks that govern the illegal wildlife trade and considers how they may be applied to disrupt the ape trade. It reviews the national laws of 17 ape range states, including domestic legislation that implements a country's obligations under the Convention on International Trade in Endangered Species of Wild Fauna and Flora (CITES), the main international agreement in this field. The chapter points out what states can do to close regulatory gaps and to increase enforcement opportunities along the entire value chain, particularly with respect to acts associated with hunting, domestic sales and advertising. It also examines the role of CITES—which uses a system of export and import permits to regulate the international trade in endangered wildlife—and other legal frameworks and international organizations that have the power to pursue cross-border enforcement action, such as INTERPOL and the World Customs Organization.

Acknowledgments

Principal authors: Josephine Head,[9] Alison White,[10] Annette Lanjouw[11] and Helga Rainer[12]

Contributors: Fiachra Kearney,[13] Vincent Nijman,[14] Johannes Refisch,[15] Maria Isabel Rodriguez Valero,[16] Lisa Rolls,[17] Pauliina Upla,[18] Penny Wallace[19] and Sabri Zain[20]

Box I.2: Pauliina Upla and Johannes Refisch

Box I.3: Vincent Nijman, Penny Wallace and Sabri Zain

Box I.4: Lisa Rolls

Box I.5: Fiachra Kearney

Box I.6: Josephine Head and Maria Isabel Rodriguez Valero

Endnotes

1   Bowen-Jones and Pendry (1999); Damania, Milner-Gulland and Crookes (2005); Fa *et al.* (2006); Meijaard *et al.* (2011); Nijman *et al.* (2011); Van Schaik, Monk and Robertson (2001); van Vliet, Nasi and Taber (2011).

2   Rosewood comprises various species in the genera *Cassia*, *Dalbergia*, *Diospyros*, *Millettia* and *Pterocarpus*.

3   Agarwood is a fragrant dark resinous wood from *Aquilaria* trees that have become infected with the *Phialophora parasitica* mold; it is used in incense, perfume and small carvings.

4   The nine languages are Arabic, Bahasa Indonesia, Chinese, English, French, Portuguese, Russian, Spanish and Vietnamese.

5   Based on feedback from the champions and internal web reports, 2018.

6   Internal web reports and agreements seen by the author, 2019.

7   Most notably Pramuka bird market in Jakarta and the Kupang bird market in Surabaya.

8   Information in this section was provided by Fiachra Kearney of the Global Eye Database.

9   Earthwatch Europe (http://earthwatch.org.uk).

10 Independent consultant.

11 Arcus Foundation (www.arcusfoundation.org).

12 Arcus Foundation (www.arcusfoundation.org).

13 Forever Wild (www.foreverwild.com.au).

14 Oxford Brookes University (www.brookes.ac.uk/social-sciences/courses/anthropology).

15 GRASP (www.un-grasp.org/).

16 Lancaster Environment Centre, Lancaster University (PhD candidate) (www.lancaster.ac.uk/lec/).

17 Wild for Life (https://wildfor.life/).

18 GRASP (www.un-grasp.org/).

19 TRAFFIC (www.traffic.org).

20 TRAFFIC (www.traffic.org).

CHAPTER 1

The Impact of Killing, Capture and Trade on Apes and their Habitat

Introduction

The hunting of apes is not a new threat: fossils and archaeological remains show that people have hunted all ape taxa since they started living in ape habitat. In Asia, hunting by humans appears to have played a part in the decline of the orangutan after the late Pleistocene, which ended about 11,700 years ago, and gibbon skeletons were discovered in a 2,000-year-old Chinese tomb (Spehar *et al.*, 2018; Turvey *et al.*, 2018).

What is new, however, is the scale of hunting, and its direct negative impact on the conservation status of apes, even though the hunting of apes is illegal in all range states. (Meijaard *et al.*, 2010b). On both continents where wild apes are found today—Africa and Asia—hunting pressure escalated with the introduction of long-distance weapons such as blowpipes and shotguns, which allow hunters to be more effective, and with the invention of snares, which permit them to cover a wider area for longer periods of time (Marshall *et al.*, 2006; Meijaard *et al.*, 2010a).

The term "hunting" is sometimes used interchangeably with "killing." In practice, however, hunting can also involve the capture of live animals. With respect to the trade in apes, hunting is the first step in a chain of illegal activities that supply meat, parts and live captures to local, national and international markets. The trade in ape meat and parts mainly meets the demand for food, medicine and fetishes; the trade in live animals, including infants captured after their

parents are killed, supplies the pet, tourism and entertainment industries. People also kill apes due to "competition for resources," to "retaliate" against animals for raiding crops or simply for being present in plantations or villages, and for perceived personal and community safety reasons. Some apes are killed or maimed unintentionally, such as when hunters inadvertently trap apes in snares set for other animals (see Box 1.1). To underscore these nuances, this volume uses the terms hunting, killing, capture and trade to refer to distinct threats to apes and their survival. It also uses the term poaching to cover illegal hunting, killing, capturing or taking of wildlife in violation of local or international wildlife conservation laws. Indirect impacts of hunting include injury and maiming,

BOX 1.1

Snaring of Chimpanzees

Snaring is a comparatively cheap, indiscriminate trapping method often aimed at small or medium-sized mammals. Snares include wire or nylon traps, as well as the more dangerous metal "mantraps" that typically trap the entire foot or leg of an animal. They are usually set either in the forest to catch game or around agricultural fields to protect crops from wildlife.

Death and mutilation resulting from snaring are relatively common in great apes, especially among the more terrestrial African apes. While there is variation across sites, mantraps tend to cause the most severe injuries. Between 2008 and 2016 in Bulindi, Uganda, five mature chimpanzees incurred injuries from large, steel mantraps (McLennan *et al.*, 2012).[1] Many more chimpanzees at various sites, especially in Budongo Forest Reserve, Uganda, have displayed injuries caused by snares (Reynolds, 2005). In the lower Kinabatangan region of Borneo, a couple of orangutans were recently caught in snares as they moved on the ground across agricultural landscapes and forest patches (HUTAN–Kinabatangan Orangutan Conservation Programme, unpublished data, 2019). Gibbons are spared snaring due to their arboreal lifestyle. Among apes, chimpanzees are the most frequently documented victims of snaring; while all subspecies of chimpanzee are affected, snaring rates vary regionally, depending on local hunting practices.

To date, there has been no evidence of the snaring of chimpanzees in Senegal, as the practice of snaring is uncommon and hunting is mainly performed using guns. In contrast,

chimpanzees in Uganda are at high risk. More than one-third of an estimated 700 chimpanzees living in the Budongo Forest Reserve—where 12% of farmers have reported using snares—have been maimed as a result of wire-snare injuries, and an estimated two to three individuals die annually as a result of snaring (Reynolds, 2005; Tumusiime and Tweheyo, 2010). Similarly, in Kibale National Park, 16 (31%) of the Sebitoli community of 51 chimpanzees exhibit limb malformations due to snare injuries (Cibot *et al.*, 2016). In Uganda's Hoima district, in the forest–agriculture matrix stretching between the Budongo and Bugoma forest reserves (that is, Bulindi), mantraps severely injured an average of at least two chimpanzees every year from 2007 to 2011; overall, these individuals had a 33% risk of dying from their wounds (McLennan *et al.*, 2012).

When caught in a snare, an individual will pull on it to remove a trapped limb or dislodge the snare. In the case of wire snares, the wire then tightens around the trapped body part, cutting off blood flow and causing an infection, which is often followed by necrosis and permanent loss of a limb or limb malformation. Severely affected adult females in Budongo spend more time in smaller parties, possibly to reduce the risk of competition with others and due to their diminished ability to follow large traveling parties (Hermans, 2011). Indeed, these females travel less, spend more time in the trees and also carry their infants less often, especially as these mature and became heavier to carry (Munn, 2006). Injured individuals—especially ones who suffered the loss of limbs—may encounter difficulties accessing and processing foods; they may also lose their social rank and hence be further limited in the competition for access to food (Byrne and Stokes, 2002; Cibot *et al.*, 2016).

which can result in an individual's death, and the social-ecological and psychological impacts of hunting activities on survivors.

The hunting of apes is one of the most important drivers of their extinction. Given that the International Union for Conservation of Nature (IUCN) lists all ape species as either "critically endangered" or "endangered"—except for the "vulnerable" eastern hoolock gibbon (*Hoolock leuconedys*)—the scale of hunting is a key determinant of their survival in the wild (Brockelman and Geissmann, 2019).

This chapter explores direct and indirect impacts of hunting, why apes are especially vulnerable to hunting and the risks of hunting to human health (see Box 1.5). It also identifies knowledge gaps that urgently need to be filled so that this threat may be tackled effectively.

The key findings include:

■ One of the most important drivers of extinction for apes is hunting, specifically when it results in the removal of apes from the wild through killing and capture.

■ People kill and capture apes for various reasons. They kill apes for their meat and parts, to facilitate the capture of infants for the live animal trade, to protect their crops or property from real or perceived threats, to feel safer, and for "sport"; they capture apes for the live animal trade, which supplies apes as pets, zoo animals, photo props and other tourism accessories, and as attractions

Photo: Death and mutilation resulting from snaring are relatively common in great apes. An elder female bonobo tries to remove a wire snare from the hand of an adolescent female as other females look on. Wamba, DRC. © Takeshi Furuichi, Wamba Committee for Bonobo Research

In addition, these individuals may experience a reduction in their immune system function, as high stress or lower-quality nutrition may affect immunocompetence in fighting disease or parasitic infections (Yersin *et al.*, 2017). Individuals are not only more susceptible to intestinal parasites, but they are also more vulnerable to external parasites such as ticks and fleas—either because they are less able to self-groom if their hands are affected, or because they tend to reuse nests (which may harbor fleas and ticks, as well as contaminated fecal matter) since they are less able to build a new nest every night, a norm among great apes (Plumptre and Reynolds, 1997; Yersin *et al.*, 2017).

Remarkably, members of some chimpanzee communities, such as Bossou in Guinea, have the ability and the knowledge to disable wire snares (Ohashi and Matsuzawa, 2011; Sugiyama and Humle, 2011). Mountain gorillas in Rwanda have exhibited similar behavior (V. Vecellio, personal communication, 2019). Since research indicates that this behavior is transmitted socially, the disappearance of primed individuals is expected to lead to a loss of knowledge that might prevent further snaring fatalities and injuries.

for amusement parks and other entertainment venues.

- Apes are particularly vulnerable to the effects of hunting because they have slow reproductive rates and a long time to maturity, which result in low growth rates that are exacerbated when even a few individuals are removed from the wild.

- Local, hunting-driven ape decline or extinction can have a severe impact on seed dispersal, which is critical to maintaining tree species diversity and ecosystem health.

- By hunting apes, people expose themselves as well as the apes to the risk of disease transmission, with serious implications for the health of both humans and apes.

- More data are needed for an accurate assessment of the scale of ape hunting and its impact on the long-term survival of intact populations and their ecosystems.

> By hunting apes, people expose themselves as well as the apes to the risk of disease transmission, with serious implications for the health of both humans and apes.

Direct Impacts of Hunting on Species Decline: Population Size and Social Consequences

Overview

Hunting has long been acknowledged as a major threat to ape populations in Africa; more recently, it was also recognized as a main driver of extinction among orangutans in Borneo and in Sumatra (Abram *et al.*, 2015; Davis *et al.*, 2013; Meijaard *et al.*, 2011a; Strindberg *et al.*, 2018; Wich *et al.*, 2012). Less is known about the impact of hunting on wild gibbon populations, but this activity has probably contributed to the decline in several populations, including the Hainan gibbon (*Nomascus hainanus*), Cao Vit gibbon (*Nomascus nasutus*), Gaoligong gibbon (*Hoolock tianxing*), Kloss's gibbon (*Hylobates*

klossii) and eastern hoolock gibbon (*Hoolock leuconedys*) (Fan *et al.*, 2013, 2017; Fellowes *et al.*, 2008; Quinten *et al.*, 2014; Wei *et al.*, 2004; Yin *et al.*, 2016). Hunting is also highly likely to affect other gibbon species, such as the Bornean white-bearded gibbon (*Hylobates albibarbis*) and moloch gibbon (*Hylobates moloch*) (Cheyne *et al.*, 2016; Smith *et al.*, 2018).

First and foremost, it is necessary to acknowledge the overall lack of understanding and knowledge concerning the actual offtake—that is, the precise number of apes removed from the wild due to hunting—and its impact for ape conservation. The direct impacts of hunting on ape populations are difficult to quantify simply because hunting is illegal and therefore its effects are challenging to measure. Nevertheless, it is important to distinguish between different types of hunting since the underlying causes are different in each case, although they may occur concurrently in a single area. The hunting of apes typically occurs for one of three reasons:

- **For wild meat**: This type of killing is largely limited to protected forests and forests that are exploited for timber or other resource extraction (Tranquilli *et al.*, 2014). While hunters generally shoot apes to supply the wild meat trade, especially in urban centers (see Chapter 3), some killings are driven by the demand for ape meat for medicinal purposes or cultural ceremonies (see Chapter 2). Hunting for meat can also result in the unplanned capture of young apes; these orphans often end up in the illegal live trade.

- **Due to "competition for resources" and other safety concerns**: This type of hunting mainly happens in non-protected forests and agricultural landscapes. It is the consequence of habitat loss and fragmentation, which displace apes or push them into people's orchards,

gardens, cultivated fields and plantations in search of food or for dispersal.
The trade in live infants is an opportunistic by-product of this type of hunting
(Meijaard *et al.*, 2011a).[2]

- **To capture infants for the trade in live
  animals**: Hunters who supply this trade
  are meeting the demand for apes that are
  to be used as pets, tourism accessories, zoo
  residents, and performers in amusement
  parks (Clough and May, 2018; Greengrass,
  2015; see Chapter 4). As noted above, the
  capture of infants can also be an unintended consequence of hunting for meat
  or in response to safety concerns.

For all ape species, the direct impacts
of hunting activities include the reduction
of the overall abundance of any hunted
population via the loss of individuals. Put
another way, hunting causes group size to
shrink and social groups to break down or
collapse. Given the dearth of information on
the offtake of apes—including the incidental
count, meaning the number of apes killed
for every targeted animal—it is difficult to
quantify the impact of hunting activities.

In human-dominated landscapes, local
people or industry players may see the presence of apes as a threat to their crops. Since
great apes spend most of their time on the
ground—much more than gibbons—they
can learn how to use mosaic agricultural
landscapes and thus survive in human-
dominated areas. Indeed, some species can
adapt their diets and their social behavior
to new ecological resources (Ancrenaz *et
al.*, 2015; McLennan and Hockings, 2014;
Meijaard *et al.*, 2010a; Seiler and Robbins,
2016). As a result, they increasingly compete
with humans for the same resources, which
can lead local people to capture or kill them
as "mitigation" measures (Ancrenaz, Dabek
and O'Neil, 2007; Baker, Milner-Gulland
and Leader-Williams, 2012).

The removal of an infant ape from the
wild generally involves the killing of the

mother. Hunters may kill several mothers
and infants to obtain one live infant for the
pet trade. Estimates range from one to ten
individuals killed to obtain a single live
infant (Stiles *et al.*, 2013). The range reflects
variations in the social organization of the
species, as well as the behavior exhibited
towards humans. For example, adult female
orangutans with unweaned offspring typically range by themselves, whereas gorillas
are found in cohesive social groups of about
ten individuals (Robbins and Robbins,
2018). Chimpanzees and bonobos live in
larger communities of 20 to more than 100
individuals, but they have a fission–fusion
grouping system, meaning that the entire
community is almost never found together,
but rather in parties (Furuichi, 2009). When
threatened by poachers, chimpanzees and
bonobos tend to flee, while an adult male
leader of a gorilla group is likely to try to
defend females and infants, increasing the
likelihood that he will be killed (Doran-
Sheehy *et al.*, 2007). The killing of a silverback of a one-male group has significant
knock-on effects, as other silverbacks are
likely to kill his unweaned offspring when
the adult females join other groups (Kalpers
et al., 2003; Robbins *et al.*, 2013; Watts, 1989).

In addition, hunting has consequences
for the socioecology of remaining individuals through social stress, loss of local
knowledge of the habitat or socially learned
behaviors (see Box 1.1), and a reduction of
the group's range if the animals start avoiding areas that are regularly hunted (Gruber
et al., 2019; Kühl *et al.*, 2019; van Schaik,
2002). While hunting can lead to the immediate death of individuals, it can also result
in injury caused by bullet wounds or snaring. Such injuries may reduce the lifespan,
breeding success and psychological well-
being of affected individuals. The extent of
the loss of injured individuals is unknown,
as apes may survive the initial injury but
succumb to it later because of wound infection or other impairments. Migration of

> " For all ape
> species, hunting
> causes group size
> to shrink and social
> groups to break down
> or collapse. "

TABLE 1.1

Number of Gibbons Held in Rescue Centers across Southeast Asia, per Species, 2015–16 (Excluding Zoos)

Rescue center location	Common name	Species	Number
Cambodia	Pileated gibbon	*Hylobates pileatus*	25
India	Western hoolock	*Hoolock hoolock*	10
Indonesia	Abbott's gray gibbon	*Hylobates abbottii*	91*
	Bornean gray gibbon	*Hylobates funereus*	
	Müller's gibbon	*Hylobates muelleri*	
	Agile gibbon	*Hylobates agilis*	100
	Bornean white-bearded gibbon	*Hylobates albibarbis*	100
	Kloss's gibbon	*Hylobates klossii*	20
	Moloch gibbon	*Hylobates moloch*	86
	Siamang	*Symphalangus syndactylus*	160
Malaysia	Siamang	*Symphalangus syndactylus*	25
Thailand	Lar gibbon	*Hylobates lar*	80
	Pileated gibbon	*Hylobates pileatus*	15
Viet Nam	*Nomascus* genus	*Nomascus* spp.	35

Note: * The starred number comprises three species; the total was not disaggregated.

Sources: Kheng *et al.* (2017); Nijman, Yang Martinez and Shepherd (2009); Smith *et al.* (2018)

bullets or pellets to organs within the body can have a significant impact on individuals' survival, as can the loss of body parts—such as fingers, toes, a hand or a foot—due to snares (see Box 1.1).

There is an urgent need to quantify the actual extent, rate and impact of killing and capture. The task requires a more global and comprehensive approach. Currently, the limited available data are drawn from a few disparate studies undertaken in localities that cannot confidently be categorized as hotspots or areas of more moderate offtake (Marshall *et al.*, 2006; Meijaard *et al.*, 2012; Quinten *et al.*, 2014; Yin *et al.*, 2016). More work is also needed to evaluate and mitigate the impact of snaring on apes, including through anti-poaching patrols, snare removal teams, and awareness raising campaigns (see Chapters 5 and 6).

Photo: The rapid growth and widespread use of social media facilitate the wildlife trade. Baby moloch gibbon for sale on social media. Source: screenshot from 2018

The Scale of Hunting Pressure: Current Knowledge per Taxon

Gibbons

The main direct threats to gibbons are habitat loss, degradation and fragmentation, infectious disease and killing, be it for wild meat or in the context of conflicts over cultivated food or other resources (Campbell, Cheyne and Rawson, 2015; Cheyne *et al.*, 2016). The relative importance of these threats varies by taxon and location. In general, gibbons are not specifically targeted for wild meat, yet poached wild meat does include gibbon meat. No one knows precisely what impact hunting for wild meat is having on wild gibbon populations. What is clear is that wild meat hunting is having a more pronounced effect on gibbons in certain countries, including China, Lao People's

Democratic Republic, Myanmar, Thailand, and Viet Nam, through habitat decline and population fragmentation.[3] Gibbon populations in the Mentawai Islands of Indonesia are more likely to be targets of cultural hunting and the pet trade (Quinten *et al.*, 2014; see Box 1.4 and Chapter 2). As described above, the killing of a mother may enable the opportunistic capture of infants, who are then supplied into the live animal trade.

A thorough understanding of local circumstances is required to address the main threats to gibbons. What is certain is that two species of gibbon—the Hainan and Gaoligong—have reached critically low numbers, in part due to hunting; urgent conservation measures are needed to protect these small, isolated populations (Bryant *et al.*, 2017; Fan *et al.*, 2017; Li *et al.*, 2018; Liu *et al.*, 1987; Wei *et al.*, 2017). Offtake data are lacking and obtaining accurate numbers for

Di jual, baby owa jawa, jantan, jinak total, antik dan langka, makan pisang penyeet, minum susu SGM minat add bbm ▮▮▮▮▮ kirim" seluruh pulau jawa

Male Javan gibbon [moloch gibbon] for sale. Funny and amusing. Eats banana and milk. Can be sent throughout the island of Java.

Gibbons for Sale on Social Media

Facebook boasts 600 million daily active users in the Asia-Pacific region, its largest market (Soto Reyes, 2019). From 2016 to 2018, the photo-sharing app Instagram gained significant momentum, reaching 1 billion monthly active accounts, most of which are in Asia (Clement, 2019; Instagram, n.d.). The rapid growth and widespread use of social media facilitate the wildlife trade, often in undetected ways. Evidence points to Indonesia and Malaysia as the two habitat countries with the most prolific trade in wildlife, predominantly of very young animals servicing the illegal pet trade. Thailand tops the list for the use of wildlife as photo props for tourist selfies on beaches and in bars (Osterberg *et al.*, 2015).

The inaccessibility of closed social media groups has implications for the control of such platforms. For security and privacy reasons, social media companies have exclusive control of the backend of their sites—that is, the data processing involved in the sending of messages, login verification, feeds, and storage. Since these companies are not technically the publishers of the content, however, they are not legally required to edit it, even if it is illegal. Nevertheless, Facebook has taken some steps to audit its content and Instagram is working with the World Wide Fund for Nature (WWF) and TRAFFIC to educate users and deter criminals from using the platform (Wagner, 2019; see Chapter 4, pp. 125–126).

The most effective ways to track the removal of gibbons is to monitor 1) sales on social media, 2) markets, 3) areas where gibbons (and other animals) are used as photo props, and 4) intake by rescue centers and zoos. It is more difficult to monitor how many individuals are kept as pets near forest sources. Preliminary surveys of gibbons for sale online in Indonesia via Facebook and Instagram found a total of 40 individual gibbons from 6 species available in a 3-month period, April–June 2017 (Smith and Cheyne, 2017). Further investigations in Malaysia and Myanmar, alongside additional research in Indonesia,[4] indicate that gibbon species for sale on social media are native species.[5]

While putting gibbons up for sale is illegal and it is clear that gibbons are being extracted from the wild, the fact that the animals are not crossing international borders means that they are not covered by the Convention on International Trade in Endangered Species of Wild Fauna and Flora (CITES). Since captured gibbons remain in their countries and CITES is not violated, it is impossible for international law enforcement agencies such as INTERPOL to intervene. Meanwhile, there is insufficient political will in these countries to pursue traders and buyers who are violating national legislation.

This large-scale online sales network is currently under-studied, and work to tackle it is under-funded. Traders have a solid online presence, their websites are openly accessible, and sales are rife across social media (Facebook, Instagram and WhatsApp); nevertheless, prosecutions are limited. To be effective, a campaign would need to bring about a reduction in the demand for gibbons. One way to reach and counter the activities of vendors and potential buyers may be through novel educational narratives.

For more information on the use of social media to trade apes, see Chapter 4.

gibbons held in rescue centers is difficult. Table 1.1 provides a general sense of the numbers based on previous publications and author interviews with gibbon rescue centers at the Orangutan Veterinary Advisory Group Meeting in July 2018 in Aceh, Indonesia; the data relate only to species held in the rescue centers (Commitante *et al.*, 2018).

The significant number of gibbons available for sale on social media and used as photo props indicates that the extraction of infants from the wild is ongoing, and possibly increasing. The demand is fueled by the proliferation of online images of gibbons as pets (Smith and Cheyne, 2017; see Box 1.2 and Chapter 4).

Orangutans

Orangutans have been part of people's diet since the Pleistocene, as suggested by fossil evidence found in the Niah caves in Sarawak, Malaysia, where humans were active as far back as 45,000 years ago (Harrisson, 1966; Spehar *et al.*, 2018). Over the following

---

BOX 1.3

Orangutan Hunting in Borneo

Recent analysis of population trends of Bornean orangutans indicates that the killing of individuals is one of the major factors leading to their decline, especially in the Indonesian part of Borneo, but also in certain parts of Sabah and Sarawak (Santika *et al.*, 2017; Voigt *et al.*, 2018).

Detailed, interview-based surveys confirm the severity of this threat. Borneo-wide social surveys of more than 5,000 respondents living in more than 500 villages—or about 10% of the villages of the entire island—show that an average of about 2,000 to 3,000 orangutans were killed annually over the average lifetime of the respondents (Davis *et al.*, 2013; Meijaard *et al.*, 2011a, 2011b). Further analysis of these data established that 750 to 1,800 individuals were killed in 2010 (Meijaard *et al.*, 2011a).

In Kalimantan nearly one-fourth of the villages sampled as part of these surveys reported the killing of an orangutan in the year before the survey was undertaken (Abram *et al.*, 2015). About 5% of all reliable respondents (232 of 4,732 persons) said that they had killed an orangutan during their lifetime (Davis *et al.*, 2013; Meijaard *et al.*, 2011a). The majority of these killings appear to have been opportunistic and very few respondents reported killing several individuals in the past, although one respondent claimed to have killed more than 70 orangutans, and another bragged about killing more than 100.

Of the villagers who asserted that they had killed an orangutan, the majority (56%) said their primary reason was securing access to meat and nearly one-fourth (23%) said they felt threatened or that the animals were destroying people's crops. Respondents who did not cite food or conflict situations as their primary driver said they had killed apes accidentally while hunting for other animals (5% of respondents), for the pet trade (3%), for traditional medicine (3%) or for "sport" hunting (3%) (Davis *et al.*, 2013).

In areas dominated by oil palm plantations and other crops, many people perceive orangutans as pests and kill them if they enter plantations (Davis *et al.*, 2013). Individuals associated with industrial and smaller oil palm plantations account for about 20–25% of the killings in Kalimantan. By far more killings—about 60% of the total—occur in protected and non-protected forests where hunters kill game (Figure 1.1). In these areas, the likelihood that orangutans will be killed increases with the proportion of resident Christians, who do not have any taboos against consuming ape meat (Abram *et al.*, 2015; Davis *et al.*, 2013; see Box 1.4).

Based on these studies, the annual killing rates are significantly above the maximum offtake levels that can be withstood by viable populations in the long term. Population viability analysis suggests that if yearly offtakes of female orangutans exceed 1%, a population will be driven towards extinction within a few decades (Marshall *et al.*, 2009). The research suggests that for many affected populations annual offtake rates exceed 1% and can be as high as 4% (Davis *et al.*, 2013; Meijaard *et al.*, 2011a). While precise annual offtake rates may not be available, newspaper reports and confiscations indicate that significant numbers of orangutans are being killed—and that this threat needs to be taken seriously.

Since the factors that lead people to kill orangutans are complex—and potentially involve ethnicity, taboos, perceptions, types of habitat, and a lack of law enforcement—measures designed to prevent killings are likely to have the greatest impact if they target specific groups with tailored messages, rather than a one-size-fits-all approach (Meijaard *et al.*, 2011b). The enforcement of relevant laws, in particular, is woefully inadequate. Convictions for killing, acquiring, and trading in orangutans are nearly non-existent, although the governments of Indonesia and Malaysia recently prosecuted a few people for killing and trading in orangutans (J. Sherman, personal communication, 2019).

FIGURE 1.1

Borneo: Plantations, Protected and Unprotected Forest

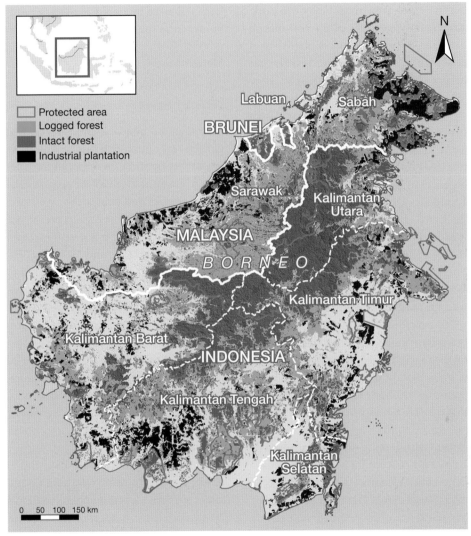

Sources: Adapted from Gaveau *et al.*, 2014, p. 6 and UNEP-WCMC and IUCN, 2019.

millennia, the proportion of orangutan fragments in prehistoric deposits increased with the development of spears and arrows (in the late Pleistocene) and with the more recent arrival of blowpipe technology (4,000 years ago) (Spehar *et al.*, 2018). During the past 300 years, powdered guns became widespread; they have played a key role in the drastic negative impact of hunting since colonial times (Goossens *et al.*, 2006). One recent analysis shows that orangutan encounter rates in Borneo have declined six-fold since the early 18th century (Meijaard *et al.*, 2010b).

Today, hunting remains a serious threat for the Bornean and Sumatran orangutans. Together with habitat loss, hunting is a major driver of extinction for all these species, with the exception of the Tapanuli orangutan (*Pongo tapanuliensis*), whose single population lives in remote areas that are mostly surrounded by people who do not hunt (Nowak *et al.*, 2017; Wich *et al.*, 2019; see the Apes Overview). One survey indicates that in Borneo alone, roughly 2,000 to 3,000 orangutans were killed every year during the lifetimes of survey respondents (Meijaard *et al.*, 2011a). The study also reveals that between 750 and 1,800 individuals were killed in Borneo in 2010 alone; these deaths represent more than 1% of the current estimated number of orangutans in the wild, a figure squarely above a "sustainable" harvest rate (see Box 1.3). Such killing estimates are higher than previously thought and are in accordance with the results of two recent studies that show a dramatic decline in orangutan numbers and abundance in Borneo between 1997 and 2015 (Santika *et al.*, 2017; Voigt *et al.*, 2018).

Unlike in Africa, there is no established wild ape meat trade in Borneo (Davis *et al.*, 2013); nevertheless, more than half of the orangutans killed on the island are hunted for their meat. Indeed, orangutans are killed in many parts of their range when hunting parties fail to kill any other animals. The fact that they are not targeted from the outset, but rather killed opportunistically, may explain why hunting was not perceived as a cause for concern for orangutan conservation until recently. About 5% of people interviewed across Borneo said that they had killed one or more orangutans (Davis *et al.*, 2013; Meijaard *et al.*, 2011a, 2011b). While the offtake rate may seem low, it is far above the sustainable level (Marshall *et al.*, 2009; see Box 1.3).

In addition to being killed for their meat, orangutans are targeted by people who compete for the same resources, particularly when apes engage in crop foraging. They are also killed by poachers who seek to obtain younger individuals or babies for the national and international live animal trade. Based on conservative data, nearly 150 orangutans from Indonesia—mostly young orphans—enter the domestic and international trade every year (Stiles *et al.*, 2013, p. 8). As late as the 1920s, orangutans were still killed by trophy hunters or head-hunters who sought their skulls, or for traditional medicinal purposes (Rijksen and Meijaard, 1999).

African Apes

African apes—bonobos, chimpanzees and gorillas—are hunted across all countries where they occur in the wild, but the drivers and extent of the problem vary spatially across species and subspecies. West and Central Africa have the highest prevalence of ape hunting, with a few regional and local exceptions (Fa and Brown, 2009; Heinicke *et al.*, 2019). While a dearth of empirical data precludes an accurate assessment of the impact of hunting on the decline of African apes, research demonstrates that hunting affects ape distribution and density and that the development of road networks, particularly in forested regions, exacerbates the problem (Hickey *et al.*, 2013; Poulsen, Clark and Bolker, 2011; Strindberg *et al.*, 2018; Vanthomme *et al.*, 2013; Walsh *et al.*, 2003).

In a few exceptional locations, cultural or religious taboos restrict the hunting and sale of ape parts for consumption, traditional medicine, fetishes and ceremonial events; in some protected areas, law enforcement or a research presence curtails such practices (Campbell *et al.*, 2011; Kortlandt, 1986; Oates *et al.*, 2007; Tagg *et al.*, 2015; see Box 1.4). These exceptional cases do not necessarily protect apes from being killed, however, as local conditions—such as the influx of people who hold different beliefs and attitudes towards apes, ape tolerance levels, the effectiveness of law enforcement measures and the presence of researchers—may change over time. In spite of taboos against killing apes, for instance, villagers in certain

" Unlike in Africa, there is no established wild ape meat trade in Borneo; nevertheless, more than half of the orangutans killed on the island are hunted for their meat. "

locations have hired "external" hunters to kill chimpanzees as a way to deter other apes from consuming their crops (Brncic, Amarasekaran and McKenna, 2010).

Villagers may also attack apes if they are perceived as threats to their property, their safety or that of their children; when such "retaliatory" killings claim the lives of mothers, they can result in the capture of infant apes (Projet Primates, n.d.; Chimpanzee Conservation Center, unpublished data, 2012). Aside from being a by-product of hunting or "conflict" situations, the capture of infants is also driven by direct demand from mainly foreign buyers. Demand varies across species; in Africa, chimpanzees top the list (Stiles *et al.*, 2013).

Chimpanzees

Of all African apes, chimpanzees have the widest distribution, as well as the largest population (see the Apes Overview). As a consequence, they also dominate the trade in live apes. An estimated 92 chimpanzees enter the live trade every year, compared to 7 bonobos and 14 gorillas (Stiles *et al.*, 2013). The capture of a single chimpanzee infant implies the death of up to ten other individuals in the community; about one-quarter of all captured infants die soon after they are caught and many more do not survive the transit to their final destination (Hicks *et al.*, 2010). Indeed, for every live chimpanzee delivered to a final recipient, 4–13 have lost their lives in the process.

The above-mentioned "retaliatory" attacks on chimpanzees can create a vicious circle, as people increasingly provoke apes, enhancing the risk that they will respond more aggressively during subsequent encounters (Hockings *et al.*, 2010; McLennan and Hockings, 2016). Outside protected areas, in landscapes shared by chimpanzees and people, such situations can escalate the killing of apes and the consequent capture of infants—unless quickly managed.

Hunting pressure on chimpanzees varies across the four subspecies and within each subspecies' range, mainly because of variations in religious or cultural taboos against the killing and capture of chimpanzees and human activities across protected and unprotected areas. The majority of western chimpanzees (*Pan troglodytes verus*) live outside protected areas, which renders them all the more vulnerable to hunting. The population—estimated at 18,000–65,000 individuals—is experiencing an annual rate of decline of 6% (Kormos *et al.*, 2003; Kühl *et al.*, 2017).

A section of the range of the Nigeria–Cameroon chimpanzee (*Pan t. ellioti*) overlaps with a region characterized by high human population density. This area, which has witnessed significant habitat destruction and fragmentation in recent years, suffers from a lack of enforcement of hunting laws. As a result, hunting has worsened, exacerbated by the increased ease of access to firearms, enhanced transport routes and growing financial incentives for supplying urban wild meat markets in the region (Morgan *et al.*, 2011). With fewer than 6,000 individuals, this subspecies will not be able to withstand the current hunting rates, which are 2–13 times higher than sustainable rates (Hughes *et al.*, 2011; Oates *et al.*, 2016).

Subsistence and especially commercial hunting have also been recognized as major threats to the conservation of central chimpanzees (*Pan t. troglodytes*), whose population comprises about 128,700 weaned individuals (Strindberg *et al.*, 2018; Tutin *et al.*, 2005). Artisanal and commercial mineral and oil extraction, transport and infrastructure development, such as roads and railways, and encroachment into forest areas via agriculture or logging activities have contributed to an increase in hunting pressure and activities across this subspecies' range (Arcus Foundation, 2014, 2015, 2018; Laurance *et al.*, 2006).

> 'Retaliatory' attacks on chimpanzees can create a vicious circle, as people increasingly provoke apes, enhancing the risk that they will respond more aggressively during subsequent encounters.

Populations of the eastern chimpanzee (*Pan t. schweinfurthii*) comprise an estimated 181,000–256,000 individuals (Plumptre *et al.*, 2016a). People hunt them across their range, primarily for meat consumption but also for traditional medicine, most prominently in the Democratic Republic of Congo (DRC) and the Central African Republic (Hicks *et al.*, 2010; Plumptre *et al.*, 2010). If mothers are killed, any infants are typically captured and kept alive to be traded. This illegal traffic of live chimpanzee orphans, from the DRC through East Africa and elsewhere on the continent, remains high, despite efforts to abate it (Hicks *et al.*, 2010).

Bonobos

The DRC is home to all bonobos (*Pan paniscus*), whose population is estimated at 15,000–20,000 (IUCN and ICCN, 2012). Although ape species are fully protected under DRC law, they continue to be killed, mostly to meet the demand for wild meat in urban centers and to facilitate the capture of infants for the live animal trade, which occurs as a direct by-product of hunting (Nasi *et al.*, 2008; Wilkie *et al.*, 2011). The high presence of rebel factions and poorly remunerated soldiers also fuels demand (Fruth, Williamson and Richardson, 2013). In only a few areas are bonobos buffered against hunting due to local cultural taboos against their killing and consumption (Inogwabini *et al.*, 2008; Lingomo and Kimura, 2009). Even in those areas, however, years of civil unrest, the movement of people across the country and poor law enforcement are weakening the influence of local taboos that protect bonobos from being killed or captured (Fruth *et al.*, 2016).

Gorillas

Available information reveals that the impact of hunting is high, yet variable, among the two species and four subspecies of gorilla. Overall, gorillas are easier to kill with guns than chimpanzees or bonobos because they are more terrestrial and live in more cohesive social groups (Plumptre *et al.*, 2016b; Strindberg *et al.*, 2018).

Over the past 20 years, Grauer's gorillas (*Gorilla beringei graueri*) have suffered the most dramatic decrease of the four gorilla subspecies, largely due to hunting. This subspecies has experienced a precipitous decline of nearly 80%, from an estimated 16,900 gorillas in the mid-1990s to around 3,800 in 2015. This sharp drop is largely due to hunting by artisanal miners in areas controlled by armed militias (Plumptre *et al.*, 2016b). In the absence of intense conservation interventions, this subspecies could go extinct in the next 20 years. The impact of hunting is exemplified by the 14 orphaned gorillas currently living in the GRACE (Gorilla Rehabilitation and Conservation Education Center) sanctuary in the eastern DRC (GRACE, n.d.).

In contrast, mountain gorillas (*Gorilla b. beringei*) experience relatively low levels of hunting, largely due to the taboo against eating gorillas and other primates in the communities surrounding their habitat (Robbins *et al.*, 2011). Mountain gorillas are the only subspecies of ape known to have a stable or increasing population size (Hickey *et al.*, 2019).[6] Nevertheless, in 1967–2008, 26 habituated gorillas were killed in the Virunga Massif; they represent 12% of all mortality during that time. These killings probably reduced the growth rate of the habituated groups by about 1% annually. Of those 26 gorillas, 3 died due to snares, 15 were shot by militias, and the remaining 8 were killed for various reasons, including the pet trade, efforts to stop crop raiding, and the wild meat trade (Robbins *et al.*, 2011). Furthermore, law enforcement confiscated six young mountain gorillas from poachers between 2004 and 2017, confirming that there is a demand for infant gorillas and that killing adults allows poachers to capture orphaned infants (Virunga Alliance, n.d.).

In recent decades, more than 1,500 snares set for duikers and other animals have been removed annually from the Virunga Massif. Between 1985 and 2008, a veterinary program removed snares from 42 habituated gorillas (Robbins *et al.*, 2011). Modeling shows that if those gorillas had died instead, the annual growth rate of the population would have been about 0.7% lower. Since the 1970s, the large difference between the growth rate of the unhabituated gorillas (-0.7%) and the habituated gorillas (4%) of that population was attributed not only to veterinary interventions, but also to daily monitoring of the habituated gorillas, which provided additional protection. The need for better protection of the unmonitored subpopulation is further demonstrated by the fact that an unhabituated gorilla was found dead in a snare during a survey of the Virunga Massif carried out in 2015–16 (Hickey *et al.*, 2019).

Hunting with snares is less widespread in and around Bwindi Impenetrable National Park, Uganda, which is home to the other population of mountain gorillas (Roy *et al.*, 2014). While this group of about 400 gorillas has required fewer veterinary snare removal interventions in the past two decades, it has not been spared illegal killings. In the mid-1990s, poachers intentionally killed four gorillas with the aim of obtaining an infant (Amooti, 1995; Roy *et al.*, 2014). An adult female gorilla was killed when a member of the local community threw a rock at her while she was eating crops outside the national park; her unweaned offspring also died (Baker, Milner-Gulland and Leader-Williams, 2012). In addition, in 2011 a blackback male was speared by a poacher who was in search of other wildlife; the perpetrator was caught but only fined a nominal amount (WWF, 2011). These seven gorillas accounted for 1.5–2% of this small population (Roy *et al.*, 2014).

Western lowland gorillas (*Gorilla gorilla gorilla*) are the most numerous of the four subspecies, with an estimated 360,000 individuals. From 2005 to 2013, the population declined at an estimated annual rate of 2.7%, due mainly to illegal killing, habitat destruction, and disease. If this rate of decline continues, the population will decrease by more than 80% in the next 60 years. The density of gorillas was significantly lower in areas that lack law enforcement guards; it also declined as the local human density increased. Both of these factors substantiate that hunting is the main cause of the lower density of gorillas. As approximately 75% of western lowland gorillas live outside protected areas, a rapid decline in population size can only be avoided through enhanced law enforcement in those areas. The density of gorillas is higher wherever there is a taboo against eating them, yet these areas account for only about 1% of their range (Strindberg *et al.*, 2018).

Several small-scale studies provide further evidence of the high impact of hunting on western lowland gorillas. Poulson, Clark and Bolker (2011) find that the density of gorillas was 61% lower in areas that had hunting and logging compared to areas with only logging. A study that compiled hunting rates from 36 sites in Central Africa estimates that 3.5 gorillas were killed per year in areas with only 0.7 gorillas per km² (70 hectares), a relatively low density (Fa, Ryan and Bell, 2005). Surveys of hunters in Cameroon found that great apes were not among the top ten species of wild meat hunted, but about 25% of the hunters had killed at least one gorilla or chimpanzee. The low rate of killing apes reflects a low number of encounters (Tagg *et al.*, 2018; Wright and Priston, 2010).

Only about 300 Cross River gorillas (*Gorilla g. diehli*) remain in the wild, scattered in a highly fragmented landscape that is characterized by high human pressure. Hunting probably contributes to the restricted range of these gorillas as much as habitat loss (Bergl *et al.*, 2012). The level of human disturbance —including hunting pressure—can determine whether Cross River gorillas occur in certain areas of suitable ecological habitat (Imong *et al.*, 2014). Modeling interventions to conserve these gorillas showed that an increase in law enforcement and a decrease in hunting pressure lead to the best scenario for recovery of this fragmented population (Imong *et al.*, 2016).

Why Apes Are Particularly Sensitive to Hunting

Slow Breeding and Population Viability Analysis

All apes are particularly sensitive to hunting because they have slow life histories and low reproductive rates (Barelli *et al.*, 2007; Cheyne, 2010; Cheyne and Chivers, 2006; Emery Thompson *et al.*, 2007; Furuichi *et al.*, 1998; Savini, Boesch and Reichard, 2008; Sugiyama and Fujita, 2011). On average, females start to reproduce between the ages of 9 and 15 years and have one offspring every 3–9 years; for infants up to 3 years, mortality rates vary from 25% to more than 50%, depending on species and populations (Mittermeier and Wilson, 2013). As a consequence, a slight increase in mortality rates —such as may be caused by hunting—can have a significant and rapid impact on population viability, including through population decline, the cumulative elimination of isolated populations and, in the most severe cases, species extinction (Carlsen *et al.*, 2012; Fan *et al.*, 2013; Smith *et al.*, 2018; Turvey *et al.*, 2015).

A recent population viability analysis (PVA) for the western chimpanzee revealed that all populations with fewer than 100 individuals have at least a 50% chance of extinction over the next 100 years if they experience a 3% annual loss of individuals—be it due to hunting, snaring, disease or other causes (Carlsen *et al.*, 2012).[7] Under these conditions, and given their slow reproductive cycles, the rate of removal of reproductive adults is greater than the rate of replacement. Viable populations of 250 to 1,000 chimpanzees may be large enough to persist with a decline in genetic diversity after 100 years, yet even these will ultimately become extinct if the annual rate of removal exceeds 2–3%, unless efforts are made to curb or eliminate the factors that influence their removal, such as hunting (Carlsen *et al.*, 2012).

BOX 1.4

Culture and Hunting of Apes

Cultural practices and religion can have a positive or negative effect on wild apes. In the many parts of Sumatra and Borneo that are dominated by Muslim communities, for example, ape hunting is less severe than in other regions (Davis *et al.*, 2013). In some areas, it is taboo to kill, eat or capture apes; such traditional taboos are often linked to the recognition of apes' resemblance to humans or their presence at sacred sites. These taboos are of particular value to the conservation of apes. Research indicates that in the absence of hunting, chimpanzees and orangutans can persist in areas of anthropogenic influence, including highly degraded landscapes dominated by agriculture and interspersed with remnant forest fragments (Blanco and Waltert, 2013; Campbell-Smith *et al.*, 2011a; Garriga *et al.*, 2019; Hockings *et al.*, 2012; Madden, 2006).

Taboos have enabled chimpanzee populations to persist outside protected areas, as is the case in some parts of Guinea, Guinea-Bissau and Sierra Leone (Bessa, Sousa and Hockings, 2015; Brncic, Amarasekaran and McKenna, 2010; Kormos *et al.*, 2003; Matsuzawa, Humle and Sugiyama, 2011). In those countries and other parts of western equatorial Africa, the densities of chimpanzees and gorillas are also much higher in areas where local communities hold taboos against eating their meat (Heinicke *et al.*, 2019; Strindberg *et al.*, 2018). In this region, such taboos benefit chimpanzees more than they do gorillas; among 59 sites surveyed, most people across 6 sites did not eat chimpanzee, while eating gorilla was generally avoided in only 3 sites (Hicks *et al.*, 2010).

Taboos may also vary with reference to local ape species; for example, in the extreme southwestern part of Gabon, one ethnic group traditionally does not eat chimpanzees, although members will consume gorilla meat. In northern Central Africa, women of certain ethnic groups reportedly refuse to cook or eat ape meat, for fear of giving birth to babies with "big ears." In other parts of the region, people have a taboo against eating chimpanzee meat, as they consider themselves to be descendants of a union of a chimpanzee and a human (Hicks *et al.*, 2010).

In some regions, the strong belief in shapeshifting or animal transformation has benefited apes. Hunters in certain parts of Cameroon are afraid to kill gorillas or chimpanzees because they are worried that they might kill a person instead (Wright and Priston, 2010). In the rare event that a chimpanzee attacks a person, such beliefs can redirect blame on people, thus minimizing any risk of retaliation for apes,[8] yet potentially fueling intrahuman conflict instead. As a result, people's attitudes and behavior towards apes may actually worsen. Indeed, with the influx of migrants who may not hold the same beliefs as the local communities, and with the growing transportation networks and access to vehicles that facilitate the supply of wild meat to urban centers, such beliefs and taboos alone cannot protect apes from being killed.

The introduction of new belief systems may also erode traditional ones. A case in point is the growing popularity of the recently established religious sect of Branhamism in the northern DRC. The sect, which adheres to the doctrine of US prophet William Branham, appears to be weakening traditional prohibitions against the consumption of chimpanzee meat (Hicks *et al.*, 2010).

In some cases, cultural practices and beliefs may also act as drivers of killing, whether for the consumption of meat or the use of body parts in traditional medicine and witchcraft. In central Sabah, some ethnic groups use orangutan parts to heal broken bones; in parts of West Africa, chimpanzee body parts are valuable fetishes that are thought to provide hunters with strength and protection; and in areas of equatorial Africa, certain gorilla body parts, namely the chest, hands and ribs, are believed to grant strength and courage, while ground chimpanzee bone is believed to cure wounds and confer strength on newborns (Hicks *et al.*, 2010; Tagg *et al.*, 2018). In the northern DRC, chimpanzee meat is a popular ingredient in stews and is sold openly in urban markets (Hicks *et al.*, 2010); meanwhile, in Indonesia's Mentawai Islands, the hunting of gibbons is embedded in local people's culture (Quinten *et al.*, 2014).

Given that cultural beliefs and practices shape behavior and attitudes, they are critical to understanding how to prevent the killing of apes. However, they are also highly dynamic and not necessarily durable: they can be modified extensively by the loss of traditional culture, new fashions and social trends, and the demand for apes and ape products. Efforts to encourage long-term positive behavior towards apes and to combat beliefs that endanger them thus require collaboration with social scientists, anthropologists and traditional leaders.

For more information on the cultural drivers behind the killing, capture and trade in apes, see Chapter 2.

Since many remnant populations of moloch gibbon are isolated and fragmented, these populations are good case studies for long-term viability under different anthropogenic pressures (Smith *et al.*, 2018). Three areas that harbor moloch gibbon populations were selected for a PVA: one that showed potential for population increase; one that comprised potentially fragmented populations; and one unprotected forest area that could experience substantial levels of poaching, such as hunting for the illegal pet trade. The PVA results indicate that all three moloch gibbon populations are likely to go extinct within 100 years if hunting and deforestation rates continue at the modeled rate—that is, if hunting costs the population 4–6 adults and 4–6 juveniles per year, and if deforestation causes their habitat to shrink by 1% per year. If both hunting and deforestation rates were to be minimized, however, all three populations would be large enough to persist and maintain high genetic diversity over the next 100 years.

A population reaches a "point of no return" when the number of apes falls beneath a given threshold, below which inbreeding, a subsequent collapse in reproduction and, ultimately, a loss of viability lead to extinction. Hainan gibbons are among the rarest mammals alive today, yet they have persisted for more than 30 years at the relatively low population size of about 25 individuals—without human intervention (Bryant *et al.*, 2015). A PVA carried out for moloch gibbons in three areas in Indonesia— the Dieng Plateau, Mount Halimun Salak National Park and Ujung Kulon National Park—modeled scenarios based on fragmented populations of 25–75 individuals. The findings suggest that such small populations face a greater risk of extinction than larger populations because they are more sensitive to increased levels of annual hunting and persistent rates of deforestation,

and because they exhibit higher rates of mortality and loss of genetic diversity (Smith *et al.*, 2018). Smaller populations would thus benefit from increased protection, and possibly from periodic genetic supplementation via translocation.

A recent population and habitat viability assessment (PHVA) conducted for orangutans establishes that a minimum population size of 150 individuals for Sumatra and 100 for Borneo is necessary to secure a viable population—one exposed to less than a 1% risk of extinction over 100 years and less than 10% over 500 years. A minimum of 200 individuals would be necessary to retain 90% of genetic diversity over a 500-year period. Based on the current knowledge of the species' ecology, the PHVA indicates that growth would be limited to 1.4% per year for the Sumatran species and 1.6% per year for the Bornean species. It shows that a rate of continuous loss of 1% or more would be unsustainable and would lead any population to its demise. In other words, an orangutan population faces a high risk of extinction if more than 1% of its individuals are killed every year (which is typically the case today); it takes a very long time for any population to recover following a hunting event (Utami-Atmoko *et al.*, 2019).

Ape Social Systems as Risk Amplifiers

Some aspects of the social systems of apes can amplify the impact of hunting. The social impacts of killings are most marked among gorillas and the other African great apes, largely because they are more social than Asian apes. As noted above, the killing of a silverback male can lead to infanticide and group disintegration (Kalpers *et al.*, 2003; Robbins *et al.*, 2013; Watts, 1989). Destabilization of the male hierarchical structure in chimpanzees can increase stress levels and intragroup lethal aggression (Pruetz *et al.*, 2017; Wilson *et al.*, 2014b). At Wamba in the DRC, an entire group of bonobos exhibited concern and distress in response to the snaring of a group member at the periphery of their home range. Some individuals tried to help dislodge the snare; failing to disentangle the injured bonobo completely, they returned to the safety of their core area for the night and traveled back 1.8 km to check on him the next day, only to find he had disappeared (Tokuyama *et al.*, 2012).

In contrast, the direct social impact of killing on semi-solitary orangutans seems to be minimal, although the killing of resident females disrupts the complex network of females in any given area. Research suggests that unrelated females may settle in a disturbed area and further destabilize the local social network.[9] Given the paucity of data available on this topic, the long-term consequences of such events on survival and breeding rates are unknown, although, as discussed above, population and habitat viability assessment simulations can offer some insight.

What is clear is that, absent hunting, great apes could persist in areas of anthropogenic influence, including fragmented forest–farm mosaics. Such has been the case for the orangutan population in Kinabatangan and several chimpanzee populations in Guinea and Sierra Leone, as well as mountain gorillas surrounded by areas of high human population density (Ancrenaz *et al.*, 2015; Brncic, Amarasekaran and McKenna, 2010; Campbell-Smith *et al.*, 2011b; Hockings and McLennan, 2012; Madden, 2006; Robbins *et al.*, 2011). Although the impact of hunting on the long-term viability of populations can be estimated using predictive models, more research is needed to build a better understanding of the social processes that support the viability of these groups and populations.

Ecological Impacts of Ape Hunting

Apes are key players in the maintenance of intact ecosystems. Due to their large size, great apes are particularly efficient dispersers of large seeds (>1 cm), which are not easily dispersed by smaller animals (Leighton, 1993; Tutin *et al.*, 1991). After feeding on large fruit and swallowing the seeds, apes regurgitate or defecate them, sometimes a distance away from the mother trees (Beaune *et al.*, 2013; Chapman and Onderdonk, 1998; Rogers *et al.*, 1998, 2004; Voysey *et al.*, 1999a, 1999b; Wilson *et al.*, 2014a; Wrangham, Chapman and Chapman, 1994). At Kibale, chimpanzees swallowed and defecated seeds from 82% of the fruit species they ate; in Borneo, gibbons did the same for at least seven plant species (Lambert, 1998; McConkey, 2000). At LuiKotale in the DRC, bonobos disperse the seeds of about 40% of the local trees; when these seeds fall straight to the ground instead of being dispersed by the apes, the vast majority fail to germinate and mature successfully, indicating that seed dispersal at this site is critical to tree conservation (Beaune, 2015).

Not only are apes good seed dispersing agents, but they also improve the germination and survival rates of seeds that they swallow and defecate for certain plant species (Ancrenaz, Lackman-Ancrenaz and Elahan, 2006; Beaune, 2015; Chapman *et al.*, 2004). In Borneo, unarmed seeds of 23 plant species were recovered from the feces of orangutans (Galdikas, 1982). In view of their role as dispersers, orangutans have been described as "gardeners or cultivators of much of their own provisions" in the forest (Rijksen and Meijaard, 1999, p. 55).

When apes are removed from the wild, so is their seed dispersing function. While it is not clear what long-term impact the removal of large, frugivorous species will have on forest ecosystems, it is evident that in many cases their disappearance would significantly impoverish flora diversity and simplify habitat structure (Beaune, 2015; Nuñez-Iturri and Howe, 2007; Petre *et al.*, 2013). Additional work is needed to better understand the ecological impacts of ape removal on ecosystems and species of potential value.

As the human impact on ape habitat grows, so does the need for data on how anthropogenic effects reshape the ecology of ape environments. For example, the impact of hunting on disease transmission between apes and humans is not well understood; additional research will need to be undertaken so that accurate risk assessments may be carried out (see Box 1.5).

Ethical, Legal and Practical Concerns

As described above, the killing of adult apes can result in the capture of orphans, be it for the live animal trade or other uses. Once rescued or confiscated, these apes cannot easily be returned to their natural habitat. Nor would it be legal to kill them or ethically acceptable to euthanize them, unless they are suffering from incurable or extreme pain. The most compelling moral argument is to provide care for these apes, either until it is possible to reintroduce them into their natural habitat, or for the rest of their lives. Despite the complexities of releasing apes back to the wild, the significant number of displaced and orphaned apes in rescue centers could contribute to restoring viable populations in areas where

Photo: Through seed dispersal, apes are key players in the maintenance of intact ecosystems. When apes are removed from the wild, so is their seed dispersing function. © Martha M. Robbins/ MPI-EVAN

apes have been extirpated, if local threats are mitigated.[10]

In spite of recent efforts to improve the enforcement of laws that forbid the trade in live apes, orphans continue to arrive at rescue centers. At least 23 sanctuaries for confiscated apes are operating in Africa and about 10 take in orangutans in Asia (PASA, 2018). The vast majority of sanctuaries are at capacity and expensive to run. While they are sometimes criticized for directing resources away from wild habitat, they provide critical support for law enforcement, animal welfare, and public education (Schoene and Brend, 2002; Sherman and Greer, 2018, pp. 227–55; Wilson et al., 2014a).

In Southeast Asia, young rescued orangutans are typically sent to rehabilitation centers, while older individuals tend to be translocated immediately, without proper assessment or monitoring (J. Sherman and D. Greer, unpublished data, 2018). Translocation often disrupts the status and hampers the connectivity of orangutan meta-populations, thereby jeopardizing their long-term viability. Moreover, it is often unclear whether the area in which orangutans are released can sustain additional individuals, and whether there is a risk of disease transmission between released animals and recipient populations (Beck et al., 2007; Campbell, Cheyne and Rawson, 2015; Tutin et al., 2001). Decisions to translocate or rescue are often driven by a fear that individuals will not survive as a result of extensive forest loss or hunting. To avoid the above-mentioned problems, however, translocation is best used as a last

BOX 1.5

Wild Meat as a Source of Major Diseases

Hunting and the consumption of wild great apes represent a major risk factor for disease emergence. Due in part to widespread hunting for wild meat, zoonotic pathogens—ones that are communicable from animals to humans—account for a large proportion of emerging infectious diseases and pose a serious threat to global human health. The risk is exacerbated by major ecological changes, greater intrusion of humans into pristine forest areas, and a human population that may be especially susceptible to disease due to poor health and pre-existing infections, such as HIV and parasites (Jones et al., 2008).

With respect to the wild meat trade and consumption, great apes are of special concern because their close evolutionary relationship with humans—along with their similar physiology—facilitates pathogen transmission. In fact, numerous zoonotic infectious agents linked to hunting great apes have had an important and sometimes global impact on human health (Gillespie, Nunn and Leendertz, 2008). The most prominent examples are simian immunodeficiency viruses, which have crossed the species barrier into humans on multiple occasions, giving rise to different human immunodeficiency virus groups and resulting in one of the most serious public health challenges—the AIDS pandemic (Hahn et al., 2000). Other viruses, such as adenoviruses, which are associated with respiratory illnesses, also originate from great apes (Hoppe et al., 2015; Richard et al., 2016). Many more transmissions have most probably occurred but have yet to be discovered and documented.

In other cases, apes are not the reservoir of a virus, but rather the victims. One example is the highly pathogenic Ebola virus, which has emerged from wild great apes on several occasions. Records show that epidemics have occurred among western lowland gorillas (Gorilla gorilla gorilla), central chimpanzees (Pan troglodytes troglodytes) and western chimpanzees (Pan t. verus) (Leendertz et al., 2016). The extent of these epidemics in great apes is not well documented, but carcass analysis and monitoring data indicate that Ebola virus infections may have led to major die-offs in several regions of Central Africa (Bermejo et al., 2006).

Numerous epidemics in humans have emerged as a consequence of exposure to great ape carcasses (individuals found dead or killed), demonstrating a direct link between epidemics in great apes and humans. The risk of spillover to humans is thus directly linked to the extent of the outbreaks in great apes (Leendertz et al., 2016). The case of the Ebola virus is just one example of the transmission of an acute disease-causing pathogen. It is highly likely that other pathogens are also transmitted to people following the same pathway; likely candidates include the monkeypox viruses and the anthrax-causing bacterium Bacillus cereus biovar anthracis (Hoffmann et al., 2017).

A reduction in the hunting and butchering of great apes is of great importance not only to their conservation, but also to public health. In addition, systematic health monitoring of great ape populations can serve as a tool for early warning and can ultimately lead to the mobilization of local and even global health resources to fight disease in great apes and humans (Calvignac-Spencer et al., 2012).

resort, if an animal's life is truly at risk. Educational and law enforcement efforts are needed to tackle the root of the problem —the removal of apes from the wild.

Hunting and snaring also raise ethical and legal issues. If a bullet or trap injures an ape, for instance, must veterinary interventions be organized? If so, by whom and using whose budget? Similarly, if apes contract a disease as a result of exposure to hunters or other people, must they be treated or vaccinated to minimize the risks of disease transmission? The use of apes for tourism purposes and for research activities raises further questions. In these contexts, responsibilities may arise given that habituated apes are more vulnerable to poachers, for instance (Macfie and Williamson, 2010).

Moreover, various groups have raised ethical considerations regarding the killing, capture and trade in apes. In view of their advanced emotional and intellectual development, some advocates propose that great apes be accorded the same rights to life, the protection of individual liberty and the prohibition of torture that humans enjoy (Cavalieri and Singer, 1993; see Chapter 8).

Ape-based Economies

In the ape range-states of Africa and Asia, people have given rise to a disparate set of ape-based economies: a legal one that comprises tourism, research and conservation, and an illegal one that revolves around the trade in meat, parts and live apes. As the illegal economy expands, it increasingly jeopardizes the legal one.

Legal Ape-based Economies

On a global scale, the extirpation of ape populations due to hunting comes at a significant socioeconomic cost. Indeed, given the iconic status of apes, their presence in an area can attract tourism or research opportunities, which can benefit local industries and create employment for local residents (Drewry, 1997; Kondgen et al., 2008; Macfie and Williamson, 2010; Marshall et al., 2016; Muehlenbein and Ancrenaz, 2009; Russell, 2001). In some countries, great ape viewing and related nature-based tourism is an important contributor to the conservation of apes and their habitat, as well as the national economy (Maekawa et al., 2015). Mountain gorillas draw nearly 50,000 people per year to Rwanda and Uganda,[11] where tourists currently pay between US$600 and US$1,500 for a one-hour visit with apes (Uganda Wildlife Authority, n.d.; Visit Rwanda, n.d.).

While such revenues may surpass those generated through agricultural land uses, there is scope to improve benefit-sharing mechanisms with local communities and to enhance the value of coexisting alongside apes and other wildlife species (Ahebwa, van der Duim and Sandbrook, 2012; Naidoo and Adamowicz, 2005). At this stage, not all ecotourism practitioners follow the IUCN Guidelines, even though doing so could help to promote ape conservation (Macfie and Williamson, 2010).

Illegal Ape-based Economies

Meanwhile, the illegal trade in apes is an increasingly profitable business. A recent report by Global Financial Integrity estimates the current rates paid for infant great apes, as well as the poachers' and retailers' cuts (Clough and May, 2018). Orangutan poachers earn between US$8 and US$121 per animal; traders operating at the village level receive between US$140 and US$385; and city-based traders can pocket US$454 (for a domestic sale) to more than US$20,000 (for an international sale). Local Indonesian consumers pay up to US$2,000 and international buyers spend up to US$70,000 per infant, indicating that the financial gain for traders up the market chain is substantial. Based on the estimated number of great apes entering the live trade every year— 7 bonobos, 14 gorillas, 92 chimpanzees and 146 orangutans (Stiles *et al.*, 2013)—the annual global market value is US$147,000 to US$301,000 for bonobos, US$560,000 to US$2.1 million for gorillas, US$1.4 million to US$6.4 million for chimpanzees and US$277,000 to US$10 million for orangutans.

These rates are not likely to decrease as long as owning an ape continues to be seen as a symbol of high social status, or as long as niche industries exploit animals for profit (J. Head, personal communication, 2018; see Chapter 4). Indeed, the demand for live captures appears to be on the rise as apes continue to be used as photo props in tourist settings, and as performers in zoos or amusement parks, particularly in Asia (Clough and May, 2018).

Similarly, killing apes for meat is associated with a substantial profit per shot, as adult ape bodies provide a lot of meat (Fa, Ryan and Bell, 2005). In Cameroon, gorillas tend to be divided into 18–20 "cuts" of meat and chimpanzees into 10–12 cuts, each of which can fetch US$2–10 (Tagg *et al.*, 2018).

All in all, the illegal trade in great apes is a lucrative and low-risk business for those operating at the middle and upper levels, in large part because governments are doing little to address the problem. The market thrives due to a host of deficiencies: significant gaps in the enforcement of the Convention on International Trade in Endangered Species of Wild Fauna and Flora (CITES), the low rate of prosecutions, the limited dissuasive effect of successful prosecutions, public- and private-sector corruption, insufficient resources for investigators in developing and developed countries, local community challenges, and abuse of social media and financial service companies. For more information on the socioeconomic drivers of the meat, parts and live animal trade, see Chapters 3 and 4.

Conclusion

The hunting of apes is a major driver of population decline and extinction. In addition to reducing the absolute size of ape populations, it has far-reaching consequences on ape habitat as well as on the human communities living alongside or near the apes and beyond. The development of adequate mitigating strategies is a complex task, one that is further complicated by the dearth of information on all aspects of the issue.

Relatively little is known about the scale of ape hunting, as it is difficult to quantify illegal activities, particularly in remote areas with limited law enforcement. While research indicates that the underlying reasons for hunting apes are multifaceted, further studies are needed to identify enablers and drivers of activities such as hunting for consumption and "retaliatory" killings. The findings could be used in modeling future trends of the impact of hunting and ways to tackle it. Additional research is also required to explain why some people are prone to consume wild ape meat, and to inform programs and policies designed to enhance people's tolerance of apes, including behavioral change campaigns, compensation schemes and alternative livelihoods activities. A better understanding of the impact of hunting on apes and their habitat is key to ensuring their survival in the wild.

Acknowledgments

Principal authors: Marc Ancrenaz,[12] Susan M. Cheyne,[13] Tatyana Humle[14] and Martha M. Robbins[15]

Contributor Box 1.5: Fabian Leendertz[16]

Endnotes

1 The cause of the injuries was presumed for three of the chimpanzees and confirmed for the other two.

2 Rankin, E., Tzanopoulos, J., Amarekaran, B., Colin, C., Cuadrado, L. and Humle, T. (manuscript in preparation). Recent deforestation drives the illegal capture of chimpanzees in West Africa.

Clake, D., Tzanopoulos, J., Amarekaran, B., Humle, T. (manuscript in preparation). Drivers of intolerance towards chimpanzee utilization of the oil palm in Sierra Leone, West Africa.

3 For details, see Chan *et al.* (2017); Fan (2017); Hallam *et al.* (2016); Hoàn, Dũng and Trường (2016); Phoonjampa and Brockelman (2008); Sarma, Krishna and Kumar (2015); Smith *et al.* (2018); Whittaker, Morales and Melnick (2003); and Yin *et al.* (2016).

4 Internal report on work undertaken by WWF Myanmar and Gibbon Protection Society Malaysia, 2018, seen by the author.

5 Cheyne, S.M., Smith, J.H., Llano Sanchez, K. and Moore, R. (manuscript in preparation) Tackling the illegal online trade of Indonesian small apes.

6 Granjon, A.C., Robbins, M.M., Arinaitwe, J., Cranfield, M.R., Eckardt, W., Mburanumwe, I., Musana, A., Robbins, A.M., Roy, J., Vigilant, L. and Hickey, J.R. (manuscript in preparation) Increased survey effort and intrinsic growth contribute to the largest recorded mountain gorilla population.

7 The model assumed equal chances of removal for adult males and females and the removal of one infant for every two adult females (Carlsen *et al.*, 2012).

8 Shapeshifting beliefs prevail among the Manon people of Bossou, Guinea (Hockings *et al.*, 2010).

9 Field observations by one of the authors and other staff members at HUTAN–Kinabatangan Orangutan Conservation Programme, Sabah, Malaysian Borneo, 2018–19.

10 See Beck *et al.* (2007); Brockelman and Osterberg (2015); Campbell, Cheyne and Rawson (2015); Cheyne, Campbell and Payne (2012); Cheyne, Chivers and Sugardjito (2008); Farmer, Buchanan-Smith and Jamart (2006); Farmer and Jamart (2002); Humle *et al.* (2011); McRae (2000); Russon (2002); Trayford and Farmer (2012); and Wilson *et al.* (2014a).

11 Visitor numbers based on author conversations with park staff (Bwindi Impenetrable Forest, Mgahinga and Volcanoes), 2018.

12 HUTAN–Kinabatangan Orang-utan Conservation Programme (www.hutan.org.my).

13 Borneo Nature Foundation (www.borneonaturefoundation.org).

14 University of Kent (www.kent.ac.uk/sac).

15 Max Planck Institute for Evolutionary Anthropology (www.eva.mpg.de).

16 Robert Koch Institute (www.rki.de).

CHAPTER 2

Understanding and Responding to Cultural Drivers of the Ape Trade

---

Introduction

This chapter explores how cultural beliefs and practices drive the trade in apes—as meat, body parts and live animals. The reasons that lead people to become involved in the trade are not always economic, indicating that addressing them requires an understanding of the behavioral nuances of specific groups of actors within and across locations. This chapter considers the trade within its localized human context, placing specific emphasis on knowledge, attitudes, beliefs and practices of individuals and their communities. It looks at the challenges in assessing impacts of the trade, especially given the dearth of research on aspects such as the use of ape parts in traditional medicine and variations in "cultural" attitudes to nature. What is known is that apes represent various resources to different people, including a product for sale, an object of entertainment, a status symbol or the focus of certain kinds of activity, such as hunting.

The chapter provides examples of both negative and positive impacts of cultural practices on ape populations; while some communities use body parts in rituals, for instance, others view apes as totem species that are not to be hunted. The chapter discusses how such practices change or vanish as rural societies in and around ape habitats undergo rapid modernization, younger generations come of age or formerly closed societies open their doors to newcomers from elsewhere.

Four case studies illustrate the need for conservationists to be sensitive to the social as well as the environmental impacts of their work. Two focus on communities in Africa, examining the demand for ape parts in Cameroon (Case Study 2.1) and how shifts in cultural practices that previously protected apes in Uganda are increasingly putting them at risk (Case Study 2.4). The other two case studies focus on Indonesian Borneo, presenting the cultural drivers of hunting in Kalimantan (Case Study 2.2) and the need for multidisciplinary analyses and interventions that situate these drivers more clearly in their anthropological and socioeconomic context (Case Study 2.3). All these studies indicate that conservation planning is most likely to be effective when it factors in the cultural practices of communities that interact with apes and their habitats.

The key findings include:

■ Far from a static concept, "culture" has context-specific meaning and value to local communities and varies across and within locations. As a result, the cultural drivers of the ape trade differ widely across communities.

> 66 Conservation planning is most likely to be effective when it factors in the cultural practices of communities that interact with apes and their habitats. 99

■ Reconciling sensitivity to cultural practices with the conservation of threatened species may require trade-offs; in turn, these trade-offs may enhance relations between conservationists and local communities as well as human–wildlife coexistence. In contrast to a single approach—such as law enforcement or the provision of alternative livelihoods for all communities—site-specific methods can help build long-term relationships on more equal terms.

■ Ethnographic and other social science research techniques can provide insights that complement traditional conservation programming.

■ While conservationists can supplement their ecological understanding through the use of social science approaches, some may need to reevaluate certain assumptions about local communities and reassess the use of widely employed Western concepts and terminology.

The Cultural Context of Human Perceptions of Apes

Today's conservation movement espouses Western principles that call for restrictive control, which is often implemented with the help of international non-governmental organizations (NGOs) (Bakels *et al.*, 2016; Dowie, 2009; Pyhälä, Osuna Orozco and Counsell, 2016). Over the past decade or so, however, this traditional approach to protecting territory and species via the exclusion of certain types of outsider or activity has raised concerns and elicited proposals of more equitable alternatives (Berkes, 2004; Brockington, 2002; Pyhälä, Osuna Orozco and Counsell, 2016). In disciplines as wide-ranging as ecology, anthropology and philosophy, practitioners and researchers are expressing a growing interest in posing normative questions about human–wildlife interaction; specifically, they are asking how a given society or community should behave towards the species with whom they share their environment (Corbey and Lanjouw, 2013; McKenna and Light, 2004). In that context, it is useful—yet challenging—to define the term "culture." Typically presented as a synonym for "tradition," culture is commonly used to refer to the characteristics, knowledge and patterns of behavior acquired by a particular group of people and transmitted by symbols, artifacts and values (Kroeber and Kluckhohn, 1952). This chapter situates these multiple meanings in the context of ape conservation and the ape trade.

Despite the fact that human development has relied on the exploitation of various species, human relations with animals are not exclusively utilitarian; connections also exist on a much broader symbolic level, depending on geography, history and faith. Culture and conservation may be imagined on spectra of beliefs and behavior that include economic and spiritual attitudes to the environment, along with types of use and consumption that are specific to a given place and time. Awareness—and integration—of these nuances can be key to conservation programming that is more equitable and sustainable than the traditional "fines and fences" approach. As discussed in this chapter, programming that reflects local knowledge and behavior related to the use of resources can further both social and environmental goals (Igoe, 2006; Pyhälä, Osuna Orozco and Counsell, 2016).

In general terms, people's connections to their environment can be grouped into four loose categories, some of which may overlap:

- People may attach **spiritual and religious values** to the environment. These may be derived from specific places, features, species and practices, and may be expressed in the selection of sites for rituals and ceremonies, shrines, cemeteries and sacred forests, rules and taboos, totems and symbols, and links to ancestors, gods or spirit worlds.

- **Cultural heritage, a sense of place and identity** may be linked to historically important landscapes, species or other valued goods. They may connect people to ancestors, practices and beliefs and evoke memories. People may derive a sense of belonging to place and time from features in the environment, which can contribute to the human need for individual and collective identity.

- The environment influences and is often the setting for **social and community relations**. It provides places for groups and institutions to gather and opportunities for communal activities, such as harvesting of food or hunting. These activities contribute to the cohesion, identity and collective well-being of a society.

- The environment contributes resources that promote **mental and physical health**. Like plant-based medicines, certain species may be seen as having specific properties related to a host of benefits that their users associate them with (Drani and Infield, 2014).

As this chapter shows, cultural practices across ape range states are diverse and multifaceted. In view of this diversity, an evolving context, and a dominant conservation ethos that has traditionally privileged science and Western doctrine over indigenous knowledge and practices, engaging with local cultural norms has emerged as a central, yet complex consideration for conservationists (Pyhälä, Osuna Orozco and Counsell, 2016). While much of this recent research supports the view that communities already conserve, it also finds that they *use* resources;

> In contrast to a single approach—such as law enforcement or the provision of alternative livelihoods for all communities—site-specific methods can help build long-term relationships on more equal terms.

Photo: Ape bones and body parts are used as preventive medicine or as fetishes, implying a belief in their magical rather than physiological or psychological properties. Konyak Naga head trophy basket decorated with western hoolock gibbon (*Hoolock hoolock*) and capped langur (*Trachypithecus pileatus*) skulls. North East India. © Pete Oxford/naturepl.com

if those resources include apes or ape parts, local practices may be placing additional pressure on already threatened populations. For those in great ape and gibbon conservation, the question then becomes how to build or retain links between people and the environment if a population's connection or attachment to it has a negative impact on the species.

Apes in Belief and Practice

Myths, legends and beliefs suggest that people feel a connection to primates that can have both positive and negative impacts

on the species themselves. Recent literature from range states reveals that communities variously see apes as protectors, reincarnated ancestors, totems or holy animals (CCFU, 2018; see Boxes 2.1 and 2.2); such beliefs are also illustrated in tales of love, magic, the protection of forest secrets and reincarnated humans (Etiendem, Hens and Pereboom, 2011). These belief systems have given rise to taboos against hunting or eating apes that may help to protect them; conversely, the use of body parts in traditional medicine and rituals can represent a significant threat to their survival (Etiendem, Hens and Pereboom, 2011; Infield, 2011).

The Use of Apes in Traditional Medicine and Rituals

Throughout human history communities around the globe have made wide use of traditional medicines derived from plant and animal sources. In areas where such practices remain strong, they are often linked to spiritual beliefs and associated cultural identities (Etiendem, Hens and Pereboom, 2011). Ape habitats tend to be remote and thus have limited access to modern pharmaceutical medicine; in these areas, people look to traditional medicine for explanations for illness and death, as well as remedies and cures for common illnesses.

While few studies examine the use of apes in traditional medicine, they demonstrate that their bones and body parts are widely used across the landscapes where these species occur—and that people who use them believe they have direct curative effects (Etiendem, Hens and Pereboom, 2011). In Lao People's Democratic Republic (PDR), for example, "primate" bones—which almost certainly include those of native gibbon species—are used to cure fevers and gonorrhea, and they may be applied as more general palliatives or tonics (Duckworth, 2008). Similarly, in Viet Nam and China, some people treat breaks or fractures with "black monkey balm," which may contain gibbon parts (J. Kempinski, personal communication, 2018). Ape bones and body parts are also used as preventive medicine or as fetishes, implying a belief in their magical rather than physiological or psychological properties. Among the Bakonjo of Uganda, for instance, there is a belief that the bones of a chimpanzee have healing power and that when placed next to the broken bone of a human, they can heal the break (CCFU, 2018; see Box 2.3). Such beliefs and practices vary widely across and within range states; Case Study 2.1 focuses on those of a particular region in Cameroon.

Data on the practices and markets within range states are scant, yet information on international demand for ape products outside those countries is even more limited. While the nature of these markets is poorly understood, recent research does suggest that demand is growing in China, Europe and ▶ p. 58

BOX 2.1

Gibbons in Myth and Folklore

One Indonesian legend holds that the female gibbon call is that of a mythical woman who roams the forest in search of her lost lover, who was killed after she betrayed him. The mournful song that rises in the morning is her song of remorse (Drani and Infield, 2014).

Another story from Indonesia tells of a young woman who was forced into an arranged marriage with a much older man. The marriage was far from happy, and the young woman would escape each day by going into the forest to collect fruits and vegetables. One day, while gathering food, she encountered a young hunter from another tribe and the two became friends. The young woman began to spend more and more time in the forest and eventually fell in love with the hunter. Her husband noticed that his meals were delayed and that his wife was often absent, so he contrived to follow her and found her with the young man. The following day, the husband gathered a large group of men from the village and followed his wife into the forest to teach the hunter a lesson. When the young lovers realized the mob was after them, they fled deeper into the forest but became separated. The great forest spirit took pity on them, lifted them up into the canopy, away from the mob, and transformed them into gibbons. So that they might always find each other in the dense forest, the great forest spirit gave them loud songs, one for the young woman and one for the young hunter, and today gibbons still sing these songs (Drani and Infield, 2014).

In Thailand, there is a story about a woman who was turned into a gibbon because she betrayed her husband. She spent the rest of her existence swinging from branch to branch, calling pua, pua, pua, which means husband in Thai. Some Thais tell this story to explain the meaning of the gibbon call (Drani and Infield, 2014).

More than 2,000 years ago, the Chinese singled out gibbons as the aristocrat among apes and monkeys. They are one of only two primates (the other being the macaques) to have been granted a special niche in Chinese culture. The gibbon is the traditional Chinese symbol of unworldly, metaphysical ideas that initiate humanity into the sciences and magic; the gibbon's call is what deepens the exalted mood of poets, painters and philosophers on misty mornings and moonlit nights (Van Gulik, 1967).

Farther south, among some ethnic minorities in Lao People's Democratic Republic, prohibitions against hunting gibbons were linked to the belief that they were reincarnated ancestors (Duckworth, 2008). These stories demonstrate a belief in familial relationships between people and apes, which may reinforce attitudes based on resemblance rather than otherness.

Cultural Drivers of the Demand for Ape Parts in Africa

Recent ethnographic studies conducted in Cameroon highlight the role that cultural beliefs and practices can play in influencing behavior around hunting and trade (Chuo and Angwafo, 2017a, 2017b). One study, which was carried out in and around Kimbi-Fungom National Park in northwestern Cameroon (see Figure 2.1), concludes that the demand for ape body parts is mainly driven by a belief that the bones and tissues have medicinal, ritualistic and even mystical properties and powers. It notes that some practitioners replace human skulls with those of apes during traditional ancestor worship (Chuo, 2018). Another study documents similar practices in southwestern Cameroon, where great ape parts are used to heal fractures and other bone dysfunctions (Bobo, Aghomo and Ntumwel, 2015).

Kimbi-Fungom National Park covers a total area of 989.8 km² (98,980 hectares) and its northern sector runs along the Cameroon–Nigeria border (Protected Planet, n.d.-a, n.d.-c). The park is home to the Nigeria–Cameroon chimpanzee (*Pan troglodytes ellioti*), the most endangered of the four subspecies of chimpanzee. During the past decade, this subspecies experienced a significant population reduction as a result of high levels of hunting, loss of habitat and habitat degradation due to human pressure; only about 6,000 individuals exist across their range today (Sesink Clee *et al.*, 2015).

In the study on Kimbi-Fungom National Park, focal villages were selected based on their proximity to the park. The majority of

FIGURE 2.1

Cameroon and Nigeria

Sources: Protected Planet (n.d.-a, n.d.-c), UNEP-WCMC (2019a, 2019c)

TABLE 2.1

Selected Conditions and the Chimpanzee Parts Used to Treat Them in Northwestern Cameroon

Ailment	Ape parts used in treatment
Bone fractures or sprains	Bones, skull
Calcium deficiency	Bone marrow, meat
Diarrhea or dysentery	Bones, skull, head, burned fur
Heart disease	Internal organs, heart, liver, chest bones
Joint pain	Bones, skull
Poisoning	Bones, gallbladder, liver, skin, fur, nails
Rheumatism, spleen trouble	Bones, fat, limbs
Stomach ache	Ground and burned bone mixed with other substances
Swollen limbs or parts	Cooked bone broth
Toothache	Ground bones
Weakness	Bones, skull

Source: Chuo (2018)

respondents reported that chimpanzee body parts and meat were used for their medicinal value, as well as in rituals and as food on special occasions. They named about 25 diseases and conditions that they said could be treated with ape body parts or meat, although they did not provide specifics on preparation, amounts or other ingredients (Chuo, 2018; see Table 2.1).

During the interviews, the researcher observed and recorded 78 chimpanzee skulls, 37 chimpanzee bones, and several bags of medicine containing ape skin and other, unidentifiable body parts. Based on the respondents' statements, the body of an adult chimpanzee typically costs CFA 75,000–250,000 (US$130–435) and skulls are the most expensive body parts, ranging from CFA 50,000 to CFA 200,000 (US$87–346), depending on age. Skin can be purchased for CFA 3,000–50,000 (US$5–85), depending on the size of the piece for sale; hands and feet cost CFA 2,000–25,000 (US$4–45). Other body parts, such as bones, testes, meat and other organs, can fetch between CFA 500 and CFA 15,000 (US$1–25), depending on the quantity and quality of the product (Chuo, 2018).

The research indicates that in northwestern Cameroon the demand for traditional medicine was particularly high, as was the use of body parts in rituals and ceremonies, such as male child circumcision, the coronation of a new chief, the burial of the dead, the transmission of power of a totem's owner, traditional title acquisition and annual feast days. Interviews suggest that the prowess of traditional doctors and healers, who reportedly heal diseases that are believed to be incurable in hospitals, is a significant factor driving the demand for meat and parts in this and other areas of the country (Chuo and Angwafo, 2017a).

A related finding is that villages and towns in northwestern Cameroon experienced a widespread influx of new beliefs and practices that utilize ape parts, both from within Cameroon and from neighboring Nigeria (Chuo and Angwafo, 2017a). This finding supports previous field research indicating that many of the individuals involved in the illegal hunting of and trade in chimpanzees in Kimbi-Fungom National Park had come across the border from neighboring Nigeria (Ekinde, Ashu and Sunderland-Groves, 2005). As Case Study 2.4 also shows, the integration of new beliefs and attitudes can increase or curb such hunting and trade. The people of Bechati, Besali and Fossimondi in southern Cameroon, for example, traditionally avoided hunting and eating gorilla due to cultural taboos and totemic beliefs (see Figure 2.1); more recently, however, they started to consume them and use their body parts for traditional medicine (Etiendem, Hens and Pereboom, 2011).

This research is mirrored in broader assessments of the ape trade in Cameroon, whose ape trafficking operations are likened to those of the ivory trade in that both are international networks that finance hunters and even provide them with motorbikes and sophisticated weapons (LAGA, 2015; Nforngwa, 2017). Ape habitat in this country continues to be fragmented by infrastructure development such as new roads, which facilitate movement and trafficking, as does the porousness of the borders. While it is not always clear whether poachers supply ape parts for use in cultural practices, law enforcement activities do provide evidence that the hunting networks are widespread. Indeed, "during a four-month period in 2015, anti-poaching and anti-trafficking squads in Cameroon arrested 22 dealers and seized 16 great ape limbs, 24 gorilla heads and 34 chimpanzee skulls in separate operations around the country" (Nforngwa, 2017). Investigators claim that whereas hunters may previously have kept meat but discarded ape limbs and heads in the forest, they now stockpile body parts in view of growing market demand (LAGA, 2015; Nforngwa, 2017). Despite the existence of adequate laws and ongoing interventions by conservation organizations, the ape trade seems to be thriving in Cameroon (Chuo, 2018; see Chapter 6).

A recent report suggests that a lucrative trade also exists in Nigeria, where it is similarly fueled by traditional beliefs and practices. It highlights that subsistence hunting has expanded into a much broader, more commercialized trade that supplies markets driven by cultural practices, such as ones that involve ancestral lore or the control of malignant spirits. Interviewees described a well-coordinated commodity chain linking local hunters to distributors and consumers in Nigeria and beyond. Due to their relative abundance, chimpanzees are commonly used in rituals; the most requested part is the left hand, which can sell for as much as US$100. Markets in the cities of Kano, Lagos and Onitsha were identified as centers of the national trade, and Nigeria appears to act as a central hub through which body parts from Central and West African countries are smuggled on to other parts of the world. Law enforcement operations may be able to disrupt supply chains and economic alternatives could help hunters to secure legal employment, yet a more nuanced approach is needed to address deep-seated traditions that fuel the trade (Sunday, 2019).

Cultural attitudes are not static, nor is the dilution of such attitudes. World-views and beliefs held by earlier generations are continually being transformed by new knowledge and information. Improving economic opportunities, formal education and access to a growing variety of capital—including natural, human and social capital—may affect and influence youths more than the practices of older generations, with both positive and negative implications for conservation (Pretty and Smith, 2004). Rapid change in the economic activities of communities can draw forest-dwellers away from the forest, diminishing their knowledge of the many values of biodiversity, and narrowing perceptions of the environment to that of an economic rather than a cultural resource. Under such circumstances, people may begin to hunt species that were not previously targeted—such as bonobos in the DRC—for wild meat and income, particularly if other species have become scarcer or access to firearms easier (Tashiro et al., 2007).

Positive counter-examples exist. In Gabon, habituating gorillas as part of research and tourism ventures has had a striking impact on communities that generally perceived these animals negatively. Those who work with gorillas increasingly see them in a more positive light. There has been a trickle-down effect to other community members, whose disapproval has also dissipated. In Rwanda, government authorities consciously contributed to such changes in attitude by linking traditional naming ceremonies to the birth of gorillas (Drani and Infield, 2014).

Ongoing and, in some cases, increasing migration across borders, as well as marriage across traditional ethnic boundaries, can result in the spreading and sharing of knowledge and values. In that sense, the identification of, association with and responsibility to protect totem animals and plants might be introduced to a growing network of people. However, cultural diffusion may also disrupt traditional knowledge. Some people, especially among the younger generations, may not know their totems and thus lack a connection to them. Case Study 2.4 returns to this issue—and how it might be rectified in a way that minimizes the trade.

BOX 2.2

Totems

Across Africa, some individuals and social groups feel a type of mystical kinship with specific totems, be they animals, trees or places. Ape totems have been documented among clans in Cameroon, Central African Republic, the Democratic Republic of Congo (DRC), Gabon, Liberia, Nigeria, Tanzania and Uganda (Drani and Infield, 2014). Taboos forbidding the consumption or other uses of animals with totemic status are part of the totemic system; such taboos can apply to wild as well as domestic animals.

Broadly speaking, research conducted in northwestern Cameroon paints a picture of unsustainable hunting of chimpanzees for body parts and meat. At the same time, it provides evidence that traditional taboos and totemic beliefs are falling by the wayside as migrants from Nigeria arrive in the area with their own belief systems— all within a context characterized by high poverty levels, a lack of access to modern medicine, and limited knowledge of and adherence to protective laws (Chuo, 2018). These conditions are common to many ape range states, where traditional belief systems and cultural norms often support day-to-day practices that affect habitat and biodiversity. Informal regulations over access and use of land can help to protect habitat. In Uganda, for example, some communities recognize specific plants as markers of places that have religious or spiritual importance, so that these may be avoided. Such regulations can protect the habitat of many species, including apes, even if they do not do so by design (Drani and Infield, 2014).

CASE STUDY 2.2

Indonesian Borneo: Dayak Tradition, the Killing of Apes and Conservation

Indigenous or traditional knowledge is an important form of ecological understanding and practice. It can be of special relevance among communities that depend on the sustainable use of natural resources for their livelihoods, such as the Dayak of Indonesian Borneo (Gadgil, Berkes and Folke, 1993). The term Dayak refers to Kalimantan's native people and comprises different ethnic groups, subgroups and indigenous communities, each with its own dialect, customs, laws and territory, although all of them share a common and identifiable culture (Rousseau, 1990). The Dayak were traditionally forest dwellers with rich indigenous knowledge of biodiversity and natural resources management; their communities are still regulated by *adat*, a customary framework of social and cultural norms, laws, ceremonies and rituals (Joshi *et al.*, 2004; Thomson, 2000). *Adat* is critically important in shaping the life and culture of Dayak communities and plays a key role in conservation and forest protection, avoiding the overexploitation of forest products and ensuring the sustainable use of natural resources (Joshi *et al.*, 2004; Mulyoutami, Rismawan and Joshi, 2009; Wadley and Colfer, 2004).

Examples of how these cultural norms have shaped conservation among Dayak communities include sacred forest sites and the use of taboos to protect forests and animals (Wadley and Colfer, 2004; Wadley, Colfer and Hood, 1997). In the Dayak traditional belief system, sacred sites are inhabited by non-human spirits, have religious meaning and are important in the preservation of natural resources (Wadley and Colfer, 2004). Taboos (*pantang*) are unwritten rules or prohibitions governing community behavior that are related to events experienced by their ancestors (Omar and Rathakrishnan, 2016); they are based on the belief that certain behaviors or objects are connected to the invisible realm (Thomson, 2000). As is the case with totems in Cameroon, Uganda and other areas of Africa, perceived connections to species and places can lead local communities in Kalimantan to show greater consideration for habitats that they share with apes.

Orangutans and Traditional Hunting

The Dayak economy is based on subsistence agriculture in the form of swidden rice cultivation and forest management, and, to a lesser extent, on hunting, which serves as an important source of protein (Eilenberg, 2012; Wadley and Colfer, 2004). While hunters target mostly larger game, such as deer and wild pigs, hunting can be opportunistic and may include other mammals or birds (Wadley and Colfer, 2004). Previously, hunters used blowguns, spears and hunting dogs, but these traditional means of hunting have since been replaced by the use of air guns, firearms and traps (Wadley and Colfer, 2004; Wadley, Colfer and Hood, 1997). Hunters usually consume animals themselves or share them with families and neighbors. Primate meat is not considered of value and is thus not sold; if trade in ape meat does take place, it occurs within close-knit cultural relations (Wadley, Colfer and Hood, 1997).

Research suggests that hunting played an important role in historic orangutan extirpations in specific areas across Borneo. While orangutan densities have undergone significant decline over the past 150 years, local extirpations have largely taken place in the past 20–50 years, particularly between 1999 and 2015, when 100,000 Bornean orangutans lost their lives due to habitat degradation and loss, as well as direct killings (Meijaard et al., 2010; Voigt et al., 2018). Arriving at an accurate estimate of the number of apes killed is difficult, but figures of orangutans received at rescue centers can provide a sense of scale. Between 2001 and 2013, nearly 1,500 orangutans arrived at only three of the seven rescue centers in Indonesia. More than half of these individuals were babies or infants, whose capture is often an unintended consequence of hunting adults, suggesting that the number of adult apes killed deserves serious consideration by conservationists (Sánchez, 2015; see Chapter 1).

Few of the studies that examine orangutan killings also explore the sociocultural factors that influence hunting behaviors or the way humans relate to orangutans (Marshall et al., 2006; Meijaard et al., 2010, 2011; Voigt et al., 2018). Such research may help to explain what processes have undermined previously common taboos that formerly protected orangutans from being hunted. It may also shed light on recent extirpations in areas where orangutans were not known to be hunted—until they disappeared.

Some Dayak communities still consider killing apes a taboo. Such protective taboos are typically based on legends according to which orangutans or gibbons either originated from humans or helped to save people's ancestors (A.I. Krisma, personal communication, 2018). Among Iban Dayak communities in West Kalimantan, similar taboos used to protect orangutans and gibbons, as people held that "a noteworthy ancestor had been helped in battle by orangutans or gibbons, and that he had been transformed into one or the other upon death" (Wadley, Colfer and Hood, 1997, p. 257).

Just as such taboos have faded away with older religious and social beliefs, so too have the protections they afforded (Wadley, Colfer and Hood, 1997). The disappearance of taboos may thus have influenced hunting practices among contemporary Dayak ethnic groups, with potentially detrimental effects for species such as orangutans or gibbons. Taboos do not vanish simply because the belief in a legend is lost; rather, they lose their meaning through the breakdown of everyday cultural practices that are based on perceived connections to the environment.

People who decide to hunt and trade in orangutans may do so for a variety of socioeconomic and cultural reasons, just as they may be influenced by social, emotional and psychological factors (see Chapter 4). The circumstances driving a subsistence hunter will differ from those that lead an individual to kill an orangutan in an oil palm plantation, opportunistically capture her baby as a pet and eventually sell the orphan into the ape trade. An awareness of these varied and complex dynamics can help conservationists tailor their interventions to communities in ways that are sensitive to their realities.

Evolving Cultural Trends as a Threat to Apes

Dayak cultural and creative rituals follow adat norms, and all forms of art have a precise cultural meaning. According to one mid-19th-century account, orangutan skulls replaced human ones as trophies after head-hunting practices were abolished in certain areas of Borneo, which may have exacerbated hunting pressure on apes (Meijaard et al., 2010). In more recent times, orangutan skulls have commonly been used as trophies at cultural events and festivals. Participants flaunt orangutan skulls as ornaments and as part of their attire, even though such elements were not previously known to be part of broader Dayak tradition or culture (A.I. Krisma, personal communication, 2018). Youths in particular have quickly adopted these trends and post pictures of such displays on social media, which may represent another threat to orangutans (see Chapter 4).

Over time, many of the traditions of Dayak people have been lost. Their animistic beliefs have been widely replaced by modern religions, such as Christianity (Thomson, 2000; Wadley and Colfer, 2004). These cultural changes, coupled with modernization, are having an impact on the conservation of natural resources in Kalimantan (Wadley and Colfer, 2004). As discussed above, the erosion of traditions and cultural practices can also bring about the loss of protective taboos, stimulate the hunting and killing of apes to supply the illegal animal trade, popularize the use of ape parts in "cultural" events, and spur interest in fad-based "tribal" art.

The trade in skulls is also associated with a rise in tourism to Indonesia. An investigation into the trade shows that wildlife products from all over the archipelago are sold in Bali. To supply the market, hunters kill apes for their skulls, which are then carved with "tribal" patterns to command higher prices. Many are fire-darkened and decorated in order to trick prospective buyers into believing that they are antiques. The study found that in one high-end antique shop in Gianyar that was offering the skulls of gibbons and orangutans, the skull of an adult female orangutan had a price tag of US$5,000. While people who kill primates for food typically break open the skull and remove the brain to eat, most primate skulls on sale in Bali are intact, indicating that these animals were not killed for food (Tenaza, 2012).

Orang-utan Skull (*Pongo pygmaeus*)
Country of Origin: Borneo Year Seized: 2004 Ref#53664
CITES Appendix I (Endangered by Trade), Pre-Convention: c.1850
CITES Permit/s Required: Pre-Convention Export Certificate

► the United States (LAGA, 2015; Nforngwa, 2017). The demand for wild meat outside range states, which is somewhat better documented than the demand for other ape products, appears to be related to cultural factors (Wood *et al.*, 2014). A study of a Liberian community living in the US state of Minnesota, for example, found that incentives for importation and consumption were multifactorial, and that nostalgia and cultural connections were significant drivers of consumption (Walz *et al.*, 2017).

Responses to the Cultural Drivers of the Trade

This chapter highlights that cultural practices do not exist in a vacuum; rather, they are embedded in the broader socioeconomic, historical and religious dynamics of a given community, reflecting how local people relate to their environment and its flora and fauna. It suggests that conservationists are more likely to design effective measures to curb the hunting and sale of apes in any

State of the Apes Killing, Capture, Trade and Conservation

location if they supplement their ecological understanding of the landscape with an awareness of cultural drivers of the trade. For some practitioners, this approach may require a reassessment of assumptions about local communities, their attitudes and their behavior. It may also call for a reframing of commonly applied concepts and terminology. The term "nature," for instance, is a Western notion for which there is no equivalent word in many ape range states (Bakels *et al.*, 2016). Its use implies that there is a distinction between nature and culture, reproducing a dichotomy that sets human communities apart from the landscapes in which they live. There are alternatives to prevailing conservation methods, however. Biocultural approaches, for example, use local cultural perspectives and recognize feedback between ecosystems and human well-being (Sterling *et al.*, 2017).

By employing a variety of social science approaches, conservationists can use community-based and participatory methods to define and assess the specific cultural factors that might influence the ape trade. As shown above, hunting is not always driven by economic incentives alone; it may have deep-seated relevance linked to identity. For some communities, the trade in meat or parts may be an offshoot of hunting rather than its central aim. Such may be the case in Viet Nam, a country notorious for its trade in wildlife. While gibbons do not appear to be targeted for their parts in Viet Nam, they are traded as pets and consumed locally; once the meat has been eaten, their bones are sometimes sold as generic "monkey" parts (J. Kempinski, personal communication, 2018). Any attempt to stage conservation interventions to curb the trade will require a nuanced understanding of this type of context.

A key issue in this context is the dearth of relevant information. With respect to Viet Nam, for instance, it is not known how many gibbons are taken as pets or killed, nor are details available on the reasons for killing them or the locations from which they are removed. What is understood is that gibbons are found only in isolated areas, that their occupancy rate is low, even within protected areas, and that many populations are still in decline. It is not clear whether extra layers of protection in certain sites are enough to dissuade people from going after them, particularly since they are not a "high-value" wildlife product, such as pangolins. Evidence points to an active trade in lorises (as pets) and regular incidents of hunting

TABLE 2.2

Methodological Approaches and Research Questions

Methodological approach	Focus	Sample research question
Biography	The meaning of an individual's lived experience	How can the lived experiences of individuals or communities in ape range states be integrated in conservation decision-making processes?
Phenomenology	Shared lived experience of a phenomenon by multiple people	How does the experience of gorilla-focused, community-led tourism in Uganda influence local perceptions of different conservation initiatives?
Case studies	What has been experienced in a given event or context	What impact does migration have on Dayak livelihoods, village politics, forms of authority and, by extension, hunting behavior that can affect apes?
Ethnography	Understanding a different culture by living or observing it	What role do beliefs about ancestors play in shaping hunting decisions among communities in western Cameroon, and how can conservationists engage with ways of seeing and managing "resources" that are relevant to local residents?

Source: McCaslin and Scott (2003)

and selling of langurs (whole or dried); rumors suggest that animals are being sold into markets in China, and gibbons may be among them (J. Kempinski, personal communication, 2018). Any interventions set to disrupt these dynamics will need to rely on newly commissioned research and take local attitudes into account.

Biocultural and participatory methods can be designed to collect qualitative data about decision-making processes as well as the unique social–ecological contexts in which they take place (Moon *et al.*, 2019). Table 2.2 presents selected methodological approaches and research questions linked to issues described in this chapter. Case Study 2.3 takes an ethnographic (or anthropological) approach to examining the killing of orangutans in Kalimantan, the subject of Case Study 2.2.

The examples in Case Study 2.3 show how different research approaches can offer unique insight into social, cultural and political decision-making contexts, rather than the processes alone. In this way, conservationists can enhance their understanding of communities in ape range states, and potentially rely on them as experts, instead of viewing them as hurdles to be overcome. An in-depth study carried out in the Nam Kading National Protected Area in Lao PDR identified key factors that play a role in driving hunting behavior in local communities:

- reliable access to markets and services;
- gradual economic development;
- a low cost of living (US$90 per month on average);
- an agriculture- and livestock-based local economy;

How Anthropological Research Can Contribute to Understanding and Addressing the Killing of Orangutans in Rural Borneo

As described in Case Study 2.2, the trade in live orangutans and, to a lesser extent, their body parts in Borneo is inseparable from a larger set of practices, including the hunting of these apes. Killing is often opportunistic rather than premeditated—an offshoot of other phenomena, such as hunting for different animals or human–orangutan conflict (Freund, Rahman and Knott, 2017; Meijaard et al., 2011; Nijman, 2005). An adult female orangutan killed in retaliation for damaging a plantation might have her flesh consumed and certain body parts retained or sold for medicinal uses, while her baby might be kept locally as a pet, before being sold on to wildlife traffickers (Nijman, 2005).

Analyses have shed light on certain dimensions of this problem, notably spatial and demographic patterns of orangutan killing, the workings of the illegal wildlife trade, and rural villagers' perceptions of orangutans, the forest and the law.[1] These unprecedented insights are the product of interviews, surveys and focus group discussions carried out across a large number of villages. Due to their inherent brevity and thematic focus, however, such methods only scratch the surface of the cultural, social, political, economic, historical and religious complexities at the village level. Yet, an inside understanding of these realities could be key to understanding and thus mitigating orangutan killing in these areas.

Anthropological Methods and Insights

Ethnographic, or sociocultural anthropological, approaches are well suited to illuminating what goes on in small-scale settings. Unlike large-scale surveys and predictive modeling, anthropological methods emphasize depth and holism, situating specific phenomena (such as orangutan killing) within their multifarious contexts (Eriksen, 2015, chapter 1; Geertz, 1973). Such research is often carried out by individual anthropologists, working solo or sometimes as part of teams.

The hallmark of sociocultural anthropology is participant observation. This means immersing oneself as both participant and observer in a particular setting—anything from a village to a global network—in order to gain an "inside" understanding of how it functions and is perceived and experienced by its members. Participant observation fundamentally entails "being there," rather than setting up formal research encounters (such as questionnaires), and being led by the day-to-day flows and informal interactions of the field (Borneman and Hammoudi, 2009).

Anthropological research typically takes place over an extended period, from several months to one or two years. This enables anthropologists to build up an everyday familiarity with their field site (including by learning local languages),

to gain the trust of their research participants—including people of different ages, sexes, social status, religions, occupations, political affiliations, and other characteristics—and to follow up on new leads and emerging insights. Participant observation is frequently carried out in conjunction with other social science methods, including semi-structured interviews, oral histories, biographical research, archival analysis, maps and censuses, and comparative research in other field sites or with other anthropologists (Bennett et al., 2017a).

Building Knowledge and Understanding

Anthropological methods generate distinctive forms of data that can fill important gaps in our understanding of the multiple dimensions of orangutan killing. First, the insights gained from fieldwork conversations tend to be more candid and honest than those elicited in the confines of structured interviews, surveys and questionnaires (Eriksen, 2015, chapter 3; Hume and Mulcock, 2004). Participants' responses to the latter might be shaped by a lack of familiarity or trust as well as their own vested interests (such as seeking financial rewards). Conversely, anthropologists' extended presence and investment in social relationships in the field often give them access to opinions and experiences that remain invisible to outsiders. This is especially important when exploring a topic as sensitive and potentially incriminating as orangutan killing, which villagers may not discuss openly with conservationists or interviewers.

Second, the holistic, open-ended nature of anthropological research can generate a fuller picture of village life than is possible through other methods. Rather than focusing on specific problems and solutions, anthropologists start by exploring the wider contexts, attending to phenomena such as gender relations, kinship, morality, economic pressures, local power structures and political formations, religion and ritual, and relationships with the state (Eriksen, 2015). These are integral to the milieu in which orangutan killing occurs and often of greater concern than biodiversity conservation to people in rural Borneo—many of whom have little interest in or experience of orangutans.

Third, anthropological methods can reveal real-life complexity, ambiguity and fluidity. People's lives and identities are as multifaceted as the problem of orangutan killing: one person can be a subsistence farmer, cash cropper, oil palm plantation employee and government official all at once—and hold multiple, even conflicting, views of orangutans, the forest, and conservation that vary situationally and evolve over time. Through their extended presence in the field, anthropologists are well equipped to trace changes and developments, and to understand their drivers, manifestations and impacts (Eriksen, 2015; Howell and Talle, 2012). Orangutan killing is not a static problem, nor is the context in which it occurs; anthropological analyses can serve to capture related vicissitudes.

The utility of anthropological insights for conservation is illustrated by research on hunting within and beyond Borneo. Studies in Africa and Papua New Guinea, for example, reveal

how hunting practices are not only utilitarian, but also structure social relationships and identities at the village level and incorporate remote places into global economies (Gordon, 2016; Sillitoe, 2003; Tadie and Fischer, 2013). Failure to acknowledge these functions and meanings of hunting has frustrated many well-intended conservation efforts (Marks, 2016; West, 2005). Conservation interventions into hunting patterns in Borneo would therefore benefit from taking seriously the deep social embeddedness of hunting practices (Puri, 2005; Wadley and Colfer, 2004; Wadley, Colfer and Hood, 1997).

Other research shows how shifting livelihoods and rural–urban migration can reshape human-wildlife interactions (Margulies and Karanth, 2018). On Borneo, these processes have a profound impact on village politics and forms of authority, which in turn influence how conservation interventions and the law are implemented at this level (Elmhirst *et al.*, 2017; Li, 2015). These processes can also generate new aspirations, forms of identity and affiliation, and religious beliefs that shape how villagers conceive of the forest, modernity and human–animal relations in general (Chua, 2012; König, 2016; Schiller, 1997; Schreer, 2016; Sillander and Alexander,

2016). Tracing how such conceptions influence social dynamics and transform over time is vital to our understanding of how villagers in rural Borneo relate to orangutans and conservation.

Formulating New Strategies

More than supplementing conservationists' understanding of the causes and contexts of orangutan killing, the above insights can inform and generate new strategies and approaches for addressing the problem at its source—the rural village level. Such strategies and approaches could also be applied to other conservation contexts involving poaching, hunting or human–wildlife conflict.

First, anthropological analysis can shed light on why certain conservation interventions succeed or fail, and how legal directives and conservation initiatives are implemented, interpreted, responded to, transformed and/or rejected on the ground (Großmann, 2018; Lounela, 2015). The approach is useful in answering a host of specific questions. For example, do people disregard wildlife protection laws out of ignorance or indifference, or due to resentment of the state, conservationists or other parties? How do they navigate the competing demands of kinship obligations, economic pressures and legal prohibitions? Did a scheme fail because of poor implementation or incompatibility with local moral ideals? Did another succeed because it converged with local agendas or through the backing of a powerful individual? By foregrounding such seemingly external considerations, anthropologists can show how they intersect with conservation in various, sometimes unexpected ways (Kockelman, 2016; Lowe, 2006; Perez, 2018; West, 2006).

Second, anthropological insights can push conservationists to consider new, contextually specific problems and possibilities when designing evidence-based interventions. Understanding local power relations, for example, can facilitate collaborations with certain networks (such as farmers' collectives, credit unions, women's groups and religious communities) or interventions at multiple levels (such as with provincial governments, customary authorities and village-based mutual assistance systems). Understanding influential cultural values and taboos, including those about reciprocity or shame, can inspire new ways of framing conservation messages in community engagement (Aini and West, 2018; Infield et al., 2018; Rubis, 2017). Moreover, understanding the circuits and technologies (such as radio and social media) through which such messages travel could give conservationists new entry points into ongoing conversations that occur beyond established channels, such as schools and "socialization" events.

Finally, anthropology can help transform the relationship between conservation and local communities. Knowledge of the diversity and complexity of life on the ground can challenge one-dimensional stereotypes about "local people" (such as forest protectors or ignorant savages) and better equip conservationists to address local concerns and priorities—some of which may have little to do with orangutans. For such contextual, evidence-based approaches to bear fruit, however, it is vital that anthropological and other social science methods be fully incorporated into the conservation mainstream, treated as primary rather than supplementary components of conservation, and allocated the time, resources and support they require to succeed (Bennett et al., 2017b).

- a close-knit community;
- protected areas and conservation of natural resources;
- a preference for wild meat consumption, mostly among hunters;
- an absence of non-local hunters in community forests (Head, 2014, p. 43).

This research revealed that while hunting was primarily a cultural activity, with wild meat almost always eaten solely by the hunter and his family, it was one of the few sources of income for adolescent boys, who do not inherit agricultural land until they are married. Head (2015) developed a number of questions that proved key to understanding the social, educational and political dynamics at play in Nam Kading. By including these questions in situational analyses of given landscapes prior to an intervention, conservationists may be able to expand their understanding of the identity and practices of local residents. The questions are:

- How is the local community structured? Who exerts the greatest degree of control over community members?
- Do local role models comprise men and women?
- How does wildlife feature in the local belief system?
- Is the area home to indigenous peoples? Do their beliefs regarding wildlife differ from those of other local residents?
- Do any local ceremonies involve the use of wildlife?
- Are social or cultural functions attributed to the consumption or hunting of wildlife?
- Is hunting apes or other species taboo? What is the origin of these taboos and how closely are they followed?
- Are community members becoming less or more likely to adhere to the taboos? Do changing attitudes to hunting or eating wild meat reflect changes in the area, such as an influx of migrants or a local extinction?

Photo: Research on hunting has revealed how hunting practices are not only utilitarian, but also structure social relationships and identities at the village level and incorporate remote places into global economies. Illegal snare in a protected area; positioned along a fence to guide animals into it. © Tim Laman/naturepl.com

- Do community members tolerate, appreciate or disapprove of ownership of wildlife and forest products?
- Could wildlife be replaced by sustainable alternatives? What obstacles would need to be overcome?
- Has the local population undergone recent cultural changes?
- Is wild meat consumption associated with different beliefs and taboos among immigrants in the area?
- What is the role of immigrants in the wild meat trade?
- Have local beliefs and taboos changed as a result of the arrival of immigrants? (Head, 2015, p. 45).

Of particular importance in this part of Lao PDR was the need to understand the social and cultural impacts of political and economic changes in rural areas. In particular, it was useful to gain an appreciation of how communities relate to the state, national and international NGOs, and other external parties, since these entities can shape their perspectives on interventions, such as wildlife protection laws and conservation initiatives. Similarly, it was valuable to keep abreast of local responses to developments such as the arrival of industrial agriculture or the emergence of extractive supply chains (Head, 2014). Case Study 2.4 discusses the importance of understanding local factors in efforts to promote conservation and engage communities in Uganda.

Intersectionality of Culture and Other Factors Relevant to the Ape Trade

This chapter suggests that effective conservation strategies rely on a solid understanding of cultural norms and practices of local communities, including hunting, and that

CASE STUDY 2.4

Integrating Culture and Conservation in Uganda

The Cross-Cultural Foundation of Uganda carried out research to establish the extent to which cultural attitudes can contribute to the conservation of chimpanzees. The work focused on two communities that exhibited a cultural affinity with apes: Uganda's Bakonzo, who are mainly found north of Lake Edward, along the border with the DRC, and the Banyoro, one of the country's largest ethnic groups, occupying forested areas east of Lake Albert (CCFU, 2018; see Figure 2.2). The study indicates that ape habitat, and land and natural resources more generally, are prized not only for their economic value, but also for their cultural and spiritual significance, which provides the community with an important sense of identity and belonging. Although many of the large forests have been gazetted as forest reserves or national parks, members of neighboring communities expressed their attachment to these natural landscapes and their wildlife. Some respondents referred to chimpanzees as "people who ran away from the community" or "relatives who should be respected" (CCFU, 2018, p. 3). In view of their similarities to humans and their obvious intelligence, as illustrated by their ability to use tools and make their own bed every night, communities have refrained from hunting or eating them (CCFU, 2018).

Both the Batangyi (of the Bakonzo ethnic group) and the Bayanja (of the Banyoro) claimed the chimpanzee as a totem (CCFU, 2018; see Box 2.3). Despite modernization, the traditional clan systems in both communities still proved to be vibrant aspects of contemporary life, with children taught at an early age not to hurt or abuse a chimpanzee, but rather to identify the animal as "grandfather" or "owner of the forest" (CCFU, 2018, p. 3). This type of identification can serve as a cultural resource in raising awareness about the importance of conserving the chimpanzee —both within and outside clans that have this species as their totem.

In certain areas, positive attitudes towards wildlife coexist with practices that have a negative impact on chimpanzee conservation. Traditional medicine practitioners in this region reported using body parts in their healing practices, allegedly due to the influence of Congolese migrants. The influx of people from elsewhere may indeed be contributing to changes in cultural practices in Uganda, where communities are not generally known to eat chimpanzee meat. In both research locations in Uganda, population growth and demographic change have led not only to the deforestation of chimpanzee habitat, but also to a shift in attitudes to the species (CCFU, 2018). Case Study 2.1 provides examples of such behavior change in Cameroon, which has seen an influx of people from diverse cultural backgrounds (CCFU, 2018; Chuo, 2018). These developments highlight the need to be sensitive to ongoing cultural changes when developing local conservation interventions.

Notwithstanding demographic changes in Uganda, cultural identity remains key to social organization and relationships within clans and beyond. Cultural institutions in both the Bakonzo and Banyoro homelands are actively engaged in the transmission of cultural values, a practice that could be amplified if undertaken in conjunction with conservation partners, the Uganda Wildlife Authority (UWA) and the district community development offices. Private forest owners in these areas are also likely to hold positive attitudes towards biodiversity and may thus be able to contribute to the preservation of chimpanzees and their habitat outside of protected areas. Together, these stakeholders are well positioned to support culturally relevant processes and practices, and thereby to promote the behavior change that is required to curb significantly both hunting and trading in apes (CCFU, 2018).

As part of the study, respondents suggested changes to the Uganda Wildlife Act, which guides UWA's conservation practice (Parliament of Uganda, 1996). In particular, they recommended that policy guidance be provided on:

- involving cultural centers in conservation activities and ensuring that indigenous knowledge and skills inform local interventions and awareness raising campaigns;

- joining forces with private forest owners to protect forests and chimpanzees, for example by setting up wildlife ranches for tourists;

- holding investors responsible for damage caused to natural and cultural heritage, and ensuring they engage in requisite restoration efforts; and

- conducting a census of chimpanzees in the country to evaluate how culture and other factors affect their endangered status (CCFU, 2018, p. 23).

Links between people and biodiversity are important aspects of individual and ethnic identity and contribute significantly to the experience of well-being. Without connections to the environment, individuals and communities may lose their sense of identity and rootedness in place and time. By going beyond the traditional fines-and-fences approach, governments and their partners can ensure that cultural heritage plays a role in promoting conservation and benefitting communities. They can do so by allowing communities to define their needs and goals in a manner that makes the most sense to them, and by identifying other ways to strengthen their ability to engage meaningfully in decision-making processes.

conservationists can best gain such an understanding by asking—rather than ascribing to or telling—people what is important to them about their natural environment. As discussed in Case Study 2.4, traditional communities pass on traditional beliefs and practices in an effort to conserve what is considered valuable. In cases where such practices—including the use of ape parts in traditional medicine—are in conflict with conservation objectives, dialog between local people and conservationists can help to identify required compromises. In the best-case scenario, such collaboration can serve to protect individual species as well people's livelihood and cultural identity, all of which depend on the ecological integrity of the local environment.

In addition to partnering with local communities, conservationists can undertake supplementary research to ensure that gender and other issues are properly factored into interventions. Wildlife conservation and management efforts often overlook gender dimensions, even though gender inequalities and differences are reflected in the use, management and conservation of wildlife at the local level (Meola, 2013; Ogra, 2012). Moreover, anecdotal evidence suggests that the roles of actors in the illegal wildlife trade are particularly gender-differentiated (L. Aguilar, personal communication, 2018). Steps to integrate gender into conservation projects can include: assessing the gender dimensions of the project and setting; developing project indicators for monitoring gender integration; and developing broader institutional processes to further this integration (L. Aguilar, personal communication, 2018).

As this chapter demonstrates, questions about ape conservation are also questions about human identity and well-being. The

FIGURE 2.2

Homelands of the Bakonzo and Banyoro Peoples of Uganda

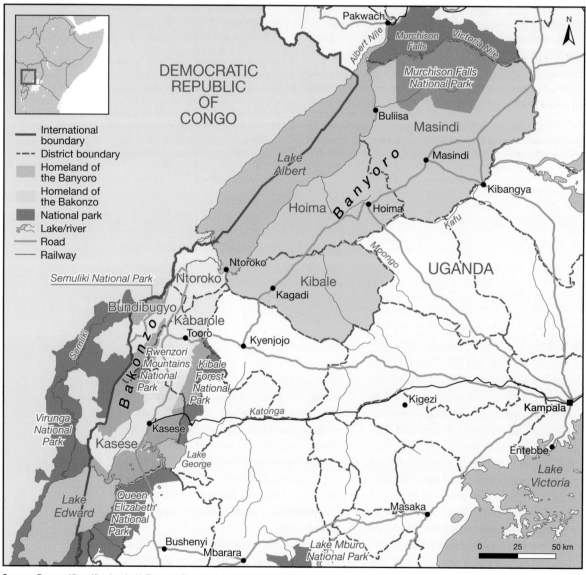

Sources: Bunyoro-Kitara Kingdom (n.d.), Protected Planet (n.d.-b), UNEP-WCMC (2019b, 2019d)

values held by local communities often reveal how they connect with their environment; conservationists who understand these values are best placed to explore how they can benefit ape conservation as well as the communities themselves.

Conclusion

Cultural attitudes and practices are among the factors that both drive and inhibit the ape trade. This chapter suggests that conservationists can benefit from a solid understanding of how these dynamic factors affect the killing and capture of apes in local contexts. Indeed, cultural behavior can be assessed alongside the economic drivers of ape population declines, and related interventions can target both via similar approaches, such as awareness raising, behavior change strategies and appropriate law enforcement (see Box I.4; Chapters 4 and 5; Annex II).

This chapter emphasizes the advantages of approaching interventions in a way that is sensitive to the identities and practices of local individuals and communities. By engaging with local people in a respectful way and identifying the co-benefits of protecting great apes and gibbons, conservationists may be able to open up avenues for compromise, such as by suggesting alternative practices that do not require the killing of apes. As Case Study 2.4 indicates, it is possible to strengthen conservation practices by better appreciating the sociocultural significance of apes among local communities —rather than seeing them purely as objects of tourism or zoology, for example. By supporting the well-being of communities— that is, their overall health and sense of identity—interventions may thus also help to secure conservation benefits.

In practice, however, it may not be possible to strike a perfect balance between the aim of curbing the ape trade and the goal of supporting local communities, their complex value systems and their socioeconomic needs. As shown in Table 2.2 and in Case Study 2.3, a number of social science methods can complement traditional ecological assessments of the ape trade and its impact, yet conservationists may not have the budgets required to carry out detailed studies of a place and its inhabitants. Moreover, while current biodiversity theory and practice suffer from certain false assumptions and misrepresentations of cultural norms, some traditional attitudes and behavior do indeed drive declines in ape and gibbon numbers. Despite these complexities, compromise and positive change are most likely to be reached if conservationists situate their interventions in local settings, in the context of social and familial relationships. In so doing, they can help to rethink narratives such that they maintain links to the past but also become more relevant to the 21st century, with outcomes that do not reinforce the traditional nature–culture dichotomy and thus have the potential to conserve biodiversity and promote well-being at the same time.

Acknowledgments

Principal author: Adam Phillipson[2]

Contributors: Liana Chua,[3] Karmele Llano Sánchez[4] and Paul Hasan Thung[5]

Case Study 2.2: Karmele Llano Sánchez

Case Study 2.3: Liana Chua and Paul Hasan Thung

Endnotes

1. Abram *et al.* (2015); Campbell-Smith, Sembiring and Linkie (2012); Campbell-Smith *et al.* (2010); Davis *et al.* (2013); Freund, Rahman and Knott (2017); Marshall *et al.* (2006); Meijaard *et al.* (2011, 2013); Nijman (2005, 2009, 2017).

2. Arcus Foundation (www.arcusfoundation.org).

3. Brunel University London (www.brunel.ac.uk/anthropology).

4. Yayasan International Animal Rescue Indonesia (www.internationalanimalrescue.or.id).

5. Brunel University London (www.brunel.ac.uk/anthropology).

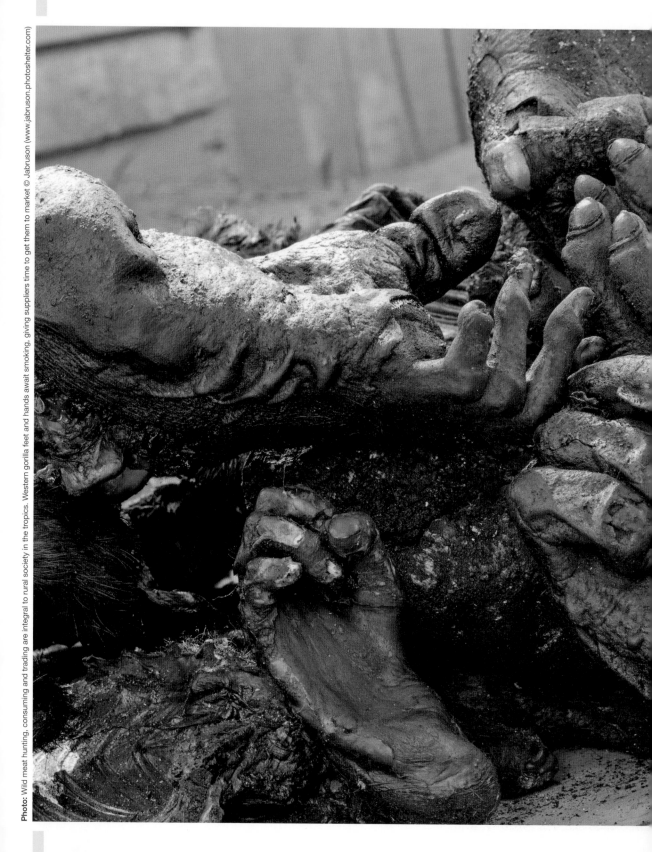

Photo: Wild meat hunting, consuming and trading are integral to rural society in the tropics. Western gorilla feet and hands await smoking, giving suppliers time to get them to market © Jabruson (www.jabruson.photoshelter.com)

CHAPTER 3

Socioeconomics and the Trade in Ape Meat and Parts

Introduction

The hunting of great apes and gibbons for their meat and parts is embedded in the overall practice of killing and capturing wild species, or wild meat hunting (Coad *et al.*, 2019). In Southeast Asian forests, for instance, hunters target a large number of species for their meat, including gibbons (Harrison *et al.*, 2016; Stokes, 2017). In considering the trade in ape meat and parts, this chapter focuses on great apes rather than gibbons, as far more information is available about the former than the latter. The chapter first outlines the scale of the problem and the general consequences of hunting great apes and primates in general. It then details the socioeconomic drivers of wild meat hunting and reviews the information available on great apes. In closing, it presents barriers to curbing the wild meat trade, as well as potential solutions.

People hunt wild animals for their meat in a large variety of ecological and cultural settings, ranging from savannah to rainforest biomes in the tropics and subtropics. While no information is available about great ape populations that lived in prehistoric times, evidence indicates that wild meat has long served as a source of protein and income for millions of people throughout the world. The emergence of lithic technology around 2.6 million years ago appears to signal increased hominid carnivory (Isaac, 1978). However, the details remain enigmatic due to sketchy zooarchaeological records and the difficulties inherent in distinguishing between scavenging and systematic hunting (Ferraro et al., 2013; Isaac, 1978).

Zooarchaeological assemblages of small bovids from about 2 million years ago, found at three sites in Kenya, possibly constitute the earliest indirect evidence of hominin hunting practices (Ferraro et al., 2013). The earliest direct evidence of systematic hunting by pre-modern hominins stems from wooden throwing spears that date back about 400,000 years; these items were discovered in Germany alongside stone tools and butchered remains of horses (Thieme, 1997). Evidence for ambush hunting of large animals comes from communities of *Homo erectus* in the Kenyan Rift Valley between about 1.2 million and 500,000 years ago (Kübler et al., 2015). The effects of hunting on wildlife abundance, distribution and extinction remain contested (Barnosky et al., 2004; Faith, 2014; Nagaoka, Rick and Wolverton, 2018).

Hunting by humans seems to have contributed to the extinction of some Pleistocene megafauna in a spatially heterogeneous manner. There is scant evidence, however, that hunting was a factor that led to the disappearance of any of the 24 large mammal species known to have become extinct in continental Africa in the late Pleistocene and early Holocene (Faith, 2014). Although it was once thought that "overkill" by early hunters caused the extinction of many species, evidence in the Americas remains ambiguous (Martin, 1958; Meltzer, 2015; Nagaoka, Rick and Wolverton, 2018). On the one hand, early people of the Americas exhibited a very broad spectrum of diets of which megafauna constituted only a small part (Dillehay et al., 2008, 2017). On the other hand, humans were implicated in the demise of megafauna from 37 genera, even though hunting evidence covers only five of the extinct taxa (mammoths, mastodons, gomphotheres, camels and horses) and the relative contribution of hunting versus other causes, such as climate change, is unresolved (Meltzer, 2015).

Orangutans were extinct in Southeast Asia and Java by the time of the Pleistocene-to-Holocene transition. Hunting is thought to have contributed to their demise, alongside other anthropogenic changes to the environment, while a low human population density might have saved orangutans from extinction in Borneo and Sumatra (Harrison, Krigbaum and Manser, 2006). In Madagascar, hunting severely impacted megafauna 2,000 to 1,000 years ago (Burney, Robinson and Burney, 2003).

There is mounting evidence that wild meat hunting was replaced by agropastoralism using zebu (*Bos indicus*) husbandry, which caused landscape changes associated with burning woodlands for pasture (Burns et al., 2016). Thus, both wild meat hunting and abandonment of hunting for agropastoralism have contributed to the extinction vortex at different points in time, highlighting the complex impacts of wild meat hunting on population dynamics (Crowley et al., 2017).

The effects of hunting and carnivory on human cultural and biological evolution have been significant. While the details remain uncertain, it is clear that hunting and meat consumption were critical in human evolution, in particular regarding brain size, learning, intelligence and social behavior (Isaac, 1978; Kaplan *et al.*, 2000; Stanford, 1999).

Wild meat hunting remains an integral part of rural human society in the tropics, as do consuming and trading meat (Atuo, O'Connell and Abanyam, 2015). However, with advances in technology, increases in human population density, encroachment into primary habitats and increasing demand from the growing commercial wild meat trade, escalating harvest rates are causing significant declines in wildlife populations and leading to local and regional extinctions (Benítez-López *et al.*, 2017). Instead of traditional hunting methods, guns and modern materials for efficient trap and snare construction are now dominant, often in com-

bination with new hunting strategies, such as the use of hunting dogs to target preferred species (Rovero *et al.*, 2012). As a consequence, hunting is a direct threat to endangered wildlife in all tropical regions and is the greatest threat facing many populations on a local scale (Harrison *et al.*, 2016; Lee *et al.*, 2014; Schwitzer *et al.*, 2014). Globally, nearly 20% of the threatened and near-threatened species on the Red List of the International Union for Conservation of Nature (IUCN) are directly affected by hunting, including more than 300 mammal species (Maxwell *et al.*, 2016; Ripple *et al.*, 2016). Wildlife hunting is also the most frequently reported threat to wildlife in protected areas in the world's tropical regions (Laurance *et al.*, 2012; Schulze *et al.*, 2018; Tranquilli *et al.*, 2014). In the case of primates, out of a total of 504 species in 79 genera, approximately 60% are threatened with extinction from hunting and trapping (Estrada *et al.*, 2017).

Photo: Forest elephants (*Loxodonta cyclotis*) are primarily poached for ivory, but their meat is an important by-product. Confiscated elephant tusks, Garamba National Park, DRC. © Jabruson (www.jabruson. photoshelter.com)

Where species are not only targeted for their meat for local and regional consumption, but are also illegally traded internationally, the consequences can be particularly severe. Forest elephants (*Loxodonta cyclotis*), for example, are primarily poached for ivory, but their meat is an important by-product (Matschie, 1900; Stiles, 2011). In a period of only ten years (2002–11), the forest elephant population declined by about 62% and its geographic range decreased by around 30% (Maisels *et al.*, 2013). Poaching of elephants for their ivory is widely supported by interwoven local, regional, national and international networks. Such widespread demand for an animal part can lead to species extinctions and—not unlike in the drug trade—can cause a cascade of devastating social consequences (Brashares *et al.*, 2014; van Uhm and Moreto, 2017).

Even where international trade has not been established, a health fad is enough to trigger either international or regional demand from an existing national network. Traditional Chinese medicine has become highly popular around the world and thus drives illegal trade in tiger body parts (Wong, 2015). In Cameroon and Nigeria, the skulls, bones, hearts and hair of the critically endangered Cross River gorilla (*Gorilla gorilla diehli*) are used in traditional medicine to treat a range of inflictions, from mental illness to rheumatism, impotence and bone fractures (Etiendem, Hens and Pereboom, 2011). For more information on cultural drivers of the ape trade, see Chapter 2.

Given the illegal nature of the trade in ape meat and parts, it is very difficult to obtain information and data on its scale and impacts. Subsistence hunters who provide food for use in the home, for instance, regularly sell their surplus, including protected species; similarly, opportunistic hunters in search of small game are likely to capture and kill protected species if the opportunity arises (Abernethy *et al.*, 2013; Coad *et al.*, 2019).

Hunters who supply the meat trade may find that selling body parts as by-products increases the profitability of wild meat hunting (Lindsey *et al.*, 2012). The trade is complex, involving a number of different actors, from the poachers at the source, to any number of actors within the source nations (see Box 3.1), including those working internationally, such as crime groups and corrupt government officials, and through to a range of facilitators involved in demand countries (Lawson and Vines, 2014). While data on the hunting of apes remain limited, they indicate that the general dynamics of the wild meat trade also apply to primates.

Although many people who live close to nature consume animals ranging from elephants to gorillas to caterpillars, terrestrial vertebrates (amphibians, reptiles, birds and mammals) make up most of the biomass extracted and eaten in the tropics (Coad *et al.*, 2019). Among vertebrates, mammals are the main source of wild meat in many regions of tropical Africa, South America and Asia (Robinson and Bennett, 2004). Three taxonomic groups account for more than three-quarters of the mammal species consumed across Africa, South America and Asia: primates (53%); ungulates, or hoofed animals (16%); and rodents (7%) (Fa *et al.*, 2013).

A comprehensive literature review indicates that wild meat hunting generally focuses on medium-sized animals but that larger species are taken opportunistically. These large species, including great apes, afford good returns simply because of the total volume of meat, thus encouraging hunters to grasp the opportunity when it arises, but not necessarily because of any particular preference for their meat. Although primates are among the taxonomic groups that are most hunted for their meat, monkeys and apes rarely account for more than 20% of the wild meat sold on African markets (Cawthorn and Hoffman, 2015; Robinson and Bennett, 2004). For most consumers

BOX 3.1

The Great Ape Commodity Chain in Cameroon

The general route of wild meat from its source to its point of consumption is well understood. In simple terms, hunters provide game to middlemen, who supply market vendors, who openly display various types of wild meat and sell them to consumers (Cowlishaw, Mendelson and Rowcliffe, 2005; Robinson, Redford and Bennett, 1999). Since great apes are protected by law, the ape meat commodity chain remains clandestine and therefore difficult to monitor. Once a middleman receives an order and a monetary deposit from a buyer, he asks a hunter in a rural part of the country to dispatch the ape meat. Having received the meat, the middleman has it delivered to the buyer at a secret location. If authorities are complicit in the deal, the trafficker can operate more openly. Traffickers typically use the same logistics to transfer live animals and wild meat orders from hunters to buyers, since poachers who hunt great apes for their meat often sell live orphaned babies (Clough and May, 2018).

A study by Tagg *et al.* (2018) used questionnaires and interviews to investigate activities and motivations of actors

involved in the ape meat trade in the northern and western periphery of the Dja Faunal Reserve, in southeastern Cameroon (see Figure 3.1). Participants included hunters, carriers and traders, as well as consumers, forestry administrators and middlemen, who facilitate the trade in different ways. Figure 3.2 illustrates the commodity chain in which these actors operate.

The hunters in this study comprised both opportunistic and specialized hunters, helped to varying extents by porters. Carriers included drivers of logging trucks, buses, taxis and private cars; some provided information about illicit means of traversing checkpoints, such as relying on the complicity of wildlife officials at checkpoints and the impunity of passengers and drivers of certain registered vehicles. Traders—including wholesalers and retailers—typically work in markets and restaurants, but they also sell from home; most of them partake in other activities, such as agriculture or bee farming. Traders can buy directly from hunters or from middlemen. Many middlemen are forestry officials who can be motivated to supply politicians and other members of the elite, and who consequently enjoy some level of impunity. Consumers, who can buy from hunters, middlemen or traders, are the final link in the chain. The part of the chain in which meat is being traded varies in length depending on the number of

FIGURE 3.1

The Dja Faunal Reserve and Environs, Cameroon

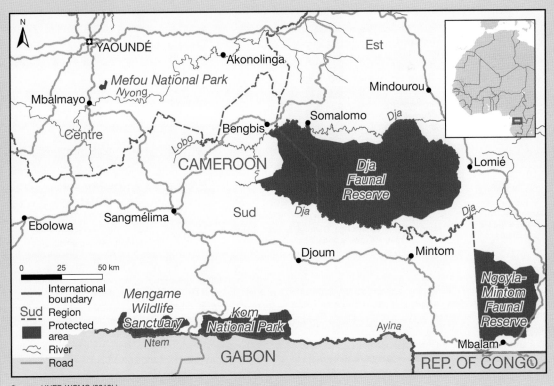

Source: UNEP-WCMC (2019b)

74

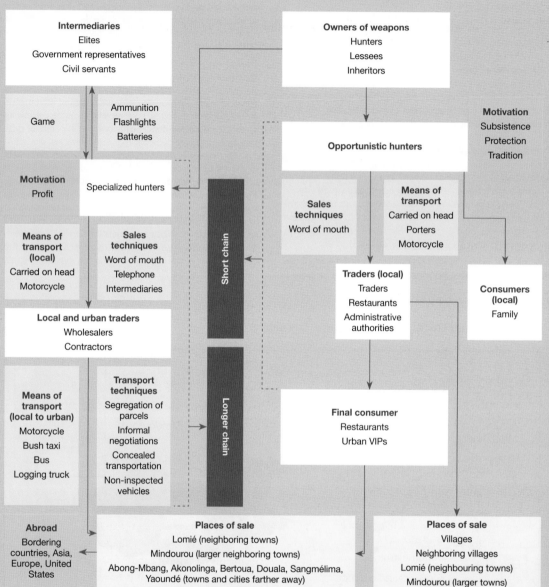

FIGURE 3.2

The Great Ape Meat Commodity Chain of the Dja Region, Cameroon

traders involved. If a trader sells meat to an individual who consumes it at home, then that consumer represents the end of the chain; if the first consumer is also a trader and sells the meat to someone else, the chain grows longer (Tagg *et al.*, 2018).

The study results indicate that most ape meat consumption occurs close to home, although some shipments are sent to international recipients. The findings also show that middle-

men reap the greatest returns, possibly because their input is very low and they enjoy some impunity. Specialized hunters earn high incomes, but they incur the risks of the hunt. Opportunistic hunters gain little because they sell quickly and at low cost to avoid being caught with illegal meat. Wholesalers have limited expenditures, but their profits are low; they prefer to buy more and spread costs across different species to minimize risk (Tagg *et al.*, 2018).

in urban areas, the origin of wild meat is rarely of importance as they tend to select the cheapest variety (Wilkie *et al.*, 2005). The opportunistic aspect of the wild meat trade is also reflected in an inverse relationship between the volume of fish and the amounts of wild meat sold in rural markets in Ghana (Brashares *et al.*, 2004).

The Scale of the Problem for Great Apes

High local, regional, national and international demand for live bonobos, chimpanzees, gorillas and orangutans—as well as their meat and body parts—leads to the killing of thousands of animals annually; however, information on market values and trade volumes remains sketchy. In the case of orangutans, adults tend to be killed, while their young enter the live animal trade. Killed orangutans are not supplied into the wild meat trade, as there is neither local nor international demand for their meat. In general, great ape meat forms part of traditional diets only in West and Central Africa, especially among non-Muslim populations (Clough and May, 2018). The wild meat and live animal trades are intertwined; meat is often obtained as a by-product when adults are killed to acquire young individuals, and vice versa.

While demand for meat and live animals is high, both locally and internationally, local subsistence hunters gain significantly less than the criminal networks and corrupt profiteers, as is also the case in the narcotics trade (van Uhm, 2018b; see the Introduction and Chapter 4). Notwithstanding this disparity in income, local commercial hunters in Africa can earn US$300–1,000 annually, which exceeds the average annual household income and competes with the income of "those responsible for regulating the trade" (Okiwelu, Ewurum and Noutcha, 2009, p. 7).

The Indonesian Market

Limited information is available both on the role of hunting in food security among rural communities in Asian tropical forest environments and on the impact of wild meat hunting and trade in orangutans (K.L. Sánchez, personal communication, 2019). Domestic demand for orangutan meat is probably insignificant in Indonesia since the country is predominantly Muslim and eating primates is considered haram (forbidden). The Sumatran orangutan (*Pongo abelii*) is mainly targeted for the domestic live animal market rather than for the international trade, as Indonesia lacks the type of illicit supply network found in West and Central Africa (Clough and May, 2018). In Borneo's Kalimantan, however, an estimated 2,000–3,000 orangutans (*Pongo pygmaeus*) are killed annually for their meat, as incidental offtake associated with the live animal trade and in human–wildlife conflicts; that figure exceeds previous estimates and is likely to be unsustainable (Meijaard *et al.*, 2011a). Small amounts of orangutan meat may be sold outside of Kalimantan's urban areas, not within them (Clough and May, 2018).

Hunting probably played an important role in the local extinction of some orangutan populations within their historical range (Marshall *et al.*, 2006; Meijaard *et al.*, 2011a, 2011b). The dramatic decrease in orangutan numbers in Borneo over the past 20 years has also been the result of changes in land cover, mainly because of habitat fragmentation and loss due to the conversion of forest to agricultural land, and associated deforestation (Voigt *et al.*, 2018; Wich *et al.*, 2008). This encroachment into orangutan habitat heightens the risk of conflict between humans and orangutans, such as retribution killing for economic loss caused by crop raiding (Marshall *et al.*, 2006).

A useful indicator of orangutan killing is the number of baby or infant orangutans rescued, handed over or confiscated by the authorities and taken in by orangutan rescue centers across Borneo and Sumatra (Nijman, 2005). In 2000–04, three of Kalimantan's seven centers took in an average of 104 individuals per year; the average climbed to 107 for the period 2005–13 (Nijman, 2005; K.L. Sánchez, personal communication, 2019). Since rescued infants represent the deaths of their mothers—and possibly of more individuals—the high rate of orangutan offtake demonstrates that the mortality rate is also high (K.L. Sánchez, personal communication, 2019).

African Markets

In the Congo Basin, most towns and cities operate regular wild meat markets (Colyn, Dudu and Mbaelele, 1987; Fa *et al.*, 2006; Juste *et al.*, 1995). In Africa, this massive degree of wildlife extraction for meat and parts represents a severe threat to bonobos (*Pan paniscus*), chimpanzees (*Pan troglodytes*), Grauer's gorilla (*Gorilla beringei graueri*) and western lowland gorillas (*Gorilla gorilla gorilla*). Research indicates this trade constitutes a sizeable—yet generally underestimated—part of the economies of many

African countries (Lescuyer and Nasi, 2016). In the range states of the affected great ape species, the combined trade is valued at anywhere between US$650,000 and US$6 million per year, which accounts for a significant proportion of the overall wild meat market (Clough and May, 2018). This broad range reflects similarly wide variations in the price of meat: from about US$1.31 to US$12 per kilogram. Urban consumers in Central and West Africa typically pay the highest prices for great ape meat, suggesting that profit margins are high for suppliers, who probably collect most of the payments in cash (Clough and May, 2018). In many locations where great ape meat is consumed regularly, it is considered a choice commodity, for various reasons. In Lomié, Cameroon, for instance, people who eat gorilla meat tend to prefer the chest, hands and ribs because they are believed to impart respect, courage, strength and skill (Tagg *et al.*, 2018).

In Cameroon's Dja Faunal landscape, costs depend in part on whether a hunter is specialized in great ape meat. While an average hunter can charge US$2–3 for a piece of smoked chimpanzee and a bit more, US$3–6, for gorilla meat, specialized poachers can earn US$9–10 (Tagg *et al.*, 2018). Similar price differences apply to whole apes. While a gorilla can generally fetch US$65–85 and a chimpanzee US$25–35, specialized poachers ask for roughly double those prices: US$135–170 and US$50–60, respectively (Tagg *et al.*, 2018). One study found that some poachers are able to sell whole chimpanzees for up to US$100 (Stiles *et al.*, 2013). A comparison with the prices of unprotected species that are commonly sold at the markets is instructive: a 10-kg duiker costs around US$13, a 6-kg monkey about US$6 and a 3-kg porcupine roughly US$4 (Tagg *et al.*, 2018).

Market surveys and reported consumption rates allow for estimates of the volume of wild meat extracted from some African forests (Fa, Peres and Meeuwig, 2002; Wilkie and Carpenter, 1999). About 4 million tons of wild meat are removed from the Congo Basin every year, yielding an extraction-to-production ratio of 2.4—which indicates that 2.4 times more biomass is extracted from the wild than is produced (that is, added to affected populations, typically via reproduction) (Fa, Peres and Meeuwig, 2002; Fa and Tagg, 2016). To counteract extraction rates, Congo Basin mammals would have to double their reproductive potential every year, which is clearly unachievable (Fa and Tagg, 2016). Hunting records and market surveys indicate that across the Congo Basin—with large regional variability—rare and vulnerable species such as great apes and elephants usually represent only a small proportion (often less than 5%) of the total number of animals hunted (Nasi, Taber and van Vliet, 2011). A study conducted in Ogooué, Gabon, reveals that primates made up just over 6% of 2,647 captures undertaken by 26 village subsistence hunters in a year (Coad, 2007). Other research, however, shows that primates account for up to 40% of harvested carcasses (Nasi, Taber and van Vliet, 2011).

Although wild meat constitutes only a small proportion of the meat consumed in large cities—typically less than 2% of the annual dietary protein requirement—the corresponding volume consumed per person is significant (Wilkie *et al.*, 2016). A recent study carried out in the Kinshasa–Brazzaville metropolitan area, which is home to around 15 million inhabitants, suggests that the local rate of wild meat consumption is high, even though the number of establishments offering wild meat for sale is low in comparison to outlets that sell other domestic meat (Fa *et al.*, 2019). A quick calculation indicates that even if each person in Kinshasa and Brazzaville eats only 1–2 kg of wild meat per year, 15–30 million kg could be consumed annually (Fa *et al.*, 2019; Wilkie and Carpenter,

1999). To get a better sense of this volume, it may be helpful to visualize the proportion accounted for by guenon monkeys (*Cercopithecus* spp.), a preferred species group in these metropolitan areas. Between 8,400 and 22,500 whole guenon monkeys are sold annually in restaurants across the two cities, yet they account for less than 1% of the total volume of wild meat entering the two cities (Fa *et al.*, 2019).

Measuring Global Offtakes

Between 2005 and 2011, more than 22,000 great apes were killed or captured in Africa and Asia to supply the wildlife trade. On average, hunters thus removed more than 3,000 individuals per year from the forests (Stiles *et al.*, 2013). The impact on ape populations is likely to be significant, especially given the species' low population densities and relatively low reproductive rates.

These data on trade volumes and values can only be seen as indicative, and mostly as minimum estimates, since accurate numbers are difficult to obtain due to the illegal nature of activities under review. Information on hunting of terrestrial species remains limited, although efforts are under way to gather, assess and monitor changes in available data sets from different studies, as demonstrated by Taylor *et al.* (2015). While the accuracy of aggregate numbers remains contested—especially since the age of most of the data, collected over 30 years, makes up-to-date assessments difficult—proxy indicators can be used to estimate regional and global offtakes (Ingram *et al.*, 2015). An example is the mean body mass indicator, which uses the mean body mass within each sample as a proxy of species composition; a drop from larger to smaller species may indicate that a habitat is experiencing defaunation. Another example is the offtake pressure indicator, which measures the offtake pressure exerted on terrestrial species, as represented by the overall trend in the number of individuals of each species killed and removed across sites and years (Dirzo *et al.*, 2014; Ingram *et al.*, 2015).

Biological Consequences of Hunting for Meat and Parts

Wildlife Reductions and Losses

A recent meta-analysis of 176 studies across the tropics shows that relative abundances in hunted areas compared to non-hunted areas were 83% lower for mammals and 58% lower for birds (Benítez-López *et al.*, 2017). A comparison of mammal species densities across 101 non-hunted and hunted sites in Amazonia points to significant population declines for 22 of the 30 considered species at high levels of hunting, with an 11-fold decrease in population biomass for the 12 hunting-sensitive species (Peres and Palacios, 2007).[1]

Long-term, detailed monitoring studies are surprisingly rare for primates in countries with prime habitat, mainly due to logistical constraints, a lack of rigor in data collection and data biases (Rovero *et al.*, 2015). A pilot study on the Angolan black-and-white colobus (*Colobus angolensis*), the Sykes' monkey (*Cercopithecus mitis* ssp. *albogularis*) and the endangered endemic Udzungwa red colobus (*Procolobus gordonorum*) in Tanzania demonstrates that trained local technicians are efficient at implementing monitoring schemes (Rovero *et al.*, 2015). Specifically, it reveals that all species inside a protected area remained stable over an 11-year period, but that two colobus populations outside the protected area suffered a marked decline, due to a combination of targeted subsistence hunting and habitat degradation (Rovero *et al.*, 2012, 2015).

In their stronghold of Kahuzi-Biega National Park in the Democratic Republic of Congo (DRC), Grauer's gorilla populations declined by 87% from 1994 to 2015, mainly due to hunting, although the trend was exacerbated by civil conflict (Plumptre *et al.*, 2016). Fifty-two percent of the total mountain gorilla (*Gorilla beringei beringei*) range lies within a 20-km radius of camps for refugees and internally displaced people (Bender and Ziegler, 2009). Across the Congo Basin, western lowland gorilla and central chimpanzee (*Pan troglodytes troglodytes*) populations are significantly negatively correlated with hunting (Strindberg *et al.*, 2018; Walsh *et al.*, 2003). The spatial patterns and intensity of losses, however, are determined by the motivations of the hunters (Kühl *et al.*, 2009).

In the northeastern Republic of Congo, nearly 7% of chimpanzees and 5% of gorillas may have been removed annually, from already low population densities of about 0.3 chimpanzees per km² and 0.2 gorillas per km². In contrast to other species that are pursued for their meat, great apes typically have low reproductive rates, which means that even low hunting pressure can lead to catastrophic population decline. Indeed, an annual offtake of 5–7% implies that the studied chimpanzee and gorilla populations were likely to be halved within 11–15 years—clearly an unsustainable rate (Kano and Asato, 1994). Even when hunting offtake diminishes

Photo: Grauer's gorilla populations, in their stronghold of Kahuzi-Biega National Park, DRC, declined by 87% from 1994 to 2015, mainly due to hunting, although the trend was exacerbated by civil conflict. Grauer's gorilla at the Gorilla Rehabilitation and Conservation Education Center (GRACE), DRC. © GRACE

with dwindling population density, it can maintain the local extinction vortex. Given their low population densities and low reproductive rates, great ape species cannot absorb such losses; instead, their survival in the wild is directly threatened. In this context, it is worth remembering that intensive hunting in fragmented forests appears to have driven Miss Waldron's red colobus (*Piliocolobus badius waldroni*) to extinction in Ghana and Ivory Coast (Oates *et al.*, 2000, 2019).

Analyses conducted in 2002 suggest that African offtake levels, which are largely driven by urban demand for wild meat, were about 50% higher than production and at least four times higher than sustainable rates (Fa, Peres and Meeuwig, 2002). Barring changes in extraction rates, Central Africa's wild meat supplies are expected to decline significantly between 2003 and 2050, with drops ranging from 61% in the Central African Republic (CAR) to 78% in the DRC (Fa, Currie and Meeuwig, 2003).

There is sufficient evidence that unsustainable hunting leads to the local decline and extirpation of wildlife populations, as well as population isolation and the resulting loss of genetic and cultural diversity. Since small populations, such as mountain gorillas, inevitably inbreed, they suffer an accumulation of deleterious mutations and a decline in the fitness of the population (Xue *et al.*, 2015). Distinct ape populations are known to exhibit a wide range of different cultural traits, many of which are being lost with local extirpations (Kühl *et al.*, 2019). Furthermore, large-bodied frugivorous primates are keystone species, which play critical functional roles, such as seed dispersal (Lambert, 2011; Nuñez-Iturri, Olsson and Howe, 2008). The loss of these kinds of ecological engineers reduces the health of an ecosystem and ultimately affects its provision of life-giving, global services, water and carbon storage (Dirzo *et al.*, 2014).

> " Great apes are keystone species, which play critical functional roles, such as seed dispersal. Their loss reduces the health of an ecosystem and ultimately affects its provision of life-giving, global services, water and carbon storage. "

Risk to and through Food Security

Humans—including rural and forest people, who rely on wild meat as their only source of animal protein, and urban dwellers, who consume wild meat as a luxury (see below)—drive unsustainable hunting throughout the tropics. Wildlife often plays an important role in rural communities, be it as a source of food, income and medicine; a target of hunting for crop protection; or as a feature of cultural traditions (Alves and van Vliet, 2018; El Bizri *et al.*, 2015; Ichikawa, Hattori and Yasuoka, 2016; Nasi *et al.*, 2008). A loss of wildlife thus results not only in the waning of a wide range of direct ecosystem services on which rural people rely, but also in the deterioration of their cultural identity. Given the scale of the current wild meat harvest and the persistent increase in human populations, it is almost inevitable that wildlife declines will continue, in turn threatening the very availability of wild meat (Ceballos, Ehrlich and Dirzo, 2017; Swamy and Pinedo-Vasquez, 2014; Wilkie *et al.*, 2011). The direct food security costs of faunal loss are expected to fall disproportionately on the millions of rural inhabitants across the tropics and subtropics—those who are the most dependent on wild meat and who have very few affordable alternatives at their disposal (Milner-Gulland and Bennett, 2003).

In Cameroon and the DRC, a high proportion of the daily protein requirement is supplied by wild meat (Fa, Currie and Meeuwig, 2003). Data from the Poverty Environment Network, representing smallholder-dominated tropical and sub-tropical landscapes across 24 developing countries, demonstrate the importance of wild foods to food security: wild animal products are collected by about 21% of households, while only about 4% of households in forested areas and 2% in non-forested areas generate cash income from the collection (Hickey *et al.*,

2016). The data also indicate that poorer households derive a higher proportion of their income from hunting; that 39% of households engage in hunting activities, more than previously assumed; that the vast majority (87%) of wild meat is consumed in hunting households; and that hunting contributes only 2% of cash income (Nielsen *et al.*, 2017).

Wild meat contributes both macronutrients and micronutrients to a diet. A rare study quantifying the importance of wild meat for micronutrient acquisition shows that 14.3% of households that consumed wild meat in the Amazon acquired significantly higher levels of iron, zinc and vitamin C than other households. Moreover, wild meat-consuming households presented a higher nutritional status, with a lower intake of carbohydrates (−10%) and a higher intake of proteins (+46%), iron (+151%) and zinc (+23%) compared to the others (Sarti *et al.*, 2015).

On the one hand, over-exploitation of wild meat destroys food security via local extinctions—a typical "tragedy of the commons" problem, as discussed below (Hardin, 1968). On the other hand, shifting food security into modern agriculture might also destroy biodiversity, affecting the same species that were previously hunted for wild meat. The rate of wild meat hunting and the importance of wild meat as a protein source are both inversely related to the consumption of alternative protein sources, such as fish or domestic livestock; as discussed below, the promotion of alternative meat sources is thus being hailed as one of the main strategies to limit the consumption of wild meat (Brashares *et al.*, 2004; Nielsen *et al.*, 2018). It needs to be stressed, however, that such studies use the term "domestic livestock" to refer to currently practiced subsistence husbandry, not to industrial, commercial agriculture (Nielsen *et al.*, 2018). This research does not address the food security of urban dwellers, who— in contrast to rural consumers—often have access to other, affordable nutritious meats and are therefore less likely to suffer nutritional hardship if they are deprived of wild meat (Bennett, 2002).

If the urban demand for wild meat is successfully curtailed, the agricultural sector will have to undergo significant changes to produce food for Africa's ever-expanding—and increasingly affluent—populations in cities and towns. The continent's urbanization trend is extraordinary: urban population density is expected to triple within the next 40 years and, by 2030, Africa will be home to as many as 9 megacities—with populations exceeding 10 million inhabitants (Güneralp *et al.*, 2017; UN DESA, 2018). Promoting the expansion and productivity of the agricultural sector to meet the demands of more urbanized populations will have devastating consequences on natural areas, even if the growth rate of Africa's agricultural sector over the past 30 years (+160%) is slower than Asia's (+212%) and South America's (+174%) (NEPAD, 2013).

Greater wealth in developing countries typically translates into increased meat consumption, as evidenced by the upsurge in China's annual per capita consumption of meat (which rose from 16 kg to 43 kg) and milk (which rose from 3 kg to 8 kg) between 1983 and 1997 (Delgado, 2003). Assuring food security outside the wild meat system is thus likely to exacerbate the loss of biodiversity and ecosystem services, which is fueled by land use changes that are designed to maximize agricultural yields for the more affluent local and global populations (Marques *et al.*, 2019). A case in point involves land use change driven by the palm oil industry, which on the one hand provides local economic development, yet on the other causes the demise of the orangutan due to habitat change and increased human–wildlife conflict (Ancrenaz *et al.*, 2015, 2016; Meijaard *et al.*, 2011a).

> " Assuring food security outside the wild meat system is likely to exacerbate the loss of biodiversity and ecosystem services, fueled by land use changes that are designed to maximize agricultural yields. "

In Central Africa, only Cameroon, CAR and Gabon could prospectively maintain their population's protein supply above the recommended daily requirements (46 g for women and 56 g for men). Maintaining current reliance on wild meat in the region not only implies that a substantial number of faunal species will become at least locally extinct relatively rapidly, but also that malnutrition will increase significantly in Central Africa unless food insecurity is promptly resolved by other means (Wicander and Coad, 2018; Wilkie *et al.*, 2016).

In some circumstances, assuring food security entails replacing wild meat and fish with industrial chicken or canned meats, which are of less nutritional value (Dounias and Froment, 2011; Nardoto *et al.*, 2011; Sarti *et al.*, 2015; van Vliet *et al.*, 2015). Overall, however, establishing food security outside the wild meat market will require an increase in locally available alternative meat and protein resources for optimal nutrition and, at the same time, a drawdown of ecologically inefficient and destructive systems, such as the farming of ruminants, as discussed below (Machovina, Feeley and Ripple, 2015; Oben, Molua and Oben, 2015).

Drivers of Wild Meat Hunting

Socioeconomic Factors

Poor societies tend to be more reliant on wild meat for survival and have fewer opportunities for developing alternative livelihoods. As poor people and hunters are more willing to participate in the illegal wild meat trade, many studies argue that profit is the main economic driver of wildlife crime (Duffy and St John, 2013; Duffy *et al.*, 2016; Harrison *et al.*, 2015; Leberatto, 2016). Sites where elephant poaching is rife, for example, have been described as suffering from relatively high levels of poverty, and people arrested for unauthorized hunting in Bwindi Impenetrable National Park in Uganda have been characterized as relatively poor (CITES, IUCN and TRAFFIC, 2013; Twinamatsiko *et al.*, 2014).

The links between poaching and poverty are not fully understood, however. Both economic and geographic drivers have been associated with wild meat consumption, as the poorest communities consume most of the wild meat in rural areas and the wealthiest eat the greatest proportion in urban areas (Brashares *et al.*, 2011). The interaction of drivers varies from one area to another, highlighting the need for interventions to be site-specific (Lindsey *et al.*, 2012). In Borneo, for example, the rate at which orangutans are hunted and killed in any area is affected by local factors such as the degree of forest cover, the proportion of land used for agriculture, income levels, religion and the rate of habitat loss (Meijaard *et al.*, 2011a; Santika *et al.*, 2017). Consideration of a site's broader context is key to an effective, socially and environmentally just approach to tackling wildlife crime (Duffy *et al.*, 2016).

As Amartya Sen points out, poverty denies people agency and the ability to lead fulfilling and meaningful lives. A hunter's decision to poach and trade in protected wildlife may thus also reflect an effort to affirm "identity, status, lifeways, custom, and local prestige" and "to define one's future and day-to-day activities" (Duffy *et al.*, 2016, p. 16; Sen, 1999). This behavior suggests there is a need to develop ways to measure human well-being while also addressing the requirements of voice, prestige and status (Milner-Gulland *et al.*, 2014; Sen, 1999). In this context, agency relates to individual choices and actions within a wider social context (Duffy *et al.*, 2016). The role of agency is commonly observed in people's responses to community initiatives, which

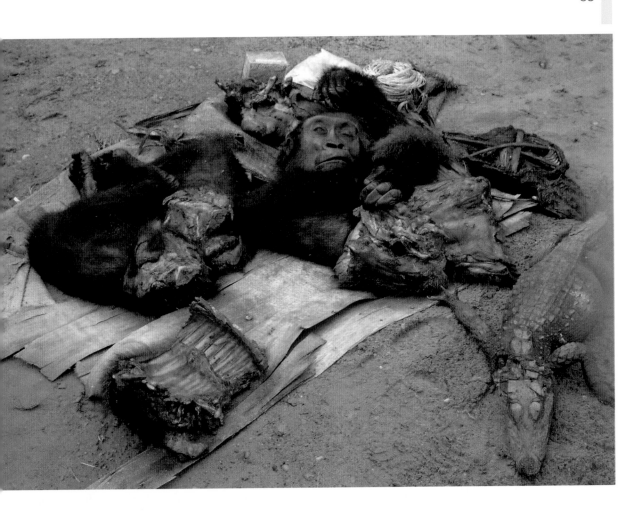

Photo: Both economic and geographic drivers have been associated with wild meat consumption, as the poorest communities consume most of the wild meat in rural areas and the wealthiest eat the greatest proportion in urban areas. Confiscated wild meat and parts, Lomié, Cameroon. © LAGA and The EAGLE Network

may be taken up by individuals who are susceptible to "carrot" solutions, but not by those who instead require "stick" solutions (Egbe, 2001). Individuals in the "stick" group may wind up fueling local hunting activities by investing extra income from community initiatives into new hunting gear or by consuming more wild meat (Damania, Milner-Gulland and Crookes, 2005; Duffy *et al.*, 2016; Milner-Gulland, 2012).

People engage in wildlife crime for a variety of reasons, and the associated goals, risks and gains vary accordingly. In some countries, licenses are required for the hunting of certain species that account for the bulk of the food on which local communities rely. In Cameroon, for instance, the law requires a license for the hunting of Class B (partially protected) species, such as some red duikers and red river hogs (*Potamochoerus porcus*) (Egbe, 2001; Pemunta, 2019). For subsistence hunters—whose families depend on wild meat from protected species for their sustenance—securing food can thus mean breaking the law. In many such cases, the law essentially threatens people's food security (Kümpel *et al.*, 2010). Wild meat is most important to communities that lack access to other sources of protein and micronutrients, such as domestic animal or staple crop production (Nielsen *et al.*, 2017). In Uganda, wildlife crime is linked to a lack of basic necessities and is correlated with population density and external pressures, such as environmental stress and social conflict (Harrison *et al.*, 2015). Overall, wild meat consumption provides substantial economic value and food security to many rural households (Reuter *et al.*, 2016).

In times of economic hardship in rural communities, wild meat can serve as a "safety net contributing to livelihood security" (Schulte-Herbrüggen *et al.*, 2013, p. 10). This idea has been proposed as an "inferior good hypothesis," according to which the poor rely on wild meat as a cheap, low-quality resource (Brashares *et al.*, 2011). The hypothesis is supported by meta-analyses, such as Nielsen *et al.* (2017), which reveal wild meat to be increasingly replaced by domestic and purchased meats as household income increases. An understanding of this hypothesis can allow for the development of effective conservation interventions, which could potentially help to avert destabilizing effects of wild meat shortages and restrictions, such as positive feedback loops that lead to increased poverty, or "poverty traps" (Sachs, 2006). Ideally, such interventions could simultaneously contribute to poverty alleviation and to the protection of biodiversity (Nielsen *et al.*, 2017).

Illegal commercial hunting, in contrast, is driven by factors such as weak law enforcement, easy access to markets (particularly for wild meat and ivory) and a lack of awareness of the law and consequences of wildlife crime (Harrison *et al.*, 2015). An increase in illegal wildlife trade can be directly related to a rise in income, suggesting that the economic drivers of commercial wildlife crime may comprise a desire for wealth, on top of meeting basic needs (Duffy and St John, 2013; Harrison *et al.*, 2015; TRAFFIC, 2008). Individuals who are exposed to consumer demand for wild meat, ivory or timber can experience a "pull factor" that may encourage them to become involved in wildlife crime; they may also succumb to "push factors," such as a lack of legitimate income sources, particularly around protected areas (Harrison *et al.*, 2015).

In other words, while poverty may encourage people to poach for commercial reasons, individuals from poor communities do so in response to demand from wealthier communities (Duffy and St John, 2013). One example is elephant poaching, which has been linked to poverty, greed, poor law enforcement and weak governance, although the recent escalation in illegal killing is correlated with a growing demand for ivory as a luxury item in Asian countries (CITES, IUCN and TRAFFIC, 2013; Wittemyer *et al.*, 2014). Similarly, in the DRC, hunting for the commercial wild meat trade is the primary threat facing primates (Estrada *et al.*, 2018). The commercial value of chimpanzees, for example, is high because they are large animals whose parts can be traded for a variety of purposes. People consume their meat, and their skin can be used for decoration, their bones for professed therapeutic qualities and their skulls in connection with traditional rituals (Downing, 2012; Prescott, Rapley and Joseph, 1993–1994).

The demand for wild meat in cities encourages more hunters to engage in commercial operations in villages (Brashares *et al.*, 2011; Coad *et al.*, 2010; Fa and Tagg, 2016; Kümpel *et al.*, 2010; Robinson, Redford and Bennett, 1999; Wilkie *et al.*, 2005). City residents consume wild meat as a luxury item, often based on personal preference (Reuter *et al.*, 2016). Since alternative meats are also more available in towns and cities than they are in rural areas, wild meat is not essential to the food security of urban consumers (Wilkie *et al.*, 2016). This finding is supported by evidence that wild meat consumption is correlated to consumer wealth (Brashares *et al.*, 2011; Fa *et al.*, 2009). Restricting access to wild meat in urban centers—by curtailing the supply from rural areas—would thus contribute to biodiversity protection without directly affecting the food security of the poor (Fa *et al.*, 2019).

Other socioeconomic forces may also be at play. The local literacy rate, as a measure of education level, is also reflected in poaching levels (de Boer *et al.*, 2013). Educated people are more likely to be involved in legal cash income activities and therefore depend less on local wildlife resources for food (Junker *et al.*, 2015).

International Trade, Data Limitations and the Wealth Effect

There is an international element to the wild meat trade, and the great ape trade in particular, with demand coming from Europe, the United States, the Middle East and Asia; however, consumption in these regions is likely to be limited compared to that of local residents in ape range states (see Box 3.2). In international markets, wild meat is always a costlier item relative to other sources of animal protein; as a result, it is considered a luxury item, served during holidays, to impress important guests or hosts, or simply to display wealth. Swiss customers, for example, pay around ten times more for great ape meat than consumers in Cameroon (Clough and May, 2018).

Since authorities rarely identify confiscated imported meat, it is not possible to determine the precise proportion of ape meat entering overseas markets as a proportion of all wild meat. About 40 tons of wild meat arrive at Geneva and Zurich airports every year, and more than 270 tons land at Charles de Gaulle in Paris, yet it is unclear how much of this volume is ape meat (Chaber *et al.*, 2010; Clough and May, 2018). Great ape body parts are also in demand around the world; chimpanzee and gorilla parts, for instance, are sold in China, Nigeria and the United States. A lack of data precludes a detailed assessment of annual trade volumes, however (Clough and May, 2018).

BOX 3.2

Wild Meat Exports from Africa: The Role of Air Travel

Recent reports about the popularity of pangolins and other endangered species may give the impression that international trade is generally driving unsustainable hunting in source countries. Research indicates, however, that of the total amount of wild meat extracted from tropical regions, only a small proportion is exported (Ingram *et al.*, 2018).

Nevertheless, the international trade in wild meat is sizeable. While accurate trade figures remain elusive, studies show that wild meat is regularly exported to Washington, DC, as well as to capitals of European countries that are home to expatriate populations from former African colonies, such as Brussels, London, Madrid and Paris (Brown, Fa and Gordon, 2007; Harris and Karamehmedovic, 2009). A systematic analysis of the scale and nature of wild meat shipped from Africa to Europe via Paris found that more than five tons are smuggled through Charles de Gaulle Airport in personal baggage on a weekly basis (see Figure 3.3). Wild meat is imported not only for personal consumption, but also as part of a lucrative organized trade in luxury goods. The meat comes from a wide range of species, many of which are listed under the Convention on International Trade in Endangered Species of Wild Fauna and Flora (CITES) (Chaber *et al.*, 2010).

A number of measures can help to curb the importation of wild meat into non-habitat countries. General steps include:

- strengthening border controls and intelligence to detect criminal hubs;
- improving meat detection at airports, such as through the use of dogs;
- training customs officers to distinguish key wild meat taxa;
- enhancing checks at ports of departure;
- appropriately fining those responsible for importing wild meat (Chaber *et al.*, 2010; see Chapter 6).

Airline companies themselves can assist by:

- informing airline passengers that:
  - carrying wild meat in their luggage is illegal, as some airline companies already do;
  - engaging in the illegal wildlife trade can lead to prosecution and substantial penalties; and
  - the unsustainable extraction of wild meat has a detrimental effect on many endangered species;
- imposing travel-related penalties on passengers who carry wild meat; and
- dismissing airline staff members who participate in or allow the carrying of wild meat (Chaber *et al.*, 2010).

FIGURE 3.3

Direct Flights to Paris, from Airports in Proximity to African Ape Ranges

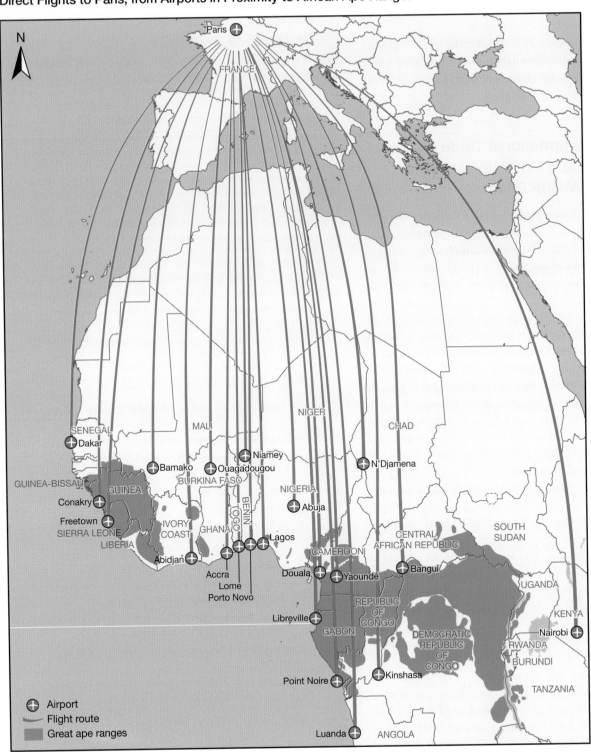

Source: Flightradar24 (n.d.)

In addition to population growth, major drivers of national and international demand for wild meat include socioeconomic changes arising from increased wealth; as noted above, such trends are exemplified by the dramatic upswing in meat consumption in China over the past few decades (Delgado, 2003). Most developing countries are expected to experience similar surges imminently; and as their greenhouse gas emissions, water consumption and land use increase, they will experience a perfect storm of highly adverse environmental effects (Henchion *et al.*, 2017).

Governance, Law Enforcement and Corruption

Weak governance facilitates wildlife crime. There are multiple, interrelated reasons why this is the case; for example, fines for poachers are often small, repeat offenses are rarely taken into consideration and neighboring countries often do not enforce the same laws or punishments (Lindsey *et al.*, 2012; Rodriguez *et al.*, 2018; see Chapter 6). Furthermore, the enforcement of laws is commonly encumbered: laws may not be adhered to voluntarily and officials often lack the resources to enforce them. For example, budget shortages and high security costs prevent authorities from employing sufficient anti-poaching patrols to deter wildlife crime in national parks (Lindsey *et al.*, 2012; Rodriguez *et al.*, 2018). Corruption within the system is a further detriment to this process. Officials can succumb to bribery and authorities may be hesitant to arrest those with links to government. Examples abound; in Central Africa, for instance, government officials have been implicated in the poaching of elephants and the ivory trade (Lindsey *et al.*, 2012; Lindsey and Bento, 2012).

Culture, Conflict and Technology

Among traditional communities, cultural or religious practices may drive hunting—or discourage it, for example through restraints on the consumption of certain types of meat (Junker *et al.*, 2015; see Chapter 2). Muslim communities in Borneo tend not to hunt orangutans for meat consumption (Santika *et al.*, 2017). Even in areas where there are local religious or cultural taboos against consuming ape meat, however, hunting can still threaten animals. In Guinea-Bissau, for instance, chimpanzee body parts are a common sight in rural and urban markets because they are used in traditional medicine to remedy disease, impotence and female infertility—despite widespread taboos against consuming chimpanzees (Sá *et al.*, 2012).

In areas that are affected by conflict and the concomitant disruption of services, conservation efforts are impossible, and poaching levels tend to be unsustainably high. The national parks in Mozambique and the Garamba National Park in the DRC witnessed the decimation of wildlife populations as a result of armed conflict (de Merode *et al.*, 2007; Hatton, Couto and Oglethorpe, 2001).

Wildlife can also suffer as a result of political uncertainty, such as land reform and the associated breakdown of law enforcement in Zimbabwe (Lindsey *et al.*, 2011). In northwestern Tanzania, illegal hunting surged after refugee camps were sited close to wildlife areas (Jambiya, Milledge and Mtango, 2007).

Modern hunting tools and technology —such as rifles and traps, night vision and thermal devices, and helicopters—have also played an important role in increasing offtake, sometimes dramatically (Coad *et al.*, 2019).

Drivers of Hunting of Great Apes

Most hunted great apes in the tropics are eaten, either close to the source, in urban areas of that country or internationally. Large-bodied mammals, including great apes, are the main source of wild meat in many tropical regions (Robinson and Bennett, 2004). Primates typically live in large groups, which renders them vulnerable and leads hunters to target them (Fa and Tagg, 2016). While poachers generally rely exclusively on firearms to hunt arboreal apes (orangutans and gibbons) in Asia, Africa's terrestrial apes—bonobos, chimpanzees and gorillas—are not only at risk of being shot, but also susceptible to being caught in indiscriminate snares (Fa, Ryan and Bell, 2005).

Apes are essentially hunted for their meat, but they are also pursued for their parts. Traditional doctors in Cameroon, Guinea and Senegal use ape heads, hands and feet, and in the DRC consuming bon-obo fingers and toes is thought to pass on magical powers (Clough and May, 2018). Similarly, due to a belief that consuming gorilla parts passes on their strength to the recipient, some partake in a practice of burning and grinding gorilla bones to make a traditional "vaccine" (Clough and May, 2018; for more on cultural drivers, see Chapter 2). Great ape parts are also used in non-medicinal ways. For example, gorilla hair is thought to boost the production of fruit and pistachio trees (Tagg *et al.*, 2018). Of note is an increasing interest in great ape skulls: the Last Great Ape Organization estimates that 900 ape skulls were trafficked in Africa in 2015 (Clough and May, 2018). Great ape skulls can be used as talismans; for example, chimpanzee skulls have been positioned in rivers to trigger rain (Tagg *et al.*, 2018). Although orangutan skulls have been used as an ornament for costumes and dresses in modern celebrations, there is no strong evidence that orangutan body parts are regularly employed for traditional

medicines, ceremonies or rituals (Clough and May, 2018; see Case Study 2.2).

Great apes may be hunted for other reasons. Studies show that orangutans in Indonesia have been killed out of fear, in self-defense, or to prevent—or retaliate for—crop-raiding (Davis *et al.*, 2013; Meijaard *et al.*, 2011a). For every individual captured for the live animal trade, collateral damage results in many more apes being killed (see Chapter 4).

As noted above, a dearth of data makes it difficult to arrive at accurate estimates of the number of apes killed for their meat; taken together, however, reports that track and document annual offtake figures provide an indication of the scale of the problem, albeit a conservative one. One study shows that, on average, more than 3,000 great apes—2,021 chimpanzees, 150 bonobos, 420 gorillas and 528 orangutans—were removed from their habitat every year during the period 2005–11. These figures are based on records of confiscated live apes, meat and parts; the estimated number of additional individuals lost per confiscated ape (1–10, depending on the species); and the estimated number of additional individuals presumed dead, based on the assumption that only 50% of all contraband is seized (Stiles *et al.*, 2013). Another study suggests that the rates of chimpanzee and gorilla extraction are more severe. Using more direct evidence collected in 2002–03, it estimates that more than 2,000 chimpanzee and more than 600 gorilla are hunted and their carcasses traded annually in 89 urban and rural markets in a 35,000-km² area between the Cross River in Nigeria and the Sanaga River in Cameroon (Fa *et al.*, 2006). If these numbers are typical throughout the range of both species, they indicate that the remaining populations in western Equatorial Africa—an estimated 128,700 chimpanzees and 361,900 gorillas—stand to be decimated by the wild meat trade (Strindberg *et al.*, 2018).

Barriers and Potential Solutions

Four main barriers thwart the transition from destructive to sustainable use of wild meat (Wilkie *et al.*, 2016). First, wild meat use is a characteristic "tragedy of the commons" problem: individuals act in their own self-interest rather than that of the community's common good, let alone that of present and future humanity. The problem is typically worse wherever communities have no legal rights, governance is inefficient and policing is weak. Neither individuals nor communities are motivated to conserve wildlife; only when people perceive a tangible stake in "their" local biodiversity do they feel that poaching is tantamount to stealing from themselves (Wilkie *et al.*, 2016).

Second, among species that are hunted for wild meat, great apes and other large-bodied species are extirpated first, while smaller-sized ones tend to be less severely impacted (see Gallego-Zamorano *et al.*, 2020). As predicted by the optimal foraging theory, even very rare large-bodied species become preferred targets when the opportunity arises, as they bring a high return in meat (Levi *et al.*, 2011; Wilkie *et al.*, 2016). The inevitable result is local extinction (Maisels *et al.*, 2001).

Third, given the exponential rate of human population growth, wildlife production cannot expand to meet the growing demand for meat, particularly in view of increasing wealth and the concomitant surge in meat consumption (Delgado, 2003; Marques *et al.*, 2019).

Fourth, wildlife habitat is lost through land use change for agriculture and land encroachment for infrastructure development and industry. This dynamic has an impact on food security, particularly among rural households in the tropics, as noted above. The pattern is complex and reliable data are only available for some habitat types, complicating the review of progress towards Aichi Biodiversity Target 5, which envisions a minimum decrease of 50% in the rate of habitat loss for the period 2011–20 (CBD, n.d.). While Africa continues to lose hundreds of thousands of hectares of rainforest per year, the rate of deforestation in 2000–10 was 37–67% lower than it was during the previous decade (Mayaux *et al.*, 2013). The Food and Agriculture Organization estimates that Africa lost 10% of its forest cover between 1990 and 2010 (FAO, 2013).

Reducing Demand

Conservationists, law enforcement agencies, communities and policymakers have variously sought to address hunting of apes for meat and parts, typically by aiming to reduce demand by bolstering the legal framework and law enforcement. Demand reduction strategies can address economic factors that drive the consumption of wild meat, for example through the provision of microcredits, affordable protein alternatives and tourism-related employment opportunities, or through public education campaigns that are designed to promote conservation and behavior change with regard to the consumption of wild meat (WCS Nigeria, n.d.; Wicander and Coad, 2018; see Box 3.3). In the longer term, school programs and awareness raising campaigns can help breed compassion and empathy (Pooley and O'Connor, 2000).

The carefully planned provision of alternative protein sources can help to establish

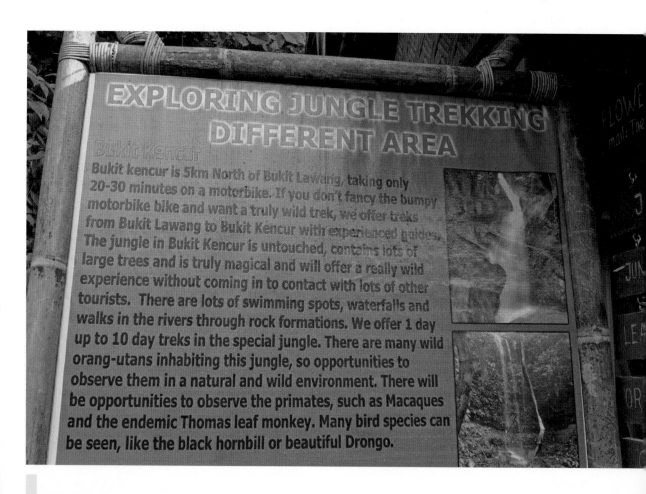

food security in rural communities and urban centers alike. Such strategies are particularly effective when they limit the use of ecologically inefficient ruminants, such as cattle, goats and sheep, in favor of more efficient sources, such as poultry and integrated aquaculture (Machovina, Feeley and Ripple, 2015). Mixed production systems that combine subsistence and cash crops with the rearing of small livestock (such as chickens or rabbits), or with the farming of fish, such as tilapia or catfish, can be a way forward (Oben, Molua and Oben, 2015). Capacity and funding shortages can undermine the implementation and effectiveness of such projects, however (Wicander and Coad, 2018).

Incentive schemes provide money or benefits to communities or individuals to encourage behavior change. Since the 1980s, efforts to incentivize local people to participate in conservation initiatives—such as integrated conservation and development projects and community-based natural resource management—have gained widespread support (see Chapter 5). Such projects can empower local people to manage wildlife sustainably while generating social and economic benefits. In a number of cases, they have successfully reduced illegal wildlife use and trade—sometimes dramatically—and incentivized strong community engagement in enforcement efforts (Roe and Booker, 2019).

Strategies for achieving community participation have focused on enhancing economic links between community members and protected areas, typically through the promotion of alternative livelihoods, including safari tourism, trophy hunting and the sale of products (Barrett and Arcese, 1995; Roe et al., 2015). The establishment of mountain gorilla tourism is an extraordinary example, as live gorillas have since become far more valuable than their meat, which has led to a reduction in hunting

pressure in Uganda's Bwindi Impenetrable National Park and the DRC's Virunga National Park. Indeed, between 1981 and 2011, the population of critically endangered Virunga mountain gorillas grew by 50% (Robbins et al., 2011).

Whatever their specific goals, strategies to reduce demand for wild meat are most likely to produce the desired results if they are custom-tailored to the targeted setting, be it a rural landscape where people and wildlife live close to each other, a town that is undergoing rapid urbanization or a megacity (Wilkie et al., 2016).

In rural, economically deprived communities that are in close proximity to wildlife, people typically rely heavily on wild meat as food. Consequently, a focus on the prohibition or cessation of wild meat hunting and consumption can undermine people's food security. A more appropriate approach is one that ensures the provision of alternative protein sources or alternative livelihoods, or one that empowers communities to participate in the sustainable management of wildlife resources by devolving rights and authority over wildlife from government bodies to local communities. The successful devolution strategies used in community conservancies in Namibia could act as models for Central Africa, but their implementation in the region would require long-term investment in capacity building (Naidoo et al., 2016). In the context of devolution strategies, the best way to avoid increasing the risk to large-bodied species through indiscriminate hunting is to establish hunting regulations that are enforced by the communities themselves.

There is limited information about how best to distribute compensation to support conservation initiatives in landscapes where people and wildlife co-occur outside protected areas (Karanth et al., 2012). Given the need to safeguard the food security and livelihoods of communities that live near wildlife—especially inside protected areas —conservationists inevitably struggle to encourage sustainable consumption of wild meat while also protecting vulnerable wildlife (Brashares et al., 2004; Kronen et al., 2010; Mavah et al., 2018). The effects of climate change are set to cause an increase in the number of demand reduction interventions designed to conserve wildlife and habitats (Kupika and Nhamo, 2016). A global issue of this scale and complexity calls for the involvement of the international community and a robust political process.

Rapidly growing towns—especially those affiliated with logging or mining activities or experiencing political unrest or war— represent a particular risk to regional wildlife. They tend to be market-isolated and wholly dependent on wild meat from the region, which can open up hundreds of square kilometers to wild meat hunting (Wilkie et al., 2016). In such towns, the provision of alternative protein sources via livestock farming becomes particularly important. These urban centers can encourage both locally emerging mixed production systems and market opportunities for the rural population.

People in cities and megacities consume wildlife because of affordability, cultural connections and perceived health advantages, or as luxury and status items. Although wild meat accounts for only a small proportion of the meat that is consumed overall, the numbers add up, as noted above. In urban centers, awareness campaigns that target the affluent—and often highly educated— drivers of the luxury market can facilitate behavior change. Regulations and the enforcement of laws are critical to tackling the illegal but tolerated wild meat market in these locations (Wilkie et al., 2016; see Chapter 6).

Despite a range of initiatives and considerable donor investment, however, it has proven difficult to provide local communities with tangible benefits from conservation, especially in sub-Saharan Africa. The assumption that market forces will protect the environment might not apply in reality because most protected areas do not create sufficient revenue to offset the costs that communities pay to maintain them (Dressler et al., 2010; Emerton, 1998; Newmark and Hough, 2000).

The arguments deployed in favor of incentives as a means of reducing illegal wildlife hunting are apparent in claims that tourism can reduce poverty, provide economic benefits to individuals and communities, and encourage people to change their behavior towards wildlife (Cooney et al., 2018). Yet, even mountain gorilla tourism, which has been exceptionally successful in terms of stopping population decline and recovering population density, is plagued by severe economic and institutional shortcomings. Such inadequacies are typically linked to a lack of real local participation; an insignificant scale of economic returns to local people relative to costs; insufficiently resourced and trained institutions in charge of planning, managing and evaluation efforts; and an institutional complexity that constrains most activities (Tumusiime and Vedeld, 2012). That said, tourism revenue sharing has the capacity to act as a key instrument for maintaining protected areas, so long as these issues are consistently addressed.

Interventions occasionally fail or lead to unexpected results. One such example involved an experiment in social marketing, which is defined as a process that seeks to develop and integrate marketing concepts with other approaches to promote behavior that benefits individuals, communities and the greater social good. In this case, one group of local residents in Brazil received an economic incentive to consume less wild meat, namely discount coupons for chickens. The result was an increase

Using a Radio Serial Drama to Change Local Behavior Regarding Cross River Gorillas in Nigeria

The critically endangered Cross River gorilla (*Gorilla gorilla diehli*) comprises at most 300 individuals. The rare subspecies is endemic to a small region on the border of Cameroon and Nigeria, which has one of the highest human population densities in Africa (see Figure 3.4; Bergl *et al*., 2016; Oates,

Bergl and Linder, 2004). The Cross River gorillas live in small, isolated populations that are very vulnerable to poaching, as their habitat is surrounded by human settlements and is being lost to agriculture and grazing.

In an effort to inspire positive change in attitudes and behavior towards Cross River gorillas, the education program of Wildlife Conservation Society (WCS) Nigeria launched the radio program *My Gorilla–My Community* (MGMC) in 2015, in collaboration with PCI Media Impact. The program features a particularly influential drama series set in a fictional area reminiscent of the geographical range of the Cross River

FIGURE 3.4

Cross River State, Nigeria

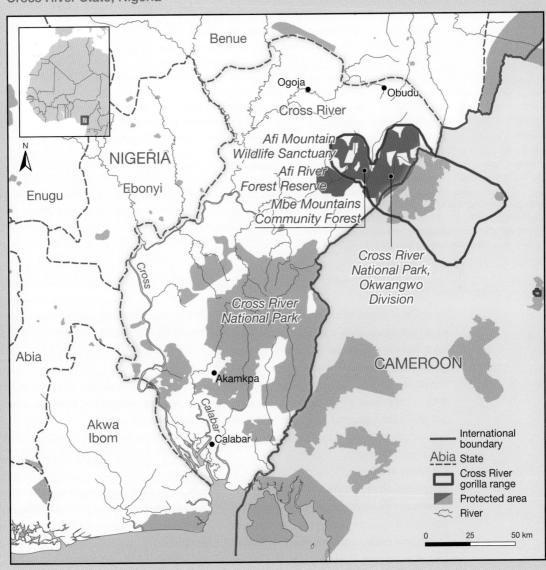

Source: UNEP-WCMC (2019b, 2019f), and Figure AO1

gorilla and neighboring human communities. By touching the heart-strings of more than 100,000 listeners in and around the Cross River gorilla's landscape—and more than 1 million in Cross River state—it was hoped that the drama would be effective in encouraging behavior change that would help protect the gorillas (Imong and Chukwu, 2019; WCS Nigeria, n.d.).

Over time, listeners form emotional ties with the fictional characters, whose thinking and behavior regarding various environmental and conservation issues positively and gradually evolve. Through this connection, the drama can have a greater influence on listeners' values and behavior than the purely cognitive information provided via documentaries or through education. The program seeks to encourage listeners to engage in protective behavior, such as: refraining from hunting protected species, hunting in areas that are properly zoned, hunting using only legal methods, supporting law enforcement authorities and protected area staff, adopting sustainable farming methods, volunteering as a gorilla guardian, using social gatherings to encourage dialog on conservation, designing social gatherings around conservation themes, and involving a broader spectrum of community members and stakeholders in decisions about the forest that affect the entire community. The drama is broadcast in parallel with community action campaigns that support the key messages through events, written materials, speaker series, school visits and other local activities (Imong and Chukwu, 2019; WCS Nigeria, n.d.).

Results of a monitoring and evaluation survey conducted in 2019 (baseline survey conducted in 2014) show that the program is successfully changing attitudes and behaviors. There was a significant increase (200%) in the number of respondents who support the protection of gorillas from hunting and habitat destruction; alongside a similar increase in the number of people who have adopted improved farming methods (190%). Additionally, more people are talking to other community members to discourage gorilla hunting and/or encourage them to take up sustainable farming methods (43%).[2]

in chicken consumption, yet without the expected decrease in wild meat consumption. In contrast, social marketing proved particularly successful among people of the same area who participated in community engagement activities but who were not offered an economic incentive: wild meat consumption dropped by 62% in this group (Chaves *et al.*, 2018).

Other studies indicate that, in practice, the provision of "alternative" livelihoods is sometimes more akin to the introduction of *additional* sources of income, particularly if projects fail to implement conditionalities or sanctions. In such cases, the financial security of a household may increase, but illegal wildlife hunting may continue, meaning that set goals were not attained. Moreover, alternative livelihoods projects, which tend to be run by local and national non-governmental organizations, are often financially constrained and inadequately monitored; as a result, they often have variable or even poor impacts (Wicander and Coad, 2018).

Enhancing the Legal Framework and Law Enforcement

A review of national laws, regulations and penalties related to killing and trafficking in apes can serve as a first step in strengthening a country's legislative framework (see Chapter 6). That process can usefully introduce or update permits and reporting systems under the Convention on International Trade in Endangered Species of Wild Fauna and Flora (CITES), as these aim to minimize forgery and falsification (Stiles *et al.*, 2013). Even where adequate wildlife legislation is in place, however, effective law enforcement is essential to addressing the wild meat trade (Holmern, Muya and Røskaft, 2007). In the absence of broader law enforcement, some laws have to be combined with targeted interventions to yield the desired effects, since laws that protect certain species of large mammal, for instance, may not actually change the choices made by commercial hunters (Rowcliffe, Merode and Cowlishaw, 2004).

When properly resourced, backed by political will and tailored to local circumstances, law enforcement can help to protect endangered species while simultaneously averting behavioral or political backlash by hunters, traffickers and local consumers (Wilkie *et al.*, 2016). In addition, it can help to reduce the illegal trade in ape meat and parts, while also safeguarding apes and their habitats, both inside and outside of protected areas. Further, the successful prosecution of individuals who violate hunting bans, anti-trafficking laws and related legislation—be they high risk-takers such as hunters, or high-level officials who abuse their positions for private gain—is key to deterring wildlife crime along the supply chain (see Chapters 5 and 6).

At the international level, actors involved in the fight against wildlife crime would benefit from reviewing lessons learned from the struggles against the narcotics trade and corruption, as multiple parallels apply (Sosnowski, 2019; van Uhm, 2018a, 2018b; van Uhm and Moreto, 2017).

Conclusion

There is mounting evidence that apes are becoming a more desired and thus more trafficked commodity (Stiles *et al.*, 2013). The potentially lucrative trade in their meat and parts represents an existential risk to these endangered species, partly because of their large body size and low reproductive rates, and partly because of the growing demand for their meat and parts. Unsustainable harvesting of apes is causing population decline, loss of genetic and cultural diversity, and, consequently, a deterioration of local and global ecosystem services and natural systems. For hundreds of millions of people in rural, tropical settings, these dynamics threaten food security and cultural identity.

The clandestine nature of the trade in ape meat and parts precludes an accurate assessment of the rate at which individuals are extracted from the wild. What is understood is that motivations for subsistence and commercial hunting vary, that rural communities tend to rely on wild meat as a source of protein and income, and that wealthier urban dwellers consume wild meat as a luxury item, even when cheaper protein

sources are available. Moreover, weak governance and corruption encourage ape hunting.

Tackling the trade in ape meat and parts requires a combination of strategies, including ones designed to reduce consumer demand by providing and promoting alternative protein sources; raise awareness of the ecological consequences of unsustainable harvesting; enhance legal frameworks and law enforcement; and provide economic incentives to stop hunting and consumption of wild meat.

Acknowledgments

Principal authors: Julia E. Fa,[3] Stephan M. Funk[4] and Nikki Tagg[5]

Contributors: Hillary Chukwu,[6] Loretta Cheung,[7] Andrew Dunn,[8] Imong Inaoyom,[9] Karmele Llano Sánchez,[10] Sean Southey[11]

Box 3.3: Hillary Chukwu, Loretta Cheung, Andrew Dunn, Imong Inaoyom, Sean Southey

Endnotes

1 Hunting levels were categorized based on local interviews, the density of households in the study areas and the number of gunshots or other hunting evidence encountered during survey periods (Peres and Palacios, 2007).

2 Survey results presented in a WCS internal report seen by the authors.

3 Manchester Metropolitan University (www.mmu.ac.uk/natural-sciences/).

4 Nature Heritage (www.natureheritage.org).

5 Born Free Foundation (www.bornfree.org.uk).

6 Wildlife Conservation Society (WCS) Nigeria (www.wcs.org).

7 PCI Media (www.pcimedia.org).

8 WCS Nigeria (www.wcs.org).

9 WCS Nigeria (www.wcs.org).

10 International Animal Rescue (IAR) (www.internationalanimalrescue.org).

11 PCI Media (www.pcimedia.org).

CHAPTER 4

Drivers of the Illegal Trade in Live Apes

Introduction

International trade in live apes is permitted only under conditions articulated in the widely ratified Convention on International Trade in Endangered Species of Wild Fauna and Flora (CITES) (CITES, 1973). The trade that takes place illegally can involve close cooperation between hunters, sellers, transporters, buyers and consumers—including audiences and pet owners. The transactional crimes between these sets of actors have been described as "victimless" because both buyers' and sellers' needs appear to be met without harm to either, which renders these violations difficult to combat (Felbab-Brown, 2017, p. 31; Sollund, Stefes and Germani, 2016, p. 6). From this perspective, the obvious victims—the apes—are not considered.

While Chapter 3 of this volume examines the socioeconomics of the trade in ape meat and parts, this chapter focuses on key drivers of the live ape trade. It comprises four main sections. The first section considers the demand for apes from zoos and wild animal parks in China, whose economic growth has been accompanied by an increase in the number of its zoological collections. The second section studies the demand for apes in the marketing and entertainment industries—including film, television, advertising and circuses—in the United States and Thailand. Specifically, it reviews factors that have led to a decrease in the use of captive apes in the entertainment industry in the United States. The following section explores the demand for orangutans as pets in Indonesian Borneo. As interviews with former ape owners reveal, misconceptions about these animals and their needs motivate some people to "save" young orphans after their mothers are killed. This section also discusses the thriving pet markets of Eastern Europe, the Middle East and former Soviet states (see Box 4.2).

The final section analyzes the role of social media as an enabler of the illegal trade in live apes. It identifies various ways in which online platforms influence demand, in particular by conferring value on ape ownership, providing access to the market and engaging new audiences. It also considers how non-governmental organizations are working with social media companies to curb online trafficking in wildlife, including by educating social media users. The section concludes by suggesting alternative and supplementary avenues for engagement with companies and consumers, as well as broader demand reduction approaches.

The key findings include:

- By cooperating with global zoological associations to enhance the welfare and well-being of their wild-caught apes,

> Evidence suggests that most live ape sales are initiated over social media, that most trafficked apes are young and transferred by air, and that demand comes mostly from private collections.

Chinese zoos could reduce their ape mortality rate and, consequently, the demand for more apes.

- Despite significant knowledge gaps regarding the scale of the illegal trade in live apes, evidence suggests that most sales are initiated over social media, that most trafficked apes are young and transferred by air, and that demand comes mostly from private collections.

- In Kalimantan, in Indonesian Borneo, where more than 100 captive orangutans are rescued every year, local residents tend to capture young orangutans opportunistically, such as after their mothers are killed for crop-raiding. They seek recognition for "saving" the orphans and do not fear legal consequences although they know orangutans are protected under the law.

- While some social media companies, such as Instagram, are monitoring images taken with wildlife, blocking access to posts that appear to sell protected species, and educating users about violations, they could have more of an impact by providing law enforcement with the details of users who violate wildlife legislation and targeting dedicated campaigns at the main potential purchasers.

- Biased and inaccurate representations of apes can affect people's perceptions of their prevalence and thus influence how concerned they are about a species' survival and how willing they are to support conservation efforts.

Apes in China's Zoos and Wild Animal Parks[1]

The increasing number of zoos and animal parks in China has fueled the demand for live apes from outside China. Indeed, China is often cited as the primary destination country in the trade (Dingfei, 2014). In the Chinese context, apes are typically found in two different types of facilities:

- "zoos," which tend to be owned and managed by the municipal or regional government; and

- privately owned "wild animal parks" (or "safari parks") and circuses.

Zoos are found in most major Chinese cities. They are generally small and typically charge low admission fees—on average US$3. Many, including Kunming Zoo in Yunnan province and Fuzhou Zoo in Fujian province, were built on undesirable terrain, such as hills or mountains deemed unsuitable for more profitable construction. In contrast, wild animal parks, such as Hangzhou Wild Animal Park in Zhejiang province, are usually located at considerable distances from cities, occupy vast areas of suburban land, and are built and maintained with substantial budgets, while charging admission fees of US$36 on average. Whereas many city zoos were established many years ago, wild animal parks have proliferated more recently, especially in wealthier coastal cities. Recent openings include those of Xiamen Central Africa Shiye Wildlife Park in Fujian province in 2016; Taizhou Bay Wildlife Park in Zhejiang province in 2018; and Jinniu Lake Wild Animal Kingdom in Jiangsu province in 2019. Others are under development, including Chimelong Qingyuan Forest Resort in Guangzhou province, which is scheduled to open in 2021.

It is difficult to estimate with any accuracy how many such facilities are in operation, not least because they are regulated by different government departments. The Chinese Ministry of Housing and Urban–Rural Development oversees city zoos, but the extent of regulations and enforcement in this area is limited. The ministry also hosts the Chinese Association of Zoological Gardens, a unifying body that counts approximately 155 zoos and wild animal parks as voluntary members but operates without any accreditation process (CAZG, n.d.). The Chinese State Forestry and Grassland Administration—which also houses the CITES Management Authority—has jurisdiction over wild animal parks and regulates the holding of all exotic species, including those in city zoos (Zuo, 2017).

The conflicting regulatory regimes of these agencies have given way to gray areas. The Ministry of Housing and Urban–Rural Development was instrumental in banning animal performances in China in 2011, for example, but it is unable to regulate performances in wild animal parks, which are administered by the Forestry and Grassland Administration. Further, some city zoos historically subcontracted animal performances to private companies, which rent space or arenas on city zoo property. Such "enclaves" also fall outside the jurisdiction of the Ministry of Housing and Urban–Rural Development; as a result, animal performances can technically continue until the expiration of contracts that were signed before 2011. In practice, pressure from the central government has led to the retirement of great apes from all but a handful of animal shows, all of which are privately operated.

The drive to establish new wild animal parks is fueled by China's economic and cultural evolution. Forty years of reforms have led to strong economic growth, lifting 800 million citizens out of poverty and transforming China into an upper-middle-income nation (International Monetary Fund, 2018). Raised in an era of economic prosperity, today's Chinese have far greater spending power than prior generations: between 2010 and 2020 alone, urban consumers' annual disposable income was expected to double to about US$8,000 (Atsmon *et al.*, 2012). As a result, they are willing and able to spend more time on leisure activities, including

> The increasing number of zoos and animal parks in China has fueled the demand for live apes from outside China.

Photo: In contrast to more traditional forms of entertainment, in Asia, leisure spending has pivoted towards novel experiences, including theme parks with wild animal attractions. Guangzhou Chimelong Tourist Resort comprises five leisure attractions, including a wild animal park, bird park, water park, circus and amusement park, plus three hotels. © PEGAS

tourism, as evidenced by an annual increase of 10% in consumer expenditure in the leisure sector since 2011. Now the second-largest in the world, China's leisure industry was valued at US$479 billion in 2017 (OC&C Strategy Consultants, 2017).

Leisure spending in China has shifted towards novel experiences, including theme parks (OC&C Strategy Consultants, 2017). Most new wild animal parks feature theme-park rides or are built around resorts that comprise multiple parks, hotels and associated infrastructure. A prime example of the latter model is the Guangzhou Chimelong Tourist Resort, which comprises five leisure attractions, including a wild animal park, bird park, water park, circus and amusement park, plus three hotels (Chimelong, n.d.). The neighboring Zhuhai Chimelong International Ocean Resort has four hotels, a circus and the largest aquarium in the world. The Chimelong Group welcomed

about 31 million visitors to these various attractions in southern China alone in 2017—almost one-fifth of the number of people who visited all Walt Disney parks and resorts worldwide during the same year. Chimelong visitors increased by 13.4% over the previous year, at roughly twice the rate of Disney visitors (TEA/AECOM, 2017). The lack of accessibility is the key barrier to increased growth in the leisure sector, a challenge that is being addressed through widespread construction of additional, multi-themed wild animal parks (OC&C Strategy Consultants, 2017). In addition to the resort model, the government incentivizes the development of wild animal parks as elements of entirely new cities and towns.

Competition-induced Fraud and Ape Trafficking

Establishing a new wild animal park is a commercial gamble, especially in areas that are already saturated with similar parks. Three new private wild animal parks were initially projected to open by 2020 in Jiangsu province, eastern China; all were expected to compete with one another and with the well-established city zoo. As of September 2019, one park had opened and a second one was under construction. It is unlikely that all three parks will be completed or prove to be financially viable.

As part of the competition, the pressure to acquire animals is high. Small city zoos with limited budgets feel this burden as they struggle to compete with large and private wild animal parks, as do smaller private operations. One zoo in Yulin, Guangxi province, displayed inflatable penguins in 2017; a few years prior, the Louhe Zoo in Henan province made international headlines by presenting a Tibetan mastiff dog as a lion (Chiu, 2013; Shen, 2017).

Since the supply of endangered species is limited, most zoos and wild animal parks

rely on Chinese animal dealers to acquire specimens for display. Dealers tend to turn to illegal sources, as was the case between 2007 and 2012, when more than 100 wild-caught chimpanzees from Guinea were trafficked to China in a CITES permit scam (see Box 6.1). The most active traffickers of wild-caught, live great apes operate in Tianjin, Hebei province, and in Dalian, Liaoning province.[2]

Limited Data on the Imports and Market Value of Apes

The financial costs associated with acquiring apes have been the subject of intense speculation. Some gibbon species are endemic to China and there is little evidence of large-scale acquisitions of gibbons from other nations. Although Chinese zoos show considerable demand for gorillas, there is no proof that any have been imported illegally, nor is it possible to assess the costs associated with such imports. The CITES Trade Database indicates that ten "captive-bred" live gorillas were imported from Guinea in 2010, yet there is no evidence that this transaction took place (CITES, n.d.-h). Ammann (2014) reports that staff members at a zoo in central China, who had prepared signage for a purported gorilla exhibit, disclosed that four gorillas had arrived in 2010 but were euthanized after two were found to be positive for hepatitis; one had bitten and infected a keeper. These reports may have confused gorillas with chimpanzees, however, as the Chinese language uses ape terms interchangeably and Chinese people are generally unfamiliar with ape species. An article in one newspaper used the Chinese characters for gorilla, chimpanzee and orangutan to describe chimpanzees (Wen Naifei and Tan Siqi, 2013).

In contrast, orangutans are known to have been imported into China, the majority of them legally (CITES, n.d.-h). Historically, they were transferred from zoos in the United States; in the 1990s, they came from Taiwan, where dozens were confiscated by the government. Many had been smuggled into Taiwan for sale in the pet trade, as demand had been fueled by a popular Taiwanese television show that featured a young orangutan (Leiman and Ghaffar, 1996). Today, most orangutans in China are controlled by a single owner who leases them to different zoos although costs and lease agreements remain undisclosed.

> In China, zookeeping is not professionalized, and while zoology and veterinary programs exist at universities, they are not focused on captive animal care and barely cover non-domestic animals.

Chimpanzees are the only apes for which documentation shows large-scale imports to Chinese zoos. Various reports have speculated on the market value of chimpanzees in China, with values ranging from US$12,500 to US$30,000 per individual (Clough and May, 2018). Dealers appear to charge each zoo a different price, most probably in line with sums that the highest bidders are prepared to pay.

Contrary to common assumptions, great apes are less popular with Chinese zoo visitors than are large carnivores. As tigers are especially important in Chinese culture, many wild animal parks house dozens or even hundreds of captive-bred tigers; the Xiongsen Bear and Tiger Mountain Village in Guilin, Guangxi autonomous region, counts about 1,800 tigers. Some parks, such as Harbin Siberian Tiger Park in Heilongjiang province, house only tigers and no other animal species. Many are farmed specifically for trade in Chinese medicines (Knowles, 2016). Among the primates, macaques carry particular cultural significance; in homage to the Ming dynasty novel *Journey to the West*, they usually live in elaborate mountain-style exhibits, while great apes are confined to much smaller enclosures in spite of their greater spatial and cognitive needs (Cheng'en Wu, 1993; Gallo and Anest, 2018). The ongoing interest in acquiring great apes may be driven less by public demand than by zoo and wild animal park managers' passion projects. It is likely that several Chinese institutions that recently acquired or expressed interest in procuring great apes did so for sentimental reasons attributed to senior staff.

Barriers to Adequate Welfare and Well-being of Captive Apes

In China, zookeeping is not professionalized, and while zoology and veterinary programs exist at universities, they are not focused on captive animal care and barely cover non-domestic animals. As a consequence, the staff in China's zoos and wild animal parks, especially the smaller and less well-resourced ones, generally lack expertise in the care of great apes. In one seemingly extraordinary case, wild animal park staff members who were not aware that orangutans are primarily frugivorous in the wild recorded buckets of fried chicken and cans of Red Bull as diets for these apes. In other cases, staff introduced two flanged males to one another, which resulted in serious injury. Chimpanzee injuries are common and deaths occur occasionally, as there is little understanding of chimpanzee behavior and sociality in the wild. Of the three institutions that house legally acquired gorillas, two have a lone silverback, contrary to natural social structure (Robbins *et al.*, 2004).[3]

The acquisition of wild-caught chimpanzees from the same or similar habitats has caused particular problems for their management in China. Inbreeding is thought to be the predominant issue: interbreeding closely related founders could be the cause of high recorded rates of stillbirth and infant mortality across the captive population. The situation is likely to persist as long as zoo managers decide on transfers and exchanges with other zoos, which typically involve deals with neighbors and friends (Banes *et al.*, 2018). Zoos may also be encouraging inbreeding by offering staff bonuses for offspring born under their care, which can cause further fetal and infant mortality as well as the hybridization of distinct ape species.

The bulk of these challenges are compounded by a lack of access to information. The Chinese government blocks or censors many online animal welfare and husbandry resources, though perhaps not always intentionally so – such resources might simply contain keywords on a blacklist. Resources of the World Association of Zoos and Aquariums (WAZA) are generally inaccessible because the Association recognizes Taiwan as an independent country (WAZA, n.d.). For this reason, Chinese zoos cannot easily affiliate with WAZA. In recent years, several Chinese zoos have individually expressed interest in joining the European Association of Zoos and Aquaria (EAZA) as observers; gorillas were sent from Rotterdam to the Shanghai Zoo in 1993 and 2007, as a result of EAZA agreements. EAZA has endorsed a proposal to send additional gorillas to at least one Chinese zoo. Chinese zoos will not be able to become accredited members of the US Association of Zoos and Aquariums (AZA) until their standards are considered adequate for accreditation.

Language barriers also stand in the way of better ape welfare in China. While AZA has made many of its online resources—including animal care manuals—accessible to non-members, none are published in Chinese.[4] Machine-translation software is commonly available and used in China, but all text to be translated must pass through a government censor, which may lead to incomprehensible translations. Machine translations of critical care information, such as veterinary guidance or drug dosages, cannot be relied upon as accurate; further, many drugs are unavailable in China. Of a total population of 1.4 billion, only around 10 million people in China are thought to be able to use English (VoiceBoxer, 2016; Yang, 2006). The lack of access to Chinese-language resources is therefore a considerable barrier to education.

Another significant challenge facing Chinese zoos is the West's critical attitude, which is often based on false allegations or gross generalizations (Banes *et al.*, 2018). Few Western organizations have been willing to engage constructively with Chinese zoos to provide training, improve conditions or address illegal trade. Antagonistic approaches are common, as evidenced by media portrayals of universally poor conditions and practices. Attempts to quantify the extent of the illegal trade—based on information that Western non-governmental organizations (NGOs) collected during surreptitious visits to Chinese zoos—have also proven problematic: the common assumption that all infant great apes were wild-caught, for example, is erroneous and has led to incorrect calculations of the scale and extent of illegal acquisitions. Such rash judgments have undermined Chinese zoo managers' confidence in Western colleagues. The Great Ape Survival Partnership (GRASP) exacerbated this problem in 2014, when it released a Facebook post about a "wild-caught," "male" orangutan at a particular facility. The infant in question was actually legally bred in captivity, female and housed at a different zoo, yet the post attracted hundreds of negative comments and reactions from its Western audience (Banes *et al.*, 2018).

In 2018, two major collaborative efforts were made to enhance orangutan welfare in China. The China National Orang-utan Workshop was hosted by the Chinese Association of Zoological Gardens from 25–30 October, at Nanjing Hongshan Forest Zoo in Jiangsu province (Sacramento Zoo, 2018), and comprised an international delegation of 136 attendees from Chinese and US zoos. A Chinese-language Orang-utan Husbandry Manual was concurrently published and

> Few Western organizations have been willing to engage constructively with Chinese zoos to provide training, improve conditions or address illegal trade.

released at the workshop, comprising 12 chapters on orangutan biology and management specifically written for a Chinese audience by 13 experts from Western zoos and universities. Both present major milestones in the Chinese zoological industry, in advancing and exceeding international standards of care. Each has set the template for similar endeavors that might now be pursued in Chinese zoos.

Further improvements in the welfare and well-being of apes in Chinese zoos are likely to reduce the mortality rate of—and thus the demand for—wild-caught apes. Similarly, better cooperation with global zoological associations might increase opportunities for legal transfers of captive-bred apes and consequently curb demand for wild-caught infants (Banes *et al.*, 2018).

Attitudes to Animal Rights as Indicators of Their Welfare

Although Buddhism and certain forms of Daoism value the sentience of non-human life, the impulse to relieve animal suffering took a backseat to 20th-century political reform. Under the leadership of Mao Zedong, China enacted what some scholars have described as a "war on nature" (Li, 2013; Shapiro, 2001). Mass starvation during the Great Leap Forward (1958–62) led to the widespread hunting of native mammals —in some cases, to near extinction—and defined animals as a means to facilitate human survival (Geng, 1998). The Four Pests Campaign of 1958—during which citizens were instructed to eliminate all sparrows, rats, mosquitoes and flies—cemented the attitude that animals had neither sentience nor value (Shapiro, 2001). More recently, Deng Xiaoping's economic reforms were developed at any cost, including that of animal welfare and environmental protection (Li and Davey, 2013).

Over the past three decades, however, interest in animal rights has steadily gained ground. The Chinese Academy of Social Sciences was among the first to introduce the concept into Chinese academia (Yang, 1993). Some Chinese scholars, however, dismissed this vision as a Western corruption (Zhao, 2002). Indeed, Western ideas appear to have had some influence—both through Western media and the activities of Western NGOs in China—but a domestic movement for animal protection has also grown substantially (Li and Davey, 2013). Although one four-year study concluded that most Chinese people do not view animals as self-aware or sentient, a second survey—this one more focused on urban residents, and thus the growing middle class—found that 61.7% of respondents said that all animals should be protected (Askue *et al.*, 2009; Zhang, Hua and Sun, 2008). More than half of the respondents (52.6%) said that animals are equal to humans and deserving of respect and protection; 81.3% expressed support for wildlife conservation (Zhang, Hua and Sun, 2008). Chinese zoos and wild animal parks could therefore play an important role in conservation education. Every year, an estimated 100 million people or more visit member institutions of the Chinese Association of Zoological Gardens, which represent only a small proportion of all zoos and wild animal parks in China (Askue *et al.*, 2009).

Given that attitudes towards animals are changing in China, pressure for zoos to improve animal welfare standards is more likely to come from the Chinese public and government than Western actors. In one survey, of things enjoyed most in theme parks, 18% of parents were interested in seeing live animals while only 2% wanted to see animal performances (OC&C Strategy Consultants, 2017). As noted above, the use of animals in circus-style shows has been illegal in city zoos since 2011; efforts to enforce related legislation appear to be intensifying. Although their use continues in private wild animal parks and circuses due to the above-mentioned conflicts in regulatory regimes, attendance at some performances is reportedly at a historic low (Agence France-Presse, 2018). As mentioned, great apes have also been eliminated from most performances following pressure from the central government.

In addition, animal abuse has drawn growing public opprobrium on social media in recent years. Repeated acid attacks on bears at the Beijing Zoo in 2002 were met with widespread condemnation; one Internet forum apparently received more comments on these incidents than on any other domestic or international event (Shuxian, Li and Su, 2005). In 2018, a keeper was fired from a zoo in Wuhan, in Hubei province, after a viral video showed him physically abusing a giant panda; another was terminated from an aquarium in Dalian, in Liaoning province, after being filmed putting lipstick on a beluga whale (Chan, 2018; Zhou, 2018). As discussed in the next section, the US experience indicates that such shifts in public perception influence the use of animals and, ultimately, the trade in wildlife.

Apes in Advertising and Entertainment in the United States and Thailand

This section reviews changes in the use of apes in the marketing and entertainment industries in the United States and Thailand. The US case focuses on the use of apes in film, television and advertising; the Thai case examines their role in circus-type facilities. The findings could inform efforts to curb the use of apes in these sectors in other countries.

> " Given that attitudes towards animals are changing in China, pressure for zoos to improve animal welfare standards is more likely to come from the Chinese public and government than Western actors. "

Great Apes in Movies, TV and Commercials in the United States

Humans have always been fascinated by wild animals, and great apes in particular. In part, this interest is due to our physical and behavioral similarity to non-human apes. The most famous early motion picture to depict a great ape was the 1932 film *Tarzan the Ape Man*, in which a chimpanzee named Jiggs played the role of Cheetah (*The Atlanta Constitution*, 1938; Van Dyke, 1932). Since then, great apes have been popular stand-ins as human caricatures in film, television shows and commercials. In 1951 a chimpanzee named Peggy starred alongside Ronald Reagan in his most popular movie, *Bedtime for Bonzo* (De Cordova, 1951; King, n.d.). An orangutan named Manis played the role of Clyde alongside Clint Eastwood in the 1978 movie *Every Which Way but Loose* (Fargo, 1978). Chimpanzees were featured in the popular 1970s spy-parody television series *Lancelot Link: Secret Chimp*, and later became fixtures of Super Bowl commercials for large US brands, such as CareerBuilder, Castrol, E*TRADE and Pepsi (Pollack, 2016; Shields, Jones and McKimson, 1970).

Unlike the early years, when chimpanzees who appeared in US films, TV shows and ads were all wild-caught, the great ape "performers" of recent years are captive-born chimpanzees and orangutans. Most were born in entertainment facilities or purchased from the Missouri Primate Foundation (MPF) in Festus, Missouri. While MPF no longer breeds or sells, it still houses chimpanzees (ChimpCARE, n.d.-a; PETA, n.d.). The cost of purchasing a great ape is not typically advertised and not likely to be standardized, but there are some indicators of their market value. A former trainer named Judie Harrison reported that she purchased an infant male chimpanzee from MPF for US$45,000 in 2002 (Schapiro, 2009a). In 2015, trainer Steve Martin valued a male chimpanzee at US$60,000 and a female one at US$25,000,[5] possibly based on physical characteristics, although female chimpanzees have generally sold for higher amounts than males in view of their breeding value. During the 1980s and 1990s in the United States, a chimpanzee typically cost US$20,000–50,000 (S. Ross, personal communication, 2019).

Much more is known today about the behavior and developmental needs of great apes than in the heyday of ape stardom. Numerous studies on ape social behavior and cognition have demonstrated that great apes are highly intelligent and emotional animals capable of psychological suffering. Researchers have observed that after experiencing traumatic events, chimpanzees may exhibit signs of post-traumatic stress disorder and depression, and that they respond to the death of a relative with behaviors similar to those of humans, including mourning (Balter, 2010; Bradshaw *et al.*, 2008; Ferdowsian *et al.*, 2011).

In order to be trained, chimpanzees and orangutans are taken from their mothers during infancy, a practice that causes distress in the mother, produces anxiety in the infant and impairs normal infant development (Baker, 2005). Training commonly involves physical abuse. Although apes can easily live to the age of 45, they are typically retired when they reach adolescence, around the age of 12, due to their great size and strength, and because their behavior may be unpredictable (Courtenay and Santow, 1989). Many former "performers" have difficulty integrating into conspecific groups after retirement, as they exhibit socially dysfunctional behaviors that are attributed to a lack of proper mothering and isolation from other apes (Freeman and Ross, 2014; Jacobsen *et al.*, 2017).

Now that US audiences are generally better informed about great apes, their use

> " Numerous studies on ape social behavior and cognition have demonstrated that great apes are highly intelligent and emotional animals capable of psychological suffering. "

BOX 4.1

Reduction in the Use of Apes in Entertainment in the United States: Advocacy, Computer-Generated Imagery (CGI) and Exhibitor Attrition

Great Ape Advocacy Campaigns

As understanding of great apes has grown from field research, and documentation of physical abuse by great ape trainers has been publicized in major campaigns starting in 1996 and 2003 by animal protection groups—together with two highly-publicized attacks on humans by "pet" chimpanzees in 2005 and 2009—public perspectives shifted on the use of apes for entertainment in the US (Friends of Washoe, n.d.; Gang, 1996; Newman, 2009; Primate Info Net, 2005; Roderick, 1990; Schapiro, 2009b).

From 2005, People for the Ethical Treatment of Animals (PETA) led focused education campaigns aimed at sensitizing the public to the plight of great apes used in entertainment, including through letter-writing initiatives targeting filmmakers and companies that were exploiting chimpanzees and orangutans (PETA, n.d.). Having garnered support from Hollywood celebrities Anjelica Huston and Pamela Anderson, PETA successfully lobbied more than 40 advertising agencies—including major players such as BBDO, DDB, Grey Group, McCann Erickson (now McCann) and Young and Rubicam (now VMLY&R)— to ban the use of great apes in their advertising (Ad Age, 2012). Several companies, including AT&T, Capital One, Dodge, Pfizer and Traveler's Insurance, pulled TV ads that featured chimpanzees and orangutans after talks with PETA and the Washington State-based organization Chimpanzee Sanctuary Northwest (Mullins, 2010; Nudd, 2010). PETA reported that between 2009 and 2016, 40 US television commercials featured great ape "performers"; 25 of them were pulled off the air soon after companies learned about the controversy associated with using great apes in advertising.[6]

Photo: In 2003, there were 87 great apes (18 orangutans and 69 chimpanzees) living in a total of 11 US facilities that provided great apes for film, television and ads. Following concerted campaigns and awareness raising, as well as developments in CGI, in 2019, there were 10 great apes (chimpanzees) living in a total of two facilities that provide apes for entertainment. Bubbles, former pet and actor, now living at the Center for Great Apes. © Center for Great Apes

Another major force responsible for shifting public opinion and corporate behavior regarding the use of great apes in entertainment and marketing was the Chimpanzee Species Survival Plan (SSP) of the Association of Zoos and Aquariums (AZA) (Lincoln Park Zoo, n.d.). The SSP wrote more than 80 letters to advertising agencies and other companies between 2002 and 2014, and engaged with many of the individuals involved in breeding, training and filming apes. In many cases, the companies and individuals confirmed that they would end their use of apes as a consequence of this engagement.

Scientists and conservationists have also served as advocates for the rights of great apes. In 2009, the *Los Angeles Times* published an opinion piece by Jane Goodall in which she condemned the use of great apes for entertainment, following an attack involving a performer-turned-pet chimpanzee in Stamford, Connecticut (Goodall, 2009). Studies published in 2008 and 2011 show that the inappropriate portrayal of chimpanzees in film and television programming hinders conservation efforts (Ross *et al.*, 2008; Ross, Vreeman and Lonsdorf, 2011; Schroepfer *et al.*, 2011; see Box 4.3). Following the first study's release, the board of directors of the AZA issued a white paper recommending that the use of all ape species in commercial entertainment and advertising be eliminated (AZA, 2008). Stephen Ross of the Lincoln Park Zoo, who co-authored two of the aforementioned studies on chimpanzee depictions, subsequently launched Project ChimpCARE, which addresses the use of chimpanzees in entertainment (ChimpCARE, n.d.-b). As part of Project ChimpCARE and in collaboration with the Chimpanzee SSP, many former "entertainment chimpanzees" were moved to zoos and accredited sanctuaries. An entire compound of 14 "actor" chimpanzees moved to zoos in Houston, Maryland and Oakland in 2010 (Bender, 2010).

Advancements in CGI

The successes ape advocates have achieved in recent years were possible in part due to the development of realistic CGI animals in motion picture productions, which provides an alternative to live animal use. The first realistic CGI animal, a white owl, was debuted in the 1986 movie *Labyrinth* (*Stuff*, n.d.). Since then, CGI has been used to create hundreds of different animal species, including chimpanzees, gorillas and orangutans. The 2011 movie *Rise of the Planet of the Apes* was a game-changer for great apes and their advocates. Weta Digital created a chimpanzee named Caesar, the movie's central character, using CGI and motion capture, thereby demonstrating that CGI could seamlessly replace a live chimpanzee in a film (Weta Digital, n.d.). Since then, the visual effects companies that employed CGI to portray an enormous orangutan in the 2016 *Jungle Book*—including Pixar, Rhythm and Hues, and Disney—have contributed to major advancements in CGI technology, which benefits animals and allows for greater versatility and control in filmmaking

(Sims, 2016). In 2005, the director of Jim Henson's Creature Shop told the *Los Angeles Times* that studios often prefer to use CGI in place of live animals because it allows "complete control over the performance" (Covarrubias, 2005). Although it is still possible to tell that CGI apes are indeed CGI, technological advances will probably make that harder to discern. It is unclear, however, how such images will affect the perception of the status and welfare of apes.

Attrition of Entertainment Providers

According to a 2003 census conducted by the Great Ape Project in the United States, 87 great apes (18 orangutans and 69 chimpanzees) were living in a total of 11 facilities that provided great apes for movies, television shows and ads (Goodall *et al.*, 2003). In April 2020, Project ChimpCARE reported that 11 chimpanzees were housed in two facilities that provide apes for entertainment (ChimpCARE, n.d.-a). These figures suggest that the number of great apes available for performances declined by 87% since the 2003 Great Ape Project census. The drop reflects two main trends: ape trainers have retired their animals and have not acquired infant apes to replace them, as was typical in previous years.

Judie Harrison, who retired two chimpanzees named Mikey and Louie to the Little Rock Zoo in 2008, cited the cost of care as a reason for retiring the animals, who were no longer "working" because of their age (Anonymous, 2009). Steve Martin of Steve Martin's Working Wildlife told the *Los Angeles Times*, "with computers and animatronics and such, there's not as much demand for chimps and live animals anymore" (Covarrubias, 2005). The youngest and last "working" chimpanzee at his facility, Eli, was most recently featured in a production in 2016. Three years later, when Eli was nine years old, Steve Martin "retired" him to Wildlife Waystation, an unaccredited sanctuary with a history of problems. The sanctuary ceased operations about a year after Eli arrived, forcing hundreds of animals to relocate. Its closure illustrates problems associated with allowing trainers to select a retirement setting for animals, as they may choose the most affordable rather than the most appropriate option. Along with another former "actor" chimpanzee named Susie, Eli was subsequently moved to Lincoln Park Zoo in Chicago, an AZA-accredited facility, where the two are being integrated into a larger social group.

as performers has become less palatable. Several factors have contributed to this shift, including advocacy campaigns by animal protection groups, advancements in computer-generated imagery (CGI) and exhibitor attrition (see Box 4.1). As a result, the entertainment and advertising landscapes have quickly changed in favor of great apes.

While it is no longer common to see great apes in movie and television productions in the United States, the practice of exploiting apes for entertainment has not been completely eradicated and is still very popular in other parts of the world. Even in the United States and Europe, images of great apes as clowns, displayed on outmoded greeting cards, are reminders of the days of "chimp shows." In 2017, a chimpanzee–bonobo hybrid named Tiby, who lives in a circus facility in France, was featured in *The Square*, a Swedish film that received critical acclaim all over the world (Östlund, 2017). Regardless of recent advances, the appearance of just one great ape in a major film or popular television show has the potential to significantly affect how humans perceive the species.

Orangutans in Thai Entertainment Facilities

Whereas the demand for apes in the entertainment industry may have declined in the United States in recent years, the opposite is true for Thailand's entertainment sector, in which demand for orangutans has recently resurfaced, following a significant drop.[7]

From around 1990, the use of orangutans became widespread in both tourist and entertainment shows in Thailand. The larger operations strove to create a Disney-like experience, combining animal theme parks with shows and targeting families in particular, such as by offering family tickets (ticket sales account for about 60% of most parks' income) (Safari World, 2017; Silom Advisory Co., 2017). Some parks, including Safari World, hired specialists from the Singapore Zoo to design and set up animal acts (former Safari World employee, personal communication, 2018). One online ad for an orangutan "boxing show" still promises visitors comical acts in which apes in boxer outfits "dazzle" audiences "with their mathematical gifts" (Safari World, n.d.). Ticket holders are also given the opportunity to hold and have photos taken with apes.

By the late 1990s, wildlife conservationists and animal rights activists had become vocal on this use of orangutans. Some of them accused Thai animal theme parks and zoos of acquiring apes from traffickers who bought them from Indonesian poachers. They also alleged that trainers mistreated apes to encourage compliant behavior during shows and interactions with visitors.[8] These outcries appeared to start reaching tourists from Japan, South Korea, the United States and Western Europe, as indicated by the absence of younger people from these countries among audiences at the shows.[9] In late 2003, the queen of Thailand added her voice to the campaign, inspiring a national crackdown on wildlife crime, which involved raids on Safari World and other establishments (ENS, 2006). Apes were seized and DNA tests provided evidence to support the allegation that more than half of the orangutans at Safari World had been smuggled from Indonesia (Reuters, 2006; S. Changtragoon, personal communication, 2006). Separately, law enforcement arrested wildlife suppliers, including one who ran a holding facility and slaughterhouse outside Bangkok, where freezers were stocked with bear paws, tiger meat and a frozen baby orangutan. Asked about the dead ape, the owner alleged that some restaurants offered orangutan to select diners on special order, adding that they did so "rarely" (L. Tiewcharoen, personal communication, 2016).

112

These raids were widely covered by local and international media, which helped create momentum to clean up Thailand's tourism business. In Bangkok, for example, mahouts stopped parading elephants down the streets —as they had done every day for more than ten years—and instead moved them to sanctuaries. By the time Thailand hosted the 13th Conference of the Parties (COP) of CITES in October 2004, the government had acknowledged its role in a global problem —at least at the senior level. Mid-level officials bristled at the criticism of Thailand and the increased work that was placed on them to eradicate the illegal trade. The prime minister offered to initiate a regional wildlife law enforcement network to stop cross-border trafficking; ministers of the Association of Southeast Asian Nations (ASEAN) who were responsible for implementing CITES agreed and launched the network within the following year (ASEAN, 2005).

Standing in the way of the proposed network, however, was an enduring disagreement between Thailand and Indonesia over the orangutan trade, namely the question of where the orangutans in Thailand's entertainment industry originated. In 2005, months after the CITES COP, Thai and Indonesian delegations met to negotiate the repatriation of Safari World's orangutans back to Indonesia. This deal was to satisfy Indonesia and pave the way for the launch of the ASEAN Wildlife Law Enforcement Network (ASEAN-WEN or WEN). During the negotiations, Thai officers placed emphasis on money and image, and on who would accept responsibility for the trafficking and the resulting public outcry. At the 13th CITES COP late in 2004, the region's ministers had agreed that the cross-border trade in orangutans and other species was a shared problem and responsibility (ClickPress, 2006). While preparing the launch of ASEAN-WEN in 2005, the Thai minister of environment intervened in the orangutan negotiations by proposing to the Indonesian delegation that Thailand would pay to fly the apes back to Indonesia on a military cargo plane. The Indonesians accepted the offer and the impasse was broken.

The next few years saw a decline in the number of orangutan shows in Thailand. National WEN task forces stepped up enforcement. Over the following decade ASEAN-WEN seized US$150 million in assets from wildlife criminals (Freeland, 2016). But some of ASEAN-WEN's funding was cut by 2015, when ASEAN member countries did not fulfil their commitments to cover the necessary financial and human resources for the WEN Secretariat. WEN law enforcement operations continued at a slower pace, while the influx of tourists into Thailand continued to grow and diversify.[10] By 2014, orangutan shows were back in full force. Seats that had been filled by South Korean, Japanese, US and Western European visitors until 2014 were subsequently filled by Chinese and Russian tourists, who may not have been exposed to awareness raising campaigns about orangutans. Shareholder reports from Safari World revealed US$58 million in revenue for 2016, prompting investors to consider constructing another park in Phuket at a cost of US$100 million; meanwhile, similar, smaller operations in Thailand, Cambodia, and Indonesia continued to source orangutans, tigers and elephants (Safari World, 2017; Silom Advisory Co., 2017).

In 2016, undercover agents working for Thai law enforcement helped Thai police to arrest traders in infant orangutans. Investigations carried out by Freeland throughout 2016 established that dealers were pricing the orangutans at US$10,000 each—probably more than local businesses would pay. The 2016 investigation that resulted in these arrests shed light on a trafficking business that supplied most of the animals sourced in Indonesia (Gettleman, 2017). As of August 2019, the case was ongoing and, like so many other wildlife cases, it was moving slowly, delayed in the face of heavy caseloads and because trafficking crimes are accorded low priority.

Although zoos and theme parks prefer captive-bred orangutans, as acquiring them is both legal and more affordable, adult apes do not always breed well. Audiences are most interested in seeing young (juvenile and adolescent) apes, which may be driving the renewed appearance of infant orangutans in Thailand.

As long as any segment of the global public enjoys orangutans in entertainment, enforcement will only be able to make temporary dents in the trade. Safari World is counting on steady growth in the influx of tourists from ASEAN countries—which are home to more than 600 million people—as well as China, the Middle East and Russia to continue to pay for such experiences. A business risk assessment for shareholders contemplating expansion of the business mentions nothing about the potential negative impact of awareness raising campaigns (Silom Advisory Co., 2017). Yet, evidence indicates that consumer awareness programs have had an impact on targeted audiences in the past, and that they can be expected to work again if they are aimed at new audiences (Burgess *et al.*, 2018; see Annex

II). Infomercials and ads that feature local influencers who tell the true story of how orangutans are acquired and treated could influence tourist expectations, which may affect demand and persuade shareholders to halt the use of orangutans in the entertainment sector.

Trafficked, "Saved" and Rescued: Pet Apes in Indonesia

In numerous countries in Asia, Eastern Europe, the Middle East and the former Soviet Union, it is not uncommon for apes to be kept as pets. International demand for apes as pets poses direct challenges for their conservation (see Box 4.2 and the Introduction to this volume). This section analyzes the demand for orangutans in Indonesia, where the trade in these species continues even though they are protected under law (Freund, Rahman and Knott, 2017; Nijman, 2017b; Republic of Indonesia, 2018; Sánchez, 2015).[11]

Rescue centers across the country are often the last destination for domesticated orangutans, many of whom are confiscated from homes where they were kept as pets. Details on the number of orangutans arriving at rescue centers provide some insight into the extent to which orangutans are being kept as pets. Data compiled from three of the seven rescue centers currently operating in Kalimantan, in Indonesian Borneo, indicate that about 1,500 orangutans were rescued between 2001 and 2013 and that up to 60% of them were known or suspected to have been pets or domesticated in local villages (Sánchez, 2015). The rescue figure is probably an underestimate, as captive live apes and apes who have died typically go unreported. From 2005 to 2013, three of Indonesia's seven operating rescue centers for orangutans rescued an average of 107 individuals per

BOX 4.2

Demand Hot Spots in the Live Ape Trade

Significant information gaps preclude an accurate assessment of the scale of the illicit ape trade as well as the number of apes kept as pets or in private collections. Most of the data is drawn from undercover investigations and analysis of the illegal trade conducted on social media and via online sales. What seems clear based on the available evidence is that the demand for illegally traded live apes stems primarily from private or personal collections (Clough and May, 2018). They are used as pets, gifts that confer status, and attractions at restaurants, hotels and private collections.

The private pet trade is principally located in Eastern Europe, the Middle East and Russia (J. Head, personal communication, 2018), and is focused almost exclusively on young animals. Most of the apes leave Africa or Asia for their destination countries smuggled on international airlines; established intermediaries and dealers whisk them through busy transit hubs and transfer them on for sale to their final buyers. In some cases, such as when the buyers are wealthy nationals from Gulf states, the apes are flown on private airplanes and pass unnoticed through border controls. The demand for protected species is also significant in the former Soviet states, where laws allow for private ownership of exotic species. Numerous private facilities, including restaurants and hotels, place acquired animals on display for the entertainment of their guests (Clough and May, 2018).

Wildlife crime specialist Mary Utermohlen reports that the United Arab Emirates (UAE) serves as a major transit hub and destination for trafficked wildlife (Utermohlen and Baine, 2018). Other major hubs include Cairo, Doha and Istanbul. In Kuwait, Qatar and the UAE, wealthy families keep young chimpanzees or gorillas as status pets. The Gulf states and Egypt are hotspots for the illegal trade in apes, partly because their location between Africa and Asia places them on the path of frequent flights and partly because they exhibit a strong demand for protected species, including live reptiles and birds, as well as wildlife products such as ivory, rhino horn and skins (Haslett, 2015).

This trade has been enabled by irregularities and corruption in the use and control of CITES permits from countries where the animals are sourced, and as a result of this greats apes such as bonobos and chimpanzees are being held by notorious wildlife traders and owners of private wildlife parks (Clough and May, 2018).

year, three more per year than reported from 2000 to 2004 (Nijman, 2005a; Sánchez, 2015). This increase points to a rise in the number of orangutans kept as pets and shows that more orangutans are arriving at rescue centers despite collective efforts by governments and organizations to protect them.

The Trade in Orangutans: Hunting, Trafficking and Market Value

Research indicates that in Kalimantan, individuals who capture orangutans tend to do so opportunistically, rather than by design, although some trade networks are known to catch and smuggle orangutans mostly for the international wildlife trade. Farmers who shoot crop-raiding adults and hunters who kill them for food may collect unweaned orphans for sale on the live animal market. Encroachment into orangutan habitat due to forest conversion and illegal logging presents hunting opportunities and drives the illegal trade by encouraging human–wildlife contact, thus increasing the likelihood of conflict between people and apes (Campbell-Smith *et al.*, 2010; Nijman, 2009; Stiles *et al.*, 2013; Utami-Atmoko *et al.*, 2017; see Box 1.3).

As part of organised trade chains, captured orangutans are transported through villages into towns and cities along the coasts of Borneo and Sumatra, from where they are sent to Jakarta or cities farther afield, using cargo services on public trains, buses and ships, or private courier services. From these international hubs, they are transported by air to Malaysia, Thailand and other destinations (Nijman, 2009; Stiles *et al.*, 2013). In 2014, customs officials intercepted a smuggling attempt of one infant orangutan and three gibbons at Jakarta International Airport (TRAFFIC, 2014). In the last few years alone, several orangutans appear to have been smuggled out of Indonesia and

discovered as far afield as Kuwait (ANTARA News, 2017).

Local prices for individual orangutans stood at IDR 1.5–2.5 million (US$100–170) in 2018; the farther an orangutan travels from the point of origin, the higher the price. In August 2017, when law enforcement officers confiscated two orangutans in a major city in Kalimantan, they revealed that traders had paid the hunter IDR 1.5 million (US$100) for one and IDR 2.5 million (US$170) for the other. The smugglers had intended to transport the two infant orangutans to the island of Java and sell them for IDR 50 million (US$3,400). On the international market, orangutans have reportedly fetched US$50,000 (Wyler and Sheikh, 2008).

Local Ownership of Pet Orangutans in West Kalimantan

The reasons and methods for acquiring pet orangutans vary across owners. In West Kalimantan, the southwestern province of Indonesian Borneo, the International Animal Rescue (IAR) Indonesia center in Ketapang conducted interviews with 127 former owners to gain insight into why and how people come to own orangutans. Fewer than one-quarter of the respondents (23%, *n*=29) said they had paid for their orangutan; nearly half (48%, *n*=61) reported having "found" them in a clearing area of an oil palm plantation or taken the animals in after they or someone else had killed the mother. Respondents who said they had paid for their orangutan reported spending anywhere between IDR 500,000 and IDR 1.8 million (US$35–US$130) for an individual from a different province of Indonesian Borneo. In descending order of frequency, respondents' declared occupations were local palm oil worker, farmer, miner, fisherman, shopper, former soldier, pastor or priest, and police officer.

Given that the average monthly wage in Indonesia is IDR 2.3 million (US$150), the price of an orangutan—an iconic, nationally protected species—is not significant (WageIndicator, n.d.). Indeed, these apes are sometimes more affordable than smaller protected primates. A slow loris (*Nycticebus* spp.), for example, can cost between IDR 300,000 and IDR 1 million (US$20–US$66) at markets in Java's main cities. Rather than acting in the interest of financial gain, people who capture orangutans are thus more likely to be focusing on removing animals from situations that can lead to conflict, such as crop-raiding.

None of the respondents indicated that they had intended to acquire a pet ape, but the majority displayed a sense of entitlement about owning an orangutan, presenting themselves as the animal's rescuer. This savior complex did not translate into the provision of adequate welfare for the apes, however; many were kept in filthy, cramped conditions, given insufficient or unsuitable food, or simply chained up outside the house without protection. Betraying an erroneous understanding of animal welfare, owners spoke about having "saved" animals as a sufficient criterion for possessing them. There is little data available to explain how this notion arose or evolved.

IAR researchers hypothesize that the respondents' behavior stems from a perception of the animals as "cute" and similar to human babies. A former owner named Tere said of the orangutan she kept:

> "He slept in our room. We made him a hammock. At night he asked for milk […] just like a human baby. I cried when we were separated from him because we cared for him deeply, as though he were our own baby."

Certain owners anthropomorphized the apes, providing them with human food, washing them and dressing them as though they were human babies (Serpell, 2002).

Some displayed pity for their pets, indicating that what they perceived as the orangutans' human-like behavior evoked a sense of affection.

Misconceptions of orangutans as tame, harmless creatures who are easy to keep may be linked to a desire to be perceived as a nurturer. Former owners appeared proud to have played this self-appointed role; they implied that doing so raised their social status among family, friends and the wider community. Yulita, another former owner, stated:

> Someone told the authorities that we were keeping an orangutan as a pet because they envied us.[12]

Owners also misunderstood the rescue, rehabilitation and release process, which they deemed to be a cruel act of abandonment whereby animals are returned to the wild and required to find their own food, fend for themselves and live without human love and compassion. After having nurtured apes for some time, many owners appeared to have blocked out or forgotten why these orphaned babies ended up in their care in the first place—namely that their mothers were killed.[13]

The majority of orangutan owners interviewed for this study kept orangutan babies and infants. Owners of larger, adult orangutans may have a different perspective, especially when their pets become aggressive and difficult to handle, at which point they may be more willing to surrender them. The study findings indicate that the local trade in orangutans is primarily opportunistic, does not involve trafficking syndicates and is not driven by significant economic incentives. Although all the respondents said they knew that orangutans were protected species, none cited that status as a reason for surrendering their pet. The lack of fear of legal consequences indicates that law enforcement is weak (Nijman, 2009; Shepherd, 2010).

Indeed, of the 229 orangutans received by the IAR center between 2009 and 2018, only three were turned over due to confiscations carried out by the authorities.

Social media plays a role in promoting the demand for live apes in Indonesia and elsewhere, in part by influencing perceptions of ape ownership. The next section explores this relationship.

Social Media: Influencing the Demand for and the Perception of Apes

The Internet enables easy, fast and ubiquitous communication and marketing that can influence behavior and desires. Growing segments of the global population have been exposed to online images and videos that present ape ownership and direct interaction with apes as desirable, affordable and attainable. While the impact of such portrayals on ape conservation may be significant, the same social media platforms present opportunities for tackling the illegal wildlife trade in apes and promoting conservation initiatives, including via social marketing designed to influence behavior (see the Introduction to this volume and Annex II).

Social Media Platforms as Hideouts for Wildlife Traffickers

Over the past few years, much of the trade in wildlife—both legal and illegal—has migrated to online forums and away from more traditional open markets (IFAW, 2008, 2014). Given the accessibility of the Internet around the world, wildlife traffickers can reach a large number of social media users very quickly (Krishnasamy and Stoner, 2016). Moreover, they can offer their goods in complete anonymity. Limited data are available

> ❝ Growing segments of the global population have been exposed to online images and videos that present ape ownership and direct interaction with apes as desirable, affordable and attainable. ❞

on the prevalence of wildlife trade in "closed" social media groups and password-protected online forums, and it is difficult to monitor related transactions or evaluate the threats with any degree of accuracy (IFAW, 2014; Krishnasamy and Stoner, 2016). Previous research largely focused on wildlife trade conducted on openly accessible platforms, such as commercial trade portals and online auction sites, which lend themselves to public monitoring (IFAW, 2014). As awareness has grown about the illegal wildlife trade and as law enforcement efforts to curb it have intensified, traffickers appear to have moved underground (Krishnasamy and Stoner, 2016).

Online trade may have a particularly pernicious effect on wildlife in Asia, a region that is not only rich in threatened and restricted-range species, but also home to more than 2.3 billion Internet users and nearly 870 million Facebook users (Internet World Stats, n.d.). The photo-sharing app Instagram has gained significant momentum and now boasts more than 1 billion monthly active accounts, most of which are in Southeast Asia (Nguyen, 2018; Yuniar, 2016).

To gain a sense of the extent to which wild animals are sold on social media, the wildlife trade monitoring network TRAFFIC monitored 14 Facebook groups in Malaysia, where about 68,000 people are active users. As most of the monitored groups were "closed," TRAFFIC relied on inside contacts, who were able to access information on transactions. The study found that, over a five-month period in 2014–15, the groups advertised the sale of more than 300 wild animals representing about 80 species, including sun bears, otters, binturong, owls and gibbons. More than 60% of the species are native to Malaysia; almost half of them are protected from all aspects of hunting or trade (Krishnasamy and Stoner, 2016). In a later report focused on the illegal wildlife trade in Thailand, TRAFFIC demonstrates that Facebook continues to be used for the sale of critically endangered wildlife (Phassaraudomsak and Krishnasamy, 2018).

Facebook responded positively when presented with the results of both reports. A spokesperson said the social networking site would work with TRAFFIC to help put an end to the illegal wildlife trade in Malaysia and that it would remove all relevant content that violates its terms of use—including groups, posts and accounts. Facebook has since joined the Coalition to End Wildlife Trafficking Online and is working with TRAFFIC and partners to tackle the illegal wildlife trade (see pp. 125–126). Despite these commitments, a growing number of wildlife traffickers appear to be active on Facebook in Malaysia, Thailand and many other places. Along with other social media platforms—such as Craigslist, eBay, Etsy, VKontakte and WeChat—Facebook could exert more control to prevent illegal sales of wildlife, including by providing law enforcement with the details of users who violate wildlife legislation.

> " Along with other social media platforms —such as Craigslist, eBay, Etsy, VKontakte and WeChat—Facebook could exert more control to prevent illegal sales of wildlife. "

Gibbons as Pets and Props in the Social Media Marketplace

The trade in gibbons, particularly in the genera *Hylobates* and *Symphalangus*, appears to be thriving at the national and international levels. The rapid growth and widespread use of social media facilitates the trade, which often occurs undetected. Evidence points to Indonesia and Malaysia as the two habitat countries with the most prolific illegal pet trade, predominantly in very young animals (see Figure 4.1).

Research conducted for this chapter from April to June 2018 identified 10 Facebook groups and 11 Instagram accounts that featured ads for gibbons, including 16 from Indonesia and 5 from Malaysia, most of them for sale in their habitat country. At least 50 individuals were selling infant gibbons.

FIGURE 4.1

Gibbons for Sale on Social Media

Sources: screenshots from 2017

A follow-up review was carried out in December 2018 (Cheyne, n.d.; see Table 4.1). In 50 reviewed ads, all gibbons were under three years of age.[14] Online comments related mostly to the price and age of gibbons, or to their "cuteness." Further questions were directed to a WhatsApp number or sent via direct message. The gibbons cost between US$150 and US$540 (Cheyne, n.d.; Smith and Cheyne, 2017).

Thailand tops the list in terms of proffering wildlife as photo props for tourist self-ies and photo opportunities on beaches and in bars (Brockelman and Osterberg, 2015; see Figure 4.2). The gibbons used in this context are typically under two years of age.

The practice of sharing tourist selfies with gibbons on social media not only perpetuates the idea that it is appropriate to have photos taken with primates, but also fuels the demand for gibbons, and thus their removal from the forest. Similarly, social media images that portray wealthy and influential individuals with their pet apes suggest that owning an endangered animal is desirable and respectable. Such pictures also demonstrate that the law is enforced selectively (Malone *et al.*, 2003). Such images may also influence the general understanding of the conservation status of apes in the wild (see Box 4.3).

A key challenge to reducing the online supply of wildlife is the inaccessibility of "closed" social media groups. For security and privacy reasons, companies retain exclusive control over the back-end of social media sites. Since these companies are not technically publishers, however, they are not required to edit content, even if it is illegal. Meanwhile, regulations and legislation governing social media lag behind online developments in the illegal wildlife trade

TABLE 4.1

Ads for Gibbons in 10 Facebook Groups and 11 Instagram Accounts

Species for sale	Number of ads	
	April–June 2018	December 2018*
Moloch gibbon (*Hylobates moloch*)	18	24
Siamang (*Symphalangus syndactylus*)	10	9
Lar gibbon (*Hylobates lar*)	6	7
Müller's gibbon (*Hylobates muelleri*)	4	4
Agile gibbon (*Hylobates agilis*)	2	2

Note: * It is not possible to determine whether any of the gibbons for sale in December 2018 were the same as those seen in April–June 2018. Some gibbons may have appeared in more than one ad.

Source: Smith and Cheyne (2017)

FIGURE 4.2

Gibbons as Photo Props for Foreign Tourists on Thai Beaches

Sources: screenshots from 2018

Portrayals of Apes and Their Influence on Conservation Action

Some research shows that large, charismatic species such as great apes receive more conservation attention and funding than smaller, less well-known taxa, such as invertebrates and amphibians (Sitas, Baillie and Isaac, 2009). At the same time, however, the widespread use of apes on social media and in the marketing and entertainment sectors has impaired efforts to conserve them (Courchamp et al., 2018). While a dearth of data makes it difficult to quantify the impact of such portrayals on the conservation of great apes and gibbons, it is clear that biased and inaccurate representations of these taxa affect people's perceptions of their prevalence. Indeed, assessments of "virtual populations" influence the degree to which the public is concerned about a species' survival (see Case Study 4.1).

In 2005, a brief visitor study conducted in accredited US zoos revealed that the public was significantly less likely to consider chimpanzees endangered in the wild than other great apes, such as gorillas (Ross et al., 2008). Respondents consistently justified their reasoning by indicating that chimpanzees were so prevalent in movies, television shows and ads that they could not possibly be under threat. Subsequent investigations demonstrated that the manner in which chimpanzees are portrayed influences the public's opinion of their conservation status (Ross, Vreeman and Lonsdorf, 2011). People who were shown digitally altered images of a chimpanzee standing in a common man-made setting, such as an office space, tended to characterize wild populations as healthy, stable and certainly not in need of conservation attention. Likewise, those who viewed images of chimpanzees in direct contact with humans concluded that they would make viable pets. These and other studies provide compelling evidence that

portrayals of apes have a substantial influence on the public's perception of these species and that they restrain support for conservation efforts (Leighty et al., 2015; Schroepfer et al., 2011).

Since that initial visitor survey in 2005, progress has been made in curtailing the use of inaccurate portrayals of primates. In the United States, virtually all of the "actor" chimpanzees who had been maintained for use in the entertainment industry have been re-homed in accredited zoos and sanctuaries (ChimpCARE, n.d.-a; Roylance, 2010). Meanwhile, the use of stock photos that display chimpanzees in unnatural poses and settings has also fallen out of favor, perhaps signaling an end to the all-too-common "grinning chimpanzee" photos on greeting cards (Cho, 2016; Djudjic, 2017). All told, the country has experienced a seismic shift in attitudes towards the use of apes in the entertainment sector (see Box 4.1).

Despite such progress, however, there is a need for continued vigilance, particularly as inappropriate portrayals of apes continue to distort public perceptions, and as ape habitats from Africa to Asia remain under threat from ongoing human encroachment and exploitation. One of the tools at the disposal of conservation advocates is holding corporate entities accountable for releasing or posting outputs that undermine conservation efforts, whether intentionally or unintentionally. Another tool is the strategic use of traditional and social media to inform and correct public perceptions of apes—and to impart an understanding of their conservaton needs (Silk et al., 2018). The revenue raised through the sale of images of threatened animals could be earmarked to pay for conservation efforts, which would help to turn "competition into cooperation between virtual and real populations" (Courchamp et al., 2018, p. 9). Such approaches can leverage the indisputable power of new media to strengthen ape conservation efforts.

British News and Social Media Portrayals of Orangutans and Threats to Their Habitat[15]

Orangutans make frequent appearances in the media in Britain, featuring regularly in national newspapers, magazines and television programs, as well as on websites and social media. While distinct in nature and oriented towards different audiences, these media outlets overlap considerably and can thus be understood as lying on the same broad continuum.

Most of these portrayals show charismatic, young orangutans juxtaposed with images of habitat destruction. The most commonly shown apes are orphans living in rescue and rehabilitation centers in Borneo or Sumatra. They are easily photographed in the open, often playing with each other or being trained in "jungle school" (Curran, 2018). They are also commonly pictured interacting with their human carers, especially when being cuddled or fed. Such images are extremely popular, drawing public attention to orangutan causes and generating donations and "adoptions" for orangutan charities (Palmer, 2018, p. 60). Portrayed as full-blown characters with names, biographies and personalities on rescue center websites, television documentaries and social media posts, these orangutans represent both the tragedy of extinction and the hope for a better future—in their case, an idealized journey "back to the wild." Their symbolic potency derives from what is often depicted as their dual nature: their simultaneous likeness to humans and their status as wild animals (Chua, 2018b; Russell, 1995).

These compelling images are commonly set against pictures of environmental destruction, which underscore the extent and urgency of the plight of orangutans. Particularly widespread are photographs of deforestation, oil palm plantations and their by-products, such as forest fires. News headlines—such as "'Now or Never' Battle to Save Indonesia's Endangered Orangutans as British Companies Still Using 'Dirty' Palm Oil"—draw a

Photo: Some facilities in Indonesia have been critised for appearing more as tourist attractions than rehabilitation centres, offering visitor opportunities to come into close contact with orangutans at feeding platforms. Although physical contact is widely prohibited, it is not uncommon for videos and photographs of tourists touching, carrying or hugging orangutans to circulate on social media. A vicious cycle thus ensues, with such images further perpetuating misleading perceptions of orangutans, while fanning demand for live apes. © Paul Hilton/Earth Tree Images

direct causal link between environmental destruction and the fate of their orangutan victims (Dalton, 2018). Unlike cute photographs, these images elicit horror and anger, with the aim of galvanizing viewers into taking action against corporations and governments. In this way, the visual tropes of cute orangutans and environmental destruction constantly invoke and reinforce each other, thereby generating a powerful narrative ("palm oil kills orangutans") that has come to dominate media portrayals of orangutans (Chua, 2018a).

Distortions and Unintended Effects

The influence of the dominant narrative can be seen in the growth of consumer movements against ("dirty") palm oil and large corporations' responses to them. A recent example is the supermarket chain Iceland's much-hyped Christmas 2018 television ad, which consists almost entirely of Greenpeace's short *Rang-tan* animation (Greenpeace, 2018; Iceland, 2018). It depicts a baby orangutan entering and messing up a girl's bedroom, before explaining that "there's a human in my forest" who is destroying the ape habitat for palm oil. The advertisement ends by reiterating Iceland's pledge to remove palm oil from all its own products "until all palm oil causes zero rainforest destruction." Denied clearance by the ad clearing body, Clearcast, because of its link to Greenpeace (classed as a body with political objectives), the ad garnered more than 65 million views online in the month after it was released on social media (Hickman, 2018). Many consumers responded with supportive messages, declaring that they were going to boycott *all* palm oil as a result.

This narrative, however, presents an oversimplified picture of current debates about palm oil and oil palm plantations; it also leaves out the many complex factors that shape the fate of orangutans and their habitat, including threats such as hunting, killing in retaliation for "crop-raiding" and the pet trade (Meijaard *et al*., 2011a, 2018; Voigt *et al*., 2018). While not unconnected to the expansion of industrial agriculture, these threats occur on a different scale and demand distinct mitigation strategies. Moreover, the media's unnuanced depiction of rehabilitation programs glosses over the controversies surrounding such projects, notably their long-term effectiveness and viability (Palmer, 2018; Rijksen and Meijaard, 1999; Wilson et al., 2014a). Although such programs represent only one component of orangutan conservation, their popularity risks channeling public attention and potential donations away from other longer-term, holistic efforts, such as habitat protection.[16]

The visual prominence of orangutans in these narratives can also have damaging knock-on effects. Although organizations strive to illuminate the wider environmental context behind these pictures, they cannot always control their dissemination and reinterpretation. Such images are frequently picked up and circulated, especially on social media, for their cuteness or amusement value. As they become unmoored from their explanatory text, two main problems arise.

First, the decontextualized circulation of "cute" orangutan images risks normalizing an already long-running perception of orangutans as performers or playthings rather than as wild animals (Aldrich, 2018; Cribb, Gilbert and Tiffin, 2014, chapters 7-8). This is compounded by the popularity of images of human–orangutan intimacy (such as orangutans clinging to carers), which risk cultivating the assumption that human–orangutan contact is acceptable or even desirable.

Although organizations try to challenge such perceptions, their messages do not always reach the wider public. As reviews on sites such as Tripadvisor suggest, many tourists arrive in Indonesia, Malaysia and elsewhere with precisely this image of cute, cuddly orangutans in mind (TripAdvisor, n.d.). Zoos and tourism-oriented wildlife centers have responded to—and arguably generated—this idea by promoting various orangutan encounters. In Indonesia, some of these facilities have been criticized for appearing more like tourist attractions than rehabilitation centers (Danaparamita, 2016). Centers such as Bukit Lawang, Semenggoh, Sepilok and Tanjung Puting offer tourists opportunities to take photographs of orangutans at their feeding platforms. Both Bali Zoo and Singapore Zoo sell "breakfast with orangutans" packages that allow visitors to have a meal a few meters away from orangutans and take photographs in close proximity to them (Singapore Zoo, n.d.; Viator, n.d.). Although physical contact is widely prohibited, this rule is difficult to enforce in practice (Palmer, 2018, chapter 6). Indeed, it is not uncommon for videos and photographs of tourists touching, carrying or hugging orangutans to circulate on social media. A vicious cycle thus ensues, with such images further perpetuating misleading perceptions of orangutans, while fanning demand for live apes to sustain these activities (Moorhouse et al., 2015). In this way, even the most well-meaning representations of orangutans can inadvertently contribute to the conditions that sustain the ape trade in Southeast Asia.

Second, the appearance of such images on television and social media can produce unintended effects among Indonesian and Malaysian audiences and users. As Meijaard and Sheil (2008) note, orangutan conservation schemes can spark resentment among villagers who see conservationists as caring more about animals than humans. Photographs of orangutans being cuddled and fed in rehabilitation centers risk aggravating such sentiments and generating accusations of double standards from local people, as well as exacerbating tensions over conservation schemes (Palmer, 2018, p. 214). In this way, such images can have detrimental consequences in the very areas where local collaboration is most needed.

Addressing the Problems

Action is needed on different fronts. First, producers of source material, such as orangutan charities and journalists, could exercise more caution with respect to potential unintended effects of their images and narratives—for example, by ensuring that the popular focus on the cute and cuddly aspects of these apes does not skew public perceptions of them. A reassessment of the extent to which images play up the human–orangutan bond is also in order, particularly in organizations that display photographs of their founders and staff interacting with orangutans—without any protection—on their websites and in publicity material. While such images can be elements of a successful marketing strategy, they can also undermine efforts to redress the misconceptions that fuel the live ape trade. Addressing these content-based issues will necessitate coordination among orangutan organizations, which currently observe varied guidelines; by joining forces, they will be better positioned to issue consistent messages and to avoid undermining each other.

Rather than changing the content of media portrayals, it is important to address the structural conditions in which they exist. For example, it is worth asking which media circuits such images and narratives travel across, and what effects they have as they move. Such an approach would require coordination between international conservation organizations and their partners in Indonesia and Malaysia. It would also involve identifying new partnerships (such as with tour operators or national celebrities) and channels for action (such as Indonesian social media campaigns) through which to disrupt misleading narratives and generate new ones. Such a joined-up approach would help tackle the effects—and not just the contents—of media distortions.

(see Box I.5). As noted above and discussed below, engagement with social media holds some promise; progress has been made with Instagram, which now monitors images taken with wildlife (see Box I.5).

Efforts are also needed to reduce consumer demand for gibbons as pets and props. Initiatives that aim to curb the pet trade can usefully target the main purchasers of apes, the emerging Indonesian and Malaysian middle classes and, in particular, 20–25 year olds who have disposable income and live in cities. Campaigns that target foreign tourists could help to reduce the use of gibbons as photo props.[17] In particular, tourists could influence perceptions and awareness of threatened species (Nekaris *et al.*, 2013).

How Online Companies Can Help to Tackle Wildlife Trafficking

As discussed above, the trade in endangered species has expanded from physical marketplaces and storefronts to web-based platforms (Kramer *et al.*, 2017). Not only does this shift allow sellers to access a far greater number of potential customers, but it also affords them a higher level of anonymity and risk mitigation since they can more readily hide behind fake accounts. Illicit sales often take place on social media platforms through posts and private messaging features, as well as through traditional e-commerce websites with built-in buying and selling functionality.

After first recognizing this issue in 2004, TRAFFIC sought to address it across online platforms starting in 2012, initially by engaging Chinese Internet giants (TRAFFIC, 2012; Williamson, 2004). By 2016, the organization was partnering with the World Wide Fund for Nature (WWF) and the International Fund for Animal Welfare (IFAW) to convene the tech sector globally and raise awareness of the illegal wildlife trade, encourage sector-wide collaboration and develop solutions (TRAFFIC, personal communication, 2019).

WWF, TRAFFIC and IFAW launched the Coalition to End Wildlife Trafficking Online on March 7, 2018 to reduce wildlife trafficking online through industry collaboration. By June 2020, the number of members had increased from 21 global companies to 36 (WWF, 2018, n.d.).[18] Through the Coalition approach, companies work with IFAW, TRAFFIC and WWF to develop an action plan tailored to their unique platforms to track progress towards reducing illegal wildlife trade on their sites. In a progress report released in March 2020, the Coalition revealed that its members had blocked or removed more than 3.3 million listings that violated wildlife policies (The Coalition, 2020).

Given social media's unique ability to influence billions of users across the globe, the Coalition's user education component is an essential part of reducing wildlife trafficking through messaging and social applications. Since many users of social media are likely to respond to and share content without fully understanding its origins, it is important to draw a connection between the use and acquisition of live animals and wildlife trafficking (TRAFFIC, personal communication, 2019).

In December 2017, TRAFFIC and WWF launched a pop-up alert system with Instagram to educate users about searched content that may be linked to the illegal trade in live animals, as well as their parts and products (Instagram, 2017). The two organizations provided about 250 hashtags (#) that may be associated with the illegal trade and related activities, including selfies with wildlife. Users who use the targeted hashtags to search for content receive an alert providing more information about the issue as well as a link to the Instagram help

FIGURE 4.3

Instagram Alert about the Illegal Wildlife Trade, Initiated on December 4, 2017

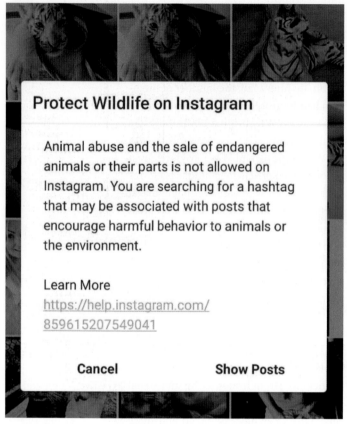

Protect Wildlife on Instagram

Animal abuse and the sale of endangered animals or their parts is not allowed on Instagram. You are searching for a hashtag that may be associated with posts that encourage harmful behavior to animals or the environment.

Learn More
https://help.instagram.com/859615207549041

Cancel   Show Posts

Source: Instagram screenshot from 2018

Photo: Awareness raising campaigns could be used to stem the demand for wild-caught apes in Thailand, particularly by targeting tourists with the aim of curbing the popularity of orangutan shows and the use of apes as props for selfies. © Paul Hilton/ Earth Tree Images

page to learn more (Instagram, n.d.-a; see Figure 4.3).

This pop-up alert has two primary objectives. The first is to educate users about posts that may be linked to wildlife trafficking. Such posts may involve the sale of unsustainably or unverifiably sourced live animals, the promotion of animal selfies at tourist sites, or trafficking of illegally sourced wildlife products. Posts that openly advertise the sale or use of animals may lead users to assume that related transactions would be legal. Such was the case when videos of a "cute" slow loris being tickled went viral. Although the species is threatened with extinction and is listed on CITES

Appendix I, these animals rode the social media wave to fame as desirable pets (CITES, n.d.-b, n.d.-d). Many viewers probably assumed the primate raised his arms to enjoy being tickled, not understanding that this natural behavior was in fact a defensive movement (Nekaris *et al.*, 2013). The pop-up alert that users receive when they search for #slowloris aims to prevent them from unknowingly facilitating this illegal trade.

The second objective of the alerts is to deter criminals from using the platform to conduct illegal activities. For sellers who previously operated with impunity, pop-ups announce Instagram's commitment to action on posts that violate company wildlife policies.

While pop-up alerts may represent a strong start to tackling online wildlife trafficking, the evolving nature of the illicit trade calls for additional, adaptable responses and preventive measures across the sector. In 2019, Facebook strengthened its wildlife policy by prohibiting advertising of all species listed on CITES Appendix I and all live animals except those for sale by verified sellers. Coalition members are advised to continue their educational efforts while strengthening policy enforcement and enhancing automated solutions to detect and prevent illegal wildlife posts.

Conclusion

Most organizations that work to combat the illegal trade in live apes have relied heavily on bans and law enforcement, with great effort invested in the prevention of poaching and the capture of poachers, traffickers, transporters and various other actors who are involved in the supply chain (World Bank Group, 2016). The continued decline in ape populations and the ongoing loss of ape habitat cast doubt on the effectiveness of this approach as a core solution. While

there is arguably a need to impose more penalties and launch more prosecutions to stem the supply of wild-caught apes, there is a pressing need to tackle the demand that drives the trade.

Most organizations that work to combat the illegal trade in live apes have relied heavily on bans and law enforcement.

As this chapter demonstrates, much of the local demand for pet orangutans in Indonesian Borneo is fueled by misperceptions of apes' basic needs, rather than hopes of financial gain. Advocacy campaigns may have a role to play here—as they did in the United States, where they helped to tackle the demand for ape performers in the entertainment industry. In Indonesia, effective demand-reduction measures would cut down on the number of orangutans caught as a by-product of hunting and forest loss. Awareness raising campaigns could similarly be used to stem the demand for wild-caught apes in Thailand, particularly by targeting tourists with the aim of curbing the popularity of orangutan shows and the use of apes as props for selfies.

Global zoological associations can partner with Chinese zoos and wildlife parks—as well as local regulatory bodies—to enhance the welfare of captive apes, such as by providing guidance on preventing hybridization and reducing fetal and infant mortality rates. Lowering these rates, and thus maintaining the desired number of infants, has the co-benefit of reducing the demand for more wild-caught infants. Emerging shifts among Chinese people's attitudes towards wildlife indicate that the country may soon favor more concerted conservation efforts and stricter policies on the welfare of apes.

By facilitating and promoting the illegal ape trade, social media present both a challenge and an opportunity. Collaboration between conservation organizations and social media companies has already led to the development of pop-up alerts and user education programs. Tougher policies and additional measures—including the reporting of violations to law enforcement authorities—

could go a long way towards reducing the demand for apes as pets, props and entertainers in today's wildlife crime hotspots and beyond.

Acknowledgments

Principal authors: Helga Rainer,[19] Annette Lanjouw,[20] Karmele Llano Sánchez[21] and Graham L. Banes[22]

Contributors: Susan M. Cheyne,[23] Liana Chua,[24] Julia Gallucci,[25] Steven Galster,[26] Giavanna Grein,[27] Steve Ross[28] and Penny Wallace[29]

Box 4.1: Julia Gallucci
Box 4.2: Annette Lanjouw
Box 4.3: Steve Ross
Case Study 4.1: Liana Chua

Endnotes

1   This section is based on the personal observations of G.L. Banes, who lived and worked in China from 2013 to 2016 and visited more than 180 zoos.

2   Based on informal conversations with zoo staff and permits seen by the author.

3   The two lone silverbacks are housed in Zhengzhou Zoo, Henan province, and in Jinan Zoo, Shandong province; the Shanghai Zoo has a group of gorillas.

4   The AZA does provide Japanese and Spanish translations of its chimpanzee care manual, however (AZA Ape TAG, 2010; TAG de Simios de la AZA, 2010).

5   Information included in Steve Martin's contract with Microsoft, 2015, seen by the authors.

6   Information from an internal tracking document at PETA, compiled by J. Gallucci.

7   This section reflects observations of Steven Galster, who, together with staff from the organization Freeland, began to monitor the use of great apes in the Thai entertainment sector in 1999 and helped broker bilateral government negotiations that led to the repatriation of smuggled orangutans from Thailand to Indonesia.

8   Based on Freeland observation of Government–NGO meetings in Jakarta and Bangkok in 2002, 2003, 2004.

9   Based on Freeland annual observations of shows in Bangkok and Phuket.

10   Freeland annual spot check surveys at shows in Bangkok and Phuket.

11 This section presents data from an ongoing study by International Animal Rescue (IAR) Indonesia that is looking at people's motivations for keeping orangutans as pets, as well as factors that influence this behavior. The data were collected during interviews with owners of pet orangutans before, while or after the apes were rescued by IAR and the BKSDA (Natural Resources Conservation Agency of the Ministry of Environment and Forestry of Indonesia). The study started in 2012.

12 This section presents data from an ongoing study by International Animal Rescue (IAR) Indonesia that is looking at people's motivations for keeping orangutans as pets, as well as factors that influence this behavior. The data were collected during interviews with owners of pet orangutans before, while or after the apes were rescued by IAR and the BKSDA (Natural Resources Conservation Agency of the Ministry of Environment and Forestry of Indonesia). The study started in 2012.

13 This section presents data from an ongoing study by International Animal Rescue (IAR) Indonesia that is looking at people's motivations for keeping orangutans as pets, as well as factors that influence this behavior. The data were collected during interviews with owners of pet orangutans before, while or after the apes were rescued by IAR and the BKSDA (Natural Resources Conservation Agency of the Ministry of Environment and Forestry of Indonesia). The study started in 2012.

14 Gibbon ages were assessed by the authors.

15 This case study draws heavily on Chua (2018a, 2018b) as well as ongoing, unpublished visual and textual research on social media engagement with orangutan causes by Liana Chua.

16 For additional information, see Palmer (2018, pp. 57–61).

17 Unpublished IAR data, seen by the authors.

18 As of June 2020, the members of the Coalition to End Wildlife Trafficking Online—which is convened by WWF, TRAFFIC and IFAW—were: 58 Group, Alibaba, Artron, Baidu, Baixing, Deine Tierwelt, eBay, Etsy, Facebook, Google, Huaxia Collection, Hantang Collection, Instagram, Kuaishou, Kupatana, Mall for Africa, Leboncoin, letgo, Microsoft, OfferUp, OLX, Pinterest, Poshmark, Qyer, Rakuten, Ruby Lane, Sapo, Shengshi Collection, Sina, Sougou, Tencent, Tortoise Friends, Wen Wan Tian Xia, Zhong Hua Gu Wan, Zhongyikupai and Zhuanzhuan (WWF, n.d.).

19 Arcus Foundation (www.arcusfoundation.org).

20 Arcus Foundation (www.arcusfoundation.org).

21 International Animal Rescue (www.internationalanimalrescue.org).

22 Wisconsin National Primate Research Center (www.primate.wisc.edu).

23 Borneo Nature Foundation (www.borneonaturefoundation.org/en/).

24 Brunel University London (www.brunel.ac.uk/anthropology).

25 People for the Ethical Treatment of Animals (www.peta.org).

26 Freeland (www.freeland.org).

27 TRAFFIC (www.traffic.org).

28 Lincoln Park Zoo (www.lpzoo.org) and Project ChimpCARE (www.chimpcare.org).

29 TRAFFIC (www.traffic.org).

CHAPTER 5

Curbing the Illegal Killing, Capture and Trade in Apes: Responses at Source

Introduction

Trafficking in apes and other endangered animals has stimulated numerous policy and strategic discussions among source and demand countries, donors and conservation organizations, as evidenced by the declarations of recent international conferences on the illegal wildlife trade (Hanoi Conference on the Illegal Wildlife Trade, 2016; Kasane Conference on The Illegal Wildlife Trade, 2015; London Conference on the Illegal Wildlife Trade, 2014, 2018). The deliberations have generated consensus on four key strategies for tackling the trade:

- reducing demand for illegal products;
- developing effective legal frameworks;
- strengthening law enforcement; and
- promoting community engagement.

The latter three approaches are particularly relevant to enhancing ape protection and curbing illegal hunting and trade at its source—at the start of the supply chain, in the specific locations where illegal activities are happening. Strengthening law enforcement and supporting sustainable livelihoods and economic development are *in situ* approaches; strengthening legal frameworks happens *ex situ* but still has an impact on the source.

These strategies for controlling the illegal wildlife trade dovetail with criminology theory and practice. In particular, they are strongly aligned with the approach of situational crime prevention, which holds that, given the opportunity, any individual is capable of committing an offense at any time. When it comes to the illegal trade in apes, local people are typically active at the start of a supply chain which can involve complex trade networks of hunters, dealers and traffickers. As predicted by situational crime prevention theory, their involvement is often opportunistic rather than organized. Approaches that recognize and respond to that dynamic are thus critical to curbing the trade at source. Situational crime prevention is based on five strategies to limit opportunism. Specifically, it aims to increase the effort required to commit a crime; increase the risks of being detected or apprehended; reduce the rewards generated by the crime; reduce the factors that provoke criminal activity; and remove excuses that potential offenders may cite for committing crimes (Clarke, 2009).

This chapter provides an overview of three of the above-mentioned approaches —developing effective legal frameworks, strengthening law enforcement and promoting community engagement—and discusses how they have been applied in the context of ape conservation. It does not seek to provide an evaluation of their effectiveness, which is beyond the scope of this chapter.

> " Where formal law contradicts customary law, even the strongest legal frameworks may not be effective if local communities do not consider them legitimate. "

Indeed, since few evaluations have been conducted, evidence remains limited on the relative effectiveness of different strategies—and that knowledge gap represents a major constraint to policy-making (Booker and Roe, 2017). As Chapter 6 provides a detailed analysis of the legislative and policy frameworks for ape conservation and protection, this chapter offers only a brief overview of legal issues and devotes more space to site-based law enforcement and community engagement.

The key findings include::

- A number of countries—including ape range states such as Gabon, Indonesia and Viet Nam—have revised their legislation to increase the severity of penalties for wildlife crimes, but weak judicial awareness of the issue and high levels of corruption hamper implementation.

- Where formal law contradicts customary law, even the strongest legal frameworks may not be effective if local communities do not consider them legitimate.

- Site-based law enforcement is key to the prevention of illegal wildlife hunting, yet flawed approaches can have deleterious social and ecological consequences, including unjust persecution of local people, human rights abuses and increased poaching pressure.

- Members of local communities are critical partners for law enforcement efforts. While their proximity to wildlife can make them more likely to engage in illegal hunting and trade, it can also enable them to help curb such activities, particularly by serving as protected area rangers.

- For wildlife conservation to prevail over wildlife crime, the expected net benefits (benefits minus costs) flowing to individuals in local communities as a result of conservation must be greater than those associated with unsustainable or illegal hunting and trade.

- To be effective, all responses to wildlife crime at the source need to reflect an understanding of the motivations of people who are involved in hunting and trading in apes.

Developing Effective Legal Frameworks

The establishment of robust legal frameworks requires a wide range of measures, including passing effective legislation; strengthening the judiciary and improving prosecutions; ensuring adequate deterrent penalties are in place; cooperating with relevant local and external authorities; and tackling corruption, money laundering and other crimes that are linked to wildlife crime (Roe and Booker, 2019; see Box 5.1).

In some cases, simply raising awareness about the law can serve as a key intervention—not just among local people, but also among government officials. A study found that in the Garamba-Bili-Chinko landscape in Central Africa, for example, there was little awareness about the protected status of chimpanzees, even among local officials, and that the killing of adults for meat and subsequent trafficking of orphaned infants was rife (Ondoua Ondoua *et al.*, 2017). Raising awareness about laws does not necessarily lead people to respect them, but it is a useful starting point and, at the very least, a strategy for removing excuses for illegal activities—one of the key principles of situational crime prevention (Clarke, 2009).

As noted above, effective legal frameworks depend in part on adequate deterrents and penalties for wildlife crime. A recent study by the United Nations Office on Drugs and Crime found that, prior to 2015, only about one-quarter of the 131 parties to the Convention on International Trade in Endangered Species of Wild Fauna and Flora (CITES) for which data were available had regulations specifying more than four years' imprisonment for involvement in the illegal wildlife trade (UNODC, 2016). Subsequently, in 2015, the UN General Assembly passed a resolution calling on member states to consider wildlife crime "serious," as per the UN Convention against Transnational Organized Crime, which stipulates that "serious crime" warrants a minimum penalty of four years' imprisonment (UNGA, 2015; UNODC, 2004). A number of countries—including ape range states such as Gabon, Indonesia, and Viet Nam—have since revised their legislation to increase the severity of penalties for wildlife crimes (Roe and Booker, 2019).

Without proper implementation, even the most comprehensive wildlife protection legislation will fall short of its desired conservation goals, especially if corruption is endemic in the judicial system. Such is the case in Indonesia, where orangutans are commonly held as pets and the first prosecutions of their owners took place as recently as 2010 in Borneo and 2012 in Sumatra—even though these apes have been strictly protected under the law since 1924 (WCS, 2012). To increase the priority given to tackling corruption, member states of the European Union and Senegal submitted a proposed resolution on wildlife trafficking and corruption at the 17th Conference of the Parties to CITES in 2016, during which it was adopted by consensus (CITES, 2016). Nevertheless, implementation remains a challenge (see Box 5.1).

Overall, the lack of effective legal frameworks is a key reason why illegal trade in apes is a lucrative and low-risk business, particularly for those operating at the middle and upper levels of the trade chain (Clough and May, 2018). Moreover, if formal law contradicts customary law, even

> " For wildlife conservation to prevail over wildlife crime, the benefits flowing to local individuals as a result of conservation must be greater than those associated with illegal hunting and trade. "

Tackling Corruption and Improving the Judicial Process in Cameroon and Beyond

In Cameroon, trafficking in live apes, skulls and meat is big business. The Last Great Ape Organization (LAGA) is a non-governmental organization that is trying to help tackle this trade, particularly by addressing the corruption that fuels it (LAGA, n.d.). In 1994, Cameroon passed a law that prohibits trade and trafficking in wildlife parts, yet no related prosecutions took place in the nine years following the law's enactment (National Assembly of Cameroon, 1994). In 2003, however, LAGA helped bring Cameroon's first wildlife crime conviction (Bale, 2016).

As one of the founding members of the Eco Activists for Governance and Law Enforcement (EAGLE) network, LAGA works with the government on arrests, legal follow-up and raising media awareness to ensure the law is properly applied (EAGLE, n.d.). In collaboration with the government, LAGA carries out undercover investigations, plans and supervises arrest operations, and follows up on court cases on behalf of the state. LAGA staff members keep a close eye on wildlife crime cases and make sure that the law is not undermined through bribery or other forms of corruption; they act as bodyguards during the entire judicial process, including during jail visits, to ensure prisoners are not released illegally. They collaborate with in-country influencers and international organizations to bring pressure to bear—such as through meetings, emails and phone calls—if judicial standards are not upheld. LAGA is credited with driving Cameroon's shift from inaction to sustained action on wildlife crime, as demonstrated by regular arrests and prosecutions of major wildlife dealers in the country.

Through the EAGLE network, LAGA's success in Cameroon has been extended to other countries in Africa—including critical great ape range states such as the Republic of Congo and Gabon (LAGA, n.d.). Like LAGA, EAGLE helps to strengthen legal frameworks for wildlife conservation by focusing on effective prosecutions of major players and by tackling corruption. The network has shown that corruption reaches into the highest levels of wildlife administration; in 2015, for instance, it helped to bring about the arrest and prosecution of the former head of the CITES Management Authority of Guinea for his role in the illegal export of chimpanzees and gorillas (PEGAS, 2015).

While increased prosecutions and arrests do not necessarily translate directly into a measurable reduction in poaching pressure on the ground, they can be effective in removing key players from complex trade chains and sending strong deterrent signals to would-be criminals.

the strongest legal frameworks may not be effective unless local populations consider them legitimate. While subsistence use and extraction of endangered wildlife is technically illegal, people may justify these activities on the basis of long-standing tradition, customary law or livelihood needs. The widespread criminalization of customary wildlife use by colonial and post-colonial administrations has, in many cases, resulted in the disenfranchisement of local communities from their land and natural resources and consequently fostered resentment of conservation efforts and authorities (Sifuna, 2012; Walters *et al.*, 2015; WIPO, 2013). In this context, recent research conducted in Central Africa and the Democratic Republic of Congo (DRC) shows that:

> Local communities are expected to respect legislation (e.g. determining which species can or cannot be hunted, when and how) that is sometimes contradictory and of which they have only superficial knowledge. Many people admit that they do not respect these laws, and that they find this legislation constraining as they rely heavily on exploiting wildlife for food and as a source of income. With high unemployment in the region, village hunters admit to poaching in the [protected areas] (Ondoua Ondoua *et al.*, 2017, p. 36).

Chapter 6 in this volume provides a wider assessment of the current status of legislative and policy frameworks with respect to ape conservation and protection. The remainder of this chapter focuses on local protection efforts: law enforcement activities, as led by government or private-sector agents, and community-based approaches.

Strengthening Law Enforcement

Management of any resource—be it timber, wildlife, water or land—requires resource users to adhere to international, national and local use rules or norms (Keane *et al.*, 2008). Successful resource management thus entails the monitoring of compliance with these rules, as well as their enforcement wherever compliance is lacking. Such enforcement involves a range of institutions and bodies, from governments to rural communities; it may be imposed on a locality by an external entity or it may have evolved locally.

The hunting, killing and commercial trade in apes—whether live or dead—is illegal in all countries. International trade is regulated by CITES, and domestic use and trade are regulated by national legislation, such as wildlife management acts and forest laws (CITES, n.d.; see Chapter 6). The dominant approach to countering illegal use and trade in apes has been focused on enforcing these regulations (Challender and MacMillan, 2014; Stiles *et al.*, 2013). Law enforcement efforts are required all along the wildlife trade chain, from source to destination, implying a need for cooperation among multiple agencies within a source country—such as park rangers, police and customs—as well as between countries. In the run-up to the international illegal wildlife trade conference in Hanoi in 2016, for example, the Ugandan government reported that it had established joint border patrols with neighboring countries, including the DRC, Kenya and Rwanda (Roe and Booker, 2019). In addition to cross-border patrols, regional wildlife enforcement networks have been established in many regions of the world. The following are of relevance to apes:

- the **Lusaka Agreement Task Force** in Kenya, Lesotho, Liberia, the Republic of Congo, Tanzania, Uganda and Zambia;
- the **Horn of Africa Wildlife Enforcement Network** in Djibouti, Eritrea, Ethiopia, Kenya, Somalia, South Sudan, Sudan and Uganda; and

- the **Association of South East Asian Nations (ASEAN) Wildlife Enforcement Network** in Brunei, Cambodia, Indonesia, Lao People's Democratic Republic, Malaysia, Myanmar, the Philippines, Singapore, Thailand and Viet Nam (EIA, 2016).

Site-based Law Enforcement: The Pros and Cons

While national and international enforcement efforts are critical, "the single most effective form of law enforcement in countering wildlife trafficking and poaching is enforcement *within areas where the species occur* to prevent animals from being killed or removed from the wild in the first place" (Felbab-Brown, 2018, emphasis added). Government and private rangers are charged with the bulk of site-level law enforcement, such as preventing the perpetration of crime, investigating crimes that have occurred and apprehending offenders. They undertake patrols, locate and remove snares, gather intelligence, conduct crime scene investigations, and pursue and arrest offenders.

Site-based law enforcement can help to curb the hunting and trade in apes but,

BOX 5.2

Militarized Conservation: A Solution or Part of the Problem?

It is claimed that greater levels of law enforcement are needed to protect wildlife and the environment, including protected areas (Moore et al., 2018). To ensure that interventions are properly tailored to local settings and contexts, however, it is useful to consider the potential utility and implications of such measures in detail.

The exploitation of natural resources—be it legal or illegal—often clashes with the interests of conservationists, environmentalists, governments and local or indigenous communities that are dependent on those resources. In response to such conflicts, governments are increasingly engaging in militarized forms of conservation, including greater use of force, counter-insurgency techniques, use of military surveillance technologies and contracting of private security services to train rangers and even to conduct patrols.[1] Many conservation organizations working with governments in state-owned protected areas have developed or support highly militarized ranger forces to protect the biodiversity and land from exploitation. As more than 1,000 rangers are known to have lost their lives over the period 2008–18, protected area authorities also consider militarization an important strategy to reduce risks to park staff (Draper, 2016; IRF, 2019).

Militarized approaches pit rangers against a variety of actors, however. In some cases, those actors are private businesses intent on industrial development or the extraction of resources; in others, they may be foreign poachers who hunt species for their parts, such as ivory, rhino horn, pangolin scales, or extract valuable timber (Global Witness, 2019). Time and again, rangers also find themselves operating in opposition to local people who depend on natural resources for water, food, shelter and other basic needs; under these circumstances, confrontations can lead to human rights abuses (Ayari and Counsell, 2017).

While militarized approaches may have led to an increased number of arrests, it is not clear whether they always lead to a decrease in

depending on how it is carried out, it can also generate problems for conservationists and local communities. From a conservation perspective, the effectiveness of law enforcement patrols has been praised as well as questioned. The utility of patrols is highlighted in a study conducted in Nyungwe National Park, Rwanda, which indicates that wildlife authorities could reduce poaching threats by adding ranger posts in areas where they do not already exist, and by increasing the number of patrols to sites where the probability of poaching activities is high (Moore *et al.*, 2018). Similarly, a study of site-based law enforcement across a range of protected areas in Africa suggests that the presence of patrols is the best predictor of great ape conservation (Tranquilli *et al.*, 2012).

Nevertheless, patrolling effectiveness is contingent on the rangers' level of training, their numbers relative to the size of the area being patrolled, and the availability of resources, equipment and salaries (Tranquilli *et al.*, 2012). As these requirements are rarely met in protected areas, patrolling effectiveness is often limited (Felbab-Brown, 2017, pp. 110–11). Another study points out that since apes are hunted and captured in diverse and dispersed ways, patrols—which tend to follow set routes and typically cannot cover

Photo: In Virunga National Park, park managers see militarization of conservation efforts as a way to improve protection and the security of local communities, but some argue that rangers also find themselves operating in opposition to local people who depend on natural resources for water, food, shelter and other basic needs; under these circumstances, confrontations can lead to human rights abuses. The Virunga volcanoes range.
© Jabruson (www.jabruson.photoshelter.com)

poaching (Carlson, Wright and Dönges, 2015). The presence of a militarized and sometimes extremely aggressive ranger force can lead to the following negative impacts, particularly for local communities living near protected areas:

- insecurity among local people, who fear getting caught in the crossfire between poachers and anti-poaching patrols;

- decreased access to land and resources, such as water, honey, meat and other non-timber forest products;

- the proliferation of firearms, especially in countries with poor arms control;

- human rights violations, including killing, rape and torture, when militarized groups lose control or state enforcement agents abuse their powers; and

- the erosion of community confidence in the government and in anti-poaching activities (Carlson, Wright and Dönges, 2015; Cooney *et al.*, 2017).

Extreme and violent behavior by park rangers against local communities in different parts of the Congo Basin, South America and parts of Southeast Asia has been well documented by academic researchers and the media alike. Factors such as contempt, insufficient training, ethnic divisions, poor rule of law, and inadequate support and supervision of rangers have led to many serious abuses (Brooks and Hopkins, 2016; Warren, Baker and Engert, 2019).

In the Democratic Republic of Congo's Virunga National Park (see Figure 5.3), park managers see militarization of conservation efforts as a way to improve protection and the security of local communities that may be vulnerable to victimization by armed militias (Draper, 2016). This is demonstrated by allowing deployment, in certain contexts, of ranger forces to communities in insecure areas close to the park (Virunga Alliance, n.d.). Broader conflict and security concerns in the region are important considerations for the conservation sector, as the use of military tactics by both rangers and armed groups could cause violence to spiral out of control (Carlson, Wright and Dönges, 2015; Marijnen and Verweijen, 2016).

more than a limited proportion of any area —are unlikely to encounter poachers (Stiles *et al.*, 2013). More worryingly, some commentators have noted that effective law enforcement can actually have the unintended effect of incentivizing poachers to step up their activities to maintain the same level of supply in the face of anticipated confiscations or arrests (Felbab-Brown, 2017, pp. 107–9).

Site-based law enforcement has also been associated with adverse social consequences, including numerous cases of heavy-handed ranger patrols, followed by persecution, harassment and human rights abuses by authorities (Corry, 2015; Warren and Baker, 2019). Of growing concern is "militarized conservation"—the use of military staff, tactics and equipment by ranger patrols (see Box 5.2). The problem is not just a one-sided issue of poorly trained rangers meting out unjust punishments on vulnerable communities; indeed, it is not uncommon for poachers and other criminals to target the rangers themselves. On average, an estimated 100 protected area rangers are killed every year (TTGLF, n.d.).

Partnerships for Law Enforcement

Local and international non-governmental organizations (NGOs) are often involved as key partners of government agencies in the management of protected areas and enforcement of conservation regulations. Organizations such as the Wildlife Conservation Society (WCS), the World Wide Fund for Nature (WWF) and the Zoological Society of London (ZSL) support a number of governments of ape range states in training and equipping rangers, for example. NGOs have also been vital in the development of new technology to support law enforcement efforts (see Box 5.3). Perhaps most prominent among the technology that is used to

support law enforcement against the illegal wildlife trade is SMART—the Spatial Monitoring and Reporting Tool (see Box 5.4). SMART was developed and is maintained by a coalition of NGO partners that comprises WCS, WWF and ZSL, as well as the Frankfurt Zoological Society, Global Wildlife

BOX 5.3

Technology for Site-based Law Enforcement against Wildlife Crime

Site-based law enforcement is making increasing use of technology to curb the illegal hunting of and trade in apes and other species. In addition to the well-known SMART software, described in Box 5.4, use of the following tools is growing:

Radio frequency identification (RFID) tags are microchips that enable the tracking of individual animals, thus greatly enhancing rapid response effectiveness. RFID tags have largely been used to protect rhinos but have also served to monitor orangutans (Hance, 2009).

Camera traps have been used as biological monitoring tools for many years; more recently, they have been adapted for anti-poaching purposes, equipped with video feeds, heat sensors, vibration detectors and acoustics (Buxton *et al.*, 2018; see Box 5.4).

Mobile phone apps—such as the award-winning apeAPP, developed by the Great Apes Survival Partnership (GRASP) (UNESCO, n.d.)—allow the general public to post sightings and report illegal activities. GRASP partners use apeAPP to post updates on confiscations and other activities, such as snare removals. Similarly, Freeland's WildScan is intended to help report illegal wildlife use (Freeland, 2018).

Online databases can be used to store information collected through mobile apps and other sources. GRASP's Apes Seizure Database is one such example.

Drones equipped with cameras and heat-sensitive infrared optics are increasingly being used to both monitor wildlife populations and to track suspected poachers (Corrigan, 2019).

Using SMART and Other Tools to Improve Law Enforcement

Since protected areas were first established, wildlife rangers have been employed to enforce the law. In undertaking patrolling, they build up deep knowledge of their site, not only with respect to the flora and fauna, but also regarding illegal activities. As this knowledge is generally underutilized and poorly shared, technology developers have sought to enhance rangers' ability to capture what they encounter in the field. These efforts have led to the development of the Spatial Monitoring and Reporting Tool (SMART), which builds on previous initiatives, such as the Management Information System (MIST), which was developed in Uganda, and CyberTracker, a South African tool (CyberTracker, n.d.; ESS, n.d.; SMART, n.d.-a).

Rangers can record data on key species and illegal activities using hand-held Global Positioning System (GPS) units or smartphones with built-in GPS capabilities. By uploading the data into SMART, they help to provide both temporal and spatial mapping of key wildlife sightings and threats. They also contribute to maps that show what areas are covered by ranger patrols, and where and when there are gaps in patrol coverage.

One of the key assumptions underlying the deployment of ranger patrols is that they act as a deterrent to hunters, yet this premise has rarely been tested. Assessments of tools such as MIST and SMART indicate that they have greatly improved patrol coverage and have been widely used to track catch per unit effort (CPUE), such as the number of snares discovered per kilometer of patrol (Critchlow et al., 2015). Analysis of CPUE methods can be vulnerable to bias, however, as the detectability of wildlife and threats can differ across observers and habitats, as well as over time (Keane, Jones and Milner-Gulland, 2011). New methods have been developed to better analyze data from SMART and MIST that incorporate measures to deal with variations in detectability (Critchlow et al., 2015; Moore et al., 2018). A recent analysis of modeled CPUE scores indicates that plotting the changes in CPUE over time against changes in patrolling efforts—that is, in the number and duration of patrols—can be used to detect where patrols provide effective deterrence against illegal activities (Dobson et al., 2019). Other tools, such as camera traps, are also starting to be incorporated in law enforcement monitoring to support rangers (see Box 5.3). With time, the growing number of SMART databases and the increasing quality of data within them will allow for enhanced analysis of the effectiveness of patrolling as a deterrence method.

In many sites that protect apes, SMART is used not only to monitor threats to their welfare and survival, but also to detect trends in their distribution and abundance. Researchers have used SMART data on sightings of signs of Grauer's gorilla (Gorilla beringei graueri) to assess the probability of occupancy across the ape's range in the eastern Democratic Republic of Congo, for example (Plumptre et al., 2016). Similarly, SMART and MIST data are being used to monitor Cross River gorilla (Gorilla gorilla diehli) occupancy.[2] SMART data are particularly useful in ranges where species are rarely encountered; over time, sufficient data can be compiled from regular patrolling to allow occupancy monitoring—an impossibility in one-off surveys.

Conservation, the North Carolina Zoo, Panthera, Peace Parks Foundation, Wildlife Protection Solutions and associates such as the CITES program Monitoring the Illegal Killing of Elephants (MIKE) (SMART, n.d.-b).

Private-sector organizations can also be key partners in law enforcement efforts, particularly those associated with natural resource sectors, such as logging, mining and industrial agriculture, including oil palm plantations. As discussed in the first two volumes of State of the Apes, the correlation between the hunting of wildlife and the influx of such industries is strong (Lanjouw, 2015; White and Fa, 2014). The link reflects not only that logging and mining operations open up forests with roads, allowing hunters to penetrate into previously inaccessible forest areas, but also that these industries bring with them large workforces that require food and thus represent a ready market for wild meat hunters.

Engaging private companies in tackling illegal hunting and the trade in apes is critical to the conservation of apes, particularly since a significant portion of their habitat lies outside of formal protected areas. Such is the case in the Congo Basin, where almost 40% of forest land has been awarded to timber enterprises, while only 12% is gazetted as protected areas (ZSL, 2014).

The International Union for Conservation of Nature (IUCN) suggests that certification through organizations such as the Forest Stewardship Council (FSC) is a potential mechanism for engaging private

companies in law enforcement efforts to protect apes from being killed (Morgan *et al.*, 2013). FSC Principle 6, for example, states that a certified organization "shall maintain, conserve and/or restore ecosystem services and environmental values of the Management Unit, and shall avoid, repair or mitigate negative environmental impacts" (FSC, 2015, p. 14). Criterion 6.6 under this principle requires that companies demonstrate that effective measures are in place to control hunting. The IUCN's FSC guidance specifically addresses companies that operate in countries that suffer from weak law enforcement capacity, emphasizing that meeting this criterion may require the companies themselves to support or finance

the protection of wildlife from illegal hunting and trafficking, and to establish strict regulations to ensure their own staff members do not become complicit in any illegal activities, such as selling or buying wild meat (Morgan *et al.*, 2013).

In Cameroon, the ZSL's Wildlife Wood Project encourages private logging companies to adopt low-impact logging practices and engage in wildlife protection. Since 2007, the project has worked with timber producers Pallisco and Rougier, which together manage more than 6,200 km² (620,000 ha) of forest. Policing illegal hunting is just one of the measures by which the companies are to mitigate the negative impact of timber concessions on wildlife (ZSL, n.d.). Similarly, schemes such as the Roundtable on Sustainable Palm Oil provide an opening for private companies to introduce strict regulations to prohibit the killing and capture of apes, but company commitment is required to translate this potential into routine practice (Ancrenaz *et al.*, 2016).

Like NGOs and private companies, local communities are critical partners for law enforcement efforts. Community buy-in can be key to making law enforcement efforts sustainable over the long term (Felbab-Brown, 2017). While their proximity to wildlife may tempt local people to engage in illegal hunting and trade, it also makes them more likely to be recruited as protected area rangers, as has been the case in Virunga National Park (Burke, 2018). Similarly, in the Lower Kinabatangan Wildlife Sanctuary in Malaysian Borneo, the Sabah Wildlife Department has recruited 24 "honorary wildlife wardens" from the local community and tasked them with conducting research, managing sanctuary resources and making arrests for illegal activities (Ancrenaz, 2019). In addition to serving as park rangers, wardens or game guards, local people can support law enforcement efforts by acting as informants and providing intelligence on planned, ongoing or completed illegal activities (Wilkie, Painter and Jacob, 2016).

The potential benefits of engaging local residents in law enforcement may seem compelling, as such a move promises to expand local authority and capacity, empower local communities, and reinforce their claims to land and resources. By participating in law enforcement efforts, however, community members may be exposed to serious risks. Specifically, individuals who are confronted by armed poachers face an immediate threat to their personal security, especially if they are not carrying weapons themselves. Further, if some community members are employed as game guards while others remain involved in poaching, the former may be perceived as aligned with external law enforcement agents rather than the community, which can cause a breakdown in social cohesion (Wilkie, Painter and Jacob, 2016). In the absence of adequate training, local guards may also undermine judicial procedures; in particular, their "arrests may not be validated by the court if they fail to follow due process or established standards for evidence collection and curation" (Wilkie, Painter and Jacob, 2016, p. 9). The potential advantages and risks inherent in involving local communities as law enforcement partners thus merit careful consideration.

Promoting Community Engagement

As discussed in the previous section, communities can bolster local law enforcement efforts to tackle illegal hunting and trade in wildlife—even if these measures on their own are not sufficient to put an end to such illegal activities. To target the root of the problem—and not just the symptoms—community members can also contribute to the development of appropriate governance and incentive structures that encourage local residents to protect rather than to poach wildlife. Such structures can take the form of income generation schemes or land and resource tenure rights, for example.

These types of measure could usefully be applied as a way to control snaring, one of the most common ways of trapping wild animals. Snaring is impossible to prevent, no matter how great the effort to identify and remove snares. These traps are easy and cheap to make, difficult to detect and indiscriminate in terms of the animals they catch. Although apes may not necessarily be the intended targets, they often get caught in snares (Wild Earth Allies, 2018; see Chapter 1). Between 2010 and 2015 almost 200,000 snares were removed from just five protected areas in Southeast Asia; during every year in that period, tens of thousands were removed from just two parks—Southern Cardamom National Park in Cambodia, and Hue and Quang Nam Saola Reserves in Viet Nam (Gray *et al.*, 2018). Snare removal and other law enforcement strategies are unlikely to be effective over the long term unless they are coupled with additional approaches, such as efforts to strengthen legal frameworks—including through provisions that criminalize the possession of snares in or near protected areas—and increased incentives for local people not to hunt.

The same factors that render local people likely to engage in poaching—their proximity to protected species and knowledge of their environment—also make them ideal candidates for participation in wildlife stewardship and conservation. Their involvement can range from being open to consulting to accepting full-on devolution of power and authority regarding conservation initiatives (Felbab-Brown, 2017, chapter 7). Regardless of the approach, the fundamental determinants of whether communities will engage in conservation—that is, whether they will protect rather than poach wildlife—are their culture, norms, beliefs, values, lifestyles and cognitive factors, as well as related financial and non-financial incentives (Milner-Gulland and Rowcliffe, 2007; Vining and Ebreo, 2002).

To be compelling, an incentive for wildlife conservation must arguably be associated with greater net benefits (benefits minus costs) to a local community than the alternative—engaging in unsustainable or illegal hunting and trade. Both benefits and costs can be tangible and intangible; they may include cash, strengthened rights, fear of arrest and other factors. The key to determining whether local people are likely to poach wildlife or to protect it is the relative significance of each of the elements in the equation depicted in Figure 5.1. Changes to any of these elements will affect the overall balance and tip the scales in favor of either poaching or protecting.

Costs and benefits vary across individuals and over time. Tipping the balance towards protection and away from poaching requires mechanisms to 1) increase or maintain the benefits from conservation while reducing—or at least not increasing—the

FIGURE 5.1

To Poach or to Protect? A Simple Equation for a Complex Issue

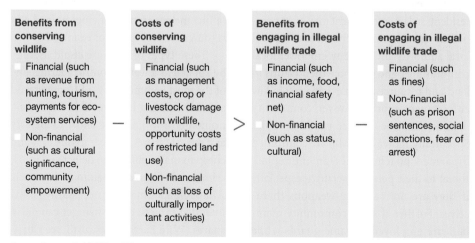

Benefits from conserving wildlife	Costs of conserving wildlife	Benefits from engaging in illegal wildlife trade	Costs of engaging in illegal wildlife trade
Financial (such as revenue from hunting, tourism, payments for ecosystem services)	Financial (such as management costs, crop or livestock damage from wildlife, opportunity costs of restricted land use)	Financial (such as income, food, financial safety net)	Financial (such as fines)
Non-financial (such as cultural significance, community empowerment)	Non-financial (such as loss of culturally important activities)	Non-financial (such as status, cultural)	Non-financial (such as prison sentences, social sanctions, fear of arrest)

Source: Cooney *et al.* (2017, p. 369)

costs, and 2) decrease the benefits and increase the costs of poaching. Different approaches to tackling illegal hunting and trade in wildlife can change the distribution of costs and benefits in unexpected ways (see Figure 5.2).

Increasing Community Benefits from Conserving Apes

Various approaches can be used to ensure that local people receive both financial and non-financial conservation benefits, either

FIGURE 5.2

Influences of Different Interventions to Combat the Illegal Wildlife Trade on Incentives for Engaging in Conservation vs. Poaching

A: How enforcement interventions seek to change incentives to conserve wildlife and engage in the illegal wildlife trade (IWT):

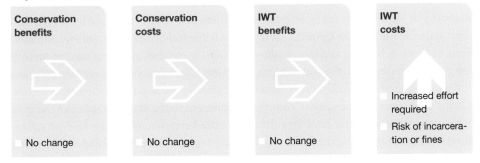

B: How enforcement interventions may inadvertently change incentives to conserve wildlife and engage in IWT:

C: How approaches that empower and engage communities may change incentives to conserve wildlife and engage in IWT:

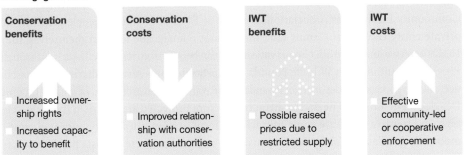

Notes: Solid arrows indicate change (increase or decrease); outlined arrows represent no change; and dotted arrows indicate possible change (increase).

Source: Cooney et al. (2017, p. 371)

of which may be derived directly or indirectly. As discussed below, the most direct method is to strengthen community land tenure and wildlife ownership rights; doing so enhances a community's capacity to use, manage and benefit from wildlife directly, such as through subsistence hunting or community-based tourism. As communities around the world have been able to secure significant benefits from wildlife use, their desire to maintain access to those benefits has provided a major incentive for them to remain engaged in conservation (Cooney et al., 2018). In Namibia, for example, returns for sustainable wildlife management—in the form of tourism, hunting and legal trade—are great enough to incentivize local communities to keep their land under conservation. Communal conservancies in the country now account for a greater land area than formal protected areas (Naidoo et al., 2016).

Given that apes are strictly protected, opportunities for direct conservation benefits are relatively limited. While the hunting of apes is prohibited, hunting of other species in ape habitat can provide an important incentive for habitat conservation and, hence, ape conservation. Ape-based tourism is another mechanism for generating conservation incentives and, in some cases, significant benefits for local people. In Rwanda, for example, the high-end Sabyinyo Silverback Lodge was developed as a joint venture between the local Kinigi and Nyange communities, as represented by the Sabyinyo Community Livelihoods Association; the private entity Governors Camps Ltd.; the NGOs International Gorilla Conservation Programme and African Wildlife Foundation; and the government department Rwanda Development Board. The lodge attracts high-end tourists who have come to track mountain gorillas in Volcanoes National Park. The local communities benefit from the joint venture in a number of different ways: equity in the business; employment;

> As communities have been able to secure significant benefits from wildlife use, their desire to maintain access to those benefits has provided a major incentive for them to remain engaged in conservation.

income for goods such as agricultural produce and services such as dancing displays; and dividends from profits (Nielsen and Spenceley, 2011).

The management of ape tourism is a delicate business, however, as apes need to be habituated and health risks properly monitored. In the case of gorilla tourism, for example, tourist groups are strictly regulated in terms of numbers, the length of time they can spend watching the gorillas and the distance they have to keep from them (Macfie and Williamson, 2010). Gorilla tourism is usually managed by government wildlife authorities rather than by communities—even when apes stray onto communal land. Community-based tourism initiatives typically focus on local culture as a complement to the main attraction of the apes; indeed, community members are not authorized to take tourists to visit apes. In Rwanda, for instance, the non-profit organization Gorilla Guardians invites tourists who are predominantly interested in gorillas to visit a traditional village on the outskirts of Volcanoes National Park, where they can speak with former poachers and learn about local crafts (Gorilla Guardians, n.d.). The HUTAN Kinabatangan Orang-utan Conservation Programme in Borneo provides a more direct link to apes, including by supporting a homestay experience and a village-run tour company, Red Ape Encounters, which escorts tourists onto an orangutan research site (HUTAN-KOCP, n.d.).

Even though local people generally do not manage ape tourism themselves, they can benefit from it indirectly, such as through protected area revenue sharing schemes. In Rwanda, for example, 5% of annual income from protected area tourism is allocated to local communities (Munanura et al., 2016). In Uganda, where tourists pay US$600 to track gorillas, US$10 of every gorilla permit sold and 20% of park entry fees are similarly allocated to the wildlife authority's revenue-

TABLE 5.1

Integrated Conservation and Development Project Approaches from 1985 To Date

Years	Approach
1985–95	**Substitution and/or compensation:** To generate support for conservation, buffer-zone communities are offered investment in infrastructure and livelihood alternatives to reduce pressure on natural resources.
1995–2000	**Benefit sharing:** Mechanisms such as tourism revenues are introduced as a means to add value to natural resources and give communities a "stake" in conservation.
2000–present	**Power sharing:** Local communities are empowered to have greater control and authority over natural resource management and the sharing of costs and benefits from conservation.

Source: Blomley *et al.* (2010)

sharing program and used to fund projects such as schools, clinics and small livestock schemes among park-adjacent villages (Franks and Twinamatsiko, 2017; UWA, n.d.; see Case Study 5.1). Additional benefits to local people include jobs in tourist lodges and small-enterprise development (such as arts and crafts/handicrafts) in and near tourist areas. Whether these benefits provide sufficient incentive for conservation over illegal use of wildlife remains debatable, however (Sabuhoro *et al.*, 2017).

Another mechanism for generating conservation incentives is through indirect benefits from ape and habitat conservation, such as alternative livelihood or, more broadly, integrated conservation and development projects (ICDPs) (see Case Study 5.1). The late 1980s and early 1990s saw the first generation of ICDPs, which were largely based on the assumption that if communities adjacent to protected areas were provided with access to alternative types of resources and income sources—in other words, if local livelihoods were "decoupled" from park resources—they would be less likely to engage in unsustainable or illegal harvesting and use of protected resources, including trees, grass and wildlife. Investing in agricultural improvements is a good example of a decoupled approach. Starting in the mid-1990s, a number of ICDPs included measures to increase benefits from

protected areas to local communities; these projects deliberately linked local livelihoods to park resources, on the assumption that people would be more willing to support conservation if they felt a direct benefit from doing so. Nature-based tourism is a good example of a linked or coupled approach. More recently, ICDPs have evolved to focus on increasing community decision-making authority over natural resources management, for example by involving them in park management committees (Blomley *et al.*, 2010). Table 5.1 summarizes this evolution in approach and Case Study 5.1 provides some insights into how ICDPs have evolved in Uganda.

Alternative livelihood initiatives, which represent a particular type of ICDP, aim to reduce threats to biodiversity by promoting:

- alternative resources, such as domestically produced cane rats or farmed fish as a source of protein to replace wild meat (Wicander and Coad, 2014);

- alternative occupations, such as tourism instead of hunting and trade, or butterfly farming instead of agricultural expansion; or

- alternative, lower-impact methods of exploiting a resource, such as the use of fuel-efficient stoves to reduce the demand for firewood (Roe *et al.*, 2015).

Using an Integrated Conservation and Development Approach to Generate Incentives for Gorilla Conservation in Uganda

Uganda was a pioneer of the integrated conservation and development (ICD) approach. In 1988, CARE International and the World Wide Fund for Nature initiated the Development through Conservation project in the country's two gorilla parks—Bwindi Impenetrable Forest Reserve and Mgahinga Forest Reserve—both of which would be gazetted as national parks three years later (see Figure 5.3). The goal of the project was to contribute to the conservation of both forests and to improve natural resource-based economic security of neighboring farming households. Prior to gazettement, local people were not allowed to live in the forests, but they had legal access to forest resources that were not commercially valuable, such as firewood, medicinal plants and wild meat. This period saw widespread illegal timber harvesting and mining, which led to concern about the future of the country's remaining population of mountain gorillas. As a result, forest authorities progressively restricted access to resources for local people, who eventually responded through acts of protest, such as arson and snaring (Blomley et al., 2010).

ICD initiatives started with an education and woodlot project in 1987 and expanded two years later with agroforestry and agriculture projects, both of which aim to replace people's dependence on forest resources with alternative sources of resources and income. In other words, the goal was to decouple livelihoods from the forest (Blomley et al., 2010).

During the 1990s, Bwindi spearheaded the expansion of ICDPs. In 1993 substitution projects aimed at decoupling were broadened into multiple-use programs, which allowed regulated harvesting of certain amounts of non-timber forest products. Then, in 1996, the government, supported by the International Gorilla Conservation Programme, introduced a revenue-sharing scheme whereby local communities could benefit from the income generated from tourism at Bwindi. Both of these "coupling interventions" were designed to provide local people with benefits from the park in order to increase their willingness to support the conservation of the gorillas (Blomley et al., 2010). The revenue-sharing program has been refined over time with successive wildlife legislation including the Wildlife Acts of 2000 and 2019 (Parliament of Uganda, 1996, 2019).

While many of Uganda's ICD initiatives have improved park–community relations, it remains unclear whether they have achieved conservation objectives, namely to reduce illegal activities (Blomley et al., 2010; Twinamatsiko et al., 2014). This lack of clarity on ICDP effectiveness reflects fundamentally flawed assumptions regarding how both coupling and decoupling interventions can generate sufficient behavior change to bring about conservation impacts; one such expectation is that people who receive benefits from conservation-linked tourism and other activities will no longer engage in illegal activities in the park (Blomley et al., 2010). Moreover, recent research points to a lack of equity in benefit sharing at Bwindi as a key motivator for continued illegal activities (Franks and Twinamatsiko, 2017; Twinamatsiko et al., 2014).

Such interventions all too often adopt the simplistic assumption that substituting one type of activity or resource for another will bring about long-term behavior change that will, in turn, bring about conservation impact (Blomley et al., 2010; Roe et al., 2015; Wright et al., 2016).

As noted above, the most effective approaches to increasing incentives for conservation are underpinned by efforts to secure land and resource rights for communities. Without such rights, local people have no long-term stake in conservation and, as a consequence, short-term, opportunistic resource exploitation is likely to prevail. Recent research suggests that a lack of formal land tenure can represent a major constraint to incentivizing people to conserve their land; in western Uganda, for instance, the absence of such rights prevented small farmers from protecting their plots as a critical element of a chimpanzee corridor between two protected areas (Lamprey, 2017).

Decreasing Conservation Costs to Communities

Efforts to promote wildlife protection are more likely to succeed if they take account of the costs associated with conserving wildlife. Potential costs to local communities include reduced access to resources in protected areas; restricted land use options

FIGURE 5.3

Bwindi Impenetrable National Park and Mgahinga Gorilla National Park, Uganda

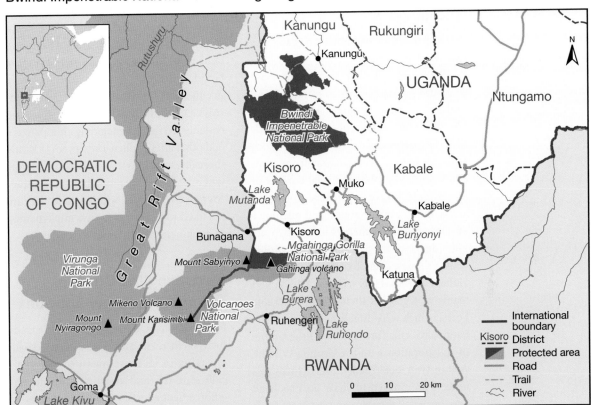

Sources: Protected areas – UNEP-WCMC (2019a, 2019b, 2019c); country boundaries – GADM (n.d.); other base map detail – OpenStreetMap (n.d., © OpenStreetMap contributors, published under Creative Commons Attribution License CC BY; for more information see http://creativecommons.org)

and potential forced resettlement; human–wildlife conflict resulting in personal injury and damage to livestock, crops and property; and disease transmission from wildlife to livestock and humans. Ape conservation can result in any combination of these costs.

In western Uganda, for example, the gazettement of Bwindi Impenetrable National Park and Mgahinga Gorilla National Park resulted in the eviction of the indigenous Batwa communities (Blomley *et al.*, 2010). Similarly, other communities have been forced to leave their homes once the areas where they live become protected (Brockington and Igoe, 2006). In and around great ape habitats, a major problem is human–wildlife conflict, and particularly incidents that involve

aggressive chimpanzees attacking and killing people, especially children (Hockings and Humle, 2009). Less extreme—yet still significant—impacts include crop raiding, particularly in areas with high densities of subsistence farmers. At Gishwati Forest in Rwanda, for instance, local farmers estimated that 10–20% of household income could be lost due to crop raiding by chimpanzees and monkeys in just one agricultural season (McGuinness and Taylor, 2014). These negative impacts can be especially significant among poor communities and can cause high levels of fear, anger and resentment, which sometimes lead to retaliation against wildlife, a park or a park authority (Twinamatsiko *et al.*, 2014). Indeed, research in Kalimantan,

Indonesia, found that there was a highly significant association between reported conflict and the killing of orangutans, as 23% of the people who reported conflict also declared that they had killed an orangutan (Meijaard *et al.*, 2011).

The IUCN and other organizations have produced guidance on how to reduce and mitigate ape-related conflict (Hockings and Humle, 2009). Interventions can include the construction of physical barriers, such as fences to keep wildlife away from crops and livestock; problem animal control or removal; planting of unpalatable crops, such as tea, in park buffer zones; and insurance or compensation schemes to compensate individuals for crops damaged by wildlife (Bowen-Jones, 2012). Examples include the Human–Gorilla (HuGo) Conflict Resolution teams in Uganda's Bwindi Impenetrable Forest, which were established by the International Gorilla Conservation Programme in collaboration with the Uganda Wildlife Authority in 1998 (Meder, 2012). HuGo volunteers are trained to chase gorillas back into the park if they appear in adjacent fields (Hockings and Humle, 2009).

Reducing the costs of and increasing the benefits from conservation are both critical to tipping the balance in favor of protection and against poaching. These interventions are unlikely to be sufficient unless simultaneous efforts are made to reduce the benefits and increase the costs of involvement in illegal hunting and trade, particularly in the context of escalating prices for illicitly sourced wildlife products (Challender and MacMillan, 2014).

Reducing the Benefits of Engaging in Illegal Activities

Efforts to render illegal activities less attractive typically rely on law enforcement interventions and initiatives to reduce demand for ape products. These include measures to reduce the likelihood of hunting success, such as through the intensification of snare detection, and education and awareness campaigns to reduce demand for (and hence the price of) live animals, animal parts and wild meat (Linkie *et al.*, 2015). The Jane Goodall Institute, for one, invests heavily in education, since many local people do not realize that it is illegal to kill and consume endangered species, including chimpanzees and other apes (Cohen-Brown, 2015). While these interventions may likewise be important in reducing the profitability and attractiveness of the illegal wildlife trade, they are not likely to be effective unless implemented in conjunction with other strategies.

Increasing the Costs of Engaging in Illegal Activities

Most responses to the illegal wildlife trade focus on increasing the costs associated with engaging in it. These measures are typically state-led (and sometimes private) law enforcement efforts, which, as noted above, can be significantly strengthened when carried out in partnership with local communities. Evidence from within and beyond the conservation sector amply shows that law enforcement and crime prevention are most effective when local residents and the police carry them out jointly (Hawdon and Ryan, 2011).

In addition, communities can apply their own cultural norms, taboos and social sanctions to increase the disincentives for engaging in illegal hunting and trade, as discussed in Chapter 2. Cultural responses vary significantly across communities. In Borneo, some Dayak subgroups see orangutans as reincarnations of respected community members and therefore will not contemplate killing or eating them. In contrast, other Dayak communities teach men not to return from the forest empty-handed lest they suffer a loss of status; to avoid such

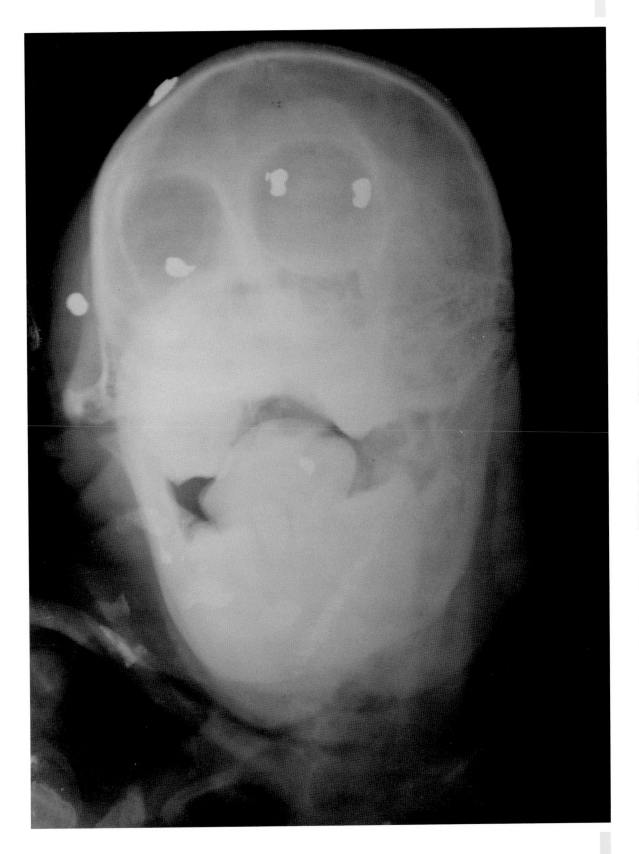

a fate, Dayak hunters may deem it acceptable to kill an orangutan. Meanwhile, religion prohibits the Malay people from eating "fanged" animals, including orangutans, but the ban on consumption does not prevent them from shooting at or killing apes that may be raiding their crops or posing a threat to their families (Yuliani *et al.*, 2018). Among the Bakweri people of Mount Cameroon, the killing and eating of chimpanzees and Cross River gorillas (*Gorilla gorilla diehli*) is culturally forbidden (Abugiche, Egute and Cybelle, 2017; Etiendem, Hens and Pereboom, 2011). Recognizing, raising awareness of and reinvigorating these cultural taboos can be an effective complement to formal law enforcement, especially where the latter is weak.

Conclusion

Tackling illegal hunting and the trade in apes at the source requires a combination of approaches. The dominant strategy to date has been to focus on site-based, top-down law enforcement. This method is unlikely to be effective on its own, however, and it can have undesirable social and ecological outcomes, including human rights abuses and local resentment of conservation agencies. Whether an individual or a community engages in the illegal wildlife trade depends on the net costs and benefits associated with conservation and illegal use, as well as prevailing norms and cultural factors. This chapter outlines selected strategies that can influence the balance of costs and benefits so as to encourage local people to be protectors rather than poachers of apes and other wildlife. Research is needed to evaluate the effectiveness of different interventions, as rigorous studies in this area are few and far between.

What is clear is that responses at the source will only be effective if they take account of the drivers and motivations of those involved in hunting and trading in

FIGURE 5.4

Drivers of Wildlife Crime in Uganda

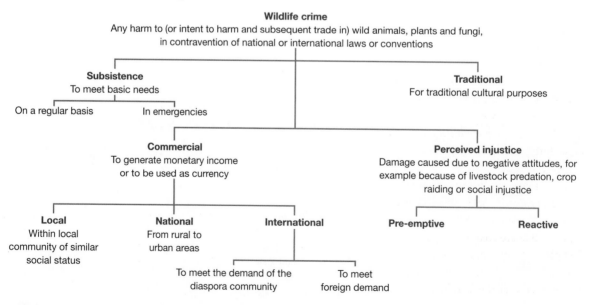

Notes: The drivers in this diagram are not mutually exclusive; they often overlap.

Source: Harrison *et al.* (2015, p. 20)

apes. Poverty is often cited as a key driver of the illegal trade in wildlife, but the reality may be far more complex (Duffy *et al.*, 2015). Incentives may also be cultural, economic, linked to resentment over conservation regulations or human–wildlife conflict, or reflective of a lack of meaningful deterrents (Milner-Gulland and Leader-Williams, 1992; Twinamatsiko *et al.*, 2014; see Chapters 2–4). A recent review of wildlife crime in Uganda, for example, indicates that people are driven by four key goals that are often interlinked:

- meeting basic subsistence needs;
- generating income;
- retaliating against perceived conservation injustices; and
- satisfying traditional cultural practices (Harrison *et al.*, 2015; see Figure 5.4).

Some of these drivers are linked to poverty, but together they illustrate that poverty is not the only motivation.

Drivers of illegal hunting and trade differ across settings, communities and individuals. Efforts to tackle wildlife crime are thus most likely to be effective if they are informed by context-specific assessments of the drivers; such assessments allow for the development of an appropriate mix of targeted responses. It would be futile, for example, to implement a project designed to replace the use of wild meat if the drivers of wildlife crime are not a desire to eat or sell meat, but rather to pursue cultural traditions. If the main motivation for illegal activities is the perception that conservation is a source of injustice, then there would similarly be no point in continuing to enforce the rules that are creating the conflict in the first place. Responses also need to factor in who in particular is undertaking illegal activities so that these individuals may be targeted effectively. For example, an intervention is not likely to bear fruit if it is aimed at local people who live near ape habitat although the biggest perpetrators of wildlife crime are transient workers attached to logging companies.

Responses that aim to tackle hunting and the trade in apes have a high chance of producing the desired impact if they are grounded in an understanding of the social, historical and political conditions that have shaped the local context. Ideally, such interventions deploy a mix of sensitive and appropriate law enforcement with community engagement strategies that not only increase the disincentives for engaging in wildlife crime, but also increase incentives for conservation, including by enhancing local perceptions of the fairness of conservation regulations. Such an approach entails maximizing local benefits from conservation, while recognizing and addressing its very real costs.

> Efforts to tackle wildlife crime are most likely to be effective if they are informed by context-specific assessments of the drivers.

Acknowledgments

Principal author: Dilys Roe[3]

Contributors: Ofir Drori[4] and Andrew J. Plumptre[5]

Box 5.1: Ofir Drori

Box 5.4: Andrew J. Plumptre

Endnotes

1   Annecke and Masubelele (2016); Barbora (2017); Buscher (2018); Duffy *et al.* (2015, 2019); Massé and Lunstrum (2016); Ramutsindela (2016); Verweijen and Marijnen (2018).

2   Plumptre, A.J., Eaton, M.J., Imong, I., *et al.* (In prep.). Trends in Cross River Gorillas across their range: using patrol data to monitor species and their threats.

3   International Institute for Environment and Development (www.iied.org).

4   The EAGLE Network (Eco Activists for Governance and Law Enforcement – www.eagle-enforcement.org).

5   KBA Secretariat (Key Biodiversity Areas – www.keybiodiversityareas.org/kba-partnership/kba-secretariat).

CHAPTER 6

Protecting Apes: The Legal and Regulatory Environment

Introduction

The preceding chapters explore a variety of issues related to the illegal wildlife trade, including its social and economic drivers, its effects on apes and their habitat, and the ways in which it may be addressed, such as through law enforcement efforts (see Chapter 5). This chapter focuses on the legal and regulatory frameworks within which ape hunters, traders and consumers operate, and considers how they may be applied to disrupt and interdict the use of and trade in live apes, their parts and their meat around the world.

The first part of the chapter looks at national laws that govern the protection of species. These laws stipulate geographical areas of protection; the conditions under which individuals may be removed from the wild, bred, held in captivity and transported; permission and reporting requirements; and fines and penalties that apply when a law is broken. The chapter also covers domestic legislation implementing a country's obligations under the Convention on International Trade in Endangered Species of Wild Fauna and Flora (CITES), the main international agreement in this field (CITES, n.d.-k).

This section draws on a detailed analysis of relevant legislation in 17 ape range states (Rodriguez et al., 2019). The Arcus Foundation commissioned the legal intelligence firm Legal Atlas to conduct the initial study in 2018 and to produce this chapter as a synthesis of the findings. Full study results are available on the Legal Atlas website, which also presents previous research findings relating to other countries' laws (Legal Atlas, n.d.).[1]

The selected countries all have a field presence of Arcus-supported programs that assisted the authors by collecting information on national laws. Since the study focuses on just 17 (55%) of the 31 total range states— 23 of which are home to great apes[2] and 11 to gibbons,[3] while 2 harbor both groups—it does not shed light on the particularities of the illegal ape trade in the 14 excluded range countries. As the aim of the study was to understand and compare the different legal architectures in place to protect apes, however, the sample does succeed in providing a representative cross-section, capturing the most common legal principles, trends and elements to consider. On average, the authors reviewed about 20 laws for each country, assessing which parts of the trade chain they regulate and how, what kinds of penalties they apply for violations and which national institutions are relevant. This kind of analysis is crucial to understanding how a national legal framework can provide an effective deterrent to the illegal removal of and trade in apes (Rodriguez et al., 2019).

The second part of the chapter examines the legal frameworks that regulate the trade in apes outside their country of origin. The main legal framework of relevance is CITES, which uses a system of export and import permits to regulate the international trade in endangered species of wildlife. In principle, CITES provides a good system, and it has had many successes, but the implementation of its obligations at the national level leaves much to be desired, whether because of a lack of capacity, the absence of political will, corruption, or a combination of the three.

While the CITES system can place pressure on non-complying parties to fulfill their obligations, CITES itself is not an enforcement agency. This section therefore reviews a range of other international organizations that do have the power—and, sometimes, the resources—to pursue enforcement action across borders, including INTERPOL and the World Customs Organization (WCO). The section also considers organizations such as the Great Apes Survival Partnership (GRASP) and the UN Office on Drugs and Crime (UNODC), which have valuable roles to play in research, awareness raising and capacity building; in addition, it reviews a number of interventions that have been coordinated across countries and between agencies.

The trade in apes is a matter of substantial concern, yet it is not the only threat to their survival; loss and fragmentation of habitats under the pressures of economic development are probably more significant. Accordingly, this section also provides a brief assessment of the main international agreements of relevance to the conservation of apes and their habitats.

The key findings include:

■ Given that the illegal wildlife trade is transnational for the most part, enforcement opportunities would increase if all countries were to include all great ape

> **Listing the genus of a species—rather than individual species—can alleviate enforcement burdens and help maintain protection for newly discovered and reclassified species.**

and gibbon species, both native and non-native, in their domestic lists of protected wildlife.

- Legislation that prohibits the removal of great apes and gibbons from the wild stands to be more effective if it explicitly criminalizes all related actions—from transport, storage and processing to exhibition, experimentation, advertising, domestic and foreign trade, use and possession.

- Countries are effective at criminalizing domestic and foreign trade of illegally taken species, but they can do more to close regulatory gaps and to increase enforcement opportunities along the entire value chain, particularly with respect to acts associated with transport, processing, storage, advertising, welfare, possession and exhibition of wildlife.

- Including non-native species in domestic lists of protected species can expand both local and international enforcement opportunities.

- Listing the genus of a species—rather than individual species—can alleviate enforcement burdens and help maintain protection for newly discovered and reclassified species.

- To adapt punishments to the type of offender and offense, jurisdictions can usefully establish differential forms of liability—that is, higher penalties for the involvement of criminal enterprises and government officials, and tougher penalties in the case of aggravating circumstances, repeat offenses and intentionality, as well as for greater volumes and values.

- International criminal networks fuel transnational wildlife crime by corrupting enforcement and justice structures across countries. Legal systems that focus on poachers can thus become more effec-

tive by expanding their scope to target these networks as well as the legal entities and governmental officials involved.

- By fully utilizing available economic and legal tools, countries could establish administrative and criminal penalties that more effectively deter and prevent wildlife crime, and that compensate for damage caused.

- None of the countries under review has established a wildlife crime task force to coordinate prevention efforts, intelligence gathering, investigations and prosecution of wildlife crimes, even though it is best practice to do so. Moreover, these states lack the legal mechanisms for effective coordination of wildlife law enforcement.

- CITES provides a largely adequate international legal framework, but it could do more to curb abuse by safaris, amusement parks and so-called zoos by rejecting all applications for trade in potentially wild-caught apes, save in exceptional circumstances.

- In the context of combating the illegal ape trade, CITES suffers less from design weaknesses than it does from the lack of capacity, resources and political will in many of its members, particularly ape range states and countries that see imports of apes for commercial purposes.

- INTERPOL and the WCO are in a position to coordinate effective enforcement action against the illegal trade in apes, but they struggle due to a shortage of resources and many competing priorities.

- Increased dedicated support from donors is needed for the implementation of CITES and cross-border enforcement operations, as well as for awareness raising activities, research and campaigning aimed at reducing the demand for illegally traded great apes and gibbons.

> " Legal systems that focus on poachers can become more effective by expanding their scope to target the criminal networks, legal entities and governmental officials involved. "

The National Legal Environment: Trend Analysis[4]

Law, Policy and Enforcement as Mutually Reinforcing

Proponents of enhancing wildlife laws are sometimes criticized for overemphasizing the role of legislation and underestimating the need for more effective policies and enforcement (Chen *et al.*, 2011). Those who argue that wildlife crime should become a priority on the policy agenda call on policy-makers to recognize illegal wildlife trade not only as a conservation matter, but also as a core governance concern (Robertson, 2017). Those who focus on enforcement point to critical limitations in implementing laws that are already on the books, and in achieving even basic conditions for the rule of law. They demand urgent action to address a host of enforcement challenges, such as corruption, insufficient capacity of field personnel, and a lack of technological and financial resources (Ariffin, 2018). Some go so far as to defend the idea that unenforced laws are worse than no laws at all (Chen, 2013).

This chapter seeks to demonstrate that the need for more effective policies and enforcement does not invalidate the call for better legislation. It argues that a comprehensive, integrated suite of legal, policy and enforcement tools is required to combat the illegal wildlife trade. In this context, it underscores the foundational role of the law. Unless policy is translated into law, it lacks enforceability and may not survive changes in political agendas. Law also defines the playing field for enforcement. This chapter is designed to promote a better understanding of how current legislation governs wildlife management and enforcement—and of how the development of more effective laws, not simply more laws, can bolster the fight against the illegal wildlife trade.

Applicable Law along the Supply Chain: From the Wild to Market to Consumer

Although the regulation of international trade in wildlife is a major concern, there are several reasons why the laws that govern domestic activities and transactions are arguably the most important. The extent to which a species is protected is almost exclusively determined by national laws that govern domestic activities and transactions. These laws define the geographical area of protection; the conditions under which wildlife may be removed from the wild, bred, held in captivity and transported; permission and reporting requirements; and fines and penalties that apply when a law is broken. Even international trade in wildlife—which is governed by CITES and other general trade agreements—must be implemented through domestic legislation. The relative importance of national legislation in this area reflects geopolitical realities: While the total length of terrestrial and maritime international borders is in the order of hundreds of thousands of kilometers, the total land area of all countries around the globe is almost 150 million km² (15 billion ha) (Worldometer, n.d.). Passing through customs and crossing a border accounts for far less time than conducting the preceding and ensuing activities within national borders—be it in the wild, on the road, through physical mail systems, or in markets, restaurants or shops. These activities are exclusively defined by national laws and mandates, few of which are directly associated with wildlife or wildlife crime. If these laws lack explicit provisions governing wildlife trade, opportunities to control detrimental trade are significantly reduced.

In reviewing how national legislation governs the trade in wildlife, it is useful to bear two points in mind. First, countries typically do not legislate solely in the interest

Chapter 6 Legal and Regulatory Environment

of a single species or group of species. There are exceptions to this general practice, but only a few. Among them are China's ban on the trade in tiger bones and rhino horn, which was approved in 1993, and the United Kingdom's 2018 ban on the ivory trade (State Council, 1993; The Stationery Office, 2018). On the whole, however, relevant laws are directed at wildlife in general. In the 17 countries under review, no legislation specifically addresses great apes or gibbons.

The second point to note is that, as illegal wildlife trade comprises a complex array of individual criminal acts, offenses may be covered by a variety of domestic laws. From the instant a hunter enters a protected area or poaches a chimpanzee anywhere to the time the captive animal is purchased or kept as a pet, any number of individuals may undertake any number of activities and transactions, all of which may be regulated by a variety of laws, sometimes simultaneously. A state's endangered species act, for example, may govern the hunting and capture of protected species, even if protected area, forestry and hunting legislation does so as well. The use of specific take methods and firearms may be proscribed by legislation on protected areas, hunting, firearms and forestry. Transport, traditional medicine, phytosanitary and animal welfare laws, among others, may govern the transport, processing, storage and use of wildlife. Laws on quarantine, customs, tax, border control, and crime may regulate transport, smuggling and associated financial transactions. In jurisdictions where wildlife trafficking is recognized as a predicate offense, anti-money-laundering statutes may apply. The falsification of documents, use of corrupt practices and involvement of criminal organizations may be covered by yet more laws.

Based on long-term research of legislation in more than 60 countries, Legal Atlas has identified 43 types of domestic law that could apply in wildlife cases, depending on the country.[5] Whatever the number of laws and particular approach, robust national legal frameworks govern all elements of the wildlife supply chain—from the wild to the final consumer. They allow for the tracking of animals, body parts and related products, such as ointments, jewelry and decorative items, from their habitat to hunters and traders, through transportation systems, to processors and the final market. In this way, they offer the greatest enforcement opportunities.

Legal Protections for Great Apes and Gibbons

Listing Status as a Cornerstone

At the domestic level, the legal protection for apes can take several forms. One of the more typical forms is a legally defined domestic list of endangered species. Species listing is the legal mechanism by which species are added to a national list and provided stricter protection. Since it is typically tied to numerous other legal instruments, species listing is a cornerstone of domestic wildlife protection and can have a pervasive impact on the control of wildlife crime.

In most jurisdictions, species status in a list is tied to legal instruments such as bans, permits, business licenses and penalties, which, in turn, are found in multiple pieces of legislation that regulate distinct parts of the trade chain, including protected areas, national markets, restaurants, airports, roads and the virtual space. Such instruments can be "triggered" by species listing; for example, the listing of an endangered species triggers the application of a hunting prohibition, as well as increased fines for those who violate the prohibition. By triggering such other instruments, species listing can expand the degree of protection afforded to particular species, while also determining punishments for a broad range of offense types. All 17 countries under review use a listing format and provide greater protection for the species included in their national list.

Approaches to listing vary across countries, however, and the lack of a standard creates inconsistencies in the process by which species are protected and the levels of protection they are given. The Red List of the International Union for Conservation of Nature (IUCN)—which is "based on an objective system for assessing the risk of extinction of a species based on past, present, and projected threats"—is the closest to a global standard for the scientific categorization of species (IUCN, 2012). It applies different categories based on criteria linked to population size, structure and trends, as well as geographic range (see Box AO1 and Annex I).

TABLE 6.1

Red List Categories and Inconsistent Classification Systems in Three Jurisdictions

Scientific Categorization of Species		
IUCN Red List Categories		
EX	Extinct	
EW	Extinct in the wild	
CE	Critically endangered	
EN	Endangered	Threatened
VU	Vulnerable	
NT	Near threatened	
LC	Least concern	

Legal Classification of Species		
Cambodia	**Viet Nam**	**Indonesia**
Endangered species	Group I-B of endangered, precious and rare species	Endangered species
Rare species		Rare species
Regional flagship species	Group II-B of endangered, precious and rare species	
Common species		

Sources: IUCN (2012); Rodriguez *et al.* (2019)

In contrast, legal categories for protected species vary widely across jurisdictions, which use terms such as "endangered species," "rare species" or "class I species"—classifications that are not necessarily consistent with the IUCN Red List categories or with each other. Table 6.1 presents terminology used in three selected countries and compares them to the Red List categories, indicating how the legal systems are not consistent with each other or with the scientific system. The "rare species" category, for example, may be based on population estimates, but it does not necessarily reflect a decreasing trend in the local population. Countries that use this category may list species that are technically rare in their jurisdiction, but not necessarily threatened by trade or habitat loss.

Countries also use different legal instruments to list species. Seven of the 17 reviewed countries list species in laws issued by a national legislative body, while the other ten use more flexible ministerial regulations (see Table 6.2). Laws issued by a national legislative body create the foundation for all subsidiary regulations and require substantial periods—sometimes many years—to be drafted, negotiated and approved. Regulations, on the other hand, are intended to implement existing laws and are generally not subject to the same level of political negotiation. Considering only time frames, species listing based on regulations thus represents a more flexible tool that can react to population studies or new CITES resolutions. The orientation of national legislative bodies also means that the listing process may not be an exclusively technical procedure, but rather one that can be compromised by political agendas and priorities.

Amending the national list also tends to be more time-consuming than passing a ministerial regulation and can therefore lag behind identified needs (EPA, n.d.). Only seven of the countries reviewed in 2018, for example, had amended their species list within

TABLE 6.2

Domestic Laws and Regulations that Protect Great Apes and Gibbons in 17 Ape Range States, 2018

Country			Uganda	Nigeria	Ivory Coast	Cambodia	Myanmar
Year of the law (L) or regulation (R)			1959 L	1985 L	1994 L	1994 R	1994 R
Great apes	Bonobo	*Pan paniscus*					
	Chimpanzee	*Pan troglodytes*[6]	◉	◉	◉		
	Eastern gorilla	*Gorilla beringei*[7]	◉				
	Western gorilla	*Gorilla gorilla*[8]		◉			
	Bornean orangutan	*Pongo pygmaeus*[9]					
	Sumatran orangutan	*Pongo abelii*					
	Tapanuli orangutan	*Pongo tapanuliensis*					
Gibbons	Hoolock gibbon	*Bunopithecus hoolock*[10]					
	Hoolock gibbon	*Hylobates hoolock*[11]					◉
	Abbott's gray gibbon	*Hylobates abbotti*					
	Agile gibbon	*Hylobates agilis*					
	Bornean gray gibbon	*Hylobates funereus*					
	Bornean white-bearded gibbon	*Hylobates albibarbis*					
	Kloss's gibbon	*Hylobates klossii*					
	Lar gibbon	*Hylobates lar*					◉
	Moloch gibbon	*Hylobates moloch*					
	Müller's gibbon	*Hylobates muelleri*					
	Pileated gibbon	*Hylobates pileatus*				◉	
	Cao Vit gibbon	*Nomascus nasutus*					
	Hainan gibbon	*Nomascus hainanus*					
	Northern white-cheeked crested gibbon	*Nomascus leucogenys*					
	Northern yellow-cheeked crested gibbon	*Nomascus annamensis*				◉	
	Southern white-cheeked crested gibbon	*Nomascus siki*					
	Southern yellow-cheeked crested gibbon	*Nomascus gabriellae*				◉	
	Western black crested gibbon	*Nomascus concolor*					
	Siamang	*Symphalangus syndactylus*					

Notes: All great apes and gibbons, except for the Tapanuli orangutan (*Pongo tapanuliensis*), are listed in CITES Appendix I, which comprises the most endangered of CITES-listed species. The Appendix does not list the Tapanuli orangutan as it pre-dates the identification of this species.

Sources: CITES (2017a); IUCN (2018); Rodriguez *et al*. (2019); UNEP-WCMC and CITES Secretariat (n.d.)

Key: ◉ Native species ● Domestic legal protection

Lao PDR	China	Cameroon	DRC	Viet Nam	Rwanda	Malaysia (Peninsular)	Republic of Congo	Tanzania	Liberia	Indonesia	Guinea
2003 R	2003 R	2006 R	2006 R	2006 R	2008 R	2010 L	2011 R	2013 L	2016 L	2018 R	2018 L
			◉								
		◉	◉		◉		◉	◉	◉		◉
			◉		◉						
		◉					◉				
						◉				◉	
										◉	
										◉	
						◉				◉	
						◉				◉	
						◉				◉	
										◉	
										◉	
◉	◉					◉				◉	
										◉	
										◉	
◉											
	◉			◉							
	◉										
◉	◉			◉							
●				●							
●				●							
●				◉							
◉	◉			◉							
						◉				◉	

the previous decade. Nigeria and Uganda represent extreme cases, with national lists that have not been amended in 34 years and 60 years, respectively. Unsurprisingly, such static national lists are highly unlikely to include all the relevant species protected under CITES, whose appendices are continually updated to reflect ongoing developments (CITES, n.d.-i).[12]

Approaches for Domestic Protection

Domestic protection of native great apes and gibbons is common, but not universal. In its review of the 17 ape range states, Legal Atlas documented the use of four approaches to the listing of great apes and gibbons. These can be ranked as either more or less inclusive and have an impact on enforcement opportunities. The most inclusive approach automatically places all species listed in CITES Appendix I on the national list, regardless of whether they are native to the country. Guinea, Malaysia and Tanzania all use this method, which guarantees that national listing shall never be out of date with respect to CITES listing. The second approach lists only some non-native great apes and gibbons. This system is used in China, which lists 15 gibbon species although only four are native to the country; the Democratic Republic of Congo (DRC), which includes one non-native gorilla;[13] Myanmar, whose list features one non-native gibbon; and Nigeria, which lists the non-native bonobo. The third approach protects exclusively native species and is employed in Indonesia, Ivory Coast, Liberia, Rwanda and Uganda. In the fourth and least inclusive method, countries list some, but not all, of their native great apes and gibbon species. This is the case for Cambodia, Lao People's Democratic Republic (PDR) and Viet Nam. The good news is that domestic protection for native great apes and gibbons is largely

granted across the study set, with the exception of the last three countries mentioned. For these, the omission of between two and three native species from their protected species lists represents a legal gap that needs to be addressed.

Listing non-native species in addition to native species increases the opportunities for law enforcement to prevent and stop illegally harvested species from being trafficked. It does so in several ways. First, it can ease enforcement burdens by eliminating the need to specifically identify species. This impact is particularly important for enforcement officials, who may have little or no training in this regard. If, for instance, road control officers in China intercept a gibbon who originated in Lao PDR, China's inclusive listing would allow the authorities to identify the genus rather than the individual species, which could require expertise or techniques that may not be readily available.

Second, listing a non-native genus offers all species within that genus protection, regardless of where they hail from; it also eliminates the potential for gaps in protection that may be inadvertently created by changes in taxonomy or new discoveries. A case in point is the recently discovered northern yellow-cheeked crested gibbon (*Nomascus annamensis*). Four of the countries under review—China, Guinea, Myanmar and Tanzania—protect the *Nomascus* gibbon genus as a whole and thus automatically provided legal protection when the new species was identified. In contrast, new species may fall into a legislative gap in countries that only protect specifically listed native or non-native species, such as Cambodia, Lao PDR and Viet Nam.

A third enforcement impact of species listing is the opportunity to use anti-money-laundering statutes against criminal organizations that profit from smuggled wildlife that is native to other jurisdictions. While such laws can only be used in prosecution

> Listing non-native species in addition to native species increases the opportunities for law enforcement to prevent and stop illegally harvested species from being trafficked.

if a predicate crime has been committed, they can serve to impose additional or higher penalties on individuals in the financial chain. If the relevant non-native species is not listed or protected in the country, there may be no case to pursue (Wingard and Pascual, 2019).

Regulating the Ape Trade along the Supply Chain

All countries under review have passed legislation that criminalizes activities at the beginning and end of the supply chain: the capture of an animal (also known as "take" in legal contexts), the final purchase and any related import or export transactions. Offenses that relate to the illegal removal of an animal from the wild are well developed in all these states; they include violations of hunting bans, detailed lists of prohibited methods, and closed areas and seasons. All 17 surveyed countries apply a complete national ban on the hunting and removal of listed great apes and gibbons (see Table 6.3); in Cambodia, Lao PDR and Viet Nam, however, a few native gibbon species remain unlisted and therefore unprotected (see Table 6.2).

As noted, all states have enacted offenses related to domestic trade as well as the import and export of endangered wildlife, to varying degrees of detail. The sale and purchase of wildlife, for example, are penalized as two separate offenses in 12 countries. The remaining jurisdictions use the generic term "trade" without defining it further. Import and export are controlled by CITES implementing laws that are present in all of the reviewed jurisdictions, as well as customs and quarantine regulations that generally prohibit the smuggling of goods, including wildlife.

When it comes to regulating other activities along the supply chain—particularly following take and trade crimes—most of the countries under review exhibit significant legal gaps. These gaps relate largely to the transport, processing and storage of wildlife, as well as to advertising, welfare, possession and exhibition. Countries that regulate one activity do not necessarily regulate the others. Rwanda, for example, has enacted offenses related to transport, but not to storage or possession. Processing (including taxidermy) is only criminalized in Cambodia, China, Malaysia and Viet Nam. To the extent that the wild meat trade involves processing, the absence of this criminal offense in areas where this type of trade is prevalent is cause for concern. Meanwhile, at a time when unregulated Internet trade is booming, only China and Malaysia have criminalized advertising of wildlife. In addition to the many difficulties that the physical trade in species presents, cyber-enabled trade adds jurisdictional challenges that most legal systems in the world have yet to address (Wingard and Pascual, 2018).

Legal systems that do not target each part of the supply chain ultimately create weaknesses that can be exploited by criminals. They also forgo opportunities to hold individuals involved in the illegal wildlife trade liable for criminal acts. For great apes and gibbons, along with other endangered species, such patchy legal regimes translate into greater vulnerability and a higher risk of being trafficked—or losing community members to the trade. These findings are consistent with those of a recent study of the great ape supply chain:

> For the illegal trade in great apes as well as the illegal wildlife trade as a whole, attention has often been directed to the ends of the supply chain—the poaching incident and the final consumer purchase—both in terms of intelligence as well as intervention. What remains relatively murky is what goes on in between, that is the "business" of the trade and more importantly the financial side of the business (GFI, 2018).

"Legal systems that do not target each part of the supply chain ultimately create weaknesses that can be exploited by criminals."

TABLE 6.3

Criminalization of Activities along the Ape Supply Chain in 17 Ape Range States, 2018

Key:
- Criminalized
- Not criminalized

	Take	Transport	Processing	Storage	Advertize	Trade	Import/export	Posession	Welfare	Exhibition
Cambodia										
Cameroon										
China										
DRC										
Guinea										
Indonesia										
Ivory Coast										
Lao PDR										
Liberia										
Malaysia										
Myanmar										
Nigeria										
Republic of Congo										
Rwanda										
Tanzania										
Uganda										
Viet Nam										

Source: Rodriguez *et al*. (2019)

Focus on Three Offense Types

This review entails an in-depth analysis of three particular types of offense—hunting, domestic sales and advertising of apes—across the 17 selected jurisdictions. The decision to limit the analysis to these offenses was made for a number of reasons. For one, it is beyond the scope of this study to analyze all offense types, especially since it is not uncommon for jurisdictions to list upwards of 100 wildlife-related crimes, including all variants. Limiting the number to three allows for some depth of analysis in this context. Offenses relating to hunting and domestic sales were selected because they are criminalized in all jurisdictions under review and regulate key points along the supply chain: the capture and the sale of apes.[14]

Offenses pertaining to advertising were chosen because they aim to control an emerging threat. Indeed, the need to curb online advertising has increased in step with the exponential growth of the virtual wildlife trade (Knowledge@Wharton, 2018). For purposes of identification and analysis, offense types selected for review were defined as follows:

- **Illegal hunting** is hunting without permission. Related penalties punish individuals for hunting both protected and unprotected species. The review excluded the criminalization of hunting in particular areas (such as national parks) and of certain hunting methods (such as night lighting), as these violations are often identified in separate provisions and typically have higher penalties due to their more serious nature. A recent ten-year study led by the Wildlife Conservation Society found that 80% of gorillas and chimpanzees in western equatorial Africa live outside protected areas (Strindberg *et al.*, 2018); based on these findings, the analysis did not apply further spatial considerations.

- **Illegal domestic sale** is the illegal sale, trade or offer for sale (excluding acts that constitute advertising, which is defined separately) of any protected or unprotected live or dead wildlife, including their parts and derivatives. Captured great apes and gibbons largely supply the wild meat trade, the pet trade and substandard zoos (Clough and May, 2018). In all cases, related prohibitions target an active market.

- **Illegal advertisement of wildlife products** is any offense related to restrictions on advertising protected, unprotected, live and dead wildlife, including their parts and derivatives, be it in print, online or through other means of communication, such as radio or television.

For each of the three selected offense types, Legal Atlas researchers examined relevant provisions and recorded detailed information on five critical elements:

- whether and how **liability** of wildlife offenders differs based on their status (individuals, corporations or government officials);
- the applicability of imposable **penalty types**—be they monetary, administrative or prison terms;
- the degree to which **intent requirements** (such as knowledge or negligence) and

aggravating circumstances are considered the basis for higher penalties;
- the criteria used to determine **fine levels**; and
- the maximum **prison terms**.

The analysis did not cover other potentially applicable penalties, forms of liability or procedural requirements contained in criminal procedure legislation.

Differential Liability by Offender Status

The analysis focused on three generic categories of offender: natural persons or individuals; legal persons (any entity recognized by law); and government officials. Some jurisdictions establish separate penalty levels for each of these categories in an effort to adapt the punishment to the type of offender and the degree of harm caused by the offender's activity.[15]

States that do not tailor liability to the type of criminal miss key opportunities to combat international criminal networks and domestic corruptive practices, which are often at the heart of illegal wildlife trade. Transnational organized criminal networks that are linked to the trade use corrupt government officials and companies in the financial, transportation and communications sectors. As the *New York Times* reports:

> A secret ape pipeline runs from the lush forests of central Africa and Southeast Asia, through loosely policed ports in the developing world, terminating in wealthy homes and unscrupulous zoos thousands of miles away. The pipeline, documents show, is lubricated by corrupt officials (several have been arrested for falsifying export permits) and run by transnational criminal gangs (Gettleman, 2017).

To deter future wrongdoing, it is thus crucial that the prosecution of ape trade crime entail specialized administrative and criminal sanctions—such as the removal of corrupt customs officers or the confiscation of assets from implicated legal entities. The application of such sanctions requires differential liability, a step beyond the more traditional approaches that treat wildlife criminals solely as individuals and, typically, as poachers. Among the 17 analyzed countries, however, individual liability is the norm for all wildlife offenses; only a handful of countries impose different or higher penalties for legal persons and even fewer do so for civil servants (see Table 6.4). China is the only country that applies the disciplinary measures enshrined in its wildlife law to government officials who fail to conduct their professional duty in accordance with the law. For the most part, in other words, primary wildlife and criminal laws do not impose heightened forms of liability on the most important players in the ape trade business.

In addition to the tools reviewed in this study, a few others are gaining attention and have the potential to promote the use of differential liability in punishing wildlife crime. A recent Legal Atlas report on anti-money-laundering statutes, for example, documents separate and substantially higher punishments for legal persons and government officials involved in money laundering activities (Wingard and Pascual, 2019).[16] The continued circulation of the proceeds of crimes recognized by such laws—which in many jurisdictions includes *any* crime and, therefore, all forms of illicit wildlife trade—constitutes money laundering. While these laws do not solve the problem of wildlife crime, they do provide greater opportunities to convict wildlife traffickers with tougher penalties than those stipulated in many wildlife laws. Similarly, organized crime legislation, another criminal law instrument with substantially higher penalties, could be leveraged in the fight against wildlife crimes.

Figure 6.1 illustrates that Cameroon's fine levels for the offense of hunting protected species are significantly higher if the crime entails money laundering, and even higher if organized crime is involved. If individual poachers are prosecuted under Cameroon's wildlife legislation, they may be fined as little as US$80.[17] If, however, investigations can prove that proceeds of the crime have been

TABLE 6.4

Differential Liability in Selected Wildlife Trade Crimes in 17 Ape Range States, 2018

	Crime	Cambodia	Cameroon	China	DRC	Guinea	Indonesia
Individuals	Illegal hunting						
	Illegal domestic sales		P		P		
	Advertising illegal products						
Legal entities	Illegal hunting						
	Illegal domestic sales				P		P
	Advertising illegal products						
Government officials	Illegal hunting	P					
	Illegal domestic sales		P				
	Advertising illegal products						

Source: Rodriguez *et al.* (2019)

laundered, then the anti-money-laundering statutes provide for fines as high as US$17,000. If the prosecution can also prove that an organized criminal network was behind the money laundering, fines can reach US$35,000 (Legal Atlas, 2018).[18]

Penalties

The legal sanctions that are available to combat the illegal wildlife trade include monetary fines, administrative sanctions and criminal penalties.

Monetary fines are imposed on guilty parties. Among the more common monetary penalties are fines and the forfeiture of the means—such as the tools and equipment used to commit a crime—and the proceeds, including the property and finances derived from the crime. Such fines are set, for example, in Viet Nam's decree on administrative penalties for forest-related violations (Decree No. 41/2017/ND-CP, 2017; Decree No. 157/2013/ND-CP, 2013, art. 21). Fines are intended to deter potential offenders, remove the capacity to commit further crime and deny the benefits of the crime to those

FIGURE 6.1

Monetary Penalties for Illegal Hunting in Cameroon

US$85–350	US$170–700	US$17,000	US$35,000
Individuals and legal entities	Government officials	If also laundering proceeds of illegal hunting	If also operating within an organized criminal network

Sources: CEMAC (2016); Legal Atlas (2018)

Key: ● Differential liability ● No liability or no differential liability ⊘ Protected species only

Ivory Coast	Lao PDR	Liberia	Malaysia	Myanmar	Nigeria	Republic of Congo	Rwanda	Tanzania	Uganda	Viet Nam
			P							
			P						P	P
			P							
		P	P							
	P		P							P
			P							
										P
	P									P

involved. Other monetary penalties include compensation and restoration, both of which address the need to repair the damage caused; while Costa Rica's wildlife conservation law imposes such fines, it does not specify how values are to be determined (Ley de Conservación de la Vida Silvestre, 1992, art. 101).

This chapter uses the term "administrative penalty" to refer to any sanction that limits an offender's rights or position held in government, whether applied by an administrative or a criminal law.[19] Among these sanctions are temporary and permanent bans on access to a resource, license suspensions and revocations, as well as suspension and removal from a government position. On the whole, such penalties are used to deny violators access to public benefits and positions. An example is Indonesia's Environmental Protection and Management Law, which stipulates which types of administrative sanctions apply to environmental offenders (Republic of Indonesia, 2009, art. 76).

For the purposes of this review, criminal penalties are limited to two types of sanctions: monetary fines and the restriction of freedom, including the imposition of prison terms and community service orders.[20] For the most part, criminal sanctions are intended to deter criminals from committing crimes

TABLE 6.5

Penalty Types for Selected Wildlife Trade Crimes in 17 Ape Range States, 2018

	Crime	Cambodia	Cameroon	China	DRC	Guinea	Indonesia
Fines	Illegal hunting						
	Illegal domestic sales		P		P		
	Advertising illegal products						
Forfeitures	Illegal hunting						
	Illegal domestic sales		P		P		P
	Advertising illegal products						
Compensation	Illegal hunting					P	
	Illegal domestic sales						
	Advertising illegal products						
Restoration	Illegal hunting						?
	Illegal domestic sales	P					
	Advertising illegal products						
Community service	Illegal hunting						
	Illegal domestic sales						
	Advertising illegal products						
Prison	Illegal hunting	P		P			P
	Illegal domestic sales	P	P	P	P		P
	Advertising illegal products						

Source: Rodriguez et al. (2019)

before they happen, remove criminals from society to minimize the threat they pose, and rehabilitate criminals.

Table 6.5 presents the types of administrative and criminal penalties that the countries under review impose for the three selected offenses. Fines and prison sentences are well represented across all jurisdictions, although they vary depending on the protection status of the relevant species. Community service is not explicitly mentioned for any of the selected crimes in any of the 17 countries.

The differences based on species status have implications for great apes and gibbons. They are listed as protected in almost all jurisdictions, yet three countries omit some species—Cambodia, Lao PDR and Viet Nam. Consequently, weaker deterrents are in place with respect to three specific ape species, which may thus be more vulnerable to being hunted and traded. In Lao PDR, the lack of prison penalties for domestic ape sales affects three species of gibbon: the northern yellow-cheeked crested gibbon (*Nomascus annamensis*), southern white-cheeked crested gibbon (*Nomascus siki*) and southern yellow-cheeked crested gibbon (*Nomascus gabriellae*). In Cambodia and Viet Nam, which apply prison terms only for the hunting of protected species, unlisted gibbons are similarly exposed

Key: ● Uses ● Does not use ◐ Protected species only

Ivory Coast	Lao PDR	Liberia	Malaysia	Myanmar	Nigeria	Republic of Congo	Rwanda	Tanzania	Uganda	Viet Nam
			P							
			P						P	P
			P							
		P	P							
			P						P	P
			P							
		P								
P										
	P		P		P					
			P	P	P		P		P	P
			P							

to higher risks. Such is the case for the northern yellow-cheeked crested gibbon and southern yellow-cheeked crested gibbon in Cambodia, and for the northern yellow-cheeked crested gibbon and southern white-cheeked crested gibbon in Viet Nam.

Intent Requirements and Aggravating Circumstances

Intent requirements and aggravating circumstances are also common elements in criminal provisions (see Table 6.6). They are an acknowledgment that as not all crimes involve the same level of guilt, they should not be treated equally.

Knowledge requirements are typically used to achieve one of two goals: 1) to lower the intentionality—and therefore the burden of proof—required for liability to be imposed; and 2) to determine penalties based on the level of criminal intent, such that lower pen-alties are imposed for negligence (including gross negligence) and higher ones for intentionality. Indonesia and Liberia are the only countries that differentiate between negligence and intentionality in their wildlife laws, increasing the economic penalties if an offense has been committed intentionally. It is unlikely that negligence plays much of a role in the great apes and gibbon trade, as involvement in the trade, by its very nature, is an intentional act—it is highly improbable that anyone would inadvertently sell a live chimpanzee. Negligence could be a factor in wild meat trade, however; correspondingly, intentionality can be considered a justification for raising fines and penalties, as applicable.

Aggravating circumstances, in contrast, are egregious aspects of a crime that can be used to increase fines and penalties. Among the countries under review, repeat offenses (recidivism) are the most common aggravat-

TABLE 6.6

Knowledge Requirements and Aggravating Circumstances in Wildlife Trade Crimes in 17 Ape Range States, 2018

	Crime	Cambodia	Cameroon	China	DRC	Guinea	Indonesia
Gross negligence	Illegal hunting						
	Illegal domestic sales						
	Advertising illegal products						
Intentionality	Illegal hunting						
	Illegal domestic sales						P
	Advertising illegal products						
Recidivism	Illegal hunting						
	Illegal domestic sales		P		P		
	Advertising illegal products						
Large amounts	Illegal hunting						
	Illegal domestic sales						
	Advertising illegal products						

Source: Rodriguez et al. (2019)

ing circumstances, while high volume and value thresholds are factors in only two of the reviewed jurisdictions, Malaysia and Viet Nam. As countries make inconsistent use of aggravating circumstances for the three selected offenses, their legal approaches are characterized by significant gaps. States that exclude the use of recidivism in their wildlife laws—in this review, Indonesia, Malaysia, Myanmar and Tanzania—exhibit the greatest regulatory gaps. Another weakness relates to the inconsistent application of aggravating circumstances across wildlife crimes. Such is the case in the DRC, which uses different laws to set out offense types, thereby creating divergent legal approaches. A less consequential limitation is the exclusive use of aggravating circumstances in offenses against protected species, an approach employed by Viet Nam. Only 6 of the 17 reviewed jurisdictions treat repeat offenses as an aggravating circumstance for all offenses contained in their wildlife laws: Cambodia, Cameroon, Ivory Coast, Guinea, Nigeria and Uganda.

On the whole, repeat offenses are probably the norm and not the exception, as indicated by the high rate of great ape and gibbon removals, as well as the involvement of criminal networks, corrupt officials and established trade pipelines (UNODC, 2016). Uniform penalty levels can only have a general effect, as they are not directed at any particular offender. In contrast, penalties that are higher for repeat offenders can help to deter individuals who are likely to commit wildlife crimes. Among the 17 countries under review, there is certainly room to expand the use of legal tools to deter people from engaging in the ape trade.

Calculating Fines

Ensuring that fine levels for wildlife crime have an appropriate deterrence value is a

Key: ● Penalty ● No Penalty ● Protected species only

Ivory Coast	Lao PDR	Liberia	Malaysia	Myanmar	Nigeria	Republic of Congo	Rwanda	Tanzania	Uganda	Viet Nam
		P								
							P			P
									P	P
			P							
										P
										P

sophisticated and complex exercise that is not yet supported by global standards. That said, three general guidelines are well established. The first is that fines should be high enough to ensure that the perceived risk or cost of being fined is higher than the perceived benefit. The second guideline is that fines should eliminate the financial gain of a crime, meaning that they should correspond to the potential or actual market value of the trafficked goods. Proportionality to the harm caused is the third guideline (OECD, 2009). In the context of the illegal wildlife trade, the ecological damage inflicted by any given take varies according to the season and the protection status, age, number and sex of the animals removed from their habitat.

The review of financial penalties for the three selected crime types—illegal hunting, selling and advertising—demonstrates that there is significant opportunity to develop greater deterrent value. Although most reviewed states impose fines that take account of a trafficked animal's protection status—only Cameroon and Ivory Coast do not—few factor in other relevant criteria. Only 7 of the 17 countries adjust fines to reflect the economic harm or ecological damage caused by the three selected wild-

TABLE 6.7

Fine Criteria Used in Wildlife Trade Crimes in 17 Ape Range States, 2018

Country	Wildlife crime penalty criteria ● Applied ● Not applied		
	Protection status	Economic damage (market or damage values)	Ecological damage (wildlife amount, age and sex)
Cambodia			
Cameroon			
China			
DRC			
Guinea			
Indonesia			
Ivory Coast			
Lao PDR			
Liberia			
Malaysia			
Myanmar			
Nigeria			
Republic of Congo			
Rwanda			
Tanzania			
Uganda			
Viet Nam			

Source: Rodriguez et al. (2019)

life crimes. Moreover, only Malaysia and Viet Nam set their fines based on the amount, sex and age of the hunted, traded and advertised wildlife (see Table 6.7).

Prison Terms

There is no global consensus on what the national minimum prison sentence should be for wildlife crimes. For illicit trafficking of endangered species, the United Nations Convention against Transnational Organized Crime (UNTOC) recommends establishing these offenses as "serious crimes"—meaning that they should carry a maximum prison sentence of at least four years (UNGA, 2000, arts. 2(b); 5).

As noted above, few countries under review have criminalized the hunting, sale or advertising of wildlife that is not on their national lists of protected species; individuals who engage in such activities are thus less likely to be served prison sentences than those who target protected wildlife. With the exception of unlisted gibbons in three countries, as detailed above, all apes are recognized as protected species in the domestic legislation of the 17 countries under review (see Table 6.2). Table 6.8 illustrates the variations in maximum prison terms for illegal hunting. For the most part, countries meet the UNTOC threshold of a four-year penalty; only four countries fail in this regard—Cameroon, Ivory Coast, Guinea and Nigeria—with terms that are substantially shorter. Viet Nam imposes the highest prison term: 15 years.

Among the countries under review, prison terms for illegal sales are largely akin to those for illegal hunting. Only three jurisdictions impose different terms for illegal sales: the penalty is lower in Liberia (1 year rather than 4) and higher in Malaysia and Tanzania (7 years rather than 6 and 30 years rather than 10, respectively). Malaysia is the only country that imposes

TABLE 6.8

Maximum Prison Terms for Illegal Hunting of Protected Species in 17 Ape Range States, 2018

Country	Maximum prison term (years)					
	<1	1	4	5	10	15
Cambodia					✓	
Cameroon	✓					
China					✓	
DRC					✓	
Guinea		✓				
Indonesia				✓		
Ivory Coast		✓				
Lao PDR				✓		
Liberia			✓			
Malaysia				✓		
Myanmar					✓	
Nigeria		✓				
Republic of Congo				✓		
Rwanda					✓	
Tanzania					✓	
Uganda				✓		
Viet Nam						✓

Source: Rodriguez et al. (2019)

prison terms for illegal advertising (seven years). The use of prison terms indicates that states generally focus on the beginning of the supply chain, ignoring the serious role played by criminal networks in the marketing and sale of endangered species. These legal gaps expose both great apes and gibbons to higher risks.

Trend Analysis: Whose Authority Is It Anyway?

Effective law enforcement requires a stable and transparent structure of national authorities. Hunters and other stakeholders need clarity regarding legal requirements on them, including where and how often they must apply for permits or licenses. Field officers need to know what their powers and limits are, with which offices they must work and with whom they need to share information. A lack of awareness about such obligations can create significant loopholes that can be exploited, compromising conservation and enforcement goals.

The kind of clarity that would help is not necessarily the natural product of the legislative process, however. One of the common characteristics of complex domestic legal frameworks is an abundance of authorities that overlap or share management and enforcement powers with respect to a particular issue. The cumulative result of multiple laws written at different times for different reasons, a legal framework pertaining to the protection of wildlife or any other issue can comprise elements that are not expressly related to that issue, such as criminal codes, criminal procedure codes and state security laws. Adding to the confusion is the periodic reorganization of management and enforcement structures in line with political events. In some jurisdictions, these changes can be so profound and frequent that legislative drafting rules prohibit the specific naming of any particular institution in the delegation of power. Instead, legislators use generic names so that the reorganization of the political structure does not require amendments of legislation (Rosenbaum, 2007).

In assessing the legislative frameworks, this study reveals that each country under review has more than six different enforcement agencies and more than five different management authorities with legal competencies related to the wildlife trade. In the most extreme case—that of Viet Nam—13 different institutions share enforcement responsibilities. In some instances, the same authority holds both managerial and enforce-

ment responsibilities. In Viet Nam, for example, the ministry of agriculture serves as the CITES management authority, but it also has inspection powers and the authority to revoke CITES permits. In all countries, the legal framework is a complex ecosystem of ministries, institutions, research bodies and enforcement authorities, such as customs, national police, military and specific wildlife enforcement bodies.

Having so many different authorities in charge of individual aspects of illegal wildlife trade is not technically inappropriate. In fact, it is to be expected given the multifaceted nature of the trade. Moving along the supply chain, the enforcement of related laws can involve rangers, specialized wildlife forces, police, customs authorities, CITES management authorities, and the judicial system, including its investigators, prosecutors and courts. In federal structures, there may even be different levels of law enforcement at which national and regional entities share competencies, as is the case in Malaysia.

The involvement of multiple institutions does, however, place a premium on coordination and sometimes makes it difficult to understand exactly who is responsible for what. By and large, the reviewed laws are short on details, defining neither formal structures for coordination, nor the exchange of information or data. One of the few exceptions is the legislation of Nigeria, which specifically tasks its National Environmental Standards and Regulations Enforcement Agency with "coordination and liaison with relevant stakeholders" (NESREA, 2007, art. 2). Malaysia confers responsibility for the national coordination of CITES enforcement on its "lead" CITES management authority, the Ministry of Water, Land and Natural Resources (Laws of Malaysia, 2008, art. 5).

Particularly important to the great apes and gibbon trade—and a critical area in law

—is the inclusion of the institutional check and balance required by CITES for the scientific and management authorities (CITES, 2007a). Pursuant to CITES, the two types of authorities must be independent from each other; the scientific authority is to hold the power to veto management authority actions, such as draft CITES legislation and export permits that may endanger the survival of a particular species. Only nine of the jurisdictions under review maintain the required independence between these authorities—Cameroon, China, Guinea, Indonesia, Ivory Coast, Lao PDR, Liberia, Uganda and Viet Nam; the other eight do not. In at least five jurisdictions, both authorities are hosted in the same ministry (Cambodia, Malaysia, Myanmar, the Republic of Congo and Rwanda), while in Nigeria and Tanzania, the management authority acts as a chair or coordinator of external entities comprising the scientific authority. More importantly, the required veto power over CITES draft legislation is missing in all countries.

The shortage of checks and balances currently endangers the transparency, functionality and purpose of CITES entities, rendering the dismissal of scientific evidence and the abuse of power more likely. Although all international commercial trade in great apes and gibbons is prohibited by CITES, trade for non-commercial purposes is still possible and must pass through this system. In this context, legal loopholes can affect the legitimacy of trade and further jeopardize species survival.

National Frameworks: Conclusions

By itself, the law cannot solve the problem of trade in great apes and gibbons. If appropriately developed and enforced within a functioning legal framework, however, it can play a critical role in addressing the complex market realities that underlie the illegal wildlife trade. Developing the law would involve identifying and criminalizing the numerous distinct activities that together constitute the wildlife supply chain —from poaching, transportation, processing, storage, advertising, and domestic and foreign trade, through to possession, exhibition and experimentation. As discussed above, the review of 17 ape range states indicates that the criminalization of domestic and foreign trade of illegally taken species is common, but that more can be done to close the regulatory gaps that leave wildlife exposed to harm.

The control of the transnational wildlife trade is not solely a function of CITES implementation. States can avail themselves of a number of legal tools to enhance domestic enforcement opportunities to address the trafficking of internationally sourced wildlife. Accordingly, some countries are recognizing both native and non-native species as domestically protected. This simple legal act has the potential to ease enforcement burdens and increase opportunities for enforcement in cases where protected wildlife has been trafficked across a border. States can also use legislation to focus on the international criminal networks and corruption that fuel trade across countries. Doing so is likely to involve expanding laws to cover not only poachers, but also legal entities, criminal networks and government officials involved in the trade. The use of related economic and legal tools—such as organized crime and anti-money-laundering statutes —can also translate into greater deterrence values and can help to target implicated entities that would otherwise escape liability.

Finally, a host of management and enforcement authorities come into play as illegal wildlife is moved from natural habitats to the market, yet many of them have no direct relation to or training in wildlife issues. Just as legislators can target all points along the trade chain, so too can they ensure that all stakeholder activities are appropriately managed, specifically by establishing formal mechanisms for effective coordination.

All told, maximizing opportunities to combat the ape trade requires the development of the law, in particular through the use of legal tools that target all activities and actors along the illegal supply chain.

International Frameworks

Individuals who transport apes, or their body parts or derivatives, across national boundaries are subject—at least potentially —to a range of laws and regulations that are designed to prevent trade in protected species and to promote wildlife conservation. This section reviews the main agreements and organizations that are most relevant to the illegal trade in apes.

CITES

The CITES Structure

The main international agreement of relevance is the 1973 Convention on International Trade in Endangered Species of Wild Fauna and Flora. CITES, which entered into force in 1975 and had 183 parties as of January 2020, aims to protect wildlife from over-exploitation by controlling international trade, under a system of import and export permits (CITES, n.d.-k).

Wildlife protected by CITES—currently about 5,800 species of animals and 30,000 species of plants (CITES, n.d.-d)—appears in different appendices:

- **Appendix I** lists species that are threatened with extinction;
- **Appendix II** lists species that are not necessarily threatened with extinction now but may become so unless trade in them is subject to strict regulation; and

■ **Appendix III** includes species listed unilaterally by parties that wish to regulate their trade and want to signal the need for international cooperation (CITES, n.d.-g).

Amendments to Appendices I and II are adopted by the CITES Conference of the Parties (CoP); individual parties may unilaterally place species on Appendix III at any time (CITES, n.d.-g).

Appendix I is effectively a black list that prohibits primarily commercial trade in endangered species, including all species of gibbon and great ape—bonobos, chimpanzees, gorillas and orangutans. Exceptions from and variations on these requirements apply to individuals, parts or derivatives that:

■ are transiting or being transshipped "while in Customs control" of a CITES member state;

■ are personal or household effects, including pets;

■ were acquired prior to the species listing under CITES;

■ were bred in captivity for commercial purposes or for non-commercial trade between scientists or scientific institutions; or

■ are part of a traveling zoo, circus or other traveling exhibition (CITES, 1973, art. VII).

Under these provisions, entities and individuals who trade in listed specimens must obtain both export and import permits; certificates are also required for re-export. All CITES parties designate one or more management authorities to administer the permit system and one or more scientific authorities to advise the management authority on the effects of trade on the status of the species. A management authority may only issue permits if two requirements are met. First, a scientific authority must issue a so-called "non-detriment" finding —a conclusion that the export of the specimen will not have a negative impact on the survival of the species in the wild. Second, the management authority must be satisfied that the specimens have been acquired legally and that the trade is not for primarily commercial purposes.

Various requirements apply to the issue of permits. For example, a separate permit is required for each consignment, and export permits are valid for a maximum of 6 months, while import permits expire after 12 months. Permits and certificates must include statements of the source of specimens—that is, whether they are wild-caught, captive-bred, ranched or artificially propagated—and the intended purpose of the import, such as commercial, scientific or educational. The requirements that apply to trade in Appendix II and III species are less strict.

The CITES CoP is the main decision-making body; its powers include adding species to and removing them from both Appendices I and II. The CITES Standing Committee, which normally meets once a year, provides policy guidance to the Secretariat concerning CITES implementation, coordinates and oversees the work of other committees and working groups, and administers the non-compliance procedure, through which recommendations can be issued for the suspension of trade in some or all listed species with parties not complying with CITES requirements (CITES, 2019a, n.d.-b, n.d.-j).

The CITES framework provides a potentially effective means of regulating the trade in endangered and threatened species of wildlife, but in practice it suffers from several weaknesses. The enforcement of CITES controls, both within a country and in regard to suspensions of trade between parties and non-complying parties, rests on parties' management authorities. In many cases these bodies do not operate effectively, typically because of insufficient capacity, a lack of willingness, corruption or, sometimes, the intricacies of international diplomacy. Permit fraud is a constant problem; especially where the traded specimens are of high value, there are incentives for fraud, theft and corruption in issuing permits, stealing or buying blank ones, or tampering with them while in use (such as by changing the numbers of specimens covered). In many cases, trade in listed specimens has been carried out for ostensibly scientific—but in reality commercial—purposes; similarly, wild-caught specimens have been falsely identified as hailing from facilities that are supposedly engaged in captive breeding (Elliott and Schaedla, 2016; Lavorgna et al., 2018; OECD, 2012; see Box 6.1).

The UN Environment World Conservation Monitoring Centre (UNEP-WCMC) maintains a database of issued import and export permits, derived from annual reports from CITES parties, but it does not systematically cross-check the documents against each other (UNEP-WCMC, n.d.).[21] Nor are the permits systematically checked against what is actually in the shipments they accompany; customs officers are not typically able to identify species as protected, particularly given the vast number listed in the CITES appendices. Claims that trade is being carried out for scientific purposes or that specimens are captive-bred frequently go unchecked by the management or customs authorities in both exporting and importing states. Many countries lack the capacity to operate the system correctly, with insufficient numbers of adequately trained or paid staff, and a lack of basic equipment; many states that do have adequate capacity simply do not operate the controls rigorously (Elliott and Schaedla, 2016; Lavorgna et al., 2018; OECD, 2012).

The CITES bodies have attempted to address these problems in various ways. The CITES Secretariat provides training and capacity building assistance; it also coordinates review missions to parties to examine their implementation of the agreement (CITES, n.d.-c). In addition, it carries out regular reviews of the status of trade in particular species. Work is currently under way to define more carefully the meaning of "legal acquisition"—that is, the requirement that specimens to be traded must have been legally caught or acquired. In 2015, against the background of a steady rise in the trade in captive-bred specimens—whose number now exceeds that of specimens traded as wild-caught—the 17th CITES CoP (CoP17) asked the Standing Committee to assess and develop solutions to the problems associated with trade in captive-bred specimens (CITES, 2015b, n.d.-a). CITES parties register commercial captive-breeding facilities in a database maintained by the CITES Secretariat, yet facilities do not need to be registered if they breed animals only for zoos or scientific purposes. The Secretariat's investigations into some of these facilities have revealed problems such as limited access and misuse of source codes (TRAFFIC, 2016).

A number of these problems could be addressed through the use of electronic permit systems rather than the paper systems that remain dominant; digitalization would help to reduce the opportunities for fraud and tampering, while facilitating monitoring of trade and communication between management authorities. In 2005, the CITES parties established a working group to explore the use of information technology, and several countries have developed and piloted, or fully implemented, electronic systems (CITES, n.d.-f). In collaboration with the World Customs Organization, the CITES Secretariat published a toolkit of common forms, protocols and standards in 2010 and updated it in 2013 (CITES, 2013a). In 2015, CoP17 decided to re-establish the working group to revise the existing documents and develop new standards and tools (CITES, n.d.-f).

CITES and Apes

As noted above, all the species of ape are listed in CITES Appendix I but, as described in this volume's Introduction, there are several ways in which CITES controls can be evaded to facilitate illegal trade. Specimens can simply be smuggled across borders without any CITES permits. Even if permits have been issued, traders often abuse the various exceptions that allow trade in Appendix I species, as noted above. Management authorities in some countries have issued export permits stating that specimens were bred in captive-breeding facilities without checking whether the named facilities even exist (see Box 6.1). Similarly, management authorities in some importing countries have issued import permits claiming that specimens are destined for zoos or scientific purposes, even though the animals are actually intended for commercial use (PEGAS, 2017, n.d.).

Apes have been discussed at many CITES CoPs and meetings of the Standing Committee. In 2004, CoP13 passed Resolution 13.4, which deals specifically with great apes and calls on CITES parties and other bodies to take a series of measures on law enforcement and conservation (CITES, 2013b).[22] Nevertheless, NGOs often argue that not enough attention is being paid to the topic, and that the relatively low number of reported seizures of trafficked great apes is a reflection of inadequate law enforcement efforts.[23] In 2015, under Decision 17.232, CoP17 directed the Secretariat to produce a report on the status of great apes and the relative impact of illegal trade and other pressures on their status, for consideration by the Standing Committee (CITES, 2017b).

GRASP, IUCN and other experts produced the requested report. In October 2018,

BOX 6.1

Permit Fraud in Guinea: A Key to Supplying Apes to China's Zoos

From 2007 onwards, chimpanzees were exported from Guinea to China under apparently valid CITES permits that indicated that the animals were captive-bred. Investigations by non-governmental organizations (NGOs) and private individuals revealed that, by 2013, at least 138 chimpanzees and 10 gorillas had been exported via travel routes established by Chinese development companies. As no captive breeding facility existed in Guinea, investigators suspected that the apes had been taken from Cameroon, Ivory Coast, Liberia, the Republic of Congo or other countries in the region, in addition to Guinea (Stiles et al., 2013). Further evidence suggested that the export of apes had been going on for years—to China, Russia, Egypt and other Middle Eastern countries (PEGAS, n.d.).

In early 2011 the CITES Secretariat responded to reports from NGOs and others by expressing concerns about this trade to the relevant management authorities, including those in China and Guinea. Dissatisfied with the response, the Secretariat set up a mission to the country, which, in September 2011, found that 69 chimpanzees had been taken out of the country during the previous year, destined for Chinese zoos or safari parks. Based on the findings made during the mission, the Secretariat issued a notification to CITES parties, highlighting concerns regarding the validity of the permits and pointing out that there was no—and that there had never been any—commercial captive breeding of specimens of CITES-listed species in Guinea (CITES, 2015a).

In 2013, after Guinea failed to respond to the Secretariat's request to improve its procedures for issuing permits, the Standing Committee recommended that all commercial trade in CITES-listed species with Guinea be suspended; this suspension remains in force. In 2015 the head of Guinea's CITES management authority was arrested for his suspected role in corrupt and fraudulent actions in the issuance of CITES export permits. Although convicted and sentenced to 18 months in prison, he was pardoned by the country's president (PEGAS, 2017).

The case illustrates the scope—and the limitations—of CITES. While the Secretariat and the Standing Committee responded to the concerns raised by NGOs and others, they are not themselves enforcement agencies; they rely on the national management authorities to ensure that the permit system is correctly implemented. While the Guinean management authority should never have issued the export permits, the Chinese management authority should equally have queried their authenticity; no captive breeding facilities exist in Guinea. In addition, many—and perhaps all—of the chimpanzees ended up in amusement and safari parks; that is, they were imported for commercial, not scientific, purposes, which is further complicated by the status afforded such establishments in the country (see Chapter 4). Since the animals were illegally transferred, they should have been confiscated and repatriated.

In addition, although China subsequently suspended imports of apes from Guinea, information in the CITES Trade Database suggests that it simply switched to importing from other countries (CITES, n.d.-e). In July 2018 correspondence was revealed from Chinese zoos to the environment minister of the Democratic Republic of Congo—which has no captive-breeding facilities either—requesting exports of mountain gorillas (Gorilla beringei beringei), bonobos (Pan paniscus), chimpanzees and other animals (Summers, 2018).

at its 70th meeting, the Standing Committee discussed the findings, including the latest information available on the distribution of great apes and their population changes over time. The report identifies the main threats to their survival as habitat loss, degradation and fragmentation; infectious disease; wild meat hunting and indiscriminate poaching; and deliberate killing due to conflicts over land. It concludes that the illegal international trade of great apes mainly involves wild meat, and mostly between neighboring countries. This type of trade tends to be less well researched and more difficult to detect and control than transcontinental trade. It also characterizes illegal trafficking of live orphans as primarily a by-product of the wild meat trade; in fact, it mentions the Guinea case outlined in Box 6.1 as the only example of great apes being targeted for capture and subsequent trade (CITES, 2018a). Some experts have questioned this finding, arguing that it underestimates the extent and drivers of illegal trade in live apes.[24]

While the report recognizes improvements in law enforcement efforts in some countries—including the spread of the Eco Activists for Governance and Law Enforcement (EAGLE) network of investigators and activists—it concludes that law enforcement efforts alone would be insufficient to halt illegal trafficking in live great apes or their body parts (CITES, 2018a; EAGLE, n.d.). It sets out 14 recommendations, including, for CITES parties, improvements in their national legal frameworks, law enforcement and data collection efforts; the adoption of transboundary agreements and collaborative judiciary proceedings; the introduction of requirements on private actors in the energy, extractive and agricultural sectors to minimize the impact of their operations on great ape populations and habitats; and efforts to promote alternatives to wild meat (CITES, 2018a). It also recommends rejecting any

applications for trade in potentially wild-caught great apes:

> Given the rarity of these taxa and the large numbers of captive-bred great apes currently held in zoos and other ex-situ collections, wild-caught great apes are not acceptable for trade among zoos, safari parks or other educational or scientific institutions except under extraordinary circumstances (CITES, 2018a, p. 23).

After discussing the report, the Standing Committee asked the Secretariat to review the provisions in Resolution 13.4 together with GRASP and IUCN, and to propose appropriate amendments for consideration at CoP18 in 2019 (CITES, 2018b, para. 52). Accordingly, the conference approved a resolution that largely repeats the conclusions of the report, including by noting that:

> as all great ape species are well represented in zoos worldwide, there consequently may not be exceptional circumstances for which the removal of further great apes from the wild would be justified (CITES, 2019b, p. 1).

If fully implemented, the recommendations of the report and resolution would go some way to controlling the illegal trade in great apes and addressing pressures on habitats. Whether they will be effectively implemented in practice remains to be seen. Meanwhile, NGOs and others have suggested additional reforms to CITES procedures, including working with international zoological associations to establish a registry of accredited zoos and scientific institutions that might house great apes, especially those with breeding programs, in order to minimize abuse of the captive-bred exception.[25] A more ambitious measure would be to require imported great apes to be registered and identified, for example through DNA profiles or inserted microchips.

International Conservation Organizations and Agreements

Great Apes Survival Partnership

An alliance of more than 100 conservation organizations, national governments, private companies, research institutions and UN agencies, GRASP was established in 2001 and is the only species-specific conservation program within the UN. Its six priorities are political advocacy, habitat protection, illegal trade, conflict-sensitive conservation, disease monitoring and the green economy. It works to promote awareness of these issues among other institutions and has been able to access funding and foster collaboration to deliver conservation projects (GRASP, n.d.-b). It has participated in technical missions with the CITES Secretariat, for example in April 2007 in Thailand and Cambodia, where the focus was on orangutans (CITES, 2007b). The publication *Stolen Apes: The Illicit Trade in Chimpanzees, Gorillas, Bonobos and Orangutans*—released in 2013 by GRASP, UNEP and GRID-Arendal—provides the first overview of the extent of the illicit global trade in great apes and includes recommendations for the mitigation of the impact of illegal trade on the remaining wild populations (Stiles *et al.*, 2013).

In September 2016, GRASP followed up on one of the recommendations in *Stolen Apes* by launching the Apes Seizure Database. Developed together with UNEP-WCMC, the database consolidates data and reports of great apes seized around the world (GRASP, n.d.-a). Much of the illegal trade in these species does not meet the requirements for inclusion in other existing databases, such as the CITES Trade Database, which does not record transactions unless they cross national borders and which may thus lead some observers to underestimate the scale of the illegal trade (CITES, n.d.-e).[26] The

Apes Seizure Database allows providers to upload records directly from the field via smartphones; a panel of experts validates each record to ensure the quality of data (GRASP, n.d.-a). On its launch, the database contained information on seizures of more than 1,800 great apes in 23 nations—almost half of which were not great ape range states—between 2005 and 2016 (UN Environment, 2016a).

Not unlike other organizations discussed in this chapter, GRASP suffers from a shortage of funding and capacity; in 2019, it was making do with just three staff members instead of the full five. Nevertheless, its research and advocacy efforts have been welcomed, and as the only intergovernmental organization dedicated to great apes, it clearly has the potential to play an important role in addressing the international illegal trade.[27]

The Convention on Migratory Species and the Gorilla Agreement

The Convention on the Conservation of Migratory Species of Wild Animals (CMS) entered into force in 1983. Operating under the aegis of UN Environment, the convention aims to conserve terrestrial, marine and avian migratory species throughout their range. CMS parties (130 as of November 2019) undertake to protect migratory species that are threatened with extinction (such as gorillas and chimpanzees), as well as species that need or would benefit significantly from international cooperation (including chimpanzees), by conserving or restoring the places where they live, mitigating obstacles to migration and controlling other factors that might endanger the animals (CMS, n.d.-a, n.d.-d, n.d.-e). The CMS effectively acts as a framework convention; more concrete commitments are entered into through specific global or regional treaties or less

formal instruments such as memorandums of understanding. Efforts are under way to develop a new compliance regime to support parties in meeting their obligations (CMS, 2018).

Species-specific treaties under the CMS include the Agreement on the Conservation of Gorillas and Their Habitats, which entered into force in 2008. Intended to cover all ten gorilla range states, the Gorilla Agreement has been ratified by seven of them—the Central African Republic, the DRC, Gabon, Nigeria, the Republic of Congo, Rwanda and Uganda; the remaining three are Angola, Cameroon and Equatorial Guinea. The agreement aims to conserve and restore gorilla populations and promote the long-term survival of their forest habitat and dependent human populations, largely through the development of subspecies-specific action plans. Activities include monitoring gorilla populations and threats; strengthening law enforcement and anti-poaching measures; promoting alternatives to forest and gorilla overexploitation as sources of income, including ecotourism; building international collaboration between range states; and developing national strategies for gorilla conservation (CMS, n.d.-b, n.d.-c).

To date, the Gorilla Agreement has not been particularly successful in achieving any of these aims. An activity report presented at the CMS conference in 2014 summarizes limited progress with regional action plans and two small projects, one to support community-based forest conservation initiatives and the other to assist governments in increasing their wildlife law enforcement capacity and monitoring the illegal wildlife trade (CMS, 2014). The equivalent report presented at the CMS conference in 2017 features only a proposal for cooperating with GRASP and information about two additional small projects (CMS, 2017). GRASP's current shortages of staff and funding may affect its ability to achieve such cooperation.[28]

The illegal international trade of great apes mainly involves wild meat, and mostly between neighboring countries. This type of trade tends to be less well researched and more difficult to detect and control than transcontinental trade.

Biodiversity Convention

The UN Convention on Biological Diversity (CBD), also known as the Biodiversity Convention, was signed in 1992 at the Rio Earth Summit and entered into force the following year. As of January 2020 it had 196 parties—almost universal participation, with the notable exception of the United States, which has signed the agreement but has not ratified it (CBD, n.d.-a, n.d.-b). The CBD has three main goals: the conservation of biodiversity, the sustainable use of its components, and the fair and equitable sharing of benefits arising from genetic resources. The convention is the first international agreement to recognize the conservation of biodiversity as "a common concern of humankind" and an integral part of the development process (Casetta, Marques da Silva and Vecchi, 2019). It covers all ecosystems, species and genetic resources; it also links traditional conservation efforts to the economic goal of using biological resources sustainably. CBD parties are required to draw up national biodiversity strategies and action plans and to ensure that they are mainstreamed into the planning and activities of all sectors whose activities can have an impact (positive or negative) on biodiversity (CBD, n.d.-a).

The requirement to draw up national strategies is legally binding, yet there are no real penalties for non-compliance or for any failure to implement meaningful policies or measures. Still, the CBD has helped to raise the profile of the issue, in part by initiating a series of studies on the economic impacts of the loss of biodiversity, which began with *The Economics of Ecosystems and Biodiversity: An Interim Report* (TEEB, 2008). The process of drawing up and implementing national strategies does appear to have assisted conservation efforts. It has also helped to mobilize financial support; from 1994 to the end of May 2016, the Global Environment Facility—a funding mechanism established

in 1992 to provide financial support to environmental initiatives, including several international conventions—provided support to about 1,300 national and regional biodiversity projects, with grants totaling US$3.4 billion, generating co-financing of US$10.2 billion (Ferreira de Souza Dias, 2016).

International Law Enforcement Organizations and Agreements

World Customs Organization

Established in 1952, the WCO aims to enhance the effectiveness and efficiency of customs administrations; as of January 2020, it had 183 members, covering 98 per cent of world trade. The WCO offers its members a forum for dialog and exchange of experiences between customs agencies, and technical assistance and training services for modernizing and building capacity in their national customs administrations (WCO, n.d.-g).

The WCO's Environment Programme focuses on combating environmental crime, including illegal trade in wildlife, timber, waste and chemicals. It tries to ensure that environmental issues are among the priorities of customs agencies, a difficult task given other calls on their resources and, often, a lack of awareness of the environmental impacts of illegal behavior (WCO, n.d.-b). The Environment Programme maintains WCO tools and instruments that are designed to facilitate enforcement, such as the Customs Enforcement Network application, which features a database of seizures and offenses as well as pictures of illicit goods (WCO, n.d.-c). In addition, it manages ENVIRONET, a real-time communication tool for information exchange among national authorities, international organizations and regional networks (WCO, n.d.-a). The WCO's annual *Illicit Trade Report* provides information on the Environment Programme's activities and an

> Wildlife crime is usually a low priority for customs agencies, particularly in developing countries, where revenue-generating activities often take priority over wildlife-related law enforcement operations.

assessment of the extent of environmental crime worldwide (WCO, n.d.-e).

With assistance from donors, the WCO has run a series of programs to raise awareness of the illegal trade in wildlife and related corruption among customs officers, including international training workshops, seminars and joint enforcement operations. One such program was Project Gapin (Great Apes and Integrity), which, in 2010–11, not only aimed to raise awareness among customs officers of the illegal trade in wildlife and related corruption, but also provided assistance to a number of customs administrations in Africa (WCO, 2012, n.d.-d). The most recent initiative, Project INAMA—funded by CITES and the German, Swedish and US governments—aims to strengthen the enforcement capacity of customs administrations in sub-Saharan Africa. An initial assessment found that most countries in the region generally accorded a low priority to the illegal wildlife trade. Many had appropriate legal provisions in place but seldom used them. Half of the administrations did not have an intelligence unit in place, and none of them had intelligence officers dedicated specifically to wildlife issues. Under Project INAMA, training sessions and workshops have been held, technical assistance has been provided for evidence handling and seizures, and joint enforcement and intelligence operations and exchange of personnel have been encouraged (WCO, 2017).

The WCO's global intelligence and information gathering functions are supported by its 11 Regional Intelligence Liaison Offices (RILOs), some of which have been active in tackling environmental crime (WCO, n.d.-f). In 2013–14, for example, RILO Asia-Pacific and RILO Eastern and Southern Africa participated in three successive global enforcement operations (CITES, 2014). Operation Cobra III, launched in 2015, was the largest global operation ever to target transnational wildlife and forest crime, including offenses involving apes.

The operation resulted in more than 300 arrests, more than 600 seizures of wildlife contraband, and tip-offs that led to the discovery of crime networks and other criminal activities (WWF, 2015).

The WCO and its RILOs are critical players in efforts to control the illegal trade in wildlife, but they are consistently hindered by a scarcity of resources and, in many national customs agencies, shortages of capacity, corruption and a lack of political will. Some of the data that national customs agencies report to the WCO are inaccurate, particularly on trade in environment-related items. As noted above, wildlife crime is usually a low priority for customs agencies, particularly in developing countries, where revenue-generating activities often take priority over wildlife-related law enforcement operations.[29]

INTERPOL

INTERPOL, the International Criminal Police Organization, was founded in 1923 and had 194 member countries in January 2020. It facilitates information exchange between national police authorities but does not investigate or prosecute cases (INTERPOL, n.d.-a). INTERPOL's Environmental Security Unit comprises four global enforcement teams, covering fisheries, forestry, pollution and wildlife. They provide national law enforcement agencies with tools and expertise, offer investigative support relating to international cases and targets, coordinate operations, and assist member countries in sharing information and studying environmental criminal networks. They are advised by an Environmental Compliance and Enforcement Committee, with four working groups that focus on the same four topics and bring together member countries to share experience and expertise and to facilitate international cooperation (INTERPOL, n.d.-b).

INTERPOL has coordinated a long series of international enforcement operations targeted at various forms of environmental crime. In 2016, for example, Operation Thunderbird, a global operation tackling the illegal trade in wildlife and timber, involved police, customs and border agencies, as well as environment, wildlife and forestry officials from 49 countries and territories and resulted in the identification of nearly 900 suspects and 1,300 seizures of illicit products worth an estimated US$5.1 million (INTERPOL, 2017). None of INTERPOL's operations appears to have targeted great apes in particular, although several have resulted in seizures of wild meat.

INTERPOL encourages each of its member countries to establish a national environmental security task force to fight environmental crime. These multi-agency cooperatives involve the police, customs, environmental agencies, other specialized bodies, prosecutors, NGOs and intergovernmental partners in pursuit of a common goal, such as the reduction of pollution, the conservation of a particular species or the protection of forests, fish stocks or other natural resources (INTERPOL, 2012).

Like the WCO, INTERPOL has done good work on environmental crime and has a potentially valuable role to play in combating the illegal trade in great apes—by identifying and apprehending offenders and raising awareness of the issue. It is constrained by a lack of resources and many other competing priorities, however, and its effectiveness is undermined by wide variations in what is legal and what is illegal in member countries, the involvement of a huge range of law enforcement agencies (not just the police) and a general lack of knowledge of environmental crimes.[30] It is most effective in coordinating national police forces that already strive to tackle wildlife crime; if a police force is not willing to do so—or is affected by corruption—there is little INTERPOL can do about it.

United Nations Office on Drugs and Crime

UNODC was established in 1997 to assist UN member states in their struggle against illicit drugs, crime and terrorism. Unlike the WCO and INTERPOL, it is not an enforcement cooperation agency. Rather, it undertakes field-based technical cooperation and capacity-building; conducts research and analytical work, partly to increase knowledge and understanding, but also to expand the evidence base for policy and operational decisions; and works with states to develop national legislation, as well as to ratify and implement relevant international treaties, such as the UN Convention against Transnational Organized Crime (UNGA, 2000). It relies on voluntary contributions for the bulk of its budget and tends to suffer from chronic funding shortages and understaffing (UNODC, n.d.-a).[31]

Within UNODC, work on wildlife crime is organized through the four-year Global Programme for Combating Wildlife and Forest Crime. Activities are undertaken together with the wildlife law enforcement community to ensure that wildlife crime, illegal logging and related offenses are treated as serious transnational organized crimes. As part of this work, UNODC delivers technical assistance and capacity building, including by training and supporting rangers, police, customs, prosecutors, investigators and the judiciary. It also supports capacity building in intelligence gathering and strengthens interagency and cross-border cooperation (UNODC, n.d.-c).

In 2012, UNODC published the *Wildlife and Forest Crime Analytic Toolkit*. Designed mainly to assist government officials, the toolkit provides a comprehensive overview and discussion of measures related to legislation, enforcement, the judiciary and prosecution, drivers and prevention, and data and analysis. Its aim is to help wildlife, forestry, customs and other enforcement agencies to conduct a comprehensive analysis of possible means and measures to protect wildlife and forests, monitor their use and identify requirements for technical assistance; more broadly, it is designed to raise awareness, bring in donor support and stimulate international cooperation (UNODC, 2012). By September 2016, the toolkit had been successfully implemented in 7 countries and was at different stages of implementation in 12 others (CITES, 2016).

In 2016, UNODC published the *World Wildlife Crime Report*, an evaluation of the extent and nature of the problem at the global level. The report includes a quantitative market assessment based on information in the World Wildlife Seizure database, which was established to enable this analysis and contains data provided by CITES and the WCO. If maintained, the database will serve to provide key indicators and a potential early warning mechanism. The report also features a series of in-depth illicit trade case studies, including one on great apes (UNODC, 2016).

United Nations Convention against Transnational Organized Crime

UNTOC entered into force in 2003 and had 190 parties as of late 2019 (UNODC, n.d.-b). Parties commit themselves to taking a series of measures against transnational organized crime—defined as offenses committed by three or more persons acting together—including by creating domestic criminal offenses; adopting frameworks for extradition, mutual legal assistance and law enforcement cooperation; and promoting training and technical assistance. In theory, UNTOC parties should be able to rely on one another in investigating, prosecuting and punishing crimes committed by organized criminal groups with some element of transnational involvement. The aim is to make it much more difficult for organized criminal groups to take advantage of gaps in national law, jurisdictional problems or a lack of accurate information about the full scope of their activities (UNGA, 2000; UNODC, n.d.-b).

According to observers, UNTOC has facilitated cooperation between enforcement agencies among different countries.[32] Its impact is inevitably limited, however, as it depends on its parties' capacity and willingness to implement its suggested framework, and the convention has no non-compliance mechanism to ensure that its parties meet their obligations.

UNTOC refers to "illicit trafficking in endangered species of wild flora and fauna" but contains no specific provisions (UNGA, 2000, preamble). The UN General Assembly and individual states have called on governments to fulfill their commitments under the terms of the convention, in particular by defining wildlife crime as a "serious crime"—meaning that it must carry a minimum penalty of at least four years' imprisonment—and also as a predicate offense for money laundering crimes (ECOSOC, 2013; London Conference on the Illegal Wildlife Trade, 2014). The evidence suggests that much of the illegal trade in great apes, particularly in high-value live specimens, is conducted by well-organized and sophisticated transnational criminal networks—groups that fall squarely within the remit of this convention (Stiles *et al.*, 2013).

International Consortium for Combating Wildlife Crime

Founded in November 2010 by the CITES Secretariat, INTERPOL, UNODC, the WCO, and the World Bank, the International Consortium on Combating Wildlife Crime (ICCWC) is a collaborative association rather than an independent organization.

Its aim is to strengthen criminal justice systems and provide coordinated support at the national, regional and international levels to combat wildlife and forest crime. A number of European countries and the United States have provided funding (CITES, 2019c, n.d.-h).

ICCWC worked together with UNODC in publishing the above-mentioned *Wildlife and Forest Crime Analytic Toolkit* in 2012 and the *World Wildlife Crime Report* in 2016 (UNODC, 2012, 2016). ICCWC has also established an indicator framework, which allows national law enforcement authorities to assess their own capacity to fight wildlife and forest crime; deployed wildlife incident support teams to assist countries that have been affected by significant poaching or that have made large-scale seizures; provided specialized training for wildlife law enforcement officers; coordinated a number of enforcement operations, such as Cobra III; developed practical tools and guidelines for forensic methods and procedures for ivory and timber sampling and analysis; and launched an anti-money laundering training course (CITES, 2015c).

To date, ICCWC has been successful in generating a high profile and attracting significant levels of funding. The involvement of the World Bank has been helpful in drawing attention to the connections between money laundering and wildlife crime. The consortium has been criticized for lacking flexibility in responding to new situations—tied as it is to its partners' agendas and institutional structures—but in general it is credited with having a positive impact, albeit not specifically on apes.[33]

Other Collaborative Initiatives

As noted above, effective action against wildlife crime benefits substantially from collaboration among several different agencies, including the police, prosecutors, customs,

> " Effective action against wildlife crime benefits substantially from collaboration among several different agencies, including the police, prosecutors, customs, wildlife and forest rangers, and environment departments. "

Photo: Effective action against the international illegal trade in apes – whether as live specimens, body parts or wild meat— requires both an adequate legal framework and the resources, capacity and political will to use it. Ranger holding a smoked gorilla hand. © Jabruson (www.jabruson.photoshelter.com)

wildlife and forest rangers, and environment departments. This is true at the international level as much as it is at the national level, and various initiatives—including ICCWC—have been undertaken to foster such collaboration. Both the WCO and INTERPOL have formal memorandums of understanding with the secretariats of relevant multilateral environmental agreements (MEAs), including CITES, and also with a number of NGOs working on the issues (CITES and ICPO-INTERPOL, 1998; CITES and WCO, 1996).

Another effort is the Green Customs Initiative, which was established in 2004 and involves INTERPOL, UN Environment, the WCO and the secretariats of several MEAs, including CITES (Green Customs, n.d.). The initiative has helped to facilitate information exchange, joint technical meetings and cooperation between environment and customs officials at the national level. It has also participated in training and awareness raising exercises, although its partners are largely responsible for organizing the workshops and providing training materials, since the initiative has very little of its own capacity (Green Customs, n.d.).[34] Some of the MEA secretariats have benefited from their newly established interaction with the customs community, but observers note that activities are limited and that momentum has been lost over the years.[35]

A number of regional wildlife enforcement networks have been established to offer a platform for regional collaboration among national environment and law enforcement agencies, CITES authorities and others. Such networks also enable countries to monitor wildlife crime, share information, develop capacity for enforcement and investigations, and learn from each other's best practices (CITES, 2019d; ICCWC, 2013, 2016). One of the best-funded networks, thanks largely to support from the United States, was the Association of Southeast Asian Nations (ASEAN) Wildlife Enforcement Network. Each of the ten ASEAN member countries was charged with setting up an interagency task force comprising police, customs and environment officials; focal points from national task forces then shared intelligence with each other throughout the region. By 2015 eight ASEAN countries had each formed a national task force, training was being offered in anti-poaching operations and wildlife crime investigations, and arrests and seizures of illegal wildlife were increasing (Freeland Foundation/ASEAN-WEN, 2016; USAID, 2015). Very few of the arrests ever led to prosecutions, however, perhaps because of bribery and corruption.[36] In 2017 the network was merged into the ASEAN Experts Group on CITES to form the ASEAN Working Group on CITES and Wildlife Enforcement (AWG CITES and WE, n.d.).

Other regional wildlife enforcement networks exist, although some are not particularly active. The Lusaka Agreement Task Force, based on a formal agreement, has powers to investigate violations of wildlife laws, undertake intelligence gathering, conduct joint investigations and enforcement actions within and across its member countries' borders, and provide training to national agencies (UN Environment, 2016b). In 2013, 2016 and 2019, the CITES Secretariat and ICCWC convened meetings of all the networks and other interested organizations, alongside the CITES CoP meetings, to promote cooperation and exchange of information (CITES, 2019d; ICCWC, 2013, 2016).

In theory, regional wildlife enforcement networks have the potential to enhance cooperation and effectiveness; in practice, however, they can be time-consuming and bureaucratic to establish, and they always require donor funding. Given that resources are limited, it may prove more valuable to target support on establishing national collaborative networks and mechanisms for direct bilateral cooperation between affected countries.

International Frameworks: Conclusions

Effective action against the international illegal trade in apes—whether as live specimens, body parts or wild meat—requires both an adequate legal framework and the resources, capacity and political will to use it.

In principle, CITES provides many elements of an adequate legal framework at the international level. It currently suffers from a number of weaknesses that could be corrected, for example if CITES parties fully implement the recommendations set out in the 2018 report to the CITES Standing Committee and included in the 2019 resolution (CITES, 2018a, 2019b). In particular, the rejection of any applications for trade in potentially wild-caught apes, except in exceptional circumstances, would help to end the current abuse of the system by safaris, amusement parks and so-called zoos.

A bigger problem than the design of CITES is the lack of capacity, resources and political will in many of its parties, particularly in the ape range states and in countries that see imports of apes for commercial purposes. Too many management authorities fail to apply the correct procedures for issuing and checking the validity of export and import permits; corruption and fraud are persistent problems.

Once apes are illegally traded, either through fraud or circumvention of the CITES permit system, several of the other organizations reviewed in this chapter come into play. The WCO and its RILOs and INTERPOL are particularly important in taking enforcement action against illegal trade; GRASP, ICCWC and UNODC all have supportive roles to play in research, data and intelligence gathering, awareness raising, training and capacity building.

All of these organizations, however, suffer from similar problems in addressing the trade in apes, including a shortage of resources, as most of them are dependent on external funding rather than a core budget to carry out activities on wildlife crime. They must also deal with many competing priorities, in terms of other species, other areas of environmental crime and other areas of crime in general. Dedicated support from donors, whether public or private, will always be needed to underpin effective action.

In the context of the illegal wildlife trade, apes have not managed to achieve the same profile and levels of public awareness as other species, such as elephants. This is the case not only in Western countries but in many range states, where it is not unusual for chimpanzees or orangutans to be kept as pets, or for trade in body parts or wild meat to be regarded as acceptable. Complicating matters is the thriving demand for live apes for commercial or private entertainment purposes in many countries (Head, 2017; see Chapter 4). Awareness raising activities, research and campaigning are therefore just as important as law enforcement activities in helping to reduce demand. While some of the organizations reviewed in this chapter, such as GRASP and UNODC, carry out these roles, many more bodies—NGOs, research institutes and universities—do so as well, and they need to be supported.

> " In the context of the illegal wildlife trade, apes have not managed to achieve the same profile and levels of public awareness as other species, such as elephants. "

Acknowledgments

Principal authors: The National Legal Environment: Jim Wingard, Maria Pascual, and Maribel Rodriguez[37] International Frameworks: Duncan Brack[38]

Endnotes

1   On the Legal Atlas website, sign up for free and select the topic "Wildlife Trade" on the top menu search bar, then the "Legal Framework" database and then any of the 17 studied jurisdictions, either by clicking on the map or by choosing from the country selector. The map indicates which other countries have also been researched (Legal Atlas, n.d.).

2   Great ape range states comprise two countries in Asia—*Indonesia* and *Malaysia*—and 21 countries in Africa—Angola, Burundi, *Cameroon*, Central African Republic, the *Democratic Republic of Congo (DRC)*, Equatorial Guinea, Gabon, Ghana, *Guinea*, Guinea Bissau, *Ivory Coast*, *Liberia*, Mali, *Nigeria*, the *Republic of Congo*, Rwanda, Senegal, Sierra Leone, South Sudan, *Tanzania* and *Uganda* (GRASP, n.d.-c). The 12 italicized states are reviewed in this legal assessment.

3   Gibbon range states comprise 11 Asian countries: Bangladesh, Brunei, *Cambodia*, *China*, India, *Indonesia*, *Lao People's Democratic Republic (PDR)*, *Malaysia*, *Myanmar*, Thailand and *Viet Nam* (https://www.iucnredlist.org). The seven italicized states form part of this legal assessment.

4   As noted in the introduction to this chapter, this section summarizes the findings of Rodriguez *et al.* (2019). Supplementary sources are cited throughout the section.

5   The Legal Atlas Research Protocol for Wildlife Trade, an internal guide for legal analysts, outlines 43 types of law and their potential relationship to the governance of wildlife trade activities and transactions.

6   Laws differentiate between species only as much as deemed necessary by the drafters. Reference to a species includes all subspecies unless otherwise indicated.

7   Laws differentiate between species only as much as deemed necessary by the drafters. Reference to a species includes all subspecies unless otherwise indicated. Eastern gorilla therefore includes both Grauer's gorilla and the mountain gorilla.

8   Laws differentiate between species only as much as deemed necessary by the drafters. Reference to a species includes all sub-species unless otherwise indicated. Western gorilla therefore includes both the Cross River gorilla and the western lowland gorilla.

9   Laws differentiate between species only as much as deemed necessary by the drafters. Reference to a species includes all subspecies unless otherwise indicated.

10 The name, *Bunopithecus hoolock* is no longer used in current taxonomy (see the Apes Overview). This change has not been reflected in the laws in China. It may only cover the eastern hoolock, as the laws pre-date the identification of the Gaoligong hoolock and the western hoolock is not native to China.

11 The name, *Hylobates hoolock* is no longer used in current taxonomy (see the Apes Overview). This change has not been reflected in the laws in Myanmar. It may only cover the eastern hoolock, as the laws pre-date the identification of the Gaoligong hoolock and the western hoolock is not native to Myanmar.

12 While there are two *Gorilla gorilla* subspecies—the western lowland gorilla (*Gorilla g. gorilla*) and the Cross River gorilla (*Gorilla g. diehli*)—the law refers only to the former.

13 See the resolutions arising from meetings of the Conference of the Parties held between 1979 and 2016. Resolutions can be used to amend Appendices I, II or III, which are "lists of species afforded different levels or types of protection from overexploitation" (CITES, n.d.-g).

14 The finding that all 17 jurisdictions regulate capture and sale is based on the assumption that the term "trade" (as used in 7 of the jurisdictions) is broad and has applicability not only to financial transactions involving captive animals, such as the sale of a gibbon, but also to the capture of those animals.

15 Costa Rica, for example, provides for three different penalty segments in its main customs law, the 1995 Ley General de Aduanas, for the crime of smuggling. Under that law, penalties for smuggling any good (including wildlife) are governed by Article 211 for individual offenders, by Article 225(b) for legal entities or corporations and by Article 225(a) for government officials (Ley General de Aduanas, 1995).

16 This review covers 110 jurisdictions and discusses the degree to which the illegal wildlife trade is a predicate for money laundering offenses (Wingard and Pascual, 2019).

17 Hunting protected species (Class A and Class B) in Cameroon carries a fine of CFA 50,000–200,000 (US$80–350) for individuals, as per the Forestry, Wildlife and Fisheries Law (National Assembly of Cameroon, 1994, arts. 78, 101, 146, 155, 162).

18 Money laundering of proceeds from wildlife trade crimes that qualify as environmental crimes carries a minimum fine of CFA 10 million (US$17,000) as per the anti-money laundering and terrorism financing regulation of the Economic and Monetary Community of Central Africa, which Cameroon and other Community members have adopted. The same regulation doubles the fine if organized criminal networks play a role in the money laundering, bringing the minimum financial penalty to CFA 20 million (US$35,000) (CEMAC, 2016, arts. 1(19), 8, 114, 116(3)).

19 Administrative penalties comprise a variety of civil sanctions, including financial penalties. In this review, the concept was limited to a subset of penalties applicable to government officials and to license or permit holders.

20 Community service is an alternative form of penalty that supports the goal of rehabilitation without incarceration. It is used in Canada, Germany, the United Kingdom and the United States, among other jurisdictions.

21 Annual reports are publicly accessible through the CITES Trade Database, enabling NGOS and independent researchers to carry out these kinds of check on an ad hoc basis (CITES, n.d.-n).

22 CoP16 amended Resolution 13.4 in 2013 (CITES, 2013b).

23 Author interviews with wildlife trade and crime experts from UN agencies, academia and NGOs, December 2017–February 2018.

24 Author interviews with wildlife trade and crime experts from UN agencies, academia and NGOs, December 2017–February 2018.

25 Author interviews with wildlife trade and crime experts from UN agencies, academia and NGOs, December 2017–February 2018.

26 Author interviews with wildlife trade and crime experts from UN agencies, academia and NGOs, December 2017–February 2018.

27 Author interviews with wildlife trade and crime experts from UN agencies, academia and NGOs, December 2017–February 2018.

28 Author interviews with wildlife trade and crime experts from UN agencies, academia and NGOs, December 2017–February 2018.

29 Author interviews with wildlife trade and crime experts from UN agencies, academia and NGOs, December 2017–February 2018.

30 Author interviews with wildlife trade and crime experts from UN agencies, academia and NGOs, December 2017–February 2018.

31 Author interviews with wildlife trade and crime experts from UN agencies, academia and NGOs, December 2017–February 2018.

32 Author interviews with wildlife trade and crime experts from UN agencies, academia and NGOs, December 2017–February 2018.

33 Author interviews with wildlife trade and crime experts from UN agencies, academia and NGOs, December 2017–February 2018.

34 Author interviews with wildlife trade and crime experts from UN agencies, academia and NGOs, December 2017–February 2018.

35 Author interviews with wildlife trade and crime experts from UN agencies, academia and NGOs, December 2017–February 2018.

36 Author interviews with wildlife trade and crime experts from UN agencies, academia and NGOs, December 2017–February 2018.

37 At the time of writing, all were at Legal Atlas (www.legal-atlas.net).

38 Independent researcher (www.dbrack.org.uk).

INTRODUCTION

Section 2: The Status and Welfare of Great Apes and Gibbons

As in previous editions of the *State of the Apes* series, this section examines broader issues that affect great apes and gibbons around the world. In this volume, **Chapter 7** features an overview of the population status of apes in the wild, as well as a deeper consideration of the relevance of evidence-based approaches to conservation; **Chapter 8** reports on the fight for personhood and rights for nonhuman animals, as well as the status of apes in captivity.

The online Abundance Annex—available at www.stateoftheapes.com—presents updated population estimates for apes across their ranges. In combination with figures provided in the previous volumes in this series, the annex allows for the tracking of population trends and patterns over time.

Chapter Highlights

Chapter 7. The Status of Apes: A Foundation for Systematic, Evidence-based Conservation

This chapter comprises two parts. The first focuses on the status of ape populations in their natural habitat, presenting statistics in the context of the various threats to apes and methods for interpreting population dynamics. The second part assesses the relevance of evidence-based conservation, highlighting the advantages of a more nuanced understanding of local contexts in the design of conservation action.

The status section is unparalleled in terms of its methodology, which aims to gather all available abundance data on all ape taxa. It collates what is understood about the main threats to apes across all ranges in Africa and Asia, namely climate breakdown, habitat loss and fragmentation, infectious disease, poaching, and human–wildlife conflict. The ubiquitous nature of these threats across all taxon highlights how global factors are at play. Identifying trends in ape distribution and density over time, this section contributes to an understanding of the impacts of these threats and allows for the design and evaluation of evidence-based conservation action. It also presents a historical overview of ape surveys, as well as current and emerging survey methods.

Photo: © Tatyana Humle

The second section demonstrates that conservation action requires accurate, site-specific socioeconomic, political and ecological data to be effective. It stresses that a thorough understanding of the complex systems at play in a conservation site is necessary if protection of nature is to be achieved. In making the case for a broader uptake of evidence-based conservation, this section presents a case study on the positive impacts of such an approach in the eastern Democratic Republic of Congo.

Chapter 8. The Campaign for Nonhuman Rights and the Status of Captive Apes

The first part of this chapter explores the struggle for personhood and rights for nonhuman animals. The second part updates and broadens the captive ape statistics that are included in each volume of the *State of the Apes* series.

The chapter begins by describing the strategic litigation campaign of the Florida-based Nonhuman Rights Project (NhRP), which argues that nonhuman animals such as chimpanzees deserve fundamental rights based on their complex cognition and autonomy. The NhRP strategy draws on the experience of the abolitionist and civil rights movements, situating the campaign for nonhuman rights in the broader context of struggles for social justice. The NhRP initially brought cases on behalf of individual captive apes in the United States, under the common law system; it subsequently expanded its campaign beyond chimpanzees to include elephants, thereby calling for an unprecedented consideration of nonhuman rights of species beyond humans' closest relatives. This section also demonstrates that the consideration of "personhood" for great apes has resulted in more explicit acknowledgment of rights in some civil law jurisdictions, including Brazil.

Photo: © Lincoln Park Zoo

The second part of this chapter presents captive ape population statistics and discusses the regulatory landscape affecting them. While data gaps and quality concerns preclude an accurate estimate of the total number of apes in captivity worldwide, available data suggest that the number of apes in most zoos is relatively static. In contrast, rescue centers and sanctuaries are taking in apes at an unsustainably high rate, suggesting that urgent measures are needed to combat the illegal trade in apes. Increases in the size or number of sanctuaries are often followed by surges in arrivals, indicating that insufficient space for seized and voluntarily released apes is a critical barrier to enforcement and compliance.

CHAPTER 7

The Status of Apes: A Foundation for Systematic, Evidence-based Conservation

Introduction

Starting in the 1970s, biodiversity loss took on the dimensions of a global conservation crisis (Junker *et al.*, 2012). In view of evidence that human activities were threatening the survival of apes, conservationists recognized the need to develop a better understanding of how many individuals remained in the wild. Scientists have been refining population survey methods ever since. By the end of the decade, systematic field survey data collection allowed for the inference of abundance, enabling large-scale systematic surveys across great ape ranges. Continuous advances in methods development and the creation of the A.P.E.S. database—a project of the International Union for Conservation of Nature (IUCN) Species Survival Commission

—have further enabled the compilation of large survey data sets to estimate total ape abundance for all 14 great ape taxa in Africa and Asia (IUCN SSC, n.d.-a). The A.P.E.S. database is currently being expanded with the aim of making reliable population estimates available for the 20 gibbon taxa.

This chapter presents and contextualizes broad abundance estimates. It reviews the main threats to all ape taxa; examines the history of surveying apes, current methodology and promising innovations; and assesses the abundance data to identify population trends. The chapter goes on to provide an overview of evidence-based conservation and its advantages. It introduces the concept of horizon scanning as a way to anticipate threats, mitigate their impacts and capitalize on opportunities (Sutherland et al., 2019b). Detailed ape abundance estimates are presented in the online Abundance Annex on the *State of the Apes* website, www.stateoftheapes.com.

The key findings include:

- Africa is home to about 730,000 great apes, including fewer than 300 mature Cross River gorillas, whose population is by far the smallest; in Asia, the total orangutan population is around 150,000, including about 800 Tapanuli individuals.

- All 20 gibbon taxa make up an estimated 600,000 individuals, one-quarter of whom are Bornean white-bearded gibbons.

- All ape taxa except the mountain gorilla are in significant decline. The population size of both Grauer's gorilla and the western chimpanzee dropped by about 80% between the 1990s and 2015. The Bornean orangutan experienced a 50% decline between 1999 and 2015; up to 80% of these great apes may vanish by 2080. All but one of the 20 gibbon taxa have suffered a reduction ranging from 50% to 80% of their populations since the 1970s.

- Urgent action is required to prevent catastrophic declines of small, isolated gibbon populations, such as the 34 remaining Hainan gibbons in on an island off southern China and the 200 Gaoligong gibbons on the Chinese mainland.

- The most pressing threats to all apes include habitat loss and fragmentation; infectious disease; poaching for wild meat and the live ape trade; and human–wildlife conflicts.

- To be accurate, assessments of conservation efforts require up-to-date information on ape populations and the threats facing them.

- The further development of an evidence-based conservation framework, building on concepts from socioecological and complex systems, is essential.

- There is a need for more systematic evaluations of conservation strategies so that effective approaches may be identified and strengthened with the aim of ensuring the survival of all ape species.

The Importance of Information on Apes

The IUCN Red List categorizes all ape taxa as "critically endangered" or "endangered," with the exception of the "vulnerable" eastern hoolock (*Hoolock leuconedys*). If apes are to avert extinction, they require immediate, effective conservation measures at the local, national and international levels (see the Apes Overview). To be able to design and evaluate such actions, conservationists principally rely on:

- baseline abundance data, which reveal how many individuals of targeted species are left in the wild at the start of an intervention;

- ongoing monitoring of ape populations —through systematic surveys and biomonitoring—to be able to infer ape population density, abundance and changes; and

- information on the distribution and the intensity of the prevailing causes of population contractions, such as hunting, habitat loss and fragmentation, and infectious diseases.

Such data allows for quantitative trend analysis as well as assessments of the importance of different habitats for the conservation of apes, including potential release sites for the reintroduction or translocation of individuals and the most appropriate sites for the creation of new protected areas (Campbell, Cheyne and Rawson, 2015; Cheyne, 2006; Plumptre and Cox, 2006). The IUCN uses such information to produce its Red List, while other conservation

organizations cite it in their reporting under the Convention on International Trade in Endangered Species of Wild Fauna and Flora (CITES) and the Great Apes Survival Partnership (GRASP) of the United Nations Environment Programme (CITES, n.d.; GRASP, n.d.; IUCN, 2019).

Threats to Apes

The most pressing threats to all apes include habitat loss and fragmentation; infectious disease; poaching for wild meat and the live animal trade;[1] and killing in human–wildlife conflict. Habitat loss exacerbates the poaching threat, while the killing of adult apes enables the opportunistic capture of infants for sale on the illegal market (Plumptre *et al.*, 2015; Singleton *et al.*, 2017).

Photo: The most pressing threats to all apes include habitat loss and fragmentation, infectious disease, poaching for wild meat or killing in conflicts. Large-scale hardwood timber extraction, Gabon. © Jabruson (www.jabruson. photoshelter.com)

TABLE 7.1

Main Threats Facing African Great Apes, by Taxon

Taxon	Main threats	Sources
Bonobo *Pan paniscus*	Disease	Fruth *et al.* (2016); Hickey *et al.* (2013); IUCN and ICCN (2012); Sakamaki, Mulavwa and Furuichi (2009)
	Habitat loss, fragmentation and degradation due to shifting agriculture, mining and infrastructure development	
	Poaching (for wild meat; traditional medicine and ritual; indiscriminate). N.B. Trafficking of live orphans is a by-product of the wild meat trade	
Central chimpanzee *Pan troglodytes troglodytes*	Disease	Maisels *et al.* (2016); Strindberg *et al.* (2018)
	Habitat loss, fragmentation and degradation due to extractive industries, commercial agriculture and infrastructure development	
	Poaching (for wild meat; indiscriminate). N.B. Trafficking of live orphans is a by-product of the wild meat trade	
Nigeria–Cameroon chimpanzee *Pan t. ellioti*	Disease	Oates *et al.* (2016)
	Habitat loss fragmentation and degradation due to shifting and commercial agriculture	
	Poaching (for wild meat; indiscriminate; human–wildlife conflict)	
Western chimpanzee *Pan t. verus*	Disease	Humle *et al.* (2016); Kühl *et al.* (2017)
	Habitat loss, fragmentation and degradation due to shifting and commercial agriculture, extractive industries and infrastructure development	
	Poaching (for wild meat; traditional medicine and ritual; indiscriminate; human–wildlife conflict; for live capture)	
	Trafficking of live animals	
Cross River gorilla *Gorilla gorilla diehli*	Disease	Bergl *et al.* (2016)
	Habitat loss, fragmentation and degradation due to shifting and commercial agriculture	
	Poaching (for wild meat; indiscriminate; human–wildlife conflict)	
Grauer's gorilla *Gorilla beringei graueri*	Disease	Plumptre *et al.* (2015, 2016b)
	Habitat loss, fragmentation and degradation due to artisanal mining, shifting cultivation and commercial agriculture	
	Poaching (for wild meat; traditional medicine and ritual; indiscriminate; human–wildlife conflict; collateral/incidental killing). N.B. Trafficking of live orphans is a by-product of the wild meat trade	
Mountain gorilla *Gorilla b. beringei*	Disease	Gray *et al.* (2010); Robbins *et al.* (2011); Roy *et al.* (2014)
	Poaching (indiscriminate; human–wildlife conflict; politically motivated/ civil unrest)	
Western lowland gorilla *Gorilla g. gorilla*	Disease	Maisels *et al.* (2018); Strindberg *et al.* (2018)
	Habitat loss, fragmentation and degradation due to extractive industries, commercial agriculture and infrastructure development	
	Poaching (for wild meat; indiscriminate; human–wildlife conflict). N.B. Trafficking of live orphans is a by-product of the wild meat trade	

Notes: This table does not quantify or compare the impact levels of listed threats. In addition to these threats, climate breakdown affects all great ape taxa (IUCN, 2020).

Source: GRASP and IUCN (2018, table 5)

This chapter compiles information on direct and indirect threats affecting ape populations from all available survey reports, both published and unpublished; from peer-reviewed publications; and based on expert opinion. Information on the conservation status of each taxon reflects the most recent assessments in the IUCN Red List (IUCN, 2019).

Threats to African Great Apes

Poaching for wild meat, habitat loss and degradation, and infectious diseases are common threats to all great apes in Africa (Butynski, 2001; GRASP and IUCN, 2018; IUCN, 2014; IUCN and ICCN, 2012; Kormos et al., 2003; Plumptre et al., 2010). In some areas, the trafficking of live infants is among the most significant threats to great apes (GRASP and IUCN, 2018).

Habitat loss can have various causes across range countries, such as industrial agriculture, extractive industries and large-scale development activities, including the construction of dams and other infrastructure projects (GRASP and IUCN, 2018; Kormos et al., 2014). The ongoing conversion of habitats into plantations threatens African great apes much as it has apes in Southeast Asia (Wich et al., 2014). Infrastructure and industrial development is proliferating throughout Africa and will exacerbate pressure on great apes and their habitats (Kormos et al., 2014).

Table 7.1 lists the threats affecting all great apes in Africa. Annex III presents threats to great ape populations in each African range country. Detailed descriptions of threats facing African great apes can be found in GRASP and IUCN (2018) and IUCN (2019).

Threats to Asian Great Apes

Forest loss due to conversion for agriculture, illegal logging, mining infrastructure and rural development; fires; and poaching are the main threats to the Bornean orangutans and are the cause of the dramatic reduction of their population in the past decades (GRASP and IUCN, 2018; Santika et al., 2017; Voigt et al., 2018; Wich et al., 2008, 2012b). Sumatran and Tapanuli orangutans are threatened by legal and illegal logging for timber and by habitat conversion for agriculture, as large areas of forests continue to be converted to oil palm plantations. Unless measures are taken to curtail the current rate of forest conversion and loss, 4,500 Sumatran orangutans will disappear by 2030 and 45,300 Bornean orangutans by 2050, as a result of habitat fragmentation and loss, alongside the killing and capture of these species (Voigt et al., 2018; Wich et al., 2016).

Habitat loss and poaching are the main causes of orangutan decline in both Indonesia and Malaysia. The development of oil palm plantations in both countries has played a major role in the destruction of great ape habitat (GRASP and IUCN, 2018).

More information on the threats facing orangutans is available in GRASP and IUCN (2018) and on the IUCN Red List website (IUCN, 2019). Threats to all orangutans are presented in Table 7.2.

Threats to Gibbons

Many threats affect gibbons. Some direct threats have a larger impact on gibbon populations than others, but no quantitative comparisons are possible. As several species cross international boundaries, threats vary even within species, based on location. In some places, gibbons are protected by local cultures and traditions, whereas in other areas the same species may be threatened. Nevertheless, all gibbons are affected by:

- **climate breakdown**, which leads to range shifts and possible changes in food availability (Dunbar et al., 2019; Struebig et al., 2015a, 2015b);

TABLE 7.2

Threats Facing Asian Great Apes, by Taxon

Species	Main threats	Source
Bornean orangutan *Pongo pygmaeus*	**Habitat loss, fragmentation and degradation** due to agriculture, extractive industries and fire	Ancrenaz *et al.* (2016a); Voigt *et al.* (2018)
	Poaching (for wild meat; human–wildlife conflict)	
Sumatran orangutan *Pongo abelii*	**Habitat loss, fragmentation and degradation** due to agriculture, extractive industries and infrastructure (roads)*	Singleton *et al.* (2017); Wich *et al.* (2012a, 2016)
	Poaching (conflict-related)	
Tapanuli orangutan *Pongo tapanuliensis*	**Habitat loss, fragmentation and degradation** due to agriculture, extractive industries and construction of large-scale infrastructure (such as hydroelectric projects)	Nowak *et al.* (2017); Wich *et al.* (2012a, 2019)
	Poaching (for wild meat; conflict-related)	Wich *et al.* (2012a, 2019)

Note: * While habitat loss is a direct threat, it results in indirect threats such as the illegal trade in apes (Singleton *et al.*, 2017). In addition to these threats, climate breakdown affects all great ape taxa (IUCN, 2020). This table does not quantify or compare the impact levels of listed threats.

Source: GRASP and IUCN (2018, table 9)

- **disease transmission**, especially as a result of contact with humans (such as through the live animal trade) and due to susceptibility to new diseases, including Covid-19 (Campbell, Cheyne and Rawson, 2015);

- **habitat loss, fragmentation and degradation** due to artisanal mining, infrastructure development, and shifting local and commercial agriculture (Ancrenaz *et al.*, 2015; Cheyne *et al.*, 2016a; Gray, Phan and Long, 2010; Kakati, 2000); and

- **poaching,** which can be either intentional or incidental, and may be related to resource conflicts; local markets; traditional medicinal practice and other customs; and subsistence hunting and the wild meat trade, whose by-products include the trafficking of live orphans

(Nijman, Yang Martinez and Shepherd, 2009; Yin *et al.*, 2016).

The volume of gibbons available for sale on social media and used as photo props indicates that the extraction of infants from the wild is ongoing, and possibly increasing. Demand for these apes is fueled by their growing exposure as pets, including online, and the proliferation of gibbons as photo props in hotels and on beaches that are frequented by tourists (Brockelman and Osterberg, 2015; Osterberg *et al.*, 2015).

While it is not possible to estimate the precise impact of hunting for wild meat on gibbons, research indicates that populations in China, the Lao People's Democratic Republic (PDR), Myanmar, Thailand and Viet Nam are particularly at risk; hunting for cultural purposes takes place in the Mentawai Islands of Indonesia; and removal of gibbons from the wild for the live animal trade (Phoonjampa and Brockelman, 2008; Quinten *et al.*, 2014; Smith *et al.*, 2018; Yin *et al.*, 2016). In general, poachers for wild meat do not specifically target gibbons. The killing of a mother may enable the opportunistic capture of infants for sale into the live animal trade (Osterberg *et al.*, 2015).

The Status of Apes

Historical Records of Ape Status

Great Apes

Historical records on the status of great apes date back to the 19th century (Schlegel and Müller, 1839–1844; Schouteden, 1930; Schwarz, 1929). Most of these sources document the distribution or commonness of great apes in different African and Asian landscapes; others comprise anecdotes from travelers and colonial officials who reported on the presence or absence of great apes in particular locations (Coolidge, 1933; Kramm, 1879).

Many provide maps or written reports of where great apes were sighted or collected for museums and zoological institutions (Coolidge, 1933; Miller, 1903).

It was only in the mid-20th century that scientists arrived at initial estimates of the number of individual apes living on the planet. At the time, broad ranges were provided as population figures for some taxa, as abundance was inferred based on experts' guesses, rather than calculated using field survey data. In 1960, scientists estimated that there were more than one million chimpanzees (*Pan troglodytes*), fewer than 100,000 western gorillas (*Gorilla gorilla*) and 3,000–15,000 eastern gorillas (*Gorilla beringei*),[2] while the size of the bonobo (*Pan paniscus*) population was thought to be about 100,000 in the 1970s (Butynski, 2001; Emlen and Schaller, 1960). For a long period, bonobos were thought to be eastern chimpanzees; they were only recognized as a separate taxon in 1929 (Schwarz, 1929). Meanwhile, primatologists with a focus on Asian great apes speculated that 15,000–90,000 Bornean orangutans (*Pongo pygmaeus*) remained in the 1970s and 1980s; they estimated that only 5,000–15,000 Sumatran orangutans (*Pongo abelii*) persisted in the wild in the 1970s and revised that figure to about 6,600 in 2000 (Rijksen, 1978; Wich *et al.*, 2008).

Scientists only began to collect field survey data systematically to infer great ape abundance in the late 1970s and early 1980s (Teleki and Baldwin, 1979; Tutin and Fernandez, 1984). In the field of primatology, the task was facilitated through the introduction of distance sampling methods, which allowed for large-scale, systematic surveys across great ape ranges (Buckland *et al.*, 2010). In the 1990s and the following decade, the development of additional techniques enabled scientists to generate abundance estimates for many species, which provided the basis for calculating population sizes of all 14 currently recognized taxa of great ape (see the Apes Overview).

Gibbons

Gibbons persist across much of their historic range, with 20 species covering 11 countries (Alfano *et al.*, 2016; Carbone *et al.*, 2014; Kheng *et al.*, 2018; see the Apes Overview).[3] Recent extinctions have occurred in China, however: two species have been extirpated in the past 50 years—the lar gibbon (*Hylobates lar*) and the northern white-cheeked crested gibbon (*Nomascus leucogenys*) (Fan, Fei and Luo, 2014). There is clear evidence that extant gibbon species occupied a larger range across China in the past and that their current distribution has been affected by human disturbance (Chatterjee, 2009; Chatterjee, Tse and Turvey, 2012; Fan, Fei and Luo, 2014; Li *et al.*, 2018). In addition, new information is coming to light about a gibbon species that went extinct in the last 2,000 years, raising questions about how many other species are waiting to be discovered in the fossil record (Turvey *et al.*, 2018).

A History of Ape Surveys

Surveying Great Apes

For a long time, field survey output on great apes was confined to the production of maps showing locations of occurrence or geographical distributions (Coolidge, 1933; Schouteden, 1930). The limitation was most probably due to the difficulty of observing great apes systematically in dense tropical rainforests, their prime habitat. One of the first attempts to quantitatively estimate the population size and density of a great ape taxon was conducted for mountain gorillas (*Gorilla berengei berengei*) in 1959, but the result suffered from considerable weaknesses (Emlen and Schaller, 1960). Initial survey methods were basic, as scientists attempted to estimate the total population size of a taxon using nest counts of different groups (Plumptre, Sterling and Buckland, 2013).

In the late 1960s, statisticians and field biologists started to develop more reliable quantitative survey methods, which facilitated more accurate estimation of animal population sizes (Plumptre and Cox, 2006). Almost all of these techniques are sample-based, which means that not all individuals of a population need to be counted. Instead, counts are done at selected locations and statistical methods are used to infer total population size. One of these methods—transect sampling—became particularly popular as it permits wildlife statisticians to estimate animal abundance reliably using a set of transects randomly placed across a study area (Plumptre, 2000; Plumptre, Sterling and Buckland, 2013).

In the early 1980s, scientists conducted the first large-scale field surveys on chimpanzees and gorillas in Gabon, using a combination of transect sampling and nest counting, as well as estimation of nest decay time and nest construction rates, to convert the number of nests into the number of apes (Tutin and Fernandez, 1984). This work was the starting point towards the systematic surveying of all great ape taxa. The initial survey method was continuously refined and the methodology, combining ape nest counts with line transect sampling, became the most commonly used approach to estimate ape population density, in view of its robustness and accuracy (Plumptre, Sterling and Buckland, 2013). Since the first large-scale surveys in Gabon, hundreds of field surveys have been conducted using this methodology over extensive areas of ape habitat in Africa and Asia; most of these studies can be found in the A.P.E.S. Portal (IUCN SSC, n.d.-b).

In recent years, developments in genetics, sensor technology and statistics led to a diversification of survey methods that can be applied to surveying great apes. For example, capture–recapture methods use the proportion of individuals identified multiple times or only once during a survey to infer

population size (Arandjelovic *et al.*, 2011; Guschanski *et al.*, 2009; White *et al.*, 1982). Nowadays, scientists use genetic capture–recapture methods—as well as camera traps—for estimating great ape abundance (Arandjelovic and Vigilant, 2018; Després-Einspenner *et al.*, 2017; McCarthy *et al.*, 2018). Capture–recapture methods provide much higher precision and accuracy than counting indirect ape signs, such as nests. Since individuals need to be identified, however, these methods are usually more time-consuming. Capture–recapture is now used in combination with genetic methods for estimating the size of the increasing population of mountain gorillas (Hickey *et al.*, 2019; Roy *et al.*, 2014). Distance sampling with camera trapping has also become a promising approach for surveying great apes (Cappelle *et al.*, 2019).

> The IUCN Section on Small Apes is working on best practice guidelines for surveying and monitoring gibbons to help alleviate some of the many practical, analytical and interpretation issues with gibbon population data.

Surveying Gibbons

The earliest surveys of gibbons were carried out using transects (Brockelman and Ali, 1987; Carpenter, 1940). Acoustic monitoring was developed in the 1980s and has since been used as the primary survey method for gibbon population surveys (Brockelman and Srikosamatara, 1993; Cheyne *et al.*, 2008, 2016a; Hamard, Cheyne and Nijman, 2010; Nijman and Menken, 2005).[4] For many fragmented gibbon populations, density information is only available from one-off surveys, and there are no long-term trend data or population monitoring, especially for populations outside of protected areas (Cheyne *et al.*, 2016a). Another challenge is estimating populations where group size is not known, and where it is easy to miss non-adult gibbons (Cowlishaw, 1992). The IUCN Section on Small Apes is working on best practice guidelines for surveying and monitoring gibbons to help alleviate some of the many practical, analytical and interpretation issues with gibbon population data (IUCN SSC PSG SSA, n.d.-b).

Future Directions in Data Collection and Analysis

Experts are developing a number of innovative technologies for surveying wildlife, in part aided by the ongoing refinement of equipment for storing and analyzing acoustic data (Corrada Bravo, Álvarez Berríos and Aide, 2017; Xie *et al.*, 2017). The following technologies in particular may allow for more precision in the estimation of population size of ape taxa:

- **Arboreal (canopy) camera traps** (Bowler *et al.*, 2017; Gregory *et al.*, 2014). Camera trapping is now a well-established method of collecting data for wildlife research and conservation, particularly for studying rare and elusive species (Ancrenaz *et al.*, 2014; Cheyne *et al.*, 2013, 2016b, 2018). Until recently, however, such traps were only placed near the ground to study terrestrial species. Using camera traps in the canopy can provide new insight into arboreal activities of gibbons and great apes, as well as many other species.

- **Passive acoustic monitoring** with autonomous recording arrays. Scientists increasingly advocate this type of monitoring in tropical ecosystems as a valuable and cost-effective tool for rapid inventories, as it has been used successfully to detect elusive species in densely forested habitats (Deichmann *et al.*, 2018; Ribeiro, Sugai and Campos-Cerqueira, 2017). In recent years, many researchers have started to use passive acoustic monitoring with audio recording devices, often referred to as autonomous recording units, to collect auditory data related to animal abundance and occupancy (Browning *et al.*, 2017; Heinicke *et al.*, 2015; Kalan *et al.*, 2015, 2016; Mellinger *et al.*, 2007). The method has also been used to facilitate anti-poaching law enforcement (Astaras *et al.*, 2017).

■ **Drones carrying acoustic recorders.** Unmanned aerial vehicles, also known as drones, have been employed in several cases to survey great ape nests (Szantoi *et al.*, 2017). Given recent improvements in flight times and the capacity to accommodate payloads—such as lighted cameras and infrared cameras—such vehicles may become increasingly useful for surveying gibbons in remote areas (Alexander *et al.*, 2018). Equipped with acoustic recorders, they could be used to conduct call surveys. The use of drones needs to be explored further before any methods can be recommended for gibbon surveys, however.

Methods for Studying Populations

Population Size Estimates

Methods for Estimating Great Ape Population Sizes

Population abundance figures in this chapter are drawn from peer-reviewed publications, published and unpublished reports, and research and conservation organizations; some are based on guesstimates from experts. Country- and taxon-level estimates were derived using combined estimates from site-level surveys conducted over the past two decades. In this context, sites include protected areas and their buffer zones, unprotected areas, and logging or mining concessions. Additional estimates are based on spatial predictions, which rely on various modeling approaches. These approaches take into consideration key environmental variables that are known to influence ape abundance, such as forest cover, human impact, topography and rainfall; they also factor in the number of nests observed along line transects in previously surveyed areas

(Plumptre *et al.*, 2010, 2016c; Strindberg *et al.*, 2018; Voigt *et al.*, 2018; Wich *et al.*, 2016). For mountain gorillas, the genetic capture–recapture method is used to arrive at estimates (Roy *et al.*, 2014).

Surveying populations of great apes and other large mammals is a challenging task since they occur at low densities and visibility in their forested habitat is low (Kouakou, Boesch and Kühl, 2009). Moreover, counting all individuals in their home range is generally not possible over large areas (Reynolds and Reynolds, 1965). Therefore, primatologists count signs of ape presence, such as nests, dung and feeding remains, rather than individual apes themselves (Kühl *et al.*, 2008). The standard method of surveying great ape populations is to count nests along line transects, since all weaned individuals build a new nest to sleep in every night (Fruth, Tagg and Stewart, 2018; Ghiglieri, 1984; Stewart, 2011). Nests remain visible for a long time and are therefore much more abundant than the individual apes.

A large proportion of the survey data used to compute the estimates was collected using systematic line transect distance sampling methods and IUCN best practice guidelines (Buckland *et al.*, 2001, 2007; Kühl *et al.*, 2008). The methods of surveying great apes are described in Kühl *et al.* (2008). They include distance sampling along line transects, but more recently, apes have also been successfully surveyed using camera traps. Cameras can be used as point transects for distance sampling, and to sample images of individuals using spatially explicit capture–recapture methods (Cappelle *et al.*, 2019; Després-Einspenner *et al.*, 2017).

Methods for Estimating Gibbon Population Size

Common methods for surveying gibbons include occupancy modelling, transect walks and fixed-point counts of songs (acoustic

> "Surveying populations of great apes and other large mammals is a challenging task since they occur at low densities and visibility in their forested habitat is low. "

monitoring).[5] If enough surveyors are available, they can use numerous fixed listening posts positioned uniformly over the survey area—for example, 500–800 m apart—for several consecutive days to detect different groups and lone individuals. They can repeat this exercise 2–3 times to confirm that they always detect the same groups and individuals. Next, they can map and triangulate the data to gain a better idea of the gibbons' locations. They can then calculate the density using a formula that takes into account the effective listening area, the calling probability of the gibbons in that survey site and the number of groups heard. The IUCN Section on Small Apes provides sample spreadsheets and a full guide on its website (IUCN SSC PSG SSA, n.d.-a).

Estimating gibbon population size presents a number of challenges. As with surveys of great apes, efforts to count gibbons are typically concentrated in protected areas, while other areas remain unsampled, which can lead to underestimates. Other complications relate to the nature of gibbons, specifically that they are highly mobile, elusive and arboreal. They are difficult to spot due to their preference for the upper canopy and may flee or hide when approached by humans (Nijman, 2001).

Statistical accuracy has improved with the development of new methods, allowing today's practitioners to expect robust research results that can withstand the scrutiny of fellow conservationists, academics, government agencies and the general public. Recent advances in statistical modelling also make possible a reassessment of historical data, which could shed additional light on gibbon population size. Even surveys that are not designed to inform conservation policies or the management of protected areas—including certain classic behavioral studies—may provide useful insights into population size and related data (Bartlett, 2009; Chivers, 1977; Srikosamatara, 1984).

Photo: Gibbons are highly-mobile, cryptic, arboreal species and this raises challenges for surveying and monitoring. © Kike Arnal/ Arcus Foundation

Population Trends

Great Apes

Population trends presented in this chapter were determined using various modeling approaches, based on nest data for sites where at least two surveys for two different time periods were available, or on a compilation of taxon-specific abundance information from available survey reports and peer-reviewed literature. All of this information was extracted from the A.P.E.S. database (IUCN SSC, n.d.-a). Arriving at rate-of-change estimates involved modeling the impact of time on ape nest encounter rates. The change in these rates, between two time periods, served as a proxy for ape population change (Kühl *et al.*, 2017; Plumptre *et al.*, 2015, 2016c; Strindberg *et al.*, 2018; Voigt *et al.*, 2018). Trends for the Tapanuli orangutans were based on different land cover and land use scenarios (Wich *et al.*, 2016).

Gibbons

For each taxon, trend data were obtained by assessing the number of individuals remaining, the decline over time, the area of habitat occupied by the species and the level of threats. As noted above, threats vary within species, particularly among the ones that cross international boundaries. Since 19 of the 20 species of gibbon are threatened, there is an urgent need to obtain accurate data on population size and density, primarily to allow practitioners to monitor trends and inform conservation actions, strategies and policies at all scales —from individual sites and protected areas to countries and regions. Estimates of gibbon population density and abundance are an essential component of conservation action because they reflect the extent and impact of threats as well as the efficacy of actions taken to combat them. Without such monitoring data, it is not possible to know whether efforts to conserve the world's gibbons are successful.

Population and Conservation Status of Apes

Taxon-Level Ape Abundance

African Great Ape Taxon-Level Estimates

Great apes are scattered across 21 African countries. They comprise nine taxa distributed among four species (see Table 7.1). With an estimated 350,000 or more individuals in the wild, the western lowland gorilla is the most abundant great ape taxon; in stark contrast, the Cross River gorilla has the smallest population, comprising fewer than 300 mature individuals. The current population figures for the western lowland gorilla, central chimpanzee and western chimpanzee are higher than they were about 20 years ago, not because of population increases, but rather as a result of more wide-ranging survey efforts (see Table 7.3).

Asian Great Ape Taxon-Level Estimates

Orangutans are found only on the islands of Sumatra and Borneo, in Indonesia and Malaysia (Wich *et al.*, 2008). They comprise three species distributed across five taxa: the three subspecies of Bornean orangutan (*Pongo pygmaeus*)—the Northeast Bornean orangutan (*Pongo p. morio*), Northwest Bornean orangutan (*Pongo p. pygmaeus*) and Southwest Bornean orangutan (*Pongo p. wurmbii*)—the Sumatran orangutan (*Pongo abelii*) and the Tapanuli orangutan (*Pongo tapanuliensis*) (Nater *et al.*, 2017). All are critically endangered.

Table 7.4 presents current population sizes for all orangutan taxa. Recent estimates for the Bornean orangutan and the Sumatran orangutan are higher than they were 15 years ago, largely due to improved survey techniques and coverage, which provide more

TABLE 7.3

African Great Ape Population Estimates and Status, in Descending Order of Abundance

Taxon	1989–2000		2018		
	Abundance	IUCN status	Abundance	IUCN status	Source
Western lowland gorilla *Gorilla gorilla gorilla*	94,500	Endangered	316,000*	Critically endangered	Strindberg *et al.* (2018)
Eastern chimpanzee *Pan troglodytes schweinfurthii*	75,200–117,700	Endangered	181,000–256,000	Endangered	Plumptre *et al.* (2010, 2016a)
Central chimpanzee *Pan t. troglodytes*	47,500–78,000	Endangered	128,760 (114,208–317,039)	Endangered	Strindberg *et al.* (2018)
Western chimpanzee *Pan t. verus*	25,500–52,900	Endangered	18,000–65,000	Critically endangered	Humle *et al.* (2016); Kühl *et al.* (2017)
Bonobo *Pan paniscus*	35,000	Endangered	15,000–20,000 minimum	Endangered	IUCN and ICCN (2012)
Grauer's gorilla *Gorilla beringei graueri*	16,900	Endangered	3,800 (1,280–9,050)	Critically endangered	Plumptre *et al.* (2015, 2016c)
Nigeria–Cameroon chimpanzee *Pan t. ellioti*	4,000–6,000	Endangered	4,400–9,345	Endangered	Mitchell *et al.* (2015); Morgan *et al.* (2011); Oates *et al.* (2016)
Mountain gorilla *Gorilla b. beringei*	324	Critically endangered	>1,000	Endangered	Hickey *et al.* (2019)
Cross River gorilla *Gorilla g. diehli*	200	Critically endangered	<300	Critically endangered	Bergl *et al.* (2016); Dunn *et al.* (2014); R. Bergl and J. Oates, personal communication, 2018

Notes: Abundance estimates for mountain gorillas include infants; all other estimates represent the number of weaned individuals capable of building nests. Estimates are derived from surveys and modelling approaches.

* Based on an estimate of 361,919 (302,973–460,093) for 2013 and an annual rate of decline of 2.7%.

Sources: population estimate 1989–2000: Butynski (2001); population estimate 2018: GRASP and IUCN (2018, table 3)

TABLE 7.4

Asian Great Ape Population Past and Recent Estimates, in Descending Order of Abundance

Taxon	Abundance	Survey period	Abundance	Survey period	Source
Southwest Bornean orangutan *Pongo p. wurmbii*	>34,975	2002	97,000 (73,800–135,000)	1999–2015	Voigt *et al.* (2018)
Northeast Bornean orangutan *Pongo p. morio*	15,842 (8,317–18,376)	2002	30,900 (22,800–44,200)	1999–2015	Voigt *et al.* (2018)
Sumatran orangutan *Pongo abelii*	12,000*	1996	13,900 (5,400–26,100)	2016	Wich *et al.* (2016)
Northwest Bornean orangutan *Pongo pygmaeus pygmaeus*	1,143–1,761	2002	6,300 (4,700–8,600)	1999–2015	Voigt *et al.* (2018)
Tapanuli orangutan *Pongo tapanuliensis*	n/a*	1996	767 (231–1,597)	2000–12	Nowak *et al.* (2017); Wich *et al.* (2019)

Notes: * The Sumatran and Tapanuli orangutans were treated as the same species until 2017. All orangutan taxa are critically endangered.

Sources: 1996: Rijksen and Meijaard (1999); 2002: Wich et al. (2008); 2016 and 2018: GRASP and IUCN (2018, table 7)

accurate data for predictions (GRASP and IUCN, 2018; Voigt *et al.*, 2018; Wich *et al.*, 2016). Tapanuli orangutans were studied as a distinct taxon for the first time in 2017 (Nater *et al.*, 2017). Prior to that, they were thought to be a population of the Sumatran orangutan.

Gibbon Taxon-Level Estimates

Taxonomic studies and surveys indicate that gibbon populations are in decline, more and more fragmented and isolated, and at increasing risk of local extinction (Fan *et al.*, 2017). There is a dearth of data for some species, such as the Gaoligong hoolock (*Hoolock tianxing*) population, some of which occurs in an area of Myanmar that is experiencing severe civil unrest (Fauna and Flora International Myanmar, personal communication, 2018). Conservation measures are urgently required to prevent small, isolated gibbon populations from declining further. An estimated 300 Gaoligong hoolocks in nine locations and all 34 Hainan gibbons (*Nomascus hainanus*) in one location are among at-risk populations whose numbers are already critically low (Fan P.-F., personal communication, 2018).

The Bornean white-bearded gibbon (*Hylobates albibarbis*)—with a population of about 120,000 individuals—Müller's gibbon (*Hylobates muelleri*), the pileated gibbon (*Hylobates pileatus*) and the siamang (*Symphalangus syndactylus*) are the most numerous taxa (see Table 7.5). An estimated 60% of large gibbon populations tend to be found outside protected areas (Cheyne *et al.*, 2016a; Guan *et al.*, 2018).

Country-Level Ape Abundance

African Great Apes

The population sizes of bonobos, chimpanzees and gorillas vary greatly across African range countries. Almost 95% of all African great apes occur in five countries; in the order of abundance, they are the Republic of Congo, the Democratic Republic of Congo (DRC), Gabon, Cameroon and Guinea. The Republic of Congo and the DRC alone host more than 50% of the cumulative population of all nine great ape taxa. The DRC is home to the greatest number of taxa (five), followed by Cameroon (four). Burundi, Ghana, Mali, Rwanda and Senegal only host a few hundred great apes (see Annex IV).

Asian Great Apes

Far more orangutans live in Indonesia than in Malaysia. The former hosts about 141,700 individuals, while the latter is home to just over 12,000 (see Annex V).

Gibbons

Gibbons exhibit great taxonomic diversity and variations in population size across the 11 countries where they occur. The estimated cumulative population size for the 20 taxa is about 600,000 individuals. Indonesia alone hosts 9 of the 20 taxa and a cumulative population of more than 330,000 individuals; Malaysia follows with 4 taxa and 100,000 individuals; then come Myanmar (with 3 taxa and more than 55,000), Thailand (with 2 taxa and 45,000) and Cambodia (with 2 taxa and 40,000). Bangladesh is home to only one taxon—the western hoolock—whose population hovers around 200 (see Annex VI).

Population Trends

Population trends and the annual rate of population change vary across ape taxa. Of all great apes and gibbons, only the mountain gorillas are increasing in number.

African Great Apes

As noted above, apart from the mountain gorillas, all great ape taxa in Africa are

TABLE 7.5

Gibbon Population Estimates and Status, in Descending Order of Abundance

Taxon	Abundance	IUCN status
Bornean white-bearded gibbon *Hylobates albibarbis*	120,000	Endangered
Müller's gibbon *Hylobates muelleri*	100,000	Endangered
Pileated gibbon *Hylobates pileatus*	60,000	Endangered
Siamang *Symphalangus syndactylus*	60,000	Endangered
Moloch gibbon *Hylobates moloch*	48,500	Endangered
Gaoligong hoolock *Hoolock tianxing*	40,000	Critically endangered
Agile gibbon *Hylobates agilis*	25,000	Endangered
Kloss's gibbon *Hylobates klossii*	25,000	Endangered
Lar gibbon *Hylobates lar*	25,000	Endangered
Western hoolock *Hoolock hoolock*	15,000	Endangered
Bornean gray gibbon *Hylobates funereus*	10,000	Endangered
Eastern hoolock *Hoolock leuconedys*	10,000	Vulnerable
Southern yellow-cheeked crested gibbon *Nomascus gabriellae*	8,000	Endangered
Northern yellow-cheeked crested gibbon *Nomascus annamensis*	6,500	Endangered
Southern white-cheeked crested gibbon *Nomascus siki*	6,000	Critically endangered
Western black crested gibbon *Nomascus concolor*	5,350	Critically endangered
Northern white-cheeked crested gibbon *Nomascus leucogenys*	2,000	Critically endangered
Cao Vit gibbon *Nomascus nasutus*	229	Critically endangered
Hainan gibbon *Nomascus hainanus*	34	Critically endangered
Abbott's gray gibbon *Hylobates abbottii*	n/a	Endangered

Notes: Estimates are based on the number of duetting or singing adults and thus exclude subadults, juveniles and infants. Estimates are derived from surveys and modelling approaches.

Source: unpublished IUCN Red List updates, seen by the authors, 2019 (now published in: Brockelman and Geissmann, 2019, 2020; Brockelman *et al.*, 2020; Brockelman, Molur and Geissmann, 2019; Cheyne and Nijman, 2020; Fan, Turvey and Bryant, 2020; Geissmann and Bleisch, 2020; Geissmann *et al.*, 2020; Liswanto *et al.*, 2020; Marshall, Nijman and Cheyne, 2020a, 2020b; Nguyen *et al.*, 2020; Nijman, 2020; Nijman, Cheyne and Traeholt, 2020; Nijman *et al.*, 2020; Pengfei *et al.*, 2020; Rawson *et al.*, 2020a, 2020b, 2020c; Thinh *et al.*, 2020)

FIGURE 7.1

Annual Population Change among African Great Apes, by Taxon

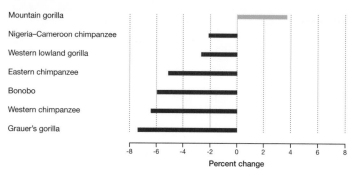

Note: For more details, see Annex VII.

Source: GRASP and IUCN (2018, table 4)

decreasing. Between 1994 and 2015, the Grauer's gorilla population declined by 7.4% per year, dropping from 16,900 to 3,800 individuals (Plumptre *et al.*, 2015, 2016c). The second largest drop was that of the western chimpanzee, whose numbers declined by 6.5% per year, with the result that their population shrank by 80.2% between 1990 and 2014 (Kühl *et al.*, 2017). In contrast, mountain gorillas experienced a growth rate of 3.7% per year between 2003 and 2010 (Gray *et al.*, 2013). The decline of the central chimpanzee between 2005 and 2013 was not statistically significant (Strindberg *et al.*, 2018). Given the extent of poaching

throughout Central Africa, however, conservationists indicate that this taxon is probably experiencing a decline that the current modeling approaches cannot detect (Maisels *et al.*, 2016). Figure 7.1 and Annex VII present an overview of the population trends in all African great apes.

Asian Great Apes

The populations of all orangutan taxa are experiencing drastic declines. The Bornean orangutan population decreased by more than 50% between 1999 and 2015; the 1999 population numbers may drop by as much as 81% by 2080 if current land cover changes continue (GRASP and IUCN, 2018; Wich *et al.*, 2015). Sumatran orangutans are expected to lose more than 30% of their current population by 2030, if the current deforestation rate continues (Wich *et al.*, 2016). The data also indicate that, by 2060, the Tapanuli orangutan population will have declined by an estimated 83% compared to 1985 levels[6] (GRASP and IUCN, 2018; Nowak *et al.*, 2017). Figure 7.2 and Annex VIII present a synthesis of the population trends in orangutans.

Gibbons

For each taxon, trend data were obtained from experts at the IUCN Red List assessment workshop held at the Singapore Zoo in November 2015 (ZOO, 2015). Collected information includes data on the number of individuals remaining, the decline over time, the area of habitat occupied by a species and the levels of threats. All gibbons are experiencing steep population declines; since 1985, 19 of the 20 taxa have lost 50–80% of their populations (see Figure 7.3 and Annex IX). Taxa with tiny populations—such as the Hainan gibbon (34 individuals left) and the Cao Vit gibbon (129 individuals remaining in China and 100 in Viet Nam)—may go extinct within a few years.

FIGURE 7.2

Annual Population Change among Asian Great Apes, by Taxon

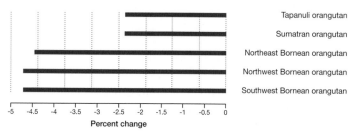

Note: For more details, see Annex VIII.

Source: GRASP and IUCN (2018, table 4)

FIGURE 7.3

Annual Population Change among Gibbons, by Taxon

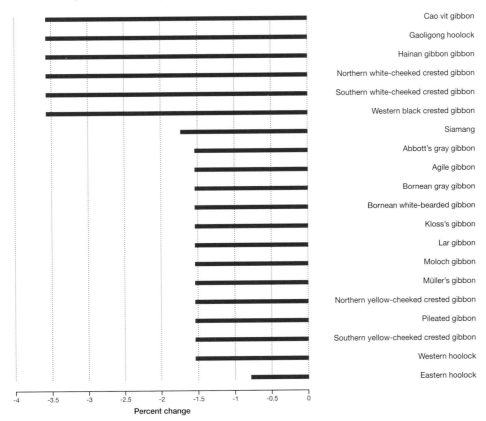

Notes: For details on survey periods, see Annex IX.

A number of taxa experienced similar levels of decline over the 45 year survey period, resulting in the same annual rate of change.

Sources: unpublished IUCN Red List updates, seen by the authors, 2019 (now published in: Brockelman and Geissmann, 2019, 2020; Brockelman *et al.*, 2020; Brockelman, Molur and Geissmann, 2019; Cheyne and Nijman, 2020; Fan, Turvey and Bryant, 2020; Geissmann and Bleisch, 2020; Geissmann *et al.*, 2020; Liswanto *et al.*, 2020; Marshall, Nijman and Cheyne, 2020a, 2020b; Nguyen *et al.*, 2020; Nijman, 2020; Nijman, Cheyne and Traeholt, 2020; Nijman *et al.*, 2020; Pengfei *et al.*, 2020; Rawson *et al.*, 2020a, 2020b, 2020c; Thinh *et al.*, 2020)

Conclusions on Ape Status

Great Apes

As discussed above, the process of assessing the status of ape populations has its roots in the 19th century, when scientists started collecting specimens for museums as part of their efforts to map ape presence. Since then, the development of various survey techniques—from distance sampling to advanced genetic, camera-trapping and statistical methods—has allowed for the surveying of vast areas across ape ranges. The A.P.E.S. database team is working with researchers and conservationists worldwide to identify, compile, update and archive all available ape survey data in a central repository, so as to facilitate reliable population estimates for all great ape taxa (IUCN SSC, n.d.-a). Available data now permit researchers to estimate the number of apes left in the wild, which was still a mystery just a few decades ago. The data indicate that:

- African habitats harbour about 730,000 great apes; and

- Asian forests are home to about 150,000 orangutans, more than 80% of whom are Bornean orangutans.

These figures—combined with the population trend data presented above and in the annexes of this chapter—underscore the urgent need for evidence-based evaluations of conservation efforts. Only through evaluations can the most effective approaches be identified and strengthened. Surveys and biomonitoring provide critical data for such evaluations, as they allow for assessments of the impacts of different approaches and tools, such as protected areas, resource management and land use schemes. When evaluation results are fed back into the redesign of conservation approaches, they can contribute to reducing the rate of decline of great ape populations.

Gibbons

Given the high rate of gibbon population decline, accurate and current data on density and abundance are urgently required so that trends may be identified and tracked. While comprehensive surveys have yet to be undertaken for many taxa, available data indicate that about 600,000 gibbons remain in the wild; the Bornean white-bearded gibbon makes up 25% of this figure. As noted above, the A.P.E.S. database is currently being expanded to cover population survey data on gibbons as well as great apes, which will enable more refined estimates for all ape taxa. Moreover, the accuracy and utility of gibbon survey and monitoring methods is likely to increase once the IUCN Section on Small Apes releases best practice guidelines.

Mitigating the threats facing gibbons throughout their ranges requires intensive, well-planned conservation actions at all scales—from individual sites and protected areas to national and regional action plans,

strategies and policy initiatives. Estimates of gibbon population density and abundance are an essential component of conservation action because they reflect the extent and impact of threats and the efficacy of actions taken to combat them. Without such biomonitoring data it is not possible to know whether conservation practices are succeeding in protecting the world's gibbons.

Urgent conservation interventions are needed to prevent small, isolated populations—such as those of the Cao Vit gibbon and Gaoligong gibbon—from reaching critically low numbers. Displaced and orphaned apes in rescue centers could potentially contribute to restoring viable populations in areas where apes have been extirpated, so long as threats can be mitigated in those locations. Since these apes are legally protected and endangered throughout their range, it can be argued that there is a legal obligation to care for them (Campbell, Cheyne and Rawson, 2015).

Evidence-Based Conservation

The Basics

For species conservation to be effective, a good understanding of the following issues is fundamental:

- species-specific needs in terms of habitat, environmental and socio-demographic requirements;

- the threats to the survival of the species and underlying drivers of those threats;

- the status of the species in terms of spatial distribution, abundance, population units and population change over time;

- ongoing conservation interventions and their effectiveness; and

- the social, economic and political factors that prevent or enable effective protection (Sutherland, 2009; see Figure 7.4).

FIGURE 7.4

Building an Understanding of Complex Socioecological Systems in Ape Habitats

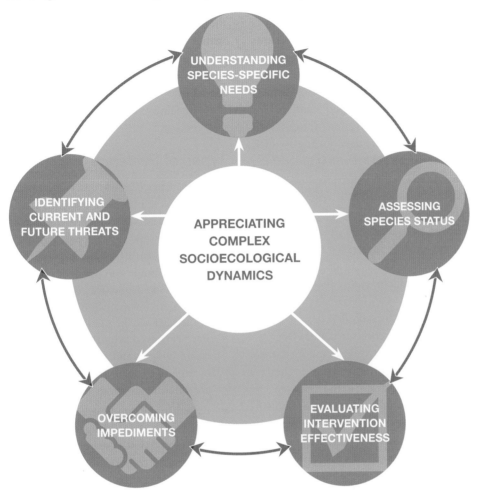

Historically, conservation was based on models established during colonial times. They tended to promote the protection of nature through national parks for reasons that were based largely on particular interests, such as to enable hunting or to preserve aesthetically pleasing landscapes or species. As a result, reserve systems throughout the world contain a biased sample of biodiversity, usually that of remote places and other areas that are unsuitable for commercial activities (Margules and Pressey, 2000). Even in the more recent past, many species conservation approaches have been based on individual experience, traditional approaches and anecdotal information. These interventions have been based on assumptions about impact and effectiveness, rather than on comprehensively designed frameworks and conservation strategies (Neugebauer, 2018). Practitioners have not made systematic use of social, economic or ecological data to inform the design of conservation responses. Nor have they methodically evaluated the effectiveness of conservation activities or shared assessments in the public domain (McKinnon *et al.*, 2015).

The first evidence-based conservation target to be specified in the literature was published in 1970 (Odum, 1970). Another three decades would pass before scientists began to employ methodical assessments of evidence as a way of furthering species conservation. A prominent example of such work is the Conservation Measures Partnership, which led to the Open Standards for the Practice of Conservation in 2004 (CMP, n.d.-a). Several scientific journals—such as *Conservation Evidence* and *Conservation Science and Practice*—also promote applied conservation knowledge. They report on the experience of researchers and conservationists who have attempted to take a systematic approach to measuring the impact of different conservation initiatives (Sutherland *et al.*, 2004; Odum, 1970, cited in Svancara *et al.*, 2005).

While the past two decades have witnessed concerted efforts to define evidence-based approaches to conservation, uptake and implementation remain limited (Junker *et al.*, 2017). The lack of enthusiasm reflects the fact that it is difficult to evaluate responses to conservation needs, which are typically complex in nature. In addition, publishing effectiveness evaluations for conservation actions can be time- and resource-intensive. If evaluations reveal that a conservation action was not effective, relevant findings may be buried in reports that do not undergo peer review and may thus remain largely unknown and inaccessible (Junker *et al.*, in press).

Conservation frameworks can inform the design of effective context-specific strategies; they can also help practitioners to overcome the institutional, social, economic and political impediments that may prevent progress towards long-lasting species conservation (Hill *et al.*, 2015). Following on from the development and implementation of a conservation framework, an essential element of evidence-based conservation is

adaptive management. This stage involves ongoing monitoring and evaluation through the collection and analysis of data; it covers the entire conservation process, which ultimately results in evidence-informed outcomes (see Figure 7.5). Ongoing monitoring of outcomes yields information that can guide the adjustment of approaches, so long as these remain flexible.

Types of Evidence

Through evidence-based conservation, practitioners look to improve the scientific basis of their work as well as their management practices. In essence, this approach involves building an evidence base and responding to it. Evidence from research, action planning and management practices is available in many different forms, including:

- **Peer-reviewed scientific journals:** To ensure a high standard of quality, panels of experts evaluate articles before they are published in these journals.

- **Expert understanding:** Scientists build up a wealth of knowledge through field studies and desk research, as do those working for conservation organizations and other civil society stakeholders, among others. The knowledge and understanding provided by these individuals can be a valuable addition to available research, especially with respect to complex habitats.

- **Gray literature:** This broad term refers to information that has not been formally published. It includes internal research and reports from non-governmental organizations (NGOs), policy institutes and think tanks; conference proceedings; government reports, policy documents and working papers; monitoring and evaluation reports; technical reports; and theses and dissertations (Haddaway and Bayliss, 2015).

FIGURE 7.5

Conservation Cycle for Project Planning, Management, Monitoring, Adaptation and Sharing

1. CONCEPTUALIZE
- Define planning purpose and project team
- Define scope, vision, targets
- Identify critical threats
- Analyze the conservation situation

2. PLAN ACTIONS AND MONITORING
- Develop goals, strategies, assumptions, and objectives
- Develop monitoring plan
- Develop operational plan

3. IMPLEMENT ACTIONS AND MONITORING
- Develop work plan and timeline
- Develop and refine budget
- Implement plans

4. ANALYZE, USE, ADAPT
- Prepare data for analysis
- Analyze results
- Adapt strategic plan

5. CAPTURE AND SHARE LEARNING
- Document learning
- Share learning
- Create learning environment

Reproduced from: CMP (2013, p. 5)

- **Indigenous knowledge:** There is growing recognition that indigenous and local knowledge can, and should, inform science and management planning to enhance the effectiveness of interventions (Raymond *et al.*, 2010).

Using an Evidence-Based Conservation Framework for Apes

An effective conservation strategy for widely distributed species, such as many ape taxa, has the following components: species protection; site/habitat conservation and management; and conservation and management in the wider landscape (such as outside protected areas or within industrial concessions). Each site has a specific cultural, political, social and economic context that not only bears influence on threats to apes, but also on how those threats affect the species and the habitat. Although conservationists generally understand broad threats, they tend to have an incomplete awareness of the complex dynamics at play in local socioecological systems; the effectiveness

TABLE 7.6

Examples of Challenges to Conservation

Category	Challenge	Example
Social	Cultural preferences	■ Great ape meat is prized among some urban communities, leading to targeted commercial hunting (Tagg *et al.*, 2018). ■ Some traditional communities depend heavily on hunting and the harvesting of natural resources (Caniago and Stephen, 1998; Loibooki *et al.*, 2002).*
Economic	Conservation costs borne mainly locally	■ Local communities bear a disproportionate share of the costs of ape conservation (Green *et al.*, 2018).
	Economic targets out-weigh conservation goals	■ When economic development clashes with conservation goals, the former is generally given priority, particularly in developing countries, where vast segments of the population live in poverty (Kormos *et al.*, 2014).
	Poverty	■ In range states, which are among the poorest in the world, many people depend on the harvesting of natural resources as a primary source of food or income. Under some circumstances, the result can be unsustainable use (Gadgil, Berkes and Folke, 1993).
	Increasing resource demand	■ Human population growth is generally high (about 3%) in African range states, which can lead to increases in levels of commercialized hunting and unsustainable use of natural resources, including endangered species (World Population Review, 2019). ■ Demand for timber, minerals and other natural resources continues to drive road expansion into remote forest areas (IUCN, 2014; Kormos *et al.*, 2014). ■ Increasing global demand for resources may lead to falling food imports to range states and result in further agricultural expansion into ape habitat (FAO, 2017).
Institutional	Lack of inclusion	■ Many conservation efforts use top–down approaches (Brechin and West, 1990). As a result, conservation planning and implementation often exclude indigenous and other local communities, inhibit the traditional use of natural resources and fail to incorporate valuable indigenous knowledge and traditional conservation practices (Becker and Ghimire, 2003).

of conservation interventions, policies and strategies; and the institutional, social, political and economic challenges to species conservation (see Table 7.6).

Ape species also vary significantly in their socioecology, demography and behavior, which has implications for their conservation and means that commonly used conservation approaches—such as co-use of areas by humans and apes—are not always viable for apes (Hockings *et al.*, 2015; Woodford, Butynski and Karesh, 2002). Unlike many other species, great apes are large-bodied, have slow life histories and exhibit low reproductive rates, such that the loss of even a few individuals has severe consequences for the persistence of populations (Duvall, 2008; Duvall and Smith, 2005; Marshall *et al.*, 2016; Wich, de Vries and Ancrenaz, 2009). Consequently, common conservation strategies that are applied for other species, including ones that feature sustainable offtake rates, are not viable options for apes (Covey and McGraw, 2014; Noutcha, Nzeako and Okiwelu, 2017).

Ape conservation practice often requires immediate action, leaving little time and resources for a systematic assessment. The

Category	Challenge	Example
Strategic	Insecure land tenure	■ Most ape range countries have insecure land tenure systems (Robinson *et al.*, 2018). Without tenure security, it can be difficult to encourage long-term, sustainable investments, such as soil conservation and tree planting (Holden, Deininger and Ghebru, 2009).
	Corruption	■ Government corruption is associated with poor environmental performance (Peh and Drori, 2010).
	Poor implementation of conservation activities outside protected areas	■ Efforts to incentivize the promotion of sustainably certified products are insufficient, especially in Asian markets (Meijaard *et al.*, 2012; Mishra *et al.*, 2003; Swarna Nantha and Tisdell, 2009).
		■ Regulation of concessions to protect apes is often ineffective (Morgan and Sanz, 2007).
	Mismatch in time scales	■ Time lags between conservation planning, implementation and tangible outcomes render investment in ape conservation uncertain and reduce the motivation of funding agencies.
	Lack of dedicated long-term funding	■ Conservation projects generally receive short-term funding, but ape conservation needs more stable investment due to the complexity and long-term nature of the issues to be addressed (Tranquilli *et al.*, 2012).
	Lack of information	■ Few policymakers and conservation practitioners have access to (translated) scientific publications or evidence that could influence their management choices (Karam-Gemael *et al.*, 2018).
Capacity	Ineffective law enforcement	■ Weak capacity in law enforcement may reflect limited knowledge, skill, staffing or equipment.
		■ Corruption and weak regulatory systems contribute to wildlife trafficking (Wyatt *et al.*, 2018).
	Lack of baselines and continuous monitoring	■ Rigorous impact evaluation studies are lacking (Ferraro and Pressey, 2015; McKinnon *et al.*, 2015).
		■ Ape population estimates are generally imprecise (Kühl *et al.*, 2008).

Note: * A thorough understanding of local cultural practices is critical to ensure that not all traditional communities are categorized as hostile to conservation goals; some communities explicitly protect habitats and species, thereby facilitating the sustainable management of ecosystems (Gadgil, Berkes and Folke, 1993; Heinicke et al., 2019; Stevens, 1997).

success rate of such interventions can be maximized if an evidence-based framework and strategies are already in place (Heinicke *et al.*, 2019). Indeed, broad uptake of evidence-based conservation would build on, and contribute to, existing ape action plans (IUCN SSC PSG, n.d.). An example of evidence-based conservation practice is provided in Case Study 7.1.

Apes, and particularly great apes, receive considerable attention from the general public, conservation initiatives and the private sector, and thus serve as flagship and umbrella species for the protection of bio-diversity (Hassan, Scholes and Ash, 2005; Wrangham *et al.*, 2008). Due to this interest, they are among the most closely monitored taxonomic groups; by keeping a close watch on them, organizations such as IUCN, GRASP and a broad spectrum of NGOs facilitate consistent updating of status and trend assessments (Heinicke *et al.*, 2019). Compared to most other species, apes are thus relatively well placed candidates for an evidenced-based conservation framework, given that the necessary data, will, interest and funding are more readily available (Robbins *et al.*, 2011).

Integrating Evidence into Conservation

The successful integration of evidence into the conservation process—from development to implementation and throughout adaptive management—relies on the collection and sharing of relevant, high-quality data, in particular through:

- **appropriate research design** that sets out best practice for rigorous testing of interventions, reporting on effectiveness, and standards of implementation, ideally as applied to research that focuses on conservation priorities and needs;

- **increased sharing of data and findings** from conservation research, practice and assessment among all stakeholders—including conservation practitioners, researchers, NGOs, governments and the private sector—in a way that is accessible to all, including through translations into relevant languages; and

- **databases of references, summaries of findings and systematic reviews**, including gray literature, to enable easy identification of relevant evidence for use in planning and decision-making.

Two examples of initiatives that are designed to integrate evidence into conservation are the Conservation Evidence Project and the Open Standards for the Practice of Conservation.

The Conservation Evidence project website was established as a central hub for evidence regarding conservation actions and their effectiveness. It is an open access, user-friendly tool that aims to facilitate decision-making by compiling field studies on different taxa, including apes (Conservation Evidence, n.d.-a; Junker *et al.*, 2017; Petrovan *et al.*, 2018). Conservation Evidence produced the free PRISM toolkit, which can help practitioners design robust studies to test interventions and report

effectiveness results (Dickson *et al.*, 2017; PRISM, n.d.). The project also started an initiative called Evidence Champions, designed to motivate companies, organizations, institutions, journals and individuals not only to increase the use of conservation evidence in project planning, but also to test interventions, publish results, provide weblinks to Conservation Evidence, and use the Conservation Evidence database as a tool for the submission of studies for publication (Conservation Evidence, n.d.-b).

The Open Standards for the Practice of Conservation website assembles guidance, tools, case studies and complementary materials from more than 600 organizations to facilitate systematic planning, implementation and monitoring of conservation initiatives (CMP, n.d.-b).

Horizon Scanning

Horizon scanning is an exercise that identifies and assesses emerging developments, opportunities and threats (Sutherland and Woodroof, 2009). It allows scientists and conservationists to undertake timely research and inform decision-makers about pressing issues and consequences of associated policies and practices. Conservationists have been using horizon scanning for more than a decade (Sutherland *et al.*, 2019b; Sutherland and Woodroof, 2009). The technique has gained traction as it allows for the anticipation and mitigation of threats that could otherwise go unnoticed, such that regular horizon scanning exercises are now undertaken to increase preparedness and capitalize on opportunities (Sutherland *et al.*, 2019b).

In the absence of horizon scanning, threats to apes can develop without adequate input from conservation researchers, practitioners and policymakers. The environmental consequences of the policy-driven switch from fossil to bio fuel, for example, received insufficient consideration (Sutherland and

CASE STUDY 7.1

Evidence-Based Conservation Practice: Targeting Wild Meat in Eastern Democratic Republic of Congo

In recent years, a consortium has emerged to conserve the entire population of Grauer's gorillas and significant numbers of chimpanzees in eastern Democratic Republic of Congo (DRC) (JGI, n.d.). Known as Ushiriki (which means "union" in Kiswahili), the consortium brings together more than 20 actors, signalling a shift from individual to collective, evidence-based planning and actions across a landscape of 268,800 km² (2.7 million ha) identified in an IUCN-validated conservation action plan (CAP) (Maldonado et al., 2012). The Ushiriki Consortium includes local, national and international NGOs, national and provincial representatives of the Congolese Ministry of Environment and Sustainable Development, and provincial and site-based representatives of the national nature conservation agency, the Institut Congolais pour la Conservation de la Nature.

A four-body coordination mechanism within the Ushiriki Consortium facilitates collaboration and adaptive management. The revision of the strategic framework and theories of change, as well as the prioritization of activities, are based on increasingly nuanced contextual and collective knowledge. In 2018, the consortium identified the need to add a wild meat committee to address knowledge gaps, such as the lack of baseline data on hunting, commerce and consumption of wild meat across the landscape. The committee also encourages partners to harmonize best practice approaches for behavior change. Based on emerging evidence and responses to focused research questions, the consortium develops best practices that can be applied in addressing stakeholders and their activities within the commercial wild meat value chain. Current shortcomings in this model revolve around data sharing and access. The consortium is therefore discussing how best to ensure access to the evidence—in the form of data, information, knowledge or wisdom—through an information-sharing platform and internal database (Salafsky et al., 2019).

Focused Research Design

The Community Conservation Zone of Lubutu and Walikale Territories

The CAP proposes a range of broad hypotheses; individual actors of the Ushiriki Consortium render these hypotheses specific and make them operational at the site level. The successful application of evidence-based decision-making to the wild meat trade is possible only if the scope of analysis is broadened from the site level to include the entire value chain.

Figure 7.6 (overleaf) shows the community conservation zone of Lubutu and Walikale Territories (CoCoLuWa) as a management unit comprising village networks and conservation sites that constitute a regional wild meat value chain. An understanding of the dynamics of this—or any other—management unit calls for an appreciation of the local ecology as well as social, economic and political nuances. The CoCoLuWa management unit, which occupies the community conservation corridor between Maiko and Kahuzi-Biega National Parks, is dominated by dense, humid, lowland forests with subalpine and seasonally inundated gallery forests in the eastern limits. The area harbors more than 20 flagship species, including endangered and endemic species, such as Grauer's gorilla.

Human activity in CoCoLuWa forests is evident through the presence of metal cable and nylon cords that are used for traps; empty cartridges; active and abandoned hunting, fishing and mining camps; and signs of non-timber forest product collection. Violent conflict in the management unit most often involves armed groups that seek to control resources, such as artisanal mining camps. Additional challenges to conservation include a lack of access to the region, which results in isolation and compromises access to markets.

Acquiring Baseline Data with Local Actors

Previous interventions attempted to mitigate threats by supporting the enforcement of laws on illegal hunting and wildlife trade, stakeholder education and awareness raising of laws and protected species, and protein replacement for wild meat. Due to a lack of baseline data, initiatives that promoted wild meat alternatives were not designed using evidence-based decision-making, nor was their impact properly assessed. Failure in these cases was indicated by a lack of uptake by the population.

In the CoCoLuWa management unit, the Ushiriki Consortium thus prioritized bridging the knowledge gap on baselines of killing and consumption of wild meat, specifically by fostering the involvement of local actors using dedicated funding. Local actors who implement priority activities of the CAP may be integrated into the consortium.

Behavior Change Best Practice

Current activities that seek to reduce the demand for wild meat include focused research on current livelihoods and the social, political and economic drivers for local participation in the commercial wild meat trade. The data are being used to inform a behavior change campaign. The revised CAP captures behavior change in new objectives, indicators and activities, as an evolution from awareness raising.

Asked what they consider the main obstacles to sustainable livelihoods, 70% of CoCoLuWa residents identified poverty—or, more specifically, a lack of financial means to invest in developing new activities—and 29% cited low agricultural productivity. More than two-thirds of the population (76%)

FIGURE 7.6

CoCoLuWa Conservation Zone

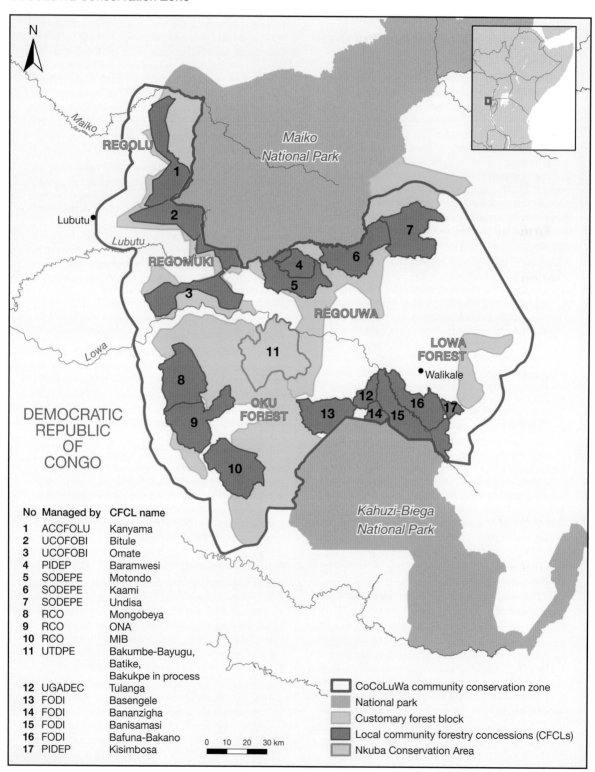

No	Managed by	CFCL name
1	ACCFOLU	Kanyama
2	UCOFOBI	Bitule
3	UCOFOBI	Omate
4	PIDEP	Baramwesi
5	SODEPE	Motondo
6	SODEPE	Kaami
7	SODEPE	Undisa
8	RCO	Mongobeya
9	RCO	ONA
10	RCO	MIB
11	UTDPE	Bakumbe-Bayugu, Batike, Bakukpe in process
12	UGADEC	Tulanga
13	FODI	Basengele
14	FODI	Bananzigha
15	FODI	Banisamasi
16	FODI	Bafuna-Bakano
17	PIDEP	Kisimbosa

Legend:
- CoCoLuWa community conservation zone
- National park
- Customary forest block
- Local community forestry concessions (CFCLs)
- Nkuba Conservation Area

0 10 20 30 km

FIGURE 7.6

Notes and Sources

Notes: ACCFOLU is the Community Association for the Conservation of Forests in Lubutu; FODI is Forest for Integral Development; PIDEP is the Integrated Program for Endogenous Development of Pygmies; RCO is the Oku Community Reserve; SODEPE is Solidarity for the Development and Protection of the Environment; UCOFOBI is the Community Union for the Conservation of Forests of Bitule; UGADEC is the Union of Associations for Gorilla Conservation and Community Development in eastern DRC; and UTDPE is the Union of Landowners for the Development and Protection of the Environment.

The managing organizations of some of the community forestry concessions are supported by other members of the Ushiriki Consortium: 1: Fauna & Flora International (FFI); 2 and 3: FFI/UGADEC; 5–7: Jane Goodall Institute: 8–10: Wildlife Conservation Society; 12–15: FODI; 17: Dian Fossey Gorilla Fund International.

Sources: Developed from shapefiles supplied by JGI.

reported that agriculture was the primary livelihood activity, while 8% said it was the main income-generating activity. In addition, 22% of the residents identified hunting as a primary revenue-generating activity, and 18% named small commerce. Approximately 45% of the respondents said they consumed wild animal protein 1–3 times per week (Ellis and Nsase, 2017).

The Jane Goodall Institute conducted studies on the drivers of wild meat commerce and demand in the CoCoLuWa management unit. Results show that wild meat commerce is often a household livelihood. Women are the buyers and sellers of wild meat, often delivering supplies to hunters who may be based in artisanal mining camps in ungoverned customary forests,[7] and trekking out the products for sale in the broader region. Hunting is generally seen as family heritage and remains a male livelihood characterized by difficult work conditions. While clandestine in nature, the sale of wild meat in the CoCoLuWa management unit occurs within a traditional female space, both in the abstract and physical sense: the market. Cultural habits, price and availability affect the demand for wild meat (Muhire and Ellis, 2018, 2019). Based on this research, The Jane Goodall Institute is openly designing and testing a behavior change campaign to reduce dependence on wild meat for food security and livelihoods.

Sharing of Data and Information

In order for this model of evidence-based conservation to succeed, increased sharing of data and information is needed. To structure and archive communications, the Ushiriki Consortium uses a Slack platform that is connected to Google Drive, in which each consortium actor, strategy, committee and priority topic has a folder. Uptake of the use of these platforms is slow, however, and thus constitutes a critical challenge towards landscape-wide, evidence-based decision-making. Presentations and discussions during biannual consortium meetings tend to serve as the main opportunities for sharing knowledge and wisdom. In the future, actors may be required to demonstrate commitment to collective objectives, including activity reporting, if they wish to participate in the consortium.

Since 2015 the Ushiriki Consortium has also struggled to identify or create a database that responds to the need for analysis at scale—via great ape distribution maps, for example. Official or unofficial organizational policies often limit the sharing of raw data. Government policies also restrict sharing of data that is deemed sensitive or high-risk. In contrast, the consortium actively promotes the sharing of analyzed data, particularly as a way to address ongoing competition, conflict and disruptions in collaboration among management unit actors.

The emerging practice of evidence-based conservation in the incredibly dynamic eastern DRC is already demonstrating the value of collaborative action. Despite challenges in relation to data collection, collation and distribution, consortium actors facilitated the official designation of an additional 5,819 km^2 (581,920 ha) of customary forests in protected area buffer zones in 2018–19. These forests are designated to reconcile forest-based livelihoods with conservation of species and habitats.

Consortium actors are also helping more than 12 community associations and more than 30 communities to increase their capacity to manage customary forests. An additional 4,422 km^2 (442,185 ha) of forests are under alternative community management structures and another 3,500 km^2 (350,000 ha) of customary forests are under participatory, inclusive, community-led processes to further extend the conservation landscape. In addition, actors in the Ushiriki Consortium manage national parks, rescue and care for apes from illegal captivity; they also engage in education, awareness raising and behavior change activities with thousands of beneficiaries. Even so, the consortium will continue to focus on how best to respond to the data and information sharing and access needs.

Woodroof, 2009). The resulting expansion of the oil palm industry into orangutan habitat in Southeast Asia massively reduced available habitat and contributed to the dramatic decline in orangutan numbers, both on Sumatra and Borneo (Gaveau *et al.*, 2014; Voigt *et al.*, 2018; Wich *et al.*, 2016). Development of industrial agriculture in African great ape range countries could follow similar trajectories. Studies on spatial dynamics and potential conservation response mechanisms need to be conducted to anticipate and alleviate future threats from such development (Ancrenaz *et al.*, 2016b; Strona *et al.*, 2018; Wich *et al.*, 2014).

For horizon scanning exercises, experts from different areas compile, research, discuss, distill and communicate a prioritized list of emergent issues relating to the question at hand. In their annual, global horizon scanning exercise for environmental issues, Sutherland *et al.* (2019a) bring together a group of experts with different backgrounds and affiliations who consult literature, their networks and social media to elicit suggestions about potential topics. They collect topics, structure them thematically and then rank them based on novelty, how likely they are to occur or be implemented, and how important they would be in that case. The experts retain the topics with the highest rank and research them further to establish their relevance and produce credible evidence. Then they revisit and discuss the issues, assign final scores and draw up a shortlist, which they share with the research community, NGOs, conservation managers and politicians.

By allowing researchers and practitioners to consider both impending threats and future opportunities, regular horizon scanning can support the move beyond reactive conservation to active conservation of ape species, all of which are at an elevated risk of extinction. The integration of experts from different fields—such as politics, social sciences, psychology and economics—can

> " Conservationists can employ systematic horizon scanning to identify nascent and future threats to ape populations, as well as conservation opportunities. "

also create a dialog and facilitate collaboration among stakeholders in other areas of conservation management, such as conservation planning and adaptive management, thereby further benefiting the conservation of ape species.

Conclusion

In view of recent and ongoing advances in conservation tools and methods, researchers and practitioners are increasingly well positioned to switch from a responsive to a vigilant, evidence-based approach to ape conservation. Such a shift would bolster their ability to identify and mitigate the increasing threats confronting ape populations throughout their ranges. In this context, a few practices and techniques hold particular promise.

First, conservationists can employ systematic **horizon scanning** to identify nascent and future threats to ape populations, as well as conservation opportunities. By integrating experts from a variety of disciplines and sectors, this process can also enhance collaboration among stakeholders.

Second, various **online communication options** allow for improved information sharing of up-to-date ape conservation data, findings, strategies, references and archives. Open platforms, for example, can be used to allow various stakeholders access to pertinent information; to structure communication among them; and, when uptake is widespread, to facilitate landscape-wide, evidence-based decision-making. When shared online in relevant languages, best practice guidelines for surveying and monitoring ape populations can help conservationists in many countries design appropriate research frameworks; avoid practical, analytical and data interpretation issues; assess the effectiveness of conservation interventions; report on standards of implementation; and overcome a variety of impediments.

Third, recent **developments in genetics, sensor technology and statistics** facilitate the surveying of great apes and gibbons. Among other approaches, capture–recapture methods, drones equipped with acoustic recorders and distance sampling with camera trapping can be used to survey vast areas and to generate more accurate abundance estimates. Passive acoustic monitoring with audio recording devices can also facilitate anti-poaching law enforcement.

Finally, evidence-based **conservation frameworks** can inform the design of effective context-specific strategies and assist practitioners in overcoming barriers to long-lasting species conservation. Such frameworks allow conservationists to complement their understanding of threats with a deeper awareness of the dynamics at play in local and regional socioecological systems; they also guide the process of evaluating the effectiveness of ongoing interventions, policies and strategies, as well as related obstacles, ideally through the collection of relevant information from peer-reviewed journals and gray literature, seasoned experts in the conservation field, and indigenous and other local communities. Basically, this type of framework enables scientists to build an evidence base and respond to it via adaptive management, with the aim of decreasing the rate of decline of ape populations.

Acknowledgments

Principal authors:[8] Tenekwetche Sop, Susan M. Cheyne,[9] Mona Bachmann, Tsegaye Gatiso, Stefanie Heinicke, Jessica Junker, Sergio Marrocoli, Elenora Neugebauer, Isabel Ordaz-Németh, Maria Voigt, Erin Wessling and Hjalmar S. Kühl

Case Study 7.1: Christina Ellis[10]

Endnotes

1   According to Ondoua Ondoua *et al.* (2017, p. viii), "The difference between hunting and poaching is the law. Poaching is the illegal killing, trapping or capture of any animal for the express purpose of either personal need or monetary gain." This chapter uses the term "poaching" to refer to the illegal killing of great apes for a number of reasons, including for wild meat; in retaliation for crop raiding or destruction; and by accident, such as through snares set for other species.

2   Note that gorilla nomenclature has changed since the 1960s. Today, the western gorilla (*Gorilla gorilla*) comprises two subspecies: the western lowland gorilla (*Gorilla g. gorilla*) and the Cross River gorilla (*Gorilla g. diehli*). In the past, the western gorilla was also referred to as "western lowland gorilla," as distinct from the eastern gorilla, today known as *Gorilla beringei* and subdivided into mountain gorilla (*Gorilla b. beringei*) and Grauer's gorilla (*Gorilla b. graueri*), a species also referred to as the eastern lowland gorilla.

3   The countries are Bangladesh, Brunei, Cambodia, China, India, Indonesia, Lao PDR, Malaysia, Myanmar, Thailand and Viet Nam.

4   For a comparison of methods, see Gilhooly, Rayadin and Cheyne (2015) and Höing *et al.* (2013).

5   Brockelman and Ali (1987); Brockelman and Srikosamatara (1993); Cheyne *et al.* (2016a); Gilhooly, Rayadin and Cheyne (2015); Hamard, Cheyne and Nijman (2010); Höing *et al.* (2013); Neilson, Nijman and Nekaris (2013).

6   In 1985, the Tapanuli orangutan was considered a subpopulation of the Sumatran orangutan (Wich *et al.*, 2016).

7   These are forests that are not allocated as CFCLs and do not have management plans, which would regulate the types of activities permitted in those spaces, and are required in CFCLs.

8   At the time of writing, all principal authors, unless otherwise stated, were affiliated with the Max Planck Institute for Evolutionary Anthropology (www.eva.mpg.de).

9   Borneo Nature Foundation (www.borneonaturefoundation.org).

10 The Jane Goodall Institute (www.janegoodall.org).

CHAPTER 8

The Campaign for Nonhuman Rights and the Status of Captive Apes

Introduction

This chapter is divided into two sections. Section I explores the fight for personhood and rights for nonhuman animals and Section II provides an update and broadening of the captive ape statistics that are included in each volume of the *State of the Apes* series.

Two millennia ago, Roman law differentiated two main categories of legal status: "person" and "thing." In more recent times, "persons" have been understood to possess the capacity for either legal rights or duties. Persons have inherent value and are visible to civil judges; they "count" in the legal system. In contrast, "things" lack the capacity for legal rights and duties. Their value is what persons give them. Things are invisible to civil judges and do not "count." In that sense, persons and things stand in complete opposition to one another, separated by a great metaphysical wall (*Byrn* v. *NYCHHC*, 1972, p. 201; Trahan, 2008).

This dichotomy between things and persons mirrors the dichotomy between welfare and rights as they presently apply to nonhuman animals.[1] Rules that govern welfare stipulate how human beings *should* treat other animals. If humans fail to abide by such rules, however, nonhuman animals lack a civil remedy. While it may be weak on its own, welfare becomes vital when combined with rights. Rights focus on how humans *must* treat other animals, and they provide nonhuman animals with a civil remedy if humans fall afoul of the law (Wise, 2017b).

The Florida-based Nonhuman Rights Project (NhRP) situates the fight to obtain fundamental legal rights for nonhuman animals in the larger context of struggles for social justice. Specifically, the NhRP utilizes a legal strategy modeled on previous and ongoing struggles in the United States: that of the abolitionists of the 18th and 19th centuries; that of the National Association for the Advancement of Colored People (NAACP) Legal Defense and Educational Fund, which began the state-by-state fight for equal rights for African Americans in 1940; and that of gay marriage advocates of the 21st century (Cole, 2016, pp. 17–93; Greenberg, 2004, pp. xi, 5; Wise, 2005).

In the United States, the NhRP has been fighting for the rights of great apes in captivity under the common law system. In a number of other countries, the same struggle is taking place under civil law. This section discusses current legal strategies and provides details on cases brought on behalf of individual apes, including Sandra, an orangutan at the Palermo Zoo in Buenos Aires, Argentina; Cecilia, a chimpanzee at Argentina's Mendoza Zoo; Hiasl, a wild-caught chimpanzee in Austria; and Suiça, a chimpanzee in the Zoological Garden of Salvador, in Bahia, Brazil. The section goes on to explore the idea of rights at the taxonomic level. The key findings include:

- In the United States, the Nonhuman Rights Project has influenced the understanding of personhood through a concerted, long-term strategic litigation campaign that argues for acknowledgment of chimpanzees' complex cognition and autonomy.

- The NhRP assumes that fair-minded judges who are persistently exposed to compelling expert evidence of chimpanzee autonomy, coupled with powerful legal arguments derived from the values and principles the judges themselves routinely espouse, will ultimately decide that nonhuman animals deserve fundamental rights that protect their fundamental interests.

- The NhRP has expanded its campaign beyond chimpanzees to include elephants, furthering unprecedented consideration of nonhuman rights in the United States beyond species that are the most closely related to humans.

- In a few civil law jurisdictions, the consideration of "personhood" for great apes has resulted in more explicit acknowledgment of rights, demonstrating value in pursuing legal campaigns.

Section II updates captive ape population statistics and discusses the regulatory landscape affecting captive apes. The key findings include:

- Details on the number, origin and welfare status of captive apes are only available for some captive settings and the quality of the data varies widely.

- Available data suggest that the number of captive apes in zoos is relatively static, although there are notable exceptions.

> **The NhRP has influenced the understanding of personhood through a concerted, long-term strategic litigation campaign that argues for acknowledgment of chimpanzees' complex cognition and autonomy.**

- Insufficient sanctuary space for seized and voluntarily released apes is a critical barrier to enforcement and compliance in many countries.

- In ape habitat countries, rescue centers and sanctuaries are taking in apes at an unsustainably high rate, indicating that urgent measures are needed to tackle the killing and capture of apes, as well as the trade in live apes.

The Struggle to Obtain Legal Rights for Non-human Animals

Background

Nowadays, under the Universal Declaration of Human Rights and the International Covenant on Civil and Political Rights, every human on Earth is considered a "person" (UN, 1948, art. 6; UN, 1966, art. 16).[2] That was not always the case. Edith Hamilton, arguably the leading classicist of the mid-20th century, reminds us of the first major turning point in the two-millennium struggle to abolish slavery. She describes slavery in ancient Greece:

> When the Greek achievement is considered, what must be remembered is that the Greeks were the first to think about slavery. To think about it was to condemn it and by the end of the second century, two thousand years before our Civil War, the great school of the Stoics, most widely spread of Greek philosophies, was denouncing it as an intolerable wrong (Hamilton, 1964, p. 24).

In the past, millions of humans—including slaves, women, children, Jews, indigenous peoples and the developmentally disabled—were treated like things. The civil rights work of the past centuries has been slow to move these humans from the "thing" side of the metaphysical wall to the "person"

side.[3] The manner in which personhood for all humans was finally established is a model for the work of the Nonhuman Rights Project (NhRP, n.d.-e). Today, all humans are legal persons, while nonhuman animals have generally remained things. For that reason, many people, judges included, erroneously believe that the metaphysical wall divides humans from other animals, rather than persons from things.

The UK's passage of the Slave Trade Act of 1807 and the Slavery Abolition Act of 1833 marked an attack on the form of slavery that rested on the "thinghood" of certain human beings (UK Parliament, 1807, 1833). The first of these acts built on a milestone judgment in the famous Somerset case, delivered 35 years prior by Lord Mansfield, who essentially abolished slavery in England (*Somerset* v. *Stewart*, 1772). The formal anti-slavery struggle did not end until 1957, with the entry into force of the Supplementary Convention on the Abolition of Slavery, the Slave Trade, and Institutions and Practices Similar to Slavery, which supplemented the League of Nations' Slavery Convention of 1926 (League of Nations, 1926; UN, 1956).

In 1976 the International Covenant on Civil and Political Rights entered into force (UN, 1966). Article 16 of the Covenant states: "Everyone shall have the right to recognition everywhere as a person before the law." It gives force to Article 6 of the Universal Declaration of Human Rights, which provides: "Everyone has the right to recognition everywhere as a person before the law" (UN, 1948).

But humans are not the only persons. Numerous kinds of nonhumans have long been considered persons in countries that use legal systems based on common law, many of which are English-speaking (*The Economist*, 2013). Well-known examples include corporations, ships and states, although the list does not end there. In 2017, the parliament of New Zealand designated the Whanganui River a person that owns its

> Details on the number, origin and welfare status of captive apes are only available for some captive settings and the quality of the data varies widely.

riverbed (New Zealand Parliament, 2017, cl. 19). It had previously designated the Te Urewera protected area a legal entity, with "all the rights, powers, duties, and liabilities of a legal person" (New Zealand Parliament, 2014, s. 11(1)). Pre-independence Indian courts designated certain Punjab mosques and a Hindu idol as "persons" with the capacity to own property or sue (*Masjid Shahid Ganj and others* v. *Shiromani Gurdwara Parbandhak Committee*, 1938; *Pramatha Nath Mullick* v. *Pradyumna Kumar Mullick*,

1925). Civil law countries, whose legal systems are derived from Roman law, are moving in similar directions (*AFADA* v. *Mendoza Zoo and City*, 2016; Tello, 2016). In 2018, the supreme court of Colombia designated the Amazon rainforest "an entity subject of rights"—that is, a "person" (Colombian Supreme Court of Justice, 2018).

Over the years, the NhRP has made numerous decisions regarding how best to mount the world's first sustained, strategic campaign for the legal rights of nonhuman

animals. The NhRP chose chimpanzees as the first plaintiffs, mainly because decades of extensive research on their highly complex cognition have revealed them to be autonomous as well as similar—and therefore more understandable—to humans. The NhRP then decided to argue that chimpanzees have legal rights under common law, which common law judges typically use while deciding cases whose outcomes are not mandated by statutes, constitutions or treaties (*NhRP* ex rel. *Tommy* v. *Lavery*,

2013). The NhRP anticipated that such judges would interpret the word "person" in the context of a statute or constitution and thus conclude, at least initially, that the term had not been intended to encompass nonhuman animals. Flexibility is touted as the glory of common law, however, and judges are required to create law in the interstices of statutes and constitutions to keep the law current with scientific discovery and the evolution of societal mores and human experience (Morrow, 2009, p. 158). The judges would need to be persuaded that, as a matter of justice, at least some nonhuman animals should be seen as persons entitled to at least some rights.

The NhRP decided that its initial lawsuits would focus on a chimpanzee's right to bodily liberty, since science has demonstrated that apes, as autonomous beings, have a fundamental interest in this freedom, and since humans can easily relate to this interest (*NhRP* ex rel. *Tommy* v. *Lavery*, 2013). The next step involved identifying persuasive legal arguments. To that end, the NhRP first studied the judicial values and principles that courts of the potential target jurisdictions—including every US jurisdiction and most other common law jurisdictions throughout the world—claimed constituted justice. Once the NhRP had decided in which jurisdictions it would first litigate, it fashioned its legal arguments accordingly.

It turns out that nearly every common law judge anywhere embraces the paramount importance of autonomy—that is, one's liberty to freely choose, within wide parameters, how one wishes to live one's life. In referring to decisions about medical treatment, for instance, New York's highest court, the Court of Appeals, states:

> In our system of a free government, where notions of individual autonomy and free choice are cherished, it is the individual who must have the final say in respect to decisions regarding his medical treatment in order to

insure that the greatest possible protection is accorded his autonomy and freedom from unwanted interference with the furtherance of his own desires (*Rivers* v. *Katz*, 1986, p. 493).

The NhRP does not claim that autonomy is a necessary condition for rights, only that it is sufficient (*NhRP* ex rel. *Tommy* v. *Lavery*, 2013). Following the legal analysis, the NhRP gathered every scientific fact that supports chimpanzee autonomy from respected experts in chimpanzee cognition and behavior worldwide. These scientists—including James Anderson, Christophe Boesch, Jennifer Fugate, Jane Goodall, Mary Lee Jensvold, James King, Tetsuro Matsuzawa, William C. McGrew, Mathias Osvath and Emily Sue Savage-Rumbaugh—filed supporting affidavits in each case (NhRP, n.d.-c).

The judicial values and principles included several senses of *equality*; the NhRP emphasizes two from the 1996 case of *Romer* v. *Evans*. It was in that case that the United States Supreme Court struck down an amendment to the Colorado Constitution that repealed existing legislation prohibiting discrimination based on sexual orientation. The Court said that, as a matter of equal protection, a classification that used a single trait to deny a class protection across the board was "at once too narrow and too broad. It identifies persons by a single trait and then denies them protection across the board" (*Romer* v. *Evans*, 1996, p. 633). Using a similar line of reasoning, the NhRP planned to argue that the inappropriate single trait was *species*. The Supreme Court also said that the amendment violated the requirement that a classification must bear a rational relationship to some "legitimate legislative end" (p. 633). The NhRP thus planned to argue that the arbitrary imprisonment of an autonomous being of any species is not a legitimate end for any government.

Finally, the NhRP decided to bring writs of habeas corpus on behalf of its plaintiffs

(*NhRP* ex rel. *Tommy* v. *Lavery*, 2013). Habeas corpus is Latin for "you have the body" and is referred to as the "great writ" (*Hamdi* v. *Rumsfeld*, 2004, p. 536). In a case the NhRP brought on behalf of two chimpanzees, Hercules and Leo, the New York County Supreme Court found:

> "The great writ of habeas corpus lies at the heart of our liberty" […] and is deeply rooted in our cherished ideas of individual autonomy and free choice […]. As "[t]he remedy against illegal imprisonment," the writ is described as "the greatest of all writs" and "the great bulwark of liberty." […] The writ of habeas corpus "has been cherished by generations of free men [sic] who had learned by experience that it furnished the only reliable protection of their freedom" (*NhRP* ex rel. *Hercules and Leo* v. *Stanley*, 2015, p. 903).

As habeas corpus writs may only be issued on behalf of a person, and not a thing, a paradox has existed whenever the writ has been wielded to demand that a thing—whether a human slave or a chimpanzee—be recognized as a person. In 18th-century England, Lord Mansfield assumed that James Somerset *might be* a person and issued the writ (*Somerset* v. *Stewart*, 1772). In the United States, however, antebellum Southern courts unanimously refused to do so whenever slaves alleged they were persons, arguing that they were things (Finkelman, 2012). The NhRP confronts this paradox whenever it demands that a court issue the writ on behalf of a nonhuman animal. It responds by urging the court to follow the example of Lord Mansfield, namely to issue the writ and then conduct the hearings, which, in Somerset's case, led Lord Mansfield to declare slavery so "odious" that common law would not support it and to order Somerset's release, thereby implicitly abolishing human slavery in England (*Somerset* v. *Stewart*, 1772, p. 19).

To alter the thinghood of a nonhuman animal, a judge must first be able to imagine that a thing could possibly be a person. Otherwise, how could a judge distinguish the claim of a chimpanzee from the claim of a chair? Lord Mansfield understood that a slave could possibly be a person. Likewise, some judges can imagine that a chimpanzee might be a person; others cannot.

Establishing Chimpanzees' Complex Cognition and Autonomy

Having established the framework for a legal strategy, the NhRP identified the above-mentioned experts, who agreed to file affidavits in which they demonstrate that chimpanzees are autonomous (NhRP,

Photo: Humans and chimpanzees demonstrate self-awareness through mirror self-recognition, alongside capacities that stem from self-awareness, such as self-reflection. Negra, CSNW © Chimpanzee Sanctuary Northwest

n.d.-c). One of them, psychology professor James King, helpfully defines autonomy as:

> behavior that reflects a choice and is not based on reflexes, innate behavior or on any conventional categories of learning such as conditioning, discrimination learning, or concept formation. Instead, autonomous behavior implies that the individual is directing the behavior based on some non-observable internal cognitive processes (King, 2013, para. 11).

> " To alter the thinghood of a nonhuman animal, a judge must first be able to imagine that a thing could possibly be a person. "

This is unsurprising, as humans and chimpanzees share almost 99% of their DNA and are evolutionarily more closely related than chimpanzees are to gorillas (IUCN SSC, n.d.; Smithsonian Institute, n.d.; Varki and Altheide, 2005; see the Apes Overview). That being the case, humans and chimpanzees share a number of attributes and traits (Anderson, 2013; Boesch, 2013; Fugate, 2013; Jensvold, 2013; King, 2013; Matsuzawa, 2013; McGrew, 2013; Osvath, 2013; Savage-Rumgaugh, 2013):

- The brains and behavior of both humans and chimpanzees are plastic, flexible and heavily dependent on learning. The brains develop and mature in similar ways, indicating that humans and chimpanzees pass through similar cognitive developmental stages.
- Both species develop "increasing levels of consciousness, awareness and self-understanding throughout adulthood, through culture and learning" (Savage-Rumgaugh, 2013, p. 6).
- Chimpanzees and humans share the "fundamental cognitive processes" that underlie their sense of being an independent agent, which is a fundamental component of autonomy (Matsuzawa, 2013, p. 7).
- Both species demonstrate self-awareness through mirror self-recognition, alongside capacities that stem from self-

awareness, such as self-monitoring and self-reflection; both are also aware of what they know and do not know.

- Chimpanzees demonstrate purposeful communication, conversation, imagination, humor and perspective-taking.
- Chimpanzees may display a sense of humor and laugh under many of the same circumstances in which humans laugh.
- Chimpanzees point and vocalize when they want another individual to notice something and can "adjust their gesturing to insure they are noticed" (Anderson, 2013, p. 5). They can communicate what they are about to do, where they are going and what assistance they want from others. They can comment on others and how they feel, answer questions about their companions' likes and dislikes, and tell researchers what other apes want. Those who understand spoken English can answer "yes/no" questions about their thoughts, plans, feelings, intentions, dislikes and likes.
- Both language-using captive chimpanzees and wild chimpanzees understand conversational give-and-take and adjust their communication to the attentional state of the other participant, using visual gestures towards an attentive partner and using more tactile and auditory gestures towards inattentive partners.
- Chimpanzees can engage in at least six forms of imaginary play, including animation, which involves pretending that an inanimate object is alive; substitution, which involves pretending that an object is something else; and imaginary private signing, in which chimpanzees lend a sign or its referent a different meaning.
- Since they possess mirror neurons that allow them "to share and relate to another's emotional state," chimpanzees can be attuned to others' experiences,

visual perspectives, knowledge states, and emotional expressions and states (Fugate, 2013, p. 5). This forms the basis for empathy—the ability to place oneself in another's situation and to identify with and understand "another's situation, feelings and motives"—which is linked to self-recognition. Thus, chimpanzees show concern for others in risky situations (Anderson, 2013, p. 4).

- Both in the wild and in captivity, chimpanzees may engage in sophisticated tactical deception, an ability related to imaginary play. This behavior, which requires attributing mental states and motives to others, allows them to devise strategies and counter-strategies designed to outwit others.

- Chimpanzees can engage in toolmaking, which implies the possession of complex problem-solving skills and evidences understanding of means–ends relations and causation. They use "tool sets"—that is, two or more tools in an obligate sequence—to achieve a goal. They might use a set of five objects—a pounder, perforator, enlarger, collector and swab—to obtain honey, for instance. Such sophisticated tool use involves choosing appropriate objects in a complex sequence to obtain a goal they keep in mind throughout the process; the sequencing and mental representation are hallmarks of intentionality, self-regulation and autonomy (McGrew, 2013, p. 6).

- At least 40 wild chimpanzee cultures exist across Africa and use combinations of more than 65 identified behaviors. Each wild chimpanzee cultural group makes and uses a unique "tool kit," which indicates that chimpanzees form mental representations of a sequence of acts aimed at achieving a goal (McGrew, 2013, p. 7). A tool kit is a unique set of about 20 different tools that chimpanzees often use in a specific sequence, such as for foraging and processing food, making comfortable and secure sleeping nests in trees, and for personal hygiene and comfort. These tool kits vary across groups; chimpanzees learn them by observing others using them.

- With respect to social culture, chimpanzees pass on widely variable social displays and social customs from one generation to the next. Thus, in one chimpanzee group, "arbitrary symbolic gestures" may communicate the desire to have sex, while in another group an entirely different symbolic gesture expresses the same desire (McGrew, 2013, p. 10).

- The most important mental abilities for culture are imitation and emulation, each of which requires learning by observation. Chimpanzees use both. They also engage in "deferred imitation," which involves copying actions that they have seen in the past. This behavior relies on capacities that are more sophisticated than direct imitation, as chimpanzees must remember the actions of another individual while replicating them in real time. These capacities for imitation and emulation are necessary for the "cumulative cultural evolution" that allows chimpanzees to build on—and maintain—customs within a group (McGrew, 2013, p. 11).

- Chimpanzees have a conscious awareness of "numerosity," which gives them a grasp of numbers.

Chimpanzees' cognitive capabilities, separately and together, have proven to be important to judges who honestly struggle to determine whether, and to what extent, chimpanzees should be legal persons with certain fundamental rights (Anderson, 2013;

> Chimpanzees demonstrate purposeful communication, conversation, imagination, humor and perspective-taking.

Boesch, 2013; Fugate, 2013; Jensvold, 2013; King, 2013; Matsuzawa, 2013; McGrew, 2013; NhRP, n.d.-c; NhRP ex rel. *Tommy* v. *Lavery*, 2018, pp. 1057–8; Osvath, 2013; Savage-Rumgaugh, 2013).

Engaging the Values and Principles of US Judges

> The NhRP's long-term strategy assumes that if fair-minded judges are persistently exposed to compelling expert evidence of a chimpanzee's complex cognition and autonomy, coupled with powerful legal arguments derived from the values and principles that the judges themselves routinely espouse, they will struggle in good faith to overcome their implicit biases.

The NhRP grounds its legal arguments in the values and principles of the judges in any jurisdiction in which it litigates, with the aim of leaving judges with four potential responses. The NhRP has grouped judges into four corresponding categories.

The "evenhanded judges" are the ones who apply their jurisdiction's fundamental values and principles of justice to the claims brought on behalf of chimpanzees. They recognize these great apes as persons with a capacity for rights, and then they fairly consider which rights chimpanzees should be entitled to.

The second category—the "temporizing judges"—are the ones who would argue that justice in their jurisdiction only *appears* to be constituted by certain fundamental values and principles, but that it actually is not. This position would have the benefit of allowing the NhRP to file new lawsuits calling for updated values and principles. To date, no US court has taken this position.

"Implicitly biased judges" may undermine their own fundamental values and principles of justice by basing their decisions on implicit bias, thereby enacting "prejudice in the form of law" (Yankwich, 1959, p. 257). Indeed:

> Present judges have been raised in a culture that pervasively views all nonhuman animals as "things." As are most of their fellow citizens, most judges are daily and routinely involved in the widespread exploitation of nonhuman animals, eating them, wearing them, hunting them, and engaging in other of the numerous

exploitive ways that the culture has long accepted. When thinking about humans, different clusters of neurons are subconsciously triggered depending upon the degree to which one identifies with the subject. Imagine how differently a judge is likely to view even such a close relative to humans as a chimpanzee (Wise, 2017a, pp. 13–14).

Many judges are therefore likely to be implicitly biased against the arguments the NhRP presents, just as they are, like everyone else, likely to be biased about race, gender, sexuality, religion, weight, age and ethnicity (Eberhardt, 2019; Project Implicit, n.d.). This bias shows that "our minds have been shaped by the culture around us. In fact, they have been invaded by it" (Banaji and Greenwald, 2014, pp. 138–9).

Implicitly biased judges bypass their own fundamental values and principles of justice to insist, *ad hoc or through the misapplication of precedent or principle,* that these cannot apply to a nonhuman animal. Rights, they say, apply only to human beings, just because they are human beings. Yet, as Martin Luther King Jr. noted, "Injustice anywhere is a threat to justice everywhere" (King, 1963). It follows that undermining the rationale for attributing rights to nonhuman animals inevitably undermines the rationale for human rights. As Robert Cover observes of judges who upheld human slavery in the 19th century, theirs is "the story of earnest, well-meaning pillars of legal respectability and of their collaboration in a system of oppression" (Cover, 1975, p. 6).

Decisions that deprive all nonhuman animals of rights merely because they are not humans are examples of biased judging. The implicit bias of US judges has long led them to undermine their own fundamental values and principles, rather than applying them to those excluded from justice. These judges once refused to grant legal rights to black people. The US Supreme Court once limited the legal right to have sex to hetero-sexuals, just as it allowed US citizens of Japanese descent to be interned in camps solely because of their ancestry (*Bowers* v. *Hardwick*, 1986; *Korematsu* v. *United States*, 1944). Courts limited personhood to men or refused to grant equal rights to women just because they were women. A case in point is that of Lavinia Goodell, who in 1875 sought admission to the Wisconsin bar, only to be refused access by the state's supreme court, on the sole grounds that she was a woman (Wisconsin Supreme Court, 1875). The court held that:

> The law of nature destines and qualifies the female sex for the bearing and nurture of the children of our race and for the custody of the homes of the world and their maintenance in love and honor. And all life-long callings of women, inconsistent with these radical and sacred duties of their sex, as is the profession of the law, are departures from the order of nature; and when voluntary, treason against it (Wisconsin Supreme Court, 1875, p. 245).

Judges in the fourth category—"deflecting judges"—want the NhRP's cases to end without being judged on their merits. They may dismiss a lawsuit seeking legal rights for chimpanzees on a procedural point or refuse to hear its arguments or issue the writ.

The NhRP's long-term strategy assumes that if fair-minded judges are persistently exposed to compelling expert evidence of a chimpanzee's complex cognition and autonomy, coupled with powerful legal arguments derived from the values and principles that the judges themselves routinely espouse, they will struggle in good faith to overcome their implicit biases. The expectation is that they will arrive at the legally, historically, politically and morally correct decision that autonomous nonhuman animals deserve the fundamental rights that can protect their fundamental interests.

The Legal Campaign Focus on Chimpanzees in New York State

In December 2013, after 28 years of preparation, the NhRP commenced its long-term strategic litigation campaign. It filed its first habeas corpus lawsuit on behalf of Tommy, a chimpanzee long imprisoned a few miles from the courthouse on a used trailer lot in Fulton County, in central New York State. There the NhRP encountered its first implicitly biased judge, who, without further explanation, stated at the hearing's conclusion:

> Your impassioned representations to the court are quite impressive. The Court will not entertain the application, will not recognize a chimpanzee as a human or as a person who can seek a writ of habeas corpus under Article 70. I will be available as the judge for any other lawsuit to right any wrongs that are done to this chimpanzee because I understand what you are saying. You make a very strong argument. However, I do not agree with the argument only insofar as Article 70 applies to chimpanzees (NYS Supreme Court, 2013c, p. 26).

The following day, the NhRP sued on behalf of a chimpanzee named Kiko, who was imprisoned in a storefront in Niagara County, New York, near the Canadian border. There it encountered its second implicitly biased judge. He desired to review the voluminous documents before holding oral argument by telephone the following week, when he concluded:

> I have to say your papers were excellent [...]. However, I'm not prepared to make this leap of faith and I'm going to deny the request for a petition for writ of habeas corpus. I think personally this is more of a legislative issue than a judicial issue (NYS Supreme Court, 2013b, p. 15).

Photo: In 2013, the NhRP filed its first unlawful imprisonment lawsuit on behalf of Tommy, a chimpanzee long caged on a used trailer lot in New York State. © "Unlocking the Cage" Pennebaker Hegedus Films

When the judge unexpectedly tried to halt the NhRP's appeal by refusing to take a necessary ministerial action, the NhRP was forced to seek action from the appellate court that oversaw this judge. Specifically, the NhRP asked for a rare writ of mandamus, a request for an order to require public officials—in this case, the judge—to do their nondiscretionary duties (*NhRP* ex rel. *Kiko* v. *Boniello and Presti*, 2014). The trial court judge then took the required action and the appeal proceeded.

Two days later, the NhRP filed suit in Suffolk County on Long Island, New York, on behalf of Hercules and Leo, two young chimpanzees who had been removed from their Louisiana-based mothers when they were two years old and then imprisoned in a cage in the basement of a Stony Brook University computer building for about six years. At the university, they were placed under general anesthesia almost monthly and had wires inserted into their muscles, all to help researchers better understand how chimpanzees develop bent legs. In this case, the judge did not see or hear the

NhRP lawyers; instead, he scrawled a two-sentence dismissal (NhRP, n.d.-d; NYS Supreme Court, 2013a).

New York State has four intermediate appellate courts that hear appeals according to geographical area. The first judicial department covers Manhattan and the Bronx; the second is responsible for the rest of New York City and the state's southern counties; the third hears appeals from central and northern counties; and the fourth deals with the western counties (NYCourts.gov, n.d.). In early 2014, the NhRP appealed Hercules and Leo's dismissal to the second judicial department, where it encountered its first deflecting court, which took the extraordinary step of dismissing the appeal without allowing the NhRP to file a brief or argue. This ruling was clearly a mistake, albeit no accident; the court affirmed its mistake even after the NhRP pointed out that it had an absolute right to appeal (NhRP, n.d.-d; NYS Supreme Court, 2014). In response, the NhRP decided to refile the case in another court at another time.

The NhRP now appealed Tommy's case to the third judicial department, which proved to be the paradigm of an implicitly biased court. The judge's disagreement with the NhRP turned mostly on whether a "person" must have the capacity to possess *either* rights *or* duties, or *both* rights *and* duties. In ruling the latter, the court partially relied upon the definition of "person" found in *Black's Law Dictionary,* the most widely used US law dictionary, which states that a person has to be able to bear both rights and duties (*People* ex rel. *NhRP* v. *Lavery*, 2014, p. 151; Garner, 2014). Had the court checked Black's sole source, it would have recognized that the source actually supported the NhRP. When the NhRP brought the error to the attention of the dictionary's editor-in-chief, he immediately promised that the next volume would carry the correct definition (B. A. Garner, personal communication, 2018; NhRP, n.d.-c).

But that was too late for Tommy. The Tommy court, without explanation or supporting scientific evidence, claimed that chimpanzees lack the capacity for duties and did not give the NhRP the opportunity to dispute its conclusion (*People* ex rel. *NhRP* v. *Lavery*, 2014, p. 152). The NhRP proceeded to prove the court wrong, again too late for Tommy. Most seriously, the Tommy court never offered any considered explanation of why the ability to bear legal duties should influence whether an autonomous being, of any species, should have the right not to be arbitrarily imprisoned; it failed to grapple with the obvious problem presented by the millions of New York infants, children, the severely cognitively disabled and other individuals who cannot bear duties, yet possess legal rights, including habeas corpus. Instead, the court disposed of the issue in a brief footnote:

> To be sure, some humans are less able to bear legal duties or responsibilities than others. These differences do not alter our analysis, as it is undeniable that, collectively, human beings possess the unique ability to bear legal responsibility. Accordingly, nothing in this decision should be read as limiting the rights of human beings in the context of habeas corpus proceedings or otherwise) (*People* ex rel. *NhRP* v. *Lavery*, 2014, p. 152, n. 3).

The result was that, for the first time in the thousand-year history of common law, a court ruled that the only type of entity that could have rights of any kind was one that could assume duties or, even more bizarrely, one that was part of some arbitrarily defined collection of entities, some of which could assume duties.

A month later, a court in the fourth judicial department ruled against Kiko. It recognized the NhRP's right to appeal and ignored the Tommy court's ruling by twice assuming, without deciding, that a chimpanzee could be a "person." The court's judges —who were both implicitly biased and deflecting—inexplicably based their decision on a fundamental misunderstanding of the NhRP's purpose and objectives. They referred to the NhRP as "an organization seeking better treatment and housing of [. . .] nonhuman primates" and one that "seeks only to change the conditions of confinement rather than the confinement itself" (*NhRP* ex rel. *Kiko* v. *Presti*, 2015, p. 1334). Consequently, the judges repeated in their ruling that "habeas corpus does not lie where a petitioner seeks only to change the conditions of confinement rather than the confinement itself" (p. 1335).

Even the Tommy court had not made this error, noting: "We have not been asked to evaluate the quality of Tommy's current living conditions in an effort to improve his welfare" (*People* ex rel. *NhRP* v. *Lavery*, 2014, p. 149). The following year, New York County Supreme Court Justice Barbara Jaffe agreed: "The conditions under which Hercules and Leo are confined are not challenged by petitioner [. . .] the sole issue is whether Hercules and Leo may be legally detained at all" (*NhRP* ex rel. *Hercules and Leo v. Stanley*, 2015, p. 901).

Unsurprisingly the New York high court declined to hear either Tommy's or Kiko's appeal, as that court hears just a small percentage of the requests to appeal brought to it. New York high court judge Eugene M. Fahey voted "no" at the time of Kiko's appeal to the fourth judicial department. He would come to regret his vote.

The NhRP refiled Hercules and Leo's habeas corpus petition in Manhattan in April 2015. Then, for the first time, a judge issued an order under a habeas corpus statute on behalf of a nonhuman animal. That order—issued by Justice Barbara Jaffe—required Stony Brook University to appear in court and present a legally sufficient reason for imprisoning the chimpanzees. Two months after that hearing, Justice Jaffe released a lengthy opinion that turned back each procedural attack on the ability of the NhRP to bring its claim. The opinion agrees that "person" is not a synonym for "human" (*NhRP* ex rel. *Hercules and Leo v. Stanley*, 2015, p. 911), that the NhRP had sought the release of Hercules and Leo and not just a change in their conditions of confinement (p. 917), and that it could choose to file a second petition on their behalf (p. 910). However, Justice Jaffe felt bound by the Tommy holding:

> Courts [...] are slow to embrace change, and occasionally seem reluctant to engage in broader, more inclusive interpretations of the law, if only to the modest extent of affording them greater consideration. As Justice Kennedy aptly observed in *Lawrence v. Texas*, albeit in a different context, "times can blind us to certain truths and later generations can see that laws once thought necessary and proper in fact serve only to oppress." [...] The pace may now be accelerating [...]. For now, however, given the precedent to which I am bound, [...] the petition for a writ of

habeas corpus is denied and the proceeding is dismissed (*NhRP* ex rel. *Hercules and Leo* v. *Stanley*, 2015, pp. 917–18).

The NhRP now gathered numerous additional scientific affidavits that demonstrated that chimpanzees routinely shoulder duties within wild chimpanzee communities, engage in lawful and rule-governed policing, cooperate, help and tend to injured or vulnerable community members, share hunting duties and food, and inform other community members about danger. These documents also testified that captive chimpanzees shoulder duties among themselves and within mixed chimpanzee–human communities, while engaging in promise-making and promise-keeping, doing chores and moral behavior (Anderson, 2015; Boesch, 2015; Goodall, 2015; Jensvold, 2015; McGrew, 2015; NhRP, n.d.-b; Savage-Rumbaugh, 2015).

The NhRP refiled Tommy and Kiko's cases in Manhattan and both were sent to Justice Jaffe, who said that the Tommy Court was the proper place to address the legality of Tommy's detention and that the NhRP could not file a second Tommy petition. When the NhRP appealed to the first judicial department, it refused to allow the appeal, just as the second department had done in 2014. This time the NhRP fought back, twice demanding its right to appeal over the next year. When its demands were refused, it took the unprecedented step of suing the first department *in* the first department and demanding that the court order *itself* to follow the law. And it did (NhRP, n.d.-b).

The price for that success was steep: the justice's questioning during oral arguments in March 2017 was unremittingly hostile. The NhRP pointed out in vain that a 1972 New York high court decision had made clear that "human" and "person" are not synonyms and that personhood is "not a question of biological or 'natural' correspondence" (*Byrn* v. *NYCHHC*, 1972, p. 201). The court ruled that the lower court had the right to dis-

miss the NhRP's case on the grounds that it was a successive petition, then noted in passing, without explanation, that Tommy and Kiko could never have any rights because rights were reserved for humans (*NhRP* ex rel. *Tommy* v. *Lavery*, 2017). This decision was so flawed that the NhRP extensively annotated its errors, sentence by sentence (Wise, 2017c). The NhRP again sought to appeal to the high court and the appeal was denied once more, without comment, in May 2018. Then something extraordinary happened.

Judge Eugene M. Fahey, who had voted in 2015 to deny Tommy and Kiko's first appeals, now became the first US high court judge to opine on the merits of the NhRP's arguments and on the merits of the adverse decisions of the first, third and fourth departments. His view was that all their decisions were incorrect (*NhRP* ex rel. *Tommy* v. *Lavery*, 2018).

In his opinion, Judge Fahey singles out for special rebuke the courts' argument that chimpanzees cannot be persons simply "because they lack 'the capacity or ability . . . to bear legal duties, or to be held legally accountable for their actions'" (*NhRP* ex rel. *Tommy* v. *Lavery*, 2018, p. 1056). His opinion goes on to say:

> Petitioner and amici law professors Laurence H. Tribe, Justin Marceau, and Samuel Wiseman question this assumption. Even if it is correct, however, that nonhuman animals cannot bear duties, the same is true of human infants or comatose human adults, yet no one would suppose that it is improper to seek a writ of habeas corpus on behalf of one's infant child [. . .] or a parent suffering from dementia [. . .]. In short, being a "moral agent" who can freely choose to act as morality requires is not a necessary condition of being a "moral patient" who can be wronged and may have the right to redress wrongs (*see generally* Tom Regan, The Case for Animal Rights 151–156 [2d ed 2004]) (*NhRP* ex rel. *Tommy* v. *Lavery*, 2018, p. 1057).

> “Chimpanzees make tools to catch insects; they recognize themselves in mirrors, photographs, and television images; they imitate others; they exhibit compassion and depression when a community member dies; they even display a sense of humor. ”

Fahey reasons that the first department's "conclusion that a chimpanzee cannot be considered a 'person' and is not entitled to habeas relief is in fact based on nothing more than the premise that a chimpanzee is not a member of the human species" (NhRP ex rel. *Tommy* v. *Lavery*, 2018, p. 1057). He goes on:

> I agree with the principle that all human beings possess intrinsic dignity and value, and have [. . .] the constitutional privilege of habeas corpus, regardless of whether they are United States citizens [. . .], but, in elevating our species, we should not lower the status of other highly intelligent species (NhRP ex rel. *Tommy* v. *Lavery*, 2018, p. 1057).

Fahey recognizes that the NhRP presented evidence that chimpanzees "are autonomous, intelligent creatures" and urges his fellow judges to address the "manifest injustice" involved in determining whether a nonhuman animal such as a chimpanzee has the right to habeas corpus when deprived of liberty (NhRP ex rel. *Tommy* v. *Lavery*, 2018, p. 1059). Fahey warns that "the question will have to be addressed eventually" and asks, "Can a nonhuman animal be entitled to release from confinement through the writ of habeas corpus? Should such a being be treated as a person or as property, in essence a thing?" (p. 1056). Referring to a "dilemma," he notes that judges will "have to recognize its complexity and confront it" (p. 1059).

Fahey further points out that the answer to the question of whether a being has the "right to liberty protected by a writ of habeas corpus":

> will depend on our assessment of the intrinsic nature of chimpanzees as a species. The record before us in the motion for leave to appeal contains unrebutted evidence, in the form of affidavits from eminent primatologists, that chimpanzees have advanced cognitive abilities, including being able to remember the

past and plan for the future, the capacities of self-awareness and self-control, and the ability to communicate through sign language. Chimpanzees make tools to catch insects; they recognize themselves in mirrors, photographs, and television images; they imitate others; they exhibit compassion and depression when a community member dies; they even display a sense of humor. Moreover, the amici philosophers with expertise in animal ethics and related areas draw our attention to recent evidence that chimpanzees demonstrate autonomy by self-initiating intentional, adequately informed actions, free of controlling influences (NhRP ex rel. *Tommy* v. *Lavery*, 2018, pp. 1057–8).

Next, he chastises both the first and fourth departments in Tommy's and Kiko's cases for mistakenly insisting that the NhRP, in the appellate division's words, "does not challenge the legality of the chimpanzees' detention, but merely seeks their transfer to a different facility" (NhRP ex rel. *Tommy* v. *Lavery*, 2018, p. 1058). He concludes that:

> In the interval since we first denied leave to the Nonhuman Rights Project [. . .], I have struggled with whether this was the right decision [. . .]. I continue to question whether the Court was right to deny leave in the first instance. The issue whether a nonhuman animal has a fundamental right to liberty protected by the writ of habeas corpus is profound and far-reaching. It speaks to our relationship with all the life around us. Ultimately, we will not be able to ignore it. While it may be arguable that a chimpanzee is not a "person," there is no doubt that it is not merely a thing (NhRP ex rel. *Tommy* v. *Lavery*, 2018, p. 1059).

A second extraordinary event followed one month later. The fourth department, which had dismissed Kiko's first case in 2014, was presented with a criminal defendant convicted of vandalizing cars owned by a car dealership. The criminal mischief statute made it a crime to damage the property of a "person" and the defendant argued only a human could be a "person." Upholding the conviction, the court cited two cases that are discussed above. One of the cases had made clear that "human" and "person" are not synonyms and that personhood is "not a question of biological or 'natural' correspondence" (*Byrn* v. *NYCHHC*, 1972, p. 201). The other case was Kiko's, which the court now cited to support the proposition that it was "*common knowledge* that personhood can and sometimes does attach to nonhuman entities like corporations or *animals*" (*People* v. *Graves*, 2018, p. 617, emphasis added).

Expanding the US Legal Campaign to Include Elephants

In October 2018, backed by affidavits filed by renowned elephant researchers Lucy Bates, Richard Byrne, Karen McComb, Cynthia Moss and Joyce Poole, which demonstrate that elephants, like chimpanzees, are extraordinarily cognitively complex and autonomous beings, the NhRP sought a writ of habeas corpus on behalf of an elephant named Happy, who had been imprisoned in the Bronx Zoo for decades (Bates, 2017; Bryne, 2016; McComb, 2016; Moss, 2017; NhRP, n.d.-a; Poole, 2016, 2018).

In New York, it is possible to file a writ of habeas corpus in any of the state's supreme courts. The NhRP filed its case in Albion, near Niagara Falls, because its appeals go to the fourth department, which had been relatively receptive to NhRP's line of argumentation. A month later, that court issued the second order under a habeas corpus statute on behalf of a nonhuman animal in New York State and the first ever on behalf of an elephant (NYS Supreme Court, 2018). After another month, however, over the NhRP's objection, the court reassigned the case to the Bronx Supreme Court.

On February 18, 2020, after hearing three hours of argument over three days, Bronx Supreme Court Justice Alison Tuitt rejected the Bronx Zoo's claim that "Happy is happy" at the Bronx Zoo and found instead that "the arguments advanced by the NhRP are extremely persuasive for transferring Happy from her solitary, lonely one-acre exhibit at the Bronx Zoo to an elephant sanctuary." Justice Tuitt also found that Happy is "an extraordinary animal with complex cognitive abilities, an intelligent being with advanced analytical abilities akin to human beings." Judge Eugene Fahey noted that he believes that a chimpanzee is likely a legal person and is certainly not a thing, and wrote that Happy "is more than just a legal thing, or property" and "is an intelligent, autonomous being who should be treated with respect and dignity, and who may be entitled to liberty" (Nonhuman Rights, 2020). Justice Tuitt, however, "regrettably" found that she could not order Happy's release to a sanctuary because she felt bound by the decision of the first department, which "held that animals are not 'persons' entitled to rights and protections afforded by the writ of habeas corpus" (*NhRP* ex rel. *Tommy* v. *Lavery*, 2017).

Meanwhile, in November 2017, the NhRP —backed by affidavits filed by the same preeminent elephant experts as in Happy's case—had sought a writ of habeas corpus on behalf of three elephants, Beulah, Karen and Minnie, who had for decades been forced to perform in a traveling circus in Connecticut (NhRP, n.d.-a). Under that state's law, the court was required to issue the writ of habeas corpus unless it lacked jurisdiction or the petition was frivolous on its face (Nonhuman Rights, 2018). The court refused to issue the writ on both grounds. Ignoring centuries of common law that permits a stranger to seek a writ of habeas corpus on behalf of an individual who is being privately detained, the court said the NhRP lacked the required standing because it did not have a preexisting relationship

with the imprisoned elephants and because it had not alleged that a pre-existing relationship was not necessary. The court also said the case was "frivolous on its face as a matter of law" as no one had ever filed such a case before; it thereby conflated "novel" with "frivolous," ignoring the fact that every new common law rule had once been sought for the first time (Choplin, 2017; NhRP, n.d.-a).

On appeal, in August 2019, the Connecticut Appellate Court affirmed the judgment of the lower court, but on entirely different grounds. It held that the NhRP lacked standing not because it had no pre-existing relationship with the elephants, but because elephants were not persons and lacked the capacity for duties required to form such relationships (*NhRP* v. *R.W. Commerford and Sons, Inc.*, 2019). As the NhRP had no

notice that the Appellate Court's decision would turn on these issues, it had not adequately briefed the court or argued the case. During the appeal, Karen died; two months later, so did Beulah.

While the appeal was pending, the NhRP sought a second writ of habeas corpus on behalf of the same three elephants, this time arguing that a pre-existing relationship with the elephants was not necessary. The lower court dismissed this second case on the grounds that it did not fundamentally differ from the first case the NhRP had litigated. The NhRP appealed that decision, contending that it had not been given the required opportunity to fully and fairly litigate anything in the first case. Only after the NhRP filed its brief in the second case did the decision in the first case issue.

Photo: In 2017, the NhRP went to court on behalf of three elephants, Beulah, Karen and Minnie. The case continues on behalf of Minnie, but both Beulah and Karen have since died. Minnie at work.
© Gigi Glendinning

In October 2019, the NhRP asked the Appellate Court for permission to file a supplemental brief in the second case, so as to be able to attack the reasoning of the court's decision in the first case. This permission was granted and the NhRP filed its supplemental brief in November 2019. The decision in the case is pending.

Until 2013, no US court had ever been presented with the claim that a nonhuman animal could be a person with the capacity for fundamental legal rights as part of a long-term, sustained, strategic litigation campaign focused on gaining personhood and rights for nonhuman animals. That year, the Nonhuman Rights Project embarked on just such a campaign to secure personhood and certain fundamental legal rights—first for chimpanzees and then for elephants, in New York and subsequently in Connecticut. It intends to file further cases in California and Colorado in 2020. This campaign is beginning to see success and the NhRP intends for it to alter the legal relationship between humans and other animals, both in captivity and in the wild.

International Paths to Personhood: Beyond the Common Law System

In the United States, the NhRP has attempted to capitalize on the common law system, in which courts can make new laws if no prior legislation exists (Garner, 2014). Should a single court uphold a writ of habeas corpus on behalf of a nonhuman animal, for example, its decision would set a new precedent for judging future applications on behalf of other nonhuman animals. While this might constitute a victory for the personhood movement, it is arguably much more difficult to secure, as the weight and scope of such a precedent in common law will be clearly apparent to judges.

In contrast, the civil law system presents more disparate challenges. In these jurisdictions, courts have no authority to act outside of preexisting and codified core principles (Garner, 2014). Consequently, if civil courts recognize only "humans" and "property," then there is no legal mechanism by which to acknowledge anything in between. Such was the case in France, where —under the 1804 Napoleonic civil code— "animals" held the same status as "furniture," and thus shared the same legal rights as an armchair (French Parliament, 1804, art. 528). Only in February 2015 did France recognize non-wild nonhuman animals as "living beings capable of sensitivity" (French Parliament, 2015, art. 2). Reportedly, this was the first time a national regulation differentiated nonhuman animals from property (Forte, 2015, p. 4).

Circumventing Civil Code for Sandra

The French decision would soon inform an Argentine judge's ruling. In November 2014, on behalf of Sandra, an orangutan at the Palermo Zoo in Buenos Aires, the Association of Officials and Attorneys for the Rights of Animals (AFADA) argued a writ of habeas corpus against the city government and zoo. Although AFADA lost the case on appeal, the nation's Federal Chamber of Criminal Cassation recognized that Sandra had limited rights and remanded the case to a lower criminal court to evaluate allegations of animal cruelty (CCC, 2014). A subsequent *amparo* legal action—an extraordinary legal remedy for the protection of constitutional rights—was considered by Judge Elena Amanda Liberatori, who proved sympathetic to Sandra's plight. Unable to change her legal recognition in the civil code, which recognizes only "people" and "possessions," Judge Liberatori categorized Sandra as a "nonhuman person," acknowledging antecedent in the French decision of 2015 (*AFADA* v. *GCBA sobre amparo*, 2015). In doing so, she made it possible for Sandra to be offered new rights beyond those awarded under civil designations. She circumvented, rather than contravened, Argentina's civil code.

Since it was issued as part of a decision in a criminal hearing, Judge Liberatori's categorization had no binding effect on Sandra's legal status. Still, the judge was empowered not only to order a committee to determine what would constitute "adequate" conditions for Sandra, but also to rule that the government must guarantee those conditions (*AFADA* v. *GCBA sobre amparo*, 2015). In practice, "adequate" conditions were found

neither in Argentina, nor in the Brazilian sanctuary to which Sandra was to be relocated, such that Judge Liberatori rejected the proposed transfer (GAP, 2017). Further, Liberatori's recognition of Sandra as a "nonhuman person" was revoked by an appellate court in 2016. The judges did not go so far as to rule that Sandra is *not* a nonhuman person; rather, they considered her status to be irrelevant, on the basis that, irrespective of the "positions that could be adopted in this regard [...] there is no dispute whatsoever in this case that this animal must be protected [and that] the suffering of animals must be proscribed" (*AFADA* v. *GCBA appeal*, 2016, pp. 1, 8).

Photo: At the age of 33, Sandra was finally transferred to the Center for Great Apes in Wauchula, Florida. © Center for Great Apes

Nonetheless, for four years, Sandra continued to exist in conditions that were legally "inadequate" under all of the judges' terms. Following the Palermo Zoo's closure in 2016, these conditions were arguably inferior to those in which she had lived at the time of AFADA's filing (Fraundorfer, 2017). Sandra's legal limbo therefore posited practical questions for other pursuits of personhood—specifically, those that call for the "release" of captive great apes. In November 2019, at the age of 33, Sandra was finally transferred to the Center for Great Apes in Wauchula, Florida (Shenoy, 2019).

Sandra Sets the Stage for Cecilia

> In a few civil law jurisdictions, the consideration of 'personhood' for great apes has resulted in more explicit acknowledgment of rights, demonstrating value in pursuing legal campaigns.

Although AFADA did not secure habeas corpus for Sandra, her case did set the stage for the group's legal argument in a later court filing. In 2016, AFADA's attorneys applied for habeas corpus—and won—on behalf of Cecilia, a chimpanzee at Argentina's Mendoza Zoo. In her landmark decision, Judge María Alejandra Mauricio stressed that her recognition of personhood could not afford Cecilia human rights; indeed, when speaking to the press, she clarified that she had not referenced "the civil rights enshrined in the civil code" (Tello, 2016). Rather, she recognized Cecilia's status as "in between" humans and objects, citing "rights specific to her species: to development, to life in her natural habitat" (*AFADA v. Mendoza Zoo and City*, 2016; Tello, 2016). For Cecilia, the Brazilian sanctuary to which Sandra's transfer was blocked qualified as "natural habitat"; by Mauricio's order, Cecilia was promptly transferred there (*AFADA v. Mendoza Zoo and City*, 2016, pp. 44–5).

It is noteworthy that neither AFADA's petitions, nor the judges' decisions, aimed to secure "human rights" for Sandra. The objectives of these cases are therefore fundamentally different from those of the NhRP. They are, conceivably, a reasonable compromise.

Personhood as a Means to an End

Civil code also presented novel challenges in Austria in February 2007, when a sanctuary that was housing Hiasl, a wild-caught chimpanzee who had been the subject of pharmaceutical research, declared bankruptcy. An Austrian businessman offered to donate "a large sum of money" to Hiasl and the Association Against Animal Factories, known by the German acronym VGT, on the condition that its president, Martin Balluch, could reach an agreement with Hiasl as to how the money should be spent. As Hiasl was incapable of reaching an agreement, VGT petitioned the Mödling district court for Balluch to be appointed as Hiasl's legal guardian. Under Austrian law, this required Hiasl to be recognized as a "person" (Balluch and Theuer, 2007).

As the funds could simply have been donated to VGT, the provision requiring Hiasl's agreement suggests that the donor may have had an additional motive, such as pushing a personhood petition. As Fraundorfer (2017) notes—and as the petitioners themselves later acknowledged—personhood would also pave the way for Hiasl to sue the pharmaceutical company responsible for capturing him from the wild in 1982, when he was an infant, and transferring him to a laboratory and later a "windowless basement" (Balluch and Theuer, 2007). Nonetheless, Eberhart Theuer, counsel for VGT, argued that the petition was simply a means to an end: "We're not talking about the right to vote here." Instead, the petition sought recognition of more basic legal rights, namely "the right to life, the right not to be tortured, the right to freedom under certain conditions" (AP, 2007).

At the first of two hearings, Judge Barbara Breit expressed frustration that Hiasl had no documents to prove his identity. After humans testified to his origins on Hiasl's behalf, Breit ruled in a second hearing that since Hiasl was neither mentally impaired nor in imminent danger, a guardian could not be appointed. As rationale for her decision, Breit also cited potential public perception that humans with court-appointed legal guardians might be considered nonhuman (Balluch and Theuer, 2007). An appeal by VGT was denied by the district court in May 2007, on the basis that only a guardian—who could not be appointed—could appeal. Citing Austria's civil code, three other courts denied subsequent appeals for the same reason: the district court did so in May 2007, the provincial court in the Wiener Neustadt in September 2007 and the Supreme Court in Vienna in January 2008 (AP, 2008; Balluch and Theuer, 2007). In all cases, technical interpretations of Austria's civil code afforded no provision to address the central question, namely whether Hiasl, as the appellant, was entitled to any legal standing (Fasel *et al.*, 2016).

A review of Hiasl's case notes that Judge Breit left open the question as to whether Hiasl is a person: "in all her decisions and correspondence, she continuously wrote as if Hiasl was a person," (Balluch and Theuer, 2007, p. 339). Indeed, the review and media reporting suggest that Breit was sympathetic to the cause, but that her hands were tied by civil code, with no potential to establish a common law precedent (Balluch and Theuer, 2007).

Historically, civil code has secured "personhood"—or at least equivalent status—when nonhuman animals were defendants. Criminal trials of farm and domestic animals were especially abundant in medieval times. In one such case, a pig was tried and convicted of murder in France in 1266, then sentenced to death by burning (Evans, 1906). In Switzerland in 1474, a chicken was tried in a "solemn" judicial proceeding and burned for the "heinous" crime of laying an egg (Walter, 1984). What has changed is

that nonhuman animals are plaintiffs, not defendants, as in these personhood cases of great apes. Yet, in civil code, such precedents do not apply. As Judge Liberatori showed in Argentina, the pursuit of personhood in civil jurisdictions will require creative solutions in the face of codified legal parameters.

Not All Cases Advance the Cause

Not all cases in civil law came as far as Sandra's or Cecilia's. In October 2005, several animal welfare organizations filed for habeas corpus on behalf of Suiça, a female chimpanzee in the Zoological Garden of Salvador, in Bahia, Brazil, in pursuit of transferring her to the Great Apes Sanctuary of Sorocaba in São Paulo. Judge Edmundo Cruz recognized that, under the law, he could terminate the proceedings immediately, but instead he chose to admit the debate "in order to provoke discussion around the event" (Cruz, 2006, p. 282). Judge Cruz even made a surreptitious visit to the zoo as part of his own research, which he documented in a lengthy opinion with intent to "arouse jurists all over the country" to address the central controversy: "Can a primate be equated with a human being or not?" (p. 284). In this case, the habeas corpus claim expired upon Suiça's unexpected death in September 2005; Judge Cruz, who had ambiguously indicated he would rule in favor of Suiça, was thus released from the obligation to issue a ruling (Cruz, 2006).

As Judge Cruz was not able to set a precedent in civil law, local justices twice took an opposite view in determining a case of habeas corpus for Jimmy, a chimpanzee in a private zoo in Niterói, Brazil. Jimmy's case was rejected outright on the basis that chimpanzees were not entitled to personhood rights. Coincidentally, before a federal appeal could be filed, the zoo was closed due to poor conditions and Jimmy was transferred to the Sorocaba sanctuary (Fraundorfer, 2017).

> " Although the government entirely ceased using chimpanzees in November 2015, invasive research on these beings is still technically legal in the United States. "

Beyond Individual Cases: Rights at the Taxonomic Level

Given that the NhRP aims to establish a common law precedent in the United States, its cases are focused on specific individuals and writs for habeas corpus on their behalf. This approach is based on an understanding that—under US law—recognition of broader rights at the taxonomic level has lagged far behind that in other nations. It was the US government, by order of Congress in 1960, that first authorized the large-scale capture and importation of wild chimpanzees for invasive research (Grimm, 2017). By 1999, following intensive captive breeding after the AIDS epidemic, their numbers had reached an all-time high of 1,500 individuals, most of whom were kept in government-run or federally sponsored laboratories (US Congress, 2000). Although the government entirely ceased using chimpanzees in November 2015, invasive research on these beings is still technically legal in the United States. Since the US Fish and Wildlife Service designated captive chimpanzees endangered in June 2015, however, permits must be obtained for such research—and no researcher is known to have applied for one (Collins, 2015).

It was a ruling effective April 2018 that truly measured how slowly US law has come to afford protections to apes (US Fish and Wildlife Service, 2018). That decision, by the US Fish and Wildlife Service, recognized two species of orangutan—a full 22 years after the two were formally accepted by the scientific community, and six months after a third new species was described in the scientific literature (Nater *et al.*, 2017; Xu and Arnason, 1996). The challenge before the NhRP is therefore significant. If US law does not acknowledge species in a timely fashion—and if invasive studies on chimpanzees are technically still legal—is it conceivable that US legislation might award specific rights to named individuals?

By contrast, many other countries are closer to recognizing personhood. With the possible exception of Gabon, the United States stood alone in its use of chimpanzees in invasive research in 2008 (Knight, 2008). By then, a number of countries had either ceased or banned such research in all great ape taxa, via law or policy. Specifically, the United Kingdom banned the use of great apes in invasive research in 1997 (having ceased using them in 1986); New Zealand in 1999; Australia and Sweden in 2003; the Netherlands in 2004; Austria and Japan in 2006; and Germany in 2013 (having ceased using them in 1992) (Federal Ministry of Food and Agriculture, n.d.; Knight, 2008). Among these bans, Austria's is the only one that explicitly prohibits experimentation on gibbons (Knight, 2008). In some nations, exceptions apply for non-invasive behavioral research, or invasive work that is intended to benefit the individual; Knight (2008) presents a useful summary of the legislation. In 2010, the European Union introduced a union-wide ban, following an earlier parliamentary declaration signed by 433 of 786 members of the European Parliament (ADI, 2007; EU, 2010). The number of signatories was the third highest recorded for any declaration, of any kind, since 2000 (ADI, 2007). This single co-decision-based legislative procedure has since advanced rights across all member states of the European Union, including in nations with no prior domestic legislation on the use of great apes in research (EU, 2010).

Some nations have arguably gone much further. Since 1999, New Zealand's Animal Welfare Act has prohibited the use of "non-human hominids" in any "research, testing, or teaching" deemed not to be in the individual's best interests, or in those of their species, limiting their use to circumstances under which the likely harm would not outweigh the overall benefits (Brosnahan, 2000, p. 190; New Zealand Parliament, 1999; see Section II of this chapter). In 2008, the

Spanish parliament approved resolutions to afford some "statutory rights" to great apes, criminalizing their killing and banning their use in medical experiments, in entertainment and in most for-profit activities, excluding zoos (*Nature*, 2008). These resolutions evolved from similar legislation passed in the Balearic Islands, an autonomous community of Spain, in 2007 (Knight, 2008).

Nonetheless, the efficacy and the value of such legislation must be appropriately weighed. Just 28 chimpanzees and six orangutans lived in New Zealand at the time the Animal Welfare Act was passed; none were used for research, testing or teaching, and there was no proposal to do so (Elder, 2019). Further, the act does not prohibit their commercial exploitation: just two months after it came into force, two chimpanzees were sold to a Pacific Island circus, and one later died in her transport cage following unforeseen delays (Brosnahan, 2000). While the precise number of great apes in Spain and the Balearic Islands a decade ago is unclear, it is known to have been a fraction of those in US biomedical laboratories.

The Status of Captive Apes: A Statistical Update

While data on the number, location, origin and welfare status of apes in captivity are needed to inform effective policies, such information cannot be obtained for all captive settings. Some detailed data are available in the form of studbooks; voluntary reporting by organizations, such as users of Species360's Zoological Information Management System (ZIMS) (Species360, n.d.); Japan's Great Ape Information Network (GAIN, n.d.); and open government records. In other cases, captive facilities themselves voluntarily publish data in reports or present them at conferences. Data on under-regulated or illegal forms of captivity are generally lacking; estimates from related activities, such as law enforcement, proxy measures, statistical models and other emerging technologies contribute to the knowledge base, but they cannot fill all of the gaps (Clough and May, 2018; Stiles *et al.*, 2013). The dearth of data is especially acute in habitat countries and surrounding

Photo: Given their social needs and capabilities, apes in captivity adjust to their surroundings better if they are part of groups of compatible individuals. Gorilla Rehabilitation and Conservation Education Center. © GRACE

areas, where captivity is more closely related to killing.

The number and status of captive apes vary in response to intrinsic and extrinsic drivers. Regulations continue to shift in a number of ways that affect how apes may be kept and used in captivity, as well as what risks they face in their natural habitats. The welfare status of captive apes varies as a function of the type of captive environment and biological traits of individuals in question. In some cases, demography can also play a role; for example, adult and geriatric individuals experience an increased risk of morbidity and mortality and might need different housing, or additional or specialized care. A range of other external factors, such as crime, corruption and income inequality, can play indirect roles as well (Clough and May, 2018; Morris, 2013).

In practice, using animal-based measures and outcomes to assess welfare and quality of life for individuals and groups is the most rigorous approach (Hemsworth *et al.*, 2015; Mellor, Hunt and Gusset, 2015;

Mellor and Webster, 2014; OIE, 2019). For broader comparisons, uniform or harmonized measures are used. The Animal Protection Index (API), a national measure that addresses risk and protective factors, is one such approach (WAP, n.d.-a). The API scores indicators under five categories that are significant to the protection and welfare status of animals: recognition, governance, standards, education and awareness. The scores are then combined into an overall API score from A to G, where A represents the highest score (WAP, n.d.-b). This section reports API scores alongside other data whenever possible.

Captive Apes in Selected Regions

Europe

In total, the European data set for 2018 contains information on 2,391 apes in 226 member institutions, whose holdings range from 1 to 54 apes per site (see Figure 8.1). Compared to the data reported in the previous volume of *State of the Apes*, the overall increase in the number of captive individuals was around 100 individuals, or less than 2% (Durham, 2018). In 2018, gibbons were the most common taxon in the sample, followed by chimpanzees, gorillas, orangutans and bonobos. The number of solitary apes in the sample was small: 23 apes, or less than 1% of the total. Given their social needs and capabilities, apes in captivity adjust to their surroundings better if they are part of groups of compatible individuals.

The API score for European countries in the data set varied considerably, from B to F (see Table 8.1). In some countries with high API scores, "white lists" are used to designate which species may be kept, and in no known cases are apes on such lists (Durham and Phillipson, 2014). A growing number of European countries have explicit bans on circuses and similar performances

FIGURE 8.1

Apes in Selected European Zoos, by Taxon, 2012, 2016, and 2018

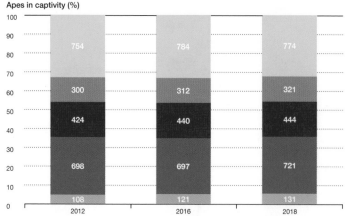

Key: ■ Bonobo ■ Chimpanzee ■ Gorilla ■ Orangutan ■ Gibbon

Note: Figures are drawn from aggregate data presented in species-holding reports submitted to Species360 in 2018. Some figures may reflect holdings from prior years.

Data sources: Durham (2015, fig. 8.1; 2018, fig. 8.3); Species360 (n.d.)

TABLE 8.1

API Score for Selected European Countries, 2020

Country	API score
Austria	B
Belarus	F
Denmark	B
France	C
Germany	C
Italy	C
Netherlands	B
Poland	C
Romania	D
Russia	D
Spain	C
Sweden	B
Switzerland	B
Turkey	D
Ukraine	E
United Kingdom	B

Source: WAP (n.d.-a)

(ADI, n.d.; Tyson, Draper and Turner, 2016). In Germany, courts initially ordered that a chimpanzee named Robby should be moved to live with other chimpanzees after his live performances in a circus were stopped, but an appeal later permitted the owner to keep him (BBC, 2018; Deutsche Welle, 2017).

Latin America

Zoos and private menageries have been maintained across Latin America for many decades (Horta Duarte, 2017). Poor welfare for captive animals is a widespread concern among the region's veterinarians and welfare groups, which cite weak regulation and enforcement as primary barriers to improve-

ment (Huertas, Gallo and Galindo, 2014; Larkin, 2010). In certain areas, however, efforts to improve protections are gaining momentum. Some countries have adopted circus and performance bans, for example, and certain courts have heard arguments for and even granted some rights for individual apes, including transfer to a sanctuary (ADI, 2019; Henao and Calatrava, 2016; Román, 2015; Samuels, 2016; Shenoy, 2019; see Section I of this chapter).

A limited number of sanctuaries operate throughout Latin America, where most captive apes are kept in zoos and other forms of exhibition. In Brazil, four sanctuaries associated with the Great Ape Project are home to 76 chimpanzees and 1 orangutan (J. Ramos, personal communication, 2018). In the absence of strong mandates for reporting and enforcement, and in view of the lack of comprehensive official figures on the number of apes in Latin America, estimates of the number of apes in captivity in this region relied on voluntarily reported data and direct inquiries (see Figure 8.2).

The API scores for Latin American countries in the data set ranged from a C in Mexico to an E in Venezuela (see Table 8.2).

FIGURE 8.2

Estimated Number of Apes in Captivity in Latin America, by Taxon, 2018

Key:
- Chimpanzee: 170 (79%)
- Gibbon: 19 (9%)
- Gorilla: 12 (6%)
- Orangutan: 13 (6%)

Note: Some figures are drawn from aggregate data presented in species-holding reports submitted to Species360 in 2018, which may reflect holdings from prior years.

Data sources: Species360 (n.d.); personal communication in 2018 with C. Alzola; H. Castelán; C. Fernandes Cipreste; L. Fernández; A. Gabriella Ioli; M.V. Josué Rángel; H. Khoshen; E. Padrón Ramos; J. Ramos; M. Rodríguez González; E.J. Sacasa; C. Silva; Zoológico Nacional del Parquemet, Santiago, Chile

TABLE 8.2

API Score for Selected Latin American Countries, 2020

Country	API score
Argentina	E
Brazil	D
Chile	D
Colombia	D
Mexico	C
Peru	D
Uruguay	D
Venezuela	E

Source: WAP (n.d.-a)

United States

More than 2,600 apes live in captivity in the United States, where chimpanzees and gibbons are more numerous than gorillas and orangutans (see Figure 8.3). Reflecting the slow life history of apes, overall numbers for 2018 show little variation compared to the numbers reported in prior volumes (Durham, 2018). The API score for the United States is D (WAP, n.d.-a).

FIGURE 8.3

Number of Apes in Captivity in the United States, by Taxon, 2018

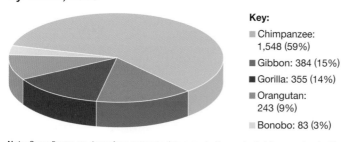

Key:
- Chimpanzee: 1,548 (59%)
- Gibbon: 384 (15%)
- Gorilla: 355 (14%)
- Orangutan: 243 (9%)
- Bonobo: 83 (3%)

Note: Some figures are drawn from aggregate data presented in species-holding reports submitted to Species360 in 2018, which may reflect holdings from prior years.

Data sources: Center for Great Apes (n.d.); ChimpCARE (n.d.); Durham (2015, fig. 8.3); Durham and Phillipson (2014, table 10.6); Species360 (n.d.); personal communication in 2018 with B. Malinsky, A. Ott, B. Richards, A. Whitely and K. Zdrojewski; author visit to the International Primate Protection League, South Carolina, 2018; author review of documents for the Bonobo Species Survival Plan (2018), Gorilla Species Survival Plan (2017), Orangutan Species Survival Plan (2017)

The majority of the apes accounted for in this data set are kept in zoos; however, disaggregation by taxon reveals that the majority of chimpanzees and gibbons are kept in other settings. With respect to chimpanzees, significant new regulatory restrictions decreased the number of individuals in US laboratories and other forms of captivity (Durham, 2015, 2018). As a result, for the first time ever in the United States, the number of chimpanzees in sanctuaries now exceeds that in any other captive setting (see Table 8.3). In 2018, the US government issued guidance on the process of transfers, which will sustain the shift from labs to sanctuaries (NIH, 2018). A small number of US ape sanctuaries, not all of which have accreditation status, provide care for chimpanzees, housing as few as 2 to more than 260. Among them is the Center for Great Apes, which is also the sole US sanctuary to house orangutans—21 were in residence as of July 2019 (Center for Great Apes, n.d.).

Although 384 captive gibbons were accounted for in the data, as reflected in Figure 8.3, an even greater number are estimated to be undocumented, mostly as pets, but also in unaccredited exhibits or roadside zoos. Nearly 300 privately owned gibbons accounted for in the first volume of *State of the Apes* fell out of the data set when the US Department of Agriculture placed new restrictions on access to records (Durham, 2018, p. 257, box 8.3). Beyond accounting for individual numbers, the restricted records include Animal Welfare Act inspection and violation details (Brulliard, 2017). Public interest is a key point in new and ongoing lawsuits to restore access (ALDF, 2018; Durham, 2018; Wadman, 2017).

Asia–Pacific

Oceania

Australia has an API score of D (WAP, n.d.-a). Its Animal Welfare Strategy and National Implementation Plan, which

TABLE 8.3

Number of Chimpanzees in Different Forms of Captivity in the United States, 2011–November 2018

Captivity type	2011[a]	2014[b]	2016[c]	2018[d]	% change 2011–18
Biomedical labs	962	794	658	464	−52%
GFAS sanctuaries*	522	525	556	585	+12%
AZA zoos**	261	258	259	236	−10%
Exhibition***	106	196	111	192	+81%
Dealer or pet owner	60	52	37	61	+2%
Entertainment	20	18	13	10	−50%
Total	**1,931**	**1,843**	**1,634**	**1,548**	**−20%**

Notes: * GFAS stands for Global Federation of Animal Sanctuaries. ** AZA stands for Association of Zoos and Aquariums. *** Exhibition comprises non-AZA zoos and other facilities that may or may not be open to the public. This category includes apes in sanctuaries that were not accredited during at least some reporting periods.

Data sources: a) Durham and Phillipson (2014, fig 10.2); b) Durham (2015, table 8.4); c) Durham (2018, table 8.1); d) ChimpCARE (n.d.)

covers all sentient animals, is informed by the Regional Animal Welfare Strategy for Asia, the Far East and Oceania (Australian Government, 2011; OIE, n.d.; WAP, n.d.-a). Laws at the territory and state levels provide greater protections for animals, in part by stipulating exhibition standards and well-being guidelines on pain, distress and positive welfare (WAP, n.d.-a). Australia is home to one of the most well-studied zoo populations of chimpanzees and, until very recently, the oldest-known orangutan in captivity lived at Perth zoo (Hart, 2018; Littleton, 2005).

New Zealand, which has an API score of C, was among the first nations to adopt legislation regarding the use of apes in laboratory experiments (Knight, 2008; Taylor, 2001; WAP, n.d.-a). New Zealand's Animal Welfare Act 1999 generally restricts research on "non-human hominids"—that is, great apes. Under the act, authorities may approve applications for proposed research on great apes only if it meets strict ethical criteria, following mandatory review by the National Animal Ethics Advisory Council and proof that the research is in the best interest of either the apes involved or their species, and so long as the benefits derived are not outweighed

by the likely harm to the individuals (New Zealand Parliament, 1999; see Section I of this chapter). The latter stipulations reflect modern bioethical principles of beneficence and justice (Beauchamp, Ferdowsian and Gluck, 2014). In 2013, a regulatory review considered how applications to exhibit apes and other animals were handled; the process was undertaken in response to concerns that

FIGURE 8.4

Apes in Captivity in Australia and New Zealand, by Taxon, 2018

Key: ■ Australia ■ New Zealand

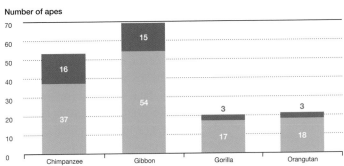

Note: Figures are drawn from aggregate data presented in species-holding reports submitted to Species360 in 2018; additional data come from the media sources cited below. Some figures may reflect holdings from prior years. No bonobos were reported.

Data sources: Durham (2015, fig. 8.1; 2018, fig. 8.3); Species360 (n.d.)

included safety and animal welfare outcomes (Environmental Protection Authority, 2013).

Overall conditions for captive apes in Oceania are stable because the numbers are small and regulations well established. The only available records for apes were for zoos and wildlife parks in Australia and New Zealand. Given the nature and scope of the region's zoo regulations and standards, few welfare risks exist beyond those associated with long-term captivity—and the occasional escape or high-profile transfer (Hart, 2018; Johnston, 2015; Lee, 2013; Mager, 2000; Pasley, 2017). Figure 8.4 shows numbers of apes in each taxon for zoos in Australia and New Zealand.

Asia

In Asia, zoos hold many captive apes. Not counting Japan, database figures for 2018 indicate that 25 gorillas, 436 gibbons, about 220 chimpanzees and 170 orangutans resided in zoos (Species360, n.d.). As noted earlier in this chapter and in prior editions of *State of the Apes*, the availability and quality of data on the number of apes in captivity and their welfare vary across countries and regions, in part because of uneven rates of access and participation in reporting and membership databases. One extensive review identified 466 orangutans in Asian zoos, considerably more than reported in the studbooks or databases (Banes *et al.*, 2018). As the study emphasizes, issues with the collection and sharing of information can be impediments for zoos, as they are for this review and other research (Banes *et al.*, 2018; Durham and Phillipson, 2014).

Detailed data have been reported for Japan in prior volumes of *State of the Apes*. The latest data show that populations in captivity in Japan are nearly static (less than 3% change since 2016): 6 bonobos, 311 chimpanzees, 21 gorillas, 47 orangutans and 178 gibbons (Durham, 2018; GAIN, n.d.; Species360, n.d.). In Japan, as in other coun-

tries where reporting is mandatory, data coverage is superior and consistent across sources (Banes *et al.*, 2018; Durham, 2018; GAIN, n.d.).

In addition, sanctuaries in Asia hold well over 600 gibbons and 1,200 orangutans (Durham, 2018; see also Table 1.1). As Chapter 1 of this volume shows, the number of apes held as pets, in amusement parks and as tourist props throughout the region appears to be on the rise, but more research is needed to produce accurate estimates per taxon (see also Chapter 4).

Africa

Zoos house a small proportion of Africa's captive apes—just over 5%. Altogether, data for the continent's zoos accounted for only 74 apes in 2018: 46 chimpanzees, 5 gorillas, 22 gibbons and 1 orangutan (Species360, n.d.). As noted earlier, the data reported here were obtained in 2018, meaning that some figures could reflect earlier reporting periods. Another consideration is data coverage; the database lists relatively few institutions for Africa, in part because participation is voluntary and may involve dues, such that reported values are likely to be underestimates.

Sanctuaries and rescue centers thus account for nearly 95% of all apes reported to be in captivity in Africa. The numbers of bonobos and gorillas held in sanctuaries are similar to those reported in the previous volume of *State of the Apes*: about 70 and 118, respectively (Durham, 2018). In contrast, the number of chimpanzees known to be in African sanctuaries has risen by more than 5% since the previous volume (see Table 8.4). That increase reflects both changes in reporting to data sources such as Species360 and a higher number of rescues, translocations and facility changes, including the following cases.

In Ivory Coast, efforts to save a lone chimpanzee named Ponso prompted planning

TABLE 8.4

Number of Chimpanzees in African Sanctuaries, 2011, 2015 and 2018

Country	Number of sanctuaries	2011	2015	2018
Cameroon	4	244	246	247
DRC	6	85	109	117
Gabon	3	20	20	20
Gambia	1	77	106	101
Guinea	1	38	50	46
Ivory Coast	1	4	1	2
Kenya	1	44	39	39
Liberia	2	76	63	99
Nigeria	1	28	30	28
Republic of Congo	3	156	145	161
Sierra Leone	1	101	75	74
South Africa	1	33	13	33
Uganda	1	45	49	49
Zambia	1	120	126	120
Total	**27**	**1,071**	**1,072**	**1,136**

Data sources: Akatia (n.d.); Chimfunshi (n.d.); CSWCT (n.d.); Durham (2018, table 8.6); Durham and Phillipson (2014, table 10.7); HELP Congo (n.d.); J.A.C.K. (n.d.); JGI South Africa (n.d.); LCRP (n.d.); Ol Pejeta Conservancy (n.d.); Projet Primates (n.d.); SYCR (n.d.); personal communication with K. Conlee, 2018; J. Desmond, 2019; G. Le Flohic, 2018

for a sanctuary (Akatia, n.d.). The sanctuary site has been selected and, while other formalities are still in process, Akatia is currently caring for one chimpanzee and three other primates (E. Raballand, personal communication, 2020).

More than 60 chimpanzees were rescued when a research laboratory was converted into a sanctuary in Liberia (Lange, 2017; K. Conlee, personal communication, 2018). Subsequently, a new and distinct initiative, Liberia Chimpanzee Rescue and Protection (LCRP), was established to accept infants and others in need of care, regardless of origin (LCRP, n.d.; J. Desmond, personal communication, 2019). The LCRP sanctuary now has more than 25 residents (J. Desmond, personal communication, 2019).

A chimpanzee from Iraq was translocated to the Sweetwaters Chimpanzee Sanctuary in Kenya, and an airlift rescue of an infant chimpanzee from Virunga National Park to the Lwiro Primates Rehabilitation Center in the Democratic Republic of Congo (DRC) also received international media attention (Brulliard, 2018; Ohanesian, 2018).

Statistical Update Conclusion

While registration and reporting practices vary considerably around the globe, available data suggest that the number of captive apes in zoos remains relatively static. The demographics of captive populations in non-habitat countries are changing, such that breeding and reproductive rates are lower overall and, as a result, the average age could increase over time.[4]

In both non-habitat and habitat countries, regulatory changes can lead to increases in the number of apes in sanctuaries in the short and intermediate term. Sanctuary capacity can thus be a critical consideration for those who make and enforce laws and for the many stakeholders with an interest in the welfare and protection of apes. A shortage of sanctuary capacity can negatively affect facility operations and practices, such as by encouraging re-release and translocation under suboptimal conditions. Increases in the size or number of sanctuaries are often followed by surges in arrivals, highlighting that insufficient space for seized and voluntarily released apes is a critical barrier to enforcement and compliance.

The past decade has seen an increase in attention to the rights of individual apes, growing scientific knowledge of the needs and capabilities of apes, and changing views on the ethics surrounding the lives of apes. These factors will continue to drive changes in welfare standards and captive care practices. They may also provide context and increase the sense of urgency around the demand for sanctuary capacity and the critical need to curb the killing and capture of apes, and the trade in apes that fuels high, often unsustainable intake rates in habitat country rescue centers and sanctuaries.

Acknowledgments

Principal authors: Steven M. Wise, Esq.,[5] Debra Durham[6] and Graham L. Banes[7]

Endnotes

1   This section uses the term "nonhuman animal" to underscore that humans are also animals and, correspondingly, to avoid implying that only nonhuman animals are "animals."

2   In practice, however, some indigenous and minority groups are regularly denied the personhood rights accorded to all humans under these international treaties.

3   In practice, however, some indigenous and minority groups are regularly denied the personhood rights accorded to all humans under these international treaties.

4   Among the main drivers of these demographic changes are the US moratorium on breeding in labs, which was followed by a major shift to sanctuaries, where sterilization and other forms of contraception are the norm. Moreover, zoos are breeding more selectively, for example by focusing on the most endangered species and excluding hybrids, as noted in prior editions of *State of the Apes* (Durham, 2015, 2018).

5   Nonhuman Rights Project (www.nonhumanrights.org/).

6   D3 Theorem (https://d3theorem.com/).

7   Wisconsin National Primate Research Center (www.primate.wisc.edu/).

Annex I

Summary of the Five Criteria (A–E) Used to Evaluate if a Taxon Belongs in an IUCN Red List Threatened Category (Critically Endangered, Endangered or Vulnerable)*

A. POPULATION SIZE REDUCTION. POPULATION REDUCTION (MEASURED OVER THE LONGER OF 10 YEARS OR 3 GENERATIONS) BASED ON ANY OF A1 TO A4		Critically Endangered	Endangered	Vulnerable
A1		≥90%	≥70%	≥50%
A2, A3 & A4		≥80%	≥50%	≥30%
A1	Population reduction observed, estimated, inferred, or suspected in the past where the causes of the reduction are clearly reversible AND understood AND have ceased.			(a) direct observation [except A3]
A2	Population reduction observed, estimated, inferred, or suspected in the past where the causes of reduction may not have ceased OR may not be understood OR may not be reversible.	based on any of the following:		(b) an index of abundance appropriate to the taxon (c) a decline in area of occupancy (AOO), extent of occurrence (EOO) and/or habitat quality
A3	Population reduction projected, inferred or suspected to be met in the future (up to a maximum of 100 years). [(a) cannot be used for A3]			(d) actual or potential levels of exploitation
A4	An observed, estimated, inferred, projected or suspected population reduction where the time period must include both the past and the future (up to a max. of 100 years in future), and where the causes of reduction may not have ceased OR may not be understood OR may not be reversible.			(e) effects of introduced taxa, hybridization, pathogens, pollutants, competitors or parasites

B. GEOGRAPHIC RANGE IN THE FORM OF EITHER B1 (EXTENT OF OCCURRENCE) AND/OR B2 (AREA OF OCCUPANCY)		Critically Endangered	Endangered	Vulnerable
B1	Extent of occurrence (EOO)	≥90%	≥70%	≥50%
B2	Area of occupancy (AOO)	≥80%	≥50%	≥30%
AND at least 2 of the following 3 conditions:				
(a)	Severely fragmented **OR** Number of locations	=1	≤5	≤10
(b)	Continuing decline observed, estimated, inferred or projected in any of: (i) extent of occurrence; (ii) area of occupancy; (iii) area, extent and/or quality of habitat; (iv) number of locations or subpopulations; (v) number of mature individuals			
(c)	Extreme fluctuations in any of: (i) extent of occurrence; (ii) area of occupancy; (iii) number of locations or subpopulations; (iv) number of mature individuals			

C. SMALL POPULATION SIZE AND DECLINE

		Critically Endangered	Endangered	Vulnerable
Number of mature individuals		**<250**	**<2,500**	**<10,000**
AND at least one of C1 or C2:				
C1	An observed, estimated or projected continuing decline of at least (up to a max. of 100 years in future):	25% in 3 years or 1 generation (whichever is longer)	20% in 5 years or 2 generations (whichever is longer)	10% in 10 years or 3 generations (whichever is longer)
C2	An observed, estimated, projected or inferred continuing decline AND at least 1 of the following 3 conditions:			
(a)	(i) Number of mature individuals in each subpopulation:	≤50	≤250	≤1,000
	(ii) % of mature individuals in one subpopulation =	90–100%	95–100%	100%
(b)	Extreme fluctuations in the number of mature individuals			

D. VERY SMALL OR RESTRICTED POPULATION

		Critically Endangered	Endangered	Vulnerable
Number of mature individuals		**<50**	**<250**	**<1,000**
D1	*Only applies to the VU category* Restricted area of occupancy or number of locations with a plausible future threat that could drive the taxon to CR or EX in a very short time.	–	–	D2. typically: AOO <20 km² or number of locations ≤5

E. QUANTITATIVE ANALYSIS

	Critically Endangered	Endangered	Vulnerable
Indicating the probability of extinction in the wild to be:	**≥50% in 10 years or 3 generations, whichever is longer (100 years max.)**	**≥20% in 20 years or 5 generations, whichever is longer (100 years max.)**	**≥10% in 100 years**

Note: * Use of this summary sheet requires full understanding of the IUCN Red List Categories and Criteria and Guidelines for Using the IUCN Red List Categories and Criteria. Please refer to both documents for explanations of terms and concepts used here.

Source: IUCN (2012, pp. 28–9)

Annex II

Reducing Demand for Wildlife Products: WildAid Campaigns in Asia

Reducing demand for wildlife products can help diminish the scale of the poaching problem while also providing a longer-term prospect of ending trade in a specific wildlife species altogether. Demand reduction can be accomplished by educating consumers and changing their behavior, introducing or enhancing policies and regulations to limit or prohibit trade, and strengthening enforcement of those measures.

Since 2000, the environmental organization WildAid has focused on bringing an end to the illegal wildlife trade by working to reduce consumption of wildlife products. Demand reduction efforts include campaigns to raise awareness and change attitudes and behavior, government outreach to change policies and regulations, and assistance designed to strengthen enforcement.

WildAid campaigns primarily focus on elephant ivory, pangolin, rhino horn, shark fin and tiger, with activities mostly under way in mainland China, Hong Kong, Taiwan, Thailand and Viet Nam. In collaboration with celebrity ambassadors and using the same techniques as high-end advertisers, WildAid creates aspirational conservation campaigns that are seen by hundreds of millions of people each year.

In recent years, WildAid campaigns have helped to:

- reduce shark fin consumption in mainland China by 50–70%, while decreasing shark fin imports and prices by 80% between 2011 and 2016. A survey conducted in 2016 shows that 93% of respondents in four major Chinese cities had not consumed shark fin in the previous six years;

- increase awareness of and affect attitudes to ivory among more than 50% of respondents in mainland China and influence both public opinion and policymakers on the need for a domestic ivory ban;

- increase awareness of and affect attitudes to rhino horn among more than 70% of respondents in Viet Nam; and

- significantly reduce the consumption of and trade in manta and mobula ray gill rakers in Guangdong province in southern coastal China, coming close to putting an end to a rapidly growing local trade (WildAid, 2017, n.d.).

Reducing Demand for Shark Fin in China

Recent economic growth in China has permitted a large group of people to buy luxury goods. China's urban population grew from 20% in 1980 to nearly 60% in 2018, and is predicted to continue rising to 80% by 2050. China has an urban population of approximately 837 million, the majority of whom are classed as upper middle class or affluent (Barton, Chen and Jin, 2013; UN DESA, 2019). The consumption of wildlife products has also grown considerably. It is estimated that the fins from 73 million sharks are used in shark fin soup each year (WildAid, 2016).

Photo: © WildAid

When WildAid began its shark fin awareness campaign in 2006, its surveys showed that public knowledge of the problem was negligible:

- 75% of Chinese survey participants were unaware that shark fin soup came from sharks (in fact, the Chinese term for shark fin soup is "fish wing soup"); and
- 19% of Chinese survey participants believed the fins grew back (WildAid, 2018a).

Very few respondents knew about the cruelty of finning and the devastating ecological impact of this trade. WildAid's premise was that increasing their awareness of the realities of the trade would help change attitudes and behavior.

Instead of playing a direct role in trying to persuade Chinese consumers to reject shark fin, WildAid enlisted dozens of popular, respected celebrities—including actor Jackie Chan and basketball star Yao Ming—to convey the message. With a limited campaign budget of a few hundred thousand dollars per year, the organization could not buy enough airtime to make a difference, so it focused on creating compelling messages that China's largely government-controlled media would agree to broadcast (WildAid, 2011, 2012, 2013, 2016, 2017).

One of WildAid's biggest campaigns centered around the Beijing Olympics in 2008, where Yao Ming led the Chinese Olympic delegation. The organization also targeted outreach activities at chief executive officers, hotels, restaurants and chefs (WildAid, 2012).

From 2008 to 2012, WildAid organized successful campaign activities with an annual budget of about US$1 million per year, while leveraging nearly US$200 million in pro bono media placements and airtime; in 2013 alone, media organizations in China donated approximately US$164 million in media activities to WildAid. The campaign's high point was a hard-hitting and widely influential segment on shark fin on Central China Television's news magazine program (similar to the US show *60 Minutes*). In 2013, as part of an anti-corruption drive, the government banned shark fin from any official banquet functions, sending a strong message to both government officials and the public (WildAid, 2013).

Campaign messages addressed multiple issues related to shark fin, including:

- the massive scale of overfishing and exploitation of sharks (up to 73 million per year);
- cruelty in how sharks are killed;
- various environmental impacts of removing large numbers of sharks from the ocean, including putting many species at risk of extinction and impacts of resulting ecosystem imbalances;
- negative health effects of eating shark fins due to their high levels of heavy metals and toxins;
- the risk of getting fake shark fin but being charged the full price; and
- the risk of ordering shark fin soup made from illegal shark fins.

In a WildAid survey in four major cities in 2013, 85% of respondents said they had stopped eating shark fin soup within the past three years and 65% cited awareness campaigns as a reason for ending their consumption (WildAid, 2014a).

After WildAid launched its shark fin campaign in China in 2006, trader interviews in 2014 and independent survey findings indicated that shark fin consumption in China had fallen by between 50% and 70%. At the September 2016 Convention on International Trade in Endangered Species of Wild Fauna and Flora (CITES) Conference of Parties, the China CITES Management Authority corroborated these findings, stating that shark fin consumption in China had declined by 80%, based on information reported in a recent publication from the China Seafood Logistic and Processing Association. Moreover, shark fin imports into China had decreased by 82% between 2011 to 2014, and estimated wholesale shark fin sales in Beijing, Guangzhou and Shanghai declined by 81% between 2010 and 2014.

Yao Ming's commercial [PSA] impact single-handedly smashed my business.

—Shark fin trader, Guangzhou (WildAid, 2014a, p. 18)

A 2016 attitudinal survey of residents in Beijing, Chengdu, Guangzhou and Shanghai found that 80% of respondents had seen WildAid's public service announcements (PSAs) and 98.8% agreed that the messages had raised their awareness of shark conservation and the need to stop consuming shark fin (WildAid, 2018a). Many restaurateurs have stopped serving shark fin soup, saying that Yao Ming changed their minds.

> Business is down by more than half, some restaurants have closed and some chefs have been laid off. Of course I know shark fin is controversial—I learned it from Yao Ming's PSAs. I feel guilty in my heart, but what else can I do?
>
> —Chen Jun, chef, Lanzhou city (Denyer, 2013)

Revulsion at the practice of finning has been steadily growing since China's best-known sports star, the basketball player Yao Ming, said on film in 2009 that he would no longer eat the soup. Yao used the slogan "*Mei yu mai mai, jiu mei yu sha hai*," meaning "when the buying stops, the killing can too."

Yao's campaign is said to have helped to reduce consumption of shark fin soup and contributed to the Chinese government's decision formally to ban the soup from all state banquets (Vidal, 2014).

Demand Reduction for Other Wildlife Products

Building on the success of the shark fin campaign, in 2012 WildAid launched a massive campaign to reduce ivory demand in China, the world's largest market, in partnership with Save the Elephants and the African Wildlife Foundation. In the first two years, public awareness of the poaching crisis increased by 50%, and 95% of those polled in 2014 supported banning the ivory trade (WildAid, 2014b). In addition, wholesale ivory prices in mainland China and Hong Kong dropped by as much as 78% between 2014 and 2016, and ivory seized coming into mainland China fell by 80% in 2016. In the greatest single step towards protecting African elephants, in late 2016 China announced that it would shut down its domestic ivory market within the year (WildAid, 2016). The ivory ban was fully implemented by December 31, 2017 (WildAid, 2017).

WildAid's rhino campaign has helped to raise awareness and reduce demand for rhino horn in China and Viet Nam. Since its peak in 2014, the price of rhino horn has fallen from US$65,000 to around US$18,000 per kilogram (WildAid, 2018b). A 2016 campaign survey in Viet Nam showed that just 23% of respondents attributed medicinal effects to rhino horn, compared with 69% in 2014—a 67% decline. Only 9.4% of respondents in 2016 said that rhino horn could cure cancer, down from 34.5% in 2014—a 73% decline. Knowledge that horn is composed of substances found in hair and fingernails increased by 258% in two years, a period during which WildAid ran the high-profile "Nail Biters" campaign featuring billionaire entrepreneur Richard Branson, actress Li Bingbing and more than 30 other prominent celebrities (WildAid, 2015, 2018b).

Separately, WildAid launched campaigns in China and Viet Nam to reduce the demand for pangolins. Over the course of two years, the organization recruited a number of Asian megastars, including martial artist Jackie Chan, singer Jay Chou and actress Angelababy, to raise awareness of the plight of pangolins and encourage the public to shun consumption of their scales and meat. Surveys of Chinese residents found that 97% of respondents stated that the Jackie Chan "Kung Fu Pangolin" PSA made them less likely to buy products made from pangolins (WildAid, 2017).

On a regional scale in Guangdong province in China, another WildAid campaign persuaded residents to cease consumption of manta and mobula ray gill rakers (*peng yu sai*). Roughly two years after launching a localized campaign in 2014, a market investigation found gill plate stocks in Guangzhou had fallen 63% in just under three years. Meanwhile, 79% of participants surveyed in 2016 had seen WildAid's PSAs and billboards. Sixty-seven percent of respondents who had first been surveyed in 2014 had stopped or reduced their consumption of *peng yu sai* by 2016, many (43%) doing so as a result of WildAid messaging (WildAid, 2016).

Making Demand Reduction Effective

The objective of demand reduction campaigns is to change behavior by raising awareness—using a variety of approaches and appeals such as "don't buy" or "stop buying." In WildAid's experience, most people change their attitudes and behavior when they learn key facts of which they were not previously aware, such as that animals are killed cruelly or illegally, that the illegal wildlife trade has devastating impacts on species and wild populations, that products are potentially unhealthy or toxic, or that they lack medicinal benefits. Not all individuals who buy or use wildlife products change their attitudes or behavior after direct exposure to campaign messages, however. WildAid anticipates that as awareness raising contributes to the creation of new social norms for the majority in society, users who do not immediately respond to campaign messages will eventually be influenced by those around them.

To be effective, demand reduction campaigns must be flexible enough to adapt to changing circumstances. It is generally not possible to plan out a campaign or reliably earmark resources for a three- or five-year period, and large funding programs that intend to support demand reduction projects can usefully recognize the need for adaptability. While a campaign needs goals and objectives, the specific series and mix of activities needs to unfold in response to short-term impacts, emerging opportunities and developing information that cannot be foreseen from the outset.

Lessons learned include the following:

- It is impossible to plan an entire campaign at the outset.
- When first phases are executed with vigor, they can serve to build momentum and create opportunities for expanded reach and new phases.
- It is important to find ways to gain attention amidst the busy marketplace.
- Definitive consumer profiles may be misleading. Consumers change as economies evolve. The uses to which wildlife products are put also change over time, often in response to traders' activities.
- Successful campaigns tend to be sustained over time; a one-year plan is not enough.
- The use of a variety of angles to address issues keeps messaging fresh and interesting.
- Perseverance is key to an effective campaign.
- While campaigns benefit from a maximum of empirical information, they also need to continue to adapt.
- By being nimble, flexible and fast to take advantage of opportunities, organizers can intensify and expand campaign momentum and impact.
- Donors and funders can support campaigns by recognizing that they will not necessarily follow linear trajectories and by allowing for step-function progress, with flexibility for adaptation and resourcefulness.

Acknowledgment

Contributor: John Baker, WildAid (http://wildaid.org/)

Annex III

Main Threats to African Great Apes, by Range Country

Country	Threats		Source
Angola (Cabinda)	Habitat loss from artisanal logging		Ron and Refisch (2013)
	Poaching		
Burundi	Disease		Hakizimana and Huynen (2013); Plumptre *et al.* (2010)
	Habitat loss and fragmentation from conversion into agricultural land		
	Habitat loss	illegal logging activities for timber and firewood	Plumptre *et al.* (2010)
		infrastructure development (such as roads and dams)	Hakizimana and Huynen (2013); Plumptre *et al.* (2010, 2016a)
	Poaching		
Cameroon	Disease		Bergl *et al.* (2016); Maisels *et al.* (2016, 2018); Oates *et al.* (2016)
	Habitat loss	conversion into agricultural land	IUCN (2014); Morgan *et al.* (2011); Walsh *et al.* (2003)
		logging activities for timber and firewood	IUCN (2014)
		resource extraction, such as mining activities	Bergl *et al.* (2016); Maisels *et al.* (2016, 2018); Oates *et al.* (2016)
		infrastructure development (such as roads and dams)	Kormos *et al.* (2014)
	Illegal wildlife trade		EAGLE (2017)
	Poaching		
Central African Republic	Disease		Maisels *et al.* (2016, 2018); Plumptre *et al.* (2016a)
	Habitat loss	conversion into agricultural land	
		infrastructure construction (such as roads and dams)	
	Poaching		
Democratic Republic of Congo	Disease		Fruth *et al.* (2016); Kirkby *et al.* (2015); Plumptre *et al.* (2015)
	Habitat loss	conversion into agricultural land	
		natural resource extraction (artisanal and industrial mining extraction, logging for timber)	
	Poaching		Plumptre, Robbins and Williamson (2019); Plumptre *et al.* (2015)

Country	Threats		Source
Equatorial Guinea	Disease		IUCN (2014)
	Poaching		Murai *et al*. (2013)
	Habitat loss	conversion into agricultural land	
		infrastructure construction (such as roads and dams)	
Gabon	Disease (Ebola)		Bermejo *et al*. (2006); IUCN (2014); Walsh *et al*. (2003)
	Habitat loss	resource extraction (such as mining extraction and logging concessions)	Maisels *et al*. (2016)
		infrastructure construction (such as roads and dams)	
	Illegal wildlife trade		EAGLE (2017)
	Poaching		Foerster *et al*. (2012); IUCN (2014)
Ghana	Disease		Humle *et al*. (2016)
	Habitat loss	conversion into agricultural land	Danquah *et al*. (2012); Kühl *et al*. (2017)
		infrastructure construction (such as roads and dams)	Humle *et al*. (2016)
	Poaching		
Guinea	Disease		Humle *et al*. (2016); Matsuzawa, Humle and Sugiyama (2011)
	Habitat loss	conversion into agricultural land	Kühl *et al*. (2017)
		resource extraction (such as mining concessions)	Kormos *et al*. (2014); Kühl *et al*. (2017)
	Illegal wildlife trade		EAGLE (2017)
	Poaching		Kühl *et al*. (2017)
Guinea-Bissau	Disease		Sá and van Schijndel (2010)
	Habitat loss	infrastructure construction (such as roads and dams)	Dias *et al*. (2019); van der Meer (2014); Wenceslau (2014)
		conversion into agricultural land	Dias *et al*. (2019); Wenceslau (2014)
		resource extraction (a mining site overlaps with chimpanzee territory)	Dias *et al*. (2019); Humle *et al*. (2016); Wenceslau (2014)
	Poaching		van der Meer (2016); Wenceslau (2014)
Ivory Coast	Disease		Campbell *et al*. (2008); Köndgen *et al*. (2008)
	Habitat loss	conversion into agricultural land	Campbell *et al*. (2008); Kühl *et al*. (2017)
		infrastructure construction (such as roads and dams)	Kühl *et al*. (2017)
	Poaching		Campbell *et al*. (2008); Kühl *et al*. (2017)

Country	Threats		Source
Liberia	Habitat loss	infrastructure construction (such as roads and dams)	Greengrass (2015); Kühl *et al.* (2017)
		conversion into agricultural land and forest concessions	Junker *et al.* (2015)
		resource extraction (logging and mining activities)	
	Poaching		Tweh *et al.* (2015)
Mali	Habitat loss and fragmentation from agriculture, fires and resource extraction (open-pit mining)		Duvall (2008); Duvall and Smith (2005)
	Poaching		
Nigeria	Habitat loss	resource extraction (such as forest logging for timber)	Bergl *et al.* (2016); Oates *et al.* (2016)
		conversion into agricultural land	Imong *et al.* (2014a, 2014b)
		infrastructure construction (such as roads and dams)	Dunn *et al.* (2014); Morgan *et al.* (2011)
	Poaching		
	Habitat loss and fragmentation from conversion into agricultural land		Bergl *et al.* (2016); Oates *et al.* (2016)
	Disease		
Republic of Congo	Disease		IUCN (2014)
	Habitat loss	infrastructure construction (such as roads and dams)	
		resource extraction (such as artisanal and industrial mining activities and logging)	
	Poaching		
Rwanda	Disease		Plumptre *et al.* (2010)
	Habitat loss and degradation	infrastructure construction (such as roads)	Gray *et al.* (2013); Plumptre, Robbins and Williamson (2019); Plumptre *et al.* (2010); Robbins *et al.* (2011)
		resource extraction	
	Poaching		
Senegal	Disease		Boyer (2011); Ndiaye (2011)
	Habitat loss, fragmentation and degradation from agriculture, bush fires, fodder extraction and drought		Ndiaye (2011); Wessling *et al.* (2018)
	Habitat loss	resource extraction (such as open-pit, small-scale and large-scale mining)	Lindshield *et al.* (2019); Ndiaye (2011)
		infrastructure construction (such as roads and dams)	Boyer (2011)
	Poaching (human–wildlife conflict)		Ndiaye (2011)

Country	Threats		Source
Sierra Leone	Disease		Brncic, Amarasekaran and McKenna (2010)
	Habitat loss	infrastructure construction (such as roads and dams)	Kühl *et al.* (2017); Kormos *et al.* (2014)
		resource extraction (such as mining)	Brncic, Amarasekaran and McKenna (2010)
	Habitat loss and fragmentation from conversion into agricultural land		Garriga *et al.* (2018); Humle *et al.* (2016)
	Poaching for meat and in retaliation for crop raiding		Garriga *et al.* (2018); Kühl *et al.* (2017)
Tanzania	Disease		Plumptre *et al.* (2016a)
	Habitat loss	bush fires	JGI *et al.* (2011)
		logging for timber and firewood	
		infrastructure development (such as roads and dams)	
	Poaching		
	Habitat loss and fragmentation from conversion into agricultural land		
Uganda	Disease		Hickey *et al.* (2018); Plumptre *et al.* (2016a); Robbins *et al.* (2009)
	Habitat loss	infrastructure construction (such as roads and dams)	Hickey *et al.* (2018); Plumptre, Robbins and Williamson (2019); Plumptre *et al.* (2016a)
		resource extraction	Plumptre, Robbins and Williamson (2019); Plumptre *et al.* (2010)
	Poaching in retaliation for crop raiding (using guns, snares, traps)		

Notes: Threats were derived from the IUCN SSC A.P.E.S. database (IUCN SSC, n.d.-b) and references. This table does not quantify or compare the impact levels of listed threats. "Poaching" includes illegal killing carried out to obtain wild meat or body parts, in human–wildlife conflict, in retaliation for crop raiding and based on fears for personal or community safety, as well as incidental trapping. In addition to the cited threats, climate breakdown affects all great ape taxa (IUCN, 2020).

Source: GRASP and IUCN, unpublished data, 2018

Annex IV

African Great Ape Populations, by Range Country, 2000 and Most Recent Estimates

Country	Taxon	2000 abundance estimates	2018 or most recent estimates		
			Abundance	Survey period	Source
Angola	Central chimpanzee *Pan troglodytes troglodytes*	200–500	1,705 (1,027–4,801)	2005–13	Strindberg *et al.* (2018)
	Western lowland gorilla *Gorilla gorilla gorilla*	Present	1,652 (1,174–13,311)	2013	Strindberg *et al.* (2018)
Burundi	Eastern chimpanzee *Pan t. schweinfurthii*	200–500	204 (122–339)	2011–13	Hakizimana and Huynen (2013)
Cameroon	Central chimpanzee	8,500–11,500	21,489 (18,575–40,408)	2005–13	IUCN SSC (n.d.-c); Strindberg *et al.* (2018)
	Cross River gorilla *Gorilla g. diehli*	100	132–194	2007–12	Dunn *et al.* (2014)
	Nigeria–Cameroon chimpanzee *Pan t. ellioti*	1,500–3,500	3,000–7,060	2004–06	Mitchell *et al.* (2015); Morgan *et al.* (2011); Oates *et al.* (2016); J.F. Oates *et al.*, personal communication, 2018
	Western lowland gorilla	15,000	38,654 (34,331–112,881)	2013	Strindberg *et al.* (2018)
Central African Republic	Central chimpanzee	800–1,000	2,843 (1,194–4,855)	2005–13	Strindberg *et al.* (2018)
	Eastern chimpanzee	n/a	907 (538–1,534)	2012–16	Aebischer *et al.* (2017)
	Western lowland gorilla	9,000	5,529 (3,635–8,581)	2015	N'Goran, Ndomba and Beukou (2016)
Democratic Republic of Congo (DRC)	Bonobo *Pan paniscus*	20,000–50,000	15,000–20,000 minimum	2010	IUCN and ICCN (2012)
	Central chimpanzee	n/a	Present	n/a	Inogwabini *et al.* (2007)
	Eastern chimpanzee	70,000–110,000	173,000–248,000	2000–10	Plumptre *et al.* (2010)
	Grauer's gorilla *Gorilla beringei graueri*	16,900	3,800	2011–15	Plumptre *et al.* (2016c)
	Mountain gorilla *Gorilla b. beringei*	183	n/a (604, including Rwanda individuals)	2015–16	Hickey *et al.* (2019)
Equatorial Guinea	Central chimpanzee	1,000–2,000	4,290 (2,894–7,985)	2005–13	Strindberg *et al.* (2018)
	Western lowland gorilla	1,500	1,872 (1,082–3,165)	2013	Strindberg *et al.* (2018)

Country	Taxon	2000 abundance estimates	2018 or most recent estimates		
			Abundance	Survey period	Source
Gabon	Central chimpanzee	27,000–53,000	43,037 (36,869–60,476)	2005–13	Strindberg et al. (2018)*
	Western lowland gorilla	35,000	99,245 (67,117–178,390)	2013	Strindberg et al. (2018)
Ghana	Western chimpanzee Pan t. verus	300–500	264	2009	Danquah et al. (2012)
Guinea	Western chimpanzee	8,100–29,000	21,210 (10,007–43,534)	2009–14	Kühl et al. (2017); WCF (2012, 2014)
Guinea-Bissau	Western chimpanzee	100–200	1,000–1,500	2016	Chimbo Foundation, unpublished data, 2017
Ivory Coast	Western chimpanzee	10,500–12,800	410 (198–743)	2007–18	IUCN SSC (n.d.-c); Kühl et al. (2017); Tiédoué et al. (2019)
Liberia	Western chimpanzee	3,000–4,000	7,008 (4,260–11,590)	2010–12	Tweh et al. (2015)
Mali	Western chimpanzee	1,800–3,500	Present	2014	Pan African Programme, unpublished data, 2014
Nigeria	Cross River gorilla	100	85–115	2007–12	Dunn et al. (2014)
	Nigeria–Cameroon chimpanzee	>2,500	730–2,095	2005–18	Morgan et al. (2011); Oates et al. (2016); J.F. Oates et al., personal communication, 2018
Republic of Congo	Central chimpanzee	10,000	55,397 (42,433–64,824)	2005–13	Strindberg et al. (2018)
	Western lowland gorilla	34,000	215,799 (180,814–263,913)	2013	Strindberg et al. (2018)
Rwanda	Eastern chimpanzee	500	430	2009–14	IUCN SSC (n.d.-c)
	Mountain gorilla	129	n/a (604, including DRC individuals)	2015–16	Hickey et al. (2019)
Senegal	Western chimpanzee	200–400	500–600	2016–17	J. Pruetz and E. Wessling, unpublished data
Sierra Leone	Western chimpanzee	1,500–2,500	5,580 (3,052–10,446)	2009	Brncic, Amarasekaran and McKenna (2010)
South Sudan	Eastern chimpanzee	200–400	Present	2011	Plumptre et al. (2016a)
Tanzania	Eastern chimpanzee	1,500–2,500	2,500	2010–12	Plumptre et al. (2016a); A. Piel and L. Pintea, unpublished data, 2018
Uganda	Eastern chimpanzee	2,800–3,800	5,000	2003	Plumptre et al. (2016a)
	Mountain gorilla	12	400–430	2011	Roy et al. (2014)

Notes: Abundance estimates for mountain gorillas include infants; all other estimates represent the number of weaned individuals capable of building nests. Figures were obtained from field surveys and predictive models. The 95% confidence intervals appear in parentheses. The western lowland gorilla population estimates presented by Strindberg et al. (2018) for the year 2013 are likely to have declined by another 13% by the end of 2018. The mountain gorilla population in Uganda is for Bwindi only (GRASP and IUCN, 2018, table 2).

Sources: 2000 estimates: Butynski (2001); recent estimates: GRASP and IUCN (2018, table 2)

Annex V

Past and Current Asian Great Ape Population Estimates, by Range Country

Country	Taxon	1996 and 2002 population estimates		Most recent population estimate		
		Abundance	Survey period	Abundance	Survey period	Source
Indonesia	**Northeast Bornean orangutan** *Pongo pygmaeus morio*	4,825	2002	24,800 (18,100–35,600)	1999–2015	Voigt *et al.* (2018)
	Northwest Bornean orangutan *Pongo p. pygmaeus*	2,000–2,500	2002	5,200 (3,800–7,200)	1999–2015	Voigt *et al.* (2018)
	Southwest Bornean orangutan *Pongo p. wurmbii*	>34,975	2002	97,000 (73,800–135,000)	1999–2015	Voigt *et al.* (2018)
	Sumatran orangutan *Pongo abelii*	12,770	1996	13,900 (5,400–26,100)	2016	Wich *et al.* (2016)
	Tapanuli orangutan *Pongo tapanuliensis*			767 (231–1,597)	2000–12	Nowak *et al.* (2017); Wich *et al.* (2019)
Malaysia	**Northeast Bornean orangutan**	11,017 (8,317–18,376)	2002	11,017 (8,317–18,376)	2002	Ancrenaz *et al.* (2005)
	Northwest Bornean orangutan	1,143–1,761	2002	1,100 (800–1,600)	1999–2015	Voigt *et al.* (2018)

Notes: All orangutans were classified as endangered at the time of the 1996 and 2002 surveys, except for the critically endangered Sumatran and Tapanuli orangutan species, which comprised one taxon. All orangutans are now critically endangered. The 95% confidence intervals appear in parentheses.

Sources: past estimates for Sumatran and Tapanuli orangutans: Rijksen and Meijaard (1999); past estimates for all other orangutans: Wich *et al.* (2008); 2018 or most recent estimates: GRASP and IUCN (2018, table 7)

Annex VI

Gibbon Population Estimates, by Range Country

Country	Taxon	Abundance	Survey period	Source
Bangladesh	**Western hoolock** *Hoolock hoolock*	c. 200	2004	Ray *et al.* (2015)
Brunei	**Bornean gray gibbon** *Hylobates funereus*	Present	2017	U.U. Temborong, personal communication, 2017
Cambodia	**Pileated gibbon** *Hylobates pileatus*	>35,000	2003	Traeholt *et al.* (2005)
	Northern yellow-cheeked crested gibbon *Nomascus annamensis*	c. 3,000	2004	Traeholt *et al.* (2005)
	Southern yellow-cheeked crested gibbon *Nomascus gabriellae*	c. 20,000	2003	Traeholt *et al.* (2005)
China	**Cao Vit gibbon** *Nomascus nasutus*	c. 110	2015	Wei *et al.* (2017)
	Gaoligong hoolock *Hoolock tianxing*	c. 200	2015–16	Fan *et al.* (2017)
	Hainan gibbon *Nomascus hainanus*	34	2020	Chan, Lo and Mo (2020)
	Western black-crested gibbon *Nomascus concolor*	c. 5,000	2010	Sun *et al.* (2012)
India	**Western hoolock**	c. 5,000	2014	Ray *et al.* (2015)
Indonesia	**Abbott's gray gibbon** *Hylobates abottii*	Present	2019	S. Cheyne, unpublished data
	Agile gibbon *Hylobates agilis*	c. 5,000	2001	O'Brien *et al.* (2004)
	Bornean gray gibbon	c. 120,000	2012–14	Cheyne *et al.* (2016a)
	Bornean white-bearded gibbon *Hylobates albibarbis*	c. 120,000	2005–15	Cheyne *et al.* (2016a)
	Kloss's gibbon *Hylobates klossii*	20,000–25,000	2005	Whittaker (2005)
	Lar gibbon *Hylobates lar*	n/a	n/a	n/a
	Moloch gibbon *Hylobates moloch*	c. 4,500	2004–11	Nijman (2004); Setiawan *et al.* (2012)
	Müller's gibbon *Hylobates muelleri*	c. 70,000	2012–14	Cheyne *et al.* (2016a)
	Siamang *Symphalangus syndactylus*	c. 22,000	2003	O'Brien *et al.* (2004)

Country	Taxon	Abundance	Survey period	Source
Lao People's Democratic Republic	Lar gibbon	Present	2011	Boonratana et al. (2011)
	Northern white-cheeked crested gibbon Nomascus leucogenys	c. 800	2006	Duckworth (2008)
	Northern yellow-cheeked crested gibbon Nomascus annamensis	c. 3,000	1994	Duckworth et al. (1995)
	Southern white-cheeked crested gibbon Nomascus siki	c. 2,000	2013	Coudrat and Nanthavong (2014)
	Southern yellow-cheeked crested gibbon	Present	2018	Rawson et al. (2020a)
	Western black crested gibbon	Present	2005–06	Brown (2009)
Malaysia	Abbott's gray gibbon	Present	2020	S. Cheyne, personal communication, 2020
	Agile gibbon	Present	1970	Khan (1970)
	Bornean gray gibbon	c. 100,000	2012–14	Cheyne et al. (2016a)
	Lar gibbon	n/a	n/a	n/a
	Siamang	n/a	n/a	n/a
Myanmar	Eastern hoolock Hoolock leuconedys	>10,000	2005	Geissmann et al. (2013); S. Htun, personal communication, 2006
	Gaoligong hoolock	c. 45,000*	2013	Geissmann et al. (2013)
	Lar gibbon	n/a	n/a	n/a
Thailand	Lar gibbon	c. 25,000	1997–2014	W. Brockelman, personal communication, 2016
	Pileated gibbon	c. 20,000	1991	R. Phoonjampa and W. Brockelman, unpublished data
Viet Nam	Cao Vit gibbon	c. 110	2007	Rawson et al. (2011)
	Northern white-cheeked crested gibbon	c. 1,200	2009	Rawson et al. (2011)
	Northern yellow-cheeked crested gibbon	c. 3,500	2009	Rawson et al. (2011)
	Southern white-cheeked crested gibbon	c. 4,000	2009	Rawson et al. (2011)
	Southern yellow-cheeked crested gibbon	c. 3,000	2008	Rawson et al. (2011)
	Western black crested gibbon	c. 300	2009	Rawson et al. (2011)

Notes: Estimates are based on the number of duetting or singing adults and thus exclude subadults, juveniles and infants. Estimates are derived from surveys and modelling approaches.

* The Gaoligong hoolock (Hoolock tianxing) was previously recognised as the eastern hoolock (Hoolock leuconedys) but was recently identified as a separate species. As the gibbon's area is experiencing civil conflict, research cannot be carried out safely and no recent data are available; consequently, the population estimate is based on extrapolation.

Annex VII

African Great Ape Population Trends by Taxon, in Descending Order of Abundance

Taxon	Abundance	Trend	Annual rate of change	Total estimated change	Period assessed	Source
Western lowland gorilla *Gorilla gorilla gorilla*	361,919 (302,973–460,093)	Declining	–2.7%	–19.4%	2005–13	Strindberg *et al.* (2018)
Eastern chimpanzee *Pan troglodytes schweinfurthii*	181,000–256,000	Declining	–5.1%	–22% to –45% in eastern DRC only	1994–2015	Plumptre *et al.* (2015, 2016a)
Central chimpanzee *Pan t. troglodytes*	128,760 (114,208–317,039)	Declining[a]	n/a	n/a	2005–13	Maisels *et al.* (2016)
Western chimpanzee *Pan t. verus*	52,800 (17,577–96,564)	Declining	–6.53%	–80.2%	1990–2014	Heinicke *et al.* (2019)
Bonobo *Pan paniscus*	15,000–20,000 minimum	Declining	–5.95%[b]	–54.9%	2003–15	Fruth *et al.* (2016)
			–1%[c]	>–50%	2003–78	
Nigeria–Cameroon chimpanzee *Pan t. ellioti*	4,400–9,345	Declining	–0.92% to –2.14%	–50% to –80%	1985–2060	R. Bergl, A. Dunn, L. Gadsby, R.A. Ikemeh, I. Imong, J.F. Oates, F. Maisels, B. Morgan, S. Nixon and E.A. Williamson, personal communication, 2018
Grauer's gorilla *Gorilla beringei graueri*	3,800 (1,280–9,050)	Declining	–7.34%	–77%	1994–2015	Plumptre *et al.* (2015, 2016c)
Mountain gorilla *Gorilla b. beringei*	>1,000	Increasing	+3.7%	+26%	2003–10	Gray *et al.* (2013); Hickey *et al.* (2018); Roy *et al.* (2014)
Cross River gorilla *Gorilla g. diehli*	<300	Declining	n/a	n/a	n/a	Dunn *et al.* (2014); R. Bergl and J. Oates, personal communication, 2000

Notes: Abundance estimates for mountain gorillas include infants; all other estimates represent the number of weaned individuals capable of building nests. Estimates are based on both surveys and spatial predictions. The 95% confidence intervals appear in parentheses.

Due to variations in modeling approaches, the taxon-specific estimates per country are not necessarily equivalent to the sums of regional estimates per country. All estimates at taxon level were derived from modeling approaches in the source publications, except for the Cross River gorilla, mountain gorilla and the Nigeria–Cameroon chimpanzee.

[a] While Strindberg *et al.* (2018) do not detect any statistically significant change in central chimpanzee numbers, they note that it is unlikely that the population remained stable between 2005 and 2013. Moreover, Maisels *et al.* (2016) observe: "Given the scale of the poaching problem across Central Africa, this taxon is likely to be experiencing declines significant in terms of the population status, which we do not have the statistical power to detect."

[b] The confidence interval for this analysis is very large, suggesting uncertainty in the data.

[c] A 1% decline per year would yield more than a 50% reduction of the bonobo population for the period 2003–78.

Source: GRASP and IUCN (2018, table 4)

Annex VIII

Asian Great Ape Population Decline by Taxon, in Descending Order of Abundance

Taxon	Abundance	Annual rate of change	Total estimated change	Survey period	Source
Southwest Bornean orangutan *Pongo pygmaeus wurmbii*	97,000 (73,800–135,000)	–4.71%	–53%	1999–2015	Voigt *et al.* (2018)
Northeast Bornean orangutan *Pongo p. morio*	30,900 (22,800–44,200)	–4.45%	–52%	1999–2015	Voigt *et al.* (2018)
Sumatran orangutan *Pongo abelii**	13,900 (5,400–26,100)	–2.37%	–30%*	2015–2030	Wich *et al.* (2016)
Northwest Bornean orangutan *Pongo p. pygmaeus*	6,300 (4,700–8,600)	–4.71%	–53%	1999–2015	Voigt *et al.* (2018)
Tapanuli orangutan *Pongo tapanuliensis*	800 (300–1,400)	–2.36%	–83%	1985–2060	Nowak *et al.* (2017)

Notes: * Temporal trends for the Sumatran orangutan are based on various forest loss scenarios (Wich *et al.*, 2016). Under the current land use scenario, as many as 4,500 individuals could disappear by 2030.

The 95% confidence intervals, which appear in parentheses, are rounded to the nearest 100.

Due to variations in modeling approaches, the taxon-specific estimates per country are not necessarily equivalent to the sums of regional estimates per country. All orangutan estimates at taxon level were derived from modeling approaches in the source publications.

Source: GRASP and IUCN (2018, table 8)

Annex IX

Small Ape Population Decline by Taxon, in Descending Order of Abundance

Taxon	Abundance	Annual rate of change	Total estimated change, 1973–2018
Bornean white-bearded gibbon *Hylobates albibarbis*	120,000	−1.54	−50%
Bornean gray gibbon *Hylobates funereus*	100,000	−1.54	−50%
Müller's gibbon *Hylobates muelleri*	100,000	−1.54	−50%
Pileated gibbon *Hylobates pileatus*	60,000	> −1.54	> −50%
Siamang *Symphalangus syndactylus*	60,000	−1.73	−50%
Moloch gibbon *Hylobates moloch*	48,500	−1.54	−50%
Gaoligong hoolock *Hoolock tianxing*	40,000	−3.57	−80%
Agile gibbon *Hylobates agilis*	25,000	> −1.54	> −50%
Kloss's gibbon *Hylobates klossii*	25,000	−1.54	−50%
Lar gibbon *Hylobates lar*	25,000	−1.54	−50%
Western hoolock *Hoolock hoolock*	15,000	−1.54	−50%
Eastern hoolock *Hoolock leuconedys*	10,000	−0.79	−30%
Southern yellow-cheeked crested gibbon *Nomascus gabriellae*	8,000	−1.54	−50%
Northern yellow-cheeked crested gibbon *Nomascus annamensis*	6,500	−1.54	−50%
Southern white-cheeked crested gibbon *Nomascus siki*	6,000	−3.57	−80%
Western black crested gibbon *Nomascus concolor*	5,350	−3.57	−80%
Northern white-cheeked crested gibbon *Nomascus leucogenys*	2,000	−3.57	−80%
Cao Vit gibbon *Nomascus nasutus*	229	−3.57	−80%

►	**Hainan gibbon** *Nomascus hainanus*	34	−3.57	−80%
	Abbott's gray gibbon *Hylobates abbottii*	n/a	−1.54	−50%

Note: A number of taxa experienced similar levels of decline over the 45 year survey period, resulting in the same annual rate of change.

Sources: unpublished IUCN Red List updates, seen by the authors, 2019 (now published in: Brockelman and Geissmann, 2019, 2020; Brockelman *et al.*, 2020; Brockelman, Molur and Geissmann, 2019; Cheyne and Nijman, 2020; Fan, Turvey and Bryant, 2020; Geissmann and Bleisch, 2020; Geissmann *et al.*, 2020; Liswanto *et al.*, 2020; Marshall, Nijman and Cheyne, 2020a, 2020b; Nguyen *et al.*, 2020; Nijman, 2020; Nijman, Cheyne and Traeholt, 2020; Nijman *et al.*, 2020; Pengfei *et al.*, 2020; Rawson *et al.*, 2020a, 2020b, 2020c; Thinh *et al.*, 2020)

ACRONYMS AND ABBREVIATIONS

A.P.E.S.	Apes, Populations, Environment, Surveys
ACCFOLU	Community Association for the Conservation of Forests in Lubutu
AFADA	Association of Officials and Attorneys for the Rights of Animals (*Asociación de Funcionarios y Abogados por los Derechos de los Animales*)
AIDS	acquired immune deficiency syndrome
ANPN	Agence Nationale des Parcs Nationaux
AOO	Area of occupancy
API	Animal Protection Index
ARU	Autonomous Recording Unit
ASEAN	Association of Southeast Asian Nations
ASEAN-WEN	Association of Southeast Asian Nations Wildlife Law Enforcement Network
asl	above sea level
AZA	Association of Zoos and Aquariums
BKSDA	Natural Resources Conservation Agency of the Ministry of Environment and Forestry of Indonesia (*Balai Konservasi Sumber Daya Alam*)
CAP	conservation action plan
CAR	Central African Republic
CBD	United Nations Convention on Biological Diversity
CFA	Central African franc
CFCL	Local Community Forestry Concession (*Concessions Forestières des Communautés Locales*)
CGI	computer-generated imagery
CITES	Convention on International Trade in Endangered Species of Wild Fauna and Flora
cm	centimeter
CMBNR	Chuxiong Management Bureau of Nature Reserves
CMP	The Conservation Measures Partnership
CMS	Convention on the Conservation of Migratory Species of Wild Animals
CoCoLuWa	community conservation zone of Lubutu and Walikale Territories
Congo	Republic of Congo
CoP	Conference of the Parties
CPUE	catch per unit effort
DRC	Democratic Republic of Congo
EAGLE	Eco Activists for Governance and Law Enforcement
EAZA	European Association of Zoos and Aquaria
EOO	extent of occurrence
EVD	Ebola virus disease
FFI	Fauna & Flora International
FMU	forest management unit
FODI	Forest for Integral Development, DRC

FR	forest reserve
FSC	Forest Stewardship Council
GDANCP	General Department of Administration for Nature Conservation and Protection, Cambodia
GFAS	Global Federation of Animal Sanctuaries
GPS	Global Positioning System
GRACE	Gorilla Rehabilitation and Conservation Education Center
GRASP	Great Apes Survival Partnership
ha	hectare
HIV	human immunodeficiency virus
HuGo	Human–Gorilla (Conflict Resolution)
IAR	International Animal Rescue
ICCN	Congolese Institute for the Conservation of Nature, DRC (*Institut Congolais pour la Conservation de la Nature*)
ICCWC	International Consortium on Combating Wildlife Crime
ICD	integrated conservation and development
ICDP	integrated conservation and development project
IDR	Indonesian rupiah
IFAW	International Fund for Animal Welfare
INTERPOL	International Criminal Police Organization
IUCN	International Union for Conservation of Nature (also *UICN: Union Internationale pour la Conservation de la Nature*)
IWT	illegal wildlife trade
JGI	Jane Goodall Institute
kg	kilogram
km	kilometer
LAGA	Last Great Ape Organization
Lao PDR	Lao People's Democratic Republic
LCRP	Liberia Chimpanzee Rescue and Protection
m	meter
MEA	multilateral environmental agreement
MGMC	My Gorilla–My Community
MINFOF	Ministry of Forestry and Wildlife, Cameroon (*Ministère des Forêts et de la Faune*)
MIST	Management Information System
MPF	Missouri Primate Foundation
NGO	non-governmental organization
NhRP	Nonhuman Rights Project
NP	national park
PAM	passive acoustic monitoring
PETA	People for the Ethical Treatment of Animals
PHVA	population and habitat viability assessment
PIDEP	Integrated Program for Endogenous Development of Pygmies
POV	point of vulnerability
PSA	public service announcement
PSG	Primate Specialist Group

PVA	population viability analysis
RCO	Oku Community Reserve, DRC
RFID	radio frequency identification
RILO	Regional Intelligence Liaison Office
SES	socio–ecological systems
SHCA	Species and Habitat Conservation Area
SMART	Spatial Monitoring and Reporting Tool
SODEPE	Solidarity for the Development and Protection of the Environment, DRC
sp.	species (singular)
spp.	species (plural)
SSA	Section on Small Apes
SSC	Species Survival Commission
ssp	sub-species
SSP	Species Survival Plan
TOC	transnational organized crime
TV	television
UAE	United Arab Emirates
UAV	unmanned aerial vehicle
UCOFOBI	Community Union for the Conservation of Forests of Bitule, DRC
UGADEC	Union of Associations for Gorilla Conservation and Community Development, DRC
UN	United Nations
UN Comtrade	United Nations International Trade Statistics Database
UNEP	United Nations Environment Programme
UNEP-WCMC	United Nations Environment Programme World Conservation Monitoring Centre
UNODC	United Nations Office on Drugs and Crime
UNTOC	United Nations Convention against Transnational Organized Crime
US	United States of America
UTDPE	Union of Landowners for the Development and Protection of the Environment, DRC
UWA	Uganda Wildlife Authority
VGT	Association Against Animal Factories (*Verein gegen Tierfabriken*)
WAZA	World Association of Zoos and Aquariums
WCF	Wild Chimpanzee Foundation
WCO	World Customs Organization
WCS	Wildlife Conservation Society
WEN	Wildlife Law Enforcement Network
WWF	World Wide Fund for Nature/World Wildlife Fund
ZSL	Zoological Society of London

GLOSSARY

Abundance: The number of individuals of a species in an area or in a population.

Acoustic monitoring: The recording of animal vocalization or threatening activities, such as gunshots, to inform on the state of a species in the area of interest.

Adaptive management: An iterative process of decision-making that is continuously informed by ecological and project monitoring and thus improved over time to meet the management objectives in the most effective way.

Administrative penalty: A sanction that limits an offender's rights or position held in government, whether applied by an administrative or a criminal law.

Advertising: The act of producing, paying for, or otherwise being engaged in announcing the sale of wildlife or wildlife products in any media or form, including online, in print, on television or on the radio.

Agency: The capacity of individuals to act independently and to make their own free choices.

Aggravating circumstances: Aspects of a crime that can be used to increase fines and penalties, such as repeat offenses (recidivism).

Agropastoralism: A way of life or a form of social organization based on the growing of crops and the raising of livestock as the primary means of economic activity.

Alternative livelihoods: An approach to conservation which seeks to reduce conservation threats to particular species or sites by providing alternatives – including alternative food options if the conservation threat is hunting for food; alternative income sources if the conservation threat is caused as a result of trying to generate income; and alternative (lower impact) methods for harvesting wildlife if the conservation threat is over-exploitation.

Anthropocene: A buzzword used to refer to the current geological epoch in view of humankind's profound impact on the Earth. The term was popularized by atmospheric chemist Paul Crutzen in 2000 and recommended for adoption by a dedicated working group of the International Union of Geological Sciences in 2016. Scholars disagree about the start date of the Anthropocene, with suggestions ranging from 8,000 years ago to about 1950.

Aquaculture (or aquafarming): The farming of animals and plants in all types of water environments.

Autonomy: One's liberty to freely choose, within wide parameters, how one wishes to live one's life.

Backend: The part of a computer application or system that stores and manipulates data to fulfill user requests and actions, but that is not visible to or accessed directly by the user.

Bimaturism: Development characterized by differing stages or timings within a species or within a sex; among orangutans, mature males are flanged or unflanged (see **flanged**).

Biodiversity: The variety of plant and animal life on Earth or in a particular habitat.

Biodiversity hotspot: A significant reservoir of biodiversity that is threatened with destruction.

Biomonitoring: Repeated surveying of the distribution and abundance of species, and of the threats they face.

Blackback: An adolescent male chimpanzee or gorilla between the ages of 8 and 12 years old. As opposed to **silverback**, as the silver on the back develops when males reach sexual maturity.

Bovid: A hoofed mammal in the family *Bovidae*, such as antelopes, sheep and bison, whose horns do not branch and are never shed.

Brachiation: Arboreal locomotion that relies exclusively on the arms to propel the body forward. Related term: brachiate.

Branhamism: The teachings of the US preacher William M. Branham (1909–65), including anti-denominationalism, the denial of eternal hell and the Serpent's Seed doctrine.

Camera trapping: The use of cameras triggered by motion or infrared sensors in animal surveys.

Capture–recapture: An analytical approach to estimating animal abundance by repeated identification and re-identification of individuals.

Catch per unit effort (CPUE): In relation to law enforcement action for conservation, it is a measure of effectiveness arrived at by calculating, for example, the number of illegal activities or items, such as snares, detected per given area or time patrolled.

Civil law: A system that dates back to Roman times and relies predominantly on comprehensive legal codes/ statutes that are updated frequently. In civil law, the judge's task is to establish the facts and decide on the appropriate action based on the laws in place. Civil law systems vary widely in procedure and substantive law.

Co-use: The intended use of an area by humans and animals. Instead of separating areas for human activity and species protection, co-use areas are meant to harmonize the co-existence of humans and other species, including great apes.

Colobine: Members of a subfamily of arboreal, leaf-eating monkeys found in forests in Africa and Asia.

Common law: A system that relies predominantly on precedent, i.e., prior decisions. It is adversarial, as opposed to investigatory, with the judge moderating between two parties, and may be influenced by the judge's values.

Community engagement: A way of developing a working relationship between public bodies and community groups.

Conditionalities: Conditions attached to the provision of benefits such as a loan, debt relief or bilateral aid.

Conservation framework: A formal concept that describes approaches to the conservation of species in a standardized and reproducible way.

Conspecific: An individual of the same species as another.

Core area: The most heavily used portion of the home range of a group or individual.

Corridor: Restricted areas of wildlife habitat that link larger patches of habitat, thereby enabling wildlife movement and supporting the viability of populations. These corridors can occur naturally, such as riparian forests, or be created through management practices.

Coupled (or linked): Characteristic of integrated conservation and development interventions that seek to link development outcomes to positive conservation outcomes, such as by making continued income from ecotourism dependent on the maintenance of the conservation status of a species or site such that tourists continue to be attracted.

Critically endangered: Facing an extremely high risk of extinction in the wild.

Deciduous: Pertaining to trees that lose their leaves for part of the year.

Decoupled: Characteristic of integrated conservation and development interventions that seek to reduce the dependence of local people on species or sites of conservation value, such as by investing in agricultural development outside of a protected area to ensure that people have sufficient food and no longer enter the protected area to secure wild meat.

Defaunation: The global, local or functional extinction of animal populations or species from ecological communities.

Devolution: The transfer or delegation of power to a lower level, especially by central government to local or regional administration.

Dichromatic: Exhibiting two color variations independent of sex and age.

Die-off: A sudden and significant decline in a population or community of organisms due to natural causes.

Differential liability: A step beyond the more traditional approaches that treat wildlife criminals solely as individuals, tailoring liability to the type of criminal by imposing different or higher penalties on legal persons and civil servants.

Dimorphic: Having two distinct forms.

Dipterocarp: A tall hardwood tree of the family *Dipterocarpaceae* that grows primarily in Asian rainforests and that is the source of valuable timber, aromatic oils and resins.

Dispersing sex: Either male or female apes who, upon reaching sexual maturity, depart from their birth area to establish their own range.

Distance sampling: A transect survey technique that calculates the distance between an observer and an animal being sampled, calculating the probability of detection.

Diurnal: Daily, or active during the day.

Driver: A factor that causes or contributes to an activity or phenomenon.

Ecosystem function: All ecological processes that occur in an ecosystem.

Elusive species: A taxon that is difficult to observe due to inconspicuous behavior and avoidance of humans.

Endangered: Facing a very high risk of extinction in the wild.

Endemic: Native to or only found in a certain place; indigenous.

Endemism: The state of being unique to a particular geographic area.

Entertainment education: A communication strategy that uses custom-tailored entertainment to alleviate a social issue or educate the public.

Exhibition: An end use component of trade, such as the display of illegally sourced apes in a circus.

Exotic: Neither domestic nor farmed.

Extinct: A species becomes 'extinct' following the death of the last individual, although the species' ability to recover/reproduce will have been lost before reaching this point. A species may become 'extinct in the wild' before being considered actually extinct, if there is one or more individual in captivity.

Extirpated: Completely destroyed/eradicated from an area.

Extraction-to-production ratio: An indicator used in wildlife studies to denote the relationship between the numbers or biomass of hunted species that can be produced (essentially through reproduction) in a particular population, to contrast against the number of animals or biomass extracted in that population based on hunter or market studies.

Extractive industry: Any operations that remove metals, minerals or aggregates from the earth for use by consumers.

Facebook: The world's largest social media platform.

Fission–fusion: Pertaining to communities whose size and composition are dynamic due to the coming together (fusion) and moving away (fission) of individuals.

Flagship species: A charismatic species that is selected to serve as ambassador for the protection of an ecosystem or an area inhabited by many species that are less well known.

Flanged: Pertaining to one of two morphs of adult male orangutan, the other being "unflanged"; characterized by large cheek pads, greater size, a long coat of dark hair on the back and a throat sac used for "long calls." See also: **unflanged**.

Flora: Plant life.

Folivore: Any chiefly leaf-eating animal. Related terms: folivorous, folivory.

Frugivore: Any chiefly fruit-eating animal. Related terms: frugivorous, frugivory.

Gazettement: The designation of an area of land for protection by the state or other public authorities according to relevant legislation.

Gill plate/raker (peng yu sai): bony or cartilaginous sieving pads in fish or other water creatures, used for feeding, by filtering zooplankton from sea water.

Gray literature: Reports that have not undergone a peer-review process and that have not been published in scientific journals.

Guenon: A long-tailed African monkey of the genus *Cercopithecus* found mainly in forests and also in savannah habitats.

Habeas corpus: Latin for "you have the body" and referred to as the "great writ." A written legal command that protects persons from being unjustly imprisoned by requiring the detainer to appear in court and provide evidence of justifiable grounds for their imprisonment.

Habitat: The natural and required environment of an animal, plant or other organism.

Habituated: Accustomed to the presence of humans. Related term: habituation.

Herbivore: Any plant-eating animal. Related terms: herbivorous, herbivory.

Holocene: The current geological epoch, which began about 10,000 years ago, at the end of the most recent ice age, when humans started to develop agriculture. Some scholars hold that the Holocene ended when the Anthropocene began, but opinion remains divided on the date. See also: **Anthropocene**.

Hominid: A member of the group that comprises all modern and extinct humans and great apes, as well as their immediate ancestors.

Hominin: A member of the group that comprises all modern human beings—*Homo sapiens*—and their extinct ancestors, including *Homo neanderthalensis* (the Neanderthals), *Homo erectus* and *Homo habilis*.

Horizon scanning: A strategic process for the early detection of developments that may have a strong impact on the environment, an ecosystem or a species.

Hunting: The pursuit, targeting, capture or killing of wildlife.

Husbandry: The care, cultivation and breeding of crops and animals.

Hybrid: The offspring of two different species or varieties of plant or animal; something that is formed by combining different elements. See also: **hybridization**.

Hybridization: Interbreeding of distinct taxa or species. See also: **hybrid**.

Immunocompetence: The ability of the body to recognize and respond to exposure to bacteria, viruses, toxins and other harmful substances.

Inbreeding: Reproduction of closely related individuals, which can cause inbreeding depression, characterized by reduced fitness and fertility in offspring.

Incidental offtake: Any capture of a species that is not the intended purpose of a hunting activity. Or, as in some legal documents, any prohibited capture of an endangered or threatened species that is not the intended purpose of an otherwise lawful activity.

Indigenous: Originating from or occurring naturally in a certain place.

Infanticide: The act of killing an infant.

Instagram: A photograph and video-sharing social networking website owned by Facebook.

Integrated conservation and development: An approach to the management of natural resources that aims to achieve lasting reconciliation between biodiversity conservation and socioeconomic development interests of different stakeholders.

Interbirth interval: The biologically determined period of time between consecutive births.

Intergroup conflict: Discord and potentially physical violence among different groups of individuals of the same species.

Internet scam: Online fraud.

Intraspecific killing: The killing of a member of the same species by one or more individuals.

Keystone species: A species that plays a crucial role in the way an ecosystem functions, and whose presence and role has a disproportionately large effect on other organisms within the ecosystem.

Life history: The length and stages of development that species pass through during their lives. Nonhuman primates grow more slowly, have their first reproduction at a later age, have lower fertility, provide extensive parental care and have longer life spans than most other mammals.

Lithic technology: The manufacture and use of stone tools.

Long call: A series of sounds made by adult male orangutans, from barking to roaring to groaning, to attract females and/or alert other orangutans to their presence and establish their personal space. Cheek flanges aid directionality of the call and the throat sac makes the sound resonate and carry further.

Macronutrients: Substances in food that are required in large amounts for growth, metabolism and other essential bodily functions.

Management unit: A well-defined area for which a management plan has been developed. In the context of the FSC this refers to a spatial area or areas submitted for certification with clearly defined boundaries and managed to a set of explicit long-term management objectives, which are expressed in a management plan.

Mantrap: A trap to catch people, usually aimed at trespassers and poachers.

Mast fruiting: The simultaneous production of fruit by a large numbers of trees every 2–10 years, without any seasonal change in temperature or rainfall.

Mean body mass indicator: A measure of defaunation, often estimated based on wild meat offtake; the value drops as the proportion of small-bodied animals in a community increases and hunters rely on ever-smaller species.

Megafauna: Extant and extinct big animals, such as elephants, giraffes, whales, cows, deer and tigers.

Micronutrients: Substances in food that are required in minuscule amounts to enable the body to produce enzymes, hormones and other substances essential for proper growth and development.

Militarized conservation: The use of military tactics, equipment and sometimes military staff to help protect flora and fauna.

Monogamy: The practice of having a single mate over a period of time. Gibbons are considered socially monogamous, having a single mate or companion over a period of time.

Morph: A distinct form of an organism or species.

Multi-male group: This refers to groups that include more than one mature (silverback) male gorilla.

Night lighting: A hunting method that is commonly criminalized and that involves the use of lights at night to help hunters see and to attract targeted animals or cause them to freeze momentarily, which assists the hunter.

Non-native species: A species that lives outside its native distributional range, having arrived there through human activity.

Occupancy: The proportion of sites at which the presence of a species has been confirmed.

Occurrence: The distribution of presence and absence of a species.

Offtake: A scientific term used to refer to the number of individuals removed from the wild through hunting, especially in the context of population trends. See also: **take**.

Offtake pressure indicator: A measure of wildlife hunting/harvest levels, estimated based on the number of individuals of a species removed from their habitat over a specific amount of time.

Optimal foraging theory: A theoretical framework that links foraging variations within and across populations to characteristics of the local ecology.

Organized crime: Criminal offenses committed by three or more persons working together over a period of time, or criminal activities planned and coordinated within a hierarchical network of people on a continuing basis.

Paleotropics: A floristic kingdom comprising tropical areas of Africa, Asia and parts of Oceania, but not Australia or New Zealand.

Parturition: The process of giving birth to offspring.

Passive acoustic monitoring: The deployment of autonomous recording devices to survey an area based on animal vocalizations and subsequent analyses to assess the state of species.

Pelage: Fur; coat.

Personhood: Is being given the legal status of a person. A "person" is a legal entity that has one or more rights, as opposed to a "thing", which has no legal rights. Historically, some humans were identified as legal "things", and you do not have to be a human being to be classified as a person, in law.

Phytosanitary: Relating to plant health and, more specifically, to rules and regulations for the control of plant diseases.

Pith: The spongy tissue in the stems and branches of many plants.

Pleistocene: The geological epoch that lasted from about 2.6 million to 10,000 years ago, when the most recent ice age ended and the Holocene began.

Poaching: Illegal hunting, killing, capturing or taking of wildlife in violation of local or international wildlife conservation laws.

Point transect: A circular area that is used as a sampling unit during a survey with a human observer, camera trap or acoustic recording device at its center to record animal observations.

Polyandrous: Pertaining to a mating system that involves one female and two or more males.

Polygynandrous: Pertaining to an exclusive mating system that involves two or more males and two or more females. The numbers of males and females are not necessarily equal.

Polygynous: Pertaining to a mating system that involves one male and two or more females.

Population and habitat viability assessment: A tool to develop population targets and a framework of conservation recommendations for a specific species.

Population viability analysis: A method of assessing the risk of extinction for a specific species.

Possession: In criminal law, the offense of being in physical control of protected wildlife or wildlife products, regardless of involvement in trafficking or related criminal activity. The criminalization of possession fills an evidentiary gap by allowing law enforcement to pursue individuals who are in control of protected species even in the absence of evidence that they are engaged in trafficking of the same. In countries where the law fails to criminalize possession, law enforcement officials are limited to arresting traffickers in the act of selling, or pursuing them based on receipts or other evidence that proves they are engaged in trafficking.

Precedent: A judgment or ruling from a previous case that is cited in a similar subsequent dispute as the justification for ruling in a specific way.

Predicate crime (or offense): A crime, or offense, that forms a part of a larger criminal activity, such as forgery, smuggling and money laundering in the context of the illegal wildlife trade.

Preputial: Relating to the foreskin or clitoral hood.

Prestige pet: An animal who is perceived as conferring status on the owner, or who reflects the owner's wealth or power.

Primary law: Various forms of legislation, statutes, regulations and decisions that are binding on the courts, government and individuals, as distinguished from commentary and other types of secondary law, which are not legally binding.

Processing: Any activity that involves the transformation of wildlife from one state or product to another.

Radio frequency identification: Technology that uses electromagnetic fields to identify and track tags attached to objects.

Range: The geographical extent of occurrence of all known populations of a species, including any unsuitable and unoccupied areas.

Reintroduction: The planned release of an organism into its natural habitat after life in captivity.

Riparian (or riverine) forest: A forest that grows alongside riverbanks.

Sanctuary: A non-profit facility dedicated to providing care for orphaned, confiscated or injured wildlife.

Shifting agriculture (or cultivation): A type of agricultural management by which farmers cultivate fields only for some time before abandoning them and creating new fields, principally to avoid decreasing harvest rates and to prevent soils from becoming increasingly impoverished.

Silverback: A mature male gorilla with silver hair on the saddle of his back.

Social first strategy: A campaign or marketing strategy that focuses on social media platforms, e.g., Facebook and Instagram, to reach and influence the target audience.

Social marketing: The application of commercial techniques to achieve social good.

Species listing: The legal mechanism by which species are added to a national or international list and provided stricter protection.

Storage: The act of keeping wildlife or wildlife products in a physical space of any kind for later use.

Strategic framework: A detailed, structured outline that spells out an overarching strategy, activities for achieving associated objectives and, in some cases, indicators for measuring progress against stated goals.

Subsistence consumption: Production of food—either grown or harvested from natural resources—at a level that is sufficient only for use or consumption by the producer and their direct family, without any surplus for trade.

Sympatric: Pertaining to species or populations that occupy the same geographic ranges.

Take: A legal term used to refer to an act that directly or indirectly results in the killing or capture of an animal. See also: **offtake** and **take method**.

Take method: A legal term used to refer to the means by which an animal is killed or captured, including the use of traps, guns, night lighting and vehicles. See also: **offtake** and **take**.

Taxon: Any unit used in the science of biological classification or taxonomy (plural: taxa).

Terrestriality: Adaptation to living on the ground.

Theory of change: A methodology that defines long-term goals and identifies strategies and activities needed to achieve the desired results.

Transect: A straight line or point used as a sampling unit in surveys to collect data on animal presence.

Transport: Any act involving the physical movement of wildlife or wildlife products, including shipping by air, sea, rail or road.

Trigger (or predicate): A circumstance or action that results in the application of additional rules and regulations. Species listing, for instance, may act as a trigger for the application of a hunting prohibition and other legal instruments.

Trophy hunting: The legal shooting of animals—frequently big game such as rhinos, elephants, lions, pumas and bears—under official government license, for pleasure. The trophy is the animal (or its head, skin or any other body part) that the hunter keeps as a souvenir.

Umbrella species: A species whose conservation leads to the protection of many other species in the same ecosystem or landscape.

Unarmed: Not having any hard and sharp projections, such as hooks, prickles, spines, thorns or other sharply pointed structures.

Ungulate: A hoofed animal.

Vulnerable: A species that has been categorized as at risk of becoming endangered if the threats to its survival are not addressed.

Wean: To accustom a young animal to nourishment other than the mother's milk.

Welfare: The state of a [nonhuman] animal's body and mind, including in terms of biological, emotional and behavioral well-being.

WhatsApp: A free messaging, voice and video call service owned by Facebook.

Wild meat: Meat from wild animals.

Wildlife trafficking: The illegal sourcing, transfer and sale or disposal of live or dead animals and plants or their parts or products, usually for commercial purposes.

Zooarcheology: The study of animal remains from archeological sites.

REFERENCES

Abernethy, K.A., Coad, L., Taylor, G., Lee, M.E. and Maisels, F. (2013). Extent and ecological consequences of hunting in Central African rainforests in the twenty-first century. *Philosophical Transactions of the Royal Society of London, Series B: Biological Sciences*, **368**(1625), 20120303. DOI: 10.1098/rstb.2012.0303.

Abram, N.K., Meijaard, E., Wells, J.A., *et al.* (2015). Mapping perceptions of species' threats and population trends to inform conservation efforts: the Bornean orangutan case study. *Diversity and Distributions*, **21**(5), 487–99. DOI: 10.1111/ddi.12286.

Abugiche, A.S., Egute, T.O. and Cybelle, A. (2017). The role of traditional taboos and custom as complementary tools in wildlife conservation within Mount Cameroon National Park Buea. *International Journal of Natural Resource Ecology and Management*, **2**(3), 60–8.

Ad Age (2012). PETA: chimp casting call. *Ad Age*, May 10, 2012. Available at: https://adage.com/creativity/work/chimp/27597.

ADI (2007). European Parliament sets historic target to end experiments on primates. *ADI: Animal Defenders International*, December 6, 2007. Available at: http://www.ad-international.org/animal_rescues/go.php?id=1135&ssi=0.

ADI (2019). Worldwide circus bans. *ADI: Animal Defenders International*. Available at: http://www.ad-international.org/animals_in_entertainment/go.php?id=281. Accessed May 9, 2019.

ADI (n.d.). Federal Circus Bill: worldwide summary. *ADI: Animal Defenders International*. Available at: http://www.federalcircusbill.org/briefings/worldwide-summary/. Accessed January 4, 2019.

Aebischer, T., Siguindo, G., Rochat, E., *et al.* (2017). First quantitative survey delineates the distribution of chimpanzees in the Eastern Central African Republic. *Biological Conservation*, **213**, 84–94. DOI: 10.1016/j.biocon.2017.06.031.

AFADA (Asociacion de Funcionarios y Abogados por los Derechos de los Animales y Otros) v. *The Government of the City of Buenos Aires (GCBA) sobre Amparo*. EXPTE A2174-2015/0 (2015). Available at: https://www.animallaw.info/sites/default/files/Sandra_%E2%80%9CASOCIACION%20DE%20FUNCIONARIOS%20Y%20ABOGADOS%20POR%20LOS%20DERECHOS%20DE%20LOS%20ANIMALES%20Y%20OTROS%20CONTRA%20GCBA%20SOBRE%20AMPARO%E2%80%9D.pdf.

AFADA (Asociacion de Funcionarios y Abogados por los Derechos de los Animales y Otros) v. *The Government of the City of Buenos Aires (GCBA)* (2016) Re: Constitutional Protection Case File No. A2174-2015/0.

AFADA (Asociacion de Funcionarios y Abogados por los Derechos de los Animales y Otros) v. *Mendoza Zoo and City*. EXPTE NRO. P-72.254/15 (2016). Available at: https://www.projetogap.org.br/wp-content/uploads/2016/11/329931683-habeas-corpus-cecilia.pdf.

Agence France-Presse (2018). Chinese circus defends using rare animals in its acts despite poor crowds at shows and constant criticism of its methods. *South China Morning Post*, July 11, 2018. Available at: https://www.scmp.com/lifestyle/travel-leisure/article/2154754/chinese-circus-defends-using-rare-animals-its-acts-despite.

Ahebwa, W.M., van der Duim, R. and Sandbrook, C. (2012). Tourism revenue sharing policy at Bwindi Impenetrable National Park, Uganda: a policy arrangements approach. *Journal of Sustainable Tourism*, **20**(3), 377–94. DOI: 10.1080/09669582.2011.622768.

Aini, J. and West, P. (2018). *Communities matter: decolonizing conservation management*. Keynote lecture presented at the International Marine Conservation Congress, Kuching, Malaysia, June 24–29. Available at: https://paige-west.com/2018/07/28/decolonizing-conservation/. Accessed October, 2018.

Akatia (n.d.). *The Sanctuary*. Abidjan, Ivory Coast: Akatia. Available at: http://www.akatia.org/the-sanctuary. Accessed October 3, 2018.

ALDF (2018). Federal appeals court to hear arguments in lawsuit concerning USDA's secrecy on animal welfare records. *Animal League Defense Fund (ALDF) Press Release*, December 13, 2018. Available at: https://aldf.org/article/federal-appeals-court-to-hear-arguments-in-lawsuit-concerning-usdas-secrecy-on-animal-welfare-records/.

Aldrich, B.C. (2018). The use of primate 'actors' in feature films 1990–2013. *Anthrozoös*, **31**(1), 5–21. DOI: 10.1080/08927936.2018.1406197.

Alexander, C., Korstjens, A.H., Hankinson, E., *et al.* (2018). Locating emergent trees in a tropical rainforest using data from an unmanned aerial vehicle (UAV). *International Journal of Applied Earth Observation and Geoinformation*, **72**, 86–90. DOI: 10.1016/j.jag.2018.05.024.

Alfano, N., Michaux, J., Morand, S., *et al.* (2016). Endogenous gibbon ape leukemia virus identified in a rodent (*Melomys burtoni* subsp.) from Wallacea (Indonesia). *Journal of Virology*, **90**(18), 8169–80. DOI: 10.1128/jvi.00723-16.

Alves, R.R.N. and van Vliet, N. (2018). Wild fauna on the menu. In *Ethnozoology*, ed. R.R. Nóbrega Alves and U.P. Albuquerque. London, UK: Academic Press, pp. 167–94. https://doi.org/10.1016/B978-0-12-809913-1.00010-7.

Ammann, K. (2014). *China and gorillas*. Unpublished report. Available at: https://www.karlammann.com/pdf/china-gorilla.pdf.

Amooti, N. (1995). Four gorillas killed in Bwindi. *Gorilla Journal*, **10**, 7. Available at: https://www.berggorilla.org/fileadmin/user_upload/pdf/journal/journal_en/gorilla-journal-10-english.pdf.

Ancrenaz, M. (2019). The HUTAN–Kinabatangan Orangutan Conservation Programme. Available at: https://www.peoplenotpoaching.org/hutan-kinabatangan-orang-utan-conservation-programme. Accessed February 20, 2019.

Ancrenaz, M., Ambu, L., Sunjoto, I., *et al.* (2010). Recent surveys in the forests of Ulu Segama Malua, Sabah, Malaysia, show that orang-utans (*P. p. morio*) can be maintained in slightly logged forests. *PLoS ONE*, **5**(7), e11510. DOI: 10.1371/journal.pone.0011510.

Ancrenaz, M., Cheyne, S.M., Humle, T. and Robbins, M.M. (2015a). Impacts of industrial agriculture on ape ecology. In *State of the Apes: Industrial Agriculture and Ape Conservation*, ed. Arcus Foundation. Cambridge, UK: Cambridge University Press, pp. 165–92. Available at: https://www.stateoftheapes.com/volume-2-industrial-agriculture/.

Ancrenaz, M., Dabek, L. and O'Neil, S. (2007). The costs of exclusion: recognizing a role for local communities in biodiversity conservation. *PLoS Biology*, **5**(11), e289. DOI: 10.1371/journal.pbio.0050289.

Ancrenaz, M., Gimenez, O., Ambu, L., *et al.* (2005). Aerial surveys give new estimates for orangutans in Sabah, Malaysia. *PLoS Biology*, **3**(1), e3. DOI: 10.1371/journal.pbio.0030003.

Ancrenaz, M., Gumal, M., Marshall, A.J., *et al.* (2016a). *Pongo pygmaeus* (errata version published in 2018). *The IUCN Red List of Threatened Species*. 2016: e.T17975A123809220. Gland, Switzerland: International Union for Conservation of Nature (IUCN). Available at: http://dx.doi.org/10.2305/IUCN.UK.2016-1.RLTS.T17975A17966347.en.

Ancrenaz, M., Lackman-Ancrenaz, I. and Elahan, H. (2006). Seed spitting and seed swallowing by wild orang-utans (*Pongo pygmaeus morio*) in Sabah, Malaysia. *Journal of Tropical Biology and Conservation*, **2**(1), 65–70.

Ancrenaz, M., Oram, F., Ambu, L., *et al.* (2015b). Of *Pongo*, palms and perceptions: a multidisciplinary assessment of Bornean orang-utans *Pongo pygmaeus* in an oil palm context. *Oryx*, **49**(3), 465–72. DOI: 10.1017/S0030605313001270.

Ancrenaz, M., Sollmann, R., Meijaard, E., *et al.* (2014). Coming down from the trees: is terrestrial activity in Bornean orangutans natural or disturbance driven? *Scientific Reports*, **4**, 4024. DOI: 10.1038/srep04024.

Ancrenaz, M., Wich, S., Meijaard, E. and Simery, J. (2016b). *Palm Oil Paradox: Sustainable Solutions to Save the Great Apes*. Nairobi, Kenya: United Nations Environment Programme (UNEP)/Great Apes Survival Partnership (GRASP). Available at: https://www.unenvironment.org/resources/report/palm-oil-paradox-sustainable-sustainable-solutions-save-great-apes.

Anderson, D.P., Nordheim, E.V. and Boesch, C. (2006). Environmental factors influencing the seasonality of estrus in chimpanzees. *Primates*, **47**(1), 43–50. DOI: 10.1007/s10329-005-0143-y.

Anderson, J.R. (2013). *Affidavit of James R. Anderson In the Matter of a Proceeding under Article 70 of the CPLR for a Writ of Habeas Corpus. The Nonhuman Rights Project, Inc., on behalf of Tommy, Petitioners, v. Patrick C. Lavery, individually and as an officer of Circle L Trailer Sales, Inc., Diane Lavery, and Circle L Trailer Sales, Inc. November 20, 2013*. Available at: https://www.nonhumanrights.org/content/uploads/Ex-4-Anderson-Affidavit-Tommy-Case.pdf. Accessed December, 2019.

Anderson, J.R. (2015). *Affidavit of James R. Anderson In the Matter of a Proceeding under Article 70 of the CPLR for a Writ of Habeas Corpus. The Nonhuman Rights Project, Inc., on behalf of Kiko, Petitioner, v. Carmen Presti, individually and as an officer and director of The Primate Sanctuary, Inc., Christie E. Presti, individually and as an officer and director of The Primate Sanctuary, Inc., and the Primate Sanctuary, Inc. November 18, 2015*. Available at: https://www.nonhumanrights.org/client-kiko/. Accessed December, 2019.

Annecke, W. and Masubelele, M. (2016). A review of the impact of militarisation: the case of rhino poaching in Kruger National Park, South Africa. *Conservation and Society*, **14**(3), 195–204. DOI: 10.4103/0972-4923.191158.

Anonymous (2009). Chimpanzees, Louie and Mikey on Kendall Project, Judie Harrison. *Chimpanzee Information Blogspot*, May 5, 2009. Available at: http://chimpanzeeinformation.blogspot.com/2009/05/mikey-and-louie-chimp-story-on-kendall.html.

ANTARA News (2017). Orangutan Dari Kuwait Kembali ke Kalteng. *ANTARA News*, September 15, 2017. Available at: https://www.antaranews.com/berita/652848/orangutan-dari-kuwait-kembali-ke-kalteng.

AP (2007). How to protect ape's rights? Make him a person. *AP: Associated Press*, May 4, 2007. Available at: http://www.nbcnews.com/id/18498435/ns/technology_and_science-science/t/how-protect-apes-rights-make-him-person/#.XTbpT_ZFyzk.

AP (2008). It's official: in Austria, a chimp is not a person. *AP: Associated Press*, January 15, 2008.

Arandjelovic, M., Head, J., Rabanal, L.I., *et al.* (2011). Non-invasive genetic monitoring of wild central chimpanzees. *PLoS ONE*, **6**(3), e14761. DOI: 10.1371/journal.pone.0014761.

Arandjelovic, M. and Vigilant, L. (2018). Non-invasive genetic censusing and monitoring of primate populations. *American Journal of Primatology*, **80**(3), e22743. DOI: 10.1002/ajp.22743.

Arcus Foundation (2014). *State of the Apes: Extractive Industries and Ape Conservation*. Cambridge, UK: Cambridge University Press. Available at: https://www.stateoftheapes.com/volume-1-extractive-industries/.

Arcus Foundation (2015). *State of the Apes: Industrial Agriculture and Ape Conservation*. Cambridge, UK: Cambridge University Press. Available at: https://www.stateoftheapes.com/volume-2-industrial-agriculture/.

Arcus Foundation (2018). *State of the Apes: Infrastructure Development and Ape Conservation*. Cambridge, UK: Cambridge University Press. Available at: https://www.stateoftheapes.com/volume-3-infrastructure-development/.

Ariffin, M. (2018). Recent challenges for the enforcement of wildlife laws in East Malaysia. *Pertanika Journal of Social Sciences and Humanities*, **26**, 167–80. Available at: http://www.pertanika.upm.edu.my/regular_issues.php?jtype=3&journal=JSSH-26-1-3.

ASEAN (2005). *ASEAN Statement on Launching of the ASEAN Wildlife Law Enforcement Network (ASEAN-WEN)*. Bangkok, Thailand: Association of Southeast Asian Nations (ASEAN). Available at: https://asean.org/?static_post=asean-statement-on-launching-of-the-asean-wildlife-law-enforcement-network-asean-wen-2.

ASEAN-WEN (2016). *ASEAN Handbook on Legal Cooperation to Combat Wildlife Crime*. Bangkok, Thailand: Freeland Foundation/Association of Southeast Asian Nations Wildlife Enforcement Network (ASEAN-WEN).

Askue, L., Heimlich, J., Yu, J.P., Wang, X. and Lakly, S. (2009). Measuring a professional conservation education training program for zoos and wildlife parks in China. *Zoo Biology*, **28**(5), 447–61. DOI: 10.1002/zoo.20210.

Astaras, C., Linder, J.M., Wrege, P., Orume, R.D. and Macdonald, D.W. (2017). Passive acoustic monitoring as a law enforcement tool for Afrotropical rainforests. *Frontiers in Ecology and the Environment*, **15**(5), 233–4. DOI: 10.1002/fee.1495.

Atsmon, Y., Magni, M., Li, L. and Liao, W. (2012). *Meet the 2020 Chinese Consumer. McKinsey Consumer & Shopper Insights*. Shanghai, China: McKinsey Insights China. Available at: https://www.mckinsey.com/~/media/mckinsey/featured%20insights/asia%20pacific/meet%20the%20chinese%20consumer%20of%202020/mckinseyinsightschina%20meetthe2020chineseconsumer.ashx.

Atuo, F.A., O'Connell, T.J. and Abanyam, P.U. (2015). An assessment of socio-economic drivers of avian body parts trade in West African rainforests. *Biological Conservation*, **191**, 614–22. DOI: 10.1016/j.biocon.2015.08.013.

Australian Government (2011). *Australian Animal Welfare Strategy (AAWS) and National Implementation Plan 2010–14*. Canberra, Australia: Department of Agriculture. Available at: http://www.agriculture.gov.au/animal/welfare/aaws/australian-animal-welfare-strategy-aaws-and-national-implementation-plan-2010-14.

AWG CITES and WE (n.d.). *ASEAN Working Group on Convention on International Trade in Endangered Species of Wild Fauna and Flora and Wildlife Enforcement*. Bangkok, Thailand: Association of Southeast Asian Nations (ASEAN) Working Group on Convention on International Trade in Endangered Species of Wild Fauna and Flora (CITES) and Wildlife Enforcement (WE). Available at: http://www.awgciteswe.org. Accessed February, 2019.

Ayari, I. and Counsell, S. (2017). *The Human Cost of Conservation in Republic of Congo: Conkouati-Douli and Nouabalé-Ndoki National Parks and their Impact on the Rights and Livelihoods of Forest Communities*. London, UK: The Rainforest Foundation UK. Available at: https://www.rainforestfoundationuk.org/media.ashx/the-human-impact-of-conservation-republic-of-congo-2017-english.pdf.

AZA (2008). *Apes in Media and Commercial Performances. AZA White Paper.* Silver Spring, MD: Association of Zoos & Aquariums (AZA). Available at: https://assets.speakcdn.com/assets/2332/ape_white_paper_approved_2_sept_08.pdf.

AZA Ape TAG (2010). *Chimpanzee (*Pan troglodytes*) Care Manual* [in Japanese]. Silver Spring, MD: Association of Zoos & Aquariums (AZA). Available at: https://assets.speakcdn.com/assets/2332/chimpanzee-care-manual-japanese.pdf.

Bakels, J., Bhagwat, S., Drani, E., Infield, M. and Kidd, C. (2016). *Culture and Conservation: Investigating the Linkages between Biodiversity Protection and Cultural Values and Practices.* Cambridge, UK: Arcus Foundation. Available at: https://www.arcusfoundation-org.s3.amazonaws.com/wp-content/uploads/2017/01/Culture-and-Conservation.pdf.

Baker, J., Milner-Gulland, E.J. and Leader-Williams, N. (2012). Park gazettement and integrated conservation and development as factors in community conflict at Bwindi Impenetrable Forest, Uganda: drivers of community conflict at Bwindi. *Conservation Biology,* **26**(1), 160–70. DOI: 10.1111/j.1523-1739.2011.01777.x.

Baker, K. (2005). *Enrichment for Non-Human Primates: Chimpanzees.* Bethesda, MD: Office of Laboratory Animal Welfare (OLAW), National Institutes of Health (NIH). Available at: https://grants.nih.gov/grants/olaw/Chimpanzees.pdf.

Baker, K., Jah, F. and Connolly, S. (2018). A radio drama for apes? An entertainment–education approach to supporting ape conservation through an integrated human behaviour, health, and environment serial drama. *The Journal of Development Communication,* **29**(1), 16–24.

Bale, R. (2016). How saving one chimp led to a new kind of anti-poaching group. *Wildlife Watch,* June 8, 2016. Available at: https://www.nationalgeographic.com/news/2016/06/0fir-drori-wildlife-corruption-laga/.

Balluch, M. and Theuer, E. (2007). Trial on personhood for chimp 'Hiasl'. *ALTEX.* Available at: http://www.altex.ch/resources/Altex_2007_4_335_342_Balluch.pdf.

Balter, M. (2010). Chimps grieve over dead relative. *Science: News.* Available at: https://www.sciencemag.org/news/2010/04/chimps-grieve-over-dead-relatives.

Banaji, M.R. and Greenwald, A.G. (2014). *Blindspot: Hidden Biases of Good People.* London, UK: Penguin Books Ltd.

Banes, G.L., Chua, W., Elder, M. and Kao, J. (2018). Orang-utans *Pongo* spp. in Asian zoos: current status, challenges and progress towards long-term population sustainability. *International Zoo Yearbook,* **52**(1), 150–63. DOI: 10.1111/izy.12178.

Barbora, S. (2017). Riding the rhino: conservation, conflicts, and militarisation of Kaziranga National Park in Assam. *Antipode,* **49**(5), 1145–63. DOI: 10.1111/anti.12329.

Barelli, C., Heistermann, M., Boesch, C. and Reichard, U.H. (2007). Sexual swellings in wild white-handed gibbon females (*Hylobates lar*) indicate the probability of ovulation. *Hormones and Behavior,* **51**, 221–30.

Barnosky, A.D., Koch, P.L., Feranec, R.S., Wing, S.L. and Shabel, A.B. (2004). Assessing the causes of Late Pleistocene extinctions on the continents. *Science,* **306**(5693), 70–5. DOI: 10.1126/science.1101476.

Barrett, C.B. and Arcese, P. (1995). Are integrated conservation–development projects (ICDPs) sustainable? On the conservation of large mammals in sub-Saharan Africa. *World Development,* **23**(7), 1073–84. DOI: 10.1016/0305-750X(95)00031-7.

Bartlett, T.Q. (2007). The Hylobatidae: small apes of Asia. In *Primates in Perspective,* ed. C. Campbell, A. Fuentes, K. C. Mackinnon, M. Panger and S. K. Bearder. New York, NY: Oxford University Press, pp. 274–89.

Bartlett, T.Q. (2009). *The Gibbons of Khao Yai: Seasonal Variation in Behavior and Ecology.* Upper Saddle River, NJ: Pearson.

Barton, D., Chen, Y. and Jin, A. (2013). Mapping China's middle class. *McKinsey Quarterly,* June 1, 2013. Available at: https://www.mckinsey.com/industries/retail/our-insights/mapping-chinas-middle-class.

Bassett, T.J. (2005). Card-carrying hunters, rural poverty, and wildlife decline in northern Côte d'Ivoire. *The Geographical Journal,* **171**(1), 24–35. DOI: 10.1111/j.1475-4959.2005.00147.x.

Bates, L. (2017). *Joint Affidavit of Lucy Bates and Richard M. Byrne. January 25, 2017.* Available at: https://www.nonhumanrights.org/client-happy/. Accessed December, 2019.

BBC (2018). Chimpanzee Robby's circus wins German court battle to keep him. *BBC News,* November 9, 2018. Available at: https://www.bbc.com/news/world-europe-46149725.

Beauchamp, T.L., Ferdowsian, H.R. and Gluck, J.P. (2014). Rethinking the ethics of research involving nonhuman animals: introduction. *Theoretical Medicine and Bioethics*, **35**(2), 91–6. DOI: 10.1007/s11017-014-9291-7.

Beaune, D. (2015). What would happen to the trees and lianas if apes disappeared? *Oryx*, **49**(3), 442–6. DOI: 10.1017/S0030605314000878.

Beaune, D., Bretagnolle, F., Bollache, L., *et al.* (2013). The bonobo–dialium positive interactions: seed dispersal mutualism. *American Journal of Primatology*, **75**(4), 394–403. DOI: 10.1002/ajp.22121.

Beck, B., Walkup, K., Rodrigues, M., *et al.* (2007). *Best Practice Guidelines for the Re-introduction of Great Apes.* Gland, Switzerland: International Union for Conservation of Nature (IUCN) Species Survival Commission (SSC), Primate Specialist Group. Available at: https://portals.iucn.org/library/sites/library/files/documents/SSC-OP-035.pdf.

Becker, C.D. and Ghimire, K. (2003). Synergy between traditional ecological knowledge and conservation science supports forest preservation in Ecuador. *Conservation Ecology*, **8**(1), e1. Available at: http://www.consecol.org/vol8/iss1/art1/

Bender, J. and Ziegler, S. (2009). GIS based threat analysis of gorilla habitat in the Congo Basin. *Zentralblatt für Geologie und Paläontologie, Teil I, Geologie*, **2009**(1/2), 97–111.

Bender, K. (2010). Oakland Zoo home to former movie star chimpanzees. *Mercury News*, August 25, 2010. Available at: https://www.mercurynews.com/2010/08/25/oakland-zoo-home-to-former-movie-star-chimpanzees/.

Benítez-López, A., Alkemade, R., Schipper, A.M., *et al.* (2017). The impact of hunting on tropical mammal and bird populations. *Science*, **356**(6334), 180–3. DOI: 10.1126/science.aaj1891.

Bennett, E.L. (2002). Is there a link between wild meat and food security? *Conservation Biology*, **16**(3), 590–2.

Bennett, N.J., Roth, R., Klain, S.C., *et al.* (2017a). Conservation social science: understanding and integrating human dimensions to improve conservation. *Biological Conservation*, **205**, 93–108. DOI: 10.1016/j.biocon.2016.10.006.

Bennett, N.J., Roth, R., Klain, S.C., *et al.* (2017b). Mainstreaming the social sciences in conservation. *Conservation Biology*, **31**(1), 56–66. DOI: 10.1111/cobi.12788.

Bergin, D. and Nijman, V. (2020). Wildlife trade research methods for lorises and pottos. In *Evolution, Ecology and Conservation of Lorises and Pottos*, ed. K.A.I. Nekaris and A. Burrows. Cambridge, UK: Cambridge University Press, pp. 339–61.

Bergl, R.A., Dunn, A., Fowler, A., *et al.* (2016). *Gorilla gorilla* ssp. *diehli* (errata version published in 2016). *The IUCN Red List of Threatened Species.* 2016: e.T39998A102326240. Gland, Switzerland: International Union for Conservation of Nature (IUCN). Available at: http://dx.doi.org/10.2305/IUCN.UK.2016-2.RLTS.T39998A17989492.en.

Bergl, R.A., Warren, Y., Nicholas, A., *et al.* (2012). Remote sensing analysis reveals habitat, dispersal corridors and expanded distribution for the critically endangered Cross River gorilla, *Gorilla gorilla diehli. Oryx*, **46**, 278–89.

Berkes, F. (2004). Rethinking community-based conservation. *Conservation Biology*, **18**(3), 621–30. DOI: 10.1111/j.1523-1739.2004.00077.x.

Bermejo, M., Rodríguez-Teijeiro, J.D., Illera, G., *et al.* (2006). Ebola outbreak killed 5000 gorillas. *Science*, **314**(5805), 1564. DOI: 10.1126/science.1133105.

Bessa, J., Sousa, C. and Hockings, K.J. (2015). Feeding ecology of chimpanzees (*Pan troglodytes verus*) inhabiting a forest-mangrove-savanna-agricultural matrix at Caiquene-Cadique, Cantanhez National Park, Guinea-Bissau. *American Journal of Primatology*, **77**(6), 651–65.

Blanco, V. and Waltert, M. (2013). Does the tropical agricultural matrix bear potential for primate conservation? A baseline study from western Uganda. *Journal for Nature Conservation*, **21**, 383–93.

Blomley, T., Namara, A., McNeilage, A., *et al.* (2010). *Development and Gorillas? Assessing Fifteen Years of Integrated Conservation and Development in South-Western Uganda.* London, UK: International Institute for Environment and Development (IIED). Available at: https://portals.iucn.org/library/sites/library/files/documents/Man-Dev-676.1-001.pdf.

Bobo, K.S., Aghomo, F.F.M. and Ntumwel, B.C. (2015). Wildlife use and the role of taboos in the conservation of wildlife around the Nkwende Hills Forest Reserve, South-west Cameroon. *Journal of Ethnobiology and Ethnomedicine*, **11**(1), 2. DOI: 10.1186/1746-4269-11-2.

Boesch, C. (2013). *Affidavit of Christophe Boesch in the Matter of a Proceeding under Article 70 of the CPLR for a Writ of Habeas Corpus. The Nonhuman Rights Project, Inc., on behalf of Tommy, Petitioners, v. Patrick C. Lavery, individually and as an officer of Circle L Trailer Sales, Inc., Diane Lavery, and Circle L Trailer Sales, Inc. November 21, 2013.* Available at: https://www.nonhumanrights.org/content/uploads/Ex-5-Boesch-Affidavit-Tommy-Case.pdf. Accessed December, 2019.

Boesch, C. (2015). *Affidavit of Christophe Boesch in the Matter of a Proceeding under Article 70 of the CPLR for a Writ of Habeas Corpus. The Nonhuman Rights Project, Inc., on behalf of Kiko, Petitioner, v. Carmen Presti, individually and as an officer and director of The Primate Sanctuary, Inc., Christie E. Presti, individually and as an officer and director of The Primate Sanctuary, Inc., and the Primate Sanctuary, Inc. October 14, 2015.* Available at: https://www.nonhumanrights.org/client-kiko/. Accessed December, 2019.

Booker, F. and Roe, D. (2017). *First Line of Defence? A Review of Evidence of the Effectiveness of Engaging Communities to Tackle Illegal Wildlife Trade.* London, UK: International Institute for Environment and Development (IIED).

Boonratana, R., Duckworth, J.W., Phiapalath, P., Reumaux, J.-F. and Sisomphane, C. (2011). The precarious status of the white-handed gibbon *Hylobates lar* in Lao PDR. *Asian Primates Journal*, **2**(1), 13–20.

Borneman, J. and Hammoudi, A. (2009). *Being There: The Fieldwork Encounter and the Making of Truth.* Berkeley, CA: University of California Press.

Bowen-Jones, E. (2012). *Tackling Human–Wildlife Conflict: A Prerequisite for Linking Conservation and Poverty Alleviation. A Decision-Makers Guide to Financial and Institutional Mechanisms.* London, UK: International Institute for Environment and Development (IIED). Available at: https://pubs.iied.org/pdfs/G03725.pdf.

Bowen-Jones, E. and Pendry, S. (1999). The threat to primates and other mammals from the bushmeat trade in Africa, and how this threat could be diminished. *Oryx*, **33**(3), 233–46. DOI: 10.1046/j.1365-3008.1999.00066.x.

Bowers v. Hardwick. 478 US 186 (1986). Available at: https://supreme.justia.com/cases/federal/us/478/186/.

Bowler, M.T., Tobler, M.W., Endress, B.A., Gilmore, M.P. and Anderson, M.J. (2017). Estimating mammalian species richness and occupancy in tropical forest canopies with arboreal camera traps. *Remote Sensing in Ecology and Conservation*, **3**(3), 146–57. DOI: 10.1002/rse2.35.

Boyer, K. (2011). *Chimpanzee conservation in light of impending iron ore mining project in SE Senegal.* Masters thesis. Ames, IA: Iowa State University. Available at: https://lib.dr.iastate.edu/etd/10215/.

Bradley, B.J., Doran-Sheehy, D.M., Lukas, D., Boesch, C. and Vigilant, L. (2004). Dispersed male networks in western gorillas. *Current Biology*, **14**(6), 510–3. DOI: 10.1016/j.cub.2004.02.062.

Bradshaw, G.A., Capaldo, T., Lindner, L. and Grow, G. (2008). Building an inner sanctuary: complex PTSD in chimpanzees. *Journal of Trauma & Dissociation*, **9**(1), 9–34. DOI: 10.1080/15299730802073619.

Brashares, J.S., Abrahms, B., Fiorella, K.J., *et al.* (2014). Wildlife decline and social conflict. *Science*, **345**(6195), 376–8. DOI: 10.1126/science.1256734.

Brashares, J.S., Arcese, P., Sam, M.K., *et al.* (2004). Bushmeat hunting, wildlife declines, and fish supply in West Africa. *Science*, **306**(5699), 1180–3. DOI: 10.1126/science.1102425.

Brashares, J.S., Golden, C.D., Weinbaum, K.Z., Barrett, C.B. and Okello, G.V. (2011). Economic and geographic drivers of wildlife consumption in rural Africa. *Proceedings of the National Academy of Sciences*, **108**(34), 13931–6. DOI: 10.1073/pnas.1011526108.

Brechin, S.R. and West, P.C. (1990). Protected areas, resident peoples, and sustainable conservation: the need to link top-down with bottom-up. *Society & Natural Resources*, **3**(1), 77–9. DOI: 10.1080/08941929009380707.

Brncic, T.M., Amarasekaran, B. and McKenna, A. (2010). *Sierra Leone National Chimpanzee Census Project August 2010.* Freetown, Sierra Leone: Tacugama Chimpanzee Sanctuary. Available at: http://www.tacugama.com/wp-content/uploads/2017/12/2010_Brncic_SLNCCP_Final_Report.pdf.

Broad, S., Mulliken, T. and Roe, D. (2003). The nature and extent of legal and illegal trade in wildlife. In *The Trade in Wildlife: Regulation for Conservation*, ed. S. Oldfield. London, UK: Earthscan, pp. 3–22.

Brockelman, W.Y. and Ali, R. (1987). Methods of surveying and sampling forest primate populations. In *Primate Conservation in the Tropical rainforest*, ed. R.A. Mittermeier and R.W. Marsh. New York, NY: Alan Liss, pp. 23–62.

Brockelman, W. and Geissmann, T. (2019). *Hoolock leuconedys. The IUCN Red List of Threatened Species. 2019:* e.T118355453A17968300. Gland, Switzerland: International Union for Conservation of Nature (IUCN). Available at: http://dx.doi.org/10.2305/IUCN.UK.2019-1.RLTS.T118355453A17968300.en.

Brockelman, W. and Geissmann, T. (2020). *Hylobates lar. The IUCN Red List of Threatened Species.* 2020: e.T10548A17967253. Gland, Switzerland: International Union for Conservation of Nature (IUCN). Available at: https://dx.doi.org/10.2305/IUCN.UK.2020-2.RLTS.T10548A17967253.en.

Brockelman, W., Geissmann, T., Timmins, T. and Traeholt, C. (2020). *Hylobates pileatus. The IUCN Red List of Threatened Species.* 2020: e.T10552A17966665. Gland, Switzerland: International Union for Conservation of Nature (IUCN). Available at: https://dx.doi.org/10.2305/IUCN.UK.2020-2.RLTS.T10552A17966665.en.

Brockelman, W., Molur, S. and Geissmann, T. (2019). *Hoolock hoolock. The IUCN Red List of Threatened Species.* 2019: e.T39876A17968083. Gland, Switzerland: International Union for Conservation of Nature (IUCN). Available at: https://dx.doi.org/10.2305/IUCN.UK.2019-3.RLTS.T39876A17968083.en.

Brockelman, W.Y. and Osterberg, P. (2015). Gibbon rehabilitation project on Phuket successfully reintroduces animals into forest. *Natural History Bulletin of the Siam Society*, **60**(2), 65–8.

Brockelman, W.Y. and Srikosamatara, S. (1993). Estimation of density of gibbon groups by use of loud songs. *American Journal of Primatology*, **29**(2), 93–108. DOI: 10.1002/ajp.1350290203.

Brockington, D. (2002). *Fortress Conservation: The Preservation of the Mkomazi Game Reserve, Tanzania.* Oxford, UK: James Currey.

Brockington, D. and Igoe, J. (2006). Eviction for conservation: a global overview. *Conservation and Society*, **4**(3), 424–70.

Brooks, C. and Hopkins, M. (2016). How protecting animals led to allegations of torture and rape. *National Geographic*, September 19, 2016. Available at: https://www.nationalgeographic.com/news/2016/09/wildlife-tanzania-poaching-human-rights-abuses/.

Brosnahan, P. (2000). New Zealand's Animal Welfare Act: what is its value regarding non-human hominids? *Animal Law*, **6**, 185–92.

Brown, D., Fa, J.E. and Gordon, L. (2007). *Assessment of Recent Bushmeat Research and Recommendations to Her Majesty's Government.* London, UK: Overseas Development Institute (ODI). Available at: http://citeseerx.ist.psu.edu/viewdoc/download;jsessionid=031C5711AC90538F2E32306418A13B1A?doi=10.1.1.617.1723&rep=rep1&type=pdf.

Brown, J. (2009). Status of the western black crested gibbon (*Nomascus concolor*) in the Nam Ha National Protected Area, Lao PDR. *Gibbon Journal*, **5**, 28–35.

Brown, S. (2006). The West develops a taste for bushmeat. *New Scientist Life*, July 8, 2006. Available at: https://www.newscientist.com/article/dn9503-the-west-develops-a-taste-for-bushmeat/.

Browning, E., Gibb, R., Glover-Kapfer, P. and Jones, K.E. (2017). *Passive Acoustic Monitoring in Ecology and Conservation.* WWF Conservation Technology Series 1 (2). Woking, UK: World Wide Fund for Nature (WWF)-UK.

Brulliard, K. (2017). USDA abruptly purges animal welfare information from its website. *The Washington Post*, February 3, 2017. Available at: https://www.washingtonpost.com/news/animalia/wp/2017/02/03/the-usda-abruptly-removes-animal-welfare-information-from-its-website/.

Brulliard, K. (2018). This pilot rescued a baby chimp and everyone swooned. *The Washington Post*, March 1, 2018. Available at: https://www.washingtonpost.com/news/animalia/wp/2018/03/01/this-pilot-rescued-a-baby-chimp-and-everyone-swooned/.

Bryant, J.V., Olson, V.A., Chatterjee, H.J. and Turvey, S.T. (2015). Identifying environmental versus phylogenetic correlates of behavioural ecology in gibbons: implications for conservation management of the world's rarest ape. *BMC Evolutionary Biology*, **15**(1), 171. DOI: 10.1186/s12862-015-0430-1.

Bryant, J.V., Zeng, X., Hong, X., Chatterjee, H.J. and Turvey, S.T. (2017). Spatiotemporal requirements of the Hainan gibbon: does home range constrain recovery of the world's rarest ape? *American Journal of Primatology*, **79**(3), e22617. DOI: 10.1002/ajp.22617.

Buckland, S.T., Anderson, D.R., Burnham, K.P., *et al.*, ed. (2001). *Introduction to Distance Sampling: Estimating Abundance of Biological Populations.* Oxford, UK: Oxford University Press.

Buckland, S.T., Anderson, D.R., Burnham, K.P., *et al.*, ed. (2007). *Advanced Distance Sampling: Estimating Abundance of Biological Populations.* Oxford, UK: Oxford University Press.

Buckland, S.T., Plumptre, A.J., Thomas, L. and Rexstad, E.A. (2010). Line transect sampling of primates: can animal-to-observer distance methods work? *International Journal of Primatology*, **31**(3), 485–99. DOI: 10.1007/s10764-010-9408-4.

Bunyoro-Kitara Kingdom (n.d.). *Bunyoro-Kitara Kingdom: profile*. Available at: www.bunyoro-kitara.org/5.html. Accessed September, 2020.

Burgess, G., Zain, S., Milner-Gulland, E.J., *et al.* (2018). *Reducing Demand for Illegal Wildlife Products: Research Analysis on Strategies to Change Illegal Wildlife Product Consumer Behaviour*. Cambridge, UK: TRAFFIC.

Burke, J. (2018). Six Virunga park rangers killed in DRC wildlife sanctuary. *The Guardian*, April 10, 2018. Available at: https://www.theguardian.com/weather/2018/apr/09/six-virunga-park-rangers-killed-in-drc-wildlife-sanctuary.

Burney, D.A., Robinson, G.S. and Burney, L.P. (2003). *Sporormiella* and the late Holocene extinctions in Madagascar. *Proceedings of the National Academy of Sciences*, **100**(19), 10800–5. DOI: 10.1073/pnas.1534700100.

Burns, S.J., Godfrey, L.R., Faina, P., *et al.* (2016). Rapid human-induced landscape transformation in Madagascar at the end of the first millennium of the Common Era. *Quaternary Science Reviews*, **134**, 92–9. DOI: 10.1016/j.quascirev.2016.01.007.

Buscher, B. (2018). From biopower to ontopower? Violent responses to wildlife crime and the new geographies of conservation. *Conservation and Society*, **16**(2), 157–69. DOI: 10.4103/cs.cs_16_159.

Butynski, T.M. (2001). Africa's great apes. In *Great Apes and Humans: The Ethics of Coexistence*, ed. B.B. Beck, T.S. Stoinski, M. Hutchins, *et al.* Washington DC: Smithsonian Institution Press.

Buxton, R.T., Lendrum, P.E., Crooks, K.R. and Wittemyer, G. (2018). Pairing camera traps and acoustic recorders to monitor the ecological impact of human disturbance. *Global Ecology and Conservation*, **16**, e00493. 10.1016/j.gecco.2018.e00493.

Byrn v. NYCHHC (New York City Health & Hospitals Corp.). 31 NY 2d 194 (1972).

Byrne, R.M. (2016). *Joint Affidavit of Lucy Bates and Richard M. Byrne. December 5, 2016*. Available at: https://www.nonhumanrights.org/client-happy/. Accessed December, 2019.

Byrne, R.W. and Stokes, E.J. (2002). Effects of manual disability on feeding skills in gorillas and chimpanzees. *International Journal of Primatology*, **23**, 539–54. DOI: 10.1023/A:1014917600198.

Caillaud, D., Ndagijimana, F., Giarrusso, A.J., Vecellio, V. and Stoinski, T.S. (2014). Mountain gorilla ranging patterns: influence of group size and group dynamics. *American Journal of Primatology*, **76**(8), 730–46. DOI: 10.1002/ajp.22265.

Caldecott, J., Miles, L. and Annan, K.A. (2005). *The World Atlas of Great Apes and their Conservation*. Berkeley and Los Angeles, CA: University of California Press.

Calvignac-Spencer, S., Leendertz, S.A.J., Gillespie, T.R. and Leendertz, F.H. (2012). Wild great apes as sentinels and sources of infectious disease. *Clinical Microbiology and Infection*, **18**(6), 521–7. DOI: 10.1111/j.1469-0691.2012.03816.x.

Campbell, C.O., Cheyne, S.M. and Rawson, B.M. (2015). *Best Practice Guidelines for the Rehabilitation and Translocation of Gibbons*. Gland, Switzerland: International Union for Conservation of Nature (IUCN) Species Survival Commission (SSC), Primate Specialist Group. Available at: https://portals.iucn.org/library/sites/library/files/documents/SSC-OP-051.pdf.

Campbell, G., Kueh, H., Diarrassouba, A., N'Goran, P.K. and Boesch, C. (2011). Long-term research sites as refugia for threatened and over-harvested species. *Biology Letters*, **7**(5), 723–6. DOI: 10.1098/rsbl.2011.0155.

Campbell, G., Kuehl, H., N'Goran P.K. and Boesch, C. (2008). Alarming decline of West African chimpanzees in Côte d'Ivoire. *Current Biology*, **18**(19), R903–R4. DOI: 10.1016/j.cub.2008.08.015.

Campbell-Smith, G., Campbell-Smith, M., Singleton, I. and Linkie, M. (2011a). Apes in space: saving an imperilled orangutan population in Sumatra. *PLoS ONE*, **6**(2), e17210. DOI: 10.1371/journal.pone.0017210.

Campbell-Smith, G., Campbell-Smith, M., Singleton, I. and Linkie, M. (2011b). Raiders of the lost bark: orangutan foraging strategies in a degraded landscape. *PLoS ONE*, **6**(6), e20962. DOI: 10.1371/journal.pone.0020962.

Campbell-Smith, G., Sembiring, R. and Linkie, M. (2012). Evaluating the effectiveness of human–orangutan conflict mitigation strategies in Sumatra. *Journal of Applied Ecology*, **49**(2), 367–75. DOI: 10.1111/j.1365-2664.2012.02109.x.

Campbell-Smith, G., Simanjorang, H.V.P., Leader-Williams, N. and Linkie, M. (2010). Local attitudes and perceptions toward crop-raiding by orangutans (*Pongo abelii*) and other nonhuman primates in northern Sumatra, Indonesia. *American Journal of Primatology*, **72**(10), 866–76. DOI: 10.1002/ajp.20822.

Caniago, I. and Stephen, F.S. (1998). Medicinal plant ecology, knowledge and conservation in Kalimantan, Indonesia. *Economic Botany*, **52**(3), 229–50. DOI: 10.1007/BF02862141.

Cappelle, N., Després-Einspenner, M.-L., Howe, E.J., Boesch, C. and Kühl, H.S. (2019). Validating camera trap distance sampling for chimpanzees. *American Journal of Primatology*, **81**(3), e22962. DOI: 10.1002/ajp.22962.

Carbone, L., Alan Harris, R., Gnerre, S., *et al.* (2014). Gibbon genome and the fast karyotype evolution of small apes. *Nature*, **513**, 195. DOI: 10.1038/nature13679.

Carlsen, F., Leus, K., Traylor-Holzer, K. and McKenna, A. (2012). *Western Chimpanzee Population and Habitat Viability Assessment for Sierra Leone: Final Report*. Copenhagen: International Union for Conservation of Nature (IUCN) Species Survival Commission (SSC) Conservation Breeding Specialist Group (CBSG)-Europe.

Carlson, K., Wright, J. and Dönges, H. (2015). In the line of fire: elephant and rhino poaching in Africa. In *Small Arms Survey 2015: Weapons and the World*, ed. Small Arms Survey. Cambridge, UK: Cambridge University Press, pp. 6–35. Available at: http://www.smallarmssurvey.org/publications/by-type/yearbook/small-arms-survey-2015.html.

Carpenter, C.R. (1940). A field study in Siam of the behaviour and social relations of the gibbon *Hylobates lar*. *Comparative Psychological Monographs*, **16**(5), 1–212.

Casetta, E., Marques da Silva, J. and Vecchi, D. (2019). Biodiversity healing. In *From Assessing to Conserving Biodiversity*, ed. E. Casetta, J. Marques da Silva and D. Vecchi. Cham, Switzerland: Springer, pp. 1–17.

Cavalieri, P. and Singer, P., ed. (1993). *The Great Ape Project: Equality Beyond Humanity*. London, UK: Fourth Estate Publishing.

Cawthorn, D.-M. and Hoffman, L.C. (2015). The bushmeat and food security nexus: a global account of the contributions, conundrums and ethical collisions. *Food Research International*, **76**, 906–25. DOI: 10.1016/j.foodres.2015.03.025.

CAZG (n.d.). *List and distribution of members* [in Chinese]. Chinese Association of Zoological Gardens (CAZG). Available at: http://www.cazg.org.cn/Home/GetArticleDetails?articleId=52&siteNodeContentSourceId=20&nodeId=bf80a4af-8645-4b60-839c-456d49e365fb&rootNodeId=bf80a4af-8645-4b60-839c-456d49e365fb. Accessed January, 2020.

CBD (n.d.-a). *Aichi Biodiversity Targets*. Convention on Biological Diversity (CBD). Available at: https://www.cbd.int/sp/targets/. Accessed August, 2019.

CBD (n.d.-b). *The Convention on Biological Diversity*. Montreal, Canada: Convention on Biological Diversity (CBD). Available at: https://www.cbd.int. Accessed January, 2020

CBD (n.d.-c). *List of parties*. Montreal, Canada: The Convention on Biological Diversity. Available at: https://www.cbd.int/information/parties.shtml. Accessed January, 2020.

CCC (2014). *Orangutana, Sandra s/ Habeas Corpus. CCC 68831/2014/CA1*. Federal Chamber of Criminal Cassation (CCC) of Argentina. Available at: https://www.animallaw.info/sites/default/files/Orangutana%2C%20Sandra%20s%3A%20Habeas%20Corpus.pdf.

CCFU (2018). *Culture and the Conservation of the Great Apes in Uganda*. Kampala: Cross-Cultural Foundation of Uganda (CCFU). Available at: http://crossculturalfoundation.or.ug/wp-content/uploads/2018/07/Culture-and-Conservation-of-the-great-apes-in-Uganda-CCFU2018.pdf.

Ceballos, G., Ehrlich, P.R. and Dirzo, R. (2017). Biological annihilation via the ongoing sixth mass extinction signaled by vertebrate population losses and declines. *Proceedings of the National Academy of Sciences*, **114**(30), E6089–96. DOI: 10.1073/pnas.1704949114.

CEMAC (2016). *Regulation No. 01/CEMAC/UMAC/CM on the Prevention and Suppression of Money Laundering and the Financing of Terrorism and Proliferation in Central Africa*. Economic and Monetary Community of Central Africa (CEMAC). Available at: http://spgabac.org/site/wp-content/uploads/2016/06/reglement_anglais.pdf.

Center for Great Apes (n.d.). *Orangutans*. Wauchula, FL: Center for Great Apes. Available at: http://www.centerforgreatapes.org/meet-apes/orangutans/. Accessed July, 2019.

Chaber, A.-L., Allebone-Webb, S., Lignereux, Y., Cunningham, A.A. and Rowcliffe, J.M. (2010). The scale of illegal meat importation from Africa to Europe via Paris. *Conservation Letters*, **3**(5), 317–21. DOI: 10.1111/j.1755-263X.2010.00121.x.

Challender, D.W.S. and MacMillan, D.C. (2014). Poaching is more than an enforcement problem. *Conservation Letters*, **7**(5), 484–94. DOI: 10.1111/conl.12082.

Chan, B.P.L., Lo, Y.F.P. and Mo, Y. (2020). New hope for the Hainan gibbon: formation of a new group outside its known range. *Oryx*, **54**(3), 296. DOI: 10.1017/S0030605320000083.

Chan, B.P.L., Mak, C.F., Yang, J.-H. and Huang, X.-Y. (2017). Population, distribution, vocalization and conservation of the Gaoligong hoolock gibbon (*Hoolock tianxing*) in the Tengchong section of the Gaoligongshan National Nature Reserve, China. *Primate Conservation*, **31**, 107–13. Available at: http://static1.1.sqspcdn.com/static/f/1200343/27795205/1515432731637/PC31_Chan_et_al_Gaoligong_Hoolock.pdf?token=vr1DVVxEAxCKKFqGsok7nJiXgdQ%3D.

Chan, E. (2018). China marine park apologises after trainer puts lipstick on beluga whale. *South China Morning Post*, June 13, 2018. Available at: https://www.scmp.com/news/china/society/article/2150576/china-marine-park-apologises-after-trainer-put-lipstick-whale.

Chan, H.-K., Zhang, H., Yang, F. and Fischer, G. (2015). Improve customs systems to monitor global wildlife trade. *Science*, **348**(6232), 291–2. DOI: 10.1126/science.aaa3141.

Chapman, C.A., Chapman, L.J., Naughton-Treves, L., Lawes, M.J. and McDowell, L.R. (2004). Predicting folivorous primate abundance: validation of a nutritional model. *American Journal of Primatology*, **62**(2), 55–69.

Chapman, C.A. and Onderdonk, D.A. (1998). Forests without primates: primate/plant codependency. *American Journal of Primatology*, **45**, 127–41.

Chatterjee, H.J. (2009). Evolutionary relationships among the gibbons: a biogeographic perspective. In *The Gibbons. Developments in Primatology: Progress and Prospects*, ed. D. Whittaker and S. Lappan. New York, NY: Springer, pp. 13–36.

Chatterjee, H.J., Tse, J.S.Y. and Turvey, S.T. (2012). Using ecological niche modelling to predict spatial and temporal distribution patterns in Chinese gibbons: lessons from the present and the past. *Folia Primatologica*, **83**(2), 85–99. DOI: 10.1159/000342696.

Chausson, A.M., Rowcliffe, J.M., Escouflaire, L., Wieland, M. and Wright, J.H. (2019). Understanding the sociocultural drivers of urban bushmeat consumption for behavior change interventions in Pointe Noire, Republic of Congo. *Human Ecology*, **47**(2), 179–91. DOI: 10.1007/s10745-019-0061-z.

Chaves, W.A., Valle, D.R., Monroe, M.C., *et al.* (2018). Changing wild meat consumption: an experiment in the Central Amazon, Brazil. *Conservation Letters*, **11**(2), e12391. DOI: 10.1111/conl.12391.

Chen, D., Jiang, D., Liang, S. and Wang, F. (2011). Selective enforcement of regulation. *China Journal of Accounting Research*, **4**(1–2), 9–27. DOI: 10.1016/j.cjar.2011.04.002.

Chen, W. (2013). Enforcement more important than law. *China Daily*, April 20, 2013. Available at: http://www.chinadaily.com.cn/opinion/2013-04/20/content_16425449.htm.

Cheng'en Wu (1993). *Journey to the West* [translation]. Beijing, China: Foreign Languages Press.

Cheyne, S.M. (2006). Wildlife reintroduction: considerations of habitat quality at the release site. *BMC Ecology*, **6**(1), 5. DOI: 10.1186/1472-6785-6-5.

Cheyne, S.M. (2008). Feeding ecology, food choice and diet characteristics of gibbons in a disturbed peat-swamp forest, Indonesia. In *XXII Congress of the International Primatological Society*, ed. P.C. Lee, P. Honess, H. Buchanan-Smith, A. MaClarnon and W.I. Sellers. Edinburgh, UK, pp. 3–8.

Cheyne, S.M. (2010). Behavioural ecology of gibbons (*Hylobates albibarbis*) in a degraded peat-swamp forest. In *Indonesian Primates*, ed. S. Gursky and J. Supriatna. New York, NY: Springer, pp. 121–56. DOI: 10.1007/978-1-4419-1560-3_8.

Cheyne, S.M. (n.d.). *The impact of social media on the trafficking of small apes*. Unpublished presentation.

Cheyne, S.M., Campbell, C.O. and Payne, K.L. (2012). Proposed guidelines for *in situ* gibbon rescue, rehabilitation and reintroduction. *International Zoo Yearbook*, **46**(1), 265–81. DOI: 10.1111/j.1748-1090.2011.00149.x.

Cheyne, S.M. and Chivers, D.J. (2006). Sexual swellings of female gibbons. *Folia Primatologica*, **77**(5), 345–52. DOI: 10.1159/000093699.

Cheyne, S.M., Chivers, D.J. and Sugardjito, J. (2008). Biology and behaviour of reintroduced gibbons. *Biodiversity and Conservation*, **17**(7), 1741–51. DOI: 10.1007/s10531-008-9378-4.

Cheyne, S.M., Gilhooly, L.J., Hamard, M.C., *et al.* (2016a). Population mapping of gibbons in Kalimantan, Indonesia: correlates of gibbon density and vegetation across the species' range. *Endangered Species Research*, **30**(1), 133–43. DOI: 10.3354/esr00734.

Cheyne, S.M. and Nijman, V. (2020). *Hylobates abbotti. The IUCN Red List of Threatened Species.* 2020: e.T39889 A17990882. Gland, Switzerland: International Union for Conservation of Nature (IUCN). Available at: https://dx.doi.org/10.2305/IUCN.UK.2020-2.RLTS.T39889A17990882.en.

Cheyne, S.M., Sastramidjaja, W.J., Muhalir, Rayadin, Y. and Macdonald, D.W. (2016b). Mammalian communities as indicators of disturbance across Indonesian Borneo. *Global Ecology and Conservation*, **7**, 157–73. DOI: 10.1016/j.gecco.2016.06.002.

Cheyne, S.M., Stark, D.J., Limin, S.H. and Macdonald, D.W. (2013). First estimates of population ecology and threats to Sunda clouded leopards *Neofelis diardi* in a peat-swamp forest, Indonesia. *Endangered Species Research*, **22**(1), 1–9.

Cheyne, S.M., Supiansyah, Adul, *et al.* (2018). Down from the treetops: red langur (*Presbytis rubicunda*) terrestrial behavior. *Primates*, **59**(5), 437–48. DOI: 10.1007/s10329-018-0676-5.

Cheyne, S.M., Thompson, C.J.H., Phillips, A.C., Hill, R.M.C. and Limin, S.H. (2008). Density and population estimate of gibbons (*Hylobates albibarbis*) in the Sabangau catchment, Central Kalimantan, Indonesia. *Primates*, **49**(1), 50–6. DOI: 10.1007/s10329-007-0063-0.

Chimelong (n.d.). *Home page* [in Chinese]. Available at: https://www.chimelong.com/. Accessed January, 2020.

Chimfunshi (n.d.). *Chimpanzees at Chimfunshi.* Hamburg, Germany: Chimfunshi Verein zum Schutz bedrohter Umwelt eV. Available at: https://www.chimfunshi.de/en/chimpanzees/. Accessed December 4, 2018.

ChimpCARE (n.d.-a). *Chimpanzees in the US.* Chicago, IL: Lincoln Park Zoo. Available at: http://www.chimpcare.org/map. Accessed October, 2019.

ChimpCARE (n.d.-b). *Project ChimpCARE.* Chicago, IL: Lincoln Park Zoo. Available at: https://chimpcare.org/. Accessed January, 2020.

Chiu, J. (2013). Henan zoo under fire for trying to pass off dog as African lion. *South China Morning Post*, August 15, 2013. Available at: https://www.scmp.com/news/china/article/1296783/henan-zoo-puts-dog-cage-labels-it-african-lion.

Chivers, D.J. (1977). The lesser apes. In *Primate Conservation*, ed. P. Rainier and G.H. Bourne. New York, NY: Academic Press, pp. 539–94.

Cho, J.H. (2016). American Greetings pulls its chimpanzee greeting cards, at PETA's request. *Cleveland.com*, December 21, 2016. Available at: https://www.cleveland.com/business/2016/12/american_greetings_pulls_its_chimpanzee_greeting_cards_after_peta_request.html.

Choplin, L. (2017). Update: Beulah, Karen, and Minnie elephant rights lawsuit. *Nonhuman Rights Blog*, December 28, 2017. Available at: https://www.nonhumanrights.org/blog/update-elephant-rights-lawsuit-12-28-17/.

Choudhury, A. (2013). Description of a new subspecies of Hoolock gibbon *Hoolock hoolock* from northeast India. *Newsletter and Journal of the Rhino Foundation for Nature in Northeast India*, **9**, 49–59.

Chua, L. (2012). *The Christianity of Culture: Conversion, Ethnic Citizenship, and the Matter of Religion in Malaysian Borneo.* New York, NY: Palgrave Macmillan.

Chua, L. (2018a). Small acts and personal politics: on helping to save the orangutan via social media. *Anthropology Today*, **34**(3), 7–11. DOI: 10.1111/1467-8322.12432.

Chua, L. (2018b). Too cute to cuddle? 'Witnessing publics' and interspecies relations on the social media-scape of orangutan conservation. *Anthropological Quarterly*, **91**(3), 873–903. DOI: 10.1353/anq.2018.0043.

Chuo, M.D. (2018). *Great Ape Program knowledge assessment on the trade in apes in Cameroon.* Unpublished report. Cambridge, UK: Arcus Foundation.

Chuo, M.D. and Angwafo, T.E. (2017a). Chimpanzee in ethno-primatological practices and its implications for biodiversity conservation: Kimbi-Fungom National Park and Kom-Wum Forest Reserve, Cameroon. *American Journal of Agriculture and Forestry*, **5**(5), 157–72. DOI: 10.11648/j.ajaf.20170505.14.

Chuo, M.D. and Angwafo, T.E. (2017b). Influence of traditional beliefs on the conservation of *Pan troglodytes ellioti*: case study, Kimbi-Fungom National Park and Kom-Wum Forest Reserve, NW Region, Cameroon. *International Journal of Forest, Animal and Fisheries Research*, **1**(3), 1–14. DOI: 10.22161/ijfaf.1.3.1.

Cibot, M., Krief, S., Philippon, J., *et al.* (2016). Feeding consequences of hand and foot disability in wild adult chimpanzees (*Pan troglodytes schweinfurthii*). *International Journal of Primatology*, **37**(4–5), 479–94. DOI: 10.1007/s10764-016-9914-0.

CITES (1973). *Convention on International Trade in Endangered Species of Wild Fauna and Flora. As amended on April 30, 1983*. Geneva, Switzerland: Convention on International Trade in Endangered Species of Wild Fauna and Flora (CITES). Available at: https://www.cites.org/eng/disc/text.php.

CITES (2007a). *Conf. 10.3* Designation and Role of the Scientific Authorities*. Geneva, Switzerland: Convention on International Trade in Endangered Species of Wild Fauna and Flora (CITES). Available at: https://www.cites.org/sites/default/files/document/E-Res-10-03_0.pdf.

CITES (2007b). *CoP14 Doc. 50 Annex 1. CITES/GRASP Orang-utan Technical Missions: Thailand and Cambodia*. Geneva, Switzerland: Convention on International Trade in Endangered Species of Wild Fauna and Flora (CITES). Available at: https://cites.org/sites/default/files/common/cop/14/doc/E14-50A01.pdf.

CITES (2007c). *CoP14 Doc. 53.2. Monitoring of Illegal Trade in Ivory and Other Elephant Products*. Geneva, Switzerland: Convention on International Trade In Endangered Species of Wild Fauna And Flora (CITES). Available at: https://cites.org/sites/default/files/eng/cop/14/doc/E14-53-2.pdf.

CITES (2013a). *CITES Electronic Permitting Toolkit*. Geneva, Switzerland: Convention on International Trade in Endangered Species of Wild Fauna and Flora (CITES). Available at: https://cites.org/sites/default/files/eng/prog/e/cites_e-toolkit_v2.pdf.

CITES (2013b). *Conf. 13.4 (Rev. CoP16). Conservation of and Trade in Great Apes*. Geneva, Switzerland: Convention on International Trade in Endangered Species of Wild Fauna and Flora (CITES). Available at: https://www.cites.org/sites/default/files/document/E-Res-13-04-R16.pdf. Accessed October, 2018.

CITES (2014). African, Asian and North American law enforcement officers team up to apprehend wildlife criminals. Operation Cobra II press release, February 10, 2014. *CITES News*. Geneva, Switzerland: Convention on International Trade in Endangered Species of Wild Fauna and Flora (CITES). Available at: https://cites.org/sites/default/files/eng/news/sundry/2014/operation_cobra_ii_pr.pdf.

CITES (2015a). CITES Secretariat confirms the arrest of former wildlife director in Guinea and applauds national authorities' work. *CITES News*. Geneva, Switzerland: Convention on International Trade in Endangered Species of Wild Fauna and Flora (CITES). Available at: https://cites.org/eng/guinea_arrest_20150903. Accessed September, 2020.

CITES (2015b). *Conf. 17.7. Review of Trade in Animal Specimens Reported as Produced in Captivity*. Geneva, Switzerland: Convention on International Trade in Endangered Species of Wild Fauna and Flora (CITES). Available at: https://cites.org/sites/default/files/document/E-Res-17-07.pdf. Accessed February, 2019.

CITES (2015c). Global alliance celebrates 5 years' achievements in combating wildlife crime. *CITES Press Release*, November 23, 2015. Available at: https://cites.org/eng/news/pr/global_alliance_celebrates_5_years_achievements_in_combating_wildlife_crime_23112015.

CITES (2016a). *CoP17 Doc. 61. Species-Specific Matters Great Apes (Hominidae spp.)*. Geneva, Switzerland: Convention on International Trade in Endangered Species of Wild Fauna and Flora (CITES). Available at: https://cites.org/sites/default/files/eng/cop/17/WorkingDocs/E-CoP17-61.pdf.

CITES (2016b). *CoP17 Inf. 33. International Consortium on Combating Wildlife Crime (ICCWC). Background Paper for Meeting of the Conference of the Parties, Johannesburg (South Africa), 24 September–5 October 2016*. Geneva, Switzerland: Convention on International Trade in Endangered Species of Wild Fauna and Flora (CITES). Available at: https://cites.org/sites/default/files/eng/cop/17/InfDocs/E-CoP17-Inf-33.pdf.

CITES (2016c). *Conf. 17.6. Prohibiting, Preventing, Detecting and Countering Corruption, which Facilitates Activities Conducted in Violation of the Convention*. Geneva, Switzerland: CITES.

CITES (2017a). *Appendices I, II and III*. Geneva, Switzerland: Convention on International Trade in Endangered Species of Wild Fauna and Flora (CITES). Available at: https://cites.org/eng/app/appendices.php.

CITES (2017b). *17.232. Great Apes (*Hominidae *spp.)*. Geneva, Switzerland: Convention on International Trade in Endangered Species of Wild Fauna and Flora (CITES). Available at: https://cites.org/eng/node/48656.

CITES (2018a). *SC70 Doc. 52. Species Specific Matters: Great Apes (*Hominidae *spp.).* Geneva, Switzerland: Convention on International Trade in Endangered Species of Wild Fauna and Flora (CITES). Available at: https://cites.org/sites/default/files/eng/com/sc/70/E-SC70-52.pdf.

CITES (2018b). *SC70 Sum. 2 (Rev. 1) (01/10/18). Summary: Monday 1 October.* Geneva, Switzerland: Convention on International Trade in Endangered Species of Wild Fauna and Flora (CITES). Available at: https://cites.org/sites/default/files/eng/com/sc/70/exsum/E-SC70-Sum-02-R1.pdf.

CITES (2019a). *Appendices I, II and III.* Valid from November 26, 2019. Geneva, Switzerland: Convention on International Trade in Endangered Species of Wild Fauna and Flora (CITES). Available at: https://cites.org/eng/app/appendices.php.

CITES (2019b). *Conf. 13.4 (Rev. CoP18). Conservation of and Trade in Great Apes.* Geneva, Switzerland: Convention on International Trade in Endangered Species of Wild Fauna and Flora (CITES). Available at: https://cites.org/sites/default/files/document/E-Res-13-04-R18.pdf.

CITES (2019c). International consortium to strengthen global action on combating wildlife crime. *Press Advisory.* Geneva, Switzerland: Convention on International Trade in Endangered Species of Wild Fauna and Flora (CITES). Available at: https://www.cites.org/eng/news/pr/International_consortium_to_strengthen_global_action_on_combating_wildlife_crime_15082019.

CITES (2019d). Wildlife enforcement networks from around the world meet to further strengthen collaborative efforts against wildlife crime. *CITES News.* Geneva, Switzerland: Convention on International Trade in Endangered Species of Wild Fauna and Flora (CITES). Available at: https://www.cites.org/eng/Wildlife_enforcement_networks_from_around_the_world_meet_to_further_strengthen_collaborative_efforts_against_wildlife_crime_26082019.

CITES (n.d.-a). *Annual report.* Convention on International Trade in Endangered Species of Wild Fauna and Flora (CITES). Available at: https://www.cites.org/eng/imp/reporting_requirements/annual_report. Accessed January, 2020.

CITES (n.d.-b). *Appendix I: included in* Nycticebus *spp.* Geneva, Switzerland: Convention on International Trade in Endangered Species of Wild Fauna and Flora (CITES). Available at: https://cites.org/eng/taxonomy/term/17486. Accessed October, 2019.

CITES (n.d.-c). *Captive-produced animals and artificially propagated plants.* Geneva, Switzerland: Convention on International Trade in Endangered Species of Wild Fauna and Flora (CITES). Available at: https://www.cites.org/eng/prog/captive-breeding. Accessed February, 2020.

CITES (n.d.-d). *The CITES Appendices.* Geneva, Switzerland: Convention on International Trade in Endangered Species of Wild Fauna and Flora (CITES). Available at: https://www.cites.org/eng/app/index.php. Accessed September, 2020.

CITES (n.d.-e). *CITES compliance procedures.* Geneva, Switzerland: Convention on International Trade in Endangered Species of Wild Fauna and Flora (CITES). Available at: https://www.cites.org/eng/res/14/14-03C15.php. Accessed February, 2020.

CITES (n.d.-f). *The CITES Secretariat.* Geneva, Switzerland: Convention on International Trade in Endangered Species of Wild Fauna and Flora (CITES). Available at: https://www.cites.org/eng/disc/sec/index.php. Accessed September, 2020.

CITES (n.d.-g). *The CITES species.* Geneva, Switzerland: Convention on International Trade in Endangered Species of Wild Fauna and Flora (CITES). Available at: https://www.cites.org/eng/disc/species.php. Accessed July, 2019.

CITES (n.d.-h). *CITES trade database.* Geneva, Switzerland: Convention on International Trade in Endangered Species of Wild Fauna and Flora (CITES). Available at: https://trade.cites.org. Accessed September, 2020.

CITES (n.d.-i). *eCITES.* Geneva, Switzerland: Convention on International Trade in Endangered Species of Wild Fauna and Flora (CITES). Available at: https://cites.org/eng/prog/ecites. Accessed October, 2018.

CITES (n.d.-j). *How CITES works.* Geneva, Switzerland: Convention on International Trade in Endangered Species of Wild Fauna and Flora (CITES). Available at: https://www.cites.org/eng/disc/how.php. Accessed September, 2020.

CITES (n.d.-k). *The International Consortium on Combating Wildlife Crime.* Geneva, Switzerland: Convention on International Trade in Endangered Species of Wild Fauna and Flora (CITES). Available at: https://www.cites.org/eng/prog/iccwc.php. Accessed September, 2020.

CITES (n.d.-l). *Resolutions of the Conference of the Parties in effect after the 17th meeting* Geneva, Switzerland: Convention on International Trade in Endangered Species of Wild Fauna and Flora (CITES). Available at: https://cites.org/eng/res/index.php. Accessed August, 2019.

CITES (n.d.-m). *Standing Committee.* Geneva, Switzerland: Convention on International Trade in Endangered Species of Wild Fauna and Flora (CITES). Available at: https://www.cites.org/eng/disc/sc.php. Accessed February, 2020.

CITES (n.d.-n). *What is CITES?* Geneva, Switzerland: Convention on International Trade in Endangered Species of Wild Fauna and Flora (CITES). Available at: https://www.cites.org/eng/disc/what.php. Accessed October, 2018.

CITES and GRASP (2006). *CITES/GRASP Orang-utan Technical Mission Indonesia. 8–12 May, 2006.* Geneva, Switzerland: Convention on International Trade in Endangered Species of Wild Fauna and Flora (CITES)–Great Apes Survival Partnership (GRASP). Available at: https://cites.org/sites/default/files/common/prog/ape/ID_mission06.pdf.

CITES and ICPO-INTERPOL (1998). *Memorandum of Understanding between the General Secretariat of ICPO-INTERPOL and the Secretariat of the Convention on International Trade in Endangered Species of Wild Fauna and Flora (CITES).* Geneva, Switzerland: Convention on International Trade in Endangered Species of Wild Fauna and Flora (CITES) and International Criminal Police Organization (ICPO-INTERPOL). Available at: https://cites.org/sites/default/files/common/disc/sec/CITES-Interpol.pdf.

CITES, IUCN and TRAFFIC (2013). *Status of African Elephant Populations and Levels of Illegal Killing and the Illegal Trade in Ivory: A Report to the African Elephant Summit.* Washington DC: Convention on International Trade in Endangered Species (CITES) Secretariat, International Union for Conservation of Nature (IUCN) Species Survival Commission (SSC) African Elephant Specialist Group and TRAFFIC International. Available at: https://www.iucn.org/sites/dev/files/import/downloads/african_elephant_summit_background_document_2013_en.pdf.

CITES and WCO (1996). *Memorandum of Understanding Between the World Customs Organization (WCO) and the CITES Secretariat.* Brussels, Belgium: Convention on International Trade in Endangered Species of Wild Fauna and Flora (CITES) Secretariat and World Customs Organization (WCO). Available at: https://cites.org/sites/default/files/eng/disc/sec/CITES-WCO.pdf.

Clarke, R.V. (2009). Situational crime prevention: theoretical background and current practice. In *Handbook on Crime and Deviance*, ed. M.D. Krohn, A.J. Lizotte and G. Penly. New York, NY: Springer, pp. 259–76.

Clement, J. (2019). Number of monthly active Instagram users from January 2013 to June 2018 (in millions). *Statista*, September 2, 2019. Available at: https://www.statista.com/statistics/253577/number-of-monthly-active-instagram-users/. Accessed October, 2019.

ClickPress (2006). Indonesian children welcome the news of the return of 54 smuggled orangutans from Thailand. *ClickPress*, April 24, 2006. Available at: https://clickpress.com/releases/Detailed/11935005cp.shtml.

Clough, C. and May, C. (2018). *Illicit Financial Flows and the Illegal Trade in Great Apes.* Washington DC: Global Financial Integrity (GFI). Available at: https://www.gfintegrity.org/wp-content/uploads/2018/10/GFI-Illicit-Financial-Flows-and-the-Illegal-Trade-in-Great-Apes.pdf.

CMP (2013). *Open Standards for the Practice of Conservation Version 3.0, April 2013.* The Conservation Measures Partnership (CMP). Available at: http://cmp-openstandards.org/wp-content/uploads/2017/06/CMP-OS-V3.0-Final-minor-update-May-2107.pdf.

CMP (n.d.-a). *Open Standards for the Practice of Conservation: History.* Conservation Measures Partnership (CMP). Available at: http://cmp-openstandards.org/about-os/history/. Accessed September, 2019.

CMP (n.d.-b). *Open Standards for the Practice of Conservation: Resources.* Conservation Measures Partnership (CMP). Available at: https://cmp-openstandards.org/resources/. Accessed September, 2020.

CMS (2014). *Progress Report on the Implementation of the Agreement on the Conservation of Gorillas (UNEP/CMS/COP11/Inf.12.1, 16 August 2014).* Bonn, Germany: Convention on the Conservation of Migratory Species of Wild Animals (CMS). Available at: https://www.cms.int/sites/default/files/document/COP11_Inf_12_1_Report_Gorilla_Agreement_Eonly.pdf.

CMS (2017). *Report on the Implementation of the CMS Gorilla Agreement (UNEP/CMS/COP12/Inf.6.5, 13 October 2017).* Bonn, Germany: Convention on the Conservation of Migratory Species of Wild Animals (CMS). Available at: https://www.cms.int/en/document/report-implementation-cms-gorilla-agreement-1.

CMS (2018). CMS Standing Committee paves way for new compliance mechanism. *CMS News*, October 31, 2018. Bonn, Germany: Convention on the Conservation of Migratory Species of Wild Animals (CMS). Available at: https://www.cms.int/en/news/cms-standing-committee-paves-way-new-compliance-mechanism.

CMS (n.d.-a). *CMS family portal.* Bonn, Germany: Convention on the Conservation of Migratory Species of Wild Animals (CMS). Available at: http://www.migratoryspecies.org. Accessed October, 2018.

CMS (n.d.-b). *Gorilla Agreement.* Bonn, Germany: Convention on the Conservation of Migratory Species of Wild Animals (CMS). Available at: http://www.cms.int/en/legalinstrument/gorilla-agreement. Accessed October, 2018.

CMS (n.d.-c). *Gorilla Agreement. Agreement on the conservation of gorillas and their habitats.* Bonn, Germany: Convention on the Conservation of Migratory Species of Wild Animals (CMS). Available at: https://www.cms.int/gorilla/. Accessed September, 2020.

CMS (n.d.-d). *Introduction to CMS.* Bonn, Germany: Convention on the Conservation of Migratory Species of Wild Animals (CMS). Available at: https://www.cms.int/en/legalinstrument/cms. Accessed October, 2018.

CMS (n.d.-e). *Parties and range states.* Bonn, Germany: Convention on the Conservation of Migratory Species of Wild Animals (CMS). Available at: https://www.cms.int/en/parties-range-states. Accessed February, 2020.

Coad, L. (2007). *Bushmeat hunting in Gabon: socio economics and hunter behaviour.* PhD thesis. Cambridge and London, UK: University of Cambridge and Imperial College London.

Coad, L., Abernethy, K., Balmford, A., *et al.* (2010). Distribution and use of income from bushmeat in a rural village, Central Gabon. *Conservation Biology*, **24**(6), 1510–8. DOI: 10.1111/j.1523-1739.2010.01525.x.

Coad, L., Fa, J., Abernethy, K., *et al.* (2019). *Towards a Sustainable, Participatory and Inclusive Wild Meat Sector.* Bogor, Indonesia: Center for International Forestry Research (CIFOR). Available at: http://www.cifor.org/publications/pdf_files/Books/BCoad1901.pdf.

Cohen-Brown, R. (2015). How JGI fights wildlife crime. *Jane Goodall's Good for All News*, March 2, 2015. Available at: https://news.janegoodall.org/2015/03/02/how-jgi-fights-wildlife-crime/.

Cole, D. (2016). *Engines of Liberty: The Power of Citizen Activists to Make Constitutional Law.* New York, NY: Basic Books.

Collins, F.S. (2015). NIH will no longer support biomedical research on chimpanzees. *The NIH Director*, November 17, 2015. Bethesda, MD: National Institutes of Health (NIH). Available at: https://www.nih.gov/about-nih/who-we-are/nih-director/statements/nih-will-no-longer-support-biomedical-research-chimpanzees.

Colombian Supreme Court of Justice (2018). *STC4360-2018 de 05 de Abril de 2018. Rad. 11001-22-03-000-2018-0 0319-01.* Bogota DC, Colombia. Available at: http://legal.legis.com.co/document/Index?obra=jurcol&document=jurcol_c947ae53aeb447bd91e8e9a315311ac5.

Colyn, M., Dudu, A. and Mbaelele, M.M. (1987). Data on small and medium scale game utilization in the rain forest of Zaire. In *International Symposium and Conference on Wildlife Management in Sub-Saharan Africa. Harare, Zimbabwe*, ed. B.D. Clers. United Nations Educational, Scientific and Cultural Organisation (UNESCO), pp. 109–45.

Commitante, R., Unwin, S., Sulistyo, F., *et al.* (2018). *Orangutan Veterinary Advisory Group Workshop 2018 Proceedings, Aceh, Indonesia.* United States and UK: Orangutan Conservancy and Chester Zoo/NEZS. Available at: https://www.ovag.org/uploads/documents/content/2018-ovag-workshop-proceedings.pdf.

Conservation Evidence (n.d.-a). *Conservation evidence: providing evidence to improve practice. Actions.* Cambridge, UK: University of Cambridge. Available at: https://www.conservationevidence.com/data/index?terms=prism. Accessed May, 2019.

Conservation Evidence (n.d.-b). *Conservation evidence: providing evidence to improve practice. Evidence champions.* Cambridge, UK: University of Cambridge. Available at: https://www.conservationevidence.com/content/page/81. Accessed October, 2019.

Cook, D., Roberts, M. and Lowther, J. (2002). *The International Wildlife Trade and Organised Crime.* World Wide Fund for Nature (WWF)/TRAFFIC report. Wolverhampton, UK: Regional Research Institute, University of Wolverhampton.

Coolidge Jr., H.J. (1933). *Pan paniscus.* Pigmy chimpanzee from south of the Congo river. *American Journal of Physical Anthropology*, **18**(1), 1–59. DOI: 10.1002/ajpa.1330180113.

Cooney, R., Roe, D., Dublin, H. and Booker, F. (2018). *Wild Life, Wild Livelihoods: Involving Communities in Sustainable Wildlife Management and Combatting the Illegal Wildlife Trade.* Nairobi, Kenya: United Nations

Environment Programme (UNEP). Available at: http://wedocs.unep.org/bitstream/handle/20.500.11822/22864/WLWL_Report_web.pdf.

Cooney, R., Roe, D., Dublin, H., *et al.* (2017). From poachers to protectors: engaging local communities in solutions to illegal wildlife trade. *Conservation Letters*, **10**(3), 367–74. DOI: 10.1111/conl.12294.

Corbey, R. and Lanjouw, A. (2013). *The Politics of Species: Reshaping our Relationships with Other Animals.* Cambridge, UK: Cambridge University Press. DOI: 10.1017/CBO9781139506755.

Corrada Bravo, C., Álvarez Berríos, R. and Aide, T. (2017). Species-specific audio detection: a comparison of three template-based detection algorithms using random forests. *PeerJ Computer Science*, **3**, e113. DOI: 10.7717/peerj-cs.113.

Corrigan, J. (2019). 8 Top anti poaching drones for critical wildlife protection. *DroneZon*, June 29, 2019. Available at: https://www.dronezon.com/drones-for-good/wildlife-conservation-protection-using-anti-poaching-drones-technology/.

Corry, S. (2015). Wildlife conservation must support, not destroy, Indigenous Peoples. *Ecologist*, February 6, 2015. Available at: https://theecologist.org/2015/feb/06/wildlife-conservation-must-support-not-destroy-indigenous-peoples.

Coudrat, C.N.Z. and Nanthavong, C. (2014). *Gibbon survey and taxonomical status in Nakai-Nam Theun National Protected Area, Laos reveals one of the largest remaining populations of white-cheeked gibbons: implications for their long-term conservation.* Presented at the XXVIth International Primatological Society Congress, Hanoi, Viet Nam.

Courchamp, F., Jaric, I., Albert, C., *et al.* (2018). The paradoxical extinction of the most charismatic animals. *PLoS Biology*, **16**(4), e2003997. DOI: 10.1371/journal.pbio.2003997.

Courtenay, J. and Santow, G. (1989). Mortality of wild and captive chimpanzees. *Folia Primatologica*, **52**(3–4), 167–77. DOI: 10.1159/000156395.

Covarrubias, A. (2005). When the show's over for Hollywood chimps. *Los Angeles Times*, March 22, 2005. Available at: https://www.latimes.com/archives/la-xpm-2005-mar-22-me-chimps22-story.html.

Cover, R.M. (1975). *Justice Accused: Antislavery and the Judicial Process.* New Haven, CT: Yale University Press.

Covey, R. and McGraw, W.S. (2014). Monkeys in a West African bushmeat market: implications for Cercopithecid conservation in eastern Liberia. *Tropical Conservation Science*, **7**(1), 115–25. DOI: 10.1177/194008291400700103.

Cowlishaw, G. (1992). Song function in gibbons. *Behaviour*, **121**(1-2), 131–53. DOI: 10.1163/156853992X00471.

Cowlishaw, G., Mendelson, S. and Rowcliffe, J.M. (2005). Evidence for post-depletion sustainability in a mature bushmeat market. *Journal of Applied Ecology*, **42**(3), 460–8. DOI: 10.1111/j.1365-2664.2005.01046.x.

Cribb, R., Gilbert, H. and Tiffin, H. (2014). *Wild Man from Borneo: A Cultural History of the Orangutan.* Honolulu, Hawaii: University of Hawai'i Press.

Critchlow, R., Plumptre, A.J., Driciru, M., *et al.* (2015). Spatiotemporal trends of illegal activities from ranger-collected data in a Ugandan national park. *Conservation Biology*, **29**(5), 1458–70. DOI: 10.1111/cobi.12538.

Crowley, B.E., Godfrey, L.R., Bankoff, R.J., *et al.* (2017). Island-wide aridity did not trigger recent megafaunal extinctions in Madagascar. *Ecography*, **40**(8), 901–12. DOI: 10.1111/ecog.02376.

Cruz, J.E. (2006). Sentença do Habeas Corpus impetrado em favor da chimpanzé Suíça. *Revista Brasileira de Direito Animal*, **1**(1), 281–5.

CSWCT (n.d.). *Chimp profiles.* Entebbe, Uganda: Chimpanzee Sanctuary and Wildlife Conservation Trust (CSWCT). Available at: https://ngambaisland.org/chimp-profiles/. Accessed October 31, 2018.

Curran, J. (2018). *Orangutan Jungle School.* Antenna Pictures, Blue Ant Media and NHNZ.

CyberTracker (n.d.). *CyberTracker software.* CyberTracker Conservation. Available at: https://www.cybertracker.org/software/introduction. Accessed September, 2020.

Dalton, J. (2018). 'Now or never' battle to save Indonesia's endangered orangutans as British companies still using 'dirty' palm oil. *The Independent*, September 18, 2018. Available at: https://www.independent.co.uk/news/uk/home-news/orangutan-indonesia-endangered-palm-oil-uk-companies-cadburys-dove-chocolate-great-apes-a8542151.html.

Damania, R., Milner-Gulland, E.J. and Crookes, D.J. (2005). A bioeconomic analysis of bushmeat hunting. *Proceedings. Biological Sciences*, **272**(1560), 259–66. DOI: 10.1098/rspb.2004.2945.

Danaparamita, A. (2016). Don't feed the orangutans – a warning unheeded at popular ecotourism stop. *Mongabay*, November 21, 2016. Available at: https://news.mongabay.com/2016/11/dont-feed-the-orangutans-a-warning-unheeded-at-popular-ecotourism-stop/.

Danquah, E., Oppong, S.K., Akom, E. and Sam, M. (2012). Preliminary survey of chimpanzees and threatened monkeys in the Bia-Goaso forest block in southwestern Ghana. *African Primates*, **7**, 163–74.

Davis, J.T., Mengersen, K., Abram, N.K., *et al.* (2013). It's not just conflict that motivates killing of orangutans. *PLoS ONE*, **8**(10), e75373. DOI: 10.1371/journal.pone.0075373.

de Boer, W.F., van Langevelde, F., Prins, H.H.T., *et al.* (2013). Understanding spatial differences in African elephant densities and occurrence, a continent-wide analysis. *Biological Conservation*, **159**, 468–76. DOI: 10.1016/j.biocon.2012.10.015.

De Cordova, F., director (1951). *Bedtime for Bonzo.* Universal International Pictures (UI). Available at: https://www.imdb.com/title/tt0043325/.

De Greef, K. and Raemaekers, S. (2014). *South Africa's Illicit Abalone Trade: An Updated Overview and Knowledge Gap Analysis.* Cambridge, UK: TRAFFIC International. Available at: https://www.traffic.org/site/assets/files/8469/south-africas-illicit-abalone.pdf.

de Merode, E. and Cowlishaw, G. (2006). Species protection, the changing informal economy, and the politics of access to the bushmeat trade in the Democratic Republic of Congo. *Conservation Biology*, **20**(4), 1262–71. DOI: 10.1111/j.1523-1739.2006.00425.x.

de Merode, E., Smith, K.H., Homewood, K., *et al.* (2007). The impact of armed conflict on protected-area efficacy in Central Africa. *Biology Letters*, **3**(3), 299–301. DOI: 10.1098/rsbl.2007.0010.

Decree No. 41/2017/ND-CP (2017). *Amendment and Supplementation to a Number of Articles of the Decree on Administrative Penalties for Violations in Fields of Aquaculture, Veterinary, Animal Breeds, Animal Feed; Forest Management, Development and Protection, and Forestry Product Management. Decree No. 41/2017/ND-CP.* Socialist Republic of Viet Nam. Available at: https://vanbanphapluat.co/decree-41-2017-nd-cp-amendment-to-decree-on-administrative-penatiles-for-violations-in-agriculture.

Decree No. 157/2013/ND-CP (2013). *Decree on Penalties for Administrative Violations Against Regulations on Forest Management, Development, Protection and Forest Product Management. No. 157/2013/ND-CP.* Socialist Republic of Viet Nam. Available at: https://vanbanphapluat.co/decree-no-157-2013-nd-cp-penalties-for-administrative-violations-against-regulations-on-forest-management.

Deichmann, J.L., Acevedo-Charry, O., Barclay, L., *et al.* (2018). It's time to listen: there is much to be learned from the sounds of tropical ecosystems. *Biotropica*, **50**(5), 713–8. DOI: 10.1111/btp.12593.

Delgado, C.L. (2003). Rising consumption of meat and milk in developing countries has created a new food revolution. *The Journal of Nutrition*, **133**(11), 3907S–10S. DOI: 10.1093/jn/133.11.3907S.

Delgado, R.A. (2010). Communication, culture and conservation in orangutans. In *Indonesian Primates*, ed. S. Gursky and J. Supriatna. New York, NY: Springer, pp. 23–40. DOI: 10.1007/978-1-4419-1560-3_3.

Delgado, R.A. and van Schaik, C.P. (2000). The behavioral ecology and conservation of the orangutan *(Pongo pygmaeus)*: a tale of two islands. *Evolutionary Anthropology: Issues, News, and Reviews*, **9**(5), 201–18. DOI: 10.1002/1520-6505(2000)9:5<201::AID-EVAN2>3.0.CO;2-Y.

Dell'amore, C. (2014). Beloved African elephant killed for ivory – 'monumental' loss. *National Geographic*, June 16, 2014. Available at: https://www.nationalgeographic.com/news/2014/6/140616-elephants-tusker-satao-poachers-killed-animals-africa-science/.

Denyer, S. (2013). In China, victory for wildlife conservation as citizens persuaded to give up shark fin soup. *The Washington Post*. October 19, 2013. Available at: https://www.washingtonpost.com/world/in-china-victory-for-wildlife-conservation-as-citizens-persuaded-to-give-up-shark-fin-soup/2013/10/19/e8181326-3646-11e3-89db-8002ba99b894_story.html.

Després-Einspenner, M.-L., Howe, E.J., Drapeau, P. and Kühl, H.S. (2017). An empirical evaluation of camera trapping and spatially explicit capture–recapture models for estimating chimpanzee density. *American Journal of Primatology*, **79**(7), e22647. DOI: 10.1002/ajp.22647.

Deutsche Welle (2017). German court orders 45-year-old circus chimp to live with other apes. *Deutsche Welle*, April 27, 2017. Available at: https://www.dw.com/en/german-court-orders-45-year-old-circus-chimp-to-live-with-other-apes/a-38618443.

Dias, F.S., Wenceslau, J.F.C., Marques, T.A. and Miller, D.L. (2019). Density and distribution of western chimpanzees around a bauxite deposit in the Boé Sector, Guinea-Bissau. *American Journal of Primatology*, **81**(9), e23047. DOI: 10.1002/ajp.23047.

Dickson, I.M., Butchart, S.H.M., Dauncey, V., *et al.* (2017). *PRISM – Toolkit for evaluating the outcomes and impacts of small/medium-sized conservation projects. Version 1*. PRISM. Available at: https://conservationevaluation.org/PRISM-Evaluation-Toolkit-V1.pdf.

Dillehay, T.D., Goodbred, S., Pino, M., *et al.* (2017). Simple technologies and diverse food strategies of the Late Pleistocene and Early Holocene at Huaca Prieta, Coastal Peru. *Science Advances*, **3**(5), e1602778. DOI: 10.1126/sciadv.1602778.

Dillehay, T.D., Ramírez, C., Pino, M., *et al.* (2008). Monte Verde: seaweed, food, medicine, and the peopling of South America. *Science*, **320**(5877), 784–6. DOI: 10.1126/science.1156533.

Dingfei, Y. (2014). China 'main destination' for illegally traded chimpanzees. *The Guardian*, October 14, 2014. Available at: https://www.theguardian.com/environment/2014/oct/14/china-main-destination-for-illegally-traded-chimpanzees.

Dirzo, R., Young, H.S., Galetti, M., *et al.* (2014). Defaunation in the Anthropocene. *Science*, **345**(6195), 401–6. DOI: 10.1126/science.1251817.

Djudjic, D. (2017). Shutterstock ban all unnatural photos of apes and monkeys after appeal from PETA. *DIYPhotography*, December 29, 2017. Available at: https://www.diyphotography.net/peta-makes-shutterstock-ban-unnatural-photos-apes-monkeys/.

Dobson, A.D.M., Milner-Gulland, E.J., Beale, C.M., Ibbett, H. and Keane, A. (2019). Detecting deterrence from patrol data. *Conservation Biology*, **33**(3), 665–75. DOI: 10.1111/cobi.13222.

Doran-Sheehy, D., Derby, A., Greer, D. and Mongo, P. (2007). Habituation of western gorillas: the process and factors that influence it. *American Journal of Primatology*, **69**, 1–16. DOI: 10.1002/ajp.20442.

Doran-Sheehy, D., Mongo, P., Lodwick, J. and Conklin-Brittain, N.L. (2009). Male and female western gorilla diet: preferred foods, use of fallback resources, and implications for ape versus old world monkey foraging strategies. *American Journal of Physical Anthropology*, **140**(4), 727–38. DOI: 10.1002/ajpa.21118.

Dounias, E. and Froment, A. (2011). From foraging to farming among present-day forest hunter-gatherers: consequences on diet and health. *International Forestry Review*, **13**(3), 294–304, 11.

Dowie, M. (2009). *Conservation Refugees: The Hundred-Year Conflict between Global Conservation and Native Peoples*. Cambridge, MA: MIT Press.

Downing, D.C. (2012). The effect of the bushmeat trade on African ape populations: critical evaluation of the evidence and potential solutions. *The Collegiate Journal of Anthropology*, **1**.

Drani, E. and Infield, M. (2014). *Cultural values in conservation: traditional values and practices that impact on ape conservation and welfare*. Unpublished background paper. Commissioned by the Arcus Foundation.

Draper, R. (2016). Inside the fight to save one of the world's most dangerous parks. *National Geographic*, July, 2016. Available at: https://www.nationalgeographic.com/magazine/2016/07/virunga-national-parks-africa-congo-rangers/.

Dressler, W., Büscher, B., Schoon, M., *et al.* (2010). From hope to crisis and back again? A critical history of the global CBNRM narrative. *Environmental Conservation*, **37**(1), 5–15. DOI: 10.1017/S0376892910000044.

Drewry, R. (1997). Ecotourism: can it save the orangutans? *Inside Indonesia*, **51**, 15–8.

Duckworth, J.W. (2008). *Preliminary gibbon status review for Lao PDR 2008*. Unpublished report. Hanoi, Viet Nam, and Cambridge, UK: Fauna and Flora International (FFI). Available at: https://www.issuelab.org/resources/10668/10668.pdf.

Duckworth, J.W., Timmins, R.J., Anderson, G.Q.A., *et al.* (1995). Notes on the conservation and status of the gibbon Hylobates (*Nomascus gabriellae*) in Laos. *Tropical Biodiversity*, **3**, 15–27.

Duffy, R., Massé, F., Smidt, E., *et al.* (2019). Why we must question the militarisation of conservation. *Biological Conservation*, **232**, 66–73. DOI: 10.1016/j.biocon.2019.01.013.

Duffy, R. and St John, F.A.V. (2013). *Poverty, poaching and trafficking: what are the links?* UK: Evidence on Demand. DOI: 10.12774/eod_hd059.jun2013.duffy.

Duffy, R., St John, F.A.V., Büscher, B. and Brockington, D. (2015). The militarization of anti-poaching: undermining long term goals? *Environmental Conservation*, **42**(4), 345–8. DOI: 10.1017/S0376892915000119.

Duffy, R., St John, F.A.V., Büscher, B. and Brockington, D. (2016). Toward a new understanding of the links between poverty and illegal wildlife hunting. *Conservation Biology*, **30**(1), 14–22. DOI: 10.1111/cobi.12622.

Dunbar, R.I.M., Cheyne, S.M., Lan, D., *et al.* (2019). Environment and time as constraints on the biogeographical distribution of gibbons. *American Journal of Primatology*, **81**(1), e22940. DOI: 10.1002/ajp.22940.

Dunn, A., Bergl, R., Byler, D., *et al.* (2014). *Revised Regional Action Plan for the Conservation of the Cross River Gorilla* (Gorilla gorilla diehli) *2014–2019*. New York, NY: International Union for Conservation of Nature (IUCN) Species Survival Commission (SSC), Primate Specialist Group, and Wildlife Conservation Society (WCS). Available at: https://portals.iucn.org/library/node/44661.

Durham, D. (2015). The status of captive apes. In *State of the Apes: Industrial Agriculture and Ape Conservation*, ed. Arcus Foundation. Cambridge, UK: Cambridge University Press, pp. 228–59. Available at: http://www.state oftheapes.com/themes/the-status-of-captive-apes/.

Durham, D. (2018). The status of captive apes: a statistical update. In *State of the Apes: Infrastructure Development and Ape Conservation*, ed. Arcus Foundation. Cambridge, UK: Cambridge University Press, pp. 255–63. Available at: https://www.stateoftheapes.com/volume-3-infrastructure-development/.

Durham, D. and Phillipson, A. (2014). Status of captive apes across Africa and Asia: the impact of extractive industry. In *State of the Apes: Extractive Industries and Ape Conservation*, ed. Arcus Foundation. Cambridge, UK: Cambridge University Press, pp. 279–305. Available at: http://www.stateoftheapes.com/volume-1-extractive-industries/.

Duvall, C.S. (2008). Human settlement ecology and chimpanzee habitat selection in Mali. *Landscape Ecology*, **23**(6), 699–716. DOI: 10.1007/s10980-008-9231-x.

Duvall, C.S. and Smith, G. (2005). Republic of Mali. In *World Atlas of Great Apes and their Conservation*, ed. J.O. Caldecott, J.G. Bennett, H.J. Ruitenbeek and L. Miles. Berkeley, CA: University of California Press, pp. 371–7.

EAGLE (2017). *The EAGLE Network Annual Report 2017.* EAGLE Network. Available at: http://www.eagle-enforcement.org/data/files/eagle-network-annual-report-2017.pdf.

EAGLE (2019). *The EAGLE Network Annual Report 2019.* Eco Activists for Governance and Law Enforcement (EAGLE). Available at: https://www.eagle-enforcement.org/data/files/eagle-network-annual-report-2019.pdf.

EAGLE (n.d.-a). *Home.* Eco Activists for Governance and Law Enforcement (EAGLE). Available at: https://www.eagle-enforcement.org/. Accessed September, 2020.

EAGLE (n.d.-b). *Our members.* Eco Activists for Governance and Law Enforcement (EAGLE). Available at: http://www.eagle-enforcement.org/members/. Accessed September, 2020.

Eberhardt, J.L. (2019). *Biased: Uncovering the Hidden Prejudice that Shapes How We Think, See, and Do.* New York, NY: Viking.

ECOSOC (2013). *E/RES/2013/40. Crime Prevention and Criminal Justice Responses to Illicit Trafficking in Protected Species of Wild Fauna and Flora. Resolution Adopted by the Economic and Social Council on 25 July 2013.* Geneva, Switzerland: United Nations Economic and Social Council (ECOSOC). Available at: https://www.un.org/ga/search/view_doc.asp?symbol=E/RES/2013/40.

Effiom, E.O., Nuñez-Iturri, G., Smith, H.G., Ottosson, U. and Olsson, O. (2013). Bushmeat hunting changes regeneration of African rainforests. *Proceedings of the Royal Society B: Biological Sciences*, **280**(1759), 20130246. DOI: 10.1098/rspb.2013.0246.

Egbe, S.E. (2001). The law, communities and wildlife management in Cameroon. *Rural Development Forestry Network Paper*, **25e**, 1–12. Available at: https://www.odi.org/sites/odi.org.uk/files/odi-assets/publications-opinion-files/1216.pdf.

EIA (2016). *Time for Action: End the Criminality and Corruption Fuelling Wildlife Crime.* London, UK: Environmental Investigation Agency (EIA). Available at: https://eia-international.org/news/time-for-action-end-the-criminality-and-corruption-fuelling-wildlife-crime/.

Eilenberg, M. (2012). The confession of a timber baron: patterns of patronage on the Indonesian–Malaysian border. *Identities*, **19**(2), 149–67. DOI: 10.1080/1070289X.2012.672841.

Ekinde, A., Ashu, M. and Sunderland-Groves, J. (2005). *Preliminary ape surveys around the Fungom Forest Reserve and Furu-Awa sub division, North West Province, Cameroon.* Unpublished report to WCS and Cross River Gorilla Project.

El Bizri, H.R., Morcatty, T.Q., Lima, J.J.S. and Valsecchi, J. (2015). The thrill of the chase: uncovering illegal sport hunting in Brazil through YouTube™ posts. *Ecology and Society*, **20**(3), 30. DOI: 10.5751/ES-07882-200330.

Elder, A.A. (2009). Hylobatid diets revisited: the importance of body mass, fruit availability, and interspecific competition. In *The Gibbons: New Perspectives on Small Ape Socioecology and Population Biology*, ed. D. Whittaker and S. Lappan. New York, NY: Springer, pp. 133–59. DOI: 10.1007/978-0-387-88604-6_8.

Elder, M. (2019). *2018 International Studbook of the Orangutan.* St Paul, MN: Como Park Zoo & Conservatory.

Ellicott, C. (2011). Meat from chimpanzees 'is on sale in Britain' in lucrative black market. *Daily Mail*, March 11, 2011. Available at: https://www.dailymail.co.uk/news/article-1361149/Chimpanzee-meat-discovered-British-restaurants-market-stalls.html.

Elliott, L. and Schaedla, W.H., ed. (2016). *Handbook of Transnational Environmental Crime.* Cheltenham, UK: Edward Elgar.

Ellis, C. and Nsase, M. (2017). *Research report: towards designing an environmentally responsible, sustainable livelihoods programme for Walikale Territory, North Kivu, Democratic Republic of Congo.* Technical report for the Jane Goodall Institute.

Elmhirst, R., Siscawati, M., Basnett, B.S. and Ekowati, D. (2017). Gender and generation in engagements with oil palm in East Kalimantan, Indonesia: insights from feminist political ecology. *The Journal of Peasant Studies*, **44**(6), 1135–57. DOI: 10.1080/03066150.2017.1337002.

Emerton, L. (1998). *Balancing the Opportunity Costs of Wildlife Conservation for the Communities Around Lake Mburo National Park, Uganda.* London, UK: International Institute for Environment and Development. Available at: https://pubs.iied.org/pdfs/7798IIED.pdf.

Emery Thompson, M. (2013). Reproductive ecology of female chimpanzees. *American Journal of Primatology*, **75**(3), 222–37. DOI: 10.1002/ajp.22084.

Emery Thompson, M., Jones, J.H., Pusey, A.E., *et al.* (2007). Aging and fertility patterns in wild chimpanzees provide insights into the evolution of menopause. *Current Biology*, **17**(24), 2150–6. DOI: 10.1016/j.cub.2007.11.033.

Emery Thompson, M. and Wrangham, R.W. (2008). Diet and reproductive function in wild female chimpanzees (*Pan troglodytes schweinfurthii*) at Kibale National Park, Uganda. *American Journal of Physical Anthropology*, **135**(2), 171–81. DOI: 10.1002/ajpa.20718.

Emery Thompson, M. and Wrangham, R.W. (2013). *Pan troglodytes* robust chimpanzee. In *Mammals of Africa. Volume II: Primates*, ed. T.M. Butynski, J. Kingdon and J. Kalina. London, UK: Bloomsbury Publishing, pp. 55–64.

Emery Thompson, M., Zhou, A. and Knott, C.D. (2012). Low testosterone correlates with delayed development in male orangutans. *PLoS ONE*, **7**(10), e47282. DOI: 10.1371/journal.pone.0047282.

Emlen, J.T. and Schaller, G.B. (1960). Distribution and status of the mountain gorilla (*Gorilla gorilla beringei*) 1959. *Zoologica*, **45**, 41–52.

Engler, M. and Parry-Jones, R. (2007). *Opportunity or Threat: The Role of the European Union in Global Wildlife Trade.* Brussels, Belgium: TRAFFIC Europe. Available at: https://www.traffic.org/publications/reports/opportunity-or-threat-the-role-of-the-european-union-in-the-global-wildlife-trade/.

ENS (2006). Orangutans seized in Bangkok will be returned to Indonesia. *Environment News Service*, April 18, 2006. Available at: http://www.ens-newswire.com/ens/apr2006/2006-04-18-01.html.

Environmental Protection Authority (2013). *APP201517: Reassessment of Approvals for New Organisms in Zoos. EPA Staff Report.* New Zealand: Environmental Protection Authority. Available at: https://www.epa.govt.nz/assets/FileAPI/hsno-ar/APP201517/c1ccb924ec/APP201517-APP201517-staff-advice-report.pdf.

EPA (n.d.). *The basics of the regulatory process.* US Environmental Protection Agency (EPA). Available at: https://www.epa.gov/laws-regulations/basics-regulatory-process. Accessed August, 2019.

Eriksen, T.H. (2015). *Small Places: Large Issues An Introduction to Social and Cultural Anthropology*, 4th edn. London, UK: Pluto Press. DOI: 10.2307/j.ctt183p184.

ESS (n.d.). *MIST.* Ecological Software Solutions (ESS). Available at: www.ecostats.com/MIST. Accessed September, 2020.

Estrada, A., Garber, P.A., Mittermeier, R.A., *et al.* (2018). Primates in peril: the significance of Brazil, Madagascar, Indonesia and the Democratic Republic of the Congo for global primate conservation. *PeerJ*, **6**, e4869. DOI: 10.7717/peerj.4869.

Estrada, A., Garber, P.A., Rylands, A.B., *et al.* (2017). Impending extinction crisis of the world's primates: why primates matter. *Science Advances*, **3**(1), e1600946-e. DOI: 10.1126/sciadv.1600946.

Etiendem, D.N., Hens, L. and Pereboom, Z. (2011). Traditional knowledge systems and the conservation of Cross River gorillas: a case study of Bechati, Fossimondi, Besali, Cameroon. *Ecology and Society*, **16**(3), 22. DOI: 10.5751/ES-04182-160322.

EU (2010). Directive 2010/63/EU of the European Parliament and of the Council of 22 September 2010 on the Protection of Animals Used for Scientific Purposes. *Official Journal of the European Union*, **L 276** (October 20, 2010), 33–79. Available at: https://eur-lex.europa.eu/LexUriServ/LexUriServ.do?uri=OJ:L:2010:276:0033:0079:en:PDF.

Evans, E.P. (1906). *The Criminal Prosecution and Capital Punishment of Animals.* London, UK: William Heinemann. Available at: https://archive.org/details/criminalprosecut00evaniala/page/n10.

Fa, J.E., Albrechtsen, L., Johnson, P.J. and Macdonald, D.W. (2009). Linkages between household wealth, bushmeat and other animal protein consumption are not invariant: evidence from Rio Muni, Equatorial Guinea. *Animal Conservation*, **12**(6), 599–610. DOI: 10.1111/j.1469-1795.2009.00289.x.

Fa, J.E. and Brown, D. (2009). Impacts of hunting on mammals in African tropical moist forests: a review and synthesis. *Mammal Review*, **39**(4), 231–64. DOI: 10.1111/j.1365-2907.2009.00149.x.

Fa, J.E., Currie, D. and Meeuwig, J. (2003). Bushmeat and food security in the Congo Basin: linkages between wildlife and people's future. *Environmental Conservation*, **30**(1), 71–8. DOI: 10.1017/S0376892903000067.

Fa, J.E., Farfán, M.A., Márquez, A.L., Duarte, J. and Vargas, J.M. (2013). Reflections on the impact and management of hunting of wild mammals in tropical forests. *Ecosistemas*, **22**(2), 76–83. DOI: 10.7818/ECOS.2013.22-2.12.

Fa, J.E., Peres, C.A. and Meeuwig, J. (2002). Bushmeat exploitation in tropical forests: an intercontinental comparison. *Conservation Biology*, **16**(1), 232–7. DOI: 10.1046/j.1523-1739.2002.00275.x.

Fa, J.E., Ryan, S.F. and Bell, D.J. (2005). Hunting vulnerability, ecological characteristics and harvest rates of bushmeat species in Afrotropical forests. *Biological Conservation*, **121**(2), 167–76. DOI: 10.1016/j.biocon.2004.04.016.

Fa, J.E., Seymour, S., Dupain, J., *et al.* (2006). Getting to grips with the magnitude of exploitation: bushmeat in the Cross–Sanaga rivers region, Nigeria and Cameroon. *Biological Conservation*, **129**(4), 497–510. DOI: 10.1016/j.biocon.2005.11.031.

Fa, J.E. and Tagg, N. (2016). Hunting and primate conservation. In *An Introduction to Primate Conservation*, ed. S.A. Wich and M.A. Marshall. Oxford, UK: Oxford University Press, pp. 143–56.

Fa, J.E., Wright, J.H., Funk, S.M., *et al.* (2019). Mapping the availability of bushmeat for consumption in Central African cities. *Environmental Research Letters*, **14**(9), 094002. DOI: 10.1088/1748-9326/ab36fa.

Faith, J.T. (2014). Late Pleistocene and Holocene mammal extinctions on continental Africa. *Earth-Science Reviews*, **128**, 105–21. DOI: 10.1016/j.earscirev.2013.10.009.

Fan, P. (2017). The past, present, and future of gibbons in China. *Biological Conservation*, **210**, 29–39. DOI: 10.1016/j.biocon.2016.02.024.

Fan, P.-F., Fei, H.-L. and Luo, A.-D. (2014). Ecological extinction of the critically endangered northern white-cheeked gibbon *Nomascus leucogenys* in China. *Oryx*, **48**(1), 52–5. DOI: 10.1017/S0030605312001305.

Fan, P., Fei, H., Xiang, Z., *et al.* (2010). Social structure and group dynamics of the Cao Vit gibbon (*Nomascus nasutus*) in Bangliang, Jingxi, China. *Folia Primatologica*, **81**(5), 245–53.

Fan, P.-F., He, K., Chen, X., *et al.* (2017). Description of a new species of hoolock gibbon (Primates: Hylobatidae) based on integrative taxonomy. *American Journal of Primatology*, **79**(5), e22631. DOI: 10.1002/ajp.22631.

Fan, P.-F. and Jiang, X.-L. (2008). Effects of food and topography on ranging behavior of black crested gibbon (*Nomascus concolor jingdongensis*) in Wuliang Mountain, Yunnan, China. *American Journal of Primatology*, **70**(9), 871–8. DOI: 10.1002/ajp.20577.

Fan, P.-F. and Jiang, X.-L. (2010). Maintenance of multifemale social organization in a group of *Nomascus concolor* at Wuliang Mountain, Yunnan, China. *International Journal of Primatology*, **31**(1), 1–13. DOI: 10.1007/s10764-009-9375-9.

Fan, P.-F., Ren, G.-P., Wang, W., *et al.* (2013). Habitat evaluation and population viability analysis of the last population of Cao Vit gibbon (*Nomascus nasutus*): implications for conservation. *Biological Conservation*, **161**, 39–47. DOI: 10.1016/j.biocon.2013.02.014.

Fan, P.F., Turvey, S.T. and Bryant, J.V. (2019). Hoolock tianxing. *The IUCN Red List of Threatened Species.* 2019: e.T118355648A118355666. Gland, Switzerland: International Union for Conservation of Nature (IUCN). Available at: https://dx.doi.org/10.2305/IUCN.UK.2019-3.RLTS.T118355648A118355666.en.

Fan, P.F., Turvey, S.T. and Bryant, J.V. (2020). *Hoolock tianxing* (amended version of 2019 assessment). *The IUCN Red List of Threatened Species.* 2020: e.T118355648A166597159. Gland, Switzerland: International Union for Conservation of Nature (IUCN). Available at: https://dx.doi.org/10.2305/IUCN.UK.2020-1.RLTS.T118355648A166597159.en.

FAO (2013). *FAO Statistical Yearbook 2013: Africa Food and Agriculture.* Accra, Ghana: Food and Agriculture Organization (FAO). Available at: http://www.fao.org/3/i3107e/i3107e.PDF.

FAO (2017). *The Future of Food and Agriculture: Trends and Challenges.* Rome, Italy: Food and Agriculture Organization of the United Nations (FAO). Available at: http://www.fao.org/3/a-i6583e.pdf.

Fargo, J., director (1978). *Every Which Way But Loose.* Warner Brothers and The Malpaso Company. Available at: https://www.imdb.com/title/tt0077523/?ref_=fn_al_tt_1.

Farmer, K.H., Buchanan-Smith, H.M. and Jamart, A. (2006). Behavioural adaptation of *Pan troglodytes troglodytes*. *International Journal of Primatology*, **27**(3), 747–65. DOI: 10.1007/s10764-006-9041-4.

Farmer, K.H. and Jamart, A. (2002). Habitat Ecologique et Liberté des Primates: a case study of chimpanzee re-introduction in the Republic of Congo. *Re-introduction News: Special Primate Issue*, **21**, 16–8.

Fasel, R., Blattner, C., Mannino, A. and Baumann, T. (2016). Fundamental rights for primates. Policy paper. *Sentience Politics*, **1**, 1–16.

Federal Ministry of Food and Agriculture (n.d.). *Improving animal welfare in Germany.* Germany: Federal Ministry of Food and Agriculture. Available at: https://www.bmel.de/EN/Animals/AnimalWelfare/_Texte/Versuchtierrichtline_Tierschutzgesetz.html. Accessed September 12, 2019.

Felbab-Brown, V. (2017). *The Extinction Market. Wildlife Trafficking and How to Counter It.* London, UK: Hurst and Company.

Felbab-Brown, V. (2018). To counter wildlife trafficking, local enforcement, not en-route interdiction, is key. *Mongabay*, January 20, 2018. Available at: https://news.mongabay.com/2018/01/to-counter-wildlife-trafficking-local-enforcement-not-en-route-interdiction-is-key-commentary/.

Fellowes, J., Chan, B., Lok, P., *et al.* (2008). Current status of the Hainan gibbon (*Nomascus hainanus*): progress of population monitoring and other priority actions. *Asian Primates Journal*, **1**(1), 2–9.

Ferdowsian, H.R., Durham, D.L., Kimwele, C., *et al.* (2011). Signs of mood and anxiety disorders in chimpanzees. *PLoS ONE*, **6**(6), e19855. DOI: 10.1371/journal.pone.0019855.

Ferraro, J.V., Plummer, T.W., Pobiner, B.L., *et al.* (2013). Earliest archaeological evidence of persistent hominin carnivory. *PLoS ONE*, **8**(4), e62174. DOI: 10.1371/journal.pone.0062174.

Ferraro, P.J. and Pressey, R.L. (2015). Measuring the difference made by conservation initiatives: protected areas and their environmental and social impacts. *Philosophical Transactions of the Royal Society B: Biological Sciences*, **370**, 4–8. DOI: 10.1098/rstb.2014.027.

Ferreira de Souza Dias, B. (2016). *GEF and the Convention on Biological Diversity.* Washington DC: Global Environment Facility (GEF). Available at: https://www.thegef.org/news/gef-and-convention-biological-diversity.

Finkelman, P. (2012). Slavery in the United States: persons or property? In *The Legal Understanding of Slavery: From the Historical to the Contemporary*, ed. J. Allain. Oxford, UK: Oxford University Press, pp. 105–34.

Flightradar24 (n.d.) *CDG/LFPG Paris Charles de Gaulle Airport France.* Stockholm, Sweden: Flightradar24. Available at: https://www.flightradar24.com/data/airports/cdg/routes. Accessed October, 2020.

Foerster, S., Wilkie, D.S., Morelli, G.A., *et al.* (2012). Correlates of bushmeat hunting among remote rural households in Gabon, Central Africa. *Conservation Biology*, **26**(2), 335–44. DOI: 10.1111/j.1523-1739.2011.01802.x.

Forte, D.L. (2015). Nonhuman animal legislation and speciesist discourse. Argentina's Pet Responsibility Act: anti-cruelty law or death row pardon? *Language and Ecology*, 1–19.

Franks, P. and Twinamatsiko, M. (2017). *Lessons Learnt from 20 Years of Revenue Sharing at Bwindi Impenetrable National Park, Uganda.* London, UK: International Institute for Environment and Development (IIED). Available at: https://pubs.iied.org/pdfs/17612IIED.pdf.

Fraundorfer, M. (2017). The rediscovery of indigenous thought in the modern legal system: the case of the great apes. *Global Policy*, **9**(1), 17–25. DOI: 10.1111/1758-5899.12517.

Freeland (2016). *USAID ARREST Program, Final Report, December 23, 2016.* Bangkok, Thailand: Freeland.

Freeland (2018). WildScan: new mobile app to help combat illegal wildlife trade in Asia. *Freeland News*, Updated October 17, 2018. Available at: https://www.freeland.org/post/wildscan-new-mobile-app-to-help-combat-illegal-wildlife-trade-in-asia.

Freeman, H.D. and Ross, S.R. (2014). The impact of atypical early histories on pet or performer chimpanzees. *PeerJ*, **2**, e579. DOI: 10.7717/peerj.579.

French Parliament (1804). *Loi no. 1804-01-25.* Paris, France: French Parliament. Available at: https://www.legifrance.gouv.fr/affichCodeArticle.do;jsessionid=151B49B8353DF7A3720BB7D18D4B4D08.tpdjo03v_3?idArticle=LEGIARTI000006428710&cidTexte=LEGITEXT000006070721&categorieLien=id&dateTexte=19990106.

French Parliament (2015). *Loi no. 2015-177 du 16 février 2015 relative à la modernisation et à la simplification du droit et des procédures dans les domaines de la justice et des affaires intérieures.* Paris, France: French Parliament. Available at: https://www.legifrance.gouv.fr/affichTexte.do?cidTexte=JORFTEXT000030248562&categorieLien=id.

Freund, C., Rahman, E. and Knott, C. (2017). Ten years of orangutan-related wildlife crime investigation in West Kalimantan, Indonesia. *American Journal of Primatology*, **79**(11), 22620. DOI: 10.1002/ajp.22620.

Friends of Washoe (n.d.). *Chimpanzees in entertainment.* Ellensburg, WA: Friends of Washoe. Available at: https://www.friendsofwashoe.org/learn/captive_chimps/entertainment.html. Accessed October, 2019.

Fruth, B., Hickey, J.R., André, C., *et al.* (2016). *Pan paniscus* (errata version published in 2016). *The IUCN Red List of Threatened Species.* 2016: e.T15932A102331567. Gland, Switzerland: International Union for Conservation of Nature (IUCN). Available at: http://dx.doi.org/10.2305/IUCN.UK.2016-2.RLTS.T15932A17964305.en.

Fruth, B. and Hohmann, G. (1996). Nest building behavior in the great apes: the great leap forward? In *Great Ape Societies*, ed. W. McGrew, L. Marchant and T. Nishida. Cambridge, UK: Cambridge University Press, pp. 225–40. DOI: 10.1017/CBO9780511752414.019.

Fruth, B., Tagg, N. and Stewart, F. (2018). Sleep and nesting behavior in primates: a review. *American Journal of Physical Anthropology*, **166**(3), 499–509. DOI: 10.1002/ajpa.23373.

Fruth, B., Williamson, E.A. and Richardson, M.C. (2013). Bonobo *Pan paniscus*. In *Handbook of the Mammals of the World. Volume 3: Primates*, ed. R.A. Mittermeier, A.B. Rylands and D.E. Wilson. Barcelona, Spain: Lynx Edicions, pp. 853–4.

FSC (2015). *FSC International Standard. FSC Principles and Criteria for Forest Stewardship. FSC-STD-01-001 V5-2 EN.* London, UK: Forest Stewardship Council (FSC). Available at: https://ic.fsc.org/file-download.fsc-principles-and-criteria-for-forest-stewardship.a-409.pdf.

Fugate, J.M.B. (2013). *Affidavit of Jennifer M. B. Fugate In the Matter of a Proceeding under Article 70 of the CPLR for a Writ of Habeas Corpus. The Nonhuman Rights Project, Inc., on behalf of Tommy, Petitioners, v. Patrick C. Lavery, individually and as an officer of Circle L Trailer Sales, Inc., Diane Lavery, and Circle L Trailer Sales, Inc. November 22, 2013.* Available at: https://www.nonhumanrights.org/content/uploads/Ex-6-Fugate-Affidavit-Tommy-Case.pdf. Accessed December, 2019.

Furuichi, T. (2009). Factors underlying party size differences between chimpanzees and bonobos: a review and hypotheses for future study. *Primates*, **50**(3), 197–209. DOI: 10.1007/s10329-009-0141-6.

Furuichi, T., Idani, G., Ihobe, H., *et al.* (1998). Population dynamics of wild bonobos (*Pan paniscus*) at Wamba. *International Journal of Primatology*, **19**(6), 1029–43. DOI: 10.1023/A:1020326304074.

Gadgil, M., Berkes, F. and Folke, C. (1993). Indigenous knowledge for biodiversity conservation. *Ambio*, **22** 151–6 DOI: www.jstor.org/stable/4314060.

GADM (n.d.). *GADM maps and data.* Available at: https://gadm.org/index.html. Accessed September, 2020.

GAIN (n.d.). *Great Ape Information Network.* Kyoto, Japan: National BioResource Project (NBRP)-Great Ape Information Network (GAIN). Available at: http://www.shigen.nig.ac.jp/gain/index.jsp. Accessed September 2, 2018.

Galdikas, B. (1982). Orangutans as seed dispersers at Tanjung Puting, Central Kalimantan: implications for conservation. In *The Orangutan: Its Biology and Conservation*, ed. L. de Boer. The Hague: Dr W. Junk Publishers.

Gallego-Zamorano, J., Benítez-López, A., Santini, L., *et al.* (2020). Combined effects of land use and hunting on distributions of tropical mammals. *Conservation Biology*, **34**, 5, 1271–80. DOI: 10.1111/cobi.13459.

Gallo, K. and Anest, K. (2018). Orang-utans in conservation education. In *Chinese-Language Orang-utan Husbandry Manual*, ed. G.L. Banes, M. Fox, C. Sodaro and Y. Bai. Beijing and Nanjing, China: Chinese Association of Zoological Gardens and Nanjing Hongshan Forest Zoo.

Ganas, J., Robbins, M.M., Nkurunungi, J.B., Kaplin, B.A. and McNeilage, A. (2004). Dietary variability of mountain gorillas in Bwindi Impenetrable National Park, Uganda. *International Journal of Primatology*, **25**(5), 1043–72. DOI: 10.1023/b:ijop.0000043351.20129.44.

Gang, B. (1996). PAWS slaps orangutan trainer Berosini with suit. *Las Vegas Sun*, March 8, 1996. Available at: https://lasvegassun.com/news/1996/mar/08/paws-slaps-orangutan-trainer-berosini-with-suit/.

GAP (2017). Argentine judge refuses to transfer orangutan Sandra to Great Apes Sanctuary of Sorocaba, Brazil. *Great Ape Project (GAP)*, July 18, 2017. Available at: http://www.projetogap.org.br/en/noticia/argentine-judge-refuses-to-transfer-orangutan-sandra-to-great-apes-sanctuary-of-sorocaba-brazil/.

Garner, B.A. (2014). *Black's Law Dictionary*, 10th edn. Eagan, MN: Thomson West, Aspatore Books.

Garriga, R., Marco, I., Casas-Díaz, E., *et al.* (2019). Factors influencing wild chimpanzee (*Pan troglodytes verus*) relative abundance in an agriculture–swamp matrix outside protected areas. *PLoS ONE*, **14**(5), e0215545. DOI: 10.1371/journal.pone.0215545.

Garriga, R.M., Marco, I., Casas-Díaz, E., Amarasekaran, B. and Humle, T. (2018). Perceptions of challenges to subsistence agriculture, and crop foraging by wildlife and chimpanzees *Pan troglodytes verus* in unprotected areas in Sierra Leone. *Oryx*, **52**(4), 761–74. DOI: 10.1017/S0030605316001319.

Gaveau, D.L.A., Sloan, S., Molidena, E., *et al.* (2014). Four decades of forest persistence, clearance and logging on Borneo. *PLoS ONE*, **9**(7), e101654. DOI: 10.1371/journal.pone.0101654.

Geertz, C. (1973). Thick description: toward an interpretive theory of culture. In *The Interpretation of Cultures: Selected Essays*, ed. C. Geertz. New York, NY: Basic Books, pp. 3–30.

Geissmann, T. (1991). Reassessment of age of sexual maturity in gibbons (*Hylobates* spp.). *American Journal of Primatology*, **23**(1), 11–22. DOI: 10.1002/ajp.1350230103.

Geissmann, T. and Bleisch, W. (2020). *Nomascus hainanus. The IUCN Red List of Threatened Species*. 2020: e.T41643A17969392. Gland, Switzerland: International Union for Conservation of Nature (IUCN). Available at: https://dx.doi.org/10.2305/IUCN.UK.2020-2.RLTS.T41643A17969392.en.

Geissmann, T., Grindley, M., Ngwe, L., *et al.* (2013). *The Conservation Status of Hoolock Gibbons in Myanmar*. Zürich, Switzerland: Gibbon Conservation Alliance. Available at: http://www.gibbonconservation.org/07_publications/book/2013_hoolock_myanmar.pdf.

Geissmann, T., Nijman, V., Boonratana, R., *et al.* (2020). *Hylobates agilis. The IUCN Red List of Threatened Species*. 2020: e.T10543A17967655. Gland, Switzerland: International Union for Conservation of Nature (IUCN). Available at: https://dx.doi.org/10.2305/IUCN.UK.2020-2.RLTS.T10543A17967655.en.

Geng, B. (1998). *Geng Biao Huiyi Lu [Geng Biao Remembers: 1949–1992]* [in Chinese]. Nanjing, China: Jiangsu People's Press.

Gettleman, J. (2017). Smuggled, beaten and drugged: the illicit global ape trade. *New York Times*, November 4, 2017. Available at: https://www.nytimes.com/2017/11/04/world/africa/ape-trafficking-bonobos-orangutans.html.

GFI (2018). New study quantifies value of illegal trade in great apes. *GFI Press Release*. Available at: https://www.gfintegrity.org/press-release/new-study-quantifies-value-of-illegal-trade-in-great-apes/.

Ghiglieri, M.P. (1984). *The Chimpanzees of Kibale Forest: A Field Study of Ecology and Social Structure*. New York, NY: Columbia University Press.

Gilhooly, L.J., Rayadin, Y. and Cheyne, S.M. (2015). A comparison of hylobatid survey methods using triangulation on Müller's gibbon (*Hylobates muelleri*) in Sungai Wain Protection Forest, East Kalimantan, Indonesia. *International Journal of Primatology*, **36**(3), 567–82. DOI: 10.1007/s10764-015-9845-1.

Gillespie, T.R., Nunn, C.L. and Leendertz, F.H. (2008). Integrative approaches to the study of primate infectious disease: implications for biodiversity conservation and global health. *American Journal of Physical Anthropology*, **137**(S47), 53–69. DOI: 10.1002/ajpa.20949.

Global Witness (2019). *Enemies of the State: How Governments and Business Silence Land and Environmental Defenders.* London, UK: Global Witness.

Goodall, J. (2009). Loving chimps to death. *Los Angeles Times,* February 25, 2009. Available at: https://www.latimes.com/archives/la-xpm-2009-feb-25-oe-goodall25-story.html.

Goodall, J. (2015). *Affidavit of Jane Goodall In the Matter of a Proceeding under Article 70 of the CPLR for a Writ of Habeas Corpus. The Nonhuman Rights Project, Inc., on behalf of Kiko, Petitioner, v. Carmen Presti, individually and as an officer and director of The Primate Sanctuary, Inc., Christie E. Presti, individually and as an officer and director of The Primate Sanctuary, Inc., and the Primate Sanctuary, Inc. September 21, 2015.* Available at: https://www.nonhumanrights.org/client-kiko/. Accessed December, 2019.

Goodall, J., Fouts, R., Patterson, F., *et al.,* ed. (2003). *The Great Ape Project Census: Recognition for the Uncounted.* Portland, OR: Great Ape Project.

Goossens, B., Chikhi, L., Ancrenaz, M., *et al.* (2006). Genetic signature of anthropogenic population collapse in orang-utans. *PLoS Biology,* **4**(2), e25. DOI: 10.1371/journal.pbio.0040025.

Goossens, B., Kapar, M.D., Kahar, S. and Ancrenaz, M. (2011). First sighting of Bornean orang-utan twins in the wild. *Asian Primates Journal,* **2**(1), 10–2.

Gordon, R. (2016). Moving targets: hunting in contemporary Africa. *Journal of Contemporary African Studies,* **34**(1), 1–6. DOI: 10.1080/02589001.2016.1196323.

Gorilla Guardians (n.d.). *Activities.* Gorilla Guardians. Available at: www.ibyiwacuvillage.org/index.php/home/about_us/activities. Accessed September, 2020.

GRACE (n.d.). *About.* North Kivu Province, DRC: Gorilla Rehabilitation and Conservation Education Center (GRACE). Available at: https://gracegorillas.org/grace-about-the-organization/. Accessed October, 2019.

Granjon, A.-C., Robbins, M.M., Arinaitwe, J., *et al.* (2020). Estimating abundance and growth rates in a wild mountain gorilla population. *Animal Conservation* **23**(4), 455–65. DOI: 10.1111/acv.12559.

GRASP (n.d.-a). *Apes Seizure Database.* Nairobi, Kenya: Great Apes Survival Partnership (GRASP). Available at: https://database.un-grasp.org/. Accessed September, 2020.

GRASP (n.d.-b). *Great Apes Survival Partnership.* Nairobi, Kenya: Great Apes Survival Partnership (GRASP). Available at: http://www.un-grasp.org. Accessed September, 2020.

GRASP (n.d.-c). *Range states.* Nairobi, Kenya: Great Apes Survival Partnership (GRASP). Available at: https://www.un-grasp.org/our-partners/range-states/. Accessed October 24, 2019.

GRASP and IUCN (2018). *Report to the CITES Standing Committee on the Status of Great Apes.* Nairobi, Kenya, and Gland, Switzerland: United Nations Environment Programme Great Apes Survival Partnership (GRASP) and International Union for Conservation of Nature (IUCN). Available at: http://www.primate-sg.org/storage/pdf/GRASP__IUCN_2018_Report_to_CITES_on_the_Status_of_Great_Apes.pdf.

Gray, M., McNeilage, A., Fawcett, K., *et al.* (2010). Censusing the mountain gorillas in the Virunga Volcanoes: complete sweep method versus monitoring. *African Journal of Ecology,* **48**(3), 588–99. DOI: 10.1111/j.1365-2028.2009.01142.x.

Gray, M., Roy, J., Vigilant, L., *et al.* (2013). Genetic census reveals increased but uneven growth of a critically endangered mountain gorilla population. *Biological Conservation,* **158**(Supplement C), 230–8. DOI: 10.1016/j.biocon.2012.09.018.

Gray, T.N.E., Hughes, A.C., Laurance, W.F., *et al.* (2018). The wildlife snaring crisis: an insidious and pervasive threat to biodiversity in Southeast Asia. *Biodiversity and Conservation,* **27**(4), 1031–7. DOI: 10.1007/s10531-017-1450-5.

Gray, T.N.E., Phan, C. and Long, B. (2010). Modelling species distribution at multiple spatial scales: gibbon habitat preferences in a fragmented landscape. *Animal Conservation,* **13**(3), 324–32. DOI: 10.1111/j.1469-1795.2010.00351.x.

Green Customs (n.d.). *The Green Customs Initiative.* Nairobi, Kenya: Green Customs Initiative Secretariat. Available at: http://www.greencustoms.org/. Accessed September, 2020.

Green, J.M.H., Fisher, B., Green, R.E., *et al.* (2018). Local costs of conservation exceed those borne by the global majority. *Global Ecology and Conservation,* **14**, e00385. DOI: 10.1016/j.gecco.2018.e00385.

Greenberg, J. (2004). *Crusaders in the Courts: Legal Battles of the Civil Rights Movement.* Northport, NY: Twelve Tables Press.

Greenfield, S. and Veríssimo, D. (2019). To what extent is social marketing used in demand reduction campaigns for illegal wildlife products? Insights from elephant ivory and rhino horn. *Social Marketing Quarterly*, **25**(1), 40–54. DOI: 10.1177/1524500418813543.

Greengrass, E. (2015). Commercial hunting to supply urban markets threatens mammalian biodiversity in Sapo National Park. *Oryx*, **50**(3), 397–404. DOI: 10.1017/S0030605315000095.

Greenpeace (2018). *Rang-tan: the story of dirty palm oil.* Greenpeace International. Available at: https://www.youtube.com/watch?v=TQQXstNh45g. Accessed October, 2019.

Gregory, T., Carrasco Rueda, F., Deichmann, J., Kolowski, J. and Alonso, A. (2014). Arboreal camera trapping: taking a proven method to new heights. *Methods in Ecology and Evolution*, **5**(5), 443–51. DOI: 10.1111/2041-210X.12177.

Grimm, D. (2017). Research on lab chimps is over. Why have so few been retired to sanctuaries? *Science News*, June 12, 2017. Available at: https://www.sciencemag.org/news/2017/06/research-lab-chimps-over-why-have-so-few-been-retired-sanctuaries.

Großmann, K. (2018). Conflicting ecologies in a 'failed' gaharu nursery program in Central Kalimantan, Indonesia. *Sojourn: Journal of Social Issues in Southeast Asia*, **33**, 319–40. DOI: 10.1355/sj33-2d.

Gruber, T., Luncz, L., Morchen, J., *et al.* (2019). Cultural change in animals: a flexible behavioural adaptation to human disturbance. *Palgrave Communications*, **5**, 9. DOI: 10.1057/s41599-019-0271-4.

Guan, Z.-H., Ma, C.-Y., Fei, H.-L., *et al.* (2018). Ecology and social system of northern gibbons living in cold seasonal forests. *Zoological Research*, **39**(4), 255–65. DOI: 10.24272/j.issn.2095-8137.2018.045.

Güneralp, B., Lwasa, S., Masundire, H., Parnell, S. and Seto, K.C. (2017). Urbanization in Africa: challenges and opportunities for conservation. *Environmental Research Letters*, **13**, 015002. DOI: 10.1088/1748-9326/aa94fe.

Guschanski, K., Vigilant, L., McNeilage, A., *et al.* (2009). Counting elusive animals: comparing field and genetic census of the entire mountain gorilla population of Bwindi Impenetrable National Park, Uganda. *Biological Conservation*, **142**(2), 290–300. DOI: 10.1016/j.biocon.2008.10.024.

Haddaway, N.R. and Bayliss, H.R. (2015). Shades of grey: two forms of grey literature important for reviews in conservation. *Biological Conservation*, **191**, 827–9. DOI: 10.1016/j.biocon.2015.08.018.

Hahn, B.H., Shaw, G.M., De Cock, K.M. and Sharp, P.M. (2000). AIDS as a zoonosis: scientific and public health implications. *Science*, **287**(5453), 607–14. DOI: 10.1126/science.287.5453.607.

Hakizimana, D. and Huynen, M.C. (2013). Chimpanzee (*Pan troglodytes schweinfurthii*) population density and abundance in Kibira National Park, Burundi. *Pan Africa News*, **20**(2), 16–9.

Hallam, C.D., Johnson, A., O'Kelly, H., *et al.* (2016). Using occupancy-based surveys and multi-model inference to estimate abundance and distribution of crested gibbons (*Nomascus* spp.) in central Laos. *American Journal of Primatology*, **78**(4), 462–72. DOI: 10.1002/ajp.22508.

Hamard, M., Cheyne, S.M. and Nijman, V. (2010). Vegetation correlates of gibbon density in the peat-swamp forest of the Sabangau catchment, Central Kalimantan, Indonesia. *American Journal of Primatology*, **72**(7), 607–16. DOI: 10.1002/ajp.20815.

Hamdi v. *Rumsfeld*. 542 US 507 (2004). Available at: https://cdn.loc.gov/service/ll/usrep/usrep542/usrep542507/usrep542507.pdf.

Hamilton, E. (1964). *The Echo of Greece*. New York, NY: W. W. Norton and Co.

Hance, J. (2009). Transmitters implanted in orangutans for tracking after release into the wild. *Mongabay*, November 23, 2009. Available at: https://news.mongabay.com/2009/11/transmitters-implanted-in-orangutans-for-tracking-after-release-into-the-wild /.

Hanoi Conference on the Illegal Wildlife Trade (2016). *Hanoi Statement on Illegal Wildlife Trade*. Hanoi, Viet Nam. Available at: http://iwthanoi.vn/wp-content/uploads/2019/09/hanoi-statement-on-illegal-wildlife-trade.pdf.

Harcourt, A.H. and Greenberg, J. (2001). Do gorilla females join males to avoid infanticide? A quantitative model. *Animal Behaviour*, **62**(5), 905–15. DOI: 10.1006/anbe.2001.1835.

Hardin, G. (1968). The tragedy of the commons. *Science*, **162**(3859), 1243–8. DOI: 10.1126/science.162.3859.1243.

Harfoot, M., Glaser, S.A.M., Tittensor, D.P., *et al.* (2018). Unveiling the patterns and trends in 40 years of global trade in CITES-listed wildlife. *Biological Conservation*, **223**, 47–57. DOI: 10.1016/j.biocon.2018.04.017.

Harris, D. and Karamehmedovic, A. (2009). Bushmeat sold on open market in US. *ABC News*, December 11, 2009. Available at: https://abcnews.go.com/Nightline/IntoTheWild/bushmeat-africa-sold-open-market-us/story?id=9312518.

Harrison, M., Roe, D., Baker, J., *et al.* (2015). *Wildlife Crime: A Review of the Evidence on Drivers and Impacts in Uganda*. London, UK: International Institute for Environment and Development (IIED). Available at: https://pubs.iied.org/pdfs/17576IIED.pdf.

Harrison, R.D., Sreekar, R., Brodie, J.F., *et al.* (2016). Impacts of hunting on tropical forests in Southeast Asia. *Conservation Biology*, **30**(5), 972–81. DOI: 10.1111/cobi.12785.

Harrison, T., Krigbaum, J. and Manser, J. (2006). Primate biogeography and ecology on the Sunda Shelf islands: a paleontological and zooarchaeological perspective. In *Primate Biogeography: Progress and Prospects*, ed. S.M. Lehman and J.G. Fleagle. Boston, MA: Springer US, pp. 331–72. DOI: 10.1007/0-387-31710-4_12.

Harrisson, T. (1966). The gibbon in west Borneo folklore and augury. *Sarawak Museum Journal*, **14**, 132–45.

Hart, M. (2018). Perth zoo keeper's heartfelt tribute after death of world's oldest Sumatran orangutan. *The West Australian*, June 18, 2018. Available at: https://thewest.com.au/news/wa/perth-zoo-keepers-heartfelt-tribute-after-death-of-worlds-oldest-sumatran-orangutan-ng-b888693972.

Haslett, C. (2015). Click to like this: is Instagram a hub for illegal ape deals? *Mongabay*, December 10, 2015. Available at: https://news.mongabay.com/2015/12/click-to-like-this-is-instagram-a-hub-for-illegal-ape-deals/.

Hassan, R., Scholes, R. and Ash, N., ed. (2005). *Ecosystems and Human Wellbeing. Volume 1. Current State and Trends*. Washington DC: Island Press, Millennium Ecosystem Assessment.

Hastie, J. and McCrea-Steele, T. (2014). *Wanted – Dead or Alive. Exposing Online Wildlife Trade*. London, UK: International Fund for Animal Welfare (IFAW). Available at: https://www.ifaw.org/uk/resources/wanted-dead-or-alive-report.

Hatton, J., Couto, M. and Oglethorpe, J. (2001). *Biodiversity and War: A Case Study of Mozambique*. Washington DC: World Wildlife Fund (WWF) Biodiversity Support Program.

Hawdon, J. and Ryan, J. (2011). Neighborhood organizations and resident assistance to police. *Sociological Forum*, **26**(4), 897–920.

Head, J. (2014). *Effecting behaviour change around bushmeat consumption: Nam Kading National Protected Area, Lao PDR*. Unpublished report. Cambridge, UK: Arcus Foundation.

Head, J. (2015). *Assessing the drivers of wild-meat hunting*. Commissioned unpublished background paper. Cambridge, UK: Arcus Foundation.

Head, J. (2017). *Knowledge Assessment on the Global Trade in Apes*. Internal report. Cambridge, UK: Arcus Foundation.

Head, J.S., Boesch, C., Makaga, L. and Robbins, M.M. (2011). Sympatric chimpanzees (*Pan troglodytes troglodytes*) and gorillas (*Gorilla gorilla gorilla*) in Loango National Park, Gabon: dietary composition, seasonality, and inter-site comparisons. *International Journal of Primatology*, **32**(3), 755–75. DOI: 10.1007/s10764-011-9499-6.

Head, J.S., Boesch, C., Robbins, M.M., *et al.* (2013). Effective sociodemographic population assessment of elusive species in ecology and conservation management. *Ecology and Evolution*, **3**(9), 2903–16. DOI: 10.1002/ece3.670.

Heinicke, S., Kalan, A.K., Wagner, O.J.J., *et al.* (2015). Assessing the performance of a semi-automated acoustic monitoring system for primates. *Methods in Ecology and Evolution*, **6**(7), 753–63. DOI: 10.1111/2041-210X.12384.

Heinicke, S., Mundry, R., Boesch, C., *et al.* (2019a). Advancing conservation planning for western chimpanzees using IUCN SSC A.P.E.S. — the case of a taxon-specific database. *Environmental Research Letters*, **14**(6), 064001. DOI: 10.1088/1748-9326/ab1379.

Heinicke, S., Mundry, R., Boesch, C., *et al.* (2019b). Characteristics of positive deviants in western chimpanzee populations. *Frontiers in Ecology and Evolution*, **7**, 16. DOI: 10.3389/fevo.2019.00016.

HELP Congo (n.d.). *Sponsorship*. Lissieu, France: Habitat Ecologique et Liberté des Primates (HELP). Available at: http://help-primates.org/en/parrainage.html. Accessed December 4, 2018.

Hemsworth, P.H., Mellor, D.J., Cronin, G.M. and Tilbrook, A.J. (2015). Scientific assessment of animal welfare. *New Zealand Veterinary Journal*, **63**(1), 24–30. DOI: 10.1080/00480169.2014.966167.

Henao, L.A. and Calatrava, A. (2016). In Argentina, freedom still distant for Sandra the orangutan. *AP: Associated Press*, September 29, 2016. Available at: https://apnews.com/e65b2d8b707b49ab85ddfa2f1e466020.

Henchion, M., Hayes, M., Mullen, A.M., Fenelon, M. and Tiwari, B. (2017). Future protein supply and demand: strategies and factors influencing a sustainable equilibrium. *Foods*, **6**(7), 53.

Herbinger, I., Boesch, C. and Rothe, H. (2001). Territory characteristics among three neighboring chimpanzee communities in the Taï National Park, Côte d'Ivoire. *International Journal of Primatology*, **22**(2), 143–67. DOI: 10.1023/a:1005663212997.

Hermans, V. (2011). *Ranging behaviour of snare-injured female chimpanzees (*Pan troglodytes schweinfurthii*) of the Sonso community in the Budongo Forest, Uganda.* MRes Primatology thesis. Roehampton, UK: University of Roehampton.

Hernandez-Castro, J. and Roberts, D. (2015). Automatic detection of potentially illegal online sales of elephant ivory via data mining. *PeerJ Computer Science*, **1**, e10. DOI: 10.7717/peerj-cs.10.

Hickey, G.M., Pouliot, M., Smith-Hall, C., Wunder, S. and Nielsen, M.R. (2016). Quantifying the economic contribution of wild food harvests to rural livelihoods: a global-comparative analysis. *Food Policy*, **62**, 122–32. DOI: 10.1016/j.foodpol.2016.06.001.

Hickey, J.R., Basabose, A., Gilardi, K.V., *et al.* (2018). *Gorilla beringei* ssp. *beringei. The IUCN Red List of Threatened Species.* 2018: e.T39999A17989719. Gland, Switzerland: International Union for Conservation of Nature (IUCN). Available at: http://dx.doi.org/10.2305/IUCN.UK.2018-2.RLTS.T39999A17989719.en.

Hickey, J.R., Granjon, A.-C., Vigilant, L., *et al.* (2019). *Virunga 2015–2016 Surveys: Monitoring Mountain Gorillas, Other Select Mammals, and Illegal Activities.* Kigali, Rwanda: Greater Virunga Transboundary Collaboration (GVTC), IGCP & Partners. Available at: http://igcp.org/wp-content/uploads/Virunga-Census-2015-2016-Final-Report-2019-with-French-summary-2019_04_24.pdf.

Hickey, J.R., Nackoney, J., Nibbelink, N.P., *et al.* (2013). Human proximity and habitat fragmentation are key drivers of the rangewide bonobo distribution. *Biodiversity and Conservation*, **22**(13), 3085–104. DOI: 10.1007/s10531-013-0572-7.

Hickman, A. (2018). Iceland's Rang-tan campaign delivers 65m views, sales and consideration lift. *PR Week*, December 3, 2018. Available at: https://www.prweek.com/article/1520088/icelands-rang-tan-campaign-delivers-65m-views-sales-consideration-lift.

Hicks, T.C., Darby, L., Hart, J., *et al.* (2010). Trade in orphans and bushmeat threatens one of the Democratic Republic of the Congo's most important populations of eastern chimpanzees (*Pan troglodytes schweinfurthii*). *African Primates*, **7**(1), 1–18.

Hill, R., Dyer, G.A., Lozada-Ellison, L.M., *et al.* (2015). A social–ecological systems analysis of impediments to delivery of the Aichi 2020 Targets and potentially more effective pathways to the conservation of biodiversity. *Global Environmental Change*, **34**, 22–34. DOI: 10.1016/j.gloenvcha.2015.04.005.

Hoàn, T.Đ., Dũng, L.V. and Trường, N.V. (2016). *Báo cáo Tổng điều tra liên khu Vượn Cao vít (Nomascus nasutus) tại Khu Bảo tồn loài và sinh cảnh Vượn Cao vít huyện Trùng Khánh, tỉnh Cao Bằng, Việt Nam và Khu bảo tồn Bằng Lượng, Trịnh Tây, Quảng Tây, Trung Quốc* [in Vietnamese]. Hanoi, Viet Nam: Flora & Fauna International (FFI).

Hockings, K. and Humle, T. (2009). *Best Practice Guidelines for the Prevention and Mitigation of Conflict Between Humans and Great Apes.* Gland, Switzerland: International Union for Conservation of Nature (IUCN) Species Survival Commission (SSC), Primate Specialist Group. Available at: https://portals.iucn.org/library/efiles/documents/ssc-op-037.pdf.

Hockings, K.J., Humle, T., Carvalho, S. and Matsuzawa, T. (2012). Chimpanzee interactions with nonhuman species in an anthropogenic habitat. *Behaviour*, **149**(3–4), 299–324.

Hockings, K.J. and McLennan, M.R. (2012). From forest to farm: systematic review of cultivar feeding by chimpanzees – management implications for wildlife in anthropogenic landscapes. *PLoS ONE*, **7**(4), e33391. DOI: 10.1371/journal.pone.0033391.

Hockings, K.J., McLennan, M.R., Carvalho, S., *et al.* (2015). Apes in the Anthropocene: flexibility and survival. *Trends in Ecology & Evolution*, **30**(4), 215–22. DOI: 10.1016/j.tree.2015.02.002.

Hockings, K.J., Yamakoshi, G., Kabasawa, A. and Matsuzawa, T. (2010). Attacks on local persons by chimpanzees in Bossou, Republic of Guinea: long-term perspectives. *American Journal of Primatology*, **72**(10), 887–96. DOI: 10.1002/ajp.20784.

Hoffmann, C., Zimmermann, F., Biek, R., *et al.* (2017). Persistent anthrax as a major driver of wildlife mortality in a tropical rainforest. *Nature*, **548**, 82. DOI: 10.1038/nature23309.

Hohmann, G., Gerloff, U., Tautz, D. and Fruth, B. (1999). Social bonds and genetic ties: kinship, association and affiliation in a community of bonobos (*Pan paniscus*). *Behaviour*, **136**(9), 1219–35. DOI: 10.1163/156853999501739.

Hohmann, G., Robbins, M.M. and Boesch, C., ed. (2006). *Feeding Ecology in Apes and Other Primates: Ecological, Physiological, and Behavioural Aspects*. Cambridge Studies in Biological and Evolutionary Anthropology Volume 48. Cambridge, UK: Cambridge University Press.

Höing, A., Quinten, M.C., Indrawati, Y.M., Cheyne, S.M. and Waltert, M. (2013). Line transect and triangulation surveys provide reliable estimates of the density of Kloss' gibbons (*Hylobates klossii*) on Siberut Island, Indonesia. *International Journal of Primatology*, **34**(1), 148–56. DOI: 10.1007/s10764-012-9655-7.

Holden, S.T., Deininger, K. and Ghebru, H. (2009). Impacts of low-cost land certification on investment and productivity. *American Journal of Agricultural Economics*, **91**(2), 359–73. DOI: 10.1111/j.1467-8276.2008.01241.x.

Holmern, T., Muya, J. and Røskaft, E. (2007). Local law enforcement and illegal bushmeat hunting outside the Serengeti National Park, Tanzania. *Environmental Conservation*, **34**(1), 55–63. DOI: 10.1017/S0376892907003712.

Hoppe, E., Pauly, M., Gillespie, T.R., *et al.* (2015). Multiple cross-species transmission events of human adeno-viruses (HAdV) during hominine evolution. *Molecular Biology and Evolution*, **32**(8), 2072–84. DOI: 10.1093/molbev/msv090.

Horta Duarte, R. (2017). Zoos in Latin America. In *Oxford Research Encyclopedia of Latin American History*, ed. Oxford Research Encyclopedias. Oxford, UK: Oxford University Press, pp. 1–20. Available at: https://oxfordre.com/latinamericanhistory/view/10.1093/acrefore/9780199366439.001.0001/acrefore-9780199366439-e-439.

Horwich, R.H., Islari, R., Bose, A., *et al.* (2010). Community protection of the Manas Biosphere Reserve in Assam, India, and the endangered golden langur *Trachypithecus geei*. *Oryx*, **44**(2), 252–60. DOI: 10.1017/S0030605310000037.

Howell, S. and Talle, A. (2012). *Returns to the Field: Multitemporal Research and Contemporary Anthropology*. Bloomington, IN: Indiana University Press.

Hrdy, S.B. (1979). Infanticide among animals: a review, classification, and examination of the implications for the reproductive strategies of females. *Ethology and Sociobiology*, **1**(1), 13–40. DOI: 10.1016/0162-3095(79)90004-9.

Huertas, S.M., Gallo, C. and Galindo, F. (2014). Drivers of animal welfare policy in the Americas. *Revue Scientifique et Technique (International Office of Epizootics)*, **33**, 67–76.

Hughes, N., Rosen, N., Gretsky, N. and Sommer, V. (2011). Will the Nigeria-Cameroon Chimpanzee go extinct? Models derived from intake rates of ape sanctuaries. In *Primates of Gashaka. Developments in Primatology: Progress and Prospects*, ed. V. Sommer and C. Ross. New York, NY: Springer, pp. 545–75. DOI: 10.1007/978-1-4419-7403-7_14.

Hume, L. and Mulcock, J. (2004). Introduction: awkward spaces, productive places. In *Anthropologists in the Field: Cases in Participant Observation*, ed. L. Hume and J. Mulcock. New York, NY: Columbia University Press, pp. xi–xxviii.

Humle, T., Boesch, C., Campbell, G., *et al.* (2016a). *Pan troglodytes* ssp. *verus* (errata version published in 2016). *The IUCN Red List of Threatened Species*. 2016: e.T15935A102327574. Gland, Switzerland: International Union for Conservation of Nature (IUCN). Available at: http://dx.doi.org/10.2305/IUCN.UK.2016-2.RLTS.T15935A17989872.en.

Humle, T., Colin, C., Laurans, M. and Raballand, E. (2011). Group release of sanctuary chimpanzees (*Pan troglodytes*) in the Haut Niger National Park, Guinea, west Africa: ranging patterns and lessons so far. *International Journal of Primatology*, **32**(2), 456–73. DOI: 10.1007/s10764-010-9482-7.

Humle, T., Maisels, F., Oates, J.F., Plumptre, A. and Williamson, E.A. (2016b). *Pan troglodytes* (errata version published in 2018). *The IUCN Red List of Threatened Species*. 2016: e.T15933A129038584. Gland, Switzerland: International Union for Conservation of Nature (IUCN). Available at: https://dx.doi.org/10.2305/IUCN.UK.2016-2.RLTS.T15933A17964454.en.

HUTAN-KOCP (n.d.). *Links*. Sabah, Malaysia: Kinabatangan Orang-utan Conservation Programme (HUTAN-KOCP). Available at: https://www.hutan.org.my/links/. Accessed: October 20, 2019

ICCWC (2013). *First Global Meeting of the Wildlife Enforcement Networks, 5 March 2013: Meeting Report*. Bangkok, Thailand: International Consortium on Combating Wildlife Crime (ICCWC). Available at: https://www.cites.org/sites/default/files/common/docs/ICCWC%20Report%20-%20First%20Global%20Meeting%20of%20the%20WENs%20-%20Final.pdf.

ICCWC (2016). *Second Global Meeting of the Wildlife Enforcement Networks, 28–29 September 2016: Meeting Report*. Johannesburg, South Africa: International Consortium on Combating Wildlife Crime (ICCWC). Available at: https://cites.org/sites/default/files/eng/prog/iccwc/WENs/Report_2nd_Global_WEN_meeting-final.pdf.

Iceland (2018). *Say hello to Rang-tan.* Iceland Foods. Available at: https://www.youtube.com/watch?v=JdpspllWI20. Accessed October, 2019.

Ichikawa, M., Hattori, S. and Yasuoka, H. (2016). Bushmeat crisis, forestry reforms and contemporary hunting among Central African forest hunters. In *Hunter-Gatherers a Changing World*, ed. V. Reyes-García and A. Pyhälä: Cham, Switzerland: Springer, pp. 59–75.

IFAW (2008). *Killing with Keystrokes.* Yarmouth Port, MA: International Fund for Animal Welfare (IFAW). Available at: https://d1jyxxz9imt9yb.cloudfront.net/resource/202/attachment/regular/Killing_with_Keystrokes.pdf.

IFAW (2014). *Wanted – Dead or Alive: Exposing Online Wildlife Trade.* London, UK: International Fund for Animal Welfare (IFAW). Available at: https://d1jyxxz9imt9yb.cloudfront.net/resource/251/attachment/original/IFAW-Wanted-Dead-or-Alive-Exposing-Online-Wildlife-Trade-2014.pdf.

Igoe, J. (2006). Measuring the costs and benefits of conservation to local communities. *Journal of Ecological Anthropology*, **10**, 72–7.

Imong, I. and Chukwu, H. (2019). Saving Cross River gorillas in Nigeria through radio drama. *Gorilla Journal*, **58**, 7–8. Available at: https://www.berggorilla.org/fileadmin/user_upload/pdf/journal/journal_en/gorilla-journal-58-english.pdf.

Imong, I.S., Kühl, H.S., Robbins, M.M. and Mundry, R. (2016). Evaluating the potential effectiveness of alternative management scenarios in ape habitat. *Environmental Conservation*, **43**(2), 161–71. DOI: 10.1017/S0376892915000417.

Imong, I., Robbins, M.M., Mundry, R., Bergl, R. and Kühl, H.S. (2014a). Distinguishing ecological constraints from human activity in species range fragmentation: the case of Cross River gorillas. *Animal Conservation*, **17**(4), 323–31. DOI: 10.1111/acv.12100.

Imong, I., Robbins, M.M., Mundry, R., Bergl, R. and Kühl, H.S. (2014b). Informing conservation management about structural versus functional connectivity: a case-study of Cross River gorillas. *American Journal of Primatology*, **76**(10), 978–88. DOI: 10.1002/ajp.22287.

Infield, M. (2011). *Cultural values and conservation delivery in Liberia. A preliminary investigation of Lake Piso multiple use reserve.* Unpublished report. Cambridge, UK: Arcus Foundation.

Infield, M., Entwistle, A., Anthem, H., Mugisha, A. and Phillips, K. (2018). Reflections on cultural values approaches to conservation: lessons from 20 years of implementation. *Oryx*, **52**(2), 220–30. DOI: 10.1017/S0030605317000928.

Ingram, D.J., Coad, L., Abernethy, K.A., *et al.* (2018). Assessing Africa-wide pangolin exploitation by scaling local data. *Conservation Letters*, **11**(2), e12389. DOI: 10.1111/conl.12389.

Ingram, D.J., Coad, L., Collen, B., *et al.* (2015). Indicators for wild animal offtake: methods and case study for African mammals and birds. *Ecology and Society*, **20**(3), 40. DOI: 10.5751/ES-07823-200340.

Inogwabini, B.-I., Bewa, M., Longwango, M., Abokome, M. and Vuvu, M. (2008). The bonobos of the Lake Tumba–Lake Maindombe hinterland: threats and opportunities for population conservation. In *The Bonobos*, ed. T. Furuichi and J. Thompson. New York, NY: Springer, pp. 273–90.

Inogwabini, B.-I., Matungila, B., Mbende, L., Abokome, M. and Tshimanga, W.T. (2007). Great apes in the Lake Tumba landscape, Democratic Republic of Congo: Newly described populations. *Oryx*, **4**, 532–8. DOI: 10.1017/S0030605307414120.

Instagram (2017). Protecting wildlife and nature from exploitation. *Info Center*, December 4, 2017. Available at: https://instagram-press.com/blog/2017/12/04/protecting-wildlife-and-nature-from-exploitation/.

Instagram (n.d.-a). *How do I learn more about wildlife exploitation?* Instagram. Available at: https://help.instagram.com/859615207549041. Accessed January, 2020.

Instagram (n.d.-b). *Our story.* Info Center, Instagram. Available at: https://instagram-press.com/our-story/. Accessed October, 2019.

International Monetary Fund (2018). *People's Republic of China: Staff Report for the 2018 Article IV Consultation.* IMF Country Reports 18/240. Washington DC: International Monetary Fund (IMF). Available at: https://www.elibrary.imf.org/doc/IMF002/25384-9781484370797/25384-9781484370797/Other_formats/Source_PDF/25384-9781484370858.pdf.

Internet World Stats (n.d.). *Internet usage in Asia.* Bogota, Colombia: Miniwatts Marketing Group. Available at: https://www.internetworldstats.com/stats3.htm. Accessed April, 2020.

INTERPOL (2012). INTERPOL launches National Environmental Security Task Force initiative. *INTERPOL News*, September 18, 2012. Lyon, France: INTERPOL. Available at: https://www.interpol.int/News-and-Events/News/2012/INTERPOL-launches-National-Environmental-Security-Task-Force-initiative.

INTERPOL (2017). Anti-wildlife trafficking operation results in global arrests and seizures. *INTERPOL News*, March 2, 2017. Lyon, France: INTERPOL. Available at: https://www.interpol.int/News-and-Events/News/2017/Anti-wildlife-trafficking-operation-results-in-global-arrests-and-seizures.

INTERPOL (n.d.-a). *About INTERPOL.* Lyon, France: INTERPOL. Available at: https://www.interpol.int/About-INTERPOL/Overview. Accessed October, 2018.

INTERPOL (n.d.-b). *Our response to environmental crime.* Lyon, France: INTERPOL. Available at: https://www.interpol.int/en/Crimes/Environmental-crime/Our-response-to-environmental-crime. Accessed January, 2020.

INTERPOL-UNEP (2016). *Strategic Report: Environment, Peace and Security – A Convergence of Threats.* Lyon, France: INTERPOL and United Nations Environment Programme (UNEP). Available at: https://wedocs.unep.org/bitstream/handle/20.500.11822/17008/environment_peace_security.pdf?sequence=1&isAllowed=y.

IRF (2019). *2009–2019: Ranger Roll of Honour In Memoriam.* International Ranger Federation (IRF). Available at: https://www.internationalrangers.org/wp-content/uploads/2019/07/2009-2019-Honour-Roll-2-1.pdf. Accessed August 23, 2019.

Isaac, G.L. (1978). The Harvey Lecture Series, 1977–1978. Food sharing and human evolution: archaeological evidence from the Plio-Pleistocene of East Africa. *Journal of Anthropological Research*, **34**(3), 311–25. DOI: 10.1086/jar.34.3.3629782.

IUCN (2012). *IUCN Red List Categories and Criteria, Version 3.1,* 2nd edn. Gland, Switzerland, and Cambridge, UK: International Union for Conservation of Nature (IUCN) Species Survival Commission (SSC). Available at: https://www.iucnredlist.org/resources/categories-and-criteria.

IUCN (2014). *Regional Action Plan for the Conservation of Western Lowland Gorillas and Central Chimpanzees 2015–2025.* Gland, Switzerland: International Union for Conservation of Nature (IUCN) Species Survival Commission (SSC), Primate Specialist Group. Available at: Available at: https://d2ouvy59p0dg6k.cloudfront.net/downloads/wea_apes_plan_2014_7mb.pdf.

IUCN (2018). *The IUCN Red List of Threatened Species. Version 2018-1.* Gland, Switzerland: International Union for Conservation of Nature (IUCN). Available at: http://www.iucnredlist.org. Accessed June, 2018.

IUCN (2019). *The IUCN Red List of Threatened Species. Version 2019-2.* Gland, Switzerland: International Union for Conservation of Nature (IUCN). Available at: https://www.iucnredlist.org. Accessed 2019.

IUCN (2020). *The IUCN Red List of Threatened Species. Version 2020-1.* Gland, Switzerland: International Union for Conservation of Nature (IUCN). Available at: https://www.iucnredlist.org. Accessed March 19, 2020.

IUCN and ICCN (2012). *Bonobo (*Pan paniscus*): Conservation Strategy 2012–2022.* Gland, Switzerland: International Union for Conservation of Nature (IUCN) Species Survival Commission (SSC), Primate Specialist Group, and Institut Congolais pour la Conservation de la Nature (ICCN). Available at: https://portals.iucn.org/library/efiles/documents/2012-083.pdf.

IUCN SSC (n.d.-a). *A.P.E.S. portal: species.* Leipzig, Germany: Max Planck Society. Available at: http://apesportal.eva.mpg.de/status/species. Accessed 2019–2020.

IUCN SSC (n.d.-b). *A.P.E.S. portal: about.* Leipzig, Germany: Max Planck Society. Available at: http://apes.eva.mpg.de. Accessed 2019–2020.

IUCN SSC (n.d.-c). *A.P.E.S. portal database: literature.* Leipzig, Germany: Max Planck Society. Available at: http://apesportal.eva.mpg.de/database/literature. Accessed 2019–2020.

IUCN SSC (n.d.-d). *A.P.E.S. portal database: data archive.* Leipzig, Germany: Max Planck Society. Available at: http://apesportal.eva.mpg.de/database/archive. Accessed 2019–2020.

IUCN SSC PSG (n.d.). *Action plans.* Arlington, VA: International Union for Conservation of Nature (IUCN) Species Survival Commission (SSC), Primate Specialist Group (PSG). Available at: http://www.primate-sg.org/action_plans/. Accessed May, 2019.

IUCN SSC PSG SSA (n.d.-a). *Category: surveys.* Oxford, UK: International Union for Conservation of Nature (IUCN) Species Survival Commission (SSC), Primate Specialist Group (PSG) Section on Small Apes (SSA). Available at: https://gibbons.asia/category/surveys/. Accessed October, 2019.

IUCN SSC PSG SSA (n.d.-b). *Resources*. Oxford, UK: International Union for Conservation of Nature (IUCN) Species Survival Commission (SSC), Primate Specialist Group (PSG) Section on Small Apes (SSA). Available at: https://gibbons.asia/resources/. Accessed October, 2019.

J.A.C.K. (n.d.). *Support a chimpanzee*. Katanga, RDC: J.A.C.K. Available at: https://jackchimp.yolasite.com/support-a-chimp.php. Accessed December 31, 2018.

Jacobsen, S., Freeman, H., Santymire, R. and Ross, S. (2017). Atypical early experiences of captive chimpanzees (*Pan troglodytes*) are associated with higher hair cortisol concentrations as adults. *Royal Society Open Science*, **4**, 170932. DOI: 10.1098/rsos.170932.

Jambiya, G., Milledge, S. and Mtango, N. (2007). *'Night Time Spinach': Conservation and Livelihood Implications of Wild Meat Use in Refugee Situations in North-Western Tanzania*. Dar es Salaam, Tanzania: TRAFFIC East/Southern Africa.

Jensvold, M.L. (2013). *Affidavit of Mary Lee Jensvold In the Matter of a Proceeding under Article 70 of the CPLR for a Writ of Habeas Corpus. The Nonhuman Rights Project, Inc., on behalf of Tommy, Petitioners, v. Patrick C. Lavery, individually and as an officer of Circle L Trailer Sales, Inc., Diane Lavery, and Circle L Trailer Sales, Inc. November 24, 2013*. Available at: https://www.nonhumanrights.org/content/uploads/Ex-7-Jensvold-Affidavit-Tommy-Case.pdf. Accessed December, 2019.

Jensvold, M.L. (2015). *Affidavit of Mary Lee Jensvold In the Matter of a Proceeding under Article 70 of the CPLR for a Writ of Habeas Corpus. The Nonhuman Rights Project, Inc., on behalf of Kiko, Petitioner, v. Carmen Presti, individually and as an officer and director of The Primate Sanctuary, Inc., Christie E. Presti, individually and as an officer and director of The Primate Sanctuary, Inc., and the Primate Sanctuary, Inc. September 29, 2015*. Available at: https://www.nonhumanrights.org/client-kiko/. Accessed December, 2019.

JGI (n.d.). *Project Ushiriki Consortium*. Vienna, VA: Jane Goodall Institute (JGI). Available at: https://www.jane goodall.org/project/africa-programs/ushiriki/. Accessed July, 2020.

JGI, TNC, CBSG, *et al.* (2011). *Tanzania Chimpanzee Conservation Action Planning Workshop Report*. Arlington, USA: Jane Goodall Institute (JGI). Available at: http://static1.1.sqspcdn.com/static/f/1200343/26917569/1458146882763/tz_c-cap_report_2012.pdf?token=jl2ekz%2fktus5fgyhhvgnusyf8pk%3d.

JGI South Africa (n.d.). *Adoptions*. Mpumalanga, South Africa: Jane Goodall Institute (JGI) South Africa. Available at: https://www.chimpeden.com/adoptions.html. Accessed December 1, 2018.

Johnston, M. (2015). Auckland Zoo puts down 'unhappy and agitated' gibbon. *New Zealand Herald*, January 22, 2015. Available at: https://www.nzherald.co.nz/nz/news/article.cfm?c_id=1&objectid=11389939.

Jones, K.E., Patel, N.G., Levy, M.A., *et al.* (2008). Global trends in emerging infectious diseases. *Nature*, **451**, 990–3. DOI: 10.1038/nature06536.

Joshi, L., Wijaya, K., Sirait, M. and Mulyoutami, E. (2004). *Indigenous Systems and Ecological Knowledge among Dayak People in Kutai Barat, East Kalimantan – A Preliminary Report*. Bogor: World Agroforestry Centre (ICRAF). Available at: http://www.worldagroforestry.org/downloads/Publications/PDFS/wp04193.pdf.

Junker, J., Arroyo-Rodríguez, V., Boonratana, R., *et al.* (2020). Severe lack of evidence limits effective conservation of the world's primates. *BioScience*, **70**(9), 794-803. DOI: 10.1093/biosci/biaa082.

Junker, J., Blake, S., Boesch, C., *et al.* (2012). Recent decline in suitable environmental conditions for African great apes. *Diversity and Distributions*, **18**(11), 1077–91. DOI: 10.1111/ddi.12005.

Junker, J., Boesch, C., Freeman, T., *et al.* (2015a). Integrating wildlife conservation with conflicting economic land-use goals in a West African biodiversity hotspot. *Basic and Applied Ecology*, **16**, 690–702.

Junker, J., Boesch, C., Mundry, R., *et al.* (2015b). Education and access to fish but not economic development predict chimpanzee and mammal occurrence in West Africa. *Biological Conservation*, **182**, 27–35. DOI: 10.1016/j.biocon.2014.11.034.

Junker, J., Kühl, H.S., Orth, L., *et al.* (2017). *Primate Conservation: Global Evidence for the Effects of Interventions*. Cambridge, UK: University of Cambridge.

Juste, J., Fa, J.E., Perez Del Val, J. and Castroviejo, J. (1995). Market dynamics of bushmeat species in Equatorial Guinea. *Journal of Applied Ecology*, **32**(3), 454–67. DOI: 10.2307/2404644.

Kakati, K. (2000). *Impact of forest fragmentation on the Hoolock gibbon (*Hylobates hoolock*) in Assam, India*. PhD thesis. Cambridge, UK: University of Cambridge.

Kalan, A.K., Mundry, R., Wagner, O.J.J., *et al.* (2015). Towards the automated detection and occupancy estimation of primates using passive acoustic monitoring. *Ecological Indicators*, **54**, 217–26. DOI: 10.1016/j.ecolind.2015.02.023.

Kalan, A.K., Piel, A.K., Mundry, R., *et al.* (2016). Passive acoustic monitoring reveals group ranging and territory use: a case study of wild chimpanzees (*Pan troglodytes*). *Frontiers in Zoology*, **13**(1), 34. DOI: 10.1186/s12983-016-0167-8.

Kalpers, J., Williamson, E.A., Robbins, M.M., *et al.* (2003). Gorillas in the crossfire: population dynamics of the Virunga mountain gorillas over the past three decades. *Oryx*, **37**(3), 326–37. DOI: 10.1017/S0030605303000589.

Kano, T. and Asato, R. (1994). Hunting pressure on chimpanzees and gorillas in the Motaba River area, northeastern Congo. *African Study Monographs*, **15**(3), 1–3.

Kaplan, H., Hill, K., Lancaster, J. and Hurtado, A.M. (2000). A theory of human life history evolution: Diet, intelligence, and longevity. *Evolutionary Anthropology: Issues, News, and Reviews*, **9**(4), 156–85. DOI: 10.1002/1520-6505(2000)9:4<156::Aid-evan5>3.0.Co;2-7.

Karam-Gemael, M., Loyola, R., Penha, J. and Izzo, T. (2018). Poor alignment of priorities between scientists and policymakers highlights the need for evidence-informed conservation in Brazil. *Perspectives in Ecology and Conservation*, **16**(3), 125–32. DOI: 10.1016/j.pecon.2018.06.002.

Karanth, K.K., Gopalaswamy, A.M., DeFries, R. and Ballal, N. (2012). Assessing patterns of human–wildlife conflicts and compensation around a central Indian protected area. *PLoS ONE*, **7**(12), e50433. DOI: 10.1371/journal.pone.0050433.

Karesh, W.B., Cook, R.A., Bennett, E.L. and Newcomb, J. (2005). Wildlife trade and global disease emergence. *Emerging Infectious Diseases*, **11**(7), 1000–2. DOI: 10.3201/eid1107.050194.

Kasane Conference on The Illegal Wildlife Trade (2015). *Kasane Conference on The Illegal Wildlife Trade 25th March 2015: Statement.* London, UK: Department for Environment, Food & Rural Affairs (Defra). Available at: https://www.gov.uk/government/publications/illegal-wildlife-trade-kasane-statement.

Keane, A., Jones, J.P.G., Edwards-Jones, G. and Milner-Gulland, E.J. (2008). The sleeping policeman: understanding issues of enforcement and compliance in conservation. *Animal Conservation*, **11**(2), 75–82. DOI: 10.1111/j.1469-1795.2008.00170.x.

Keane, A., Jones, J.P.G. and Milner-Gulland, E.J. (2011). Encounter data in resource management and ecology: pitfalls and possibilities. *Journal of Applied Ecology*, **48**(5), 1164–73. DOI: 10.1111/j.1365-2664.2011.02034.x.

Kemp, S. (2019). *The Global State of Digital in 2019 Report.* Canada: Hootsuite, We Are Social. Available at: https://hootsuite.com/pages/digital-in-2019. Accessed August 1, 2019.

Kerr, M. (2017). Great apes in Asian circus-style shows on rise – so is trafficking. *Mongabay*, April 12, 2017. Available at: https://news.mongabay.com/2017/04/great-apes-in-asian-circus-style-shows-on-rise-so-is-trafficking/. Accessed March 25, 2020.

Khan, M.K.M. (1970). Distribution and population of siamang and gibbons in the state of Perak. *Malayan Nature Journal*, **24**, 3–8.

Kheng, V., Zichello, J.M., Lumbantobing, D.N., *et al.* (2018). Phylogeography, population structure, and conservation of the Javan gibbon (*Hylobates moloch*). *International Journal of Primatology*, **39**(1), 5–26. DOI: 10.1007/s10764-017-0005-7.

King, J. (2013). *Affidavit of James King In the Matter of a Proceeding under Article 70 of the CPLR for a Writ of Habeas Corpus. The Nonhuman Rights Project, Inc., on behalf of Tommy, Petitioners, v. Patrick C. Lavery, individually and as an officer of Circle L Trailer Sales, Inc., Diane Lavery, and Circle L Trailer Sales, Inc. November 21, 2013.* Available at: https://www.nonhumanrights.org/content/uploads/Ex-8-King-Affidavit-Tommy-Case.pdf. Accessed December, 2019.

King, M.L., Jr (1963). Letter from Birmingham Jail [The Negro Is Your Brother]. *The Atlantic Monthly*, Available at: https://web.cn.edu/kwheeler/documents/Letter_Birmingham_Jail.pdf. Accessed September, 2019.

King, S. (n.d.). Cinema simians. *Los Angeles Times.* Available at: https://www.latimes.com/entertainment/la-et-monkeymovies-pg-photogallery.html. Accessed January, 2020.

Kirkby, A., Spira, C., Bahati, B., *et al.* (2015). *Investigating Artisanal Mining and Bushmeat Around Protected Areas: Kahuzi-Biega National Park and Itombwe Reserve.* New York, NY: Wildlife Conservation Society (WCS).

Knight, A. (2008). The beginning of the end for chimpanzee experiments? *Philosophy, Ethics, and Humanities in Medicine*, **3**(1), 16. DOI: 10.1186/1747-5341-3-16.

Knott, C.D. (1998). Changes in orangutan caloric intake, energy balance, and ketones in response to fluctuating fruit availability. *International Journal of Primatology*, **19**(6), 1061–79. DOI: 10.1023/a:1020330404983.

Knott, C.D. (2005). Energetic responses to food availability in the great apes: implications for hominin evolution. In *Seasonality in Primates: Studies of Living and Extinct Human and Non-Human Primates*, ed. D.K. Brockman and C.P. van Schaik. New York, NY: Cambridge University Press, pp. 351–78.

Knott, C.D., Scott, A.M., O'Connell, C.A., *et al.* (2019). Possible male infanticide in wild orangutans and a re-evaluation of infanticide risk. *Scientific Reports*, **9**(1), 7806. DOI: 10.1038/s41598-019-42856-w.

Knowledge@Wharton (2018). How tech companies are helping to curb wildlife trafficking. *Knowledge@Wharton*, March 14, 2018. Available at: https://knowledge.wharton.upenn.edu/article/how-tech-companies-are-helping-to-curb-wildlife-trafficking/.

Knowles, G. (2016). Why 1,800 tigers are in a rundown China park: to be made into wine. *South China Morning Post*, April 21, 2016. Available at: https://www.scmp.com/magazines/post-magazine/travel-leisure/article/1937522/why-1800-tigers-are-rundown-china-park-be.

Kockelman, P. (2016). *The Chicken and the Quetzal: Incommensurate Ontologies and Portable Values in Guatemala's Cloud Forest.* Durham, NC: Duke University Press.

Köndgen, S., Kühl, H., N'Goran, P.K., *et al.* (2008). Pandemic human viruses cause decline of endangered great apes. *Current Biology*, **18**(4), 260–4. DOI: 10.1016/j.cub.2008.01.012.

König, A. (2016). Identity constructions and Dayak ethnic strife in West Kalimantan, Indonesia. *The Asia Pacific Journal of Anthropology*, **17**(2), 121–37. DOI: 10.1080/14442213.2016.1146917.

Korematsu v. United States. 324 US 885 (1944). Available at: http://cdn.loc.gov/service/ll/usrep/usrep323/usrep323214/usrep323214.pdf.

Kormos, R., Boesch, C., Bakarr, M.I. and Butynski, T.M. (2003). *West African Chimpanzees: Status, Survey and Conservation Action Plan.* Gland, Switzerland: International Union for Conservation of Nature (IUCN) Species Survival Commission (SSC). Available at: https://portals.iucn.org/library/sites/library/files/documents/2003-059.pdf.

Kormos, R., Kormos, C.F., Humle, T., *et al.* (2014). Great apes and biodiversity offset projects in Africa: the case for national offset strategies. *PLoS ONE*, **9**(11), e111671. DOI: 10.1371/journal.pone.0111671.

Kortlandt, A. (1986). The use of stone tools by wild living chimpanzees and earliest hominids. *Journal of Human Evolution*, **15**, 77–132. DOI: 10.1016/S0047-2484(86)80068-9.

Kouakou, C.Y., Boesch, C. and Kühl, H. (2009). Estimating chimpanzee population size with nest counts: validating methods in Taï National Park. *American Journal of Primatology*, **71**(6), 447–57. DOI: 10.1002/ajp.20673.

Kramer, R., Sawyer, R., Amato, S. and LaFontaine, P. (2017). *The US Elephant Ivory Market: A New Baseline.* Washington DC: TRAFFIC. Available at: http://www.trafficj.org/publication/17_The_US_Elephant_Ivory_Market.pdf.

Kramm, W. (1879). Tochtjes in Tapanoeli. *Sumatra-Courant*, **20**, 1–2.

Krishnasamy, K. and Stoner, S. (2016). *Trading Faces: A Rapid Assessment on the use of Facebook to Trade Wildlife in Peninsular Malaysia.* Petaling Jaya, Malaysia: TRAFFIC. Available at: https://www.traffic.org/site/assets/files/2434/trading-faces-facebook-malasia.pdf.

Kroeber, A.L. and Kluckhohn, C. (1952). *Culture: A Critical Review of Concepts and Definitions.* Papers of the Peabody Museum of American Archeology and Ethnology, Vol. XLVII, No. 1. Cambridge, MA: Harvard University.

Kronen, M., Vunisea, A., Magron, F. and McArdle, B. (2010). Socio-economic drivers and indicators for artisanal coastal fisheries in Pacific island countries and territories and their use for fisheries management strategies. *Marine Policy*, **34**(6), 1135–43. DOI: 10.1016/j.marpol.2010.03.013.

Kübler, S., Owenga, P., Reynolds, S.C., Rucina, S.M. and King, G.C.P. (2015). Animal movements in the Kenya Rift and evidence for the earliest ambush hunting by hominins. *Scientific Reports*, **5**, 14011. DOI: 10.1038/srep14011.

Kühl, H.S., Boesch, C., Kulik, L., *et al.* (2019). Human impact erodes chimpanzee behavioral diversity. *Science*, **363**(6434), 1453. DOI: 10.1126/science.aau4532.

Kühl, H., Maisels, F., Ancrenaz, M. and Williamson, E.A. (2008). *Best Practice Guidelines for Surveys and Monitoring of Great Ape Populations.* Gland, Switzerland: International Union for Conservation of Nature (IUCN) Species Survival Commission (SSC), Primate Specialist Group. Available at: https://portals.iucn.org/library/efiles/documents/ssc-op-036.pdf.

Kühl, H.S., Nzeingui, C., Yeno, S.L.D., *et al.* (2009). Discriminating between village and commercial hunting of apes. *Biological Conservation*, **142**(7), 1500–6. DOI: 10.1016/j.biocon.2009.02.032.

Kühl, H.S., Sop, T., Williamson, E.A., *et al.* (2017). The critically endangered western chimpanzee declines by 80%. *American Journal of Primatology*, **79**(9), e22681-e. DOI: 10.1002/ajp.22681.

Kümpel, N.F., Milner-Gulland, E.J., Cowlishaw, G. and Rowcliffe, J.M. (2010). Incentives for hunting: the role of bushmeat in the household economy in rural Equatorial Guinea. *Human Ecology*, **38**(2), 251–64. DOI: 10.1007/s10745-010-9316-4.

Kupika, O. and Nhamo, G. (2016). Mainstreaming biodiversity and wildlife management into climate change policy frameworks in selected east and southern African countries. *Jàmbá: Journal of Disaster Risk Studies*, **8**(3). DOI: 10.4102/jamba.v8i3.254.

LAGA (2015). *Annual Report January – December 2015*. Cameroon: Last Great Ape Organization (LAGA). Available at: http://www.laga-enforcement.org/en/annual-report-2015-R.

LAGA (n.d.). *Home.* Cameroon: Last Great Ape Organization (LAGA). Available at: http://www.laga-enforcement.org. Accessed September, 2020.

Lambert, J.E. (1998). Primate frugivory in Kibale National Park, Uganda, and its implications for human use of forest resources. *African Journal of Ecology*, **36**(3), 234–40. DOI: 10.1046/j.1365-2028.1998.00131.x.

Lambert, J.E. (2011). Primate seed dispersers as umbrella species: a case study from Kibale National Park, Uganda, with implications for Afrotropical forest conservation. *American Journal of Primatology*, **73**(1), 9–24. DOI: 10.1002/ajp.20879.

Lamprey, R. (2017). *Community-based restoration of ecological corridors between chimpanzee forests in Uganda's Albertine rift.* Unpublished background paper. Commissioned by the Arcus Foundation.

Lange, K.E. (2017). Sanctuary. *The Humane Society*, May 1, 2017. Available at: https://www.humanesociety.org/news/abandoned-chimps-find-sanctuary.

Lanjouw, A. (2015). Economic development and conservation of biodiversity: understanding the interface of ape conservation and industrial agriculture. In *State of the Apes: Industrial Agriculture and Ape Conservation*, ed. Arcus Foundation. Cambridge, UK: Cambridge University Press, pp. 13–39.

Lappan, S. (2008). Male care of infants in a siamang (*Symphalangus syndactylus*) population including socially monogamous and polyandrous groups. *Behavioral Ecology and Sociobiology*, **62**(8), 1307–17. DOI: 10.1007/s00265-008-0559-7.

Lappan, S. (2009). Flowers are an important food for small apes in southern Sumatra. *American Journal of Primatology*, **71**(8), 624–35. DOI: 10.1002/ajp.20691.

Larkin, M. (2010). Latin America's welfare issues prevalent yet ignored. *JAVMA News*, January 15, 2010. Available at: https://www.avma.org/News/JAVMANews/Pages/100115e.aspx.

Laurance, W.F., Carolina Useche, D., Rendeiro, J., *et al.* (2012). Averting biodiversity collapse in tropical forest protected areas. *Nature*, **489**, 290. DOI: 10.1038/nature11318.

Laurance, W.F., Croes, B.M., Tchignoumba, L., *et al.* (2006). Impacts of roads and hunting on central African rainforest mammals. *Conservation Biology*, **20**(4), 1251–61. DOI: 10.1111/j.1523-1739.2006.00420.x.

Lavorgna, A., Rutherford, C., Vaglica, V., Smith, M.J. and Sajeva, M. (2018). CITES, wild plants, and opportunities for crime. *European Journal on Criminal Policy and Research*, **24**(3), 269–88. DOI: 10.1007/s10610-017-9354-1.

Laws of Malaysia (2008). *International Trade in Endangered Species Act 2008 [Act 686] (as at 1 October 2018).* Malaysia: Laws of Malaysia. Available at: http://www.agc.gov.my/agcportal/uploads/files/Publications/LOM/EN/Act%20686.pdf.

Lawson, K. and Vines, A. (2014). *Global Impacts of the Illegal Wildlife Trade: The Costs of Crime, Insecurity and Institutional Erosion.* London, UK: Chatham House (The Royal Institute of International Affairs). Available at: https://www.chathamhouse.org/sites/default/files/public/Research/Africa/0214Wildlife.pdf.

LCRP (n.d.). *Our story.* Liberia Chimpanzee Rescue and Protection (LCRP). Available at: http://www.liberia chimpanzeerescue.org/our-story.html. Accessed November 1, 2018.

League of Nations (1926). *The Convention to Suppress the Slave Trade and Slavery.* Geneva, Switzerland: League of Nations. Available at: https://ec.europa.eu/anti-trafficking/legislation-and-case-law-international-legislation-united-nations/1926-slavery-convention_en.

Leberatto, A.C. (2016). Understanding the illegal trade of live wildlife species in Peru. *Trends in Organized Crime*, **19**(1), 42–66. DOI: 10.1007/s12117-015-9262-z.

Lee, F. (2013). Gibbons escape at Christchurch's Orana Park. *Stuff*, September 8, 2013. Available at: https://www.stuff.co.nz/the-press/news/9138922/Gibbons-escape-at-Christchurchs-Orana-Park.

Lee, T., Sigouin, A., Pinedo-Vasquez, M. and Nasi, R. (2014). *The Harvest of Wildlife for Bushmeat and Traditional Medicine in East, South and Southeast Asia: Current Knowledge Base, Challenges, Opportunities and Areas for Future Research.* Bogor, Indonesia: Center for International Forestry Research (CIFOR). Available at: http://www.cifor.org/publications/pdf_files/OccPapers/OP-115.pdf.

Leendertz, S., Wich, S., Ancrenaz, M., *et al.* (2016). Ebola in great apes: current knowledge, possibilities for vaccination, and implications for conservation and human health. *Mammal Review*, **47**(2), 98–111. DOI: 10.1111/mam.12082.

Legal Atlas (2018). *Legis-Apes Project.* Presented at the Congress of the International Primatology Society, August, 2018, Nairobi, Kenya.

Legal Atlas (n.d.). *Home.* Missoula, MT: Legal Atlas. Available at: https://www.legal-atlas.com/. Accessed September, 2020.

Leighton, D.S.R. (1987). Gibbons: territoriality and monogamy. In *Primate Societies*, ed. B.B. Smuts, D.L. Cheyney, R.M. Seyfarth, R.W. Wrangham and T.T. Struhsaker. Chicago IL: University of Chicago Press.

Leighton, M. (1993). Modelling dietary selectivity by Bornean orangutans: evidence of multiple criteria in fruit selection. *International Journal of Primatology*, **14**(2), 257–313.

Leighty, K.A., Valuska, A.J., Grand, A.P., *et al.* (2015). Impact of visual context on public perceptions of non-human primate performers. *PLoS ONE*, **10**(2), e0118487. DOI: 10.1371/journal.pone.0118487.

Leiman, A. and Ghaffar, N. (1996). Use, misuse, and abuse of the orang-utan: exploitation as a threat or the only real salvation? In *The Exploitation of Mammal Populations*, ed. V.J. Taylor. London, UK: Chapman & Hall, pp. 345–57. DOI: 10.1007/978-94-009-1525-1_20.

Lescuyer, G. and Nasi, R. (2016). Financial and economic values of bushmeat in rural and urban livelihoods in Cameroon: inputs to the development of public policy. *International Forestry Review*, **18**(s1), 93–107, 15. DOI: 10.1505/146554816819683726.

Levi, T., Lu, F., Yu, D.W. and Mangel, M. (2011). The behaviour and diet breadth of central-place foragers: an application to human hunters and Neotropical game management. *Evolutionary Ecology Research*, **13**, 171–85. Available at: http://www.evolutionary-ecology.com/issues/v13/n02/ggar2663.pdf.

Ley de Conservación de la Vida Silvestre (1992). *Ley de Conservación de la Vida Silvestre 7317/1992, As amended October 4, 1995.* La Asamblea Legislativa de la República de Costa Rica. Available at: https://studylib.es/doc/697346/ley-de-conservacion-de-la-vida-silvestre--n°-7317.

Ley General de Aduanas (1995). *Ley General de Aduanas No. 7557* La Asamblea Legislativa de la República de Costa Rica. Available at: https://www.crecex.com/asesoria-juridica/legislacion-consulta/aduanas/ley-aduanas.pdf.

Li, B., Li, M., Li, J., *et al.* (2018). The primate extinction crisis in China: immediate challenges and a way forward. *Biodiversity and Conservation*, **27**(13), 3301–27.

Li, P.J. (2013). Explaining China's wildlife crisis: cultural tradition or politics of development. In *Ignoring Nature No More: The Case for Compassionate Conservation*, ed. M. Bekoff. Chicago, IL: The University of Chicago Press, pp. 317–30.

Li, P.J. and Davey, G. (2013). Culture, reform politics, and future directions: a review of China's animal protection challenge. *Society & Animals*, **21**(2013), 34–53. DOI: 10.1163/15685306-12341264.

Li, T.M. (2015). *Social Impacts of Oil Palm in Indonesia: A Gendered Perspective from West Kalimantan.* Bogor, Indonesia: Center for International Forestry Research (CIFR). DOI: 10.17528/cifor/005579.

Lincoln Park Zoo (n.d.). *Chimpanzee SSP.* Chicago, IL: Lincoln Park Zoo. Available at: https://www.lpzoo.org/conservation-science/projects/chimpanzee-ssp. Accessed January, 2020.

Lindsey, P., Balme, G., Becker, M., *et al.* (2012). *Illegal Hunting and the Bush-Meat Trade in Savanna Africa: Drivers, Impacts and Solutions to Address the Problem.* New York, NY: Panthera.

Lindsey, P. and Bento, C. (2012). *Illegal Hunting and the Bushmeat Trade in Central Mozambique. A Case-Study from Coutada 9, Manica Province.* Harare, Zimbabwe: TRAFFIC East/Southern Africa. Available at: https://www.traffic.org/site/assets/files/7163/bushmeat-trade-mozambique.pdf.

Lindsey, P.A., Romañach, S.S., Matema, S., *et al.* (2011). Dynamics and underlying causes of illegal bushmeat trade in Zimbabwe. *Oryx*, **45**(1), 84–95. DOI: 10.1017/S0030605310001274.

Lindshield, S., Bogart, S.L., Gueye, M., Ndiaye, P.I. and Pruetz, J.D. (2019). Informing protection efforts for critically endangered chimpanzees (*Pan troglodytes verus*) and sympatric mammals amidst rapid growth of extractive industries in Senegal. *Folia Primatologica*, **90**(2), 124–36. DOI: 10.1159/000496145.

Lingomo, B. and Kimura, D. (2009). Taboo of eating bonobo among the Bongando people in the Wamba region, Democratic Republic of Congo. *African Study Monographs*, **30**(4), 209–25.

Linkie, M., Martyr, D.J., Harihar, A., *et al.* (2015). Editor's choice: safeguarding Sumatran tigers: evaluating effectiveness of law enforcement patrols and local informant networks. *Journal of Applied Ecology*, **52**(4), 851–60. DOI: 10.1111/1365-2664.12461.

Liswanto, D., Whittaker, D., Geissmann, T. and Whitten, T. (2020). *Hylobates klossii. The IUCN Red List of Threatened Species.* 2020: e.T10547A17967475. Gland, Switzerland: International Union for Conservation of Nature (IUCN). Available at: https://dx.doi.org/10.2305/IUCN.UK.2020-2.RLTS.T10547A17967475.en.

Littleton, J. (2005). Fifty years of chimpanzee demography at Taronga Park Zoo. *American Journal of Primatology*, **67**(3), 281–98. DOI: 10.1002/ajp.20185.

Liu, Z.H., Jiang, H.S., Zhang, R.Z., *et al.* (1987). Field report on the Hainan gibbon. *Primate Conservation*, **8**, 49–50.

Loibooki, M., Hofer, H., Campbell, K.L. and East, M.L. (2002). Bushmeat hunting by communities adjacent to the Serengeti National Park, Tanzania: the importance of livestock ownership and alternative sources of protein and income. *Environmental Conservation*, **29**(3), 391–8. DOI: 10.1017/S0376892902000279.

Loken, B., Boer, C. and Kasyanto, N. (2015). Opportunistic behaviour or desperate measure? Logging impacts may only partially explain terrestriality in the Bornean orang-utan *Pongo pygmaeus morio*. *Oryx*, **49**(3), 461–4. DOI: 10.1017/S0030605314000969.

Loken, B., Spehar, S. and Rayadin, Y. (2013). Terrestriality in the Bornean orangutan (*Pongo pygmaeus morio*) and implications for their ecology and conservation. *American Journal of Primatology*, **75**(11), 1129–38. DOI: 10.1002/ajp.22174.

London Conference on the Illegal Wildlife Trade (2014). *London Conference on the Illegal Wildlife Trade 12–13 February 2014: Declaration.* London, UK: Department for Environment, Food & Rural Affairs (Defra), Department for International Development (DFID), Foreign & Commonwealth Office (FCO) and Home Office. Available at: https://assets.publishing.service.gov.uk/government/uploads/system/uploads/attachment_data/file/281289/london-wildlife-conference-declaration-140213.pdf.

London Conference on the Illegal Wildlife Trade (2018). *London Conference on the Illegal Wildlife Trade (October 2018): Declaration.* London, UK: Department for Environment, Food & Rural Affairs (Defra), Department for International Development (DFID), Foreign & Commonwealth Office (FCO) and Home Office. Available at: https://www.gov.uk/government/publications/declaration-london-conference-on-the-illegal-wildlife-trade-2018/london-conference-on-the-illegal-wildlife-trade-october-2018-declaration.

Lounela, A. (2015). Climate change disputes and justice in Central Kalimantan, Indonesia. *Asia Pacific Viewpoint*, **56**(1), 62–78. DOI: 10.1111/apv.12088.

Lowe, C. (2006). *Wild Profusion: Biodiversity Conservation in an Indonesian Archipelago.* Princeton, NJ: Princeton University Press.

Macfie, E.J. and Williamson, E.A. (2010). *Best Practice Guidelines for Great Ape Tourism.* Gland, Switzerland: International Union for Conservation of Nature (IUCN) Species Survival Commission (SSC), Primate Specialist Group. Available at: https://portals.iucn.org/library/efiles/documents/SSC-OP-038.pdf.

Machovina, B., Feeley, K.J. and Ripple, W.J. (2015). Biodiversity conservation: the key is reducing meat consumption. *Science of The Total Environment*, **536**, 419–31. DOI: 10.1016/j.scitotenv.2015.07.022.

Madden, F. (2006). Gorillas in the garden: human–wildlife conflict at Bwindi Impenetrable National Park. *Policy Matters*, **14**, 180–90.

Maekawa, M., Lanjouw, A., Rutagarama, E. and Sharp, D. (2015). Mountain gorilla ecotourism: supporting macroeconomic growth and providing local livelihoods. In *Livelihoods, Natural Resources, and Post-Conflict Peacebuilding*, ed. H. Young and L. Goldman. Abingdon, UK: Taylor and Francis, pp. 167–86.

Mager, D. (2000). Freed orphan happy at last. *New Zealand Herald*, June 30, 2000. Available at: https://www.nzherald.co.nz/nz/news/article.cfm?c_id=1&objectid=129664.

Maisels, F., Bergl, R.A. and Williamson, E.A. (2018). *Gorilla gorilla* (amended version of 2016 assessment). *The IUCN Red List of Threatened Species*. 2018: e.T9404A136250858. Gland, Switzerland: International Union for Conservation of Nature (IUCN). Available at: http://dx.doi.org/10.2305/IUCN.UK.2018-2.RLTS.T9404A136250858.en.

Maisels, F., Keming, E., Kemei, M. and Toh, C. (2001). The extirpation of large mammals and implications for montane forest conservation: the case of the Kilum-Ijim Forest, North-west Province, Cameroon. *Oryx*, **35**(4), 322–31. DOI: 10.1046/j.1365-3008.2001.00204.x.

Maisels, F., Strindberg, S., Blake, S., *et al.* (2013). Devastating decline of forest elephants in central Africa. *PLoS ONE*, **8**(3), e59469. DOI: 10.1371/journal.pone.0059469.

Maisels, F., Strindberg, S., Breuer, T., *et al.* (2018). *Gorilla gorilla* ssp. *gorilla* (amended version of 2016 assessment). *The IUCN Red List of Threatened Species*. 2018: e.T9406A136251508. Gland, Switzerland: International Union for Conservation of Nature (IUCN). Available at: http://dx.doi.org/10.2305/IUCN.UK.2016-2.RLTS.T9406A136251508.en.

Maisels, F., Strindberg, S., Greer, D., *et al.* (2016). *Pan troglodytes* ssp. *troglodytes* (errata version published in 2016). *The IUCN Red List of Threatened Species*. 2016: e.T15936A102332276. Gland, Switzerland: International Union for Conservation of Nature (IUCN). Available at: http://dx.doi.org/10.2305/IUCN.UK.2016-2.RLTS.T15936A17990042.en.

Maldonado, O., Aveling, C., Cox, D., *et al.* (2012). *Grauer's Gorillas and Chimpanzees in Eastern Democratic Republic of Congo (Kahuzi-Biega, Maiko, Tayna and Itombwe Landscape): Conservation Action Plan 2012–2022*. Gland, Switzerland: International Union for Conservation of Nature (IUCN) Species Survival Commission (SSC), Primate Specialist Group, Ministry of Environment, Nature Conservation & Tourism, Institut Congolais pour la Conservation de la Nature & the Jane Goodall Institute. Available at: https://www.iucn.org/content/grauers-gorillas-and-chimpanzees-eastern-democratic-republic-congo-kahuzi-biega-maiko-tayna-and-itombwe-landscape-conservation-action-plan-2012-2022.

Malone, N.M., Fuentes, A., Purnama, A.R. and Adi Putra, I.M.W. (2003). Displaced Hylobatids: biological, cultural, and economic aspects of the primate trade in Java and Bali, Indonesia. *Tropical Biodiversity*, **8**(1), 41–9.

Margules, C.R. and Pressey, R.L. (2000). Systematic conservation planning. *Nature*, **405**(6783), 243–53. DOI: 10.1038/35012251.

Margulies, J.D. and Karanth, K.K. (2018). The production of human–wildlife conflict: a political animal geography of encounter. *Geoforum*, **95**, 153–64. DOI: 10.1016/j.geoforum.2018.06.011.

Marijnen, E. and Verweijen, J. (2016). Selling green militarization: The discursive (re)production of militarized conservation in the Virunga National Park, Democratic Republic of the Congo. *Geoforum*, **75**, 274–85. DOI: 10.1016/j.geoforum.2016.08.003.

Marks, S.A. (2016). *Life as a Hunt: Thresholds of Identities and Illusions on an African Landscape.* New York and Oxford: Berghahn.

Marques, A., Martins, I.S., Kastner, T., *et al.* (2019). Increasing impacts of land use on biodiversity and carbon sequestration driven by population and economic growth. *Nature Ecology & Evolution*, **3**(4), 628–37. DOI: 10.1038/s41559-019-0824-3.

Marshall, A., Lacy, R., Ancrenaz, M., *et al.* (2009a). Orangutan population biology, life history, and conservation: perspectives from population viability analysis models. In *Orangutans: Geographic Variation in Behavioral Ecology and Conservation*, ed. S.A. Wich, S.S. Utami-Atmoko, T. Mitra Setia and C.P. van Schaik. Oxford, UK: Oxford University Press, pp. 311–26. DOI: 10.1093/acprof:oso/9780199213276.001.0001.

Marshall, A.J., Ancrenaz, M., Brearley, F.Q., *et al.* (2009b). The effects of forest phenology and floristics on populations of Bornean and Sumatran orangutans. In *Orangutans: Geographic Variation in Behavioral Ecology and Conservation*, ed. S.A. Wich, S.S. Utami-Atmoko, T. Mitra Setia and C.P. van Schaik. Oxford, UK: Oxford University Press, pp. 97–117.

Marshall, A.J. and Leighton, M. (2006). How does food availability limit the population density of white-bearded gibbons? In *Feeding Ecology in Apes and Other Primates: Ecological, Physiological and Behavioural Aspects*, ed. G. Hohmann, M. Robbins and C. Boesch. Cambridge Studies in Biological and Evolutionary Anthropology Volume 48. Cambridge, UK: Cambridge University Press, pp. 313–35.

Marshall, A.J., Meijaard, E., Van Cleave, E. and Sheil, D. (2016). Charisma counts: the presence of great apes affects the allocation of research effort in the paleotropics. *Frontiers in Ecology and the Environment*, **14**(1), 13–9. DOI: 10.1002/14-0195.1.

Marshall, A.J., Nardiyono, Engström, L.M., *et al.* (2006). The blowgun is mightier than the chainsaw in determining population density of Bornean orangutans (*Pongo pygmaeus morio*) in the forests of East Kalimantan. *Biological Conservation*, **129**(4), 566–78. DOI: 10.1016/j.bibcon.2005.11.025.

Marshall, A.J., Nijman, V. and Cheyne, S. (2020a). *Hylobates albibarbis. The IUCN Red List of Threatened Species.* 2020: e.T39879A17967053. Gland, Switzerland: International Union for Conservation of Nature (IUCN). Available at: https://dx.doi.org/10.2305/IUCN.UK.2020-2.RLTS.T39879A17967053.en.

Marshall, A.J., Nijman, V. and Cheyne, S.M. (2020b). *Hylobates muelleri. The IUCN Red List of Threatened Species.* 2020: e.T39888A17990934. Gland, Switzerland: International Union for Conservation of Nature (IUCN). Available at: https://dx.doi.org/10.2305/IUCN.UK.2020-2.RLTS.T39888A17990934.en.

Martin, P.S. (1958). Pleistocene ecology and biogeography of North America. In *Zoogeography*, ed. C.L. Hubbs. Washington DC: American Association for the Advancement of Science, pp. 375–420.

Masi, S., Cipolletta, C. and Robbins, M.M. (2009). Western lowland gorillas (*Gorilla gorilla gorilla*) change their activity patterns in response to frugivory. *American Journal of Primatology*, **71**(2), 91–100. DOI: 10.1002/ajp.20629.

Masjid Shahid Ganj and others v. *Shiromani Gurdwara Parbandhak Committee.* Amritsar, AIR 1938 369, 15 (Lahore High Court, Full Bench) (1938). Available at: https://www.casemine.com/judgement/uk/5b4dc2642c94e07cccd24247.

Massé, F. and Lunstrum, E. (2016). Accumulation by securitization: commercial poaching, neoliberal conservation, and the creation of new wildlife frontiers. *Geoforum*, **69**, 227–37. DOI: 10.1016/j.geoforum.2015.03.005.

Matschie, P. (1900). Über geographische Abarten des afrikanischen Elefanten. *Sitzungsberichte der Gesellschaft Naturforschender Freunde zu Berlin*, **8**, 189–97.

Matsuzawa, T. (2013). *Affidavit of Tetsuro Matsuzawa In the Matter of a Proceeding under Article 70 of the CPLR for a Writ of Habeas Corpus. The Nonhuman Rights Project, Inc., on behalf of Tommy, Petitioners, v. Patrick C. Lavery, individually and as an officer of Circle L Trailer Sales, Inc., Diane Lavery, and Circle L Trailer Sales, Inc. November 23, 2013.* Available at: https://www.nonhumanrights.org/content/uploads/Ex-9-Matsuzawa-Affidavit-Tommy-Case.pdf. Accessed December, 2019.

Matsuzawa, T., Humle, T. and Sugiyama, Y., ed. (2011). *The Chimpanzees of Bossou and Nimba.* Tokyo, Japan: Springer. DOI: 10.1007/978-4-431-53921-6_3.

Mavah, G.A., Funk, S.M., Child, B., *et al.* (2018). Food and livelihoods in park-adjacent communities: the case of the Odzala Kokoua National Park. *Biological Conservation*, **222**, 44–51. DOI: 10.1016/j.biocon.2018.03.036.

Maxwell, S.L., Fuller, R.A., Brooks, T.M. and Watson, J.E. (2016). Biodiversity: the ravages of guns, nets and bulldozers. *Nature*, **536**(7615), 143–5.

Mayaux, P., Pekel, J.-F., Desclée, B., *et al.* (2013). State and evolution of the African rainforests between 1990 and 2010. *Philosophical Transactions of the Royal Society B: Biological Sciences*, **368**(1625), 20120300. DOI: 10.1098/rstb.2012.0300.

Mc Guinness, S. and Taylor, D. (2014). Farmers' perceptions and actions to decrease crop raiding by forest-dwelling primates around a Rwandan forest fragment. *Human Dimensions of Wildlife*, **19**(2), 179–90. DOI: 10.1080/10871209.2014.853330.

McCarthy, M.S., Després-Einspenner, M.-L., Samuni, L., *et al.* (2018). An assessment of the efficacy of camera traps for studying demographic composition and variation in chimpanzees (*Pan troglodytes*). *American Journal of Primatology*, **80**(9), e22904. DOI: 10.1002/ajp.22904.

McCaslin, M.L. and Scott, K.W. (2003). The five-question method for framing a qualitative research study. *The Qualitative Report*, **8**(3), 447–61. Available at: https://nsuworks.nova.edu/tqr/vol8/iss3/6.

McComb, K. (2016). *Affidavit of Karen McComb. December 22, 2016.* Available at: https://www.nonhumanrights.org/client-happy/. Accessed December, 2019.

McConkey, K.R. (2000). Primary seed shadow generated by gibbons in the rain forests of Barito Ulu, central Borneo. *American Journal of Primatology*, **52**(1), 13–29. DOI: 10.1002/1098-2345(200009)52:1<13::AID-AJP2>3.0.CO;2-Y.

McGraw, W.S. (2007). Vulnerability and conservation of the Taï monkey flora. In *Monkeys of the Taï Forest: An African Primate Community*, ed. W.S. McGraw, K. Zuberbühler and R. Noë. Cambridge, UK: Cambridge University Press, pp. 290–316.

McGrew, W.C. (2013). *Affidavit of William C. McGrew In the Matter of a Proceeding under Article 70 of the CPLR for a Writ of Habeas Corpus. The Nonhuman Rights Project, Inc., on behalf of Tommy, Petitioners, v. Patrick C.*

Lavery, individually and as an officer of Circle L Trailer Sales, Inc., Diane Lavery, and Circle L Trailer Sales, Inc. November 21, 2013. Available at: https://www.nonhumanrights.org/content/uploads/Ex-10-McGrew-Affidavit-Tommy-Case.pdf. Accessed December, 2019.

McGrew, W.C. (2015). *Affidavit of William C. McGrew In the Matter of a Proceeding under Article 70 of the CPLR for a Writ of Habeas Corpus. The Nonhuman Rights Project, Inc., on behalf of Kiko, Petitioner, v. Carmen Presti, individually and as an officer and director of The Primate Sanctuary, Inc., Christie E. Presti, individually and as an officer and director of The Primate Sanctuary, Inc., and the Primate Sanctuary, Inc. October 9, 2015.* Available at: https://www.nonhumanrights.org/client-kiko/. Accessed December, 2019.

McKenna, E. and Light, A. (2004). *Animal Pragmatism: Rethinking Human-Nonhuman Relationships.* Bloomington, IN: Indiana University Press.

McKinnon, M.C., Mascia, M.B., Yang, W., Turner, W.R. and Bonham, C. (2015). Impact evaluation to communicate and improve conservation non-governmental organization performance: the case of Conservation International. *Philosophical Transactions of the Royal Society B: Biological Sciences*, **370**(1681), 20140282. DOI: doi:10.1098/rstb.2014.0282.

McLennan, M.R. and Hockings, K.J. (2014). Wild chimpanzees show group differences in selection of agricultural crops. *Scientific Reports*, **4**, 5956. DOI: 10.1038/srep05956.

McLennan, M.R. and Hockings, K.J. (2016). The aggressive apes? Causes and contexts of great ape attacks on local persons. In *Problematic Wildlife: A Cross-Disciplinary Approach*, ed. F.M. Angelici. Cham, Switzerland: Springer, pp. 373–94. DOI: 10.1007/978-3-319-22246-2_18.

McLennan, M.R., Hyeroba, D., Asiimwe, C., Reynolds, V. and Wallis, J. (2012). Chimpanzees in mantraps: lethal crop protection and conservation in Uganda. *Oryx*, **46**(4), 598–603. DOI: 10.1017/S0030605312000592.

McRae, M. (2000). Central Africa's orphan gorillas. *National Geographic*, **197**(2), 84–97.

Meder, A. (2012). Buffer zone and human–wildlife conflict management. *Gorilla Journal*, **44**, 17–9.

Meijaard, E., Abram, N.K., Wells, J.A., *et al.* (2013). People's perceptions about the importance of forests on Borneo. *PLoS ONE*, **8**(9), e73008. DOI: 10.1371/journal.pone.0073008.

Meijaard, E., Albar, G., Nardiyono, *et al.* (2010a). Unexpected ecological resilience in Bornean orangutans and implications for pulp and paper plantation management. *PLoS ONE*, **5**(9), e12813. DOI: 10.1371/journal.pone.0012813.

Meijaard, E., Buchori, D., Hadiprakarsa, Y., *et al.* (2011a). Quantifying killing of orangutans and human–orangutan conflict in Kalimantan, Indonesia. *PLoS ONE*, **6**(11), e27491. DOI: 10.1371/journal.pone.0027491.

Meijaard, E., Buchori, D., Hadiprakarsa, Y., *et al.* (2012a). Correction: Quantifying killing of orangutans and human–orangutan conflict in Kalimantan, Indonesia. *PLoS ONE*, **7**(3). DOI: 10.1371/annotation/7b65cf64-9fd5-4b95-baf2-8824c4785ab1.

Meijaard, E., Garcia-Ulloa, J., Sheil, D., *et al.*, ed. (2018). *Oil Palm and Biodiversity. A Situation Analysis by the IUCN Oil Palm Task Force.* Gland, Switzerland: International Union for Conservation of Nature (IUCN) Oil Palm Task Force. Available at: https://portals.iucn.org/library/sites/library/files/documents/2018-027-En.pdf.

Meijaard, E., Mengersen, K., Buchori, D., *et al.* (2011b). Why don't we ask? A complementary method for assessing the status of great apes. *PLoS ONE*, **6**(3), 1–10. DOI: 10.1371/journal.pone.0018008.

Meijaard, E. and Sheil, D. (2008). Cuddly animals don't persuade poor people to back conservation. *Nature*, **454**(7201), 159. DOI: 10.1038/454159b.

Meijaard, E., Welsh, A., Ancrenaz, M., *et al.* (2010b). Declining orangutan encounter rates from Wallace to the present suggest the species was once more abundant. *PLoS ONE*, **5**(8), e12042. DOI: 10.1371/journal.pone.0012042.

Meijaard, E., Wich, S., Ancrenaz, M. and Marshall, A.J. (2012b). Not by science alone: why orangutan conservationists must think outside the box. *Year in Ecology and Conservation Biology*, **1249**, 29–44. DOI: 10.1111/j.1749-6632.2011.06288.x.

Mellinger, D.K., Stafford, K.M., Moore, S.E., Dziak, R.P. and Matsumoto, H. (2007). An overview of fixed passive acoustic observation methods for cetaceans. *Oceanography*, **20**(4), 36–45. DOI: 10.5670/oceanog.2007.03.

Mellor, D.J., Hunt, S. and Gusset, M. (2015). *Caring for Wildlife: The World Zoo and Aquarium Animal Welfare Strategy.* Gland, Switzerland: World Association of Zoos and Aquariums (WAZA) Executive Office. Available at: https://www.waza.org/priorities/animal-welfare/animal-welfare-strategies/.

Mellor, D.J. and Webster, J.R. (2014). Development of animal welfare understanding drives change in minimum welfare standards. *Revue Scientifique et Technique (International Office of Epizootics)*, **33** (1), 121–30.

Meltzer, D.J. (2015). Pleistocene overkill and North American mammalian extinctions. *Annual Review of Anthropology*, **44**(1), 33–53. DOI: 10.1146/annurev-anthro-102214-013854.

Meola, C.A. (2013). Navigating gender structure: women's leadership in a Brazilian participatory conservation project. *Forests, Trees and Livelihoods*, **22**(2), 106–23. DOI: 10.1080/14728028.2013.798947.

Miller, G.S. (1903). Mammals collected by Dr. W. L. Abbott on the coast and islands of northwest Sumatra. *Proceedings of the United States National Museum*, **26**(1317), 437–83. DOI: 10.5479/si.00963801.26-1317.437.

Milliken, T. and Shaw, J. (2012). *The South Africa–Viet Nam Rhino Horn Trade Nexus: A Deadly Combination of Institutional Lapses, Corrupt Wildlife Industry Professionals and Asian Crime Syndicates*. Johannesburg, South Africa: TRAFFIC. Available at: https://www.traffic.org/publications/reports/the-south-africa-viet-nam-rhino-horn-trade-nexus/.

Milner-Gulland, E.J. (2012). Interactions between human behaviour and ecological systems. *Philosophical Transactions of the Royal Society B: Biological Sciences*, **367**(1586), 270–8. DOI: doi:10.1098/rstb.2011.0175.

Milner-Gulland, E.J. and Bennett, E.L. (2003). Wild meat: the bigger picture. *Trends in Ecology & Evolution*, **18**(7), 351–7. DOI: 10.1016/S0169-5347(03)00123-X.

Milner-Gulland, E.J. and Leader-Williams, N. (1992). A model of incentives for the illegal exploitation of black rhinos and elephants: poaching pays in Luangwa Valley, Zambia. *Journal of Applied Ecology*, **29**(2), 388–401. DOI: 10.2307/2404508.

Milner-Gulland, E.J., McGregor, J.A., Agarwala, M., *et al.* (2014). Accounting for the impact of conservation on human well-being. *Conservation Biology*, **28**(5), 1160–6. DOI: 10.1111/cobi.12277.

Milner-Gulland, E.J. and Rowcliffe, J.M. (2007). *Conservation and Sustainable Use*. Oxford, UK: Oxford University Press.

Ministry of Forestry (1990). *Act of the Republic of Indonesia No. 5 of 1990. Concerning Conservation of Living Resources and Their Ecosystems*. Republic of Indonesia. Available at: http://extwprlegs1.fao.org/docs/pdf/ins3867.pdf.

Mishra, C., Allen, P., Mccarthy, T., *et al.* (2003). The role of incentive programs in conserving the snow leopard. *Conservation Biology*, **17**(6), 1512–20. DOI: 10.1111/j.1523-1739.2003.00092.x.

Mitani, J.C. (2009). Male chimpanzees form enduring and equitable social bonds. *Animal Behaviour*, **77**(3), 633–40. DOI: 10.1016/j.anbehav.2008.11.021.

Mitani, J.C., Watts, D.P. and Amsler, S.J. (2010). Lethal intergroup aggression leads to territorial expansion in wild chimpanzees. *Current Biology*, **20**(12), R507–R8. DOI: 10.1016/j.cub.2010.04.021.

Mitchell, M.W., Locatelli, S., Ghobrial, L., *et al.* (2015). The population genetics of wild chimpanzees in Cameroon and Nigeria suggests a positive role for selection in the evolution of chimpanzee subspecies. *BMC Evolutionary Biology*, **15**(1), 3. DOI: 10.1186/s12862-014-0276-y.

Mittermeier, R.A., Rylands, A.B. and Wilson, D.E., ed. (2013). *Handbook of the Mammals of the World. Volume 3: Primates*. Barcelona, Spain: Lynx Edicions.

Moon, K., Blackman, D.A., Adams, V.M., *et al.* (2019). Expanding the role of social science in conservation through an engagement with philosophy, methodology, and methods. *Methods in Ecology and Evolution*, **10**(3), 294–302. DOI: 10.1111/2041-210x.13126.

Moore, J.F., Mulindahabi, F., Masozera, M.K., *et al.* (2018). Are ranger patrols effective in reducing poaching-related threats within protected areas? *Journal of Applied Ecology*, **55**(1), 99–107. DOI: 10.1111/1365-2664.12965.

Moorhouse, T.P., Dahlsjö, C.A.L., Baker, S.E., D'Cruze, N.C. and Macdonald, D.W. (2015). The customer isn't always right – conservation and animal welfare implications of the increasing demand for wildlife tourism. *PLoS ONE*, **10**(10), e0138939. DOI: 10.1371/journal.pone.0138939.

Morgan, B., Adeleke, A., Bassey, T., *et al.* (2011). *Regional Action Plan for the Conservation of the Nigeria-Cameroon Chimpanzee (*Pan troglodytes ellioti*)*. New York, NY: International Union for Conservation of Nature Species (IUCN) Species Survival Commission (SSC), Primate Specialist Group, and Zoological Society of San Diego, CA. Available at: https://portals.iucn.org/library/sites/library/files/documents/2011-123-En.pdf.

Morgan, D. and Sanz, C. (2006). Chimpanzee feeding ecology and comparisons with sympatric gorillas in the Goualougo Triangle, Republic of Congo. In *Feeding Ecology in Apes and Other Primates: Ecological, Physiological and Behavioural Aspects*, ed. G. Hohmann, M. Robbins and C. Boesch. Cambridge Studies in Biological and Evolutionary Anthropology Volume 48. Cambridge, UK: Cambridge University Press, pp. 97–122.

Morgan, D. and Sanz, C. (2007). *Best Practice Guidelines for Reducing the Impact of Commercial Logging on Great Apes in Western Equatorial Africa*. Gland, Switzerland: International Union for Conservation of Nature (IUCN) Species Survival Commission (SSC), Primate Specialist Group. Available at: https://portals.iucn.org/library/node/9059.

Morgan, D.B., Sanz, C., Greer, D., *et al.* (2013). *Great Apes and FSC: Implementing 'Ape Friendly' Practices in Central Africa's Logging Concessions*. Gland, Switzerland: International Union for Conservation of Nature (IUCN). Available at: https://portals.iucn.org/library/sites/library/files/documents/SSC-OP-049.pdf.

Morris, M.C. (2013). Improved nonhuman animal welfare is related more to income equality than it is to income. *Journal of Applied Animal Welfare Science*, **16**(3), 272–93. DOI: 10.1080/10888705.2013.768921.

Morrow, K. (2009). United Kingdom. In *The Role of the Judiciary in Environmental Governance: Comparative Perspectives*, ed. L.J. Kotzé and A.R. Paterson. Alphen aan den Rijn, the Netherlands: Kluwer Law International, pp. 151–79.

Moss, C.J. (2017). *Affidavit of Cynthia J. Moss. May 6, 2017*. Available at: https://www.nonhumanrights.org/client-happy/. Accessed December, 2019.

Muehlenbein, M.P. and Ancrenaz, M. (2009). Minimizing pathogen transmission at primate ecotourism destinations: the need for input from travel medicine. *Journal of Travel Medicine*, **16**(4), 229–32. DOI: 10.1111/j.1708-8305.2009.00346.x.

Muhire, B. and Ellis, C. (2018). *Analyse de la chaine de valeur du commerce de la viande de brousse: Walikale, Lubutu, Kisangani et Kindu*. Technical report for the Jane Goodall Institute.

Muhire, B. and Ellis, C. (2019). *Analyse des facteurs de consommation de la viande de brousse: Acteurs et moteurs determinants—Province du Tshopo, Maniema et Nord Kivu (RDC)*. Technical report for the Jane Goodall Institute.

Mullins, A. (2010). Dodge makes chimp disappear in TV ad. *OpposingViews*, August 16, 2010. Available at: https://www.opposingviews.com/category/dodge-s-disappearing-ape.

Mulyoutami, E., Rismawan, R. and Joshi, L. (2009). Local knowledge and management of simpukng (forest gardens) among the Dayak people in East Kalimantan, Indonesia. *Forest Ecology and Management*, **257**(10), 2054–61. DOI: 10.1016/j.foreco.2009.01.042.

Munanura, I.E., Backman, K.F., Hallo, J.C. and Powell, R.B. (2016). Perceptions of tourism revenue sharing impacts on Volcanoes National Park, Rwanda: a Sustainable Livelihoods framework. *Journal of Sustainable Tourism*, **24**(12), 1709–26. DOI: 10.1080/09669582.2016.1145228.

Munn, J. (2006). Effects of injury on the locomotion of free-living chimpanzees in the Budongo Forest Reserve, Uganda. In *Primates of Western Uganda*, ed. N.E. Newton-Fisher, H. Notman, J.D. Paterson and V. Reynolds. New York: Springer, pp. 259–317.

Murai, M., Ruffler, H., Berlemont, A., *et al.* (2013). Priority areas for large mammal conservation in Equatorial Guinea. *PLoS ONE*, **8**(9), e75024. DOI: 10.1371/journal.pone.0075024.

Nagaoka, L., Rick, T. and Wolverton, S. (2018). The overkill model and its impact on environmental research. *Ecology and Evolution*, **8**(19), 9683–96. DOI: 10.1002/ece3.4393.

Naidoo, R. and Adamowicz, W.L. (2005). Biodiversity and nature-based tourism at forest reserves in Uganda. *Environment and Development Economics*, **10**(2), 159–78. DOI: 10.1017/S1355770X0400186X.

Naidoo, R., Weaver, L.C., Diggle, R.W., *et al.* (2016). Complementary benefits of tourism and hunting to communal conservancies in Namibia. *Conservation Biology*, **30**(3), 628–38. DOI: 10.1111/cobi.12643.

Nardoto, G.B., Murrieta, R.S.S., Prates, L.E.G., *et al.* (2011). Frozen chicken for wild fish: nutritional transition in the Brazilian Amazon region determined by carbon and nitrogen stable isotope ratios in fingernails. *American Journal of Human Biology*, **23**(5), 642–50. DOI: 10.1002/ajhb.21192.

Nasi, R., Brown, D., Wilkie, D., *et al.* (2008). *Conservation and Use of Wildlife-Based Resources: The Bushmeat Crisis*. Montreal, Canada, and Bogor, Indonesia: Secretariat of the Convention on Biological Diversity, and Center for International Forestry Research (CIFOR). Available at: https://www.cbd.int/doc/publications/cbd-ts-33-en.pdf.

Nasi, R., Taber, A. and van Vliet, N. (2011). Empty forests, empty stomachs? Bushmeat and livelihoods in the Congo and Amazon Basins. *International Forestry Review*, **13**(3), 355–68. Available at: http://www.cifor.org/publications/pdf_files/articles/ANasi1101.pdf.

Nater, A., Mattle-Greminger, M.P., Nurcahyo, A., *et al.* (2017). Morphometric, behavioral, and genomic evidence for a new orangutan species. *Current Biology*, **27**(22), 3487–98.e10. DOI: 10.1016/j.cub.2017.09.047.

National Assembly of Cameroon (1994). *Law 94/01 of 20 January 1994 to Lay Down Forestry, Wildlife and Fisheries Regulations*. Yaoundé, Cameroon: Republic of Cameroon. Available at: https://sherloc.unodc.org/res/cld/document/law-no--94-01-of-20-january-1994-to-lay-down-forestry--wildlife-and-fisheries-regulations-en_html/Law_No._94-01_on_Forestry_Wildlife_and_Fisheries_EN.pdf.

Nature (2008). News in Brief: Spain awards apes legal rights. *Nature*, **454**, 15.

Ndiaye, S. (2011). *Conservation du Chimpanzé au Sénégal. Etat des Connaissances et Réactualisation du Plan d'Actions*. Report for USAID/Wula Nafaa.

Neilson, E., Nijman, V. and Nekaris, K.A.I. (2013). Conservation assessments of arboreal mammals in difficult terrain: occupancy modeling of pileated gibbons (*Hylobates pileatus*). *International Journal of Primatology*, **34**(4), 823–35. DOI: 10.1007/s10764-013-9688-6.

Nekaris, B.K.A.-I., Campbell, N., Coggins, T.G., Rode, E.J. and Nijman, V. (2013). Tickled to death: analysing public perceptions of 'cute' videos of threatened species (slow lorises – *Nycticebus* spp.) on web 2.0 sites. *PLoS ONE*, **8**(7), e69215. DOI: 10.1371/journal.pone.0069215.

NEPAD (2013). *Agriculture in Africa: Transformation and Outlook*. Johannesburg, South Africa: NEPAD Agency for the African Union. Available at: http://nepad.org/caadp/publication/agriculture-africa-transformation-and-outlook.

NESREA (2007). *National Environmental Standards and Regulations Enforcement Agency (Establishment) Act, 2007, No. 25*. National Assembly of the Federal Republic of Nigeria. Available at: http://extwprlegs1.fao.org/docs/pdf/nig120569.pdf.

Neugebauer, E. (2018). *Evaluating conservation efforts to inform future management decisions for western chimpanzees*. MSc thesis. Frankfurt, Germany: University of Frankfurt, Institute for Ecology, Evolution & Diversity.

New Zealand Parliament (1999). *Animal Welfare Act 1999. Public Act 1999 No. 142. Reprint as at 8 September 2018*. Wellington, New Zealand: Parliamentary Counsel Office. Available at: http://www.legislation.govt.nz/act/public/1999/0142/latest/DLM49664.html.

New Zealand Parliament (2014). *Te Urewera Act 2014. Public Act 2014 No. 51. Reprint as at 1 October 2018*. Wellington, New Zealand: Parliamentary Counsel Office. Available at: www.legislation.govt.nz/act/public/2014/0051/latest/DLM6183601.html.

New Zealand Parliament (2017). *Te Awa Tupua (Whanganui River Claims Settlement) Act 2017. Public Act 2017 No. 7*. Wellington, New Zealand: Parliamentary Counsel Office. Available at: www.legislation.govt.nz/act/public/2017/0007/latest/whole.html.

Newman, A. (2009). Pet chimpanzee attacks woman in Connecticut. *New York Times*, February 17, 2009. Available at: https://www.nytimes.com/2009/02/17/world/americas/17iht-chimp.1.20241928.html.

Newmark, W.D. and Hough, J.L. (2000). Conserving wildlife in Africa: integrated conservation and development projects and beyond. *BioScience*, **50**(7), 585–92. DOI: 10.1641/0006-3568(2000)050[0585:Cwiaic]2.0.Co;2.

Newton, A.C. and Cantarello, E. (2014). *An Introduction to the Green Economy: Science, Systems and Sustainability*. Abingdon, UK: Routledge.

Nforngwa, E. (2017). Trade in skulls, body parts severely threatens Cameroon's great apes. *Mongabay*, January 19, 2017. Available at: https://news.mongabay.com/2017/01/trade-in-skulls-body-parts-severely-threatens-cameroons-great-apes/.

N'Goran, K.P., Ndomba, D.L. and Beukou, G.B. (2016). *Rapport de l'inventaire des grands et moyens mammifères dans le segment RCA du paysage trinational de la Sangha*. Unpublished report. Bayanga, Central African Republic: Bureau Régional du WWF pour l'Afrique.

Nguyen, J. (2018). How Instagram is changing advertising in Southeast Asia. *e27*, December 17, 2018. Available at: https://e27.co/how-instagram-is-changing-advertising-in-southeast-asia-20181217/.

Nguyen, M.H., Coudrat, C.N.Z., Roos, C., Rawson, B.M. and Duckworth, J.W. (2020). *Nomascus siki. The IUCN Red List of Threatened Species*. 2020: e.T39896A17968765. Gland, Switzerland: International Union for Conservation of Nature (IUCN). Available at: https://dx.doi.org/10.2305/IUCN.UK.2020-2.RLTS.T39896A17968765.en.

NhRP (n.d.-a). *Client, Happy (elephant): first elephant to pass mirror self-recognition test; held alone at the Bronx Zoo.* Coral Springs, FL: Nonhuman Rights Project (NhRP). Available at: https://www.nonhumanrights.org/client-happy/. Accessed September 9, 2019.

NhRP (n.d.-b). *Client, Kiko (chimpanzee): a former animal "actor," partially deaf from past physical abuse.* Coral Springs, FL: Nonhuman Rights Project (NhRP). Available at: https://www.nonhumanrights.org/client-kiko/. Accessed September 9, 2019.

NhRP (n.d.-c). *Client, Tommy (chimpanzee): the NhRP's first client.* Coral Springs, FL: Nonhuman Rights Project (NhRP). Available at: https://www.nonhumanrights.org/client-tommy/. Accessed September 9, 2019.

NhRP (n.d.-d). *Clients, Hercules and Leo (chimpanzees): two former research subjects and the first nonhuman animals to have a habeas corpus hearing.* Coral Springs, FL: Nonhuman Rights Project (NhRP). Available at: https://www.nonhumanrights.org/hercules-leo/. Accessed September 9, 2019.

NhRP (n.d.-e). *Litigation: confronting the core issue of nonhuman animals' legal thinghood.* Coral Springs, FL: Nonhuman Rights Project (NhRP). Available at: https://www.nonhumanrights.org/litigation-2/. Accessed September, 2020.

NhRP (Nonhuman Rights Project, Inc.) ex rel. Hercules and Leo v. Stanley. 16 NYS 3d 898 (NY Sup Ct) (2015). Available at: https://casetext.com/case/nonhuman-rights-project-inc-ex-rel-hercules-v-stanley.

NhRP (Nonhuman Rights Project, Inc.) ex rel. Kiko v. Boniello and Presti (4th Dept) (2014). Available at: https://www.nonhumanrights.org/content/uploads/4.-Petition-for-Mandamus-Kikos-Appeal.pdf.

NhRP (Nonhuman Rights Project, Inc.) ex rel. Kiko v. Presti. 124 AD 3d 1334 (4th Dept) (2015).

NhRP (Nonhuman Rights Project, Inc.) ex rel. Tommy v. Lavery. (2013). Available at: https://www.nonhumanrights.org/content/uploads/Petition-re-Tommy-Case-Fulton-Cty-NY.pdf.

NhRP (Nonhuman Rights Project, Inc.) ex rel. Tommy v. Lavery. 54 NYS 3d 392, 394, 396 (1st Dept) (2017).

NhRP (Nonhuman Rights Project, Inc.) ex rel. Tommy v. Lavery. 31 NY 3d 1054 (2018). Available at: http://courts.state.ny.us/Reporter/3dseries/2018/2018_03309.htm.

NhRP (Nonhuman Rights Project, Inc.) v. R.W. Commerford and Sons, Inc. 192 Conn App 36 (2019). Available at: https://static.lettersblogatory.com/wp-content/uploads/2019/09/192AP408.pdf.

Nielsen, H. and Spenceley, A. (2011). The success of tourism in Rwanda: gorillas and more. In *Yes Africa Can: Success Stories from a Dynamic Continent*, ed. P. Chuhan-Pole and M. Angwafo. Washington DC: The World Bank.

Nielsen, M.R., Meilby, H., Smith-Hall, C., Pouliot, M. and Treue, T. (2018). The importance of wild meat in the Global South. *Ecological Economics*, **146**, 696–705. DOI: 10.1016/j.ecolecon.2017.12.018.

Nielsen, M.R., Pouliot, M., Meilby, H., Smith-Hall, C. and Angelsen, A. (2017). Global patterns and determinants of the economic importance of bushmeat. *Biological Conservation*, **215**, 277–87. DOI: 10.1016/j.biocon.2017.08.036.

NIH (2018). *Council of Councils Working Group on Assessing the Safety of Relocating At-Risk Chimpanzees.* Bethesda, MD: National Institutes of Health (NIH). Available at: https://dpcpsi.nih.gov/sites/default/files/CoC_May_2018_WG_Report_508.pdf.

Nijman, V. (2001). Effect of behavioural changes due to habitat disturbance on density estimation of rain forest vertebrates, as illustrated by gibbons (Primates: Hylobatidae). In *The Balance between Biodiversity Conservation and Sustainable Use of Tropical Rain Forests*, ed. P.J.M. Hillegers and H.H. de Longh. Wageningen, the Netherlands: Tropenbos International, pp. 217–25.

Nijman, V. (2004). Conservation of the Javan gibbon *Hylobates moloch*: population estimates, local extinctions and conservation priorities. *Raffles Bulletin of Zoology*, **51**(1), 271–80.

Nijman, V. (2005a). *Hanging in the Balance: An Assessment of Trade in Orang-Utans and Gibbons on Kalimantan, Indonesia.* Petaling Jaya, Malaysia: TRAFFIC Southeast Asia. Available at: https://portals.iucn.org/library/sites/library/files/documents/Traf-092.pdf.

Nijman, V. (2005b). *In Full Swing: An Assessment of trade in Orang-utans and Gibbons on Java and Bali, Indonesia.* Petaling Jaya, Selangor, Malaysia: TRAFFIC Southeast Asia. Available at: https://www.traffic.org/site/assets/files/3984/in_full_swing.pdf.

Nijman, V. (2009). *An Assessment of Trade in Gibbons and Orang-Utans in Sumatra, Indonesia.* Petaling Jaya, Malaysia: TRAFFIC Southeast Asia. Available at: https://www.traffic.org/site/assets/files/3986/sumatran-gibbons-orangutans.pdf.

Nijman, V. (2010). An overview of international wildlife trade from Southeast Asia. *Biodiversity and Conservation*, **19**(4), 1101–14. DOI: 10.1007/s10531-009-9758-4.

Nijman, V. (2017a). North Africa as a source for European eel following the 2010 EU CITES eel trade ban. *Marine Policy*, **85**, 133–7. DOI: 10.1016/j.marpol.2017.06.036.

Nijman, V. (2017b). Orangutan trade, confiscations, and lack of prosecutions in Indonesia. *American Journal of Primatology*, **79**(11), 22652. DOI: 10.1002/ajp.22652.

Nijman, V. (2020). *Hylobates moloch. The IUCN Red List of Threatened Species*. 2020: e.T10550A17966495. Gland, Switzerland: International Union for Conservation of Nature (IUCN). Available at: https://dx.doi.org/10.2305/IUCN.UK.2020-2.RLTS.T10550A17966495.en.

Nijman, V., Cheyne, S. and Traeholt, C. (2020). *Hylobates funereus. The IUCN Red List of Threatened Species*. 2020: e.T39890A17990856. Gland, Switzerland: International Union for Conservation of Nature (IUCN). Available at: https://dx.doi.org/10.2305/IUCN.UK.2020-2.RLTS.T39890A17990856.en.

Nijman, V. and Geissmann, T. (2008). *Symphalangus syndactylus. The IUCN Red List of Threatened Species*. 2008: e.T39779A10266335. Gland, Switzerland: International Union for Conservation of Nature (IUCN).

Nijman, V., Geissmann, T., Traeholt, C., Roos, C. and Nowak, M.G. (2020). *Symphalangus syndactylus. The IUCN Red List of Threatened Species*. 2020: e.T39779A17967873. Gland, Switzerland: International Union for Conservation of Nature (IUCN). Available at: https://dx.doi.org/10.2305/IUCN.UK.2020-2.RLTS.T39779A17967873.en.

Nijman, V. and Healy, A. (2016). Present-day international primate trade in historical context. In *An Introduction to Primate Conservation*, ed. S. Wich and A. Marshall. Cambridge, UK: Cambridge University Press, pp. 129–42.

Nijman, V. and Menken, S.B. (2005). Assessment of census techniques for estimating density and biomass of gibbons (Primates: Hylobatidae). *Raffles Bulletin of Zoology*, **53**(1), 169–79.

Nijman, V., Nekaris, K.A.I., Donati, G., Bruford, M. and Fa, J. (2011). Primate conservation: measuring and mitigating trade in primates. *Endangered Species Research*, **13**(2), 159–61.

Nijman, V., Spaan, D., Rode-Margono, E.J., Wirdateti and Nekaris, K.A.I. (2017). Changes in the primate trade in Indonesian wildlife markets over a 25-year period: fewer apes and langurs, more macaques, and slow lorises. *American Journal of Primatology*, **79**(11), e22517. DOI: 10.1002/ajp.22517.

Nijman, V., Yang Martinez, C.F. and Shepherd, C.R. (2009). Saved from trade: donated and confiscated gibbons in zoos and rescue centres in Indonesia. *Endangered Species Research*, **9**, 151–7.

Nonhuman Rights (2018). Second petition filed on behalf of captive elephants in Connecticut. *Nonhuman Rights Blog*, June 11, 2018. Available at: https://www.nonhumanrights.org/blog/second-petition-connecticut /.

Nonhuman Rights (2020). Tuitt decision in Happy's elephant rights case: FAQ. *Nonhuman Rights Blog*, February 25, 2020. Available at: https://www.nonhumanrights.org/blog/tuitt-decision-in-happys-elephant-rights-case-faq /.

Normand, E. and Boesch, C. (2009). Sophisticated Euclidean maps in forest chimpanzees. *Animal Behaviour*, **77**(5), 1195–201. DOI: 10.1016/j.anbehav.2009.01.025.

Noutcha, M.A.E., Nzeako, S.O. and Okiwelu, S.N. (2017). Offtake numbers at 5-yearly intervals over a 10 year-period in the catchment area of a rural bushmeat market, Rivers State, Nigeria. *Journal of Scientific Research & Reports*, **13**(3), 1–5. DOI: 10.9734/JSRR/2017/31600.

Nowak, M.G., Rianti, P., Wich, S.A., Meijaard, E. and Fredriksson, G.M. (2017). *Pongo tapanuliensis. The IUCN Red List of Threatened Species*. 2017: e.T120588639A120588662. Gland, Switzerland: International Union for Conservation of Nature (IUCN). Available at: http://dx.doi.org/10.2305/IUCN.UK.2017-3.RLTS.T120588639A120588662.en.

Nudd, T. (2010). Under fire, Dodge makes a chimp disappear. *Adweek*, August 12, 2010. Available at: https://www.adweek.com/creativity/under-fire-dodge-makes-chimp-disappear-12368/.

Nuñez-Iturri, G. and Howe, H.F. (2007). Bushmeat and the fate of trees with seeds dispersed by large primates in a lowland rain forest in western Amazonia. *Biotropica*, **39**(3), 348–54. DOI: 10.1111/j.1744-7429.2007.00276.x.

Nuñez-Iturri, G., Olsson, O. and Howe, H.F. (2008). Hunting reduces recruitment of primate-dispersed trees in Amazonian Peru. *Biological Conservation*, **141**(6), 1536–46. DOI: 10.1016/j.biocon.2008.03.020.

NYCourts.gov (n.d.). *Appellate Courts: Appellate Divisions*. New York, NY: New York State Unified Court System. Available at: https://www.nycourts.gov/courts/appellatedivisions.shtml. Accessed September, 2019.

NYS Supreme Court (2013a). *Order to Show Cause and Writ of Habeas Corpus. Index No. 13-32098. December 5, 2013.* Suffolk County, New York State (NYS). Available at: https://www.nonhumanrights.org/content/uploads/Transcript-of-Suffolk-County-Decision-re-Hercules-Leo-12.5.13.pdf. Accessed December, 2019.

NYS Supreme Court (2013b). *Transcript in the Matter of a Proceeding under Article 10 of the CPLR for a Writ of Habeas Corpus, The Nonhuman Rights Project, Inc., ex rel. Kiko Petitioners, against Carmen Presti, Individually and as an Officer and Director of The Primate Sanctuary, Inc., Christie Presti, Individually and as an Officer and Director of The Primate Sanctuary, Inc., and the Primate Sanctuary, Inc., Respondents. Index No. 15L125. December 9, 2013.* Niagara County, New York State (NYS). Available at: https://www.nonhumanrights.org/content/uploads/Transcript_of_Oral_Argument-_Niagara_County_12-9-13.pdf. Accessed December, 2019.

NYS Supreme Court (2013c). *Transcript in the Matter of a Proceeding under Article 70 of the CPLR for a Writ of Habeas Corpus, Petitioners, against Index No. 02051 Patrick C. Lavery, Individually and as an Officer of Circle L Trailer Sales, Inc., Diane Lavery and Circle L Trailer Sales, Inc., Respondents. December 2, 2013.* Fulton County, New York State (NYS): Montgomery County Courthouse. Available at: https://www.nonhumanrights.org/content/uploads/Fulton-Cty-hearing-re.-Tommy-12-2-13.pdf. Accessed December, 2019.

NYS Supreme Court (2014). *Petitioners-Appellants' Memorandum of Law in Support of Motion for Reargument. Index No. 2014-01825. April 16, 2014.* Supreme Court of the State of New York (NYS) Appellate Division: Second Judicial Department. Available at: https://www.nonhumanrights.org/content/uploads/5.-Memorandum-of-law-in-support-of-motion-for-reargument-Hercules-Leo.pdf. Accessed December, 2019.

NYS Supreme Court (2018). *Order to Show Cause. Index No. 18-45164. November 16, 2018.* Orleans County, New York State (NYS). Available at: https://www.nonhumanrights.org/content/uploads/Order-to-Show-Cause-Happy.pdf. Accessed December, 2019.

O'Brien, T.G., Kinnaird, M.F., Nurcahyo, A., Iqbal, M. and Rusmanto, M. (2004). Abundance and distribution of sympatric gibbons in a threatened Sumatran rain forest. *International Journal of Primatology*, **25**(2), 267–84. DOI: 10.1023/B:IJOP.0000019152.83883.1c.

Oates, J.F., Abedi-Lartey, M., McGraw, W.S., Struhsaker, T.T. and Whitesides, G.H. (2000). Extinction of a west African red colobus monkey. *Conservation Biology*, **14**(5), 1526–32. DOI: 10.1046/j.1523-1739.2000.99230.x.

Oates, J.F., Bergl, R.A. and Linder, J.M. (2004). *Africa's Gulf of Guinea Forests: Biodiversity Patterns and Conservation Priorities.* Washington DC: Conservation International. Available at: http://www.bioone.org/doi/book/10.1896/1-881173-82-8.

Oates, J.F., Doumbe, O., Dunn, A., *et al.* (2016). *Pan troglodytes* ssp. *ellioti. The IUCN Red List of Threatened Species.* 2016: e.T40014A17990330. Gland, Switzerland: International Union for Conservation of Nature (IUCN). Available at: http://dx.doi.org/10.2305/IUCN.UK.2016-2.RLTS.T40014A17990330.en.

Oates, J.F., Koné, I., McGraw, S. and Osei, D. (2019). *Piliocolobus waldroni. The IUCN Red List of Threatened Species.* 2019: e.T18248A92650711. Gland, Switzerland: International Union for Conservation of Nature (IUCN). Available at: https://dx.doi.org/10.2305/IUCN.UK.2019-1.RLTS.T18248A92650711.en.

Oates, J.F., Sunderland-Groves, J., Bergl, R., *et al.* (2007). *Regional Action Plan for the Conservation of the Cross River Gorilla (Gorilla gorilla diehli).* Gland, Switzerland and Arlington, VA: International Union for Conservation of Nature (IUCN) Species Survival Commission (SSC), Primate Specialist Group, and Conservation International. Available at: https://portals.iucn.org/library/sites/library/files/documents/2007-012.pdf.

Oben, B.O., Molua, E.L. and Oben, P.M. (2015). Profitability of small-scale integrated fish-rice-poultry farms in Cameroon. *Journal of Agricultural Science*, **7**(11), 232–44. DOI: 10.5539/jas.v7n11p232.

OC&C Strategy Consultants (2017). *Taking a Serious Look at Fun: The Growth of the Leisure Industry in China.* London, UK: OC&C Strategy Consultants. Available at: https://www.occstrategy.com/media/1327/occ-taking-a-serious-look-at-fun.pdf.

Odum, E.P. (1970). Optimum population and environment: a Georgia microcosm. *Current History*, **58**, 355–9.

OECD (2009). *Determination and Application of Administrative Fines for Environmental Offences: Guidance for Environmental Enforcement Authorities in EECCA Countries.* Paris, France: Organisation for Economic Co-operation and Development (OECD). Available at: https://www.oecd.org/env/outreach/42356640.pdf.

OECD (2012). *Illegal Trade in Environmentally Sensitive Goods. OECD Trade Policy Studies.* Paris, France: Organisation for Economic Co-operation and Development (OECD) Publishing. Available at: http://dx.doi.org/10.1787/9789264174238-en.

Ogra, M.V. (2012). Gender mainstreaming in community-oriented wildlife conservation: experiences from non-governmental conservation organizations in India. *Society & Natural Resources*, **25**(12), 1258–76. DOI: 10.1080/08941920.2012.677941.

Ohanesian, A. (2018). Kenya's Sweetwaters sanctuary: chimpanzees without borders. *Al Jazeera*, May 9, 2018. Available at: https://www.aljazeera.com/indepth/inpictures/kenya-sweetwaters-sanctuary-chimpanzees-borders-180508100626979.html.

Ohashi, G. and Matsuzawa, T. (2011). Deactivation of snares by wild chimpanzees. *Primates*, **52**(1), 1–5.

OIE (2019). *Terrestrial Animal Health Code*, 28th edn. Paris, France: World Organisation for Animal Health (OIE). Available at: http://www.oie.int/en/standard-setting/terrestrial-code/.

OIE (n.d.). *Regional Animal Welfare Strategy (RAWS) for Asia, the Far East and Oceania*. Paris, France: World Organisation for Animal Health (OIE). Available at: https://rr-asia.oie.int/en/projects/animal-welfare/. Accessed December, 2019.

Okiwelu, S., Ewurum, N. and Noutcha, A.E. (2009). Wildlife harvesting and bushmeat trade in Rivers State, Nigeria. I. Species composition, seasonal abundance and cost. *Scientia Africana*, **8**(2), 1–8.

Ol Pejeta Conservancy (n.d.). *Sweetwaters Chimpanzee Sanctuary*. Nanyuki, Kenya: Ol Pejeta Conservancy. Available at: https://www.olpejetaconservancy.org/wildlife/chimpanzees/sweetwaters-chimpanzee-sanctuary/. Accessed December 31, 2018.

Olupot, W., McNeilage, A.J. and Plumptre, A.J. (2009). *An Analysis of Socioeconomics of Bushmeat Hunting at Major Hunting Sites in Uganda*. Working Paper No. 38. Bronx, NY: Wildlife Conservation Society (WCS).

Omar, S. and Rathakrishnan, M. (2016). *Pantang larang makanan masyarakat Melanau Sarawak*. Presented at the International Conference on Social Sciences and Humanities (PASAK 2016), 20–21 April 2016, KUIS Convention Center, International Islamic University College Selangor (KUIS).

Ondoua Ondoua, G., Beodo Moundjim, E., Mambo Marindo, J.C., *et al.* (2017). *An Assessment of Poaching and Wildlife Trafficking in the Garamba-Bili-Chinko Transboundary Landscape*. Cambridge, UK: TRAFFIC. Available at: https://www.traffic.org/site/assets/files/1591/garamba-bili-chinko-xxs.pdf.

OpenStreetMap (n.d.). *OpenStreetMap*. Available at: https://www.openstreetmap.org/#map=5/54.910/-3.432. Accessed September, 2020.

Osterberg, P., Samphanthamit, P., Maprang, O., Punnadee, S. and Brockelman, W.Y. (2015). Gibbon (*Hylobates lar*) reintroduction success in Phuket, Thailand, and its conservation benefits. *American Journal of Primatology*, **77**(5), 492–501. DOI: 10.1002/ajp.22367.

Östlund, R., director (2017). *The Square*. Plattform Produktion. Available at: https://www.imdb.com/title/tt4995790/.

Osvath, M. (2013). *Affidavit of Mathias Osvath In the Matter of a Proceeding under Article 70 of the CPLR for a Writ of Habeas Corpus. The Nonhuman Rights Project, Inc., on behalf of Tommy, Petitioners, v. Patrick C. Lavery, individually and as an officer of Circle L Trailer Sales, Inc., Diane Lavery, and Circle L Trailer Sales, Inc. November 19, 2013*. Available at: https://www.nonhumanrights.org/content/uploads/Ex-11-Osvath-Affidavit-Tommy-Case.pdf. Accessed December, 2019.

Palmer, A. (2018). *Saving and sacrificing: ethical questions in orangutan rehabilitation*. PhD thesis. London, UK: University College London.

Palombit, R.A. (1992). *Pair bonds and monogamy in wild siamang (*Hylobates syndactylus*) and white-handed gibbon (*Hylobates lar*) in northern Sumatra*. PhD thesis. Davis, CA: University of California Davis.

Palombit, R.A. (1994). Dynamic pair bonds in Hylobatids: implications regarding monogamous social systems. *Behaviour*, **128**(1), 65–101. DOI: 10.1163/156853994X00055.

Palombit, R.A. (1997). Inter- and intraspecific variation in the diets of sympatric siamang (*Hylobates syndactylus*) and Lar gibbons (*Hylobates lar*). *Folia Primatologica*, **68**(6), 321–37. DOI: 10.1159/000157260.

Parliament of Uganda (1996). *Uganda Wildlife Act, Chapter 200*. Uganda Legal Information Institute. Available at: https://ulii.org/ug/legislation/consolidated-act/200.

Parliament of Uganda (2019). *The Uganda Wildlife Act, 2019*. Available at: https://ulii.org/system/files/legislation/act/2019/2019/Uganda-Wildlife-Act-2019.pdf.

PASA (2018). *Pan African Sanctuary Alliance Annual Report 2018*. Portland, OR: Pan African Sanctuary Alliance (PASA). Available at: https://pasa.org/wp-content/uploads/2019/04/PASA_2018_Annual_Report.pdf.

Pasley, J. (2017). Two siamang gibbons escape from Auckland Zoo enclosure. *Stuff*, December 13, 2017. Available at: https://www.stuff.co.nz/auckland/local-news/central-leader/99771325/two-siamang-gibbons-escape-from-enclosure-in-auckland-zoo.

Payne, J. (1988). *Orang-utan Conservation in Sabah. Report 3759.* Kuala Lumpur, Malaysia: World Wide Fund for Nature (WWF), Malaysia International.

PEGAS (2015). Former head of CITES in Guinea arrested. *PEGAS News*, August 24, 2015. Nanyuki, Kenya: Project to End Great Ape Slavery (PEGAS). Available at: https://freetheapes.org/2015/08/24/former-head-of-cites-in-guinea-arrested/.

PEGAS (2017). *Presidential pardon: former head of Guinea CITES office pardoned before his case was finalized. PEGAS News,* January 29, 2017. Nanyuki, Kenya: Project to End Great Ape Slavery (PEGAS). Available at: https://freetheapes.org/2017/01/29/presidential-pardon-former-head-of-guinea-cites-office-pardoned-before-his-case-was-finalized/.

PEGAS (n.d.). *Reply to 'Great apes exported from Guinea to China from 2009 to 2011' SC65 Doc. 34.1 Annex.* Nanyuki, Kenya: Project to End Great Ape Slavery (PEGAS). Available at: http://danstiles.org/publications/wildlife/39.%20PEGAS%20reply.pdf. Accessed September, 2020.

Peh, K.S.-H. and Drori, O. (2010). Fighting corruption to save the environment: Cameroon's experience. *Ambio*, **39**(4), 336–9. DOI: 10.1007/s13280-010-0053-0.

Pemunta, N.V. (2019). Fortress conservation, wildlife legislation and the Baka Pygmies of southeast Cameroon. *GeoJournal*, **84**(4), 1035–55. DOI: 10.1007/s10708-018-9906-z.

Pengfei, F., Nguyen, M.H., Phiaphalath, P., *et al.* (2020). *Nomascus concolor. The IUCN Red List of Threatened Species.* 2020: e.T39775A17968556. Gland, Switzerland: International Union for Conservation of Nature (IUCN). Available at: https://dx.doi.org/10.2305/IUCN.UK.2020-2.RLTS.T39775A17968556.en.

People ex rel. NhRP (Nonhuman Rights Project, Inc.) v. *Lavery.* 124 AD 3d 148 (3rd Dept) (2014). Available at: https://www.leagle.com/decision/innyco20141204335.

People v. *Graves, 78 NYS 3d 613* (4th Dept) (2018). Available at: https://casetext.com/case/people-v-graves-297?resultsNav=false.Peres, C.A. and Palacios, E. (2007). Basin-wide effects of game harvest on vertebrate population densities in Amazonian forests: implications for animal-mediated seed dispersal. *Biotropica*, **39**(3), 304–15. DOI: 10.1111/j.1744-7429.2007.00272.x.

Peres, C.A. and Palacios, E. (2007). Basin-wide effects of game harvest on vertebrate population densities in Amazonian forests: implications for animal-mediated seed dispersal. *Biotropica*, **39**(3), 304–15. DOI: 10.1111/j.1744-7429.2007.00272.x.

Perez, P.L. (2018). *Green Entanglements: Nature Conservation and Indigenous Peoples' Rights in Indonesia and the Philippines.* Quezon City: University of the Philippines Press.

PETA (n.d.). *PETA's milestones for animals.* Norfolk, VA: People for the Ethical Treatment of Animals (PETA). Available at: https://www.peta.org/about-peta/milestones/. Accessed January, 2020.

Petre, C.-A., Tagg, N., Haurez, B., *et al.* (2013). Role of the western lowland gorilla (*Gorilla gorilla gorilla*) in seed dispersal in tropical forests and implications of its decline. *Biotechnology, Agronomy, Society and Environment*, **17**(3), 517–26.

Petrovan, S.O., Junker, J., Wordley, C.F.R., *et al.* (2018). Evidence-based synopsis of interventions, a new tool in primate conservation and research. *International Journal of Primatology*, **39**(1), 1–4. DOI: 10.1007/s10764-018-0017-y.

Phassaraudomsak, M. and Krishnasamy, K. (2018). *Trading Faces: A Rapid Assessment on the Use of Facebook to Trade in Wildlife in Thailand.* Petaling Jaya, Malaysia: TRAFFIC. Available at: https://www.traffic.org/site/assets/files/11073/trading_faces_thailand_2019.pdf.

Phelps, J., Webb, E.L., Bickford, D., Nijman, V. and Sodhi, N.S. (2010). Boosting CITES. *Science*, **330**(6012), 1752–3. DOI: 10.1126/science.1195558.

Phoonjampa, R. and Brockelman, W. (2008). Survey of pileated gibbon *Hylobates pileatus* in Thailand: populations threatened by hunting and habitat degradation. *Oryx*, **42**(4), 600–6. DOI: 10.1017/S0030605308000306.

Plumptre, A.J. (2000). Monitoring mammal populations with line transect techniques in African forests. *Journal of Applied Ecology*, **37**(2), 356–68. DOI: 10.1046/j.1365-2664.2000.00499.x.

Plumptre, A.J. and Cox, D. (2006). Counting primates for conservation: primate surveys in Uganda. *Primates*, **47**(1), 65–73. DOI: 10.1007/s10329-005-0146-8.

Plumptre, A., Hart, J.A., Hicks, T.C., *et al.* (2016a). *Pan troglodytes* ssp. *schweinfurthii* (errata version published in 2016). *The IUCN Red List of Threatened Species.* 2016: e.T15937A102329417. Gland, Switzerland: International Union for Conservation of Nature (IUCN). Available at: http://dx.doi.org/10.2305/IUCN.UK.2016-2.RLTS.T15937A17990187.en.

Plumptre, A., Nixon, S., Caillaud, D., *et al.* (2016b). *Gorilla beringei* ssp. *graueri* (errata version published in 2016). *The IUCN Red List of Threatened Species.* 2016: e.T39995A102328430. Gland, Switzerland: International Union for Conservation of Nature (IUCN). Available at: http://dx.doi.org/10.2305/IUCN.UK.2016-2.RLTS.T39995A17989838.en.

Plumptre, A.J., Nixon, S., Critchlow, R., *et al.* (2015). *Status of Grauer's Gorilla and Chimpanzees in Eastern Democratic Republic of Congo: Historical and Current Distribution and Abundance.* New York, NY: Wildlife Conservation Society (WCS), Fauna & Flora International (FFI) and Institut Congolais pour la Conservation de la Nature (ICCN). Available at: http://fscdn.wcs.org/2016/04/04/inbumeq9_Status_of_Grauers_gorilla_and_eastern_chimpanzee_Report_Final.pdf.

Plumptre, A.J., Nixon, S., Kujirakwinja, D.K., *et al.* (2016c). Catastrophic decline of world's largest primate: 80% loss of Grauer's gorilla (*Gorilla beringei graueri*) population justifies critically endangered status. *PLoS ONE*, **11**(10), e0162697. DOI: 10.1371/journal.pone.0162697.

Plumptre, A.J. and Reynolds, V. (1997). Nesting behavior of chimpanzees: implications for censuses. *International Journal of Primatology*, **18**, 475–85.

Plumptre, A., Robbins, M.M. and Williamson, E.A. (2019). *Gorilla beringei. The IUCN Red List of Threatened Species.* 2019: e.T39994A115576640. Gland, Switzerland: International Union for Conservation of Nature (IUCN). Available at: http://dx.doi.org/10.2305/IUCN.UK.2019-1.RLTS.T39994A115576640.en.

Plumptre, A.J., Rose, R., Nangendo, G., *et al.* (2010). *Eastern Chimpanzee (*Pan troglodytes schweinfurthii*): Status Survey and Conservation Action Plan 2010–2020.* Gland, Switzerland: International Union for Conservation of Nature (IUCN). Available at: https://portals.iucn.org/library/sites/library/files/documents/2010-023.pdf.

Plumptre, A.J., Sterling, E.J. and Buckland, S.T. (2013). Primate census and survey techniques. In *Primate Ecology and Conservation: A Handbook of Techniques*, ed. E.J. Sterling, N. Bynum and M.E. Blair. Oxford, UK: Oxford University Press, pp. 10–26.

Pollack, J. (2016). Goodbye, Mr. Chimps: a look at monkeys past in Super Bowl ads. *Ad Age*, January 29, 2016. Available at: https://adage.com/article/special-report-super-bowl/video-compilation-super-bowl-ads-monkeys/302367.

Poole, J. (2016). *Affidavit of Joyce Poole. December 2, 2016.* Available at: https://www.nonhumanrights.org/client-happy/. Accessed December, 2019.

Poole, J. (2018). *Supplemental Affidavit of Joyce Poole. October 1, 2018.* Available at: https://www.nonhumanrights.org/client-happy/. Accessed December, 2019.

Pooley, J.A. and O'Connor, M. (2000). Environmental education and attitudes: emotions and beliefs are what is needed. *Environment and Behavior*, **32**(5), 711–23. DOI: 10.1177/0013916500325007.

Poulsen, J.R., Clark, C.J. and Bolker, B.M. (2011). Decoupling the effects of logging and hunting on an Afrotropical animal community. *Ecological Applications*, **21**(5), 1819–36.

Pramatha Nath Mullick v. *Pradyumna Kumar Mullick.* 52 Indian Appeals 245, 264 (1925). Available at: https://indiankanoon.org/doc/290902/.

Prescott, J., Rapley, W.A. and Joseph, M.M. (1993–1994). Status and conservation of chimpanzee and gorilla in Cameroon. *Primate Conservation*, **14–15**, 7–12. Available at: http://www.primate-sg.org/primate_conservation/.

Pretty, J. and Smith, D. (2004). Social capital in biodiversity conservation and management. *Conservation Biology*, **18**(3), 631–8. DOI: 10.1111/j.1523-1739.2004.00126.x.

Primate Info Net (2005). *Chimpanzee Collaboratory.* Madison, WI: University of Wisconsin-Madison. Available at: http://pin.primate.wisc.edu/idp/idp/entry/547. Accessed January, 2020.

PRISM (n.d.). *Toolkit for Evaluating the Outcomes and Impacts of Small/Medium-Sized Conservation Projects.* PRISM. Available at: https://conservationevaluation.org. Accessed July, 2020.

Project Implicit (n.d.). *Project Implicit: social attitudes.* Project Implicit. Available at: https://implicit.harvard.edu/implicit/. Accessed December, 2019.

Projet Primates (n.d.-a). *CCC Chimps: chimps of the Chimpanzee Conservation Center.* Projet Primates. Available at: https://www.projetprimates.com/ccc-chimps/. Accessed December 1, 2018.

Projet Primates (n.d.-b). *Chimpanzee Conservation Center.* Projet Primates. Available at: https://www.projetprimates.com/chimpanzee-conservation-center. Accessed October, 2019.

Protected Planet (n.d.-a). *Kimbi-Fungom in Cameroon.* Cambridge, UK: UN Environment Programme World Conservation Monitoring Centre (UNEP-WCMC) and International Union for Conservation of Nature (IUCN). Available at: https://www.protectedplanet.net/kimbi-fungom-national-park. Accessed October, 2019.

Protected Planet (n.d.-b). *Rwenzori Mountains in Uganda.* Cambridge, UK: UN Environment Programme World Conservation Monitoring Centre (UNEP-WCMC) and International Union for Conservation of Nature (IUCN). Available at: https://www.protectedplanet.net/rwenzori-mountains-national-park. Accessed October, 2019.

Protected Planet (n.d.-c). *Tofala in Cameroon.* Cambridge, UK: UN Environment Programme World Conservation Monitoring Centre (UNEP-WCMC) and International Union for Conservation of Nature (IUCN). Available at: https://www.protectedplanet.net/555622120. Accessed October, 2019.

Pruetz, J.D. and Herzog, N.M. (2017). Savanna chimpanzees at Fongoli, Senegal, navigate a fire landscape. *Current Anthropology*, **58**(S16), S337–S50. DOI: 10.1086/692112.

Pruetz, J.D., Ontl, K.B., Cleaveland, E., *et al.* (2017). Intragroup lethal aggression in west African chimpanzees (*Pan troglodytes verus*): inferred killing of a former alpha male at Fongoli, Senegal. *International Journal of Primatology*, **38**(1), 31–57. DOI: 10.1007/s10764-016-9942-9.

Puri, R.K. (2005). *Deadly Dances in the Bornean Rainforest: Hunting Knowledge of the Penan Benalui.* Royal Netherlands Institute of Southeast Asian and Caribbean Studies Monograph Series. Leiden, the Netherlands: KITLV Press.

Pyhälä, A., Osuna Orozco, A. and Counsell, S. (2016). *Protected Areas on the Congo Basin: Failing Both People and Biodiversity?* London, UK: Rainforest Foundation-UK. Available at: https://www.rainforestfoundationuk.org/media.ashx/protected-areas-in-the-congo-basin-failing-both-people-and-diversity-english.pdf.

Quinten, M.C., Stirling, F., Schwarze, S., Dinata, Y. and Hodges, K. (2014). Knowledge, attitudes and practices of local people on Siberut Island (West-Sumatra, Indonesia) towards primate hunting and conservation. *Journal of Threatened Taxa*, **6**(11), 6389–98. DOI: 10.11609/JoTT.o3963.6389-98.

Ramutsindela, M. (2016). Wildlife crime and state security in south(ern) Africa: an overview of developments. *Politikon*, **43**(2), 159–71. DOI: 10.1080/02589346.2016.1201376.

Rawson, B.M., Hoang, M.D., Roos, C., Van, N.T. and Nguyen, M.H. (2020a). *Nomascus gabriellae. The IUCN Red List of Threatened Species.* 2020: e.T128073282A17968950. Gland, Switzerland: International Union for Conservation of Nature (IUCN). Available at: https://dx.doi.org/10.2305/IUCN.UK.2020-2.RLTS.T128073282A17968950.en.

Rawson, B.M., Insua-Cao, P., Nguyen, M.H., *et al.* (2011). *The Conservation Status of Gibbons in Vietnam.* Hanoi, Viet Nam: Fauna & Flora International (FFI) and Conservation International. Available at: http://www.gibbons.de/main/books/2011gibbons-vietnam.pdf.

Rawson, B.M., Nguyen, M.H., Coudrat, C.N.Z., *et al.* (2020b). *Nomascus leucogenys. The IUCN Red List of Threatened Species.* 2020: e.T39895A17969139. Gland, Switzerland: International Union for Conservation of Nature (IUCN). Available at: https://dx.doi.org/10.2305/IUCN.UK.2020-2.RLTS.T39895A17969139.en.

Rawson, B.M., Roos, C., Nguyen, M.H., *et al.* (2020c). *Nomascus nasutus. The IUCN Red List of Threatened Species.* 2020: e.T41642A17969578. Gland, Switzerland: International Union for Conservation of Nature (IUCN). Available at: https://dx.doi.org/10.2305/IUCN.UK.2020-2.RLTS.T41642A17969578.en.

Ray, P.C., Kumar, A., Devi, A., *et al.* (2015). Habitat characteristics and their effects on the density of groups of western hoolock gibbon (*Hoolock hoolock*) in Namdapha National Park, Arunachal Pradesh, India. *International Journal of Primatology*, **36**(3), 445–59. DOI: 10.1007/s10764-015-9834-4.

Raymond, C.M., Fazey, I., Reed, M.S., *et al.* (2010). Integrating local and scientific knowledge for environmental management. *Journal of Environmental Management*, **91**(8), 1766–77. DOI: 10.1016/j.jenvman.2010.03.023.

Reichard, U. (1995). Extra-pair copulations in a monogamous gibbon (*Hylobates lar*). *Ethology*, **100**(2), 99–112. DOI: 10.1111/j.1439-0310.1995.tb00319.x.

Reinartz, G., Ingmanson, E.J. and Vervaecke, H. (2013). *Pan paniscus gracile* chimpanzee (bonobo, pygmy chimpanzee). In *Mammals of Africa. Volume II: Primates*, ed. T. Butynski, J. Kingdon and J. Kalina. London, UK: Bloomsbury Publishing, pp. 64–9.

Republic of Indonesia (2009). *Environmental Protection and Management Law no. 32/ 2009, dated October 3, 2009*. Republic of Indonesia. Available at: http://extwprlegs1.fao.org/docs/pdf/ins97643.pdf.

Republic of Indonesia (2018). *Regulation of the Ministry of Environment and Forestry Number P.20/MENLHK/ SETJEN/KUM.1/6/2018 on the Drawn up List of Protected Plant and Animal Species*. Republic of Indonesia.

Reuter, K.E., Randell, H., Wills, A.R. and Sewall, B.J. (2016). The consumption of wild meat in Madagascar: drivers, popularity and food security. *Environmental Conservation*, **43**(3), 273–83. DOI: 10.1017/S0376892916000059.

Reuters (2006). Kick boxing orangutans get to go home. *NBC News World Environment*, November 21, 2006.

Reynolds, V. (2005). *The Chimpanzees of the Budongo Forest: Ecology, Behaviour and Conservation*. Oxford, UK: Oxford University Press.

Reynolds, V. and Reynolds, F. (1965). Chimpanzees of Budongo Forest. In *Primate Behaviour: Field Studies of Monkeys and Apes*, ed. I. Devore. New York, NY: Holt, Rinehart & Winston, pp. 368–424.

Ribeiro, J.W., Sugai, L.S.M. and Campos-Cerqueira, M. (2017). Passive acoustic monitoring as a complementary strategy to assess biodiversity in the Brazilian Amazonia. *Biodiversity and Conservation*, **26**(12), 2999–3002. DOI: 10.1007/s10531-017-1390-0.

Richard, L., Mouinga-Ondeme, A., Betsem, E., *et al.* (2016). Zoonotic transmission of two new strains of human T-lymphotropic virus type 4 in hunters bitten by a gorilla in Central Africa. *Clinical Infectious Diseases*, **63**(6), 800–3. DOI: 10.1093/cid/ciw389.

Rijksen, H.D. (1978). *A field study on Sumatran orangutans (*Pongo pygmaeus abelii *Lesson 1827). Ecology, behaviour and conservation*. Doctoral thesis. Wageningen, The Netherlands: Nature Conservation Department, Agricultural University Wageningen.

Rijksen, H.D. and Meijaard, E. (1999). *Our Vanishing Relative? The Status of Wild Orangutans at the Close of the Twentieth Century*. Dordrecht, the Netherlands: Kluwer Academic.

Ripple, W.J., Abernethy, K., Betts, M.G., *et al.* (2016). Bushmeat hunting and extinction risk to the world's mammals. *Royal Society Open Science*, **3**(10), 160498. DOI: 10.1098/rsos.160498.

Rivers v. Katz. 67 NY 2d 485 (1986). Available at: https://www.leagle.com/decision/198655267ny2d4851500.

Robbins, A.M., Gray, M., Basabose, A., *et al.* (2013). Impact of male infanticide on the social structure of mountain gorillas. *PLoS ONE*, **8**(11), 1–10. DOI: 10.1371/journal.pone.0078256.

Robbins, A.M., Stoinski, T., Fawcett, K. and Robbins, M.M. (2011a). Lifetime reproductive success of female mountain gorillas. *American Journal of Physical Anthropology*, **146**(4), 582–93. DOI: 10.1002/ajpa.21605.

Robbins, M.M. (2011). Gorillas: diversity in ecology and behavior. In *Primates in Perspective*, ed. C.J. Campbell, A. Fuentes, K.C. MacKinnon, S. Bearder and R.M. Stumpf. Oxford, UK: Oxford University Press, pp. 326–39.

Robbins, M.M., Bernejo, M., Cipoletta, C., *et al.* (2004). Social structure and life-history patterns in western gorillas (*Gorilla gorilla gorilla*). *American Journal of Primatology*, **64**, 145–59.

Robbins, M.M., Gray, M., Fawcett, K.A., *et al.* (2011b). Extreme conservation leads to recovery of the Virunga mountain gorillas. *PLoS ONE*, **6**, 1–10. DOI: 10.1371/journal.pone.0019788.

Robbins, M.M., Gray, M., Kagoda, E. and Robbins, A.M. (2009). Population dynamics of the Bwindi mountain gorillas. *Biological Conservation*, **142**(12), 2886–95. DOI: 10.1016/j.biocon.2009.07.010.

Robbins, M.M. and Robbins, A.M. (2018). Variation in the social organization of gorillas: life history and socioecological perspectives. *Evolutionary Anthropology: Issues, News, and Reviews*, **27**, 218–33. DOI: 10.1002/evan.21721.

Robbins, M.M. and Sawyer, S. (2007). Intergroup encounters in mountain gorillas of Bwindi Impenetrable National Park, Uganda. *Behaviour*, **144**(12), 1497–519. DOI: 10.1163/156853907782512146.

Robertson, S. (2017). Why law enforcement is essential to stopping illegal wildlife trade. *World Bank Blogs*, July 27, 2017. Available at: https://blogs.worldbank.org/voices/why-law-enforcement-essential-stopping-illegal-wildlife-trade.

Robinson, B.E., Masuda, Y.J., Kelly, A., *et al.* (2018). Incorporating land tenure security into conservation. *Conservation Letters*, **11**(2), e12383. DOI: 10.1111/conl.12383.

Robinson, J.G. and Bennett, E.L. (2004). Having your wildlife and eating it too: an analysis of hunting sustainability across tropical ecosystems. *Animal Conservation*, **7**(4), 397–408. DOI: 10.1017/s1367943004001532.

Robinson, J.G., Redford, K.H. and Bennett, E.L. (1999). Wildlife harvest in logged tropical forests. *Science*, **284**(5414), 595–6. DOI: 10.1126/science.284.5414.595.

Robson, S.L. and Wood, B. (2008). Hominin life history: reconstruction and evolution. *Journal of Anatomy*, **212**(4), 394–425. DOI: 10.1111/j.1469-7580.2008.00867.x.

Roderick, K. (1990). Spectacle, complete with apes, in Vegas courtroom: animal rights: Stardust headliner Bobby Berosini is suing after tapes showed him hitting his orangutans. *Los Angeles Times*, August 8, 1990. Available at: https://www.latimes.com/archives/la-xpm-1990-08-08-mn-161-story.html.

Rodriguez, M., Pascual, M., Wingard, J., *et al.* (2019). *Legal Protection of Great Apes & Gibbons: Country Profiles for 17 Range Countries.* Missoula, MT: Legal Atlas. Available at: https://www.legal-atlas.com/uploads/2/6/8/4/26849604/apes_legal_protection__feb_2019_.pdf.

Roe, D. and Booker, F. (2019a). Engaging local communities in tackling illegal wildlife trade: a synthesis of approaches and lessons for best practice. *Conservation Science and Practice*, **1**(5), e26. DOI: 10.1111/csp2.26.

Roe, D. and Booker, F. (2019b). *More Than Words: Are Commitments to Tackle Illegal Wildlife Trade Being Met?* Godalming, UK: World Wide Fund for Nature (WWF)-UK. Available at: https://www.wwf.org.uk/sites/default/files/2019-08/WWF_IWT_Report_v8.pdf.

Roe, D., Booker, F., Day, M., *et al.* (2015). Are alternative livelihood projects effective at reducing local threats to specified elements of biodiversity and/or improving or maintaining the conservation status of those elements? *Environmental Evidence*, **4**(1), 22. DOI: 10.1186/s13750-015-0048-1.

Rogers, M.E., Abernethy, K., Bermejo, M., *et al.* (2004). Western gorilla diet: a synthesis from six sites. *American Journal of Primatology*, **64**(2), 173–92. DOI: 10.1002/ajp.20071.

Rogers, M.E., Voysey, B.C., McDonald, K.E., Parnell, R.J. and Tutin, C.E.G. (1998). Lowland gorillas and seed dispersal: the importance of nest sites. *American Journal of Primatology*, **45**(1), 45–68. DOI: 10.1002/(sici)1098-2345(1998)45:1<45::Aid-ajp5>3.0.Co;2-w.

Román, V. (2015). Argentina grants an orangutan human-like rights. *Scientific American*, January 9, 2015. Available at: https://www.scientificamerican.com/article/argentina-grants-an-orangutan-human-like-rights/.

Romer v. Evans. 517 US 620 (1996). Available at: https://web.stanford.edu/~mrosenfe/Romer_v_Evans_SC_1996.pdf.

Ron, T. and Refisch, J. (2013). *Towards a Transboundary Protected Area Complex in the Mayombe Forest Ecosystems: Strategic Plan.* United Nations Environment Programme (UNEP), Great Apes Survival Partnership (GRASP) and International Union for Conservation of Nature (IUCN). Available at: https://portals.iucn.org/library/sites/library/files/documents/2013-029-En.pdf.

Rosen, G.E. and Smith, K.F. (2010). Summarizing the evidence on the international trade in illegal wildlife. *EcoHealth*, **7**(1), 24–32. DOI: 10.1007/s10393-010-0317-y.

Rosenbaum, K. (2007). *Legislative Drafting Guide: A Practitioner's View, A Resource for People Working on International Technical Assistance Projects.* FAO Legal Papers Online 64. Rome, Italy: Food and Agriculture Organization (FAO). Available at: http://www.fao.org/3/a-bb097e.pdf.

Rosenbaum, S., Vecellio, V. and Stoinski, T. (2016). Observations of severe and lethal coalitionary attacks in wild mountain gorillas. *Scientific Reports*, **6**(1), 37018. DOI: 10.1038/srep37018.

Ross, S.R., Lukas, K.E., Lonsdorf, E.V., *et al.* (2008). Inappropriate use and portrayal of chimpanzees. *Science*, **319**(5869), 1487. DOI: 10.1126/science.1154490.

Ross, S.R., Vreeman, V.M. and Lonsdorf, E.V. (2011). Specific image characteristics influence attitudes about chimpanzee conservation and use as pets. *PLoS ONE*, **6**(7), e22050. DOI: 10.1371/journal.pone.0022050.

Rousseau, J. (1990). *Central Borneo: Ethnic Identity and Social Life in a Stratified Society.* Oxford, UK: Clarendon Press.

Rovero, F., Mtui, A., Kitegile, A., *et al.* (2015). Primates decline rapidly in unprotected forests: evidence from a monitoring program with data constraints. *PLoS ONE*, **10**(2), e0118330. DOI: 10.1371/journal.pone.0118330.

Rovero, F., Mtui, A.S., Kitegile, A.S. and Nielsen, M.R. (2012). Hunting or habitat degradation? Decline of primate populations in Udzungwa Mountains, Tanzania: an analysis of threats. *Biological Conservation*, **146**(1), 89–96. DOI: 10.1016/j.biocon.2011.09.017.

Rowcliffe, J.M., de Merode, E. and Cowlishaw, G. (2004). Do wildlife laws work? Species protection and the application of a prey choice model to poaching decisions. *Proceedings of the Royal Society of London, Series B: Biological Sciences*, **271**(1557), 2631–6. DOI: doi:10.1098/rspb.2004.2915.

Roy, J., Vigilant, L., Gray, M., *et al.* (2014). Challenges in the use of genetic mark–recapture to estimate the population size of Bwindi mountain gorillas (*Gorilla beringei beringei*). *Biological Conservation*, **180**(Supplement C), 249–61. DOI: 10.1016/j.biocon.2014.10.011.

Roylance, F.D. (2010). Retired show biz chimps come to Maryland Zoo. *The Baltimore Sun*, August 16, 2010. Available at: https://www.baltimoresun.com/maryland/bs-xpm-2010-08-16-bs-md-chimps-maryland-zoo-20100816-story.html.

Rubis, J.M. (2017). Ritual revitalisation as adaptation to environmental stress: skull-blessing in Bidayuh communities of Borneo. *Third World Thematics: A TWQ Journal*, **2**(2–3), 356–75. DOI: 10.1080/23802014.2017.1402667.

Russell, C. (2001). Primate-focused ecotourism: proceed with caution. *Laboratory Primate Newsletter*, **40**(4), 7–8.

Russell, C.L. (1995). The social construction of orangutans: an ecotourist experience. *Society & Animals*, **3**(2), 151–70. DOI: 10.1163/156853095X00134.

Russon, A.E. (2002). Return of the native: cognition and site-specific expertise in orangutan rehabilitation. *International Journal of Primatology*, **23**(3), 461–78.

Russon, A.E., Wich, S.A., Ancrenaz, M., *et al.* (2009). Geographic variation in orangutan diets. In *Orangutans: Geographic Variation in Behavioral Ecology and Conservation*, ed. S.A. Wich, S. Utami-Atmoko, T. Mitra Setia and C.P. van Schaik. Oxford, UK: Oxford University Press, pp. 135–56.

Sá, R. and van Schijndel, J. (2010). *Gastrointestinal parasites of chimpanzees (*Pan troglodytes verus*) in the Boé sector, Republic of Guinea-Bissau. Preliminary survey and mid report.* Unpublished report. Chimbo Foundation.

Sá, R.M.M., Ferreira da Silva, M., Sousa, F.M. and Minhós, T. (2012). The trade and ethnobiological use of chimpanzee body parts in Guinea-Bissau. *TRAFFIC Bulletin*, **24**(1), 31–4.

Sabuhoro, E., Wright, B., Munanura, I.E., Nyakabwa, I.N. and Nibigira, C. (2017). The potential of ecotourism opportunities to generate support for mountain gorilla conservation among local communities neighboring Volcanoes National Park in Rwanda. *Journal of Ecotourism*, 1–17. DOI: 10.1080/14724049.2017.1280043.

Sachs, J.D. (2006). *The End of Poverty.* London, UK: Penguin Books.

Sacramento Zoo (2018). Sacramento Zoo primate expert travels to China to help lead the country's first orangutan husbandry workshop. *Sacramento Zoo News*, November 28, 2018. Available at: https://www.saczoo.org/2018/11/sacramento-zoo-primate-expert-travels-to-china-to-help-lead-the-countrys-first-orangutan-husbandry-workshop/.

Safari World (2017). *Minutes of Annual Shareholders Meeting, April 24, 2017.* Bangkok, Thailand: Safari World Public Co. Ltd. Available at: http://www.safariworld.com/investor/home/pdf/2560_e/2.pdf.

Safari World (n.d.). *Orangutan boxing show.* Bangkok, Thailand: Safari World Public Co. Ltd. Available at: http://www.safariworld.com/oran.html. Accessed October, 2019.

Sakamaki, T., Mulavwa, M. and Furuichi, T. (2009). Flu-like epidemics in wild bonobos (*Pan paniscus*) at Wamba, the Luo Scientific Reserve, Democratic Republic of Congo. *Pan Africa News*, **16**, 1–4.

Salafsky, N., Boshoven, J., Burivalova, Z., *et al.* (2019). Defining and using evidence in conservation practice. *Conservation Science and Practice*, **1**(5), e27. DOI: 10.1111/csp2.27.

Samuels, G. (2016). Chimpanzees have rights, says Argentine judge as she orders Cecilia be released from zoo. *The Independent*, November 7, 2016. Available at: http://www.independent.co.uk/news/world/americas/argentina-judge-says-chimpanzee-poor-conditions-has-rights-and-should-be-freed-from-zoo-a7402606.html.

Sánchez, K. (2015). *Oil palm industry and orangutan rescues.* Unpublished background paper commissioned by Arcus Foundation. Indonesia: International Animal Rescue (IAR).

Santika, T., Ancrenaz, M., Wilson, K.A., *et al.* (2017). First integrative trend analysis for a great ape species in Borneo. *Scientific Reports*, **7**(1), 1–16. DOI: 10.1038/s41598-017-04435-9.

Sarma, K., Krishna, M. and Kumar, A. (2015). Fragmented populations of the vulnerable eastern hoolock gibbon *Hoolock leuconedys* in the Lower Dibang Valley district, Arunachal Pradesh, India. *Oryx*, **49**(1), 133–9. DOI: 10.1017/S0030605312001299.

Sarti, F.M., Adams, C., Morsello, C., *et al.* (2015). Beyond protein intake: bushmeat as source of micronutrients in the Amazon. *Ecology and Society*, **20**(4), 22. DOI: 10.5751/ES-07934-200422.

Sas-Rolfes, M.T., Challender, D.W.S., Hinsley, A., Veríssimo, D. and Milner-Gulland, E.J. (2019). Illegal wildlife trade: scale, processes, and governance. *Annual Review of Environment and Resources*, **44**(1), 201–28. DOI: 10.1146/annurev-environ-101718-033253.

Savage-Rumgaugh, E.S. (2013). *Affidavit of Emily Sue Savage-Rumbaugh In the Matter of a Proceeding under Article 70 of the CPLR for a Writ of Habeas Corpus. The Nonhuman Rights Project, Inc., on behalf of Tommy, Petitioners, v. Patrick C. Lavery, individually and as an officer of Circle L Trailer Sales, Inc., Diane Lavery, and Circle L Trailer Sales, Inc. November 22, 2013.* Available at: https://www.nonhumanrights.org/content/uploads/Ex-12-Savage-Rumbaugh-Affidavit-Tommy-Case.pdf. Accessed December, 2019.

Savage-Rumgaugh, E.S. (2015). *Affidavit of Emily Sue Savage-Rumbaugh In the Matter of a Proceeding under Article 70 of the CPLR for a Writ of Habeas Corpus. The Nonhuman Rights Project, Inc., on behalf of Kiko, Petitioner, v. Carmen Presti, individually and as an officer and director of The Primate Sanctuary, Inc., Christie E. Presti, individually and as an officer and director of The Primate Sanctuary, Inc., and the Primate Sanctuary, Inc. December 1, 2015.* Available at: https://www.nonhumanrights.org/client-kiko/. Accessed December, 2019.

Savini, T., Boesch, C. and Reichard, U.H. (2008). Home-range characteristics and the influence of seasonality on female reproduction in white-handed gibbons (*Hylobates lar*) at Khao Yai National Park, Thailand. *American Journal of Physical Anthropology*, **135**(1), 1–12. DOI: 10.1002/ajpa.20578.

Schapiro, R. (2009a). All it takes is $45,000 and a phone call to get a pet chimp. *New York Daily News*, February 21, 2009. Available at: https://www.nydailynews.com/news/takes-45-000-phone-call-pet-chimp-article-1.369397.

Schapiro, R. (2009b). The worst story I ever heard. *Esquire*, November 11, 2009. Available at: https://www.esquire.com/news-politics/a5609/chimpanzee-attack-0409/.

Scheffers, B.R., Oliveira, B.F., Lamb, I. and Edwards, D.P. (2019). Global wildlife trade across the tree of life. *Science*, **366**(6461), 71–6. DOI: 10.1126/science.aav5327.

Schiller, A. (1997). *Small Sacrifices: Religious Change and Cultural Identity Among the Ngaju of Indonesia.* New York and Oxford: Oxford University Press.

Schlegel, H. and Müller, S. (1839–1844). Bijdragen tot de natuurlijke historie van den orang-oetan (*Simia satyrus*). In *Verhandelingen over de Natuurlijke Geschiedenis der Nederlandsche Overzeesche Bezittingen: Zoologie*, ed. C.J. Temminck. Leiden, the Netherlands: Luchtmans, pp. 1–28.

Schoene, C.U.R. and Brend, S.A. (2002). Primate sanctuaries: a delicate conservation approach. *South African Journal of Wildlife Research*, **32**(2), 109–13.

Schouteden, H. (1930). Le chimpanzee de la rive gauche du Congo. *Bulletin du Cercle Zoologique Congolais*, **VI**(4), 114–9.

Schreer, V. (2016). *Longing for prosperity in Indonesian Borneo.* PhD thesis. Canterbury, UK: University of Kent.

Schroepfer, K.K., Rosati, A.G., Chartrand, T. and Hare, B. (2011). Use of 'entertainment' chimpanzees in commercials distorts public perception regarding their conservation status. *PLoS ONE*, **6**(10), e26048. DOI: 10.1371/journal.pone.0026048.

Schulte-Herbrüggen, B., Cowlishaw, G., Homewood, K. and Rowcliffe, J.M. (2013). The importance of bushmeat in the livelihoods of west African cash-crop farmers living in a faunally-depleted landscape. *PLoS ONE*, **8**(8), e72807. DOI: 10.1371/journal.pone.0072807.

Schulze, K., Knights, K., Coad, L., *et al.* (2018). An assessment of threats to terrestrial protected areas. *Conservation Letters*, **11**(3), e12435. DOI: 10.1111/conl.12435.

Schwarz, E. (1929). Das Vorkommen des Schimpansen auf den linken Kongo-Ufer. *Revue de Zoologie et de Botanique Africaine*, **16**(4), 425–6.

Schwitzer, C., Mittermeier, R.A., Johnson, S.E., *et al.* (2014). Averting lemur extinctions amid Madagascar's political crisis. *Science*, **343**(6173), 842–3. DOI: 10.1126/science.1245783.

Seiler, N., Boesch, C., Mundry, R., Stephens, C. and Robbins, M.M. (2017). Space partitioning in wild, non-territorial mountain gorillas: the impact of food and neighbours. *Royal Society Open Science*, **4**(11), 170720. DOI: 10.1098/rsos.170720.

Seiler, N., Boesch, C., Stephens, C., *et al.* (2018). Social and ecological correlates of space use patterns in Bwindi mountain gorillas. *American Journal of Primatology*, **80**(4), e22754. DOI: 10.1002/ajp.22754.

Seiler, N. and Robbins, M.M. (2016). Factors influencing ranging on community land and crop raiding by mountain gorillas. *Animal Conservation*, **19**(2), 176–88. DOI: 10.1111/acv.12232.

Sen, A. (1999). *Development as Freedom.* Oxford, UK: Oxford University Press.

Serckx, A., Huynen, M.-C., Bastin, J.-F., *et al.* (2014). Nest grouping patterns of bonobos (*Pan paniscus*) in relation to fruit availability in a forest-savanna mosaic. *PLoS ONE*, **9**(4), e93742. DOI: 10.1371/journal.pone.0093742.

Serpell, J.A. (2002). Anthropomorphism and anthropomorphic selection – beyond the 'cute response'. *Society & Animals*, **10**(4), 437–54. DOI: 10.1163/156853002320936926.

Sesink Clee, P.R., Abwe, E.E., Ambahe, R.D., *et al.* (2015). Chimpanzee population structure in Cameroon and Nigeria is associated with habitat variation that may be lost under climate change. *BMC Evolutionary Biology*, **15**(1), 2. DOI: 10.1186/s12862-014-0275-z.

Setiawan, A., Nugroho, T.S., Wibisono, Y., Ikawati, V. and Sugardjito, J. (2012). Population density and distribution of Javan gibbon (*Hylobates moloch*) in Central Java, Indonesia. *Biodiversitas*, **13**, 23–32.

Shapiro, J. (2001). *Mao's War Against Nature: Politics and the Environment in Revolutionary China.* Cambridge, UK: Cambridge University Press.

Shen, A. (2017). Visitors to Chinese zoo feel deflated after discovering new penguin display consists of blow-up toys. *South China Morning Post*, December 1, 2017. Available at: https://www.scmp.com/news/china/society/article/2122445/visitors-chinese-zoo-feel-deflated-after-discovering-new-penguin.

Shenoy, R. (2019). This orangutan's 'personhood' victory brings hope to US animal rights movement. *PRI*, November 20, 2019. Available at: https://www.pri.org/stories/2019-11-20/orangutan-s-personhood-victory-brings-hope-us-animal-rights-movement.

Shepherd, C. (2010). Illegal primate trade in Indonesia exemplified by surveys carried out over a decade in North Sumatra. *Endangered Species Research*, **11**(3), 201–5. DOI: 10.3354/esr00276.

Sherman, J. and Greer, D. (2018). The status of captive apes. In *State of the Apes: Infrastructure Development and Ape Conservation*, ed. Arcus Foundation. Cambridge, UK: Cambridge University Press, pp. 225–55. Available at: https://www.stateoftheapes.com/themes/ch-8-the-status-of-captive-apes/.

Shields, P., Jones, C. and McKimson, R., directors (1970). *Lancelot Link: Secret Chimp.* American Broadcasting Company (ABC) and Sandler-Burns-Marmer Productions. Available at: https://www.imdb.com/title/tt0065309/fullcredits?ref_=ttco_sa_1.

Shukman, D. and Piranty, S. (2017). The secret trade in baby chimps. *BBC News Science and Environment*, January 30, 2017. Available at: https://www.bbc.co.uk/news/resources/idt-5e8c4bac-c236-4cd9-bacc-db96d733f6cf.

Shuxian, Z., Li, P.J. and Su, P.-F. (2005). Animal welfare consciousness of Chinese college students: findings and analysis. *China Information*, **19**(1), 67–95. DOI: 10.1177/0920203X05051020.

Sifuna, N. (2012). The future of traditional customary uses of wildlife in modern Africa: a case study of Kenya and Botswana. *Advances in Anthropology*, **2**, 31–8. DOI: 10.4236/aa.2012.21004.

Silk, M.J., Crowley, S.L., Woodhead, A.J. and Nuno, A. (2018). Considering connections between Hollywood and biodiversity conservation. *Conservation Biology*, **32**(3), 597–606. DOI: 10.1111/cobi.13030.

Sillander, K. and Alexander, J. (2016). Belonging in Borneo: refiguring Dayak ethnicity in Indonesia. *The Asia Pacific Journal of Anthropology*, **17**(2), 95–101. DOI: 10.1080/14442213.2016.1152882.

Sillitoe, P. (2003). *Managing Animals in New Guinea: Preying the Game in the Highlands.* Studies in Environmental Anthropology Vol. 7. New York, NY: Routledge.

Silom Advisory Co. (2017). *Opinion of the Independent Financial Advisor regarding to the asset acquisition of Safari World Company Limited* [translation]. Prepared by Silom Advisory Company Limited. Available at: https://www.safariworld.com/investor/home/pdf/2560_e/4.pdf.

Sims, D. (2016). *The Jungle Book* points toward a CGI future. *The Atlantic*, April 18, 2016. Available at: https://www.theatlantic.com/entertainment/archive/2016/04/the-jungle-book-and-the-uncanny-valley/478767/.

Singapore Zoo (n.d.). *Special experiences: jungle breakfast with wildlife.* Singapore: Singapore Zoo. Available at: https://www.wrs.com.sg/en/singapore-zoo/animals-and-zones/orangutan.html. Accessed September, 2020.

Singleton, I., Knott, C.D., Morrogh-Bernard, H.C., Wich, S.A. and van Schaik, C.P. (2009). Ranging behavior of orangutan females and social organization. In *Orangutans: Geographic Variation in Behavioral Ecology and Conservation*, ed. S.A. Wich, S. Utami-Atmoko, T. Mitra Setia and C.P. van Schaik. Oxford, UK: Oxford University Press, pp. 205–13.

Singleton, I., Wich, S.A., Nowak, M., Usher, G. and Utami-Atmoko, S.S. (2017). *Pongo abelii* (errata version published in 2018). *The IUCN Red List of Threatened Species*. 2017: e.T121097935A123797627. Gland, Switzerland: International Union for Conservation of Nature (IUCN). Available at: http://dx.doi.org/10.2305/IUCN.UK.2017-3.RLTS.T121097935A115575085.en.

Sitas, N., Baillie, J.E.M. and Isaac, N.J.B. (2009). What are we saving? Developing a standardized approach for conservation action. *Animal Conservation*, **12**(3), 231–7. DOI: 10.1111/j.1469-1795.2009.00244.x.

SMART (n.d.-a). *Home*. Spatial Monitoring and Reporting Tool (SMART). Available at: https://smartconservation tools.org. Accessed September, 2020.

SMART (n.d.-b). *SMART Partnership*. Spatial Monitoring and Reporting Tool (SMART). Available at: https://smartconservationtools.org/smart-partnership. Accessed September, 2020.

Smith, J. and Cheyne, S.M. (2017). *Investigating the extent and prevalence of gibbons being traded online in habitat countries: a preliminary report for Arcus Foundation*. Oxford, UK: Oxford Brookes University.

Smith, J.H., King, T., Campbell, C., Cheyne, S.M. and Nijman, V. (2018). Modelling population viability of three independent Javan gibbon (*Hylobates moloch*) populations on Java, Indonesia. *Folia Primatologica*, **88**(6), 507–22. DOI: 10.1159/000484559.

Smithsonian Institute (n.d.). *What does it mean to be human?* Washington DC: Smithsonian Institution. Available at: http://humanorigins.si.edu/evidence/genetics. Accessed December, 2019.

Sollund, R., Stefes, C.H. and Germani, A.R., ed. (2016). *Fighting Environmental Crime in Europe and Beyond: The Role of the EU and Its Member States*. London, UK: Palgrave Macmillan.

Somerset v. *Stewart*. 1 Lofft 1 (KB) (1772). Available at: http://www.commonlii.org/int/cases/EngR/1772/57.pdf.

Sosnowski, M. (2019). Black markets: a comparison of the illegal ivory and narcotic trades. *Deviant Behavior*, 1–10. DOI: 10.1080/01639625.2019.1568360.

Soto Reyes, M. (2019). Scandals and teen dropoff weren't enough to stop Facebook's growth. *Business Insider*, April 26, 2019. Available at: https://www.businessinsider.com/facebook-grew-monthly-average-users-in-q1-2019-4?r=US&IR=T.

Species360 (n.d.). *Zoological Information Management System (ZIMS). Species holding reports 2018*. Minneapolis, MN: Species360. Available at: https://zims.species360.org. Accessed November, 2018.

Spehar, S.N., Sheil, D., Harrison, T., *et al.* (2018). Orangutans venture out of the rainforest and into the Anthropocene. *Science Advances*, **4**(6), 1–13. DOI: 10.1126/sciadv.1701422.

Srikosamatara, S. (1984). Ecology of pileated gibbons in South-East Asia. In *The Lesser Apes: Evolutionary and Behavioural Biology*, ed. H.H. Preuschoft, D.J. Chivers, W.Y. Brockelman and N. Creel. Edinburgh, UK: Edinburgh University Press, pp. 242–57.

Stanford, C.B. (1999). *The Hunting Apes: Meat Eating and the Origins of Human Behavior*. Princeton, NJ: Princeton University Press.

State Council (1993). *Circular of the State Council on Banning the Trade of Rhinoceros Horn and Tiger Bone*. Beijing, China: State Council of the People's Republic of China. Available at: https://sherloc.unodc.org/cld/document/chn/1993/circular_of_the_state_council_on_banning_the_trade_of_rhinoceros_horn_and_tiger_bone.html.

Sterling, E.J., Filardi, C., Toomey, A., *et al.* (2017). Biocultural approaches to well-being and sustainability indicators across scales. *Nature Ecology & Evolution*, **1**(12), 1798–806. DOI: 10.1038/s41559-017-0349-6.

Stevens, S.F. (1997). *Conservation through Cultural Survival: Indigenous Peoples and Protected Areas*. Washington DC: Island Press.

Stewart, F.A. (2011). Why sleep in a nest? Empirical testing of the function of simple shelters made by wild chimpanzees. *American Journal of Physical Anthropology*, **146**(2), 313–8. DOI: 10.1002/ajpa.21580.

Stewart, K. (1988). Suckling and lactational anoestrus in wild gorillas (*Gorilla gorilla*). *Journal of Reproduction and Fertility*, **83**(2), 627–34.

Stiles, D. (2011). *Elephant Meat Trade in Central Africa: Summary Report.* Gland, Switzerland: International Union for Conservation of Nature (IUCN).

Stiles, D. (2016). *The Illegal Trade in Great Apes. A Report Prepared by the Project to End Great Ape Slavery (PEGAS).* Johannesburg, South Africa. Available at: https://freetheapes.files.wordpress.com/2014/11/cop17-report.pdf.

Stiles, D. (2017). Social media trafficking of great apes raises concern. *SWARA Magazine*, May 25, 2017.

Stiles, D., Redmond, I., Cress, D., Nellemann, C. and Formo, R.K. (2013). *Stolen Apes: The Illicit Trade in Chimpanzees, Gorillas, Bonobos and Orangutans. A Rapid Response Assessment.* Arendal, Sweden: United Nations Environment Programme and GRID-Arendal. Available at: https://www.grida.no/publications/191.

Stokes, D. (2017). Pileated gibbons poached as bushmeat to feed illegal rosewood loggers. *Mongabay*, January 17, 2017. Available at: https://news.mongabay.com/2017/01/pileated-gibbons-poached-as-bushmeat-to-feed-illegal-rosewood-loggers/.

Strindberg, S., Maisels, F., Williamson, E.A., *et al.* (2018). Guns, germs, and trees determine density and distribution of gorillas and chimpanzees in western Equatorial Africa. *Science Advances*, **4**(4), eaar2964. DOI: 10.1126/sciadv.aar2964.

Strona, G., Stringer, S.D., Vieilledent, G., *et al.* (2018). Small room for compromise between oil palm cultivation and primate conservation in Africa. *Proceedings of the National Academy of Sciences*, **115**(35), 8811–6. DOI: 10.1073/pnas.1804775115.

Struebig, M.J., Fischer, M., Gaveau, D.L.A., *et al.* (2015a). Anticipated climate and land-cover changes reveal refuge areas for Borneo's orang-utans. *Global Change Biology*, **21**(8), 2891–904. DOI: 10.1111/gcb.12814.

Struebig, M.J., Wilting, A., Gaveau, D.L.A., *et al.* (2015b). Targeted conservation to safeguard a biodiversity hotspot from climate and land-cover change. *Current Biology*, **25**(3), 372–8. DOI: 10.1016/j.cub.2014.11.067.

Stuff (n.d.). 25 best movie CGI effects ever. *Stuff*. Available at: https://www.stuff.tv/news/25-best-movie-cgi-effects-ever/labyrinth-1986. Accessed January, 2020.

Sugiyama, Y. and Fujita, S. (2011). The demography and reproductive parameters of Bossou chimpanzees. In *The Chimpanzees of Bossou and Nimba*, ed. T. Matsuzawa, T. Humle and Y. Sugiyama. Tokyo, Japan: Springer, pp. 23–34. DOI: 10.1007/978-4-431-53921-6_4.

Sugiyama, Y. and Humle, T. (2011). A wild chimpanzee uses a stick to disable a snare at Bossou, Guinea. *Pan Africa News*, **18**(1), 3–4.

Summers, H. (2018). Outrage over alleged plan to export rare animals from Congo to China. *The Guardian*, July 2, 2018. Available at: https://www.theguardian.com/global-development/2018/jul/02/outrage-alleged-plan-export-rare-animals-democratic-republic-congo-china-gorillas-endangered-species-zoos.

Sun, G.Z., Ni, Q.Y., Huang, B., *et al.* (2012). Population, distribution and conservation status of western black crested gibbon. *Forest Conservation*, **1**, 38–43.

Sunday, O. (2019). What is magic without ape parts? Inside the illicit trade devastating Nigeria's apes. *Mongabay*, May 29, 2019. Available at: https://news.mongabay.com/2019/05/what-is-magic-without-ape-parts-inside-the-illicit-trade-devastating-nigerias-apes/?fbclid=IwAR0vKf8vBiKh5ystWSIPv792CoX1qOtOrjEafkZU3BsPayCI_1z0994VgCY.

Sutherland, W.J., ed. (2009). *Conservation Science and Action.* Oxford, UK: Wiley-Blackwell.

Sutherland, W.J., Broad, S., Butchart, S.H.M., *et al.* (2019a). A horizon scan of emerging issues for global conservation in 2019. *Trends in Ecology & Evolution*, **34**(1), 83–94. DOI: 10.1016/j.tree.2018.11.001.

Sutherland, W.J., Fleishman, E., Clout, M., *et al.* (2019b). Ten years on: a review of the first global conservation horizon scan. *Trends in Ecology & Evolution*, **34**(2), 139–53. DOI: 10.1016/j.tree.2018.12.003.

Sutherland, W.J., Pullin, A.S., Dolman, P.M. and Knight, T.M. (2004). The need for evidence-based conservation. *Trends in Ecology & Evolution*, **19**(6), 305–8. DOI: 10.1016/j.tree.2004.03.018.

Sutherland, W.J. and Woodroof, H.J. (2009). The need for environmental horizon scanning. *Trends in Ecology & Evolution*, **24**(10), 523–7. 10.1016/j.tree.2009.04.008.

Svancara, L.K., Brannon J., R., Scott, M., *et al.* (2005). Policy-driven versus evidence-based conservation: a review of political targets and biological needs. *BioScience*, **55**(11), 989–95. DOI: 10.1641/0006-3568(2005)055[0989:pvecar]2.0.co;2.

Swamy, V. and Pinedo-Vasquez, M. (2014). *Bushmeat Harvest in Tropical Forests: Knowledge Base, Gaps and Research Priorities.* Bogor, Indonesia: Center for International Forestry Research (CIFOR).

Swarna Nantha, H. and Tisdell, C. (2009). The orangutan–oil palm conflict: economic constraints and opportunities for conservation. *Biodiversity and Conservation*, **18**(2), 487–502. DOI: 10.1007/s10531-008-9512-3.

SYCR (n.d.). *Our sanctuary.* Portland, OR: Sanaga Yong Chimpanzee Rescue (SYCR). Available at: https://www.sychimprescue.org/our-sanctuary/. Accessed December 31, 2018.

Szantoi, Z., Smith, S.E., Strona, G., Koh, L.P. and Wich, S.A. (2017). Mapping orangutan habitat and agricultural areas using Landsat OLI imagery augmented with unmanned aircraft system aerial photography. *International Journal of Remote Sensing*, **38**(8–10), 2231–45. DOI: 10.1080/01431161.2017.1280638.

Tadie, D. and Fischer, A. (2013). Hunting, social structure and human–nature relationships in Lower Omo, Ethiopia: people and wildlife at a crossroads. *Human Ecology*, **41**(3), 447–57. DOI: 10.1007/s10745-012-9561-9.

TAG de Simios de la AZA (2010). *Manual para cuidado de chimpancés (*Pan troglodytes*).* Silver Spring, MD: Association of Zoos & Aquariums (AZA). Available at: https://assets.speakcdn.com/assets/2332/chimpanzee_care_manual_spanish_alpza.pdf.

Tagg, N., Maddison, N., Dupain, J., *et al.* (2018). A zoo-led study of the great ape bushmeat commodity chain in Cameroon. *International Zoo Yearbook*, **52**(1), 182–93. DOI: 10.1111/izy.12175.

Tagg, N., Willie, J., Duarte, J., Petre, C.A. and Fa, J.E. (2015). Conservation research presence protects: a case study of great ape abundance in the Dja region, Cameroon. *Animal Conservation*, **18**(6), 489–98. DOI: 10.1111/acv.12212.

Tashiro, Y., Idani, G.I., Kimura, D. and Bongori, L. (2007). Habitat changes and decreases in the bonobo population in Wamba, Democratic Republic of the Congo. *African Study Monographs*, **28**(2), 99–106.

Taylor, G., Scharlemann, J.P.W., Rowcliffe, M., *et al.* (2015). Synthesising bushmeat research effort in West and Central Africa: a new regional database. *Biological Conservation*, **181**, 199–205. DOI: 10.1016/j.biocon.2014.11.001.

Taylor, R. (2001). A step at a time: New Zealand's progress toward hominid rights. *Animal Law*, **7** (35), 35–43.

TEA/AECOM (2017). *Theme Index and Museum Index: The Global Attractions Attendance Report.* Burbank, CA: Themed Entertainment Association (TEA). Available at: http://www.teaconnect.org/images/files/TEA_268_653730_180517.pdf.

TEEB (2008). *The Economics of Ecosystems and Biodiversity – An Interim Report. European Communities.* Geneva, Switzerland: The Economics of Ecosystems and Biodiversity (TEEB).

Teleki, G. and Baldwin, L. (1979). *Known and Estimated Distributions of Extant Chimpanzee Populations (*Pan troglodytes *and* Pan paniscus*) in Equatorial Africa.* The World Conservation Union (IUCN) Species Survival Commission (SSC), Primate Specialist Group.

Tello, I.Z. (2016). En una decisión judicial inédita, la mona Cecilia será trasladada de Mendoza a Brasil. *Los Andes*, November 3, 2016.

Tenaza, R. (2012). *The primate skull trade in Bali.* Unpublished presentation. University of the Pacific, California/ International Union for Conservation of Nature (IUCN) Species Survival Commission (SSC) Primate Specialists Group.

The Atlanta Constitution (1938). Famous chimpanzee, Jiggs, dies on coast. *The Atlanta Constitution*, March 2, 1938.

The Coalition (2020). *Offline and in the Wild: A Progress Report of the Coalition to End Wildlife Trafficking Online.* Coalition to End Wildlife Trafficking Online. Available at: https://www.endwildlifetraffickingonline.org/our-progress.

The Economist (2013). What is the difference between common and civil law? *The Economist*, July 17, 2013. Available at: https://www.economist.com/the-economist-explains/2013/07/16/what-is-the-difference-between-common-and-civil-law.

The Stationery Office (2018). *Ivory Act 2013, Chapter 30.* Norwich, UK: The Stationery Office. Available at: http://www.legislation.gov.uk/ukpga/2018/30/pdfs/ukpga_20180030_en.pdf.

Thieme, H. (1997). Lower Palaeolithic hunting spears from Germany. *Nature*, **385**(6619), 807–10. DOI: 10.1038/385807a0.

Thinh, V.N., Mootnick, A.R., Thanh, V.N., Nadler, T. and Roos, C. (2010). A new species of crested gibbon, from the central Annamite mountain range. *Vietnamese Journal of Primatology*, **4**, 1–12.

Thinh, V.N., Roos, C., Rawson, B.M., *et al.* (2020). *Nomascus annamensis. The IUCN Red List of Threatened Species.* 2020: e.T120659170A120659179. Gland, Switzerland: International Union for Conservation of Nature (IUCN). Available at: https://dx.doi.org/10.2305/IUCN.UK.2020-2.RLTS.T120659170A120659179.en.

Thomson, L.K. (2000). *The effect of the Dayak worldwide, customs, traditions, and customary law (Adat-Istiadat) on the interpretation of the Gospel in West Kalimantan, Indonesian Borneo.* PhD thesis. Glenside, PA: Faculty of Theology, Arcadia University.

Tiédoué, M.R., Kone, S.S., Diarrassouba, A. and Tondossama, A. (2019). *Etat de conservation du Parc national de Taï : Résultats du suivi* écologique, *Phase 13.* Soubré, Côte d'Ivoire: Office Ivoirien des Parcs et Réserves/ Direction de Zone Sud-ouest.

Timmins, B. (2019). Facial recognition tool tackles illegal chimp trade. *BBC News*, January 22, 2019. Available at: https://www.bbc.com/news/science-environment-46945302.

Tokuyama, N., Emikey, B., Bafike, B., *et al.* (2012). Bonobos apparently search for a lost member injured by a snare. *Primates*, **53**(3), 215–9.

Traeholt, C., Bunthoeun, R., Rawson, B., *et al.* (2005). *Status Review of Pileated Gibbon,* Hylobates pileatus, *and Yellow-Cheeked Crested Gibbon,* Nomascus gabriellae, *in Cambodia.* Phnom Penh, Cambodia: Fauna & Flora International (FFI) Cambodia Programme Office.

TRAFFIC (2008). *What's Driving the Wildlife Trade? A Review of Expert Opinion on Economic and Social Drivers of the Wildlife Trade and Trade Control Efforts in Cambodia, Indonesia, Lao PDR and Vietnam. East Asia and Pacific Region Sustainable Development Discussion Papers.* Washington DC: East Asia and Pacific Region Sustainable Development Department, World Bank. Available at: http://www.trafficj.org/publication/08_what%27s_driving_the_wildlife_trade.pdf.

TRAFFIC (2012). e-Commerce companies declare zero-tolerance towards illegal online wildlife trading. *TRAFFIC News*, June 8, 2012. Available at: https://www.traffic.org/news/e-commerce-companies-declare-zero-tolerance-towards-illegal-online-wildlife-trading/.

TRAFFIC (2014). Orangutan, gibbons and other animals seized at Soekarno-Hatta International Airport Jakarta, Indonesia. *TRAFFIC News*, June 17, 2014. Available at: https://www.traffic.org/news/orangutan-gibbons-and-other-animals-seized-at-soekarno-hatta-international-airport/.

TRAFFIC (2016). *Captive Breeding and Ranching: The Case for a New CITES Mechanism for Reviewing Trade.* TRAFFIC Briefing. Cambridge, UK: TRAFFIC. Available at: https://www.traffic.org/site/assets/files/7515/cites-cop17-ranching-captive-breeding.pdf.

TRAFFIC International (2018). *Wildlife Trade Information System.* Cambridge, UK: TRAFFIC International.

Trahan, J.R. (2008). The distinction between persons and things: an historical perspective. *Journal of Civil Law Studies*, **1**(1), 9–20.

Tranquilli, S., Abedi-Lartey, M., Abernethy, K., *et al.* (2014). Protected areas in tropical Africa: assessing threats and conservation activities. *PLoS ONE*, **9**(12), e114154. DOI: 10.1371/journal.pone.0114154.

Tranquilli, S., Abedi-Lartey, M., Amsini, F., *et al.* (2012). Lack of conservation effort rapidly increases African great ape extinction risk. *Conservation Letters*, **5**(1), 48–55. DOI: 10.1111/j.1755-263X.2011.00211.x.

Trayford, H.R. and Farmer, K.H. (2012). An assessment of the use of telemetry for primate reintroductions. *Journal for Nature Conservation*, **20**, 311–25.

TripAdvisor (n.d.). *Cuddle an orangutan – Bali Zoo.* UK: TripAdvisor. Available at: https://www.tripadvisor.co.uk/ShowUserReviews-g2646686-d1793975-r420737290-Bali_Zoo-Sukawati_Gianyar_Regency_Bali.html. Accessed October, 2019.

TTGLF (n.d.). *Our story.* South Melbourne, Australia: The Thin Green Line Foundation (TTGLF). Available at: https://thingreenline.org.au/story/. Accessed July, 2019.

Tumusiime, D.M.E.G. and Tweheyo, M.B.F. (2010). Wildlife snaring in Budongo Forest Reserve, Uganda. *Human Dimensions of Wildlife*, **15**(2), 129–44.

Tumusiime, D. and Vedeld, P. (2012). False promise or false premise? Using tourism revenue sharing to promote conservation and poverty reduction in Uganda. *Conservation and Society*, **10**(1), 15–28. DOI: 10.4103/0972-4923.92189.

Turvey, S.T., Bruun, K., Ortiz, A., *et al.* (2018). New genus of extinct Holocene gibbon associated with humans in Imperial China. *Science*, **360**(6395), 1346–9. DOI: 10.1126/science.aao4903.

Turvey, S.T., Traylor-Holzer, K., Wong, M.H.G., *et al.* (2015). *International Conservation Planning Workshop for the Hainan Gibbon: Final Report.* London/Apple Valley, MN: Zoological Society of London/International Union for Conservation of Nature (IUCN) Species Survival Commission (SSC) Conservation Breeding Specialist Group. Available at: https://www.cpsg.org/sites/cbsg.org/files/documents/Hainan_Gibbon_Workshop_Report.pdf.

Tutin, C.E.G., Ancrenaz, M., Paredes, J., *et al.* (2001). Conservation biology framework for the release of wild-born orphaned chimpanzees into the Conkouati Reserve, Congo. *Conservation Biology*, **15**(5), 1247–57. DOI: 10.1111/j.1523-1739.2001.00046.x.

Tutin, C.E.G. and Fernandez, M. (1984). Nationwide census of gorilla (*Gorilla g. gorilla*) and chimpanzee (*Pan t. troglodytes*) populations in Gabon. *American Journal of Primatology*, **6**(4), 313–36. DOI: 10.1002/ajp.1350060403.

Tutin, C.E.G., Fernandez, M., Rogers, M.E., *et al.* (1991). Foraging profiles of sympatric lowland gorillas and chimpanzees in the Lope Reserve, Gabon. *Philosophical Transactions of the Royal Society of London, Series B: Biological Sciences*, **334**(1270), 179–86. DOI: 10.1098/rstb.1991.0107.

Tutin, C., Stokes, E., Boesch, C., *et al.* (2005). *Regional Action Plan for the Conservation of Chimpanzees and Gorillas in Western Equatorial Africa.* Washington DC: Conservation International. Available at: https://portals.iucn.org/library/sites/library/files/documents/2005-115.pdf.

Tweh, C.G., Lormie, M.M., Kouakou, C.Y., *et al.* (2015). Conservation status of chimpanzees *Pan troglodytes verus* and other large mammals in Liberia: a nationwide survey. *Oryx*, **49**(4), 710–8. DOI: 10.1017/S0030605313001191.

Twinamatsiko, M., Baker, J., Harrison, M., *et al.* (2014). *Linking Conservation, Equity and Poverty Alleviation: Understanding Profiles and Motivations of Resource Users and Local Perceptions of Governance at Bwindi Impenetrable National Park.* London, UK: International Institute for Environment and Development (IIED). Available at: https://pubs.iied.org/pdfs/14630IIED.pdf.

Tyson, L., Draper, C. and Turner, D. (2016). *The Use of Wild Animals in Performance 2016.* Born Free Foundation.

UK Parliament (1807). *An Act for the Abolition of the Slave Trade.* 47 Geo III Sess. 1 c. 36. London, UK: UK Parliament. Available at: https://www.pdavis.nl/Legis_06.htm.

UK Parliament (1833). *Slavery Abolition Act 1833.* 3 & 4 Will. IV c. 73. London, UK: UK Parliament. Available at: https://www.pdavis.nl/Legis_07.htm.

UN (1948). *Universal Declaration of Human Rights. United Nations General Assembly Resolution 217 A. Paris, 10 December.* Geneva, Switzerland: United Nations (UN) General Assembly. Available at: https://www.un.org/en/universal-declaration-human-rights/.

UN (1956). *Supplementary Convention on the Abolition of Slavery, the Slave Trade, and Institutions and Practices Similar to Slavery. Adopted by a Conference of Plenipotentiaries convened by Economic and Social Council Resolution 608(XXI) of 30 April 1956.* Geneva, Switzerland: United Nations (UN). Available at: https://www.ohchr.org/EN/ProfessionalInterest/Pages/SupplementaryConventionAbolitionOfSlavery.aspx.

UN (1966). *International Covenant on Civil and Political Rights.* Geneva, Switzerland: United Nations (UN). Available at: https://www.ohchr.org/en/professionalinterest/pages/ccpr.aspx.

UN DESA (2018). *The World's Cities in 2018—Data Booklet.* ST/ESA/ SER.A/417. New York, NY: United Nations (UN) Department of Economic and Social Affairs (DESA) Population Division. Available at: https://www.un.org/en/events/citiesday/assets/pdf/the_worlds_cities_in_2018_data_booklet.pdf.

UN DESA (2019). *World Urbanization Prospects 2018: Highlights.* ST/ESA/SER.A/421. New York, NY: United Nations (UN), Department of Economic and Social Affairs (DESA), Population Division. Available at: https://population.un.org/wup/Publications/Files/WUP2018-Highlights.pdf.

UN Environment (2016a). Apes Seizure Database reveals true extent of illegal trade. *UN Environment Programme – Environment for Development News*, September 29, 2016. Capacity4dev. Available at: https://europa.eu/capacity4dev/unep/blog/apes-seizure-database-reveals-true-extent-illegal-trade.

UN Environment (2016b). *Implementing the African Strategy on Combating Illegal Exploitation and Trade in Wild Fauna and Flora: The Role and Contribution of the Lusaka Agreement.* Brussels, Belgium: United Nations Environment Programme (UN Environment).

UNEP (2016). *UNEP/EA.2/Res.14. Illegal Trade in Wildlife and Wildlife Products (4 August 2019). Resolution 2/14.* Nairobi, Kenya: United Nations Environment Programme (UNEP). Available at: http://wedocs.unep.org/bitstream/handle/20.500.11822/17508/K1607258_UNEPEA2_RES14E.pdf?sequence=8&isAllowed=y.

UNEP-WCMC (2019a). *Protected Area Profile for Brunei Darussalam from the World Database of Protected Areas, November 2019.* Cambridge, UK: United Nations Environment Programme World Conservation Monitoring Centre (UNEP-WCMC) and International Union for Conservation of Nature (IUCN). Available at: www.protectedplanet.net.

UNEP-WCMC (2019b). *Protected Area Profile for Cameroon from the World Database of Protected Areas, October 2019.* Cambridge, UK: United Nations Environment Programme World Conservation Monitoring Centre (UNEP-WCMC) and International Union for Conservation of Nature (IUCN). Available at: www.protectedplanet.net.

UNEP-WCMC (2019c). *Protected Area Profile for Democratic Republic of Congo from the World Database of Protected Areas, November 2019.* Cambridge, UK: United Nations Environment Programme World Conservation Monitoring Centre (UNEP-WCMC) and International Union for Conservation of Nature (IUCN). Available at: www.protectedplanet.net.

UNEP-WCMC (2019d). *Protected Area Profile for Indonesia from the World Database of Protected Areas, October 2019.* Cambridge, UK: United Nations Environment Programme World Conservation Monitoring Centre (UNEP-WCMC) and International Union for Conservation of Nature (IUCN). Available at: www.protectedplanet.net.

UNEP-WCMC (2019e). *Protected Area Profile for Malaysia from the World Database of Protected Areas, October 2019.* Cambridge, UK: United Nations Environment Programme World Conservation Monitoring Centre (UNEP-WCMC) and International Union for Conservation of Nature (IUCN). Available at: www.protectedplanet.net.

UNEP-WCMC (2019f). *Protected Area Profile for Nigeria from the World Database of Protected Areas, October 2019.* Cambridge, UK: United Nations Environment Programme World Conservation Monitoring Centre (UNEP-WCMC) and International Union for Conservation of Nature (IUCN). Available at: www.protectedplanet.net.

UNEP-WCMC (2019g). *Protected Area Profile for Rwanda from the World Database of Protected Areas, October 2019.* Cambridge, UK: United Nations Environment Programme World Conservation Monitoring Centre (UNEP-WCMC) and International Union for Conservation of Nature (IUCN). Available at: www.protectedplanet.net.

UNEP-WCMC (2019h). *Protected Area Profile for Uganda from the World Database of Protected Areas, October 2019.* Cambridge, UK: United Nations Environment Programme World Conservation Monitoring Centre (UNEP-WCMC) and International Union for Conservation of Nature (IUCN). Available at: www.protectedplanet.net.

UNEP-WCMC (n.d.-a). *CITES Trade Database.* Cambridge, UK: United Nations Environment World Conservation Monitoring Centre (UNEP-WCMC). Available at: https://www.unep-wcmc.org/resources-and-data/cites-trade-database. Accessed October, 2018.

UNEP-WCMC (n.d.-b). *Our expertise.* Cambridge, UK: United Nations Environment Programme (UNEP)-World Conservation Monitoring Centre (WCMC). Available at: https://www.unep-wcmc.org/expertise. Accessed September, 2020.

UNEP-WCMC and CITES Secretariat (n.d.). *Species+.* United Nations Environment World Conservation Monitoring Centre (UNEP-WCMC) and Convention on International Trade in Endangered Species of Wild Fauna and Flora (CITES) Secretariat. Available at: https://www.speciesplus.net/species. Accessed September, 2019.

UNESCO (n.d.). *Great apes app wins MobileWebAward for best environmental mobile application.* United Nations Educational, Scientific and Cultural Organization (UNESCO). Available at: https://en.unesco.org/news/great-apes-app-wins-mobilewebaward-best-environmental-mobile-application-0. Accessed September, 2020.

UNGA (2000). *A/RES/55/25. United Nations Convention against Transnational Organized Crime. Resolution 55/25. Adopted November 15.* New York, NY: United Nations General Assembly (UNGA). Available at: https://treaties.un.org/doc/source/docs/A_RES_55_25-E.pdf.

UNGA (2015). *A/RES/69/314. Tackling Illicit Trafficking in Wildlife (19 August 2015). Resolution 69/314.* New York, NY: United Nations General Assembly (UNGA). Available at: https://undocs.org/en/A/RES/69/314.

UNODC (2004). *United Nations Convention Against Transnational Organized Crime and the Protocols Thereto.* Vienna, Austria: United Nations Office on Drugs and Crime (UNODC). Available at: https://www.unodc.org/documents/treaties/UNTOC/Publications/TOC%20Convention/TOCebook-e.pdf.

UNODC (2012). *Wildlife and Forest Crime Analytic Toolkit.* Vienna, Austria: United Nations Office on Drugs and Crime (UNODC). Available at: http://www.unodc.org/documents/Wildlife/Toolkit_e.pdf.

UNODC (2016). *World Wildlife Crime Report: Trafficking in Protected Species.* Vienna, Austria: United Nations Office on Drugs and Crime (UNODC). Available at: https://www.unodc.org/documents/data-and-analysis/wildlife/World_Wildlife_Crime_Report_2016_final.pdf.

UNODC (n.d.-a). *About UNODC*. Vienna, Austria: United Nations Office on Drugs and Crime (UNODC). Available at: http://www.unodc.org/unodc/en/about-unodc/index.html?ref=menutop. Accessed October, 2018.

UNODC (n.d.-b). *United Nations Convention against Transnational Organized Crime and the Protocols Thereto*. Vienna, Austria: United Nations Office on Drugs and Crime (UNODC). Available at: https://www.unodc.org/unodc/en/organized-crime/intro/UNTOC.html. Accessed October, 2018.

UNODC (n.d.-c). *Wildlife and forest crime*. Vienna, Austria: United Nations Office on Drugs and Crime (UNODC). Available at: http://www.unodc.org/unodc/en/wildlife-and-forest-crime/index.html. Accessed October, 2018.

US Congress (2000). *Chimpanzee Health Improvement, Maintenance and Protection Act (2000). Senate Report 106-494*. Washington DC: Government Printing Office (GPO). Available at: https://congress.gov/106/crpt/srpt494/CRPT-106srpt494.pdf.

US Fish and Wildlife Service (2018). Endangered and threatened wildlife and plants; taxonomical update for orangutan (83 FR 2085). *Federal Register*, **83**(10), 2085. Available at: https://www.federalregister.gov/documents/2018/01/16/2018-00610/endangered-and-threatened-wildlife-and-plants-taxonomical-update-for-orangutan.

USAID (2015). *Asia's Regional Response to Endangered Species Trafficking*. Bangkok, Thailand: US Agency for International Development (USAID) Regional Development Mission for Asia (RDMA). Available at: https://www.usaid.gov/asia-regional/fact-sheets/asias-regional-response-endangered-species-trafficking.

Utami-Atmoko, S.S., Mitra Setia, T., Goossens, B., *et al.* (2009a). Orangutan mating behaviour and strategy. In *Orangutans: Geographic Variation in Behavioral Ecology and Conservation*, ed. S.A. Wich, S.S. Utami-Atmoko, T. Mitra Setia and C.P. van Schaik. Oxford, UK: Oxford University Press, pp. 235–44.

Utami-Atmoko, S.S., Singleton, I., van Noordwijk, M.A., van Schaik, C.P. and Mitra Setia, T. (2009b). Male–male relationships in orangutans. In *Orangutans: Geographic Variation in Behavioral Ecology and Conservation*, ed. S.A. Wich, S.S. Utami-Atmoko, T. Mitra Setia and C.P. van Schaik. Oxford, UK: Oxford University Press, pp. 225–33.

Utami-Atmoko, S., Traylor-Holzer, K., Rifqi, M.A., *et al.*, ed. (2017). *Orangutan Population and Habitat Viability Assessment: Final Report*. Apple Valley, MN: International Union for Conservation of Nature (IUCN) Species Survival Commission (SSC) Conservation Breeding Specialist Group.

Utami-Atmoko, S., Traylor-Holzer, K., Rifqi, M.A., *et al.*, ed. (2019). *Orangutan Population and Habitat Viability Assessment: Final Report*. Jakarta, Indonesia, and Apple Valley, MN: Ministry of Environment and Forestry of Indonesia, and International Union for Conservation of Nature (IUCN) Species Survival Commission (SSC) Conservation Planning Specialist Group.

Utermohlen, M. and Baine, P. (2018). *In Plane Sight: Wildlife Trafficking in the Air Transport Sector*. Washington DC: Center for Advanced Defense (C4ADS). Available at: https://www.traffic.org/publications/reports/in-plane-sight.

UWA (n.d.). *Conservation Tariff: January 2018 to December 2019*. Kampala, Uganda: Uganda Wildlife Authority (UWA). Available at: https://ugandawildlife.org/images/pdfs/UWA-Tariff-2018-2019.pdf. Accessed September, 2019.

van der Meer, D. (2016). *Can the random encounter model be a useful tool in estimating chimpanzee density?* Internship report. The Netherlands: VHL University of Applied Sciences and Chimbo Foundation.

van der Meer, I.P. (2014). *Inventory of the vegetation structure and food availability for the Western chimpanzee (Pan troglodytes verus) in the Boé region, Guinea-Bissau*. Internship report. Wageningen, the Netherlands: Wageningen University.

Van Dyke, W.S., director (1932). *Tarzan the Ape Man*. Metro-Goldwyn-Mayer (MGM). Available at: https://www.imdb.com/title/tt0023551/fullcredits/?ref_=tt_ov_st_sm.

Van Gulik, R.H. (1967). *The Gibbon in China: An Essay in Chinese Animal Lore*. Leiden: E. J. Brill.

van Noordwijk, M.A., Sauren, S.E.B., Nuzuar, *et al.* (2009). Development of independence: Sumatran and Bornean orangutans compared. In *Orangutans: Geographic Variation in Behavioral Ecology and Conservation*, ed. S.A. Wich, S.S. Utami-Atmoko, T. Mitra Setia and C. P. van Schaik. Oxford, UK: Oxford University Press, pp. 189–203.

van Noordwijk, M.A., Utami-Atmoko, S.S., Knott, C.D., *et al.* (2018). The slow ape: high infant survival and long interbirth intervals in wild orangutans. *Journal of Human Evolution*, **125**, 38–49. DOI: 10.1016/j.jhevol.2018.09.004.

van Noordwijk, M.A., Willems, E.P., Utami-Atmoko, S.S., Kuzawa, C.W. and van Schaik, C.P. (2013). Multi-year lactation and its consequences in Bornean orangutans (*Pongo pygmaeus wurmbii*). *Behavioral Ecology and Sociobiology*, **67**(5), 805–14. DOI: 10.1007/s00265-013-1504-y.

van Schaik, C. (2002). Fragility of traditions: the disturbance hypothesis for the loss of local traditions in orangutans. *International Journal of Primatology*, **23**(3), 527–38. DOI: 10.1023/A:1014965516127.

van Schaik, C.P., Monk, K.A. and Robertson, J.M.Y. (2001). Dramatic decline in orang-utan numbers in the Leuser ecosystem, northern Sumatra. *Oryx*, **35**(1), 14–25. DOI: 10.1046/j.1365-3008.2001.00150.x.

van Uhm, D.P. (2018a). The social construction of the value of wildlife: a green cultural criminological perspective. *Theoretical Criminology*, **22**(3), 384–401. DOI: 10.1177/1362480618787170.

van Uhm, D.P. (2018b). Wildlife and laundering: Interaction between the under and upper world. In *Green Crimes and Dirty Money*, ed. T. Spapens, R. White, D. van Uhm and W. Huisman. London, UK: Routledge, pp. 197–214. DOI: 10.4324/9781351245746.

van Uhm, D.P. and Moreto, W.D. (2017). Corruption within the illegal wildlife trade: a symbiotic and antithetical enterprise. *The British Journal of Criminology*, **58**(4), 864–85. DOI: 10.1093/bjc/azx032.

van Vliet, N. and Mbazza, P. (2011). Recognizing the multiple reasons for bushmeat consumption in urban areas: a necessary step toward the sustainable use of wildlife for food in Central Africa. *Human Dimensions of Wildlife*, **16**(1), 45–54. DOI: 10.1080/10871209.2010.523924.

van Vliet, N., Nasi, R. and Taber, A. (2011). From the forest to the stomach: bushmeat consumption from rural to urban settings in Central Africa. In *Non-Timber Forest Products in the Global Context*, ed. S. Shackleton, C. Shackleton and P. Shanley. Berlin, Heidelberg: Springer, pp. 129–45. DOI: 10.1007/978-3-642-17983-9_6.

van Vliet, N., Quiceno-Mesa, M.P., Cruz-Antia, D., *et al.* (2015). From fish and bushmeat to chicken nuggets: the nutrition transition in a continuum from rural to urban settings in the Tri frontier Amazon region. *Ethnobiology and Conservation*, **4**(6), 1–12. DOI: 10.15451/ec2015-7-4.6-1-12

Vanthomme, H., Kolowski, J., Korte, L. and Alonso, A. (2013). Distribution of a community of mammals in relation to roads and other human disturbances in Gabon, central Africa. *Conservation Biology*, **27**(2), 281–91. DOI: 10.1111/cobi.12017.

Varki, A. and Altheide, T.K. (2005). Comparing the human and chimpanzee genomes: searching for needles in a haystack. *Genome Research*, **15**(12), 1746–58. DOI: 10.1101/gr.3737405.

Vermeulen, C., Julve, C., Doucet, J.-L. and Monticelli, D. (2009). Community hunting in logging concessions: towards a management model for Cameroon's dense forests. *Biodiversity and Conservation*, **18**(10), 2705–18. DOI: 10.1007/s10531-009-9614-6.

Verweijen, J. and Marijnen, E. (2018). The counterinsurgency/conservation nexus: guerrilla livelihoods and the dynamics of conflict and violence in the Virunga National Park, Democratic Republic of the Congo. *The Journal of Peasant Studies*, **45**(2), 300–20. DOI: 10.1080/03066150.2016.1203307.

Viator (n.d.). *Breakfast with the orangutans at Bali Zoo.* Viator. Available at: https://www.viator.com/tours/Ubud/Breakfast-with-the-Orangutans-at-Bali-Zoo/d5467-22460P10. Accessed September, 2020.

Vidal, J. (2014). This could be the year we start to save, not slaughter, the shark. *The Guardian.* January 11, 2014. Available at: https://www.theguardian.com/environment/2014/jan/11/shark-finning-in-decline-in-far-east.

Vining, J. and Ebreo, A. (2002). Emerging theoretical and methodological perspectives on conservation behavior. In *Handbook of Environmental Psychology*, ed. R.B. Bechtel and A. Churchman. Hoboken, NJ: John Wiley & Sons Inc., pp. 541–58.

Virunga Alliance (n.d.-a). *Gorilla Orphans Project.* DRC: Virunga Alliance. Available at: https://virunga.org/alliance/gorilla-orphans. Accessed September, 2020

Virunga Alliance (n.d.-b). *Rangers Project.* DRC: Virunga Alliance. Available at: https://virunga.org/alliance/rangers-project. Accessed September, 2020

Visit Rwanda (n.d.). *Gorilla tracking.* Kigali, Rwanda: Rwanda Development Board. Available at: https://www.visitrwanda.com/interests/gorilla-tracking/. Accessed October, 2019.

VoiceBoxer (2016). What about English in China? *VoiceBoxer*, February 25, 2016. Available at: http://voiceboxer.com/english-in-china/.

Voigt, M., Wich, S.A., Ancrenaz, M., *et al.* (2018). Global demand for natural resources eliminated more than 100,000 Bornean orangutans. *Current Biology*, **28**(5), 761–9. DOI: 10.1016/j.cub.2018.01.053.

Voysey, B.C., McDonald, K.E., Rogers, M.E., Tutin, C.E.G. and Parnell, R.J. (1999a). Gorillas and seed dispersal in the Lopé Reserve, Gabon. I. Gorilla acquisition by trees. *Journal of Tropical Ecology*, **15**(1), 23–38. DOI: 10.1017/S0266467499000656.

Voysey, B.C., McDonald, K.E., Rogers, M.E., Tutin, C.E.G. and Parnell, R.J. (1999b). Gorillas and seed dispersal in the Lope Reserve, Gabon. II. Survival and growth of seedlings. *Journal of Tropical Ecology*, **15**(1), 39–60.

Wadley, R.L. and Colfer, C.J.P. (2004). Sacred forest, hunting, and conservation in West Kalimantan, Indonesia. *Human Ecology*, **32**(3), 313–38. DOI: 10.1023/B:HUEC.0000028084.30742.do.

Wadley, R.L., Colfer, C.J.P. and Hood, I.G. (1997). Hunting primates and managing forests: the case of Iban forest farmers in Indonesian Borneo. *Human Ecology*, **25**(2), 243–71. DOI: 10.1023/a:1021926206649.

Wadman, M. (2017). More groups sue to force USDA to restore online animal welfare records. *Science News*, February 22, 2017. Available at: http://www.sciencemag.org/news/2017/02/breaking-reversal-usda-reposts-some-animal-welfare-records-it-had-scrubbed-website.

WageIndicator (n.d.). *Salaries*. WageIndicator Foundation. Available at: https://wageindicator.org/salary. Accessed December, 2018.

Wagner, K. (2019). Wildlife traffickers use Facebook, Instagram to find black-market buyers. *Bloomberg*, July 11, 2019. Available at: https://www.bloomberg.com/news/articles/2019-07-11/wildlife-traffickers-use-facebook-instagram-to-find-black-market-buyers.

Walker, K.K., Walker, C.S., Goodall, J. and Pusey, A.E. (2018). Maturation is prolonged and variable in female chimpanzees. *Journal of Human Evolution*, **114**, 131–40. DOI: 10.1016/j.jhevol.2017.10.010.

Wallis, J. (1997). A survey of reproductive parameters in the free-ranging chimpanzees of Gombe National Park. *Journal of Reproduction and Fertility*, **109**, 297–307. DOI: 10.1530/jrf.0.1090297.

Walsh, P.D., Abernathy, K.A., Bermejo, M., *et al.* (2003). Catastrophic ape decline in western equatorial Africa. *Nature*, **422**, 611–4. DOI: 10.1038/nature01566.

Walter, E.V. (1984). Nature on trial: the case of the rooster that laid an egg. In *Methodology, Metaphysics and the History of Science. Boston Studies in the Philosophy of Science 84*, ed. R.S. Cohen and M.W. Wartofsky. Dordrecht, the Netherlands: Springer, pp. 295–321. Available at: https://link.springer.com/chapter/10.1007/978-94-009-6331-3_13.

Walters, G., Schleicher, J., Hymas, O. and Coad, L. (2015). Evolving hunting practices in Gabon: lessons for community-based conservation interventions. *Ecology and Society*, **20**(4), 31. DOI: 10.5751/ES-08047-200431.

Walz, E., Wilson, D., Stauffer, J.C., *et al.* (2017). Incentives for bushmeat consumption and importation among West African immigrants, Minnesota, USA. *Emerging Infectious Disease Journal*, **23**(12), 2095. DOI: 10.3201/eid2312.170563.

WAP (n.d.-a). *Animal Protection Index*. London, UK: World Animal Protection (WAP). Available at: https://api.worldanimalprotection.org. Accessed April, 2020.

WAP (n.d.-b). *Methodology*. London, UK: World Animal Protection (WAP). Available at: https://api.worldanimalprotection.org/methodology. Accessed December, 2019.

Warren, T. and Baker, K.J.M. (2019). WWF's secret war. *Buzzfeed News*, March 4, 2019. Available at: https://www.buzzfeednews.com/article/tomwarren/wwf-world-wide-fund-nature-parks-torture-death.

Warren, T., Baker, K.J.M. and Engert, M. (2019). Leaked report: WWF-backed guards raped pregnant women and tortured villagers at a wildlife park funded by the US government. *Buzzfeed News*, July 11, 2019. Available at: https://www.buzzfeednews.com/article/tomwarren/leaked-report-wwf-backed-guards-raped-pregnant-women.

Watts, D.P. (1984). Composition and variability of mountain gorilla diets in the central Virungas. *American Journal of Primatology*, **7**(4), 323–56. DOI: 10.1002/ajp.1350070403.

Watts, D.P. (1989). Infanticide in mountain gorillas: new cases and a reconsideration of the evidence. *Ethology*, **81**(1), 1–18. DOI: 10.1111/j.1439-0310.1989.tb00754.x.

Watts, D.P., Muller, M., Amsler, S.J., Mbabazi, G. and Mitani, J.C. (2006). Lethal intergroup aggression by chimpanzees in Kibale National Park, Uganda. *American Journal of Primatology*, **68**(2), 161–80. DOI: 10.1002/ajp.20214.

WAZA (n.d.). *About WAZA*. World Association of Zoos and Aquariums (WAZA). Available at: https://www.waza.org/about-waza/. Accessed January, 2020.

WCF (2012). *Etat de la faune et des menaces dans les aires protégées terrestres et principales zones de forte biodiversité de République de Guinée*. Conakry, Guinea: Wild Chimpanzee Foundation (WCF). Available at: https://rris.biopama.org/sites/default/files/2019-03/2012WCFBiodivGn.pdf.

WCF (2014). *Study of a key area for the preservation of chimpanzee in West Africa: preliminary inventory along the Bafing River, Republic of Guinea*. Unpublished report. Conakry, Guinea: Wild Chimpanzee Foundation (WCF).

WCO (2012). *Illicit Trade Report 2012.* Brussels, Belgium: World Customs Organization (WCO). Available at: http://www.wcoomd.org/-/media/wco/public/global/pdf/topics/enforcement-and-compliance/activities-and-programmes/illicit-trade-report/itr_2012_en.pdf?db=web.

WCO (2017). Project INAMA: situation analysis and first results. *WCO News,* **82**, February 2017. Available at: http://www.wcoomd.org/-/media/wco/public/global/pdf/topics/enforcement-and-compliance/activities-and-programmes/environmental-crime/wco-news-article/project-inama-situation-analysis-and-first-results.pdf?db=web.

WCO (n.d.-a). *ENVIRONET.* Brussels, Belgium: World Customs Organization (WCO). Available at: http://www.wcoomd.org/-/media/wco/public/global/pdf/topics/enforcement-and-compliance/activities-and-programmes/environmental-crime/environment/concept-note-en.pdf?la=en. Accessed October, 2018.

WCO (n.d.-b). *Environment programme.* Brussels, Belgium: World Customs Organization (WCO). Available at: http://www.wcoomd.org/en/topics/enforcement-and-compliance/activities-and-programmes/environment-programme.aspx. Accessed October, 2018.

WCO (n.d.-c). *National Customs Enforcement Network (nCEN).* Brussels, Belgium: World Customs Organization (WCO). Available at: http://www.wcoomd.org/en/topics/enforcement-and-compliance/instruments-and-tools/cen-suite/ncen.aspx. Accessed September, 2020.

WCO (n.d.-d). *Project GAPIN.* Brussels, Belgium: World Customs Organization (WCO). Available at: http://www.wcoomd.org/en/topics/integrity/resources/project-gapin.aspx. Accessed October, 2018.

WCO (n.d.-e). *Publications.* Brussels, Belgium: World Customs Organization (WCO). Available at: http://www.wcoomd.org/en/topics/enforcement-and-compliance/resources/publications.aspx. Accessed October, 2018.

WCO (n.d.-f). *Regional intelligence liaison offices.* Brussels, Belgium: World Customs Organization (WCO). Available at: http://www.wcoomd.org/en/about-us/wco-regional-bodies/rilo.aspx. Accessed September, 2020.

WCO (n.d.-g). *WCO in brief.* Brussels, Belgium: World Customs Organization (WCO). Available at: http://www.wcoomd.org/en/about-us/what-is-the-wco.aspx. Accessed October, 2018.

WCS (2012). Illegal orangutan trader prosecuted. *ScienceDaily,* February 23, 2012. Available at: www.sciencedaily.com/releases/2012/02/120223142430.htm.

WCS Nigeria (n.d.). *My Gorilla – My Community.* Calabar, Nigeria: Wildlife Conservation Society (WCS) Nigeria. Available at: https://nigeria.wcs.org/Global-Initiatives/My-Gorilla-My-Community.aspx. Accessed July, 2019.

Wei, S., Ma, C., Tan, W., *et al.* (2017). Discovery of a new formed group and current population status of eastern black crested gibbon in Bangliang National Nature Reserve, Guangxi, China. *Acta Theriologica Sinica,* **37**, 233–40.

Wei, W., Wang, X., Claro, F., *et al.* (2004). The current status of the Hainan black-crested gibbon *Nomascus* sp. cf. *nasutus hainanus* in Bawangling National Nature Reserve, Hainan, China. *Oryx,* **38**(4), 452–6. DOI: 10.1017/S0030605304000845.

Wen Naifei and Tan Siqi (2013). Changsha is so hot, even African gorillas can't stand it. *Xiaoxiang Morning News,* August 7, 2013.

Wenceslau, J.F.C. (2014). *Bauxite mining and chimpanzees population distribution, a case study in the Boé sector, Guinea-Bissau.* Masters thesis. The Netherlands: VHL University of Applied Sciences and Chimbo Foundation.

Wessling, E.G., Deschner, T., Mundry, R., *et al.* (2018). Seasonal variation in physiology challenges the notion of chimpanzees (*Pan troglodytes verus*) as a forest-adapted species. *Frontiers in Ecology and Evolution,* **6**, 60. DOI: 10.3389/fevo.2018.00060.

West, P. (2005). Translation, value, and space: theorizing an ethnographic and engaged environmental anthropology. *American Anthropologist,* **107**(4), 632–42. DOI: 10.1525/aa.2005.107.4.632.

West, P. (2006). *Conservation is our Government Now: The Politics of Ecology in Papua New Guinea.* Durham, NC: Duke University Press.

Westphal, M.I., Browne, M., MacKinnon, K. and Noble, I. (2008). The link between international trade and the global distribution of invasive alien species. *Biological Invasions,* **10**(4), 391–8. DOI: 10.1007/s10530-007-9138-5.

Weta Digital (n.d.). *Caesar.* Wellington, New Zealand: Weta Digital. Available at: https://www.wetafx.co.nz/films/case-studies/caesar /. Accessed January, 2020.

White, A. and Fa, J.E. (2014). The bigger picture: indirect impacts of extractive industries on apes and ape habitat. In *State of the Apes: Extractive Industries and Ape Conservation,* ed. Arcus Foundation. Cambridge, UK: Cambridge University Press, pp. 197–225.

White, G.C., Anderson, D.R., Burnham, K.P. and Otis, D.L. (1982). *Capture–Recapture and Removal Methods for Sampling Closed Populations.* Los Alamos, NM: Los Alamos National Laboratory.

Whittaker, D.J. (2005). New population estimates for the endemic Kloss's gibbon *Hylobates klossii* on the Mentawai Islands, Indonesia. *Oryx*, **39**(4), 458–61. DOI: 10.1017/S0030605305001134.

Whittaker, D.J., Morales, J.C. and Melnick, D.J. (2003). *Conservation biology of Kloss's gibbons (*Hylobates klossii*).* Presented at the Seventy-Second Annual Meeting of the American Association of Physical Anthropologists, April 23–26, 2003 Tempe, AZ.

Wicander, S. and Coad, L. (2014). *Learning Our Lessons: A Review of Alternative Livelihood Projects in Central Africa.* Gland, Switzerland: International Union for Conservation of Nature (IUCN). Available at: https://www.iucn.org/sites/dev/files/import/downloads/english_version.pdf.

Wicander, S. and Coad, L. (2018). Can the provision of alternative livelihoods reduce the impact of wild meat hunting in west and central Africa? *Conservation and Society*, **16**(4), 441–58. DOI: 10.4103/cs.cs_17_56.

Wich, S.A., de Vries, H. and Ancrenaz, M. (2009). Orangutan life history variation. In *Orangutans: Geographic Variation in Behavioral Ecology and Conservation*, ed. S.A. Wich, S.S. Utami-Atmoko, T. Mitra Setia and C.P. van Schaik. Oxford, UK: Oxford University Press, pp. 65–75.

Wich, S.A., Fredriksson, G., Usher, G., Kühl, H.S. and Nowak, M.G. (2019). The Tapanuli orangutan: status, threats, and steps for improved conservation. *Conservation Science and Practice*, **1**(6), e33. DOI: 10.1111/csp2.33.

Wich, S.A., Fredriksson, G.M., Usher, G., *et al.* (2012a). Hunting of Sumatran orang-utans and its importance in determining distribution and density. *Biological Conservation*, **146**(1), 163–9. DOI: 10.1016/j.biocon.2011.12.006.

Wich, S.A., Garcia-Ulloa, J., Kühl, Hjalmar S., *et al.* (2014). Will oil palm's homecoming spell doom for Africa's great apes? *Current Biology*, **24**(14), 1659–63. DOI: 10.1016/j.cub.2014.05.077.

Wich, S.A., Gaveau, D., Abram, N., *et al.* (2012b). Understanding the impacts of land-use policies on a threatened species: is there a future for the Bornean orang-utan? *PLoS ONE*, **7**(11), e49142. DOI: 10.1371/journal.pone.0049142.

Wich, S.A., Geurts, M.L., Mitra Setia, T. and Utami-Atmoko, S.S. (2006). Influence of fruit availability on Sumatran orangutan sociality and reproduction. In *Feeding Ecology in Apes and Other Primates: Ecological, Physiological and Behavioral Aspects*, ed. G. Hohmann, M.M. Robbins and C. Boesch. Cambridge Studies in Biological and Evolutionary Anthropology Volume 48. Cambridge, UK: Cambridge University Press, pp. 337–58.

Wich, S.A., Meijaard, E., Marshall, A.J., *et al.* (2008). Distribution and conservation status of the orang-utan (*Pongo* spp.) on Borneo and Sumatra: how many remain? *Oryx*, **42**(3), 329–39. DOI: 10.1017/S003060530800197X.

Wich, S.A., Singleton, I., Nowak, M.G., *et al.* (2016). Land-cover changes predict steep declines for the Sumatran orangutan (*Pongo abelii*). *Science Advances*, **2**(3), e1500789. DOI: 10.1126/sciadv.1500789.

Wich, S.A., Struebig, M., Refisch, J., *et al.* (2015). *The Future of the Bornean Orangutan: Impacts of Change in Land Cover and Climate.* Nairobi, Kenya: UNEP/GRASP. Available at: https://www.unenvironment.org/resources/report/future-bornean-orangutan-impacts-change-land-cover-and-climate.

Wich, S.A., Utami-Atmoko, S., Mitra Setia, T. and van Schaik, C.P., ed. (2009). *Orangutans: Geographic Variation in Behavioral Ecology and Conservation.* Oxford, UK: Oxford University Press.

WildAid (2011). *Annual Report 2011.* San Francisco, CA: WildAid. Available at: https://wildaid.org/wp-content/uploads/2017/10/2011-Annual-Report.pdf.

WildAid (2012). *Annual Report 2012.* San Francisco, CA: WildAid. Available at: https://wildaid.org/wp-content/uploads/2017/10/2012-Annual-Report-WildAid_Layout_web.pdf.

WildAid (2013). *Annual Report 2013.* San Francisco, CA: WildAid. Available at: https://wildaid.org/wp-content/uploads/2017/10/WildAid_Annual_Report_2013_Final_Low-Res.pdf.

WildAid (2014a). *Evidence of Declines in Shark Fin Demand China.* San Francisco, CA: WildAid. Available at: https://wildaid.org/wp-content/uploads/2017/09/SharkReport_Evidence-of-Declines-in-Shark-Fin-Demand_China.pdf.

WildAid (2014b). *Ivory Demand in China 2012–2014.* San Francisco, CA: WildAid. Available at: https://wildaid.org/wp-content/uploads/2017/09/Print_Ivory-Report_Final_v3.pdf.

WildAid (2015). *Rhino Horn Demand 2012–2014.* San Francisco, CA: WildAid. Available at: https://wildaid.org/wp-content/uploads/2017/09/Rhino-Horn-Report_Final_v2.pdf.

WildAid (2016). *2016 Annual Report*. San Francisco, CA: WildAid. Available at: https://wildaid.org/wp-content/uploads/2017/10/Annual-Report_2016-2.pdf.

WildAid (2017). *2017 Annual Report*. San Francisco, CA: WildAid. Available at: https://wildaid.org/wp-content/uploads/2018/04/Annual-Report-2017.pdf.

WildAid (2018a). *Sharks in Crisis: Evidence of Positive Behavioral Change in China as New Threats Emerge*. San Francisco: WildAid, CA. Available at: https://wildaid.org/wp-content/uploads/2018/02/WildAid-Sharks-in-Crisis-2018.pdf.

WildAid (2018b). *25 Years After China's Rhino Horn Ban, Poaching Persists*. San Francisco, CA: WildAid. Available at: https://wildaid.org/wp-content/uploads/2018/09/25-Years-After-Chinas-Ban.pdf.

WildAid (n.d.). *Programs*. San Francisco, CA: WildAid. Available at: https://wildaid.org/program. Accessed September, 2020.

Wild Earth Allies (2018). Snares: an unintended threat to great apes. *Wild Earth Allies*, June 1, 2018. Available at: https://wildearthallies.org/snares-unintended-threat-great-apes/.

Wild for Life (n.d.). *Champions*. Wild for Life. Available at: https://wildfor.life/champions.

Wildlife Watch (2018). Exclusive: an inside look at Cecil the lion's final hours. *National Geographic*, March 5, 2018. Available at: https://www.nationalgeographic.co.uk/animals/2018/03/exclusive-inside-look-cecil-lions-final-hours.

Wilkie, D.S., Bennett, E.L., Peres, C.A. and Cunningham, A. (2011). The empty forest revisited. *Annals of the New York Academy of Sciences*, **1223**, 120–8. DOI: 10.1111/j.1749-6632.2010.05908.x.

Wilkie, D.S. and Carpenter, J.F. (1999). Bushmeat hunting in the Congo Basin: an assessment of impacts and options for mitigation. *Biodiversity and Conservation*, **8**(7), 927–55. DOI: 10.1023/a:1008877309871.

Wilkie, D.S., Painter, M. and Jacob, A. (2016). *Rewards and Risks Associated with Community Engagement in Anti-Poaching and Anti-Trafficking*. Washington DC: US Agency for International Development (USAID). Available at: https://pdf.usaid.gov/pdf_docs/PA00M3R4.pdf.

Wilkie, D.S., Starkey, M., Abernethy, K., *et al.* (2005). Role of prices and wealth in consumer demand for bushmeat in Gabon, Central Africa. *Conservation Biology*, **19**(1), 268–74. DOI: 10.1111/j.1523-1739.2005.00372.x.

Wilkie, D.S., Wieland, M., Boulet, H., *et al.* (2016). Eating and conserving bushmeat in Africa. *African Journal of Ecology*, **54**(4), 402–14. DOI: 10.1111/aje.12392.

Willcox, A.S. and Nambu, D.M. (2007). Wildlife hunting practices and bushmeat dynamics of the Banyangi and Mbo people of Southwestern Cameroon. *Biological Conservation*, **134**(2), 251–61. DOI: 10.1016/j.biocon.2006.08.016.

Williams, J.M., Lonsdorf, E.V., Wilson, M.L., *et al.* (2008). Causes of death in the Kasekela chimpanzees of Gombe National Park, Tanzania. *American Journal of Primatology*, **70**(8), 766–77. DOI: 10.1002/ajp.20573.

Williamson, D.F. (2004). *Tackling the Ivories: The Status of the US Trade in Elephant and Hippo Ivory*. Washington DC: TRAFFIC North America and World Wildlife Fund (WWF). Available at: https://www.traffic.org/site/assets/files/4054/tackling_the_ivories.pdf.

Williamson, E.A. (2014). Mountain gorillas: a shifting demographic landscape. In *Primates and Cetaceans: Field Research and Conservation of Complex Mammalian Societies*, ed. J. Yamagiwa and L. Karczmarsk. Tokyo, Japan: Springer, pp. 273–87.

Williamson, E.A. and Butynski, T.M. (2013a). *Gorilla beringei* eastern gorilla. In *Mammals of Africa. Volume II: Primates*, ed. T.M. Butynski, J. Kingdon and J. Kalina. London, UK: Bloomsbury Publishing, pp. 45–53.

Williamson, E.A. and Butynski, T.M. (2013b). *Gorilla gorilla* western gorilla. In *Mammals of Africa. Volume II: Primates*, ed. T.M. Butynski, J. Kingdon and J. Kalina. London, UK: Bloomsbury Publishing, pp. 39–45.

Williamson, E.A., Maisels, F.G., Groves, C.P., *et al.* (2013). Hominidae. In *Handbook of the Mammals of the World. Volume 3: Primates*, ed. R.A. Mittermeier, A.B. Rylands and D.E. Wilson. Barcelona, Spain: Lynx Edicions, pp. 792–854.

Wilson, D. and Reeder, D. (2005). *Mammal Species of the World: A Taxonomic and Geographic Reference*, 3rd edn. Baltimore, MD: Johns Hopkins University Press.

Wilson, H.B., Meijaard, E., Venter, O., Ancrenaz, M. and Possingham, H.P. (2014a). Conservation strategies for orangutans: reintroduction versus habitat preservation and the benefits of sustainably logged forest. *PLoS ONE*, **9**(7), e102174. DOI: 10.1371/journal.pone.0102174.

Wilson, M.L., Boesch, C., Fruth, B., *et al.* (2014b). Lethal aggression in *Pan* is better explained by adaptive strategies than human impacts. *Nature*, **513**, 414–7. DOI: 10.1038/nature13727.

Wingard, J. and Pascual, M. (2018). *Catch Me If You Can: Legal Challenges to Illicit Wildlife Trafficking over the Internet. Policy Brief Prepared by Legal Atlas on behalf of the Global Initiative against Transnational Organized Crime.* Geneva, Switzerland: The Global Initiative Against Transnational Organized Crime. Available at: https://www.legal-atlas.com/uploads/2/6/8/4/26849604/digital-dangers-catch-me-if-you-can-july-2018.pdf.

Wingard, J. and Pascual, M. (2019). *Following the Money: Wildlife Crimes in Anti-Money Laundering Laws, revised edn.* Missoula, MT: Legal Atlas. Available at: https://www.legal-atlas.com/uploads/2/6/8/4/26849604/following_the_money__feb_11_.pdf.

WIPO (2013). *Customary Law, Traditional Knowledge and Intellectual Property: An Outline of the Issues.* World Intellectual Property Organization (WIPO). Available at: https://www.wipo.int/export/sites/www/tk/en/resources/pdf/overview_customary_law.pdf.

Wisconsin Supreme Court (1875). *Motion to Admit Miss Lavinia Goodell to the Bar of this Court, 39 Wis. 232 August 1, 1875.* Wisconsin Supreme Court. Available at: https://cite.case.law/wis/39/232/.

Wise, S. (2005). *Though the Heavens May Fall: The Landmark Trial that Led to the End of Human Slavery.* Cambridge, MA: Da Capo Press.

Wise, S. (2017a). Introduction to animal law book. *Syracuse Law Review*, **67**(1), 7–30.

Wise, S. (2017b). A proposal for a new taxonomy of animal law. *Nonhuman Rights Blog*, December 12, 2017. Available at: https://www.nonhumanrights.org/blog/new-taxonomy-animal-law/.

Wise, S. (2017c). Why the First Department's decision in our chimpanzee rights cases is wildly wrong. *Nonhuman Rights Blog*, June 22, 2017. Available at: https://www.nonhumanrights.org/blog/first-department-wildly-wrong/.

Wittemyer, G., Northrup, J.M., Blanc, J., *et al.* (2014). Illegal killing for ivory drives global decline in African elephants. *Proceedings of the National Academy of Sciences*, **111**(36), 13117–21. DOI: 10.1073/pnas.1403984111.

Wong, R.W.Y. (2015). The organization of the illegal tiger parts trade in China. *The British Journal of Criminology*, **56**(5), 995–1013. DOI: 10.1093/bjc/azv080.

Wood, K.L., Tenger, B., Morf, N. and Kratzer, A. (2014). Bushmeat trafficking in Switzerland. *Gorilla Journal*, **48**, 27–33. Available at: https://www.berggorilla.org/en/journal/issues/journal-no-48/article-view/bushmeat-trafficking-in-switzerland/.

Woodford, M.H., Butynski, T.M. and Karesh, W.B. (2002). Habituating the great apes: the disease risks. *Oryx*, **36**(2), 153–60. DOI: 10.1017/S0030605302000224.

World Bank Group (2016). *Analysis of International Funding to Tackle Illegal Wildlife Trade.* Washington DC: World Bank. Available at: https://openknowledge.worldbank.org/handle/10986/25340.

World Customs Organization (2017). *HS Nomenclature 2017 Edition.* Brussels, Belgium: World Customs Organization. Available at: http://www.wcoomd.org/en/topics/nomenclature/instrument-and-tools/hs-nomenclature-2017-edition.aspx.

World Population Review (2019). *Africa population 2019.* World Population Review. Available at: http://worldpopulationreview.com/continents/africa/. Accessed October, 2019.

Worldometer (n.d.). *Largest countries in the world (by area).* Worldometer. Available at: https://www.worldometers.info/geography/largest-countries-in-the-world. Accessed August, 2020.

Wrangham, R.W. (1986). Ecology and social relationships in two species of chimpanzee. In *Ecological Aspects of Social Evolution: Birds and Mammals*, ed. D.I. Rubenstein and R.W. Wrangham. Princeton, NJ: Princeton University Press, pp. 352–78.

Wrangham, R.W., Chapman, C.A. and Chapman, L.J. (1994). Seed dispersal by forest chimpanzees in Uganda. *Journal of Tropical Ecology*, **10**, 355–68. DOI: 10.1017/S0266467400008026.

Wrangham, R.W., Hagel, G., Leighton, M., *et al.* (2008). The Great Ape World Heritage Species Project. In *Conservation in the 21st Century: Gorillas as a Case Study*, ed. T.S. Stoinski, H.D. Steklis and P.T. Mehlman. New York, NY: Springer Science and Business Media, pp. 282–95. DOI: 10.1007/978-0-387-70721-1_14.

Wright, A.J., Veríssimo, D., Pilfold, K., *et al.* (2015a). Competitive outreach in the 21st century: why we need conservation marketing. *Ocean & Coastal Management*, **115**, 41–8. DOI: 10.1016/j.ocecoaman.2015.06.029.

Wright, E., Grueter, C.C., Seiler, N., *et al.* (2015b). Energetic responses to variation in food availability in the two mountain gorilla populations (*Gorilla beringei beringei*). *American Journal of Physical Anthropology*, **158**(3), 487–500. DOI: 10.1002/ajpa.22808.

Wright, J. and Priston, N. (2010). Hunting and trapping in Lebialem Division, Cameroon: bushmeat harvesting practices and human reliance. *Endangered Species Research*, **11**, 1–12. DOI: 10.3354/esr00244.

Wright, J.H., Hill, N.A.O., Roe, D., *et al.* (2016). Reframing the concept of alternative livelihoods. *Conservation Biology*, **30**(1), 7–13. DOI: 10.1111/cobi.12607.

WWF (2011). Arrests made in Uganda mountain gorilla death. *WWF News*, June 22, 2011. Available at: http://wwf. panda.org/?200728/Arrests-made-in-Uganda-mountain-gorilla-death.

WWF (2015). Major successes for largest ever global operation against wildlife crime. *WWF Press Release*, June 19, 2015. Available at: http://wwf.panda.org/?248311/Major-successes-for-largest-global-operation-ever-against-wildlife-crime.

WWF (2018). Leading tech companies unite to stop online wildlife traffickers. *WWF Press Release*, March 7, 2018. Available at: https://www.worldwildlife.org/press-releases/leading-tech-companies-unite-to-stop-online-wildlife-traffickers.

WWF (n.d.). *Coalition to End Wildlife Trafficking Online.* Washington DC: World Wildlife Fund (WWF). Available at: https://www.worldwildlife.org/pages/coalition-to-end-wildlife-trafficking-online. Accessed October, 2019.

Wyatt, T., Johnson, K., Hunter, L., George, R. and Gunter, R. (2018). Corruption and wildlife trafficking: three case studies involving Asia. *Asian Journal of Criminology*, **13**(1), 35–55. DOI: 10.1007/s11417-017-9255-8.

Wyler, L.S. and Sheikh, P.A. (2008). *International Illegal Trade in Wildlife: Threats and U.S. Policy. DTIC Document.* Washington DC: Library of Congress. Available at: https://apps.dtic.mil/dtic/tr/fulltext/u2/a479399.pdf.

Xie, J., Towsey, M., Zhu, M., Zhang, J. and Roe, P. (2017). An intelligent system for estimating frog community calling activity and species richness. *Ecological Indicators*, **82**, 13–22. DOI: 10.1016/j.ecolind.2017.06.015.

Xu, X. and Arnason, U. (1996). The mitochondrial DNA molecule of Sumatran orangutan and a molecular proposal for two (Bornean and Sumatran) species of orangutan. *Journal of Molecular Evolution*, **43**(5), 431–7. DOI: 10.1007/bf02337514.

Xue, Y., Prado-Martinez, J., Sudmant, P.H., *et al.* (2015). Mountain gorilla genomes reveal the impact of long-term population decline and inbreeding. *Science*, **348**(6231), 242–5. DOI: 10.1126/science.aaa3952.

Yamagiwa, J. and Basabose, A.K. (2009). Fallback foods and dietary partitioning among *Pan* and *Gorilla*. *American Journal of Physical Anthropology*, **140**(4), 739–50. DOI: 10.1002/ajpa.21102.

Yang, J. (2006). Learners and users of English in China. *English Today*, **22**(2), 3–10. DOI: 10.1017/S0266078406002021.

Yang, T. (1993). The animal rights theory and the eco-centric arguments [in Chinese]. *Journal of Studies in Dialectics of Nature*, **8**, 54–48.

Yankwich, L.R. (1959). Social attitudes as reflected in early California law. *Hastings Law Journal*, **10**(3), 250–70.

Yersin, H., Asiimwe, C., Voordouw, M.J. and Zuberbühler, K. (2017). Impact of snare injuries on parasite prevalence in wild chimpanzees (*Pan troglodytes*). *International Journal of Primatology*, **38**(1), 21–30. DOI: 10.1007/s10764-016-9941-x.

Yin, L.Y., Fei, H.L., Chen, G.S., *et al.* (2016). Effects of group density, hunting, and temperature on the singing patterns of eastern hoolock gibbons (*Hoolock leuconedys*) in Gaoligongshan, southwest China. *American Journal of Primatology*, **78**(8), 861–71. DOI: 10.1002/ajp.22553.

Yuliani, E.L., Adnan, H., Achdiawan, R., *et al.* (2018). The roles of traditional knowledge systems in orang-utan *Pongo* spp. and forest conservation: a case study of Danau Sentarum, West Kalimantan, Indonesia. *Oryx*, **52**, 156–65. Available at: http://www.cifor.org/publications/pdf_files/articles/AYuliani1601.pdf.

Yuniar, R.W. (2016). In Southeast Asia, Facebook and Instagram are where people shop. *Wall Street Journal*, December 6, 2016. Available at: https://www.wsj.com/articles/where-facebook-and-instagram-are-about-shopping-1481023577.

Zainol, M.Z., Fadzly, N., Rosely, N. and Ruppert, N. (2018). *Assessment of illegal online primate trade in Malaysia.* Poster presented at the Congress of the International Primatological Society, Nairobi, Kenya.

Zhang, D., Fei, H.-L., Yuan, S.-D., *et al.* (2014). Ranging behavior of eastern hoolock gibbon (*Hoolock leuconedys*) in a northern montane forest in Gaoligongshan, Yunnan, China. *Primates*, **55**(2), 239–47. DOI: 10.1007/s10329-013-0394-y.

Zhang, L., Hua, N. and Sun, S. (2008). Wildlife trade, consumption and conservation awareness in southwest China. *Biodiversity and Conservation*, **17**(6), 1493–516. DOI: 10.1007/s10531-008-9358-8.

Zhao, N. (2002). *The essence of the animal rights arguments is anti-humanity* [in Chinese]. Available at: https://view.news.qq.com/a/20120118/000013.htm. Accessed October 28, 2019.

Zhou, J. (2018). Chinese zoo suspends keeper over 'mistreatment' of giant panda. *South China Morning Post*, June 21, 2018. Available at: https://www.scmp.com/news/china/society/article/2151720/chinese-zoo-suspends-keeper-over-mistreatment-giant-panda.

Zhou, J., Wei, F., Li, M., *et al.* (2005). Hainan black-crested gibbon is headed for extinction. *International Journal of Primatology*, **26**(2), 453–65. DOI: 10.1007/s10764-005-2933-x.

Zhou, J., Wei, F., Li, M., Pui Lok, C.B. and Wang, D. (2008). Reproductive characters and mating behaviour of wild *Nomascus hainanus*. *International Journal of Primatology*, **29**(4), 1037–46. DOI: 10.1007/s10764-008-9272-7.

ZOO (2015). *IUCN/SSC Asian Primates Red List Assessment Workshop, November 19–24, 2015.* Tamil Nadu, India: Zoo Outreach Organization (ZOO). Available at: https://zooreach.org/ZOO_WILD_Activities/2015/APA2015.htm.

ZSL (2014). Sustainable wildlife management in timber concessions. *The Wildlife Wood Project. ZSL Conservation.* London, UK: Zoological Society of London (ZSL). Available at: https://www.zsl.org/sites/default/files/document/2014-01/Wildlife%20Wood%20Project%20-%20Info%20Sheet%20English.pdf.

ZSL (n.d.). *Wildlife Wood Project.* London, UK: Zoological Society of London (ZSL). Available at: https://www.zsl.org/conservation/regions/africa/wildlife-wood-project. Accessed October 18, 2019.

Zuo, M. (2017). China's terrible zoos and why they're still thriving. *South China Morning Post*, July 1, 2017. Available at: https://www.scmp.com/news/china/society/article/2100775/chinas-terrible-zoos-and-why-theyre-still-thriving.

Index

H

O

P

R

Z